GRAPHICS GEMS V

This is a volume in

The Graphics Gems Series

A Collection of Practical Techniques
for the Computer Graphics Programmer

Series Editor

Andrew Glassner
Microsoft
Redmond, Washington

GRAPHICS GEMS V

Edited by Alan W. Paeth

Computer Science Department
Okanagan University College
Kelowna, British Columbia

An Imprint of Elsevier

San Diego San Francisco New York Boston
London Sydney Tokyo

This book is printed on acid-free paper

ACADEMIC PRESS
An Imprint of Elsevier

525 B Street, Suite 1900, San Diego, CA 92101-4495 USA
http://www.academicpress.com

Academic Press
24-28 Oval Road, London NW1 7DX United Kingdom
http://www.hbuk/ap/

Morgan Kaufmann
340 Pine Street, Sixth Floor, San Francisco, CA 94104-3205
http://mkp.com

Library of Congress Cataloging-in-Publication Data
Graphics Gems V / edited by Alan W. Paeth.
     p. cm. —(The graphics gems series)
   Includes bibliographical references and index.
   ISBN 0-12-543455-3 (with IBM disk)
   ISBN 0-12-543457-X (with Macintosh disk)
   1. Computer Graphics. I. Paeth, Alan W. II. Graphics Gems 5.
 III. Title: Graphics Gems five. IV. Series.
 T385.G6935 1995
 006.6'6—dc20
                          93-41849
                            CIP

Printed and bound by CPI Group (UK) Ltd, Croydon, CR0 4YY
Transferred to Digital Print 2011

◊ Contents

Foreword *by Andrew S. Glassner* ix

Preface xiii

Author Index xvii

I.   Algebra and Arithmetic   1

I.1. Solving Quartics and Cubics for Graphics   3
Don Herbison-Evans

I.2. Computing the Inverse Square Root 16
Ken Turkowski

I.3. Fixed-Point Square Root 22
Ken Turkowski

I.4. Rational Approximation 25
Ken Shoemake

II.   Computational Geometry 33

II.1. Efficient Computation of Polygon Area and Polyhedron Volume . . 35
Allen Van Gelder

II.2. Point in Polyhedron Testing Using Spherical Polygons 42
Paulo Cezar Pinto Carvalho and Paulo Roma Cavalcanti

II.3. Clipping a Concave Polygon 50
Andrew S. Glassner

II.4. Rotations for *N*-Dimensional Graphics 55
Andrew J. Hanson

II.5. Parallelohedra and Uniform Quantization 65
Robert Buckley

II.6. Matrix-based Ellipse Geometry 72
Kenneth J. Hill

II.7. Distance Approximations and Bounding Polyhedra 78
Alan Wm. Paeth

III. Modeling and Transformation **89**

III.1. The Best Least-Squares Line Fit 91
David Alciatore and Rick Miranda

III.2. Surface Models and the Resolution of N-Dimensional
Cell Ambiguity 98
Steve Hill and Jonathan C. Roberts

III.3. Tricubic Interpolation 107
Louis K. Arata

III.4. Transforming Coordinates from One Coordinate Plane
to Another 111
Robert D. Miller

III.5. A Walk through BSP Trees 121
Norman Chin

III.6. Generic Implementation of Axial Deformation Techniques 139
Carole Blanc

IV. Curves and Surfaces **147**

IV.1. Identities for the Univariate and Bivariate Bernstein
Basis Functions 149
Ronald N. Goldman

IV.2. Identities for the B-Spline Basis Functions 163
Ronald N. Goldman

IV.3. Circular Arc Subdivision 168
Ken Turkowski

IV.4. Adaptive Sampling of Parametric Curves 173
Luiz Henrique de Figueiredo

IV.5. Fast Generation of Ellipsoids 179
Jaewoo Ahn

IV.6. Sparse Smooth Connection between Bézier/B-Spline Curves 191
Chandrajit Bajaj and Guoliang Xu

IV.7. The Length of Bézier Curves 199
Jens Gravesen

IV.8. Quick and Simple Bézier Curve Drawing 206
Robert D. Miller

IV.9. Linear Form Curves 210
Ken Shoemake

V. **Ray Tracing and Radiosity** **225**

 V.1. Computing the Intersection of a Line and a Cone 227
   Ching-Kuang Shene

 V.2. Ray Intersection of Tessellated Surfaces: Quadrangles
   versus Triangles 232
   Christophe Schlick and Gilles Subrenat

 V.3. Faster Ray Tracing Using Scanline Rejection 242
   Tomas Möller

 V.4. Ray Tracing a Swept Sphere 258
   Andreas Leipelt

 V.5. Acceleration of Ray Tracing via Voronoi Diagrams 268
   Gábor Márton

 V.6. Direct Lighting Models for Ray Tracing with Cylindrical Lamps . . 285
   Kurt Zimmerman

 V.7. Improving Intermediate Radiosity Images Using Directional Light . 290
   Martin Feda

VI. **Halftoning and Image Processing** **295**

 VI.1. Improved Threshold Matrices for Ordered Dithering 297
   Werner Purgathofer, Robert F. Tobler, and Manfred Geiler

 VI.2. Halftoning with Selective Precipitation and Adaptive Clustering . . 302
   Tien-tsin Wong and Siu-chi Hsu

 VI.3. Faster "Pixel-Perfect" Line Clipping 314
   Steven Eker

 VI.4. Efficient and Robust 2D Shape Vectorization 323
   Jean-François Doué and Ruben Gonzalez Rubio

 VI.5. Reversible Straight Line Edge Reconstruction 338
   S. C. Hsu and I. H. H. Lee

 VI.6. Priority-based Adaptive Image Refinement 355
   Rajesh Sharma

 VI.7. Sampling Patterns Optimized for Uniform Distribution of Edges . . 359
   Robert A. Cross

VII. Utilities **365**

 VII.1. Wave Generators for Computer Graphics 367
   Christophe Schlick

VII.2. Fast Polygon–Cube Intersection Testing 375
Daniel Green and Don Hatch

VII.3. Velocity-based Collision Detection 380
William Bouma and George Vaněček, Jr.

VII.4. Spatial Partitioning of a Polygon by a Plane 386
George Vaněček, Jr.

VII.5. Fast Polygon Triangulation Based on Seidel's Algorithm 394
Atul Narkhede and Dinesh Manocha

VII.6. Accurate Z-Buffer Rendering 398
Raghu Karinthi

VII.7. A Survey of Extended Graphics Libraries 400
Alan Wm. Paeth, Ferdi Scheepers, and Stephen May

Index 407

Volume I–V Cumulative Index 411

Foreword

Andrew S. Glassner

Computer graphics exists because people have messages to communicate. As our tools for rendering, modeling, and animation become more sophisticated, we find it ever easier to create meaningful statements. But the tools of graphics are rarely the point of our enterprise; our goal is to enable meaningful communication of important ideas. To create meaning we must make creative choices, and this leads us to the creation of art.

There are many ways to define art, and perhaps no definition will ever work universally. For now, I will use a broad definition that includes all "technical" creations and say that any creative act can result in art, whether it produces a painting, a song, a video showing tidal forces on Saturn, or a daydream. The last example is something created purely to entertain its creator; all other forms of art are vehicles for communication. Every image we produce with computer graphics that is ultimately destined to be shown to another person contains a message: the image is simply the vehicle for communicating that underlying idea. That idea may be very simple (*e.g.*, a restful arrangement of colors), or very complex (*e.g.*, particle flow in turbulent water), but the image is always subservient to the message: without its intended message, the image has no intrinsic value.

For these reasons, I believe that as we develop our tools we must keep in mind how they help people create, refine, and present their ideas. Each new option in a paint program, each new method for interpolating 3D keyframes, and indeed every new technique, should be evaluated in terms of not just its technical performance, but also in terms of whether it improves people's ability to communicate.

The point of view that images exist to carry messages is quite far from the idea that computers should be generating their own images. The concept of computer-generated art (as opposed to computer-assisted art, which is what we have now) has been around as long as computers and science fiction have been around. Sometimes hailed as a good and sometimes couched as a warning, the idea that computers might start creating images, films, sculptures, and other artifacts in the same form as traditional media carries with it some interesting questions for those of us who create images to express our ideas and who create new tools for that purpose.

The computer is the perfect simulator and imitator, but only along one axis of the human experience: intellectual analysis. This is an essential part of what it is to be human, but not the whole thing. It is, however, the only tool at our disposal as creators of new hardware and software, because the computer is inherently a logical, rational device. We have no way of writing an intuitive or spiritual program; those ideas just don't fit into the computer model. We can force these ideas onto the Procrustean bed of computers and try to create an algorithmic model of intuition, but I believe this does more harm than good: it means distorting the very nature of something not based on reason to codify it using the tools of reason. Perhaps someday there will be a way to emulate intuition and imagination and soul, but I see no hope of doing that with the machines and ideas that form the field of computers as we know them now.

Without these essential human characteristics, a computer by itself cannot produce art that carries anywhere near the levels of meaning that a human artist can provide. An artifact produced by a person carries within it many layers of conscious and unconscious thought, imagination, filtering, selection, phrasing, shaping, and so on. Artists struggle to find the right way to present something, to find the essential core of the message they are communicating. Even practical artists, for example, those who produce images of traffic flow on urban streets, select shapes and colors and compositions that work best, as judged by both objective and subjective criteria. We can try to codify our processes for these selections and judgments, but so many of them happen so deeply inside us that often the best we can do is create a behaviorist's paradise: a book of rules that, when obeyed, usually produces a reasonable result. Music composed by mechanically following the rules of theory is nothing like what a five-year-old makes when banging on a piano, but which has more heart? Which speaks more directly to us as people?

Returning to computer graphics, I believe that the best images and films are the ones that are made by people with something to say, and that we should address our tools to helping those people with their message. We ought not to try to place layers of computer-generated art over their message in order to make it look more sophisticated, creative, or artistic in some way, because this creates information without meaning.

Let us take as an example an imaginary lighting system (unimplemented to my knowledge) that attempts to provide lighting for scene designers. Someone creates an image or animation that appears splotchy; that is, there are some large dark regions and everything else is about evenly lit. The person invokes the lighting system, which inserts a new light to illuminate the dark regions. Is this a good thing? Consider that the new light may create new highlights if the surfaces are shiny—do those highlights draw a viewer's eye away from a region of more importance? Does the new light create shadows that change how the surface appears to move? Is it simply out of place in some way? Perhaps. The computer can't answer these questions, because they are vague and hard to define—two of the characteristics of a problem ill-suited for computerization. It is better to leave the creator of the image to define and place that light than to do it automatically. This has very little to do with expertise and experience, and everything to do with the complex job of trading off countless vague and intuitive decisions when we create anything. Whatever the person decides, it will have been a decision formed and evaluated by someone with intent, and, like the five-year-old on the piano, the message, even if imperfectly stated, is always more important than whether or not the rules were followed. To break the rules we sometimes need tools more powerful than the ones we've had in the past. And when we share those tools, the entire community gains as we discover each other's insights. Part of the inspiration for the *Graphics Gems* series was to provide some of the small and large tools that would prove useful to creative people working on creative tasks.

So it is with great pleasure that I welcome you to *Graphics Gems V*, a volume of new and useful tools for you to apply to your work as you create images, films, and the systems that help people create them. My goal in this series has been to provide programmers with tools that have been forged by necessity, shaped by experience, and shared through a sense of community.

When I had the original idea for the first *Graphics Gems*, I was inspired by a wallet-sized card one of my college professors carried, which had the entire APL language (with examples!) printed on its two sides. I thought *Gems* would be a small paperback book that you could just carry around casually; in fact, we were uncertain that we could fill enough pages, even with large type and wide margins, to make it financially sound to print the book. The flood of high-quality submissions I received in response to the original solicitation quickly changed that premise, and now we have produced five large, densely packed volumes.

It gives me particular pleasure to note that all of the source code for all the *Gems* books is freely available to the public through many different channels. This is important to me, and I thank AP Professional for supporting this approach. You can now find much of the *Gems* source code on disk and CD-ROM, as well as through anonymous ftp, the World Wide Web, and other Internet servers.

The tools in this book are yours, to extend your reach, conserve your time, and encourage you to reach for ever-higher dreams. Enjoy!

◇ Preface

As with previous volumes of the *Graphics Gems* series, this book ultimately serves a number of purposes. First, it provides a recognized, moderated forum of computer graphics dialogue, allowing emerging techniques to come to light before a large audience. Where possible, it places evolving methods within their historical context through its choice of entries and through interactions between the technical editor and each contributor. My emphasis on the latter, which took the form of providing citations lists, related articles, and copyediting for many authors, proved to be both a major undertaking and a rewarding task.

Second, the book serves as a means of dissemination and distribution of this information across a broad and secure domain. Today, the contents of this book "in any form and by any means, electronic or mechanical" is circulating in libraries lacking the benefits of Internet access. Tomorrow, it will be in libraries that will abandon that network. I regard my floppy disk from Volume III as both a landmark step in publishing and a 5 1/4″ historical keepsake. [As an electronic document, the diskette included with this book contains code from all five volumes. The original authors have in some cases revised their entries to correct bugs or to cite related work; see, for example, the code that accompanies Volume IV's "Point in Polygon Strategies." This decision in not running previous code verbatim also keeps the diskettes up to publication date with respect to their anonymous FTP mirrors at Princeton.edu (see under /pub/Graphics/GraphicsGems) and elsewhere.]

Finally, the book provides information in a medium that will never be outmoded. Good gems and good books are worthy of rereading simply on their own merit. The best implementations appearing here either transcend the C language in which they were first coded or are presently reembodied in C merely for the time being. Ultimately, this volume is not a summary of past work but a congress of ideas looking toward the electronic frontier.

Notable entries include Herbison-Evans' noniterative root solver, which opens the volume. Its code has perhaps the oldest pedigree of any gem, having begun life on an English Electric KDF9 in Algol-60 before migrating to an IBM 7040 (Fortran), thence to a PDP11/34. Other feature-length entries include the surveys. Chin's illustrative binary space partition "walk-through" is detailed to the point of a complete implementation, making it a welcome contribution for even the casual graphics programmer. Of similar value is the book's concluding survey of four extended graphics libraries. Owing to the extreme code length of these and a few other gems, only excerpts appear in print, though such gems *in toto* may truly be said to exist between the book's covers. Gems lacking code (the other extreme) are more rare; Goldman provides a remarkably concise summary of curve and surface basis identities annotated with a valuable citations list. Finally, most of the entries in Part VI collectively describe advances in halftoning and image processing at the state of the art that beckon for further experimentation.

The editor wishes to acknowledge two who helped make this work possible: Eric Haines served as an external reviewer for four submissions and also provided editorial assistance in rewriting a portion of one contribution. Special thanks go to MIT's resident expert in communication policy, Dr. Branko Gerovak, who ran a make-shift Mass Ave *sneaker net* one late Cambridge afternoon in early Fall and to the AP PROFESSIONAL staff—Jenifer Niles, sponsoring editor, Cindy Kogut, production editor, and Jacqui Young, editorial assistant—who coordinated and managed the entire project.

◇ **Afterword** ◇

Five years ago a friend and fellow PARC alumnus conceived of a computer graphics text unlike any previous. A collected work, its appendices would contain full implementations—in C and placed in the public domain—of the algorithms it described. For many of us, Glassner's book offered the perfect niche for the mathematical tools and tricks accumulated over years of graphics programming, whose essential design details would fit neither a short note nor a journal article. Hitherto, our gems-in-the-rough were strewn across the backs of envelopes, among disk subdirectories, and within desk-side shoe boxes. We polished what we had, contributed liberally, then waited. The book proved a runaway success.

An evolution of volumes followed. In the second, Arvo captured many more gems not already in hardback (together, those texts total nearly fifteen hundred pages). Color plates were added. While the form and style of the book remained unchanged per se, the accompanying code was already ensconced on an Internet-based repository at Yale by the time the edition appeared in print.

The third volume retained the color plates while the FTP mirror migrated from Yale to Princeton. More important, the code was reproduced on floppy disk attached to the back cover, wherein it became a physical portion of Kirk's volume. Not coincidentally, a book leading the edge in graphics content was also pushing the envelope in methods of electronic publishing, as suggested by the four ISBN numbers that catalogue both the printed pages and IBM/Macintosh diskettes.

These advances, plus the sizable niche market of literate computer professionals, helped give rise to AP PROFESSIONAL. The fourth volume, edited by Heckbert, became a founding entry. The Internet was more widely employed for manuscript submission as well as correspondence. Accordingly, a standardized typesetting language (LaTeX) was chosen and a book style sheet provided. As a consequence, that volume—and this which follows—underwent an appendectomy in that the code listings now accompany their respective gems. In short, gems publication has became a desktop enterprise for nearly all parties involved.

This is the fifth collection of graphics gems, those practical programming essentials. The fifth volume in a series traditionally provides a summary of work to date. With this in mind, the gems were solicited (electronically) with two requests. First, that they constitute summary works. Second, that they satisfy my benchmark for a good gem: Would the author look up their own work? What came over the transom were over one hundred highly diverse submissions. Herein are four dozen shining examples from contributors who span four continents and who have widely diverse professional backgrounds. While there are only a few summary gems, each entry is unique, at times scintillating, and worth reading carefully many times over, as I have already done.

To the gems!

Alan Paeth
Kelowna, British Columbia

LIMITED WARRANTY AND DISCLAIMER OF LIABILITY

◊ Author Index

Numbers in parentheses indicate pages on which authors' gems begin.

Jaewoo Ahn (179), *Systems Engineering Research Institute, K/ST, PO Box 1, Yusong, Taejon 305-600, South Korea*

David G. Alciatore (91), *Department of Mechanical Engineering, Colorado State University, Fort Collins, Colorado 80523, dga@lance.colostate.edu*

Louis K. Arata (107), *Picker International, Ohio Imaging, Nuclear Medicine Division, 23130 Miles Road, Bedford Heights, Ohio 44128-5443, arata@nm.picker.com*

Chandrajit Bajaj (191), *Department of Computer Sciences, Purdue University, West Lafayette, Indiana 47906-1398*

Carole Blanc (139), *Laboratoire Bordelais de Recherche en Informatique, 351, cours de la Libération, 33405 Talence, France, blanc@labri.u-bordeaux.fr*

William Bouma (380), *Department of Computer Sciences, Purdue University, West Lafayette, Indiana 47906-1398*

Robert Buckley (65), *Xerox Corporation, MS 0128-27E, 800 Phillips Road, Webster, New York 14580, buckley.wbst128@xerox.com*

Paulo Cezar Pinto Carvalho (42), *Instituto de Matemática Pura e Aplicada, Universidade Federal do Rio de Janeiro, Estrada Dona Castorino, 110, 22460-320 Rio de Janeiro, Brazil, pcezar@visgraf.impa.br*

Paulo Roma Cavalcanti (42), *Instituto de Matemática Pura e Aplicada, Universidade Federal do Rio de Janeiro, Estrada Dona Castorino, 110, 22460-320 Rio de Janeiro, Brazil, proma@visgraf.impa.br*

Norman Chin (121), *Silicon Graphics, Inc., 2011 North Shoreline Boulevard, Mountain View, California 94043, nc@sgi.com*

Robert A. Cross (359), *Department of Computer Science, Indiana University, Lindley Hall 215, Bloomington, Indiana 47405, rcross@cs.indiana.edu*

Luiz Henrique de Figueiredo (173), *Instituto de Matemática Pura e Aplicada, Universidade Federal do Rio de Janeiro, Estrada Dona Castorino, 110, 22460-320 Rio de Janeiro, Brazil, lhf@visgraf.impa.br*

Jean-François Doué (323), *Gerencia Comercial, Aguos Argentinos, Av. Cordoba 1950, CP1120, Buenos Aires, Argentina*

Steven Eker (314), *Department of Computer Science, Brunel University, Uxbridge, Middlesex UB8 3PH, United Kingdom, Steven.Eker@brunel.ac.uk*

Martin Feda (290), *Institute of Computer Graphics, Technical University of Vienna, Karlsplatz 13/186, A-1040 Vienna, Austria, feda@cg.tuwien.ac.at*

Manfred Geiler (297), *Institute of Computer Graphics, Technical University of Vienna, Karlsplatz 13/186, A-1040 Vienna, Austria*

Andrew S. Glassner (50), *Microsoft, 16011 Northeast 36th Way, Redmond, Washington 98052-6399*

Ronald N. Goldman (149, 163), *Department of Computer Science, Rice University, PO Box 1892-MS 132, Houston, Texas 77251-1892, rng@cs.rice.edu*

Jens Gravesen (199), *Mathematical Institute, Technical University of Denmark, Building 303, DK-2800 Lyngby, Denmark*

Daniel Green (375), *Autodesk, Inc., Multimedia Division, 111 McInnis Parkway, San Rafael, California 94903, daniel.green@autodesk.com*

Andrew J. Hanson (55), *Department of Computer Science, Indiana University, Lindley Hall 215, Bloomington, Indiana 47405, hanson@cs.indiana.edu*

Don Hatch (375), *Silicon Graphics, Inc., 2011 North Shoreline Boulevard, Mountain View, California 94043, hatch@sgi.com*

Don Herbison-Evans (3), *Central Queensland University, Bundaberg Campus, PO Box 5424, Bundaberg West, Queensland, Australia 4670, herbisod@musgrave.cqu.edu.au*

Kenneth J. Hill (72), *Evolution Computing, 885 North Granite Reed Road #49, Scottsdale, Arizona 85257, 76667.2576@compuserve.com*

Steve Hill (98), *Computing Laboratory, University of Kent, Canterbury, Kent CT2 7NF, United Kingdom*

Siu-chi Hsu (302, 338), *Computer Science Department, The Chinese University of Hong Kong, Shatin, New Territories, Hong Kong, schsu@acm.org*

Raghu Karinthi (398), *Department of Statistics and Computer Science, West Virginia University, PO Box 6330, Knapp Hall, Morgantown, West Virginia 26506, raghu@cs.wvu.edu*

I. H. H. Lee (338), *Creature House, Ltd., Hong Kong, creature@acm.org*

Andreas Leipelt (258), *Mathematisches Seminar der Universität Hamburg, Bundesstrasse 55, D-20146 Hamburg, Germany, leipelt@GEOMAT.math.uni-hamburg.de*

Dinesh Manocha (394), *Department of Computer Science, University of North Carolina at Chapel Hill, CB# 3175, Sitterson Hall, Chapel Hill, North Carolina 27599, manocha@cs.unc.edu*

Gábor Márton (268), *Process Control Department, Technical University of Budapest, Müegyetem Rkp. 9/R, Budapest, H-1111, Hungary, marton@seeger.fsz.bme.hu*

Stephen May (400), *Department of Computer Science, The Ohio State University, Columbus, Ohio 43210, smay@cgrg.ohio-state.edu*

Robert D. Miller (111, 206), *1837 Burrwood Circle, East Lansing, Michigan 48823*

Rick Miranda (91), *Department of Mathematics, Colorado State University, Fort Collins, Colorado 80523*

Tomas Möller (242), *Lund Institute of Technology, Ulrikedalsvagen 4C:314, 224 58 Lund, Sweden, d91tm@efd.lth.se*

Atul Narkhede (394), *Department of Computer Science, University of North Carolina at Chapel Hill, CB# 3175, Sitterson Hall, Chapel Hill, North Carolina 27599, narkhede@cs.unc.edu*

Alan Wm. Paeth, editor (78, 400), *Department of Computer Science, Okanagan University College, 3333 College Way, Kelowna, British Columbia, V1V 1V7 Canada, awpaeth@okanagan.bc.ca*

Werner Purgathofer (297), *Institute of Computer Graphics, Technical University of Vienna, Karlsplatz 13/186, A-1040 Vienna, Austria*

Jonathan C. Roberts (98), *Computing Laboratory, University of Kent, Canterbury, Kent CT2 7NF, United Kingdom*

Ruben Gonzalez Rubio (323), *University of Sherbrooke, 2500 University Boulevard, Sherbrooke G1T 2RE, Quebec, Canada*

Ferdi Scheepers (400), *Department of Computer Science, The Ohio State University, Columbus, Ohio 43210, ferdi@cgrg.ohio-state.edu*

Christophe Schlick (232, 367), *Laboratoire Bordelais de Recherche en Informatique, 351, cours de la Libération, 33405 Talence, France, schlick@labri.u-bordeaux.fr*

Rajesh Sharma (355), *Indiana University, Lindley Hall 310, Bloomington, Indiana 47405, rsharma@cs.indiana.edu*

Ching-Kuang Shene (227), *Department of Math and Computer Science, Northern Michigan University, 1401 Presque Isle Avenue, Marquette, Michigan 49855, shene@nmu.edu*

Ken Shoemake (25, 210), *Computer Science Department, University of Pennsylvania, 220 S. 33rd Street, Philadelphia, Pennsylvania 19104, shoemake@graphics.cis.upenn.edu*

Gilles Subrenat (232), *Laboratoire Bordelais de Recherche en Informatique, 351, cours de la Libération, 33405 Talence, France, subrenat@labri.u-bordeaux.fr*

Robert F. Tobler (297), *Institute of Computer Graphics, Technical University of Vienna, Karlsplatz 13/186, A-1040 Vienna, Austria*

Ken Turkowski (16, 22, 168), *Apple Computer, Inc., 1 Infinite Loop, MS 301-3J, Cupertino, California 95014, turk@apple.com*

Allen Van Gelder (35), *Baskin Computer Science Center, 225 A.S., Computer and Information Sciences, University of California, Santa Cruz, California 95064*

George Vaněček, Jr. (380, 386), *Department of Computer Sciences, Purdue University, West Lafayette, Indiana 47906-1398*

Tien-tsin Wong (302), *Computer Science Department, The Chinese University of Hong Kong, Shatin, New Territories, Hong Kong, ttwong@cs.cuhk.hk*

Guoliang Xu (191), *Department of Computer Sciences, Purdue University, West Lafayette, Indiana 47906-1398*

Kurt Zimmerman (285), *Indiana University, Lindley Hall 215, Bloomington, Indiana 47405, kuzimmer@cs.indiana.edu*

$\diamond$ **I** $\diamond$

Algebra and Arithmetic

The gems in this section describe general mathematical techniques having ready application to computer graphics. The methods are crafted with both efficiency and numerical stability in mind.

Herbison-Evans' root finder (I.1) offers the penultimate word in polynomial root finding for computationally closed forms. One immediate gem application generalizes the efficient 3D eigenvalue finder (gem III.2 in volume IV) onto the 4D case. Turkowski (I.2, I.3) provides two elegant and efficient (inverse) square root finders. The first is optimized for use with floating-point hardware and requires no divisions; the second is suitable for integer hardware and features a fixed binary point having adjustable position. Shoemake (I.4) discusses the utility of rational approximation and derives an implementation more stable than one based upon first principles. The availability of his code makes it a useful tool in crafting well-tuned software, as when finding the integer coefficients for the code that concludes gem II.7.

I.1

Solving Quartics and Cubics for Graphics

Don Herbison-Evans
Central Queensland University
Bundaberg Campus
herbisod@musgrave.cqu.edu.au

◇ Introduction ◇

In principle, quartic and cubic equations can be solved without using iterative techniques. In practice, most numerical algorithms based directly upon analytic solutions of these equations are neither well-behaved nor efficient. This gem[1] derives a robust C-language implementation based upon the solutions of Neumark and Ferrari. Its superiority in controlling both round-off error and overflow is also demonstrated.

◇ Background ◇

Quartic equations need to be solved when ray tracing fourth-degree surfaces, e.g., a torus. Quartics also need to be solved in a number of problems involving quadric surfaces. Quadric surfaces (e.g., ellipsoids, paraboloids, hyperboloids, cones) are useful in computer graphics for generating objects with curved surfaces (Badler and Smoliar 1979). Fewer primitives are required than with planar surfaces to approximate a curved surface to a given accuracy (Herbison-Evans 1982b).

Bicubic surfaces may also be used for the composition of curved objects. They have the advantage of being able to incorporate recurves: lines of inflection. There is a problem, however, when drawing the outlines of bicubics in the calculation of hidden arcs. The visibility of an outline can change where its projection intersects that of another outline. The intersection can be found as the simultaneous solution of the two projected outlines. For bicubic surfaces, these outlines are cubics, and the simultaneous solution of two of these is a sextic which can be solved only by iterative techniques. For quadric surfaces, the projected outlines are quadratic. The simultaneous solution of two of these leads to a quartic equation.

---

[1]This gem updates a prior technical report (Herbison-Evans 1986).

The need to solve cubic equations in computer graphics arises in the solution of the quartic equations mentioned above. Also, a number of problems that involve the use of cubic splines require the solution of cubic equations.

One simplifying feature of the computer graphics problem is that often only the real roots (if there are any) are required. The full solution of the quartic in the complex domain (Nonweiler 1967) is then an unnecessary use of computing resources. (See also "Ellipse Intersections" in gem II.6.)

Another simplification in the graphics problem is that displays have a limited resolution, so that only a limited number of accurate digits in the solution of a cubic or quartic may be required. A resolution of one in one million should in principle be achievable using single-precision floating-point (thirty-two bit) arithmetic, which would be more than adequate for most current displays.

◇ Iterative Techniques ◇

The roots of quartic and cubic equations can be obtained by iterative techniques. These techniques can be useful in animation where scenes change little from one frame to the next. Then the roots for the equations in one frame are good starting points for the solution of the equations in the next frame. There are two problems with this approach.

One problem is storage. For a scene composed of n quadric surfaces, $4n(n-1)$ roots may need to be stored between frames. A compromise is to store pointers to those pairs of quadrics that give no roots. This trivial idea can be used to halve the number of computations within a given frame, for if quadric "a" has no intersection with quadric "b," then "b" will not intersect "a."

The other problem is more serious: It is the problem of deciding when the number of roots changes. There appears to be no simple way to find the number of roots of a cubic or quartic. The best-known algorithm for finding the number of real roots, the Sturm sequence (Hook and McAree 1990), involves approximately as much computation as solving the equations directly by radicals (Ralston 1965). Without information about the number of roots, iteration where a root has disappeared can waste a lot of computer time, and searching for new roots that may have appeared becomes difficult.

Even when a root has been found, deflation of the polynomial to the next lower degree is prone to severe round-off exaggeration (Conte and de Boor 1980).

Thus there may be an advantage in examining the techniques available for obtaining the real roots of quartics and cubics analytically.

◇ Quartic Equations ◇

Quartics are the highest-degree polynomials that can be solved analytically in general by the method of radicals, that is, operating on the coefficients with a sequence of operators from the set: sum, difference, product, quotient, and the extraction of an integral order root. An algorithm for doing this was first published in the sixteenth century (Cardano 1545). A number of other algorithms have subsequently been published. The question that arises is which algorithm is best to use on a computer for finding the real roots, in terms of speed and stability for computer graphics.

Very little attention appears to have been given to a comparison of the algorithms. They have differing properties with regard to overflow and the exaggeration of round-off errors. Where a picture results from the computation, any errors may be rather obvious. Figures 1, 2, and 3 show a computer bug composed of ellipsoids with full outlines, incorrect hidden outlines, and correct hidden outlines, respectively. In computer animation, the flashing of incorrectly calculated hidden arcs is most disturbing.

Many algorithms use the idea of first solving a particular cubic equation, the coefficients of which are derived from those of the quartic. A root of the cubic is then used to factorize the quartic into quadratics, which may then be solved. The algorithms may then be classified according to the way the coefficients of the quartic are combined to form the coefficients of the subsidiary cubic equation. For a general quartic equation of the form

$$x^4 + ax^3 + bx^2 + cx + d = 0,$$

the subsidiary cubic can be one of the following forms:

Ferrari–Lagrange (Turnbull 1947):

$$y^3 + by^2 + (ac - 4d)y + (a^2d + c^2 - 4bd) = 0.$$

Descartes–Euler–Cardano (Strong 1859):

$$y^3 + (2b - \tfrac{3}{4}a^2)y^2 + (\tfrac{3}{16}a^4 - a^2b + ac + b^2 - 4d)y + \left(abc - \frac{a^6}{64} + \frac{a^4b}{8} - \frac{a^3c + a^2b^2}{4} - c^2\right) = 0.$$

Neumark (Neumark 1965):

$$y^3 - 2by^2 + (ac + b^2 - 4d)y + (a^2d - abc + c^2) = 0.$$

The casual user of the literature may be confused by variations in the presentation of quartic and cubic equations. Sometimes the coefficients are labeled from the lowest-degree term to the highest. Sometimes the highest-degree term has a nonunit coefficient, or the numerical factors of 3, 4, and 6 are included. There are also a number of trivial changes to the cubic caused by the following:

$$
\begin{aligned}
\text{if} \quad & y^3 + py^2 + qy + r = 0 \\
\text{then} \quad & z^3 - pz^2 + qz - r = 0 \quad \text{for} \quad z = -y \\
\text{and} \quad & z^3 + 2pz^2 + 4qz + 8r = 0 \quad \text{for} \quad z = 2y.
\end{aligned}
$$

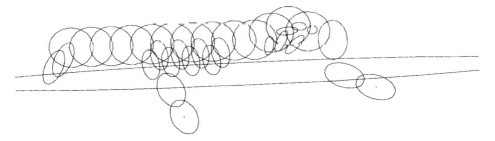

Figure 1. The polyellipsoid caterpillar.

Figure 2. Hidden arcs solved using first-principles quartics.

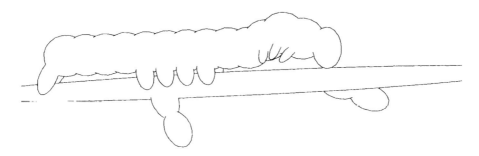

Figure 3. Hidden arcs solved using methods described here.

Table 1, lines one through three (both panels) shows the stable combinations of signs of the quartic coefficients for the computation of the coefficients of these subsidiary cubics. For instance, row three, column two indicates that given a quartic with coefficients $a, b, c > 0$ and $d < 0$, then under Neumark's algorithm the coefficients p and q of the subsidiary cubic are stable.

Table 1. Quartic, subsidiary cubic, and intermediate coefficient stability.

Variable	$a+$							
	$b+$				$b-$			
	$c+$		$c-$		$c+$		$c-$	
	$d+$	$d-$	$d+$	$d-$	$d+$	$d-$	$d+$	$d-$
Ferrari (subsid.)	p	$p\,q$	$p\,q$	p	$p\,r$	$p\,q$	$p\,q\,r$	p
Descartes (subsid.)					$p\,r$	$p\,q\,r$	p	p
Neumark (subsid.)	p	$p\,q$	$p\,r$	p	$p\,r$	$p\,q$	p	p
Ferrari ($y>0$)	ef	$ef\,f^2$		f^2	ef	$ef\,f^2$		f^2
Ferrari ($y<0$)		f^2	ef	$ef\,f^2$	e^2	$e^2\,f^2$	$ef\,e^2$	$ef\,e^2$
Neumark ($y>0$)	g_1	g_1	g_1	g_1	$g_1\,h_1$	$g_{1,2}h_{1,2}$	$g_1\,h_1$	$g_{1,2}h_{1,2}$
Neumark ($y<0$)	$g_{1,2}h_1$	$g_{1,2}h_{1,2}$	$g_{1,2}h_{1,2}$	$g_{1,2}h_{1,2}$	$g_{1,2}$	$g_{1,2}$	$g_{1,2}$	$g_{1,2}$

	$a-$							
	$b+$				$b-$			
	$c+$		$c-$		$c+$		$c-$	
	$d+$	$d-$	$d+$	$d-$	$d+$	$d-$	$d+$	$d-$
Ferrari (subsid.)	$p\,q$	p	p	$p\,q$	$p\,q\,r$	p	$p\,r$	$p\,q$
Descartes (subsid.)					p	p	$p\,r$	$p\,q\,r$
Neumark (subsid.)	$p\,r$	p	p	$p\,q$	p	p	$p\,r$	$p\,q$
Ferrari ($y>0$)		f^2	ef	$ef\,f^2$		f^2	ef	$ef\,f^2$
Ferrari ($y<0$)	ef	$ef\,f^2$		f^2	$ef\,e^2$	$ef\,e^2\,f^2$	e^2	$e^2\,f^2$
Neumark ($y>0$)	g_1	g_1	g_1	g_1	$g_1\,h_1$	$g_1\,h_{1,2}$	$g_1\,h_1$	$g_{1,2}h_{1,2}$
Neumark ($y<0$)	$g_{1,2}h_{1,2}$	$g_{1,2}h_{1,2}$	$g_{1,2}h_1$	$g_{1,2}h_1$	$g_{1,2}$	$g_{1,2}$	$g_{1,2}$	$g_{1,2}$

Ferrari's Algorithm

Of the three subsidiary cubics, that from Ferrari's algorithm has two stable combinations of signs of a, b, c, and d for the derivation of all of the coefficients of the cubic, p, q, and r. For this reason, attempts were made initially (see Figures 1 and 2) to use Ferrari's method for finding quadric outline intersections (Herbison-Evans 1982a).

The coefficients of the subsequent quadratics depend on two intermediate quantities, e and f, where

$$e^2 = a^2 - b - y,$$
$$f^2 = \tfrac{1}{4}y^2 - d,$$
$$ef = \tfrac{1}{4}ay + \tfrac{1}{2}c.$$

The signs of each of the quartic coefficients a, b, c, d, and y, the cubic root, may be positive or negative, giving thirty-two possible combinations of signs. Of these, only twelve can be clearly solved in a stable fashion for e and f by the choice of two out of the three equations involving them. Two are from the stable cases for the calculation of p, q, and r. In the remaining twenty cases, the most stable choices are unclear. This is shown in Table 1, lines four and five.

The quadratic equations are then

$$x^2 + Gx + H = 0,$$
$$x^2 + gx + h = 0,$$

where

$$G = +\tfrac{1}{2}a + e, \quad g = +\tfrac{1}{2}a - e,$$
$$H = -\tfrac{1}{2}y + f, \quad h = -\tfrac{1}{2}y - f.$$

If a and e are the same sign, and b and y are the same sign, then g may be more accurately computed using

$$g = (b + y)/G.$$

If a and e are opposite signs, G can be more accurately computed from g in a similar fashion.

If y and f are the same sign, then H may be more accurately computed using

$$H = d/h.$$

If y and f are opposite in sign, then h can be computed similarly from H more accurately.

The solution of the quadratic equations requires the evaluation of the discriminants

$$g^2 - 4h \quad \text{and} \quad G^2 - 4H.$$

Unless h and H are negative, one or both of these evaluations will be unstable. Unfortunately, positive h and H values are incompatible with the two stable cases for the evaluation of p, q, r, e, and f, so there is no combination of coefficients for which Ferrari's algorithm can be made entirely stable.

It might appear that the problem can be alleviated by observing that reversing the signs of a and c simply reverses the signs of the roots, but may alter the stability of the intermediate quantities. However, all the algorithms appear to have identical stabilities under this transformation.

Descartes–Euler–Cardano Algorithm

This algorithm also has two combinations of quartic coefficients for which the evaluation of the subsidiary cubic coefficients is stable. However, the calculation of these coefficients involves significantly more operations than Ferrari's or Neumark's algorithms. Also, the high power of a in the coefficients makes this algorithm prone to loss of precision and also overflow.

In this algorithm, if the greatest root of the cubic, y, is negative, the quartic has no real roots. Otherwise, the coefficients of the quadratics involve the quantities m, n_1, and n_2:

$$X^2 + mX + n_1 = 0, \quad X^2 - mX + n_2 = 0, \quad \text{and} \quad x = X - \tfrac{1}{4}a$$

where

$$m = \sqrt{y},$$
$$n_1 = \tfrac{1}{2}(y + A + B/m),$$
$$n_2 = \tfrac{1}{2}(y + A - B/m),$$

and

$$A = b - \tfrac{3}{8}a^2 d,$$
$$B = c + \tfrac{1}{8}a^3 - \tfrac{1}{2}ab.$$

There appears to be no way of making the evaluation of A, B, n_1, and n_2 stable. Some quantities are bound to be subtracted, leading to possible loss of precision.

Neumark's Algorithm

Attempts were also made to stabilize the algorithm of Neumark. In this, the coefficients of the quadratic equations are parameters g, G, h, and H, where:

$$G = \frac{1}{2}\left[a + \sqrt{a^2 - 4y}\right], \quad g = \frac{1}{2}\left[a - \sqrt{a^2 - 4y}\right],$$
$$H = \frac{1}{2}\left[b - y + \frac{a(b - y) - 2c}{\sqrt{a^2 - 4y}}\right], \quad h = \frac{1}{2}\left[b - y - \frac{a(b - y) - 2c}{\sqrt{a^2 - 4y}}\right].$$

Some cancellations due to the additions and subtractions can be eliminated by writing

$$G = g_1 + g_2, \quad g = g_1 - g_2,$$
$$H = h_1 + h_2, \quad h = h_1 - h_2,$$

where

$$g_1 = \tfrac{1}{2}a, \quad g_2 = \tfrac{1}{2}\sqrt{a^2 - 4y},$$
$$h_1 = \tfrac{1}{2}(b - y), \quad h_2 = \frac{a(b - y) - 2c}{2\sqrt{a^2 - 4y}},$$

and using the identities

$$G \cdot g = y, \quad H \quad h = d.$$

Thus, if g_1 and g_2 are the same sign, G will be accurate, but g will lose significant digits by cancellation. Then the value of g can be better obtained using

$$g = y/G.$$

If g_1 and g_2 are of opposite signs, then g will be accurate, and G better obtained using

$$G = y/g.$$

Similarly, h and H can be obtained without cancellation from h_1, h_2, and d.

The computation of g_2 and h_2 can be made more stable under some circumstances using the alternative formulation:

$$h_2 = \frac{1}{2}\sqrt{(b-y)^2 - 4d}.$$

Furthermore,

$$g_2 = \frac{ah_1 - c}{\sqrt{(b-y)^2 - 4d}}.$$

Thus, g_2 and h_2 can both be computed either using

$$m = (b-y)^2 - 4d$$

or using

$$n = a^2 - 4y.$$

If y is negative, n should be used. If y is positive and b and d are negative, m should be used. Thus, seven of the thirty-two sign combinations give stable results with this algorithm. These are shown in Table 1, lines six and seven. For other cases, a rough guide to which expression to use can be found by assessing the errors of each of these expressions by summing the moduli of the addends:

$$e(m) = b^2 + 2\,|by| + y^2 + 4\,|d|,$$
$$e(n) = a^2 + 4\,|y|.$$

Thus, if

$$|m| \cdot e(n) \; > \; |n| \cdot e(m),$$

then m should be used; otherwise, n is more accurate.

◇   **The Cubic**   ◇

Let the cubic equation be

$$y^3 + py^2 + qy + r = 0.$$

The solution may be expressed (Littlewood 1950) using

$$u = q - p^2,$$
$$v = r - \tfrac{1}{3}pq + \tfrac{2}{27}p^3,$$

and the discriminant

$$j = 4\left(\frac{u}{3}\right)^3 + v^2.$$

If this is positive, then there is one root, y, to the cubic, which may be found using

$$y = \sqrt[3]{\frac{w-v}{2}} - \frac{u}{3}\sqrt[3]{\frac{2}{w-v}} - \frac{p}{3},$$

where

$$w = \sqrt{j}.$$

This formulation is suitable if v is negative. The calculation in this form can lose accuracy if v is positive. This problem can be overcome by the rationalization

$$\frac{w-v}{2} = \frac{w^2 - v^2}{2(w+v)} = \frac{2}{w+v}\left(\frac{u}{3}\right)^3,$$

giving the alternative formulation of the root:

$$y = \sqrt[3]{\frac{w+v}{2}} - \frac{u}{3}\sqrt[3]{\frac{2}{w+v}} - \frac{p}{3}.$$

A computational problem with this algorithm is overflow while calculating w, for

$$O(j) = O(p^6) + O(q^3) + O(r^2).$$

If the cubic is the subsidiary cubic of a quartic, then the different algorithms each have differing overflow behaviors:

Ferrari: $O(j) = O(a^4 d^2) + O(a^3 c^3) + O(b^6) + O(c^4) + O(d^3),$
Descartes: $O(j) = O(a^{12}) + O(b^6) + O(c^4) + O(d^3),$
Neumark: $O(j) = O(a^4) + O(b^6) + O(c^4) + O(d^3).$

Before evaluating the terms of w, it is useful to test p, q, and r against the appropriate root of the maximum number represented on the machine ("M"). The values of u and v should similarly be tested. In the event that some value is too large, various approximations can be employed, for example,

$$\text{if} \quad |p| > \tfrac{27}{2}\sqrt[3]{M}, \quad \text{then} \quad y \approx -p,$$

$$\text{if} \quad |v| > \sqrt{M}, \quad \text{then} \quad y \approx -\tfrac{1}{3}p + \sqrt[3]{|v|},$$

$$\text{if} \quad |u| > \tfrac{27}{4}\sqrt[3]{M}, \quad \text{then} \quad y \approx -\tfrac{1}{3}p.$$

If the discriminant j is negative, then there are three real roots to the cubic. These real roots of the cubic may then be obtained via parameters s, t, and k:

$$s = \sqrt{-\tfrac{1}{3}u},$$
$$t = -v/(2s^3),$$
$$k = \tfrac{1}{3}\arccos t,$$

giving

$$y_1 = 2s \cdot \cos k - \tfrac{1}{3}p,$$
$$y_2 = s(-\cos k + \sqrt{3}\sin k) - \tfrac{1}{3}p,$$
$$y_3 = s(-\cos k - \sqrt{3}\ \sin k) - \tfrac{1}{3}p.$$

Note that if the discriminant is negative, then u must also be negative, guaranteeing a real value for s. This value may be taken as positive without loss of generality. Also, k will lie in the range 0 to 60 degrees, so that $\cos(k)$ and $\sin(k)$ are both positive. Thus,

$$y_1 \geq y_2 \geq y_3.$$

If the cubic is a subsidiary of a quartic, either y_1 or y_3 may be the most useful root. Unfortunately, $p = -2b$ in Neumark's algorithm, so although y_1 may be the largest root, it may not be positive. Then if b and d are both negative, it would be advantageous to use the most negative root: y_3.

The functions sine and cosine of $\tfrac{1}{3}\arccos(t)$ may be tabulated to speed the calculation (Herbison-Evans 1982a, Cromwell 1994). Sufficient accuracy (1 in 10^7) can be obtained with a table of two hundred entries with linear interpolation, requiring four multiplications, eight additions, and two tests for each function. When t is near its extremes, the asymptotic forms may be useful:

for $t \to 0$:
$$\sin(\tfrac{1}{3}\arccos t) \approx \tfrac{1}{2} - (\tfrac{1}{6}\sqrt{3})t + O(t^2),$$
$$\cos(\tfrac{1}{3}\arccos t) \approx \tfrac{1}{2}\sqrt{3} + \tfrac{1}{6}t + O(t^2);$$

for $t \to 1$:
$$\sin(\tfrac{1}{3}\arccos t) \approx \tfrac{2}{3}\sqrt{(1-t)} + O((1-t)^{3/2}),$$
$$\cos(\tfrac{1}{3}\arccos t) \approx 1 - \tfrac{1}{9}(1-t) + O((1-t)^2).$$

Table 2. Operation counts (min[max]) for best combination of stabilized algorithms.

	Additions and subtractions	Multiplications and divisions	Functions e.g. root, sine	Tests
Cubic	9 [12]	11 [15]	2 [3]	15 [15]
Quartic	5 [14]	6 [22]	0 [2]	1 [36]
Quadratic (×2)	1 [2]	2 [4]	0 [1]	1 [3]
Totals	**16 [30]**	**21 [45]**	**2 [7]**	**18 [57]**

If the discriminant j is expanded in terms of the coefficients of the cubic, it has ten terms. Two pairs of terms cancel and another pair coalesce, leaving five independent terms. In principle, any pair of subsets of these may cancel catastrophically, leaving an incorrect value or even an incorrect sign for the discriminant. This problem can be alleviated by calculating the five terms separately, and then combining them in increasing order of magnitude (Wilkinson 1963). When quartics are solved, the discriminant should be expanded in terms of the quartic coefficients directly. This gives fifteen terms that can be sorted by modulus and combined in increasing order.

◇ **Conclusion** ◇

There have been many algorithms proposed for solving quartic and cubic equations, but most have been proposed with aims of generality or simplicity rather than error minimization or overflow avoidance. The work described here gives a low rate of error using single-precision floating-point arithmetic for the computer animation of quadric surfaces.

The operation counts of the best combination of stabilized algorithms are summarized in Table 2.

A further comment may be useful here concerning the language used to implement these algorithms. Compilers for the C language often perform operations on single-precision variables (`float`) in double precision, converting back to single precision for storage. Thus, there might be little speed advantage in using `float` variables compared with using `double` for these algorithms. Fortran compilers may not do this. For example, using a VAX8600, the time taken to solve 10,000 different quartics was 6.3 seconds for Fortran single precision (using `f77`), 15.5 seconds for C single precision (using `cc`), and 16.1 seconds for C using double precision.

A check on the accuracy of the roots can be done at the cost of more computation. Each root may be substituted back into the original equation and the residual calculated. This can then be substituted into the derivative to give an estimate of the error of the root, or used for a Reguli–Falsi or, better still, a Newton–Raphson correction.

A comparison of the stabilities of the three algorithms for the solution of quartic equations was made. Quartics were examined that had all combinations and permutations of coefficients from the ten-element set:

$$\pm 10^8, \ \pm 10^4, \ \pm 1, \ \pm 10^{-4}, \ \pm 10^{-8}.$$

Of the 10,000 equations, the three algorithms agreed on the number of real roots in 8,453 cases. Of these, 1,408 had no real roots. Of the remaining 7,045 equations, Ferrari's algorithm had the least worst error in 1,659 cases, Neumark's in 2,918, Descartes' in 88, and in the other 2,380 cases, two or more algorithms had equal worst errors.

It may be observed that four of the seven stable cases for Neumark's algorithm coincide with four of the twelve stable cases for Ferrari's algorithm, making only fifteen stable cases in all out of the thirty-two possible sign combinations. Further work on this topic may be able to increase the number of stable cases.

◇ Acknowledgments ◇

Thanks are due to the Departments of Computer Science at the Universities of Sydney (Australia) and Waterloo (Canada) where much of this work was done. Initial investigations on which the work was based were made by Charles Prineas. Thanks are also due to the late Alan Tritter for discussions, to Zoë Kaszas for the initial preparation of this paper, to Professor John Bennett for his continual encouragement, and finally to Alan Paeth for turning the paper into such an elegant LaTeX document.

◇ Bibliography ◇

(Badler and Smoliar 1979) Norman I. Badler and S. W. Smoliar. Digital representations of human movement. *ACM Computing Surveys*, 11(1):24–27, 1979.

(Cardano 1545) Girolamo Cardano. *Ars Magna*. University of Pavia, 1545.

(Conte and de Boor 1980) S. D. Conte and C. de Boor. *Elementary Numerical Analysis*. McGraw-Hill, New York, 1980.

(Cromwell 1994) Robert L. Cromwell. Efficient eigenvalues for visualization. In Paul Heckbert, editor, *Graphics Gems IV*, pages 193–198. AP Professional, Boston, 1994.

(Herbison-Evans 1982a) Don Herbison-Evans. Caterpillars and the inaccurate solution of cubic and quartic equations. *Australian Computer Science Communications*, 5(1):80–89, 1982.

(Herbison-Evans 1982b) Don Herbison-Evans. Real time animation of human figure drawings with hidden lines omitted. *IEEE Computer Graphics and Applications*, 2(9):27–33, 1982.

(Herbison-Evans 1986) Don Herbison-Evans. Solving quartics and cubics for graphics. Technical Report CS-86-56, University of Waterloo, November 1986. (out of print).

(Hook and McAree 1990) D. G. Hook and P. R. McAree. Using Sturm sequences to bracket real roots of polynomial equations. In Andrew Glassner, editor, *Graphics Gems*, pages 416–422. AP Professional, Boston, 1990.

(Littlewood 1950) D. E. Littlewood. *A University Algebra*, page 173. Heineman, London, 1950.

(Neumark 1965) S. Neumark. *Solution of Cubic and Quartic Equations*. Pergamon Press, Oxford, 1965.

(Nonweiler 1967) T. R. F. Nonweiler. Roots of low order polynomial equations. In *Collected Algorithms of the ACM*. C2 edition, 1967. Algorithm 326.

(Ralston 1965) A. Ralston. *A First Course in Numerical Analysis*, page 351. McGraw-Hill, New York, 1965.

(Strong 1859) T. Strong. *Elementary and Higher Algebra*, page 469. Pratt and Oakley, 1859.

(Turnbull 1947) H. W. Turnbull. *Theory of Equations*, fourth edition, page 130. Oliver and Boyd, London, 1947.

(Wilkinson 1963) J. J. Wilkinson. *Rounding Errors in Algebraic Processes*, page 17. Prentice-Hall, London, 1963.

 **1.2**

Computing the Inverse
Square Root

Ken Turkowski
Apple Computer, Inc.
Cupertino, California
turk@apple.com

◊ Introduction ◊

In computer graphics calculations, the square root is often followed by a division, as when normalizing vectors:

$$\frac{\mathbf{v}}{\|\mathbf{v}\|} = \mathbf{v} \left(\sum_i v_i^2 \right)^{1/2}.$$

This adds a significant amount of computational overhead, as a floating-point division typically costs much more than multiplication.

The cost of division may be mitigated by a *reciprocation*. This gem derives the method and provides an implementation for directly computing the *inverse* square root, $f(x) = x^{-1/2}$.

◊ Description of the Algorithm ◊

The algorithm is noteworthy, as no divisions are required. It is based upon the method of successive approximations (Ralston and Rabinowitz 1978). The square root may also be computed at the cost of one additional multiplication, as $\sqrt{x} = x \cdot f(x)$.

The algorithm has two parts: computing an initial estimate, and refining the root by using a fixed number of iterations.

Initialization

The initial estimate, or *seed*, is determined by table look-up. The inverse square root of a floating-point number $m \cdot 2^e$ is given by

$$(m \cdot 2^e)^{-1/2} = m^{-1/2} \cdot 2^{-e/2}.$$

IBM ISBN 0-12-543455-3
Macintosh ISBN 0-12-543457-X

16

The exponent e is adjusted by negation and halving (or shifting if radix-2) to form the seed exponent. If the seed exponent $-\frac{e}{2}$ is to be an integer, then e must be even. When e is odd, the next smaller even value is considered and the mantissa is doubled (that is, $[1 \ldots 4)$ becomes its domain of representation). The extended mantissa indexes a lookup table whose entries contain the inverse square root on the restricted domain. The final seed value is formed by merging the seed mantissa and seed exponent.

Single-precision floating-point numbers typically employ a 24-bit mantissa (with the most significant one bit "hidden"), an eight-bit excess-127 exponent, and a sign bit.[1] Since the iteration we have chosen has quadratic convergence, the number of significant bits roughly doubles with each iteration. This suggests a seed table indexed by a twelve-bit mantissa, requiring just one iteration. However, the table length ($2 \cdot 2^{12}$ two-byte entries, hence 16,384 bytes) becomes prohibitive. Additional iterations allow for a much more relaxed table length, described later.

The Iteration

Given an approximate inverse square root y_n, a better one, y_{n+1}, may be found using the iteration[2]

$$y_{n+1} = \frac{y_n \left(3 - xy_n^2\right)}{2}.$$

An implementation is presented below.

◇   C Implementation   ◇

```
/* Compute the Inverse Square Root
 * of an IEEE Single Precision Floating-Point number.
 *
 * Written by Ken Turkowski.
 */

/* Specified parameters */
#define LOOKUP_BITS     6    /* Number of mantissa bits for lookup */
#define EXP_POS        23    /* Position of the exponent */
#define EXP_BIAS      127    /* Bias of exponent */
/* The mantissa is assumed to be just down from the exponent */

/* Type of result */
```

---

[1] IEEE arithmetic (Donovan and Van Hook 1994) supports 24 (53) bit single (double) precision mantissas; calculation employs such features as "round-to-nearest" or "even-if-tie," a guard bit, a round bit, and a sticky bit.

[2] This algorithm was inspired by the Weitek technical note "Performing Floating-Point Square Root with the WTL 1032/1033."

```
#ifndef DOUBLE_PRECISION
 typedef float FLOAT;
#else /* DOUBLE_PRECISION */
 typedef double FLOAT;
#endif /* DOUBLE_PRECISION */


/* Derived parameters */
#define LOOKUP_POS   (EXP_POS-LOOKUP_BITS) /* Position of mantissa lookup */
#define SEED_POS     (EXP_POS-8)           /* Position of mantissa seed */
#define TABLE_SIZE   (2 << LOOKUP_BITS)    /* Number of entries in table */
#define LOOKUP_MASK  (TABLE_SIZE - 1)            /* Mask for table input */
#define GET_EXP(a)   (((a) >> EXP_POS) & 0xFF)   /* Extract exponent */
#define SET_EXP(a)   ((a) << EXP_POS)            /* Set exponent */
#define GET_EMANT(a) (((a) >> LOOKUP_POS) & LOOKUP_MASK)  /* Extended mantissa
                                                  * MSB's */
#define SET_MANTSEED(a) (((unsigned long)(a)) << SEED_POS)  /* Set mantissa
                                                  * 8 MSB's */

#include <stdlib.h>
#include <math.h>

static unsigned char *iSqrt = NULL;

union _flint {
    unsigned long    i;
    float            f;
} fi, fo;

static void
MakeInverseSqrtLookupTable(void)
{
    register long f;
    register unsigned char *h;
    union _flint fi, fo;

    iSqrt = malloc(TABLE_SIZE);
    for (f = 0, h = iSqrt; f < TABLE_SIZE; f++) {
        fi.i = ((EXP_BIAS-1) << EXP_POS) | (f << LOOKUP_POS);
        fo.f = 1.0 / sqrt(fi.f);
        *h++ = ((fo.i + (1<<(SEED_POS-2))) >> SEED_POS) & 0xFF; /* rounding */
    }
  \ iSqrt[TABLE_SIZE / 2] = 0xFF;    /* Special case for 1.0 */
}

/* The following returns the inverse square root */
FLOAT
InvSqrt(float x)
{
    register unsigned long a = ((union _flint*)(&x))->i;
    register float arg = x;
    union _flint seed;
    register FLOAT, r;
```

```
    if (iSqrt == NULL) MakeInverseSqrtLookupTable();

    seed.i = SET_EXP(((3*EXP_BIAS-1) - GET_EXP(a)) >> 1)
            | SET_MANTSEED(iSqrt[GET_EMANT(a)]);

    /* Seed: accurate to LOOKUP_BITS */
    r = seed.f;

    /* First iteration: accurate to 2*LOOKUP_BITS */
    r = (3.0 - r * r * arg) * r * 0.5;

    /* Second iteration: accurate to 4*LOOKUP_BITS */
    r = (3.0 - r * r * arg) * r * 0.5;

#ifdef DOUBLE_PRECISION
    /* Third iteration: accurate to 8*LOOKUP_BITS */
    r = (3.0 - r * r * arg) * r * 0.5;
#endif /* DOUBLE_PRECISION */
    return(r);
}
```

◇ Numerical Accuracy (Empirical Results) ◇

This procedure has been exhaustively tested for all single-precision IEEE mantissas lying between 0.5 and 2.0 using IEEE arithmetic. Empirical results appear in Table 1.

Note that the minimum of the maximum errors is one least significant bit; that is, perfect accuracy is never achieved for all possible numbers. This is due to numerical roundoff in intermediate computations. However, in the case of two single-precision iterations from a six-, seven-, and eight-bit seed, an "exact" result is computed for nearly all numbers (except for one-bit errors in 0.7%, 0.04%, and 0.007% of all numbers, respectively).

From Table 1 it can be seen that the techniques producing the highest accuracy with the minimum memory and computation are a six-bit seed with two iterations or a three-bit seed with three iterations for single precision, and a seven-bit seed with three iterations for double precision. Obviously, a smaller table or fewer iterations can be used if less precision is adequate for a given task. Note that single precision may be employed to compute the first twenty-three bits of double-precision calculations.

A slight increase in overall accuracy may be achieved by judicious choice of seed values. The method for determining the seed value in this algorithm was found superior to that used in the Weitek technical note, but there is still room for further improvement. In particular, the computed exponent for numbers just slightly greater than or equal to one is too small, so the mantissa is set to the largest value in the table to compensate for this. Additionally, up to one more effective bit of seed precision could be achieved by setting the table value equal to the *average* of the range for the entry, rather than the edge of the range as is done in this implementation.

Table 1. Effect of seed precision on resultant precision.

Itera-tions	Single precision	
	Seed bits	Final bits
1	8	16
1	7	14
1	6	12
2	8	23
2	7	23
2	6	23
2	5	21
2	4	17
3	4	23
3	3	23
	Double precision	
2	8	32
2	7	29
2	6	25
2	5	21
3	8	52
3	7	52
3	6	51
3	5	43
3	4	35
3	3	27

◇ Implementation Notes ◇

Certain compilers do not pass single-precision values as procedure parameters but instead promote them to double or extended precision. In such cases, pointers may be passed instead. The multiplication by 0.5 amounts to a decrement of the exponent, as supported by the IEEE-defined operation `scalb`. Unless hand-coding, the machine multiply is faster than the subroutine overhead lost in invoking `ldexp()`, `scalb()`, or related routines to effect the change.

The code is highly portable: non-IEEE (e.g., radix-16) floating-point hardware merely requires new macros for proper seed construction. A 128-byte table is small enough to be hard-coded into the sources; this also assures that the correct table entries (to the LSB) are evaluated and further allows for more carefully tuned/tweaked entries whose defining formula might be complex.

Previous gems (Lalonde and Dawson 1990, Hill 1992) use a similar method for constructing and indexing a mantissa table. However, these solve instead for the conventional square root and omit the iteration step.

◇ **Bibliography** ◇

(Donovan and Van Hook 1994) Walt Donovan and Tim Van Hook. Direct outcode calculation for faster clip testing. In Paul Heckbert, editor, *Graphics Gems IV*, page 126. AP Professional, Boston, 1994.

(Hill 1992) Steve Hill. IEEE fast square root. In David Kirk, editor, *Graphics Gems III*, page 48. AP Professional, Boston, 1992.

(Hwang 1979) Kai Hwang. *Computer Arithmetic: Principles, Architecture, and Design*, pages 360–379. Wiley, 1979.

(Lalonde and Dawson 1990) Paul Lalonde and Robert Dawson. A high-speed, low-precision square root. In Andrew Glassner, editor, *Graphics Gems*, pages 424–426. AP Professional, Boston, 1990.

(Ralston and Rabinowitz 1978) Anthony Ralston and Philip Rabinowitz. *A First Course in Numerical Analysis*, pages 344–347. McGraw-Hill, 1978.

I.3

Fixed-Point Square Root

Ken Turkowski

Apple Computer, Inc.
Cupertino, California
turk@apple.com

◇ Introduction ◇

Many graphics algorithms rely upon fixed-point arithmetic and its inherent speed advantage over floating point. Often, a fixed-point algorithm requires the evaluation of a square root. This gem describes an algorithm that computes the square root directly in its fixed-point representation, saving the expense of (re)converting and evaluating in floating point. A related gem (Musial 1991) computes an approximate integer square root through the use of integer divisions, but the following algorithm uses more elementary operations.

◇ The Algorithm ◇

The algorithm is based upon a fixed-point format having two integer and thirty fractional bits, operated upon using conventional machine (integer) arithmetic. This choice gives a domain of representation $[-2.0, 2.0)$ suitable for representing normals, colors, and other graphic quantities whose magnitude is bounded by unity.

This algorithm is based upon a method, similar to longhand decimal division, that was taught in schools before the advent of electronic calculators (Gellert *et al.* 1975). This implementation, called the "binary restoring square root extraction," substitutes binary digits (bits), further streamlining the algorithm.

A radical r (the square root of the radicand x) is constructed a bit at a time such that $r^2 \le x$ is always preserved by application of the identity

$$(r + 1)^2 = r^2 + 2r + 1,$$

in which the $(2r + 1)$ term is subtracted from the radicand x at each step. If the result is non-negative, a "1" is generated; otherwise, a "0" is generated and the radicand is unaltered (i.e., restored).

Two radicand bits are consumed and one radical bit generated with each loop iteration. Although this algorithm has only $O(n)$ (linear) convergence, the loop is so simple that it executes quickly, making it amenable to hardware implementation.

◇ **C Implementation** ◇

```
/* The definitions below yield 2 integer bits, 30 fractional bits */
#define FRACBITS 30     /* Must be even! */
#define ITERS    (15 + (FRACBITS >> 1))
typedef long TFract;

TFract
FFracSqrt(TFract x)
{
    register unsigned long root, remHi, remLo, testDiv, count;

    root = 0;          /* Clear root */
    remHi = 0;         /* Clear high part of partial remainder */
    remLo = x;         /* Get argument into low part of partial remainder */
    count = ITERS;     /* Load loop counter */

    do {
        remHi = (remHi << 2) | (remLo >> 30); remLo <<= 2;  /* get 2 bits of arg */
        root <<= 1;    /* Get ready for the next bit in the root */
        testDiv = (root << 1) + 1;    /* Test radical */
        if (remHi >= testDiv) {
            remHi -= testDiv;
            root += 1;
        }
    } while (count-- != 0);

    return(root);
}
```

◇ **Discussion** ◇

A nonrestoring version of the algorithm (Hwang 1979) may run slightly faster at the expense of a slightly more complicated inner loop.

This algorithm may be modified to return the square root of a 32-bit *integer* by redefining FRACBITS as zero, producing a variant requiring one additional iteration (count = 15). Other formats having even numbers of fractional bits can be accommodated simply by adjusting these values. Note that the square root of a long int (thirty-two bits) yields a short int (sixteen bits).

◇ **Bibliography** ◇

(Gellert *et al.* 1975) W. Gellert, H. Küstner, M. Hellwich, and H. Kästner. *The VNR Concise Encyclopedia of Mathematics*, pages 52–53. Van Nostrand Reinhold, 1975.

(Hwang 1979) Kai Hwang. *Computer Arithmetic: Principles, Architecture, and Design*, pages 360–366. Wiley, 1979.

(Musial 1991) Christopher Musial. An integer square root algorithm. In James Arvo, editor, *Graphics Gems II*, pages 387–388. AP Professional, Boston, 1991.

I.4

Rational Approximation

Ken Shoemake
University of Pennsylvania
Philadelphia, Pennsylvania
shoemake@graphics.cis.upenn.edu

◇ Introduction ◇

One way to combat accuracy losses in graphical algorithms such as intersection testing is to use rational numbers instead of floating point. For these and other purposes, the following discussion (accompanied by code) presents a way to construct a rational approximation to a floating-point number, optionally limiting the size of the integers used. The mathematical theory of best rational approximations is a necessary ingredient, but because it assumes perfect real numbers, it is not sufficient. Floating-point arithmetic must be avoided even during conversion!

Rational approximation with limits is surprisingly difficult. Consider the number 0.84375 (which has an exact IEEE floating-point representation). Its only best rational approximations are these few values:

$$1, \frac{3}{4}, \frac{4}{5}, \frac{5}{6}, \frac{11}{13}, \frac{16}{19}, \frac{27}{32}.$$

Approximations not on the list (such as 8/9) are bigger, but not better.

Before reading more, readers might like to challenge themselves by trying to devise a mathematical procedure that finds exactly these values (without attempting exhaustive search). For a greater challenge, try to find the best approximation given a limit. Given the limit 9, say, the procedure should return 5/6. For the ultimate challenge, try to write a C program that does this for an arbitrary floating-point number using 32-bit arithmetic, without generating floating-point exceptions.

Those who attempt any of these challenges will appreciate this gem most. Those with "a lazy attitude" (Knuth 1973, p. 73) must be content with less.

◇ Best Rational Approximations ◇

A *best rational approximation* to a real number x is a rational number n/d (with positive denominator d) that is closer to x than any approximation with a smaller denominator.

A (regular) *continued fraction* (Behnke *et al.* 1974) is a fraction of the form

$$c_0 + \cfrac{1}{c_1 + \cfrac{1}{c_2 + \cfrac{1}{\ddots}}}$$

with positive c_k for $k > 0$. This expression will be abbreviated below as

$$\mathcal{F}[c_0, c_1, c_2, \ldots].$$

Every real number has a unique continued fraction (possibly infinite), which is the key to its best rational approximations. (More precisely, finite continued fractions must absorb any trailing 1 to be unique.)

For example, the continued fraction for 0.84375 is

$$0.84375 = \mathcal{F}[0, 1, 5, 2, 2].$$

Continued fractions for its best rational approximations are

$$1 = \mathcal{F}[0, 1],$$
$$3/4 = \mathcal{F}[0, 1, 3],$$
$$4/5 = \mathcal{F}[0, 1, 4],$$
$$5/6 = \mathcal{F}[0, 1, 5],$$
$$11/13 = \mathcal{F}[0, 1, 5, 2],$$
$$16/19 = \mathcal{F}[0, 1, 5, 2, 1],$$
$$27/32 = \mathcal{F}[0, 1, 5, 2, 2].$$

It is evident that knowing the continued fraction of x is a big step toward knowing its best rational approximations, though mysteries remain. (Why, for instance, does the list not include $\mathcal{F}[0, 1, 2]$ or $\mathcal{F}[0, 1, 5, 1]$?) The most basic rule is this:

Rule 1 *All best rational approximations of x can be obtained by truncating the continued fraction for x, and possibly decrementing its last term.*

The option of decrementing large terms (such as the 292 in $\pi = \mathcal{F}[3, 7, 15, 1, 292, \ldots]$) permits many best approximations. But as the exceptions indicate, restrictions apply. The basic rule of decrementing is this:

Rule 2 *The decremented value of the last term must be at least half its original value.*

This explains why $\mathcal{F}[0, 1, 2]$ did not appear on the list, since 2 is less than half of 5. Any decremented value greater than half the original is always permissible, but there is one final rule. When the decremented value is exactly half the original value, sometimes it is allowed, and sometimes it is not. (Consider $\mathcal{F}[0, 1, 5, 1]$ versus $\mathcal{F}[0, 1, 5, 2, 1]$.) Taking the last term to be c_k, the rule for discrimination is this:

Rule 3 *When c_k is even, using the decremented value $c_k/2$ gives a best rational approximation just when $\mathcal{F}[c_k, c_{k-1}, c_{k-2}, \ldots, c_1] > \mathcal{F}[c_k, c_{k+1}, c_{k+2}, \ldots]$.*

Although this form of the rule is easy to state, a more convenient form to implement will appear in the algorithm given later. In any case, since

$$\mathcal{F}[2, 5, 1] = 2\tfrac{1}{6} < 2\tfrac{1}{2} = \mathcal{F}[2, 2]$$

but

$$\mathcal{F}[2, 2, 5, 1] = 2\tfrac{6}{13} > 2 = \mathcal{F}[2],$$

no mysteries remain in the example above.

◇ **Continued Fraction Calculations** ◇

In the realm of ideal mathematics, continued fractions are easy to calculate. First, set $c_0 = \lfloor x \rfloor$. Now, since $x - c_0$ is less than 1, set $x_1 = 1/(x - c_0)$, and repeat. That is, set $c_1 = \lfloor x_1 \rfloor$, and $x_2 = 1/(x_1 - c_1)$, and so on. If x_k happens to be an integer, c_k is the last term (and x was a rational number).

The trouble with this version of the algorithm is that it loses accuracy when implemented using floating-point arithmetic. However, an accurate integer version can be derived from Euclid's GCD algorithm, because floating-point numbers are integers divided by a power of 2. Let $x = a_{-2}/a_{-1}$, so that $c_0 = \lfloor a_{-2}/a_{-1} \rfloor$ and $a_0 = a_{-2} \bmod a_{-1}$. Then iterate with $c_1 = \lfloor a_{-1}/a_0 \rfloor$ and $a_1 = a_{-1} \bmod a_0$, and so on. After the first nonzero term (c_0 if $x \geq 1$, otherwise c_1), all subsequent values of c_k and a_k are sure to fit in 32-bit integers if x is an IEEE 32-bit floating-point number. Best of all, full accuracy is retained at every step.

Applying this to 0.84375, which happens to be exactly 27/32, gives

$$
\begin{aligned}
c_0 &= \lfloor 27/32 \rfloor = 0 & a_0 &= 27 \bmod 32 = 27, \\
c_1 &= \lfloor 32/27 \rfloor = 1 & a_1 &= 32 \bmod 27 = 5, \\
c_2 &= \lfloor 27/5 \rfloor = 5 & a_2 &= 27 \bmod 5 = 2, \\
c_3 &= \lfloor 5/2 \rfloor = 2 & a_3 &= 5 \bmod 2 = 1, \\
c_4 &= \lfloor 2/1 \rfloor = 2 & a_4 &= 2 \bmod 1 = 0.
\end{aligned}
$$

Converting a continued fraction to an ordinary fraction is easily done incrementally. Begin with the dummy initial fractions $n_{-2}/d_{-2} = 0/1$ and $n_{-1}/d_{-1} = 1/0$. Then fold the c_k term into the numerator and denominator using

$$n_k = n_{k-2} + n_{k-1}c_k$$

and

$$d_k = d_{k-2} + d_{k-1}c_k.$$

This makes it possible to monitor the size of the numerator and denominator as they grow with each new term. With a little care, accumulation can stop before either one grows beyond a given limit.

For the example above, pure truncation gives the following:

c_k		0	1	5	2	2
n_k	0	1	0	1	5	11	27
d_k	1	0	1	1	6	13	32

◇ **Complications** ◇

Computer programs frequently contain a small amount of heavily used code and a much larger amount of special case handling. This routine is no exception, with an inner loop of only ten lines (of which three merely shuffle variables). Most of the remaining code is devoted to careful handling of the first continued fraction term, and to getting the exactly half case right.

There are two potential problems with the first nonzero term. The simplest is that it could be too large to fit in a 32-bit integer. But then it must exceed the limit (which necessarily fits), so a floating-point comparision against some constants can "pretest" the floating-point value of x. The more awkward problem is that even though $\lfloor 1/x \rfloor$ may fit (when $x < 1$), the floating-point computation of $1/x$ loses accuracy. A custom multiple-precision fixed-point divide solves this problem, though it is inelegant.

A little care is needed in testing approximations against the limit. The algorithm sets up the inner loop so the denominator is always larger, to avoid testing the numerator. But if the denominator increases one step too many, it may not fit in a 32-bit integer. Testing $c_k \geq (l - d_{k-2})/d_{k-1}$, not $d_{k-2} + d_{k-1}c_k \geq l$, avoids this hazard.

The final problem is to discriminate the exactly half case. Since it should rarely occur, one option is to "just say no"—which is safe, if not accurate. But there is a better solution using data already at hand: Allow $c_k/2$ whenever $d_{k-2}/d_{k-1} > a_k/a_{k-1}$, or (since floating-point division would lose accuracy) whenever $d_{k-2}a_{k-1} > d_{k-1}a_k$. (Equations (6.131) and (6.135) of *Concrete Mathematics* (Graham *et al.* 1989) are the basis for a proof.) This involves generating and comparing two 64-bit integer results, but that is not so hard (Knuth 1981, p. 253).

Readers interested in learning more about continued fractions are encouraged to seek out Item 101 in the unusual collection known as HAKMEM (Beeler *et al.* 1972). Not explored here are connections to computational complexity (Shallit 1991) and to Bresenham's line drawing algorithm. (As a final challenge, find the next term in the sequence $1, 3, 29, 545, 6914705085169818401684631, \ldots$ —Ed.)

◇   **Code**   ◇

```
/****** rat.h ******/
/* Ken Shoemake, 1994 */

#ifndef _H_rat
#define _H_rat

#include <limits.h>
typedef int BOOL;
#define TRUE 1
#define FALSE 0
#define BITS (32-1)
#if (INT_MAX>=2147483647)
    typedef int INT32;
    typedef unsigned int UINT32;
#else
    typedef long INT32;
    typedef unsigned long UINT32;
#endif
typedef struct {INT32 numer,denom;} Rational;

Rational ratapprox(float x, INT32 limit);
#endif

/****** rat.c ******/
/* Ken Shoemake, 1994 */

#include <math.h>
#include "rat.h"

static void Mul32(UINT32 x, UINT32 y, UINT32 *hi, UINT32 *lo)
{
    UINT32 xlo = x&0xFFFF, xhi = (x>>16)&0xFFFF;
    UINT32 ylo = y&0xFFFF, yhi = (y>>16)&0xFFFF;
    UINT32 t1, t2, t3, s;
    UINT32 lolo, lohi, t1lo, t1hi, t2lo, t2hi, carry;
    *lo = xlo * ylo; *hi = xhi * yhi;
    t1 = xhi * ylo; t2 = xlo * yhi;
    lolo = *lo&0xFFFF; lohi = (*lo>>16)&0xFFFF;
    t1lo = t1&0xFFFF; t1hi = (t1>>16)&0xFFFF;
    t2lo = t2&0xFFFF; t2hi = (t2>>16)&0xFFFF;
    t3 = lohi + t1lo + t2lo;
    carry = t3&0xFFFF; lohi = (t3<<16)&0xFFFF;
    *hi += t1hi + t2hi + carry; *lo = (lohi<<16) + lolo;
};

/* ratapprox(x,n) returns the best rational approximation to x whose numerator
    and denominator are less than or equal to n in absolute value. The denominator
    will be positive, and the numerator and denominator will be in lowest terms.
    IEEE 32-bit floating point and 32-bit integers are required.
    All best rational approximations of a real x may be obtained from x's
    continued fraction representation, x = c0 + 1/(c1 + 1/(c2 + 1/(...)))
```

```
   by truncation to k terms and possibly "interpolation" of the last term.
   The continued fraction expansion itself is obtained by a variant of the
   standard GCD algorithm, which is folded into the recursions generating
   successive numerators and denominators. These recursions both have the
   same form: f[k] = c[k]*f[k-1] + f[k-2]. For further information, see
   Fundamentals of Mathematics, Volume I, MIT Press, 1983.
 */
Rational ratapprox(float x, INT32 limit)
{
    float tooLargeToFix = ldexp(1.0, BITS);        /* 0x4f000000=2147483648.0 */
    float tooSmallToFix = ldexp(1.0, -BITS);       /* 0x30000000=4.6566e-10 */
    float halfTooSmallToFix = ldexp(1.0, -BITS-1); /* 0x2f800000=2.3283e-10 */
    int expForInt = 24;      /* This exponent in float makes mantissa an INT32 */
    static Rational ratZero = {0, 1};
    INT32 sign = 1;
    BOOL flip = FALSE;       /* If TRUE, nk and dk are swapped */
    int scale;               /* Power of 2 to get x into integer domain */
    UINT32 ak2, ak1, ak;     /* GCD arguments, initially 1 and x */
    UINT32 ck, climit;       /* ck is GCD quotient and c.f. term k */
    INT32 nk, dk;            /* Result num. and den., recursively found */
    INT32 nk1 = 0, dk2 = 0;  /* History terms for recursion */
    INT32 nk2 = 1, dk1 = 1;
    BOOL hard = FALSE;
    Rational val;

    if (limit <= 0) return (ratZero);        /* Insist limit > 0 */
    if (x < 0.0) {x = -x; sign = -1;}
    val.numer = sign; val.denom = limit;
    /* Handle first non-zero term of continued fraction,
       rest prepared for integer GCD, sure to fit.
     */
    if (x >= 1.0) {/* First continued fraction term is non-zero */
          float rest;
          if (x >= tooLargeToFix || (ck = x) >= limit)
             {val.numer = sign*limit; val.denom = 1; return (val);}
          flip = TRUE;         /* Keep denominator larger, for fast loop test */
          nk = 1;  dk = ck;    /* Make new numerator and denominator */
          rest = x - ck;
          frexp(1.0,&scale);
          scale = expForInt - scale;
          ak = ldexp(rest, scale);
          ak1 = ldexp(1.0, scale);
       } else {/* First continued fraction term is zero */
          int n;
          UINT32 num = 1;
          if (x <= tooSmallToFix) {        /* Is x too tiny to be 1/INT32 ? */
             if (x <= halfTooSmallToFix) return (ratZero);
             if (limit > (UINT32)(0.5/x)) return (val);
             else return (ratZero);
          }
          /* Treating 1.0 and x as integers, divide 1/x in a peculiar way
             to get accurate remainder
           */
```

```
        frexp(x,&scale);
        scale = expForInt - scale;
        ak1 = ldexp(x, scale);
        n = (scale<BITS)?scale:BITS;      /* Stay within UINT32 arithmetic */
        num <<= n;
        ck = num/ak1;                     /* First attempt at 1/x */
        ak = num%ak1;                     /* First attempt at remainder */
        while ((scale -= n) > 0) {/* Shift quotient, remainder until done */
            n = (scale<8)?scale:8;        /* The 8 is 24 bits of x in 32 bits */
            num = ak<<n;
            ck = ck<<n + num/ak1;
            ak = num%ak1;                 /* Reduce remainder */
        }
        /* All done with divide */
        if (ck >= limit) {                /* Is x too tiny to be 1/limit ? */
            if (2*limit > ck)
                return (val);
            else return (ratZero);
        }
        nk = 1;  dk = ck;                 /* Make new numer and denom */
    }
while (ak != 0) {                         /* If possible, quit when have exact result */
    ak2 = ak1;  ak1 = ak;                 /* Prepare for next term */
    nk2 = nk1;  nk1 = nk;                 /* (This loop does almost all the work) */
    dk2 = dk1;  dk1 = dk;
    ck = ak2/ak1;                         /* Get next term of continued fraction */
    ak = ak2 - ck*ak1;                    /* Get remainder (GCD step) */
    climit = (limit - dk2)/dk1;           /* Anticipate result of recursion on denom */
    if (climit <= ck) {hard = TRUE; break;} /* Do not let denom exceed limit */
    nk = ck*nk1 + nk2;                    /* Make new result numer and denom */
    dk = ck*dk1 + dk2;
}
if (hard) {
    UINT32 twoClimit = 2*climit;
    if (twoClimit >= ck) {               /* If climit < ck/2 no improvement possible */
        nk = climit*nk1 + nk2;           /* Make limited numerator and denominator */
        dk = climit*dk1 + dk2;
        if (twoClimit == ck) {           /* If climit == ck improvement not sure */
            /* Using climit is better only when dk2/dk1 > ak/ak1 */
            /* For full precision, test dk2*ak1 > dk1*ak */
            UINT32 dk2ak1Hi, dk2ak1Lo, dk1akHi, dk1akLo;
            Mul32(flip?nk2:dk2, ak1, &dk2ak1Hi, &dk2ak1Lo);
            Mul32(flip?nk1:dk1, ak, &dk1akHi, &dk1akLo);
            if ((dk2ak1Hi < dk1akHi
               || ((dk2ak1Hi == dk1akHi) && (dk2ak1Lo <= dk1akLo)))
                { nk = nk1;  dk = dk1; }    /* Not an improvement, so undo step */
        }
    }
}
if (flip) {val.numer = sign*dk;  val.denom = nk;}
else      {val.numer = sign*nk;  val.denom = dk;}
return (val);
```

◇ **Bibliography** ◇

(Beeler *et al.* 1972) M. Beeler, R.W. Gosper, and R. Schroeppel. HAKMEM. Artificial Intelligence Memo 239, Massachusetts Institute of Technology, Cambridge, MA, February 1972.

(Behnke *et al.* 1974) H. Behnke, F. Bachmann, K. Fladt, and W. Süss. *Foundations of Mathematics: The Real Number System and Algebra*, Volume 1 of *Fundamentals of Mathematics*. The MIT Press, Cambridge, MA, 1974.

(Graham *et al.* 1989) Ronald L. Graham, Donald E. Knuth, and Oren Patashnik. *Concrete Mathematics*. Addison-Wesley, Reading, MA, 1989.

(Knuth 1973) Donald E. Knuth. *Sorting and Searching*, Volume 3 of *The Art of Computer Programming*. Addison-Wesley, Reading, MA, 1973.

(Knuth 1981) Donald E. Knuth. *Seminumerical Algorithms*, 2nd edition, Volume 2 of *The Art of Computer Programming*. Addison-Wesley, Reading, MA, 1981.

(Shallit 1991) Jeffrey Outlaw Shallit. Description of generalized continued fractions by finite automata. Technical Report CS-91-44, University of Waterloo, September 1991.

◇ **II** ◇

Computational Geometry

The gems in this section describe abstract geometric models having practical graphics application. Their use in rendering is not limited to merely the spatial but includes colorimetric operations within (Euclidean) color space, as when r, g, and b replace x, y, and z.

Van Gelder's polyhedron volume and area finders (II.1) employ both computational optimizations and a mathematical reformulation not previously appearing in print. The latter's derivation is illustrated clearly, the former defended through empirical tables. The spherical geometry reviewed by Carvalho and Cavalcanti (II.2) rederives Girard's method of spherical excesses, ultimately yielding a point-in-polygon test while squelching a bug in a previous gem. Glassner (II.3) offers a reentrant polygon clipper whose edge traverse includes a nonsequential step, yielding a compact algorithm not prone to unnecessary object fragmentation. Hanson, who previously described the geometry of 4D space in practical terms, now derives and describes (II.4) their rotation. A practical application (trackball manipulation) keeps the related application well in hand. Buckley (II.5) provides an insightful nearest lattice point test. Based upon the properties of space close packing, it is first conceived as a geometric color quantizer having possible spatial applications. Hill (II.6) derives a method of ellipse–ellipse intersection not requiring quartic polynomials by application of quadratic matrix forms. Both the intersection methods *per se* and the treatment of the linear algebra provide valuable graphics tools. The distance approximations by Paeth (II.7) are treated in essentially geometrical terms, offering insight into the nature of both cubic symmetry and spherical surfaces while producing a useful set of N-dimensional containment heuristics.

II.1

Efficient Computation of Polygon Area and Polyhedron Volume

Allen Van Gelder
University of California
Santa Cruz, California

◇ Introduction ◇

This gem describes new methods to obtain the area of a planar polygon and the volume of a polyhedron, in three-dimensional space. They provide substantial speed-ups (factors ranging from two to sixteen) over previously reported methods. In most cases, the new methods are also easier to program.

Implementers should be familiar with basic vector operations, particularly the *cross product* (Foley *et al.* 1990, Appendix). This gem assumes a right-handed coordinate system; for a left-handed coordinate system, define the cross product to be the negative of its usual definition. Some derivations require slightly more advanced knowledge of vector calculus (Marsden *et al.* 1993). Derivations are sketched separately in the section "Derivations and Proofs."

◇ Background ◇

Formulas for polyhedral area and volume are older than computers, but their computational efficiency is seldom addressed. A previous gem has adapted 3D methods for area and volume computation from standard sources (Goldman 1991); for conciseness, they are referred to here as the "Goldman method." Formulas for polygonal area in 2D have also been summarized (Eves 1968, Glassner 1990, Rokne 1991).

Area Vectors

The most important observation for the formulas to be obtained is that area is most productively thought of as a *vector*, particularly if further calculations are to be done with it. This point of view is well known in vector calculus. For example, the dot product

Operation	add	scale	dot prod.	cross prod.	magnitude
Notation	$\mathbf{v} + \mathbf{w}$	$c\mathbf{v}$	$\mathbf{v} \cdot \mathbf{w}$	$\mathbf{v} \times \mathbf{w}$	$\|\mathbf{v}\|$
Cost symbol	α	σ	δ	γ	M
Floating Mpy's	0	3	3	6	~ 17

Figure 1. Cost of vector operations.

of an area vector with a direction vector yields the (scalar) area of the projection in that direction.

Assume a bounded surface lies in a plane in 3D, having normal vector $\mathbf{n}$. The interior of the surface is denoted as S and the boundary is denoted as ∂S. It is not necessary to know the normal vector to compute the area vector:

$$\mathbf{A} = \tfrac{1}{2} \oint_{\partial S} \mathbf{r} \times d\mathbf{s}, \tag{1}$$

where $\mathbf{r}$ is the position vector, $d\mathbf{s}$ is the differential arc length vector, and "$\times$" denotes the cross product. The boundary curve ∂S is traversed in counterclockwise order when viewed from the half space into which the normal vector points.

It can also be shown that the vectors $\mathbf{A}$ and $\mathbf{n}$ are collinear. This observation allows the program to avoid computing normal vectors separately.

This gem treats the case in which the boundary of S is a planar polygon. Its vertices are $\mathbf{P}_0, \mathbf{P}_1, \ldots, \mathbf{P}_{k-1}, \mathbf{P}_0$, listed in counterclockwise order when viewed from the half space into which the normal vector points. Equation (1) can be reduced to

$$2\mathbf{A} = \sum_{i=0}^{k-2} \mathbf{P}_i \times \mathbf{P}_{i+1} + \mathbf{P}_{k-1} \times \mathbf{P}_0, \tag{2}$$

which is essentially that given by Goldman (*op. cit.*). Improvements are described in the section "Polygon Area Calculation."

Computational Cost Model

Computational costs will be estimated symbolically in terms of the costs of the various 3D vector operations (see Figure 1). Floating-point multiplies, usually the dominant instruction, appear in the last row. *Vector magnitude* consists of a dot product followed by a square root.

Equation (2) costs $(k\gamma + (k-1)\alpha)$ in general, which becomes $(4\gamma + 3\alpha)$ for a quadrilateral.

◇   **Polygon Area Calculation**   ◇

This section describes how Equation (1) can be reformulated based on geometric insight, and computed much more efficiently. The same idea applies to 2D polygons. Observe the following:

Proposition.   The area of a planar quadrilateral is one-half the cross product of its diagonals, that is, using the counterclockwise indexing convention,

$$\mathbf{A}(\text{quad}) = \tfrac{1}{2}(\mathbf{P}_2 - \mathbf{P}_0) \times (\mathbf{P}_3 - \mathbf{P}_1). \tag{3}$$

To exploit the proposition, partition a k-sided polygon into a series of quadrilaterals formed between $\mathbf{P}_0$ and three consecutive vertices. For k odd, a triangle completes the sequence. To express the formula in an easily coded form, some additional notation is useful: Let $h = \lfloor \tfrac{1}{2}(k-1) \rfloor$, and let $\ell = 0$ if k is odd, or $\ell = k-1$ if k is even. Then

$$2\mathbf{A} = \sum_{i=1}^{h-1} (\mathbf{P}_{2i} - \mathbf{P}_0) \times (\mathbf{P}_{2i+1} - \mathbf{P}_{2i-1}) + (\mathbf{P}_{2h} - \mathbf{P}_0) \times (\mathbf{P}_{\ell} - \mathbf{P}_{2h-1}). \tag{4}$$

This can also be derived formally from Equation (2).

The cost of Equation (4) is $(h\gamma + (3h - 1)\alpha)$. Roughly speaking, half of the cross products in Equation (2) have been replaced by vector subtractions. A quadrilateral now costs only $(\gamma + 2\alpha)$, which is nearly a factor of four better.

◇   **Polyhedron Volume Calculation**   ◇

Let R be a polyhedron with N vertices and m faces, labeled $F_0, \ldots, F_{m-1}$. For each face F_j, choose an arbitrary vertex of that face, which is called its *representative vertex* and is denoted by $\mathbf{P}_{F_j}$. The volume of R is given by

$$V = \tfrac{1}{3} \sum_{j=0}^{m-1} \mathbf{P}_{F_j} \cdot \mathbf{A}_j = \tfrac{1}{6} \sum_{j=0}^{m-1} \mathbf{P}_{F_j} \cdot (2\mathbf{A}_j), \tag{5}$$

where $\mathbf{A}_j$ is the vector area of F_j. Again, this is a "mathematician's formula," which makes no attempt to optimize computational costs.[1] However, it still offers a substantial

---

[1] Consider this illustrative joke. Question 1: How does a mathematician make a cup of tea, given a kettle of water at room temperature? Answer 1: *He puts the kettle on the stove. When the water boils, he pours some into a cup with tea leaves.* Question 2: How does a mathematician make a cup of tea, given a kettle of boiling water? Answer 2: *He sets the kettle aside until the water cools to room temperature, thereby reducing the problem to one previously solved.*

improvement over the Goldman formula by eliminating vector-magnitude calculations and by using the more efficient Equation (4) to evaluate the vectors $(2\mathbf{A}_0)\ldots(2\mathbf{A}_{m-1})$.

For example, on a hexahedron having quadrilateral faces (a deformed cube), the Goldman method would cost $(12M + 30\gamma + 6\delta + 6\sigma + 30\alpha)$, while Equation (5) costs $(6\gamma + 6\delta + 12\alpha)$. A further optimization for hexahedra is described later.

The mystically inclined may ponder the following fact: If a polyhedron has rational vertices, then it may have sides of irrational length, and it may have faces of irrational (scalar) area, but its volume is surely rational!

Optimizations and Special Cases

This section describes two optimization techniques for volume calculations and applies them to obtain further improvements on all polyhedra with four to six faces. Such figures arise frequently in finite element analysis, 3D flow simulations, and related graphics applications.

The first economy of computation is to use a small set of representative vertices in Equation (5). One vertex can represent all the faces upon which it is incident. The area vectors of those faces can be added together first, and then just one dot product is taken with their common representative vertex.

A second possible economy is (conceptually) to translate the origin to one of the representative vertices. Then the contribution of all faces containing that vertex becomes zero in Equation (5). The program need not compute the area vectors for those faces. The actual cost of the translation operation is one vector subtraction per *remaining* representative vertex. It is important to notice that the translation operation need not actually be applied to vectors participating in the area calculations of Equation (4), because they already appear as differences. If there are thirty or more representative vertices, this step may not be cost-effective.

Application of these optimizations depends on the topology of the polyhedron, so this gem can only give specifics for special cases. The remainder of this section describes optimizations for all polyhedra of four to six faces.

First, consider a tetrahedron. Assume the orientation is such that $\mathbf{P}_1, \mathbf{P}_2, \mathbf{P}_4$ appear in *clockwise* order when viewed from $\mathbf{P}_0$ (see Figure 2). The second optimization makes it unnecessary to compute the areas of three of its faces, giving

$$V(\text{tetra}) = \tfrac{1}{6}(\mathbf{P}_1 - \mathbf{P}_0) \cdot \big((\mathbf{P}_2 - \mathbf{P}_1) \times (\mathbf{P}_4 - \mathbf{P}_1)\big). \tag{6}$$

This special case is well known, of course. Its cost is $(\gamma + \delta + 3\alpha)$. (By omitting the factor of $\tfrac{1}{6}$, Equation (6) gives the volume of a parallelepiped. This also computes a 3×3 determinant efficiently.)

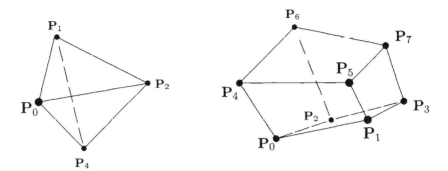

Figure 2. Orientations of tetrahedral vertices for Equation (6) and hexahedral vertices for Equation (8).

More surprisingly, Equation (6) can be extended at no cost to the hexahedron formed by two abutting tetrahedra. To the above tetrahedron, add vertex $\mathbf{P}_7$ with edges to $\mathbf{P}_1$, $\mathbf{P}_2$, and $\mathbf{P}_4$. The volume of this polyhedron is

$$V(\text{dbl-tetra}) = \tfrac{1}{6}(\mathbf{P}_7 - \mathbf{P}_0) \cdot \left((\mathbf{P}_2 - \mathbf{P}_1) \times (\mathbf{P}_4 - \mathbf{P}_1)\right). \tag{7}$$

Now consider a hexahedron with quadrilateral faces, that is, a deformed cube. Let the vertices be labeled as for a cube: $\mathbf{P}_0, \dots, \mathbf{P}_7$ appear in the orientation shown in Figure 2. Observe that all five-faced polyhedra can be obtained by coalescing appropriate vertices of this figure.

Now choose $\mathbf{P}_0$ and $\mathbf{P}_7$ as the representative vertices. After translating the origin to $\mathbf{P}_0$, only the faces containing $\mathbf{P}_7$ require their areas to be calculated. The formula then reduces to

$$V(\text{hexa}) = \tfrac{1}{6}(\mathbf{P}_7 - \mathbf{P}_0) \cdot \left(P_1 \times (P_3 - P_5) + P_2 \times (P_6 - P_3) + P_4 \times (P_5 - P_6)\right). \tag{8}$$

To the best of the author's knowledge, this formula has not previously appeared in print. Its cost is $(3\gamma + \delta + 6\alpha)$. This saves another factor of two over straightforward application of Equations (5) and (4).

Basing costs on the number of multiplies (except $\alpha = 1$, not 0), the Goldman method would cost 450. Equation (8) costs 27. The ratio of $450/27$ gives the factor of sixteen promised in the introductory sentence.

◇ Derivations and Proofs ◇

All facts about vector calculus mentioned in this section can be found in standard texts (Marsden *et al.* 1993).

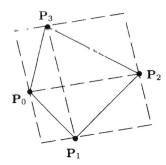

Figure 3.   Parallelogram based on diagonals of an arbitrary quadrilateral.

Equation (1).   The author has not seen this coordinate-independent formulation in print, but it is easily verified. Recall that the cross product commutes with rotation, that is, $R(a \times b) = (Ra) \times (Rb)$, where R is a rotation transformation. Therefore it suffices to consider the case in which the surface normal is $\mathbf{k}$, the unit vector in the positive z direction. Then the z component of $\mathbf{r}$ is constant on the curve ∂S, and the integral simplifies to

$$\tfrac{1}{2} \oint_{\partial S} (x\,dy - y\,dx)\,\mathbf{k}.$$

The magnitude is known to be the area of S by Green's theorem. Also, the area vector is collinear with the surface normal.

Equation (2).   Mathematically, only the component of $\mathbf{r}$ orthogonal to $d\mathbf{s}$ contributes to the cross product, and this component does not change along the line segment from $\mathbf{P}_i$ to $\mathbf{P}_{i+1}$. The contribution of this segment is $P_i \times (P_{i+1} - P_i)$. But $P_i \times P_i = 0$.

As seen geometrically, the right side is the vector sum of the areas of k triangles with vertices $(\mathbf{0}, P_i, P_{i+1})$.)

Equation (3).   Circumscribe the quadrilateral by a parallelogram whose sides are parallel to the diagonals of the quadrilateral (Figure 3). The area of the parallelogram is $(\mathbf{P}_2 - \mathbf{P}_0) \times (\mathbf{P}_3 - \mathbf{P}_1)$. The triangles are congruent in pairs.

Equation (5).   Mathematically, by the divergence theorem, the volume of a 3D region R bounded by the surface ∂R is

$$V = \tfrac{1}{3} \iint_{\partial R} \mathbf{r} \cdot d\mathbf{A}, \tag{9}$$

where $d\mathbf{A}$ is the outwardly oriented differential area vector. When R is a polyhedron, let F_j be any face, and let $\mathbf{P}$ be any fixed point on that face. Then $\mathbf{r} \cdot d\mathbf{A} = \mathbf{P} \cdot d\mathbf{A}$ for all points $\mathbf{r}$ on F_j. Choose a *representative vertex* $\mathbf{P}_{F_j}$ as $\mathbf{P}$, and the integral on that face simplifies to $\mathbf{P}_{F_j} \cdot \iint_{F_j} d\mathbf{A}$.

Geometrically, the right side is the algebraic sum of the volumes of m pyramids with bases $F_0 \ldots F_{m-1}$ and common apex at the origin. (If the origin is outside the volume, some volumes are negative.) Each pyramid's altitude is $\mathbf{P}_{F_j} \cdot (\mathbf{A}_j / \|\mathbf{A}_j\|)$.

Equation (8). The intermediate formula for the deformed cube, after translating the origin to P_0 in Equation (5), is

$$\tfrac{1}{6}(P_7 - P_0) \cdot \Big((P_1 - P_7) \times (P_3 - P_5) + (P_2 - P_7) \times (P_6 - P_3) + (P_4 - P_7) \times (P_5 - P_6) \Big)$$

All the cross products involving P_7 cancel.

◇ **Conclusions** ◇

The discrete equations of area and volume, when derived by first principles, describe an underlying geometry of mensuration based upon triangles. An algebraic rederivation substituting the quadrilateral provides added computational efficiency. Factors of improvement may be estimated based upon machine costs of select operations. The derivation is faster regardless of machine specifics because scalar sums and differences replace slower vector-based operations, including the cross product and absolute value.

◇ **Bibliography** ◇

(Eves 1968) Howard Eves. Analytical geometry. In William H. Beyer, editor, *CRC Handbook of Mathematical Sciences*, 5th edition. CRC Press, Boca Raton, FL, 1968.

(Foley *et al.* 1990) James D. Foley, Andries Van Dam, Steven Feiner, and John Hughes. *Computer Graphics: Principles and Practice*, 2nd edition. Addison-Wesley, Reading, MA, 1990.

(Glassner 1990) Andrew S. Glassner. Useful 2D geometry. In Andrew S. Glassner, editor, *Graphics Gems*, pages 3–11. AP Professional, Boston, 1990.

(Goldman 1991) Ronald N. Goldman. Area of planar polygons and volume of polyhedra. In James Arvo, editor, *Graphics Gems II*, pages 170–171. AP Professional, Boston, 1991.

(Marsden *et al.* 1993) Jerrold E. Marsden, Anthony J. Tromba, and Alan Weinstein. *Basic Multivariate Calculus*. Springer-Verlag, New York, 1993.

(Rokne 1991) Jon Rokne. Area of a simple polygon. In James Arvo, editor, *Graphics Gems II*, pages 5–6. AP Professional, Boston, 1991.

II.2

Point in Polyhedron Testing Using Spherical Polygons

Paulo Cezar Pinto Carvalho
IMPA, Instituto de Matemática Pura e Aplicada
UFRJ, Universidade Federal do Rio de Janeiro
Rio de Janeiro, Brazil
pcezar@visgraf.impa.br

Paulo Roma Cavalcanti
IMPA, Instituto de Matemática Pura e Aplicada
UFRJ, Universidade Federal do Rio de Janeiro
Rio de Janeiro, Brazil
proma@visgraf.impa.br

◇ Introduction ◇

This gem presents a method based on spherical polygons to determine if a given point is inside or outside a three-dimensional polyhedron, given by its face list. This approach extends a well-known 2D technique (Haines 1994) to 3D.

In two dimensions, one can decide whether a point p is inside a simple polygon P by computing the signed angle around p determined by each side of P. If p is not on the boundary of P, the sum S of all such signed angles is necessarily -2π, 0, or 2π. If $S = 0$, p is exterior to P. Otherwise, p is interior to P. Usually, this method is considered to be inferior to the one that is based on counting the number of intersections with P of a ray through p. However, it deserves attention for its elegance and simplicity.

Below, it is shown how to extend the signed angle method to the 3D problem. It is assumed that P is a simple polyhedron, given by its face list, in which the faces are consistently oriented.

◇ Method of Solution ◇

First observe that the measure of the signed angle corresponding to an edge is (in the 2D case) the measure of the directed arc obtained by projecting that edge onto the unit circle whose center is the point p being tested. The arc is positive if its orientation is counterclockwise and negative otherwise. The corresponding operation in three dimensions is to project each face of the polyhedron onto a unit sphere of center p and compute the signed area of the spherical polygon thus determined. The sign is positive if the spherical polygon has counterclockwise orientation and negative otherwise (Figure 1). In analogy to the 2D case, the following holds:

Theorem. *The sum S of the signed areas of the projections of all faces of the simple polyhedron P onto the unit sphere of center p is necessarily 0, 4π, or -4π.*

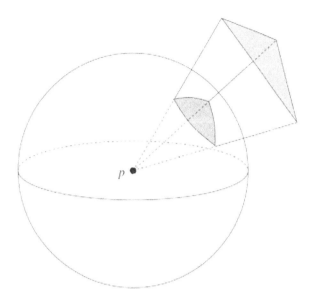

Figure 1. Projecting faces in 3D.

If $S = 0$, then p is exterior to P; otherwise, p is interior to P.

Proof. The projections of all edges of P partition the surface of the unit sphere into a finite family $Q = \{Q_1, Q_2, \ldots, Q_m\}$ of spherical polygons. The projection of a face of P is a finite union of elements of Q. Each element of Q may appear in the projection of several faces, and in each case its area may contribute positively or negatively to the total signed area S, depending on the face orientation. Hence, S can be expressed as $S = \sum_{i=1}^{m} \alpha_i \cdot \text{area}(Q_i)$, where α_i is the *net contribution* of Q_i. Assume that p is interior to P and that the faces of P have counterclockwise orientation. Let us compute the contribution α_i of a spherical polygon Q_i to S. Consider a ray defined by p and an arbitrary point interior to Q_i. This ray may cross several faces of P. The first crossing goes from the inside to the outside of P (Figure 2). As a consequence, the orientation of the projection of the first face crossed is counterclockwise, and the area of Q_i is counted positively. If there is another crossing, then it goes from the outside to the inside, and so the corresponding face projects onto a clockwise spherical polygon. Since p is interior, the total number of crossings is odd, and the ray goes from the inside to the outside once more often than it goes the other way. So, the net contribution of Q_i is positive and $\alpha_i = 1$. Since this happens for every Q_i, S is equal to the area of the sphere, which is given by 4π.

If the faces of P have clockwise orientation, then $S = -4\pi$. Finally, if p is exterior, the number of crossings is even, and the total contribution of each spherical polygon is zero, regardless of the orientation of the faces of P. Thus, in this case $S = 0$. ∎

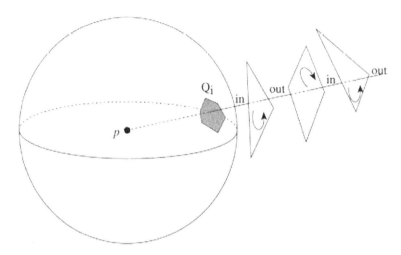

Figure 2.   Crossing faces.

Computing Signed Areas of Spherical Projections of Polygons

To use the previous theorem to locate a point p with respect to a polyhedron P, it is necessary to find the signed area of the projection of each face F of P onto the unit sphere of center p. It is possible to project each vertex onto the sphere and employ the routine presented in a previous gem (Miller 1994) to compute[1] the signed area of the spherical polygon thus obtained. A more practical approach avoids the projection of faces onto the sphere. Presented below, it is based upon the classical formula of Girard for the area of a spherical triangle.

According to Girard's formula (Coxeter 1961, Lines 1965, Bian 1992), the area of a spherical triangle on the unit sphere is given by $S = A + B + C - 2\pi$, where A, B, and C are the (spherical) angles at each vertex, and 2π is the spherical excess. This is readily extended for spherical polygons by adjusting the excess. If a spherical n-gon is triangulated into $n - 2$ spherical triangles, its area may be expressed by

$$S = \left(\sum_i A_i \right) - 2(n - 2)\pi. \tag{1}$$

The spherical angle at a given vertex A is the angle α determined by the tangents to two great circles corresponding to the sides that cross at A. But α is also the angle formed by the planes containing those two great circles. Thus, α can be determined from the normal vectors to each of these planes, which can be computed without actually projecting the vertices onto the sphere (Figure 3).

---

[1] A correction to his implementation concludes this work.

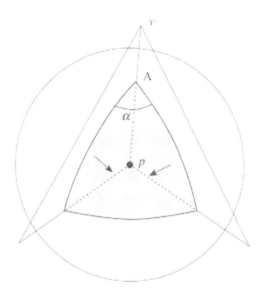

Figure 3.   Computing spherical angles.

Note, however, that the corresponding angle A of the spherical polygon may be either α or $2\pi - \alpha$, depending on whether A is the projection of a convex or concave angle. This can be ascertained by computing the vector product of the two corresponding face edges and comparing the resulting vector with the normal vector to the plane. If they have the same orientation, the angle is convex and $A = \alpha$; otherwise, $A = 2\pi - \alpha$.

This procedure is executed for each vertex of the polygon, and Equation (1) then gives the area of the spherical polygon. Finally, it is necessary to find the sign to be attributed to this area. It suffices to compute the inner product of the face normal vector and the vector pv that joins the center p of the sphere to an arbitrary vertex v of the face. If this product is positive, the projection of F is counterclockwise and its signed area is positive. Otherwise, the area takes a negative value.

Code Revision for Computing the Area of a Spherical Polygon

The published routine (*op. cit.*, page 136) used to compute the area of a spherical polygon does not work in every case. The error lies in the statement

```
if (Lam2 < Lam1) Excess - - Excess;
```

appearing as the penultimate line of the final **if** statement. The method fails when the polygon crosses the 0° meridian (the case is analogous to crossing the international date line). It should be replaced by

```
    double Lam;
    Lam = (Lam2 + Lam1 > 0) ? Lam2   Lam1 . Lam2   Lam1 + 4*HalfPi;
    if (Lam > 2*HalfPi) Excess= -Excess;
```

With this revision in place the routine may be used to find the correct orientation of the projected face and hence the correct signed area.

◇   ANSI C Code   ◇

The code given below reads the face list of a polyhedron (description of each face, consisting of the number of vertices and the coordinates of each vertex) and tests an arbitrary point for inclusion in the polyhedron. To keep it short, the code does not test whether a given point is too close to a polygon plane. In practice, should this happen, the code should check for proximity to the polygon and return *point on the boundary*.

```c
#include <math.h>
#include <stdlib.h>
#include <stdio.h>

#ifndef max
#define max(a,b)  ((a)>(b)?(a):(b))
#define min(a,b)  ((a)<(b)?(a):(b))
#endif
#define PI 3.141592653589793324
#define GeoZeroVec(v)  ((v).x = (v).y = (v).z = 0.0)
#define GeoMultVec(a,b,c)  \
  do {(c).x = a*(b).x;  (c).y = a*(b).y;  (c).z = a*(b).z; } while (0)
#define Geo_Vet(a,b,c)  \
  do {(c).x = (b).x-(a).x;  (c).y = (b).y-(a).y;  (c).z = (b).z-(a).z;} while (0)

typedef double Rdouble;
typedef float  Rfloat;
typedef struct _GeoPoint { Rfloat x, y, z; } GeoPoint;

/*========================= Geometrical Procedures  ======================== */

Rdouble GeoDotProd ( GeoPoint *vec0, GeoPoint *vec1 )
{
 return ( vec0->x * vec1->x + vec0->y * vec1->y + vec0->z * vec1->z );
}

void GeoCrossProd ( GeoPoint *in0, GeoPoint *in1, GeoPoint *out )
{
 out->x = (in0->y * in1->z) - (in0->z * in1->y);
 out->y = (in0->z * in1->x) - (in0->x * in1->z);
 out->z = (in0->x * in1->y) - (in0->y * in1->x);
}

Rdouble GeoTripleProd ( GeoPoint *vec0, GeoPoint *vec1, GeoPoint *vec2 )
{
```

```
 GeoPoint tmp;

 GeoCrossProd ( vec0, vec1, &tmp );
 return ( GeoDotProd( &tmp, vec2 ) );
}

Rdouble GeoVecLen ( GeoPoint *vec )
{
 return sqrt ( GeoDotProd ( vec, vec ) );
}

int GeoPolyNormal ( int n_verts, GeoPoint *verts, GeoPoint *n )
{
 int      i;
 Rfloat   n_size;
 GeoPoint v0, v1, p;

 GeoZeroVec ( *n );
 Geo_Vet ( verts[0], verts[1], v0 );
 for ( i = 2; i < n_verts; i++ )
     {
      Geo_Vet ( verts[0], verts[i], v1 );
      GeoCrossProd ( &v0, &v1, &p );
      n->x += p.x; n->y += p.y; n->z += p.z;
      v0 = v1;
     }

 n_size = GeoVecLen ( n );
 if ( n_size > 0.0 )
    {
     GeoMultVec ( 1/n_size, *n, *n );
     return 1;
    }
 else
     return 0;
}

/*========================= geo_solid_angle  =========================*/
/*
  Calculates the solid angle given by the spherical projection of
  a 3D plane polygon
*/

Rdouble geo_solid_angle (
        int     n_vert,  /* number of vertices */
        GeoPoint *verts,  /* vertex coordinates list */
        GeoPoint *p )     /* point to be tested */
{
 int      i;
 Rdouble  area = 0.0, ang, s, l1, l2;
 GeoPoint p1, p2, r1, a, b, n1, n2;
 GeoPoint plane;
```

```
  if ( n_vert < 3 ) return 0.0;

  GeoPolyNormal ( n_vert, verts, &plane );

  /*
     WARNING: at this point, a practical implementation should check
     whether p is too close to the polygon plane. If it is, then
     there are two possibilities:
       a) if the projection of p onto the plane is outside the
          polygon, then area zero should be returned;
       b) otherwise, p is on the polyhedron boundary.
  */

  p2 = verts[n_vert-1];  /* last vertex */
  p1 = verts[0];         /* first vertex */
  Geo_Vet ( p1, p2, a ); /* a = p2 - p1 */

  for ( i = 0; i < n_vert; i++ )
      {
       Geo_Vet(*p, p1, r1);
       p2 = verts[(i+1)%n_vert];
       Geo_Vet ( p1, p2, b );
       GeoCrossProd ( &a, &r1, &n1 );
       GeoCrossProd ( &r1, &b, &n2 );

       l1 = GeoVecLen ( &n1 );
       l2 = GeoVecLen ( &n2 );
       s  = GeoDotProd ( &n1, &n2 ) / ( l1 * l2 );
       ang = acos ( max(-1.0,min(1.0,s)) );
       s = GeoTripleProd( &b, &a, &plane );
       area += s > 0.0 ? PI - ang : PI + ang;

       GeoMultVec ( -1.0, b, a );
       p1 = p2;
       }

 area -= PI*(n_vert-2);

 return ( GeoDotProd ( &plane, &r1 ) > 0.0 ) ? -area : area;
}

/* ====================== main ========================= */

int main ( void )
{
 FILE    *f;
 char    s[32];
 int     nv, j;
 GeoPoint verts[100], p;
 Rdouble  Area =0.0;

 fprintf ( stdout, "\nFile Name: " );
 gets ( s );
```

```
if ( (f = fopen ( s, "r" )) == NULL )
    {
    fprintf ( stdout, "Can not open the Polyhedron file \n" );
    exit ( 1 );
    }
fprintf ( stdout, "\nPoint to be tested: " );
fscanf( stdin, "%f %f %f", &p.x, &p.y, &p.z );

while ( fscanf ( f, "%d", &nv ) == 1 )
        {
        for ( j = 0; j < nv; j++ )
            if ( fscanf ( f, "%f %f %f",
                &verts[j].x, &verts[j].y, &verts[j].z ) != 3 )
                {
                fprintf ( stdout, "Invalid Polyhedron file \n" );
                exit ( 2 );
                }

        Area += geo_solid_angle ( nv, verts, &p );
        }

fprintf ( stdout, "\n  Area = %12.4lf spherical radians.\n", Area);
fprintf ( stdout, "\n  The point is %s",
        ( (Area > 2*PI) || (Area < -2*PI) )? "inside" : "outside" );
fprintf ( stdout, "the given polyhedron \n" );
return 1;
}
```

◇ **Bibliography** ◇

(Bian 1992) Buming Bian. Hemispherical projection of a triangle. In David Kirk, editor, *Graphics Gems III*, Chapter 6.8, page 316. AP Professional, Boston, 1992.

(Coxeter 1961) H. S. M. Coxeter. *Introduction to Geometry*. John Wiley and Sons, New York, 1961.

(Haines 1994) Eric Haines. Point in polygon strategies. In Paul Heckbert, editor, *Graphics Gems IV*, pages 24–46. AP Professional, Boston, 1994.

(Lines 1965) L. Lines. *Solid Geometry*. Dover Publications, New York, 1965.

(Miller 1994) Robert D. Miller. Computing the area of a spherical polygon. In Paul Heckbert, editor, *Graphics Gems IV*, pages 132–137. AP Professional, Boston, 1994.

◊ II.3

Clipping a Concave Polygon

Andrew S. Glassner
Microsoft Corp.
Redmond, Washington

◊ Introduction ◊

Polygons are a popular modeling primitive. Polygon *clipping* against a line or a plane is one of the most common[1] rendering operations. The classic reentrant method (Sutherland and Hodgman 1974) clips a convex polygon against a line, yielding a pair of polygons lying on either side of the line. The algorithm is conceptually elegant and easy to program for convex polygons, but becomes difficult to implement for concave ones. Although it can be patched up to treat these cases (Foley *et al.* 1990), the patching becomes complicated, involving the detection of degenerate edges.

This gem presents a simple yet robust method for clipping concave polygons. The method considers that often one merely needs the polygon lying to one side of the line. In the general case, both polygons are returned, suggesting an algorithm that can accommodate multiple polygons such as those produced when a concave polygon is split into many fragments (which may also be concave).

◊ The Algorithm ◊

Following standard convention, discussion is phrased in terms of a clipping line, which may also represent the line of intersection between a clipping plane and the polygon. The line is *oriented*: It has a positive side and a negative side. Points (or polygon parts) on the positive side of the clipping line are *inside*, otherwise *outside*.

Consider Figure 1(a), which shows a polygon and a clipping line. The vertices of the polygon are labeled 1 through 8; assume vertex 1 is *inside*. To recapitulate the operations of the Sutherland–Hodgman algorithm, first traverse the polygon's vertices (in either order). Test the current edge for intersection against the clipping line. If it does intersect, compute the point of intersection and insert it into the vertex list between the two endpoints. Continuing for all edges results in the new points labeled *A* through *H*. For purposes of discussion, this will be called a *prepared* polygon (now having sixteen vertices).

---

[1] A basic utility supporting this operation for general polygons appears on page 386.

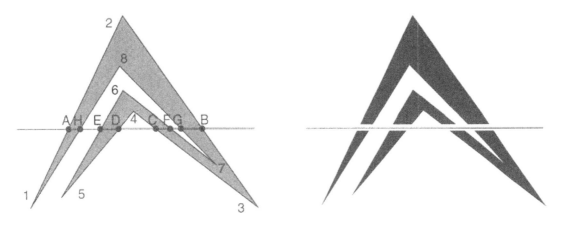

Figure 1. Reentrant clipping of a concave polygon

The Sutherland–Hodgman approach considers vertex 1 as *inside* and creates the A on exit, the point B on reentry includes vertex 3, and so on, constructing the polygon $(1, A, B, 3, \ldots)$. But points A and B *do not* belong to the same final polygons, so this is not an auspicious beginning.

The gem's approach is based on the observation that the new intersection points necessarily come in pairs that exactly correspond to edges. (This is the famous Jordan Curve theorem in action.) That is, it considers the sequential points of intersection along the cutting edge while evaluating consecutive vertices along the polygon.

In the example, points G and B represent a pair, though they were generated at different times during the edge traverse. To find such pairs, pick any two intersection points X and Y at random. All points of intersection lie along the line through X and Y. Treating this as a directed line, find the signed distance of each intersection point from X. For example, if one used D and F as the pair of points, with D at the origin of the line and F lying in the positive direction, then points C, F, and G lie at increasingly positive distances from D, and E, H, and A lie at increasingly negative distances. In a second structure, sort these distance–point pairs by distance to create a second list, for example, A, H, E, D, C, F, G, B. Return to the polygon (the primary data structure) and create links between adjacent pairs, beginning at the head of the list. In the example, this generates the pairs (A, H), (E, D), (C, F), and (G, B).

Note that pair production always requires an even number of points. This can be a problem for vertices lying directly upon (or edges coincident with) the clipping line. The solution borrows a technique from ray tracing (Haines 1989). The heart of the method is that all vertices are classified as *inside* or *outside* in an initial pass before clipping begins, and any vertex that is on the line is considered to be *inside*. This approach has the desirable property that if a polygon is clipped against the same line twice in a row, it will not be changed.

◇   **Pseudocode Implementation**   ◇

```
ConcaveClip(Polygon polygon, Line clipper)

        for each vertex V in polygon.vertices
                V.link := NULL
                u := signed distance of V to clipper
                if (u < 0) then V.inside := FALSE
                        else V.inside := TRUE
                        endif
                endfor
        createdList := NULL
        vertex V := polygon.vertices
        do
                N := V.next
                if (V.inside <> N.inside) then
                        compute location of intersection point P
                        insert P in polygon.vertices between V and N
                        append P to createdList
                        V := P
                        endif
                V := N
                while (V <> first vertex in polygon)
        A := first vertex in createdList
        B := second vertex in createdList
        for each vertex V in createdList
                V.distance := distance from A along line AB
                end for
        sort createdList by distance
        for each consecutive pair of vertices A and B in createdList
                A.link := B
                B.link := A
                end for
        for each vertex V in polygon.vertices
                V.visited := FALSE
                end for
        while any V.visited in polygon.vertices is FALSE
                /* start of a new polygon */
                find first unvisited vertex U
                V := U
                do
                        V.visited := TRUE
                        /* emit V as a vertex of the polygon */
                        if (V.link = TRUE)
                                V = V.link
                                V.visited := TRUE
                                /* emit V as a vertex of the polygon */
                                endif
                        V := V.next
                        while (V <> U)
                end while
        end ConcaveClip
```

Program Data Structures

The implementation assumes that a polygon's vertices are stored as records in a linked list, with the *next* field locating successive records. Additional fields are used for internal bookkeeping: The boolean `inside` is true for a vertex on the positive side of the clipping line. New vertices employ a distance field for sorting and a `link` field that locates its mated pair. The latter serves double duty in identifying the (non) original vertices as the field is then (not) NULL. The `visited` flag assures that all original vertices are accounted for in the output. The sorting step employs a vertex list called `createdList`.

Program Operation

The code first evaluates each polygon vertex with respect to the clipping line and sets the `inside` field FALSE for all vertices having a nonpositive distance. The `createdList` is also cleared. The polygon traverse now commences. Two successive (original) vertices having differing `inside` fields cross the clipping line. When encountered, compute the point of intersection, insert it into the list of vertices, and add it to `createdList`. It is important to advance the walking vertex pointer so that this newly created vertex is not revisited on the next trip around the loop.

The next step picks any two points in `createdList` (e.g., the first two) and assigns signed distances to all the other points based on the oriented line they define. The points are sorted by this distance, and the `link` fields set so that the vextex in each pair points to its mate.

The last step creates the new polygons. Since there may be multiple fragments, the code first sets the `visited` field of all vertices FALSE. This loop begins with any unvisited vertex and walks around the polygon in order, emitting each vertex (and marking it visited). When a new vertex with non-NULL link is encountered, its mate is picked up before continuing around the polygon. The polygon construction loop runs as long as unvisited vertices remain. When it is done, all new polygons have been built. Note that each new vertex on the clipping line will be output twice, while an original vertex is only output once.

The algorithm is simple to implement, and robust because the only classification concerns the intersection of an edge and a clipping line. When the number of vertices in the polygon is small, a simple sorting procedure will often work well. Note that even a relatively simple polygon can quickly become complicated after a few clips, as seen in Figure 1(b).

◇   **Bibliography**   ◇

(Foley *et al.* 1990) James D. Foley, Andries van Dam, Steven K. Feiner, and John F. Hughes. *Computer Graphics: Principles and Practice*, 2nd edition. Addison-Wesley, Reading, MA, 1990.

(Haines 1989) Eric Haines. Essential ray tracing algorithms. In Andrew Glassner, editor, *An Introduction to Ray Tracing*. Academic Press, New York, 1989.

(Sutherland and Hodgman 1974) Ivan E. Sutherland and Gary W. Hodgman. Reentrant polygon clipping. *CACM*, 17(1):32–42, January 1974.

Rotations for *N*-Dimensional Graphics

Andrew J. Hanson
Computer Science Department
Indiana University
Bloomington, Indiana
hanson@cs.indiana.edu

◇ Introduction ◇

A previous gem[1] (Hanson 1994) described a family of techniques for dealing with the geometry of *N*-dimensional models in the context of graphics applications. Here, that framework is used to examine rotations in *N*-dimensional Euclidean space in greater detail. In particular, a natural *N*-dimensional extension is created both for the 3D rolling ball technique described in an earlier gem (Hanson 1992) and for its analogous virtual sphere method (Chen *et al.* 1988). This work also addresses practical methods for specifying and understanding the parameters of *N*-dimensional rotations. The gem concludes by presenting explicit 4D extensions of the 3D quaternion orientation splines.

Additional details and insights are available in the classic sources (see, for example, Sommerville 1985, Coxeter 1991, Hocking and Young 1961, Efimov and Rozendorn 1975).

◇ The *N*-Dimensional Rolling Ball ◇

Basic Intuition of the Rolling Ball

The defining property of any *N*-dimensional rolling ball (or *tangent space*) rotation algorithm is that it takes a unit vector $\hat{\mathbf{v}}_0 = (0, 0, \ldots, 0, 1)$ pointing purely in the *N*th direction (towards the "north pole" of the ball) and tips it in the direction of an orthogonal unit vector $\hat{\mathbf{n}} = (n_1, n_2, \ldots, n_{N-1}, 0)$ lying in the $(N-1)$-plane tangent to the ball at the north pole, thus producing a new, rotated unit vector $\hat{\mathbf{v}}$, where

$$\hat{\mathbf{v}} = M_N \cdot \hat{\mathbf{v}}_0 = \hat{\mathbf{n}} \sin\theta + \hat{\mathbf{v}}_0 \cos\theta,$$

---

[1]The reader is referred to "Geometry for *N*-Dimensional Graphics" in Volume IV of this series.

IBM ISBN 0-12-543455-3
Macintosh ISBN 0-12-543457-X

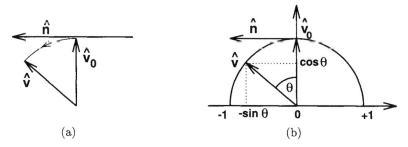

Figure 1.   The "north pole" vector $\hat{\mathbf{v}}_0$ pulled toward the tangent vector $\hat{\mathbf{n}}$, as by an unseen finger.

as indicated schematically in Figure 1(a). (Note: for notational simplicity the components of column vectors appear as horizontal lists.)

By the conventional right-hand rule, a positive rotation (e.g., one that moves the x onto the y axis) moves the north pole into the negative direction of the remaining axes of the rotation plane. That is, if the 2D "rolling circle" acts on $\hat{\mathbf{v}}_0 = (0, 1)$ and $\hat{\mathbf{n}} = (-1, 0)$ as shown in Figure 1(b), then

$$\hat{\mathbf{v}} = M_2 \cdot \hat{\mathbf{v}}_0 = \hat{\mathbf{n}} \sin\theta + \hat{\mathbf{v}}_0 \cos\theta = (-\sin\theta, \cos\theta) \, ,$$

where the rotation matrix M_2 can be written

$$M_2 = \begin{bmatrix} \cos\theta & -\sin\theta \\ +\sin\theta & \cos\theta \end{bmatrix} = \begin{bmatrix} c & -s \\ +s & c \end{bmatrix}$$

$$= \begin{bmatrix} c & +n_x s \\ -n_x s & c \end{bmatrix} \, . \tag{1}$$

If the right-handed coordinate frame is adopted, the sign of $\hat{\mathbf{n}}$ will follow standard convention.

The intuitive model may be summarized in kinesthetic terms. If one is looking straight down at the north pole, the rolling ball *pulls* the unseen Nth component of a vector along the direction $\hat{\mathbf{n}}$ of the $(N-1)$-dimensional controller motion, bringing the unseen component gradually into view.

Implementation.   In practice, one chooses a radius R for the ball containing the object or scene to be rotated and moves the controller[2] a distance r in the tangent direction $\hat{\mathbf{n}}$, as indicated in Figure 2(a). Working from the simplified diagram in Figure 2(b), we define $D^2 = R^2 + r^2$ and choose the rotation parameters $c = \cos\theta = R/D$ and $s = \sin\theta = r/D$.

For interactive systems, this choice has the particular advantage that, however rapidly the user moves the controller, $0 \le (r/D) < +1$, so $0 \le \theta < \pi/2$. Depending upon the

---

[2]The "controller" may include a slider, 2D mouse, 3D mouse, or other physical or virtual device.

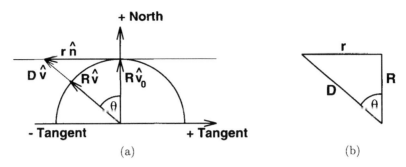

Figure 2. The notation used in implementing the rolling ball rotation model for *N* dimensions.

desired interface behavior, an alternative choice would be to take $\theta = r/R$. This requires computing a trigonometric function instead of a square root, and it may cause large discontinuities in orientation for large controller motion.

3D

The explicit 3D rolling ball formula can be derived starting from an arbitrary 2D mouse displacement $\vec{r} = (x, y, 0) = (rn_x, rn_y, 0)$, where $n_x^2 + n_y^2 = 1$. Then one replaces Equation (1) with $n_x = +1$ by the analogous 3×3 matrix R_0 for (x, z) rotations and encloses this in a conjugate pair of rotations R_{xy} that transform the 2D mouse displacement $\vec{r}$ into the strictly positive x-direction and back. Since even $\vec{r} = (-1, 0, 0)$ is rotated to the positive x-direction before R_0 acts, all signs are correct. With the explicit matrices

$$R_{xy} = \begin{bmatrix} n_x & -n_y & 0 \\ n_y & n_x & 0 \\ 0 & 0 & 1 \end{bmatrix}, \quad R_0 = \begin{bmatrix} c & 0 & +s \\ 0 & 1 & 0 \\ -s & 0 & c \end{bmatrix},$$

one thereby finds an alternative derivation of the author's formula in a previous gem (Hanson 1992):

$$
\begin{aligned}
M_3 &= R_{xy} R_0 (R_{xy})^{-1} \\
&= \begin{bmatrix} c + (n_y)^2(1-c) & -n_x n_y(1-c) & n_x s \\ -n_x n_y(1-c) & c + (n_x)^2(1-c) & n_y s \\ -n_x s & -n_y s & c \end{bmatrix} \\
&= \begin{bmatrix} 1 - (n_x)^2(1-c) & -n_x n_y(1-c) & n_x s \\ -n_x n_y(1-c) & 1 - (n_y)^2(1-c) & n_y s \\ -n_x s & -n_y s & c \end{bmatrix}.
\end{aligned}
\tag{2}
$$

4D

The 4D case takes as input a 3D mouse motion $\vec{r} = (x, y, z, 0) = (rn_x, rn_y, rn_z, 0)$, with $n_x^2 + n_y^2 + n_z^2 = 1$. Then one first transforms (n_y, n_z) into a pure y-component, rotates that result to yield a pure x-component, performs a rotation by θ in the (x, w)-plane, and reverses the first two rotations. Defining the required matrices as

$$
R_{yz} = \begin{bmatrix} 1 & 0 & 0 & 0 \\ 0 & \frac{n_y}{r_{yz}} & -\frac{n_z}{r_{yz}} & 0 \\ 0 & \frac{n_z}{r_{yz}} & \frac{n_y}{r_{yz}} & 0 \\ 0 & 0 & 0 & 1 \end{bmatrix}, \quad R_{xy} = \begin{bmatrix} n_x & -r_{yz} & 0 & 0 \\ r_{yz} & n_x & 0 & 0 \\ 0 & 0 & 1 & 0 \\ 0 & 0 & 0 & 1 \end{bmatrix}, \quad R_0 = \begin{bmatrix} c & 0 & 0 & +s \\ 0 & 1 & 0 & 0 \\ 0 & 0 & 1 & 0 \\ -s & 0 & 0 & c \end{bmatrix}, \quad (3)
$$

where $r_{yz}^2 = n_y^2 + n_z^2$, we find

$$
\begin{aligned}
M_4 &= R_{yz} R_{xy} R_0 (R_{xy})^{-1} (R_{yz})^{-1} \\
&= \begin{bmatrix} 1 - (n_x)^2(1-c) & -(1-c)n_x n_y & -(1-c)n_x n_z & sn_x \\ -(1-c)n_x n_y & 1 - (n_y)^2(1-c) & -(1-c)n_y n_z & sn_y \\ -(1-c)n_x n_z & -(1-c)n_y n_z & 1 - (n_z)^2(1-c) & sn_z \\ -sn_x & -sn_y & -sn_z & c \end{bmatrix}.
\end{aligned} \quad (4)
$$

ND

The extension of this procedure to any dimension is accomplished by having the controller interface supply an $(N-1)$-dimensional vector $\vec{r} = (rn_1, rn_2, \ldots, rn_{N-1}, 0)$ with $\vec{r} \cdot \vec{r} = r^2$ and $\hat{n} \cdot \hat{n} = 1$ and applying the rotation

$$
\begin{aligned}
M_N &= R_{N-2,N-1} R_{N-3,N-2} \cdots R_{1,2} R_0 (R_{1,2})^{-1} \cdots (R_{N-3,N-2})^{-1} (R_{N-2,N-1})^{-1} \\
&= \begin{bmatrix} 1 - (n_1)^2(1-c) & -(1-c)n_2 n_1 & \cdots & -(1-c)n_{N-1}n_1 & sn_1 \\ -(1-c)n_1 n_2 & 1 - (n_2)^2(1-c) & \cdots & -(1-c)n_{N-1}n_2 & sn_2 \\ \vdots & \vdots & \ddots & \vdots & \vdots \\ -(1-c)n_1 n_{N-1} & -(1-c)n_2 n_{N-1} & \cdots & 1 - (n_{N-1})^2(1-c) & sn_{N-1} \\ -sn_1 & -sn_2 & \cdots & -sn_{N-1} & c \end{bmatrix}.
\end{aligned} \quad (5)
$$

Recall that the controller input $\vec{r} = r\hat{n}$ that selects the direction to "pull" also determines $c = \cos\theta = R/D$, $s = \sin\theta = r/D$, with $D^2 = R^2 + r^2$, or, alternatively, $\theta = r/R$.

◇ **Controlling the Remaining Rotational Degrees of Freedom** ◇

There are $N(N-1)/2$ parameters in a general N-dimensional orthogonal rotation matrix, one parameter for each possible pair of axes specifying a *plane of rotation* (the 3D intuition about "axes of rotation" does not extend simply to higher dimensions). The matrix M_N in Equation (5) has only $(N-1)$ independent parameters: One must now account for the remaining $(N-1)(N-2)/2$ degrees of freedom needed for arbitrary rotations.

In fact, the noncommutativity of the rotation group allows us to generate all the other rotations by *small circular motions* of the controller in the $(N-1)$-dimensional subspace of $\vec{r} = r\hat{n}$. Moving the controller in circles in the $(1,2)$-plane, $(1,3)$-plane, etc., of the $(N-1)$-dimensional controller space exactly generates the missing $(N-1)$ $(N-2)/2$ rotations required to exhaust the full parameter space. In mathematical terms, the additional motions are generated by the commutation relations of the $SO(N)$ Lie algebra for $i,j = 1, \ldots, N-1$,

$$[R_{iN}, R_{jN}] = \delta_{ij}R_{NN} - \delta_{jN}R_{iN} + \delta_{iN}R_{jN} - \delta_{NN}R_{ij}$$
$$= -R_{ij} \ .$$

The minus sign in the preceding equation means that *clockwise* controller motions in the (i,j)-plane inevitably produce *counterclockwise* rotations of the object, and vice versa. Thus, the philosophy (Hanson 1992) of achieving the full set of context-free rotation group transformations with a limited set of controller moves extends perfectly to N dimensions. *Implementation Note*: In practice, the effectiveness of this technique varies considerably with the application; the size of the counterrotation experienced may be relatively small for parameters that give appropriate spatial motion sensitivity with current 3D mouse technology.

Alternative Context Philosophies

The rolling ball interface is a *context-free* interface that allows the user of a virtual reality application to ignore the absolute position of the controller and requires no supplementary cursor context display; thus, one may avoid distractions that may disturb stereography and immersive effects in a virtual reality environment. However, some applications are better adapted to *context-sensitive* interfaces such as the Arcball method (Shoemake 1994) or the virtual sphere approach (Chen *et al.* 1988). The virtual sphere approach in particular can be straightforwardly extended to higher dimensions by using the rolling ball equations inside a displayed spatial context (typically a sphere) and changing over to an $(N-1)$-dimensional rolling ball outside the context; that is, as the controller approaches and passes the displayed inner domain context sphere, the rotation action changes to one that leaves the Nth coordinate fixed but changes the remaining $(N-1)$ coordinates as though an $(N-1)$-dimensional rolling ball controller were attached to the nearest point on the sphere. Similar flexibility can be achieved by using a different controller state to signal a discrete rather than a continuous context switch to the $(N-1)$-dimensional controller.

◇   Handy Formulas for *N*-Dimensional Rotations   ◇

For some applications, the incremental orientation control methods described above are not as useful as knowing a single matrix for the entire N-dimensional orientation frame for an object. The following subsections describe three ways to represent such an orientation frame.

Columns Are New Axes

One straightforward construction simply notes that if the default coordinate frame is represented by the orthonormal set of unit vectors $\hat{\mathbf{x}}_1 = (1, 0, \ldots, 0)$, $\hat{\mathbf{x}}_2 = (0, 1, 0, \ldots, 0)$, $\ldots$, $\hat{\mathbf{x}}_N = (0, \ldots, 0, 1)$, and the desired axes of the new (orthonormal) coordinate frame are known to be $\hat{\mathbf{a}}_1 = (a_1^{(1)}, a_1^{(2)}, \ldots, a_1^{(N)})$, $\hat{\mathbf{a}}_2$, $\ldots$, $\hat{\mathbf{a}}_N$, then the rotation matrix that transforms any vector to that frame just has the new axes as its columns:

$$M = \begin{bmatrix} \hat{\mathbf{a}}_1 & \hat{\mathbf{a}}_2 & \cdots & \hat{\mathbf{a}}_N \end{bmatrix}.$$

The orthonormality constraints give M the required $N(N-1)/2$ degrees of freedom.

Concatenated Subplane Rotations

Rotations in the plane of a pair of coordinate axes $(\hat{\mathbf{x}}_i, \hat{\mathbf{x}}_j)$, $i, j = 1, \ldots, N$ can be written as the block matrix

$$R_{ij}(\theta_{ij}) = \begin{bmatrix} 1 & \cdots & 0 & 0 & \cdots & 0 & 0 & \cdots & 0 \\ \vdots & \ddots & \vdots & \vdots & \ddots & \vdots & \vdots & \ddots & \vdots \\ 0 & \cdots & \cos\theta_{ij} & 0 & \cdots & 0 & -\sin\theta_{ij} & \cdots & 0 \\ 0 & \cdots & 0 & 1 & \cdots & 0 & 0 & \cdots & 0 \\ \vdots & \ddots & \vdots & \vdots & \ddots & \vdots & \vdots & \ddots & \vdots \\ 0 & \cdots & 0 & 0 & \cdots & 1 & 0 & \cdots & 0 \\ 0 & \cdots & \sin\theta_{ij} & 0 & \cdots & 0 & \cos\theta_{ij} & \cdots & 0 \\ \vdots & \ddots & \vdots & \vdots & \ddots & \vdots & \vdots & \ddots & \vdots \\ 0 & \cdots & 0 & 0 & \cdots & 0 & 0 & \cdots & 1 \end{bmatrix}, \tag{6}$$

and thus the $N(N-1)/2$ distinct $R_{ij}(\theta_{ij})$ may be concatenated in some order to produce a rotation matrix such as

$$M = \prod_{i<j} R_{ij}(\theta_{ij})$$

with $N(N-1)/2$ degrees of freedom parametrized by $\{\theta_{ij}\}$. However, since the matrices R_{ij} do not commute, different orderings give different results, and it is difficult to intuitively understand the global rotation. In fact, as is the case for 3D Euler angles, one may even repeat some matrices (with distinct parameters) and omit others, and still not miss any degrees of freedom.

Quotient Space Decomposition

Another useful decomposition relies on the classic quotient property of the topological spaces of the orthogonal groups (Helgason 1962),

$$SO(N)/SO(N-1) = S^{N-1} , \tag{7}$$

where S^K is a K-dimensional topological sphere. In practical terms, this means that the $N(N-1)/2$ parameters of $SO(N)$, the mathematical group of N-dimensional orthogonal rotations, can be viewed as a nested family of points on spheres. The 2D form is the matrix (1) parameterizing the points on the circle S^1; the 3D form reduces to the standard matrix

$$M_3(\theta, \hat{\mathbf{n}}) = \begin{bmatrix} c + (n_1)^2(1-c) & n_1 n_2 (1-c) - sn_3 & n_3 n_1 (1-c) + sn_2 \\ n_1 n_2 (1-c) + sn_3 & c + (n_2)^2(1-c) & n_3 n_2 (1-c) - sn_1 \\ n_1 n_3 (1-c) - sn_2 & n_2 n_3 (1-c) + sn_1 & c + (n_3)^2(1-c) \end{bmatrix} , \tag{8}$$

where the two free parameters of $\hat{\mathbf{n}} \cdot \hat{\mathbf{n}} = (n_1)^2 + (n_2)^2 + (n_3)^2 = 1$ describe a point on the two-sphere. These two parameters plus a third from the S^1 described by $c^2 + s^2 = 1$ (i.e., $c = \cos\theta$, $s = \sin\theta$) yield the required total of three free parameters equivalent to the three Euler angles. The 4D and higher forms are already too unwieldy to be conveniently written as single matrices.

◇ **Interpolating *N*-Dimensional Orientation Frames** ◇

To define a uniform-angular-velocity interpolation between two N-dimensional orientation frames, one might either consider independently interpolating each angle in Equation (6), or might take the quotient space decomposition given by the hierarchy of points on the spheres $(S^{N-1}, \ldots, S^2, S^1)$ and apply a constant angular velocity spherical interpolation to each spherical point in each successive dimension using the "Slerp"

$$\hat{\mathbf{n}}_{12}(t) = \text{Slerp}(\hat{\mathbf{n}}_1, \hat{\mathbf{n}}_2, t) = \hat{\mathbf{n}}_1 \frac{\sin((1-t)\theta)}{\sin(\theta)} + \hat{\mathbf{n}}_2 \frac{\sin(t\theta)}{\sin(\theta)}$$

where $\cos\theta = \hat{\mathbf{n}}_1 \cdot \hat{\mathbf{n}}_2$. (This formula is simply the result of applying a Gram–Schmidt decomposition while enforcing unit norm in any dimension.)

Either of these methods often achieves the goal of smooth appearance, but the solutions are neither unique nor mathematically compelling, since the curve is not guaranteed to be a geodesic in $SO(N)$.

In general, specification of geodesic curves in $SO(N)$ (Barr *et al.* 1992) is a difficult problem; fortunately, the two most important cases for interactive systems, $N = 3$ and $N = 4$, have elegant solutions using the covering or "Spin" groups. For $SO(3)$, geodesic interpolations and suitable corresponding splines are definable using Shoemake's quaternion splines (Shoemake 1985), which can be simply formulated using Slerps on S^3 as follows: Let $\hat{\mathbf{n}}$ be a unit 3-vector, so that

$$q_0 = \cos(\theta/2), \quad \vec{\mathbf{q}} = \hat{\mathbf{n}}\sin(\theta/2)$$

is automatically a point on S^3 due to the constraint $(q_0)^2 + (q_1)^2 + (q_2)^2 + (q_3)^2 = 1$. Then each point on S^3 corresponds to an $SO(3)$ rotation matrix

$$R_3 = \begin{bmatrix} q_0^2 + q_1^2 - q_2^2 - q_3^2 & 2q_1q_2 - 2q_0q_3 & 2q_1q_3 + 2q_0q_2 \\ 2q_1q_2 + 2q_0q_3 & q_0^2 + q_2^2 - q_1^2 - q_3^2 & 2q_2q_3 - 2q_0q_1 \\ 2q_1q_3 - 2q_0q_2 & 2q_2q_3 + 2q_0q_1 & q_0^2 + q_3^2 - q_1^2 - q_2^2 \end{bmatrix}, \tag{9}$$

which the reader can verify reduces exactly to the nested-sphere form in Equation (8). Note that the quaternions q and $-q$ each correspond to the same 3D rotation. Slerping q generates sequences of matrices $R_3(t)$ that are geodesic interpolations. Arbitrary splines can be defined using the method of Schlag (Schlag 1991).

Quaternions in Four Dimensions

In four dimensions, the correspondence between the rotation group $SO(4)$ and the spin group Spin(4) that is its double covering may be computed by extending quaternion multiplication to act not just on three-vectors ("pure" quaternions) $v = (0, \vec{\mathbf{V}})$, but on full four-vector quaternions v^μ in the following way:

$$\sum_{\nu=0}^{3} R^\mu{}_\nu v^\nu = q \cdot v^\mu \cdot p^{-1} .$$

Thus, the general double-quaternion parameterization for 4D rotation matrices takes the form

$$
R_4 = \begin{bmatrix}
q_0p_0 + q_1p_1 + q_2p_2 + q_3p_3 & -q_1p_0 + q_0p_1 + q_3p_2 - q_2p_3 \\
+q_1p_0 - q_0p_1 + q_3p_2 - q_2p_3 & q_0p_0 + q_1p_1 - q_2p_2 - q_3p_3 \\
+q_2p_0 - q_0p_2 + q_1p_3 - q_3p_1 & q_1p_2 + q_2p_1 + q_0p_3 + q_3p_0 \\
+q_3p_0 - q_0p_3 + q_2p_1 - q_1p_2 & q_1p_3 + q_3p_1 - q_0p_2 - q_2p_0
\end{bmatrix}
$$

$$
\begin{bmatrix}
-q_2p_0 + q_0p_2 + q_1p_3 - q_3p_1 & -q_3p_0 + q_0p_3 + q_2p_1 - q_1p_2 \\
q_1p_2 + q_2p_1 - q_3p_0 - q_0p_3 & q_1p_3 + q_3p_1 + q_2p_0 + q_0p_2 \\
q_0p_0 + q_2p_2 - q_1p_1 - q_3p_3 & q_2p_3 + q_3p_2 - q_0p_1 - q_1p_0 \\
q_2p_3 + q_3p_2 + q_1p_0 + q_0p_1 & q_0p_0 + q_3p_3 - q_1p_1 - q_2p_2
\end{bmatrix} . \quad (10)
$$

One may check that Equation (9) is just the lower right-hand corner of the degenerate $p = q$ case of Equation (10).

Shoemake-style interpolation between two distinct 4D frames is now achieved by applying the desired Slerp-based interpolation method independently to a set of quaternion coordinates $q(t)$ on one three-sphere, and to a separate set of quaternion coordinates $p(t)$ on another. The resulting matrix $R_4(t)$ gives geodesic interpolations for simple Slerps and can be used as the basis for corresponding spline methods (Schlag 1991, Barr *et al.* 1992). Analogues of the $N = 3$ and $N = 4$ approaches for general N involve computing Spin(N) geodesics and thus are quite complex.

Controls

As pointed out by Shoemake (Shoemake 1994), the Arcball controller can be adapted with complete faithfulness of spirit to the 4D case, since one can pick *two* points in a three-sphere to specify an initial 4D frame, and then pick *two more* points in the three-sphere to define the current 4D frame. Equation (10) gives the complete form of the effective 4D rotation. Alternately, one can replace the 4D rolling ball or virtual sphere controls described earlier by a pair (or more) of 3D controllers (Hanson 1992).

◇ **Acknowledgment** ◇

This work was supported in part by NSF grant IRI-91-06389.

◇ **Bibliography** ◇

(Barr *et al.* 1992) Alan H. Barr, Bena Currin, Steven Gabriel, and John F. Hughes. Smooth interpolation of orientations with angular velocity constraints using quaternions. *Computer Graphics*, 26(2):313–320, 1992.

(Chen *et al.* 1988) Michael Chen, S. Joy Mountford, and Abigail Sellen. A study in interactive 3-D rotation using 2-D control devices. In *Proceedings of Siggraph 88*, Volume 22, pages 121–130, 1988.

(Coxeter 1991) H. S. M. Coxeter. *Regular Complex Polytopes*, second edition. Cambridge University Press, 1991.

(Efimov and Rozendorn 1975) N.V. Efimov and E.R. Rozendorn. *Linear Algebra and Multi-Dimensional Geometry*. Mir Publishers, Moscow, 1975.

(Hanson 1992) Andrew J. Hanson. The rolling ball. In David Kirk, editor, *Graphics Gems III*, pages 51–60. AP Professional, Boston, 1992.

(Hanson 1994) Andrew J. Hanson. Geometry for *N*-dimensional graphics. In Paul Heckbert, editor, *Graphics Gems IV*, pages 149–170. AP Professional, Boston, 1994.

(Helgason 1962) Sigurdur Helgason. *Differential Geometry and Symmetric Spaces*. Academic Press, New York, 1962.

(Hocking and Young 1961) John G. Hocking and Gail S. Young. *Topology*. Addison-Wesley, 1961.

(Schlag 1991) John Schlag. Using geometric constructions to interpolate orientations with quaternions. In James Arvo, editor, *Graphics Gems II*, pages 377–380. AP Professional, Boston, 1991.

(Shoemake 1985) Ken Shoemake. Animating rotation with quaternion curves. In *Computer Graphics*, Volume 19, pages 245–254, 1985. Proceedings of SIGGRAPH 1985.

(Shoemake 1994) Ken Shoemake. Arcball rotation control. In Paul Heckbert, editor, *Graphics Gems IV*, pages 172–192. AP Professional, Boston, 1994.

(Sommerville 1958) D. M. Y. Sommerville. *An Introduction to the Geometry of N Dimensions*. Reprinted by Dover Press, 1958.

II.5

Parallelohedra and Uniform Quantization

Robert Buckley
Xerox Digital Imaging Technology Center
Webster, New York
buckley.wbst128@xerox.com

This gem describes a method of quantizing values (locating the nearest neighbor) in 3-space. The method was originally intended as an optimal means of color coding, using a non-Cartesian partitioning of space. The solution, based upon the geometry of the truncated octahedron, has general applications, as in heuristics for intersection testing.

◇ Original Problem ◇

More and more, color image, interchange, and management applications are using the 1976 CIE $L^*a^*b^*$ or "CIELAB" color space to represent color data. CIELAB (together with CIELUV) comprises CIE recommendations defining approximately uniform color spaces useful in calculating color differences. The recommendations are based upon the good correlation between the perceptual difference of two colors compared to the Euclidean distance between the two points representing these colors in CIELAB three-space.

In a digital system where a color is represented or quantized in CIELAB space, the usual practice is to quantize each coordinate L^*, a^*, b^* independently and uniformly. As a result, the collection of all quantized points or codewords lies on the simple cubic lattice shown in Figure 1, and quantizing a point is equivalent to selecting the nearest lattice point. In each dimension, the lattice points are separated by a distance equal to the quantization step.

Associated with each lattice point is a Dirichlet or Voronoi region, containing the points that are closer to that lattice point than to any other. In this application, this region is called a quantization or Q region and contains the points that after quantization are represented by the associated lattice point or codeword. In the case of the simple cubic lattice, the Q regions are cubes centered on the lattice points; the Q region for a lattice point is shown in Figure 1. The edge length e of the cube corresponds to the quantization step. A cube is a parallelohedron: a polyhedron that can fill three-

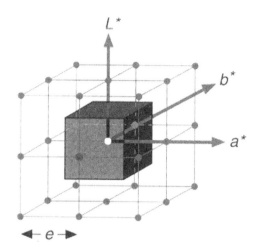

Figure 1.   Simple cubic lattice and cubic *Q* region.

space by translations alone. In effect, the quantizer is filling CIELAB space with cubic Q regions.

One criterion for choosing the size of the quantization step e is the maximum quantization error. Quantization error is the difference or distance $\|v - Q(v)\|$ between a value v and the codeword $Q(v)$ used to represent it. In CIELAB space, this is the difference between the actual color and the color used to represent it. For a cubic Q region, this is equivalent to the radius of the sphere (the circumsphere) that circumscribes a cube with edge length e. In Figure 1, the maximum quantization error is half the length of the body diagonal, or $e\sqrt{3}/2$.

Another criterion for choosing the size of the quantization step is minimizing the visibility of quantization contours (the two are correlated in CIELAB space) so that quantizing a smooth color gradient or color sweep will not introduce spurious contours, which are the color space analogue of jaggies. Because a color gradient can have any orientation in color space, two colors that are nearly the same could be encoded by CIELAB values separated by a distance equal to the body diagonal of the cube that is the Q region. This is the maximum distance between adjacent codewords or neighboring lattice points, which are ones whose Q regions have a common point. In Figure 1, this distance is $e\sqrt{3}$, or twice the maximum quantization error. (As will be noted in a moment, the two criteria are not so simply related for other lattice quantizers.) It determines the worst-case visibility of quantization contours, as two colors that are nearly the same could be represented by colors separated by this distance.

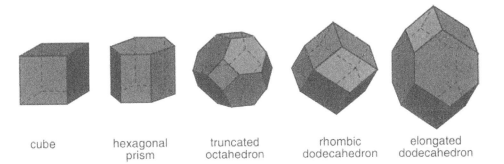

cube   hexagonal   truncated   rhombic   elongated
        prism   octahedron   dodecahedron   dodecahedron

Figure 2.   The five parallelohedra.

◇ **Geometric Quantization** ◇

A more economical quantizer would achieve the same quantization criterion using fewer codewords or equivalently larger Q regions to cover the entire color space (Buckley 1981, 1993). Thus, the largest uniform volume surrounding any codeword is sought, as this provides the most efficient means to partition a space in the fewest number of lattice points. The unique solutions are known to crystallography and lattice theory and necessarily have opposing faces that are parallel and congruent. The five space-filling convex polyhedra or parallelohedra are shown in Figure 2: the cube, hexagonal prism, rhombic dodecahedron, truncated octahedron, and elongated dodecahedron (Coxeter 1973). Of these five, only the first four need be considered, as the rhombic dodecahedron is the limiting case of an elongated dodecahedron: Collapsing the edges shared by pairs of hexagonal faces of the latter results in the former.

Each of these four parallelohedra is the Q region for a different lattice and consequently a different quantizer. From Figure 1, the cube is the Q region for a simple cubic lattice. The rhombic dodecahedron is the Q region for the face-centered cubic lattice (Figure 3a). This parallelohedron has twelve rhombic faces and fourteen vertices. The truncated octahedron is the Q region for the body-centered cubic lattice. It has six square faces, eight hexagonal faces, and twenty-four vertices. The hexagonal prism is the Q region for two-dimensional hexagonal lattices, stacked one above the other.

If the quantizer criterion is minimizing the quantizer error r, then the most economical quantizer is the one whose Q region has the largest volume for a given r, because it will use the fewest Q regions, and consequently the fewest lattice points or codewords, to cover the space. The volume of the cube, rhombic dodecahedron, and truncated octahedron can be described in terms of the radius r of their circumspheres. For the hexagonal prism, the prism height h must also be considered. However, $h = \sqrt{r}$ maximizes its volume with respect to its circumsphere.

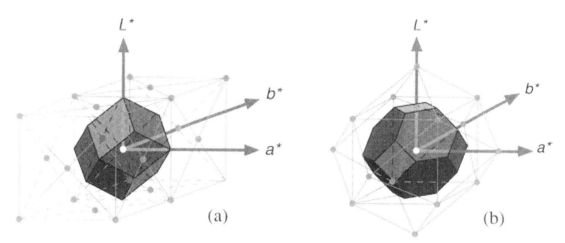

Figure 3. Cubic lattices: face centered (a) and body centered (b).

Table 1 compares the metrics of the four parallelohedra. Column 2 gives the ratio of the maximum distance d between adjacent lattice points (which is equivalent to the quantization step size) to the circumsphere radius r (which is equivalent to the quantization error). Columns 3 and 4 give the volume, normalized for the quantization error r and the maximum adjacent distance d.

According to the table, the truncated octahedron has the largest volume for a given r. If a truncated octahedron and a cube are inscribed inside the same sphere, the volume of the truncated octahedron would be $12\sqrt{3}/5\sqrt{5}$, or 1.86 times that of the cube. This means that a uniform quantizer based on a body-centered cubic lattice would use 53.8% as many codewords to achieve the same minimum error as a quantizer based on a simple cubic lattice.

Similarly, if the quantizer criterion is minimizing the quantization step size (the maximum distance d between adjacent codewords), then the most economical quantizer is

Table 1. Metrics of parallelohedra.

Parallelohedron	d/r ratio	Normalized volume	
		$V(r)/r^3$	$V(d)/d^3$
cube	2	$8/(3\sqrt{3}) \approx 1.54$	$1/(3\sqrt{3}) \approx 0.19$
rhombic dodecahedron	2	2	$1/4 = 0.25$
truncated octahedron	$4/\sqrt{5}$	$32/(5\sqrt{5}) \approx 2.86$	$1/2 = 0.5$
hexagonal prism	$\sqrt{5}$	2	$2/(5\sqrt{5}) \approx 0.18$

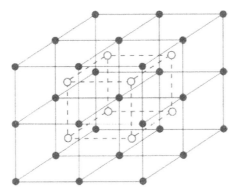

Figure 4.   Body-centered cubic lattice.

the one whose Q region has the largest volume for a given d. Again, it will use the fewest Q regions, and consequently the fewest lattice points or codewords, to cover the space. The table shows that the truncated octahedron has the largest volume for a given d. For the same d, the ratio of the volume of a truncated octahedron to the volume of a cube is $3\sqrt{3}/2$ or 2.60. Therefore, a body-centered cubic lattice quantizer requires 38.5% of the codewords used by a simple cubic lattice quantizer while meeting the same worst-case visibility criterion for quantization contours.

◇   Implementation   ◇

Implementing a body-centered cubic lattice quantizer (Conway and Sloane 1982) is a straightforward task. Figure 4 shows that a body-centered cubic lattice is equivalent to two interlaced simple cubic lattices, A and B, whose lattice points are represented by filled and open circles. The given color is quantized first on lattice A in the usual way by independently quantizing the L^*, a^*, and b^* coordinates. The color is then quantized on lattice B in the same way. If the lattice point on A that is closest to the color is closer to it than the closest lattice point on B, then the closest lattice point on A is returned. Otherwise, the closest lattice point on B is returned. So a body-centered cubic lattice quantizer is equivalent to a program that compares the quantization errors of two simple cubic lattice quantizers.

◇   Related Work   ◇

Color quantization traditionally employs a spatial partitioning, most often the Cartesian product (Paeth 1990b) of three unit intervals of irregular subdivision (Heckbert 1982). These define a cubic lattice formed by parallel cutting planes and having irregular spacing (Paeth 1989). Determination of axis quantization is described in previous gems (Gervautz and Purgathofer 1990, Wu 1990) and elsewhere. A non-Cartesian method based upon the geometry of the cuboctahedron was also described in other gems (Paeth 1990a, 1991). Other geometrical explorations of color quantization are also known (Turkowski 1986). Recent color research at the University of Waterloo explored the OSA space by applying semiregular solids (Lai 1991); reflective color space models based upon parallelotopes and zonotopes have also been employed (Paeth 1994).

◇ Bibliography ◇

(Buckley 1981) Robert Buckley. *Digital Color Image Coding and the Geometry of Color Space*. PhD thesis, Massachusetts Institute of Technology, 1981.

(Buckley 1993) Robert Buckley. The quantization of the CIE uniform color spaces using cubic lattices. In *Colour 93; 7th Congress of the AIC*, pages 246–247. International Colour Association (AIC), June 1993.

(Conway and Sloane 1982) J. H. Conway and N. J. A. Sloane. Fast quantizing and decoding algorithms for lattice quantizers and codes. *IEEE Trans. Inform. Theory*, IT-28(2):227–232, March 1982.

(Coxeter 1973) H. S. M. Coxeter. *Convex Polytopes*. Dover Publications, New York, 1973.

(Gervautz and Purgathofer 1990) Michael Gervautz and Werner Purgathofer. A simple method for color quantization: Octree quantization. In Andrew Glassner, editor, *Graphics Gems*, pages 287–293. AP Professional, Boston, 1990.

(Heckbert 1982) Paul S. Heckbert. Color image quantization for frame buffer display. *Computer Graphics (ACM SIGGRAPH '82 Proceedings)*, 16(3):297–307, July 1982.

(Lai 1991) James W. Lai. Implementation of colour design tools using the OSA Uniform Colour System. Master's thesis, University of Waterloo, 1991.

(Paeth 1989) Alan Wm. Paeth. Algorithms for fast color correction. In *Int. Symp. Digest of Technical Papers*, Volume 30, pages 169–175. Society for Information Display (SID), 3Q 1989.

(Paeth 1990a) Alan Wm. Paeth. Mapping RGB triples onto four bits. In Andrew Glassner, editor, *Graphics Gems*, Chapter 4, pages 233–245. AP Professional, Boston, 1990.

(Paeth 1990b) Alan Wm. Paeth. Proper treatment of pixels as integers. In Andrew Glassner, editor, *Graphics Gems*, pages 254–256. AP Professional, Boston, 1990.

(Paeth 1991) Alan Wm. Paeth. Mapping RGB triples onto 16 distinct values. In James Arvo, editor, *Graphics Gems II*, Chapter 3.5, pages 143–146. AP Professional, Boston, 1991.

(Paeth 1994) Alan Wm. Paeth. *Linear Models of Reflective Colour*. PhD thesis, University of Waterloo, 1994.

(Turkowski 1986) Kenneth Turkowski. Anti-aliasing in topological color spaces. *Computer Graphics (ACM SIGGRAPH '86 Proceedings)*, 20(4), August 1986.

(Wu 1990) Xiaolin Wu. Efficient statistical computations for optimal color quantization. In James Arvo, editor, *Graphics Gems III*, pages 287–293. AP Professional, Boston, 1990.

◊ II.6

Matrix-based Ellipse Geometry

Kenneth J. Hill
Evolution Computing
Scottsdale, Arizona
76667.2576@compuserve.com

This gem introduces the matrix form of the general planar conic section equation. This form is then used to extend the familiar transformation by homogeneous matrices to ellipses, and to find intersections of pairs of ellipses without reference to quartic equations.

◊   Matrix Form of a Planar Conic   ◊

All conic sections (including degenerate forms) can be expressed as a second-degree equation:

$$Ax^2 + 2Bxy + Cy^2 + 2Dx + 2Ey + F = 0. \tag{1}$$

Equation (1) can be written as a matrix equation,

$$\mathbf{X}\mathbf{S}\mathbf{X}^{\mathrm{T}} = 0. \tag{2}$$

Here $\mathbf{S}$ is the symmetric "characteristic matrix" (Rogers and Adams 1990, Hosaka 1990) given by

$$\mathbf{S} = \begin{bmatrix} A & B & D \\ B & C & E \\ D & E & F \end{bmatrix} \quad \text{and} \quad \mathbf{X} = [x \; y \; 1]. \tag{3}$$

◊   Transformation of Ellipses   ◊

One use of the characteristic matrix is to transform conic sections. The most important conic section in computer graphics (excluding the line–a degenerate conic) is the ellipse (including circles). Techniques to transform ellipses are detailed here, although one may extend these methods to parabolas and hyperbolas.

Transformation of Points

Transformation of a point (x, y) to a point (x', y') by equations

$$\begin{aligned} x' &= ax + cy + m \\ y' &= bx + dy + n \end{aligned} \tag{4}$$

is expressed (*op. cit.*) as

$$\mathbf{X'} = \mathbf{XT}, \tag{5}$$

with

$$\mathbf{T} = \begin{bmatrix} a & b & 0 \\ c & d & 0 \\ m & n & 1 \end{bmatrix}, \ \mathbf{X} = \begin{bmatrix} x & y & 1 \end{bmatrix}, \text{ and } \mathbf{X'} = \begin{bmatrix} x' & y' & 1 \end{bmatrix}. \tag{6}$$

The added dimensionality (3×3 for planar operations) allows the expression of translation by vector (m, n) as

$$T_{m,n} = \begin{bmatrix} 1 & 0 & 0 \\ 0 & 1 & 0 \\ m & n & 1 \end{bmatrix}. \tag{7}$$

Forms for rotation, scaling, and shearing resemble their 2×2 analogues, with zeros introduced on the off-diagonal, and unity on the diagonal, that is, rotation by φ:

$$R_\varphi = \begin{bmatrix} \cos\varphi & \sin\varphi & 0 \\ -\sin\varphi & \cos\varphi & 0 \\ 0 & 0 & 1 \end{bmatrix}. \tag{8}$$

Multiplying these elementary matrices together allows one to create more complex transformations. For example, one can rotate by φ around an arbitrary point (m, n) with the transformation

$$\mathbf{X'} = \mathbf{X} T_{-m,-n} R_\varphi T_{m,n}. \tag{9}$$

This equation can be interpreted as: translate from the pivot point to the origin; rotate by φ; translate back.

Transformation of Conics

Conic sections can be transformed using transformation matrices. Consider a point X on a conic section and its image X' under the transformation T (i.e., $\mathbf{X'} = \mathbf{XT}$). Such a point (X) must satisfy $\mathbf{X}\mathbf{S}\mathbf{X}^{\mathrm{T}} = 0$. Assuming that the transformation is invertable,

$\mathbf{X} = \mathbf{XT}^{-1}$ and $\mathbf{X}^{\mathsf{T}} = (\mathbf{XT}^{-1})^{\mathsf{T}} = (\mathbf{T}^{-1})^{\mathsf{T}}\mathbf{X}^{\mathsf{T}}$. Substituting these expressions into (2) gives

$$0 = \mathbf{XT}^{-1}\mathbf{S}(\mathbf{T}^{-1})^{\mathsf{T}}\mathbf{X}^{\mathsf{T}}; \tag{10}$$

hence, the transformed characteristic matrix is $\mathbf{S} = \mathbf{T}^{-1}\mathbf{S}(\mathbf{T}^{-1})^{\mathsf{T}}$. The result of this matrix product is still symmetric, since

$$\mathbf{S}^{\mathsf{T}} = \left[\mathbf{T}^{-1}\mathbf{S}\left(\mathbf{T}^{-1}\right)^{\mathsf{T}}\right]^{\mathsf{T}} = \left(\mathbf{T}^{-1}\right)^{\mathsf{T}\mathsf{T}} \mathbf{S}^{\mathsf{T}} \left(\mathbf{T}^{-1}\right)^{\mathsf{T}} = \mathbf{T}^{-1}\mathbf{S}\left(\mathbf{T}^{-1}\right)^{\mathsf{T}} = \mathbf{S}.$$

Thus, ellipses remain ellipsoidal under general transformation, an important property.

Computing the Characteristic Matrix from Ellipse Parameters

The defining properties of general ellipses may now be examined under arbitrary transformation. Without loss of generality, consider an ellipse symmetric about the origin having semimajor and semiminor axes r_x and r_y parallel to the coordinate axes. That is, the unit circle defined by characteristic matrix

$$\mathbf{S}_u = \begin{bmatrix} 1 & 0 & 0 \\ 0 & 1 & 0 \\ 0 & 0 & -1 \end{bmatrix} \tag{11}$$

is scaled in x by r_x, in y by r_y (matrix σ), and rotated (inclined) by φ (matrix $\mathbf{R}$), giving

$$\mathbf{S}_e = \left(\sigma_{r_x,r_y}\mathbf{R}_\varphi\right)^{-1}\mathbf{S}_u\left[\left(\sigma_{r_x,r_y}\mathbf{R}_\varphi\right)^{-1}\right]^{\mathsf{T}}. \tag{12}$$

Expansion yields

$$\mathbf{S}_e = \begin{bmatrix} \frac{\cos^2\varphi}{r_x^2} + \frac{\sin^2\varphi}{r_y^2} & \left(\frac{1}{r_x^2} - \frac{1}{r_y^2}\right)\sin\varphi\cos\varphi & 0 \\ \left(\frac{1}{r_x^2} - \frac{1}{r_y^2}\right)\sin\varphi\cos\varphi & \frac{\cos^2\varphi}{r_x^2} + \frac{\sin^2\varphi}{r_y^2} & 0 \\ 0 & 0 & -1 \end{bmatrix}. \tag{13}$$

Retrieving Ellipse Parameters from the Characteristic Matrix

Conversely, a characteristic matrix may be converted into ellipse parameters. First select the rotation that diagonalizes the characteristic matrix. It is

$$\varphi = \frac{1}{2} \tan^{-1} \left(\frac{2B}{A - C} \right).$$
(14)

Rotating by $-\varphi$ yields the diagonal characteristic matrix

$$\begin{bmatrix} A & 0 & 0 \\ 0 & B & 0 \\ 0 & 0 & -1 \end{bmatrix},$$
(15)

which represents a coaxial, rectilinear ellipse with semiaxes

$$r_x = A^{-1/2}, \ r_y = C^{-1/2}.$$
(16)

◇ **Intersections of Ellipses** ◇

Unlike finding intersections of two circles or of a line and circle, there is no obvious geometric method to find ellipse–ellipse intersections. One might imagine that one must solve a quartic equation to arrive at the four possible intersection points, but not so. Once again, characteristic matrices offer an elegant means of solution.

Given conic characteristic matrices $\mathbf{S}_1$ and $\mathbf{S}_2$, any point X on their intersection must satisfy both $\mathbf{X}\mathbf{S}_1\mathbf{X}^T = 0$ and $\mathbf{X}\mathbf{S}_2\mathbf{X}^T = 0$. Taking an arbitrary linear combination gives $\alpha\mathbf{X}\mathbf{S}_1\mathbf{X}^T + \beta\mathbf{X}\mathbf{S}_2\mathbf{X}^T = 0$. Factoring out $\mathbf{X}$ and $\mathbf{X}^T$ gives

$$\mathbf{X}(\mathbf{S}_1 + \mu\mathbf{S}_2)\mathbf{X}^T = 0,$$
(17)

where $\mu = \frac{\beta}{\alpha}$. Note that $\mathbf{S}_1 + \mu\mathbf{S}_2$ is symmetric (as any linear combination of symmetric matrices will be), and hence it, too, is a conic characteristic matrix. Thus, the (potentially four) points of intersection lie upon a third conic. Now, $\mathbf{S}_1 + \mu\mathbf{S}_2$ need not define an ellipse, in fact choosing μ so that $S_1 + \mu S_2$ is degenerate is best. This reduces the problem of finding the intersections between two conics to the problem of finding the intersections between a set of lines and a conic (Hosaka 1990).

The algorithm contains four steps:

1. *Transformation*

    Create the conic characteristic matrix as described above. The formulas of the preceding section assume the ellipse center is at the origin, so one must translate both characteristic matrices to their correct centers using

    $$\mathbf{S} = \mathbf{T}_{m,n}^{-1}\mathbf{S}(\mathbf{T}_{m,n}^{-1})^T, \quad \mathbf{T}_{m,n} = \begin{bmatrix} 1 & 0 & 0 \\ 0 & 1 & 0 \\ m & n & 1 \end{bmatrix},$$
    (18)

    where (m, n) is an ellipse center. (This offset will be reapplied to the final solutions.)

2. *Degeneration*

   Solve for μ such that $|\mathbf{S}_1 + \mu \mathbf{S}_2| = 0$ (conics having zero determinant are degenerate). The cubic equation in μ is easily solved using the algorithms presented in gem I.1.

3. *Linearization*

   For each μ found above, interpret the elements (3) of $\mathbf{S}_1 + \mu \mathbf{S}_2$ as a system of lines. The matrix takes three possible forms based on zero elements. To accommodate numerical imprecision, a value V is "approximately zero" when $|V| < \varepsilon$; $\varepsilon = 10^{-3} \operatorname{Min}(r_x, r_y)$ is typical.

   (a) Single Line, $A = B = C = 0$

   $S_1 + \mu S_2$ represents a line having equation $Dx + Ey + F = 0$. Calculate two points on this line: If $-1 \leq -\frac{D}{E} \leq 1$, substitute $x = \{-1, 1\}$ into $y = -\frac{Dx+F}{E}$ to obtain corresponding values of y; otherwise, use $y = \{-1, 1\}$ in $x = -\frac{Ey+F}{D}$ to produce values of x.

   (b) Parallel Lines, $B^2 - AC = 0$

   Rotate by

   $$\varphi = -\frac{1}{2} \tan^{-1} \left(\frac{2B}{A - C} \right) \tag{19}$$

   to make the lines parallel to one of the axes, yielding a matrix of the form

   $$\begin{bmatrix} A & 0 & D \\ 0 & 0 & 0 \\ D & 0 & F \end{bmatrix} \quad \begin{bmatrix} 0 & 0 & 0 \\ 0 & B & E \\ 0 & E & F \end{bmatrix}. \tag{20}$$

   These matrices represent the quadratic equations $Ax^2 + Dx + F = 0$ or $By^2 + Ey + F = 0$ whose roots (r_1 and r_2) determine where the lines cross the x (y) axis. Compute two points on each line [e.g., $(r_1, -1)$, $(r_1, 1)$], and rotate these points by $-\varphi$ back to their original position.

   (c) Crossing Lines, $B^2 - AC > 0$

   $S_1 + \mu S_2$ represents a pair of crossing lines. Rotate by φ as in (b), then translate the intersection to the origin using

   $$m = -\frac{CD - BE}{B^2 - AC},$$

   $$n = -\frac{AE - BD}{B^2 - AC}, \tag{21}$$

   with m and n computed with the rotated coefficients (Rogers and Adams 1990). After the translation, $(0,0)$ and $\left(|A|^{-1/2}, |B|^{-1/2} \right)$ are points on the first line, and $(0, 0)$ and $\left(|A|^{-1/2}, -|B|^{-1/2}\right)$ are points on the second. Again, transform each of these points back to the original position (translate by $(-m, -n)$, rotate by $-\varphi$).

(d) (Else)

Ignore; continue with next μ.

4. *Intersection*

For each line found in (c), calculate the intersections of that line with the first ellipse. This is easily done by transforming the ellipse–line system into a circle–line system, finding the intersections and transforming the points back. Test each intersection point to determine if it is on the second ellipse (again turn the second ellipse into a circle and test against the circle). If so, one of the intersections of the ellipses has been found.

There are several details and optimizations that we leave to the source code listing. The source code can be found in the file `CONMAT.C` on the accompanying disk.

◇ **Acknowledgments** ◇

Thanks are due to Alan Paeth, whose suggestions greatly improved this gem, and to Michael Riddle and Susan Montooth for their support of this effort.

◇ **Bibliography** ◇

(Farin 1988) G. Farin. *Curves and Surfaces for Computer Aided Geometric Design: A Practical Guide*. Academic Press, New York, 1988.

(Hosaka 1990) M. Hosaka. *Modeling of Curves and Surfaces in CAD/CAM*, pages 48–49. Springer, Berlin, 1990.

(Rogers and Adams 1990) D. F. Rogers and J. A. Adams. *Mathematical Elements for Computer Graphics*, pages 87–88, 236–242. McGraw-Hill, New York, 1990.

II.7

Distance Approximations and Bounding Polyhedra

Alan Wm. Paeth
Department of Computer Science
Okanagan University College
Kelowna, British Columbia
awpaeth@okanagan.bc.ca

◇ Introduction ◇

This gem presents an n-dimensional linear approximation that can only overestimate distance, preserving the valuable containment property of the previous 2D method (Paeth 1990a). Whereas the latter was solved using trigonometry, this gem employs geometric methods to derive a family of semiregular polytopes having cubic symmetry. These solids provide a nested sequence of bounding that encases the n-sphere: that locus of points in n-space lying at a unit distance from the origin. As a bonus, the gem provides geometric insight and illustration of the symmetries of the n-dimensional "hypercube" measure solid.

◇ Background ◇

The n-dimensional Manhattan[1] $||\mathbf{X}||_1 = |x_1| + \cdots + |x_n|)$ norm and infinity norm $||\mathbf{X}||_\infty = \lim_{n \to \infty}(|x_1|^n + \cdots + |x_n|^n)^{1/n}$ are computationally attractive. Both may be evaluated using integer arithmetic; the first sums the first n components of $\mathbf{X}$, the second is $\text{Max}(|x_1|, \ldots, |x_n|)$. Each consistently over- and underestimates the distance described by the Euclidean norm $||\mathbf{X}||_2$, as seen in Figure 1.

A linear approximation is a compromise sharing properties of the other two norms: It ranks the component magnitudes (instead of finding merely the maximum), then sums these Manhattan-style subject to weights:

$$||\mathbf{X}||_{approx} = c_1|x_1| + \cdots + c_n|x_n|. \tag{1}$$

In particular, given weight vectors $\mathbf{W}$ with values $(1, 0, \ldots, 0)$ and $(1, \ldots, 1)$ the norms $||X||_\infty$ and $||X||_1$ are rederived, respectively. Previously (*op. cit.*), the tightest solution possible in 2D used the weight set $\mathbf{W} = (1, \tan(\pi/8)) \approx (1, \frac{1}{2})$. The last form

---

[1]This is also known as the "taxicab" norm.

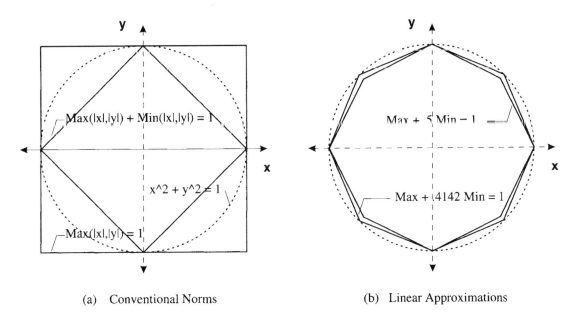

(a) Conventional Norms   (b) Linear Approximations

Figure 1.   Distance metrics in 2D.

rederives the rule-of-thumb method long known in graphics circles; since $\tan(\pi/8) < \frac{1}{2}$, increasing the weight of c_2 can only loosen the approximation, thereby increasing the overestimation and contracting the surface of unit distance, as seen in Figure 1(b).

◇   **Methods of Extension**   ◇

Algebraic Extension

In the first volume of *Graphics Gems* (Glassner 1990), the editor asserts that higher-dimensional distance approximations may be formed by nesting smaller ones. Procedurally, this suggests that dist3(...) may be defined in terms of dist2(...) using two variants:

$$\text{dist3}(x_1, x_2, x_3) = \text{dist2}[\text{dist2}(x_1, x_2), x_3],$$
$$\text{dist3}(x_1, x_2, x_3) = \text{dist2}[x_1, \text{dist2}(x_2, x_3)]. \tag{2}$$

Substituting the previous approximation

$$\text{dist2}(x_1, x_2) = \max(|x_1|, |x_2|) + \tfrac{1}{2} \min(|x_1|, |x_2|) \tag{3}$$

and expanding yields the two candidate approximations

$$\text{dist3}(x_1, x_2, x_3) = \max(|x_1|, |x_2|, |x_3|) + \text{med}(|x_1|, |x_2|, |x_3|) + \tfrac{1}{2}\min(|x_1|, |x_2|, |x_3|),$$
$$\text{dist3}(x_1, x_2, x_3) = \max(|x_1|, |x_2|, |x_3|) + \tfrac{1}{2}\text{med}(|x_1|, |x_2|, |x_3|) + \tfrac{1}{2}\min(|x_1|, |x_2|, |x_3|).$$

$$(4)$$

Remarkably, the conjecture holds for the traditional metrics, provides excellent solutions in the approximate 3D case, and is false. To disprove the assertion, consider the form in (4b) above in 4D, operating on the vector $\mathbf{X} = (1, 1, 1, 1)$. The vector defines the body diagonal of a hypercube and has a (Euclidean) length of two. The approximation employs the weight set $\mathbf{W} = (1, \tfrac{1}{2}, \tfrac{1}{4}, \tfrac{1}{8})$, giving an estimated length of $15/8 < 2$, underestimating the length, and the assertion fails. (In higher dimensions the length of the body diagonal grows arbitrarily large, while the approximation is still bounded by the value two.)

The underlying reason for failure is subtle: The partial component magnitudes computed by the nested dist2() in (4b) have a range that is sufficient to alter their proper position in the terms. Put another way, ranking all n component magnitudes constitutes a sort, requiring $O(n \log n)$ steps. However, unrolling the sequence of nested function calls would provide a straight-line implementation requiring only $O(n)$ max and min operations, which are insufficient to support the sort having an $O(n \log n)$ bound.

Geometric Extension

The geometric extension to 3D considers the locus of points $\mathbf{X} = (x_1, x_2, x_3)$ having a unit length under the approximation. Substituting the weight vector linear sum is a dot product, giving the equation of a plane not passing through the origin:

$$\mathbf{W} \cdot \mathbf{X} = 1 \quad \text{with} \quad x_1 \geq x_2 \geq x_3. \tag{5}$$

The left-hand side (5a) defines a plane; the right-hand (5b) sets limits on the range of coordinates within the plane, forming a polygon. Moreover, (5a) admits solutions having eightfold symmetry ($\pm x_1, \pm x_2, \pm x_3$). Likewise, (5b) admits the sixfold symmetry created when permuting the three components. In general, the defining (hyper)plane for any solution remains valid as long as the component ordering is preserved. At its limits, when two components are equal (e.g., $x_1 = x_2$), the original ordering in (5b) also holds for a second limit, for example, $x_2 \geq x_1 \geq x_3$. Since both hold concurrently, these define a line of intersection of the weight plane $W \cdot X = 1$ with the symmetry plane $x_1 = x_2$.

The symmetry planes seen above are present in any n-space. Sign complementation yields the 2^n-fold cubic symmetry planes related to the (nonunit) hypercube having vertices $(\pm 1, \ldots, \pm 1)$, which is the regular measure solid (Coxeter 1973) present in any n-space. The second set are the $(n!)$-fold symmetry planes that describe an irregular cross solid, the dual (*op. cit.*) of an n-dimensional rectangular brick.[2]

With both this geometric symmetry and the original overestimation constraint, an analytical solution may now be constructed. In 1D, all norms are equivalent and $w_1 = 1$, trivially. In 2D, the "fold-over" point where the components of $\mathbf{X}$ change order occurs along the line $x_1 = x_2$, accounting for the exact solution appearing in Figure 1(b). This introduces the new weight $w_2 = \sqrt{2} - 1$.

In 3D the solution is a polyhedron. Cartesian symmetry indicates that a regular octagon lying in the z (flatland) plane appearing in Figure 1(b) must occupy the x and y planes as well—that is, the evaluation of dist3$(1, 1, 0)$ must be invariant under parameter permutation. This constraint ensures that any solution in a higher dimension rederives one in the lower where trailing components are elided. Geometrically, this zero substitution projects the figure onto a plane containing the Cartesian axes.

The trial polyhedron created in this fashion has eighteen vertices ($3 \times 8 - 6$; less six because each octahedral vertex is counted twice). This is not the desired solid, which by the previous symmetry conditions should have additional vertices (this vertex tally is not rigorous: A large number of redundant vertices could be present). Its convex hull shows that its greatest departure from the sphere occurs near the body diagonals of an encasing cube. In fact, the missing vertices are the extreme crossover points found when $x_1 = x_2 = x_3$ along the body diagonal of an encasing cube. When one solves for correct distance, the ones-vector $\mathbf{V} = (1, 1, 1)$ has a distance of $\sqrt{3}$. The exact fit may now be found by determining the value of w_3 that admits this solution, thus providing both an exact fit along the symmetry planes while preserving the lower-dimensional solutions. Based on previous weights, the required value is $w_3 = \sqrt{3} - \sqrt{2}$.

In all dimensions, the length estimation of $x = (\pm 1, \ldots, \pm 1)$ invokes the solution of the plane equation (5) regardless of component permutation. That is, this vertex is common to all the weight planes and hence is the extreme point not present in the trial solid now introduced by dimensional increase. Put another way, changing any of the n components of this ones-vector by ϵ crosses over to one of n plane equations, whose intersection is n-space. Since multiplicity reduces dimensionality, these define a feature of dimension $n - n$, a (nondegenerate) point.

---

[2]The regular cross solid in three-space is the octahedron, whose vertices are the permutations of $(\pm 1, 0, 0)$.

Table 1.		Exact weights for encasing polytopes.			
n	1	2	3	4	5
$\sqrt{n}$	1	1.4142	1.7321	2.0000	2.2362
$\mathbf{w_n}$	**1**	**.4142**	**.3178**	**.2679**	**.2361**
error	1.0	1.082	1.128	1.159	1.183

The complete solution may be created by computing the exact lengths of the ones-vector $\mathbf{V}$ and adjusting the succession of weight accordingly, giving the exact solution

$$w_n = \sqrt{n} - \sqrt{n-1}. \tag{6}$$

These are presented in Table 1.

◇   Geometrical Analysis   ◇

In the 3D case, the hull of the solid formed by three mutually perpendicular and interlocking octagons accommodates these eight additional vertices of cubic symmetry. The new solid has twenty-six vertices and may be regarded as the superposition of the cube's mid-faces (six), mid-edges (twelve), and vertices (eight), in which each point group (in the first octant) lies along the respective vectors $(1,0,0)$, $(1,1,0)$, and $(1,1,1)$. Adding the origin $(0,0,0)$ as a twenty-seventh point forms a $3 \times 3 \times 3$ point lattice and demonstrates the decomposition of the three-cube into its forty-eight ($2^n n!$) Dirichlet cells, which are tetrahedra whose four vertices are taken from the vector set presented immediately above. This may be easily generalized. For instance, the four-cube contains cells having the five vertices $(0,0,0,0)$ through $(1,1,1,1)$ (ones are shifted in from the left); the related sum is

$$2^1 C(n,1) + 2^2 C(n,2) + 2^3 C(n,3) + 2^4(n,3) = 3^n - 1 = 80, \tag{7}$$

as expected. (Here C(i,j) is the choose function.)

Adjusting the vertices so that each is a unit-length vector is akin to a spherical projection of the vertices of the Dirichlet cell (see also page 68). This forms a solid having vertices

$$(1,0,0), \quad (\sqrt{2},\sqrt{2}), \quad (\sqrt{3},\sqrt{3},\sqrt{3}) \tag{8}$$

taking under all permutations and sign alternations. The solid is a hexakis octahedron having twenty-six vertices (Color Plate II.7). Through largely geometrical means, its vertex components have been presented in exact form, as with related gems (Paeth 1990c, 1991).

Substitution of other weights forms distinct yet related solids, as seen in Figure 2. For example, setting $w_2 = w_3$ yields coincident vertices by symmetry, thereby reducing the total number of faces. Put another way, the points defining a triangle converge to a

Family of surfaces (r,s) which solve

$$Max(|x|,|y|,|z|) + r\,Med(,,,) + s\,Min(,,,) = 1,$$

The vertices of the surfaces' convex hull are

$$(1,0,0), \quad (u,u,0), \quad (v,v,v),$$

in all sign alternations and permutations, with

$$u = 1/(r+1), \quad v = 1/(r+s+1).$$

Legend

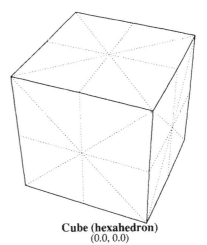

Cube (hexahedron)
(0.0, 0.0)

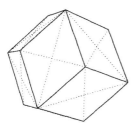

Rhombic Dodecahedron
(1.0, 0.0)

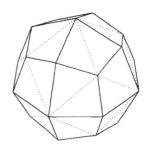

Trapezoidal Icositetrahedron
(sqrt(2)-1, sqrt(2)-1)

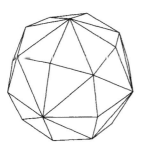

Hexakis Octahedron
(sqrt(2)-1, sqrt(3)-sqrt(2))

Octahedron
(1.0, 1.0)

Figure 2.   Semiregular solids of cubic symmetry in 3D.

single vertex, "collapsing" the face. Setting $w_2 = w_3 = \sqrt{2} - 1$ forms the dual of a cubic rhombidodecahedron, called a trapezoidal icositetrahedron, seen in Figure 2(d). Coxeter regards $\mathbf{W} - (1, 1, 0)$ as "nearly" a Platonic solid analogous to the regular 24-cell.[3]

◇ **Error Estimation** ◇

Error estimation is elegantly supported by the geometric method. Previously, the 2D case found the point of greatest deviation at 22.5°, for which the maximum error is $\tan(\pi/8) = \sqrt{2} - 1$. Although this point can be located by symmetry considerations of the solution in Figure 1(b), this does not generalize easily to higher dimensions. (That is, the trigonometric solution previously employed is now a minimization in multiple variables.)

Geometrically, a surface reaches its extrema relative to some point when the segment spanning the point's segment is perpendicular to the surface. The encasing unit sphere lies at a constant distance and hence is everywhere perpendicular to an origin vector. In contrast, the bounding solid has faces whose point minimum distance is indicated by the normal vector of their defining plane equation, as in (5a). Since this vector is perpendicular both to the face and to the sphere, it defines the span of greatest deviation between both. The normal vector is the weight vector, so the distance ratio of a (nonunit) vector $\mathbf{W}$ is $\|\mathbf{W}\|_{approx}/\|W\|_2$. These appear as the "max dev." ratios appearing in Table 1. As the relative length is in reference to a unit sphere, the absolute deviation (span length) can be found by subtracting these values into one (the sphere's radius).

The point of closest approach exists on every face on the solid circumscribed by the sphere. Moreover, each lies at the same origin distance: A smaller sphere may be inscribed. In fact, these points of contact can serve as vertices defining the convex hull of the (inscribed) dual. The solid is the dual rhombidodecahedron having forty-eight vertices. Through largely geometrical means, the components of its vertices have been determined. These are

$$(\pm 1, \pm[\sqrt{2} - 1], \pm[\sqrt{3} - \sqrt{2}]) \quad \text{(all permutations)}. \tag{9}$$

The number of faces is necessarily twenty-six; dualization is a self-complementary operation that exchanges the meaning of face and vertex and in/circum-sphere. Both solids have seventy-two edges by Euler's formula $F + V = E - 2$, which is invariant under dualization. (The edges may be grouped together in space and are oriented at right angles to each other.)

---

[3]This self-dual analogue can be related both to the weight set $\mathbf{W} = (1, 1, 0, 0)$ and to the quaternions.

Implementation

The best solution has irrational values (these define the vertex positions of the unit cubic rhombidodecahedron). Although valuable in its own right, the related code embodies floating-point calculations, thereby defeating the gem's original purpose: to provide a fast approximation using integer[4] arithmetic.

Instead, the coefficients c_i may be increased at will. This loosens slightly the exact containment (which is an inexact approximation) and thus allows integral and rational solutions (see also Figure 1). By inspection, the weight set $W = (1, 0.5)$ is a good choice in 2D. In 3D, the weight set $\mathbf{W} = (1, 0.5, 0.25)$ is particularly attractive, because $\|(1, 1, 1)\| = \sqrt{3} \approx 1.732 < 1.75$ is a good fit and the method may take advantage of bit shifts to have components of diminishing magnitude.

In four dimensions, methods of rational approximation (see also page 25) may be used to find computationally attractive forms. Exhaustive searching is still required because the continuants for each weight tend to have distinct denominators and the GCD of the weight set tends to form unattractively large values. Hand analysis yields the particularly compelling weights

$$w_1 = 1, \quad w_2 = \frac{5}{12}, \quad w_3 = \frac{19}{60}, \quad w_4 = \frac{4}{15}. \tag{10}$$

Note that $w_3 = 3.1\bar{6}$ slightly underestimates $\sqrt{3} - \sqrt{2} = .3178+$. However, the previous overestimation in $w_2 = 4.1\bar{6}$ versus $.41421+$ is enough to overcome the loss. That is, the bounding solid draws in from the sphere along the axes $(1, 1, 0, 0)$, providing for an otherwise oversize weight when dist4 is evaluated with $(1, 1, 1, 0)$. As a final bonus, the four-vector $(1, 1, 1, 1)$ has integral length, so an exact fit is possible as the numerator of w_4 has an exact integral value. The program code is then

$$\text{dist4}(x_1, x_2, x_3, x_4) = |x_1| + 1/60(25 |x_2| + 19 |x_3| + 16 |x_4|), \tag{11}$$

where it is assumed that the components of $\mathbf{X}$ are sorted by magnitude, an operation that may take place in five comparisons (the minimum) using merely swap operations; the swap/sort operations are borrowed from the implementation appearing in a previous gem (Paeth 1990b), and are employed below.

◇ C Implementation ◇

```
#define absv(x) if (x < 0) x = -x
#define inorder(x,y) {int t; if ((t = a - b) < 0) {a -= t; b += t; } }
```

---

[4]The admission of floating point allows an exact Euclidean norm at a cost of only $n+6$ multiplications, with n the cost of the dot product and 6 the overhead for an efficient square root, as on page 16.

```
len4(a, b, c, d)
{
        absv(a); absv(b);                  /* get the absolute values */
        absv(c); absv(d);                  /* (component magnitudes) */
        inorder(a, b); inorder(c, d);      /* everyone has a chance to play */
        inorder(a, c); inorder(b, d);      /* (a,d) are big (winner, loser) */
        inorder(b, c);                     /* playoff for 2nd and 3rd slots */
        a += (25*b + 19*c + 16*d)/60;      /* compute 4D approximate length */
        a++;                               /* Roundoff -> underestimation */
        return(a);                         /* omit the above one bit jitter */
}
```

◇ Conclusions ◇

In higher dimensions the weight equation (6) shows that weights diminish slowly, and the added complexity of both magnitude computation and element sorting strongly favor the use of the Euclidean norm in floating point. Finally, the values for 3D linear approximation provided by Ritter (*op. cit.*) were created by empirical testing.[5] This method provides a means of exact computation.

◇ Bibliography ◇

(Coxeter 1973) H. S. M. Coxeter. *Regular Polytopes.* Dover, New York, 1973.

(Glassner 1990) Andrew Glassner. Distance measures summary (section introduction). In Andrew Glassner, editor, *Graphics Gems*, page 423. AP Professional, Boston, 1990.

(Paeth 1990a) Alan Wm. Paeth. A fast approximation to the hypotenuse. In Andrew Glassner, editor, *Graphics Gems*, Chapter 8, pages 427–431. AP Professional, Boston, 1990.

(Paeth 1990b) Alan Wm. Paeth. Median finding on a 3 × 3 grid. In Andrew Glassner, editor, *Graphics Gems*, Chapter 3, pages 171–175. AP Professional, Boston, 1990.

(Paeth 1990c) Alan Wm. Paeth. Trigonometric functions at select points. In Andrew Glassner, editor, *Graphics Gems*, Chapter 1, pages 18–19. AP Professional, Boston, 1990.

---

[5]The authors exchanged ideas by telephone in collaboration after the back-to-back publication of their independent gems.

(Paeth 1991) Alan Wm. Paeth. Exact dihedral metrics for common polyhedra. In James Arvo, editor, *Graphics Gems II*, Chapter 4.3, pages 1–2. AP Professional, Boston, 1991.

(Ritter 1990) Jack Ritter. An efficient bounding sphere. In Andrew Glassner, editor, *Graphics Gems*, Chapter 5, pages 301–303. AP Professional, Boston, 1990.

◇ **III** ◇
Modeling and
Transformation

The gems in this section describe algebraic models and their transformations. In most cases a linear algebra underlies the derivations, supporting a natural extension to higher dimensions, as with gems II.4 and II.7 of the previous section.

In the first gem (III.1), Alciatore and Miranda apply the method of least squares to fit a line to a set of points. What is unique is that perpendicular distance is chosen to create a true isotropic fit, not a conventional fit by abscissa. Hill and Roberts (III.2) review modeling methods related to the marching cubes method in which slope discontinuities and their ambiguities arise. These occur at the adjoining boundaries between the discrete cells that collectively approximate a continuous surface. Arata provides a straightforward study of tri-cubic interpolation, whereby a set of gridded data takes on a higher dimensional fit (compared with commonplace tri-linear methods). Catmull-Rom splines are the model of choice; their coefficients suggest particularly fast evaluation. Miller (III.4) describes the affine mapping between related point sets on two distinct Cartesian planes. This overdetermined problem arises with noisy data. His first-principles approach illustrates matrix-based singular value decomposition (SVD) while providing a freestanding C implementation requiring no external matrix library. Chin provides a thorough description of BSP trees (III.5). The worked examples are carefully illustrated and treat all the conventional cases (e.g, preprocessing interpenetrating data; locating the tree's root) plus a number of optimizations. A C-language suite (excerpted throughout the text) completes the work. Blanc's discussion of axial deformation techniques (III.6) describes the procedural manipulation of data sets by transformations more intuitive than the mathematician's. Based upon a model that minimizes artifacts of the underlying coordinate system, the axial deformations include bending, twisting, and pinching.

III.1

The Best Least-Squares Line Fit

David Alciatore

Mechanical Engineering Department
Colorado State University
Fort Collins, Colorado

Rick Miranda

Mathematics Department
Colorado State University
Fort Collins, Colorado

◇ Introduction ◇

Traditional approaches for fitting least-squares lines to a set of two-dimensional data points involve minimizing the sum of the squares of the minimum vertical distances between the data points and the fitted line. That is, the fit is against a set of independent observations in the range[1] y. This gem presents a numerically stable algorithm that fits a line to a set of ordered pairs (x, y) by minimizing its least-squared distance to each point without regard to orientation. This is a true 2D point-fitting method exhibiting rotational invariance.

◇ Background ◇

The classical formula for the univariate case based on vertical error measurement is

$$y = m_y x + b_y, \tag{1}$$

$$m_y = \frac{N \sum x_i y_i - \sum x_i \sum y_i}{N \sum x_i^2 - \left(\sum x_i\right)^2},$$

$$b_y = \frac{\sum y_i \sum x_i^2 - \sum x_i \sum x_i y_i}{N \sum x_i^2 - \left(\sum x_i\right)^2}.$$

Though well known, and presented in many numerical, statistical, and analytical texts (Charpra and Canale 1988, Chatfield 1970, Kryszig 1983), the method is not acceptable as a general line-fitting tool. Its frequent misapplication gives poor results when both coordinates are uncertain or when the line to be fit is near vertical ($m_y \to \infty$). Reversing the axes merely disguises the problem: The method still remains sensitive to the orientation of the coordinate system.

A least-squares line-fitting method that is insensitive to coordinate system orientation can be constructed by minimizing instead the sum of the squares of the perpendicular

---

[1]Horizontal distances can also be used by reversing the roles of the variables.

distances between the data points and their nearest points on the target line. (The perpendiculars are geometric features of the model independent of the coordinate system.) Such an algorithm has been presented in the literature (Ehrig 1985), but the algorithm is based on a slope–intercept form of the line resulting in solution degeneracy and numerical inaccuracies; as the line approaches vertical, the slope and intercept grow without bound. Also, the equations provided (*op. cit.*) have two solutions, and the user must perform a test to determine the correct one.

The algorithm presented in the next section uses a θ–ρ (line angle, distance from the origin) parameterization of the line that results in no degenerate cases and gives a unique solution. This parameterization has been used for statistical fitting of noisy data with outlying points as in image data (Weiss 1988, Rosenfeld and Sher 1986), but the parameterization has not been applied to a least-squares line fit.

The perpendicular error measurement least-squares technique is also readily applied to circular arc fitting. Several robust solutions to this problem have been presented in the literature (Karimaki 1992, Moura and Kitney 1991, Chernov and Ososkov 1984).

◇ Optimal Least-Squares Fit ◇

The problem may now be stated. Given an arbitrary line defined by parameters (θ, ρ) and the sum of the squares of the related perpendicular distances r_i between points (x_i, y_i) and their nearest points to this line (Figure 1), then find the values of θ and ρ that minimize this sum. That is, minimize the value

$$Z = \sum_{i=1}^{N} r_i^2(\rho, \theta); \tag{2}$$

where N is the number of data points to be fitted and r_i is a function of the chosen line. Locating the zeros of the derivative of this function forms the method of solution.

To simplify the analysis and to avoid degeneracies, the parameter ρ is chosen to be the length of a perpendicular erected between the line and the origin, and θ is chosen to be its orientation with respect to the x axis (Figure 1). From simple plane geometry, the parametric equation for the line is given by

$$x s_\theta + y c_\theta + \rho = 0, \tag{3}$$

where

$$c_\theta = \cos(\theta) \text{ and } s_\theta = \sin(\theta). \tag{4}$$

The perpendicular distance r_i is given by

$$r_i = y_i c_\theta - x_i s_\theta - \rho. \tag{5}$$

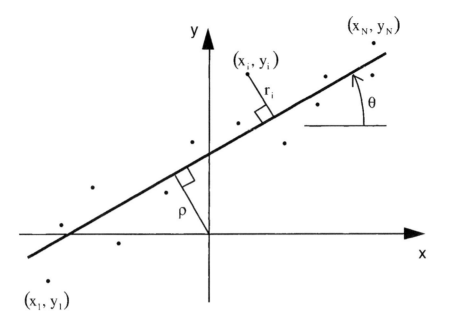

Figure 1. Least-squares line fit geometry.

To minimize the sum of errors Z in (2), the following must hold:

$$\frac{\partial Z}{\partial \theta} = 0 \text{ and } \frac{\partial Z}{\partial \rho} = 0. \tag{6}$$

Taking derivatives of (2) using (5) results in the following expressions:

$$ac_\theta s_\theta + b(s_\theta^2 - c_\theta^2) + c\rho c_\theta + d\rho s_\theta = 0 \tag{7}$$

and

$$dc_\theta - cs_\theta = N\rho, \tag{8}$$

where

$$a = \sum_{i=1}^{N} x_i^2 \quad \sum_{i=1}^{N} y_i^2, b \quad \sum_{i=1}^{N} s_i y_i, c = \sum_{i=1}^{N} x_i, \text{ and } d = \sum_{i=1}^{N} y_i. \tag{9}$$

Equation (8) can be written as

$$\overline{x} s_\theta - \overline{y} c_\theta + \rho = 0, \tag{10}$$

where $(\bar{x}, \bar{y})$ is the centroid of the data set $\{(x_i, y_i)\}$. Since (10) appears in the form presented in (3), the fit necessarily passes through the centroid of the data.

Equation (7) can be simplified if the original data are translated so that the centroid is located at the origin, by setting

$$x_i' = x_i - \bar{x} \text{ and } y_i' = y_i - \bar{y}. \tag{11}$$

This translation results in

$$c' = d' = \rho' = 0, \tag{12}$$

and (7) reduces to

$$a' c_\theta s_\theta + b'(s_\theta^2 - c_\theta^2) = 0, \tag{13}$$

where

$$a' = \sum_{i=1}^{N} (x_i')^2 - \sum_{i=1}^{N} (y_i')^2 \text{ and } b' = \sum_{i=1}^{N} x_i' y_i'. \tag{14}$$

Equation (13) is a quadratic equation that can be solved for the ratio c_θ / s_θ, giving

$$\frac{c_\theta}{s_\theta} = \frac{\alpha \pm \gamma}{\beta}, \tag{15}$$

where

$$\alpha = a', \beta = 2b', \text{ and } \gamma = \sqrt{\alpha^2 + \beta^2}. \tag{16}$$

Equation (15) can be written as

$$c_\theta = t(\alpha \pm \gamma) \text{ and } s_\theta = t\beta, \tag{17}$$

where t is a constant satisfying the condition $s_\theta^2 + c_\theta^2 = 1$. One of these solutions is the minimum of (2) representing the best-fit line, and the other is a maximum representing the worst-fit line passing through the centroid of the data. It should be noted that this worst-fit line is always perpendicular to the best-fit line since the solutions of Equation (15) (which represent the line slopes) are negative reciprocals of each other. To determine which solution represents the best-fit line (other than by graphical inspection of the data), the second-derivative test can be employed. The following must hold:

$$\frac{\partial^2 Z}{\partial \theta^2} > 0. \tag{18}$$

The second derivative of the error function gives

$$\frac{\partial^2 Z}{\partial \theta^2} = 2\alpha(c_\theta^2 - s_\theta^2) + 4\beta c_\theta s_\theta. \tag{19}$$

After substituting (17) and simplifying, the second-derivative test (18) reduces to

$$t^2 \gamma^2 (\alpha \pm \gamma) > 0. \tag{20}$$

This forces $\alpha \pm \gamma > 0$, and since $\gamma > \alpha$, the $\alpha + \gamma$ solution represents the best-fit line. Therefore, the best-fit line [in the form of (3) and (17)] is defined by

$$\beta x - (\alpha + \gamma)y = -\rho/t = C, \tag{21}$$

where C is a constant that can be determined (10) by requiring that the line pass through the centroid:

$$C = \beta \bar{x} - (\alpha + \gamma)\bar{y}. \tag{22}$$

Therefore, from (16) and (21), the constants defining the best-fit line in standard form are

$$A = 2b', \tag{23}$$

$$B = -\left(a' + \sqrt{(a')^2 + 4(b')^2}\right),$$

$$C = A\bar{x} + B\bar{y}.$$

◇ **Example** ◇

The following data will be used to demonstrate the results of the method:

i	x_i	y_i
1	0.237	−1.000
2	0.191	−0.833
3	0.056	−0.667
4	0.000	−0.500
5	0.179	−0.333
6	0.127	−0.167
7	0.089	0.000
8	0.136	0.167
9	0.202	0.333
10	0.085	0.500
11	0.208	0.667
12	0.156	0.833
13	0.038	1.000

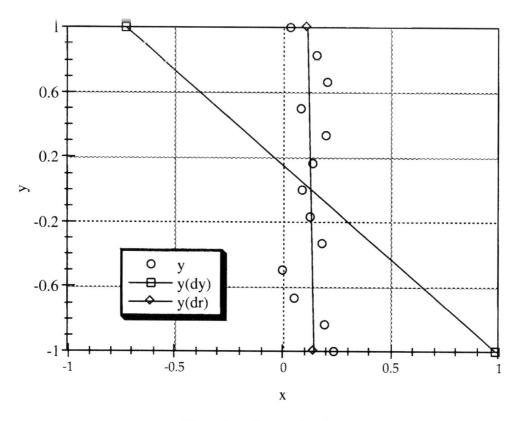

Figure 2.   Example line fit.

The centroid of this data is located at

$$\bar{x} = 0.131, \bar{y} = 0.000.$$

Expressed in tems of (14), this gives

$$a' = -4.992 \quad \text{and} \quad b' = -0.075,$$

and so from (23) the final solution is

$$A = -0.149, B = -0.002, \text{ and } \quad C = -0.020.$$

This line $(Ax + By = C)$ is plotted in Figure 2 along with the results from Equation (1) for purposes of comparison. The original $y = m_y x + b_y$ fit afforded by (1) is extremely poor since the data lie near a vertical line.

◇ **Conclusions** ◇

The method for determining the line passing through a two-dimensional data set and having best least-squares fit was derived. This line's orientation minimizes the sum of the squares of the perpendicular distances between the data and the line. A ρ-θ parameterization of the line resulted in a fairly straightforward analysis. The results, which were expressed in standard $(Ax + By = C)$ form, provide a unique, general, and robust solution that is free of degenerate cases. The only possible indeterminacy occurs when $a' = b' = 0$. However, this case can occur only when the data exhibit a perfect circular symmetry (isomorphism under arbitrary rotation). In this case, there is no line of "best fit" because all lines passing through the centroid have a fit that is equally good or bad.

◇ **Bibliography** ◇

(Charpra and Canale 1988) S. Charpra and R. Canale. *Numerical Methods for Engineers*, 2nd ed. McGraw-Hill, 1988.

(Chatfield 1970) C. Chatfield. *Statistics for Technology*. Penguin Books, 1970.

(Chernov and Ososkov 1984) N. Chernov and G. Ososkov. Effective algorithm for circle fitting. *Computer Physics Communications*, 33:329–333, 1984.

(Ehrig 1985) H. Ehrig. 45th annual meeting of the ACMS. Technical report, ACMS, 1985.

(Karimaki 1992) V. Karimaki. Fast code to fit circular arcs. *Computer Physics Communications*, 69:133–141, 1992.

(Kryszig 1983) E. Kryszig. *Advanced Engineering Mathematics*, 5th ed. John Wiley and Sons, 1983.

(Moura and Kitney 1991) L. Moura and R. Kitney. A direct method for least-squares circle fitting. *Computer Physics Communications*, 64:57–63, 1991.

(Rosenfeld and Sher 1986) A. Rosenfeld and A. Sher. Direction weighted line fitting to edge data. Technical Report CAR-TR-189, Computer Vision Laboratory, University of Maryland, 1986.

(Weiss 1988) I. Weiss. Straight line fitting in a noisy image. In *Proceedings of IEEE Conference on Computer Vision and Pattern Recognition*, pages 647–652, 1988.

◊ III.2

Surface Models and the Resolution of *N*-Dimensional Cell Ambiguity

Steve Hill
Computing Laboratory
University of Kent
United Kingdom

Jonathan C. Roberts
Computing Laboratory
University of Kent
United Kingdom

◊ Introduction ◊

The representation of n-dimensional continuous surfaces often employs a discrete lattice of n-dimensional cube cells. For instance, the marching cubes method locates the surface lying between adjacent vertices of the n-cube edges in which the cell vertices represent discrete sample values (Lorensen and Cline 1987). The volume's surface exists at a point of zero value: It intersects any cube edge whose vertex values have opposing sign.

Ambiguities occur in the cells whose vertex sets show many sign alternations. Geometrically, the surface intersects one face of the n-cube through each of its four edges. It is these special cases that engender the need for resolution as a central concern in surface modeling. This gem reviews and illustrates the disambiguation strategies described in the literature.

◊ Background ◊

In an ideal surface algorithm, the features of the surface geometry should match those of the underlying surface. In particular, if the original surface is continuous, the representational model must preserve this continuity. Most practical algorithms create spurious holes (false negatives) or additional surfaces (false positives) depending on the "eagerness" of the algorithm in joining pieces of the surface model along adjacent cube faces. This is the consequence known as the "ambiguous face" n-cube present in any dimension $n \geq 2$ whose vertex signs resemble a spatial "checkerboard" (Figure 1). The abutting of two cubes having such faces then introduces the possibility of false positives or negatives (Figure 2).

In this gem, we refer to the vertex classification with respect to the threshold as *inside* or *outside* the surface. The surface intersects the edge between an *inside* and an

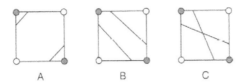

Figure 1.   Ambiguous face choices.

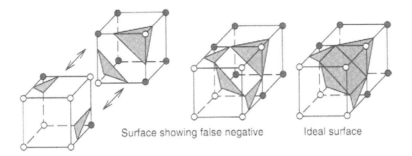

Surface showing false negative   Ideal surface

Figure 2.   Ambiguous face.

outside vertex, shown gray on the diagrams; linear interpolation is used to calculate this position. The ambiguous face can be estimated using the vertex classification, but can never be completely disambiguated.

The local surface contours can be represented by sections of a hyperbola and the ambiguous face can be one of three orientations (Figure 1); therefore, the cross representation is the other orientations taken to the limit and is normally discarded.

The cells can be subdivided into further *n*-cubes or into simplices. A simplex is the simplest nondegenerate object in *n* dimensions (Hanson 1994, Moore 1992a), for example, a triangle in two dimensions and a tetrahedron in three dimensions. A simplex is always unambiguous and so can be used in an *n*-cube disambiguation strategy.

◇ Static Analysis ◇

To disambiguate the ambiguous face, the static techniques consider only the vertex classification points; they do not introduce extra classification points. These methods are generally fast, but they do not guarantee an ideal or faithful surface.

Uniform Orientation

Always present the surface at a common orientation whenever the evaluation of an ambiguous face is encountered. Computation of orientation can be implemented using a lookup table (Lorensen and Cline 1987) or by algorithm (Wyvill *et al.* 1986, Bloomenthal 1988, Bloomenthal 1994). If the data resolution is high, the surface segments will be

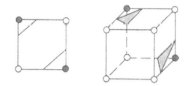

Figure 3. Uniform orientation.

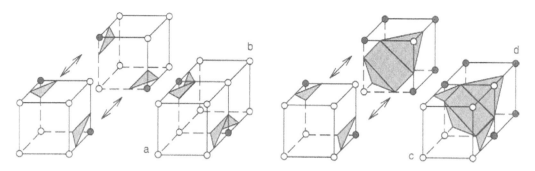

Figure 4. Adjacent cell disambiguation.

small and the anomalies unnoticeable (unless the surface is zoomed). This method is simple to implement and is fast to execute (Figure 3).

Face Adjacency

In some cases the adjacent cell configuration can be used to disambiguate the n-cube (Duurst 1988, Zahlten 1992); for example, if an "inverted" cube and a "normal" cube orientation are adjacent, then the surface should be added (Figure 4). The new surface intersects the diagonal between the nonadjacent vertices c and d, where vertex d is *inside* and vertex c is *outside* the surface.

Simplex Decomposition

In two dimensions the square can be decomposed into two triangle segments and treated as by the uniform orientation method. In three dimensions the cube has many decompositions into tetrahedra (Moore 1992b, 1992a) (Figure 5); examples of five tetrahedra (Ning and Bloomenthal 1993) and six tetrahedra (Zahlten 1992) behave like the fixed orientation method in that they add an extra diagonal that affects the connectivity of the surface. The orientation of the diagonal is determined by the simplex decomposition. To maintain surface consistency, neighboring n-cubes should have the same diagonal orientation (mirrored simplex orientation).

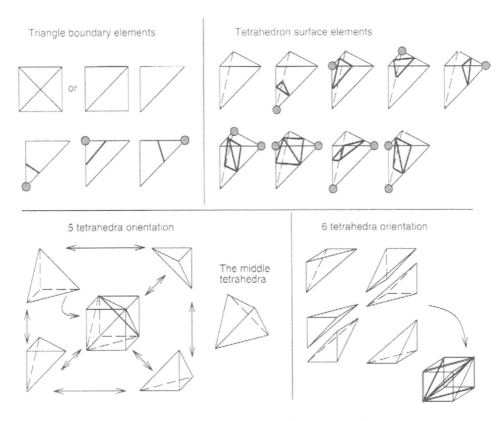

Figure 5. Simplex decompositions, and surfaces.

◇ Interpolation Analysis ◇

This section reviews disambiguation techniques that require the computation of additional values or vertices for the decision. The values are often created by methods of trilinear interpolation (Hill 1994). Other interpolation techniques may also be considered (e.g., tricubic interpolation, gem III.3).

Closest Orientation

The four face intersection points are located by linear interpolation, the total length of the connecting paths calculated, and the orientation having the shortest path is chosen (Mackerras 1992). If both paths are the same length, then the cross configuration is chosen (Cottifava and Moli 1969). In Figure 1, the closest orientation technique would select configuration A.

Resampling

The data are resampled at a higher resolution and solution reattempted. This is possible only when the data are algorithmically obtained or readily resampled. Moreover, ambiguities may still remain at the higher resolution.

Interpolation

The data resolution is doubled using a trilinear interpolation (Hill 1994) or a tricubic interpolation. The tricubic interpolation considers points outside the local neighbors. As with the resampling technique, ambiguities may still occur at the finer resolution. (A variation reinterpolates merely the ambiguous cells.)

Subdivision

All the n-cubes that are on the surface are subdivided (using linear interpolation) until a predefined limit is reached. The limit can be the pixel size, for example, dividing cubes (Cline *et al.* 1988), or smaller (Cook *et al.* 1987). Each subcube is *inside*, *outside*, or *on* the surface and may be shaded and projected onto the view plane. Trilinear interpolation cannot introduce an ambiguous case, but might not (therefore) faithfully model the surface. However, adaptive subdivision techniques (using interpolation or resampling methods) can be used at points of great interest or high curvature (Bloomenthal 1988).

Simplex Decomposition

In two dimensions the two-cube can be decomposed into two or four triangles (Figure 5); with two triangles the method is similar to the uniform orientation strategy, but with four triangles an extra center vertex is required. This can be obtained by averaging the four vertices (that is, from bilinear interpolation). If the center value is *inside* the threshold, then orientation *B* is chosen; otherwise, orientation *A* is used (Figure 1). This method is often named "facial average" and can be used on any n-cube face when $n > 1$ (Wyvill *et al.* 1986, Wilhelms and Gelder 1990, Hall 1990).

In three dimensions the three-cube can be divided into twelve tetrahedra (Figure 6) and the required value at the center of the cube found using trilinear interpolation.

Bilinear Contours

The contours of the image can be represented (locally) by parts of a hyperbola (Nielson and Hamann 1991). The ambiguous face occurs when both parts of the hyperbola

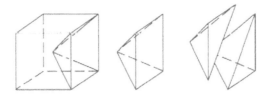

Figure 6.   Twelve-tetrahedra orientation in a cube.

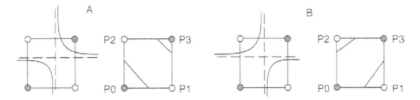

Figure 7.   Bilinear contours.

intersect a face; therefore, the topology of the hyperbola equals the connection of the contour. The correct orientation (Figure 7) is achieved by comparing the threshold with the bilinear interpolation at the crossing point of the asymptotes of the hyperbola, given by $\frac{P0P3+P2P1}{P0+P3-P1-P2}$. If the interpolation value is less than the threshold, then use orientation A; otherwise, use orientation B.

Gradient

Disambiguation of the cell can be achieved by calculating the gradient contribution (Ning and Bloomenthal 1993, Wilhelms and Gelder 1990) from the neighboring faces that point toward the center of the ambiguous face. These gradient contributions can be added to the four face vertex values and used to create a better approximation for the center of that face. This center value can then be used to disambiguate the cell (Figure 8).

Quadratic

Disambiguation can be achieved by fitting a quadratic curve to the local values (using the method of least squares). The orientation of the curve is then used to disambiguate the face (Wilhelms and Gelder 1990, Ning and Bloomenthal 1993).

◇   **Summary**   ◇

The n-cube with an ambiguous face can never be disambiguated by the vertex classification alone; however, at high resolutions the anomalies become unnoticeable.

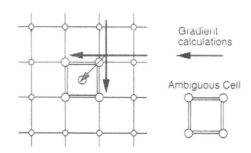

Figure 8. Gradient disambiguation.

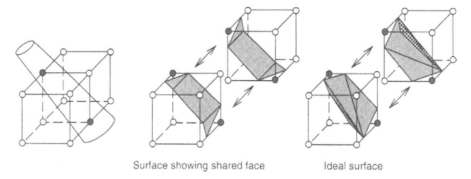

Surface showing shared face   Ideal surface

Figure 9. Concave triangle surfaces

The simplex decomposition strategies work well if a center vertex is calculated, but they accrue many triangle elements.

Subdivision techniques can be used to view an enlargement of the image without false positives and negatives appearing, and the pixel-sized cubes are then projected onto the viewing plane using a gradient shading based upon the four vertices. Subdivision techniques also eliminate degenerate triangle segments. Degenerate segments (very small triangle pieces) occur when the data resolution is high, or at the edge of the evaluation mesh. The degenerate triangles degrade the rendering efficiency. Degenerate triangles can also be reduced by using a "bending" technique (Moore and Warren 1992).

The gradient and quadratic methods are more accurate and more expensive than other methods, but they are useful if the sampling rate is low and if the data cannot be resampled.

Most disambiguation strategies, after deciding on the face orientation, place an extra surface section on the face. However, two such adjacent surfaces may share a common face. To resolve this, concave surfaces (Nielson and Hamann 1991) are used (Figure 9).

In the choice of disambiguation strategy there is a contention between speed and fidelity. Static methods are generally faster but can lead to erroneous surfaces. When the data resolution is sufficiently high, these artifacts are not significant.

◇ **Bibliography** ◇

(Bloomenthal 1988) Jules Bloomenthal. Polygonization of implicit surfaces. *Computer Aided Geometric Design*, 5:341–355, 1988.

(Bloomenthal 1994) Jules Bloomenthal. An implicit surface polygonizer. In Paul S. Heckbert, editor, *Graphics Gems IV*, pages 324–349. AP Professional, Boston, 1994.

(Cline *et al.* 1988) H. E. Cline, W. E. Lorensen, S. Ludke, C. R. Crawford, and B. C. Teeter. Two algorithms for the three-dimensional reconstruction of tomograms. *Medical Physics*, 15(3):320–327, May/June 1988.

(Cook *et al.* 1987) Robert L. Cook, Loren Carpenter, and Edwin Catmull. The Reyes image rendering architecture. *Computer Graphics*, 21(4):95–102, July 1987.

(Cottifava and Moli 1969) G. Cottifava and G. Le Moli. Automatic contour map. *Communications of the ACM*, 12(7):386–391, 1969.

(Duurst 1988) M. J. Duurst. Additional reference to marching cubes. *Computer Graphics*, 22(2):72–73, April 1988.

(Hall 1990) Mark Hall. Defining surface from sampled data. In Andrew S. Glassner, editor, *Graphics Gems*, pages 552–557. AP Professional, Boston, 1990.

(Hanson 1994) Andrew J. Hanson. Geometry of n-dimensional graphics. In Paul S. Heckbert, editor, *Graphics Gems IV*, pages 149–170. AP Professional, Boston, 1994.

(Hill 1994) Steve Hill. Tri-linear interpolation. In Paul S. Heckbert, editor, *Graphics Gems IV*, pages 521–525. AP Professional, Boston, 1994.

(Lorensen and Cline 1987) William E. Lorensen and Harvey E. Cline. Marching cubes: A high resolution 3D surface construction algorithm. *Computer Graphics*, 21(4):163–169, July 1987.

(Mackerras 1992) Paul Mackerras. A fast parallel marching-cubes implementation on the Fujitsu AP1000. Technical Report TR-CS-92-10, Australian National University, Department of Computer Science, August 1992.

(Moore and Warren 1992) Doug Moore and Joe Warren. Compact isocontours from sampled data. In David Kirk, editor, *Graphics Gems III*, pages 23–28. AP Professional, Boston, 1992.

(Moore 1992a) Doug Moore. Subdividing simplices. In David Kirk, editor, *Graphics Gems III*, pages 244–249. AP Professional, Boston, 1992.

(Moore 1992b) Doug Moore. Understanding simploids. In David Kirk, editor, *Graphics Gems III*, pages 250–255. AP Professional, Boston, 1992.

(Nielson and Hamann 1991) Gregory M. Nielson and Bernd Hamann. The asymptotic decider: Resolving the ambiguity in the marching cubes. In *Proceedings Visualization '91 – sponsored by the IEEE Computer Society*, pages 83–91, 1991.

(Ning and Bloomenthal 1993) Paul Ning and Jules Bloomenthal. An evaluation of implicit surface tilers. *IEEE Computer Graphics and Applications*, 13(6):33–41, November 1993.

(Wilhelms and Gelder 1990) Jane Wilhelms and Allen Van Gelder. Topological considerations in isosurface generation – extended abstract. *Computer Graphics*, 24(5):79–86, November 1990.

(Wyvill *et al.* 1986) Geoff Wyvill, Craig McPheeters, and Brian Wyvill. Data structure for soft objects. *The Visual Computer*, 2(4):227–234, 1986.

(Zahlten 1992) Cornelia Zahlten. Piecewise linear approximation of isovalued surfaces. In F. H. Post and A. J. S. Hin, editors, *Advances in Scientific Visualization*, pages 105–118. Springer-Verlag, 1992.

III.3

Tricubic Interpolation

Louis K. Arata

Picker International
Ohio Imaging
Nuclear Medicine Division
Bedford Heights, Ohio
arata@nm.picker.com

◇ Introduction ◇

In many cases, linear interpolation provides a very good compromise between speed and accuracy. However, when the data volume is nonisotropic, linear interpolation may introduce objectionable artifacts. In these cases cubic interpolation may be substituted (Pokorny and Gerald 1989; a generous treatment appears in Chapters seven and eight).

This gem reviews tricubic interpolation and provides a C code implementation. Additional information on bilinear and bicubic interpolation is available in the literature (Andrews and Patterson III 1976).

◇ The Implementation ◇

This implementation uses Catmull–Rom interpolating curves. For the one-dimensional case, these curves can be expressed by the following matrix formula:

$$C(u) = \begin{bmatrix} u^3 & u^2 & u & 1 \end{bmatrix} \begin{bmatrix} -0.5 & 1.5 & -1.5 & 0.5 \\ 1.0 & -2.5 & 2.0 & -0.5 \\ -0.5 & 0 & 0.5 & 0 \\ 0 & 1 & 0 & 0 \end{bmatrix} \begin{bmatrix} p_{i-1} \\ p_i \\ p_{i+1} \\ p_{i+2} \end{bmatrix},$$

where $C(u)$ is the interpolated value, p_{i-1}, p_i, p_{i+1}, p_{i+2} are four consecutive data points, and $u \in [0, 1]$ is a parameter that defines the fractional position between p_i and p_{i+1}. Certain run-time optimizations can be employed to reduce the number of floating-point multiplications required by the above equation (see source code).

Tricubic interpolation is done by cascading the one-dimensional operations in the X, Y, then Z directions. Sixteen interpolations using sixty-four original data values are performed in the X direction (in the inner loop of the code). Four interpolations using the prior sixteen values are then done in the Y direction. Finally, the data from the previous four interpolations are combined in the Z direction for the final value. As with trilinear interpolation (Hill 1994), the order of combination is not important; the interpolated value is unique.

The application as a whole must treat cases where the value requiring interpolation has a reduced set of neighboring points p_i (edge effects). There are two possible ways of handling these edge effects. A range check can be applied before the interpolation function is called, and if the position of this computed value is next to an edge point, trilinear interpolation can be used (the preferred implementation). Alternatively, the function can be modified to do the range checking itself and arbitrarily set (to some background value) the neighboring points that fall outside of the data set before doing the tricubic interpolation.

◇ C Code ◇

```c
typedef struct
{
  float           x, y, z;
}               Point;


/*
 * TriCubic - tri-cubic interpolation at point, p.
 *    inputs:
 *       p - the interpolation point.
 *       volume - a pointer to the float volume data, stored in x,
 *                y, then z order (x index increasing fastest).
 *       xDim, yDim, zDim - dimensions of the array of volume data.
 *    returns:
 *       the interpolated value at p.
 *    note:
 *       NO range checking is done in this function.
 */


float           TriCubic (Point p, float *volume, int xDim, int yDim, int zDim)
{
  int           x, y, z;
  register int  i, j, k;
  float         dx, dy, dz;
  register float *pv;
  float         u[4], v[4], w[4];
  float         r[4], q[4];
  float         vox = 0;
  int           xyDim;

  xyDim = xDim * yDim;

  x = (int) p.x, y = (int) p.y, z = (int) p.z;
  if (x < 0 || x >= xDim || y < 0 || y >= yDim || z < 0 || z >= zDim)
    return (0);
```

```
  dx = p.x - (float) x, dy = p.y - (float) y, dz = p.z - (float) z;
  pv = volume + (x - 1) + (y - 1) * xDim + (z - 1) * xyDim;

# define CUBE(x)   ((x) * (x) * (x))
# define SQR(x)    ((x) * (x))
/*
 #define DOUBLE(x) ((x) + (x))
 #define HALF(x)    ...
 *
 * may also be used to reduce the number of floating point
 * multiplications. The IEEE standard allows for DOUBLE/HALF
 * operations.
 */

  /* factors for Catmull-Rom interpolation */

  u[0] = -0.5 * CUBE (dx) + SQR (dx) - 0.5 * dx;
  u[1] = 1.5 * CUBE (dx) - 2.5 * SQR (dx) + 1;
  u[2] = -1.5 * CUBE (dx) + 2 * SQR (dx) + 0.5 * dx;
  u[3] = 0.5 * CUBE (dx) - 0.5 * SQR (dx);

  v[0] = -0.5 * CUBE (dy) + SQR (dy) - 0.5 * dy;
  v[1] = 1.5 * CUBE (dy) - 2.5 * SQR (dy) + 1;
  v[2] = -1.5 * CUBE (dy) + 2 * SQR (dy) + 0.5 * dy;
  v[3] = 0.5 * CUBE (dy) - 0.5 * SQR (dy);

  w[0] = -0.5 * CUBE (dz) + SQR (dz) - 0.5 * dz;
  w[1] = 1.5 * CUBE (dz) - 2.5 * SQR (dz) + 1;
  w[2] = -1.5 * CUBE (dz) + 2 * SQR (dz) + 0.5 * dz;
  w[3] = 0.5 * CUBE (dz) - 0.5 * SQR (dz);

  for (k = 0; k < 4; k++)
  {
    q[k] = 0;
    for (j = 0; j < 4; j++)
    {
      r[j] = 0;
      for (i = 0; i < 4; i++)
      {
        r[j] += u[i] * *pv;
        pv++;
      }
      q[k] += v[j] * r[j];
      pv += xDim - 4;
    }
    vox += w[k] * q[k];
    pv += xyDim - 4 * xDim;
  }
  return (vox < 0 ? 0.0 : vox);
}
```

◇ **Bibliography** ◇

(Andrews and Patterson III 1976) Harry C. Andrews and Claude L. Patterson III. Digital interpolation of discrete images. *IEEE Transactions on Computers*, 25(2):196–202, February 1976.

(Hill 1994) Steve Hill. Tri-linear interpolation. In Paul Heckbert, editor, *Graphics Gems IV*, pages 521–525. AP Professinal, Boston, 1994.

(Pokorny and Gerald 1989) Cornel K. Pokorny and Curtis F. Gerald. *Computer Graphics: The Principles Behind the Art and Science.* Franklin, Beedle and Associates, Irvine, California, 1989, Chapters 7 and 8.

III.4

Transforming Coordinates from One Coordinate Plane to Another

Robert D. Miller
East Lansing, Michigan

◇ Introduction ◇

A common problem in graphics requires converting Cartesian coordinates from one reference system to corresponding points on a different reference frame. Other applications might include registration of overlays on an existing map or drawing in which the coordinate systems of each can only be determined empirically. The conversion of local (digitized) coordinates to a common world coordinate system may be done with the procedures outlined in this gem.

◇ Method ◇

To find a general transformation between 2D coordinate systems, coordinates of some corresponding points are known. A transformation will be determined that will then map any other point from one system to the other. Schematically, one wishes to convert the position of any point on A to its corresponding position on B as shown (Figure 1) by finding equations that convert (x_i, y_i) to (ζ_i, η_i).

In the simplest case, the transformation determines an origin offset between the two systems, a scale factor difference, and a relative rotation. To solve for these unknowns (three in each coordinate), at least three pairs of corresponding points are required in order to determine a unique transformation.

The equations to convert from (x, y) to (ζ, η) are

$$\zeta_i = ax_i + by_i + c,$$
$$\eta_i = dx_i + ey_i + f \quad \text{for } i = 1, 2, 3.$$

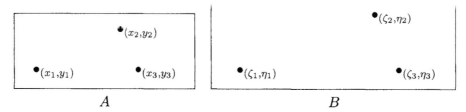

Figure 1. Coordinate plane transformation from *A* to *B*.

Using homogeneous coordinates to recast in matrix form, these equations become

$$
\begin{bmatrix} \zeta_1 \\ \zeta_2 \\ \zeta_3 \end{bmatrix} = \begin{bmatrix} x_1 & y_1 & 1 \\ x_2 & y_2 & 1 \\ x_3 & y_3 & 1 \end{bmatrix} \begin{bmatrix} a \\ b \\ c \end{bmatrix}, \quad
\begin{bmatrix} \eta_1 \\ \eta_2 \\ \eta_3 \end{bmatrix} = \begin{bmatrix} x_1 & y_1 & 1 \\ x_2 & y_2 & 1 \\ x_3 & y_3 & 1 \end{bmatrix} \begin{bmatrix} d \\ e \\ f \end{bmatrix}.
$$

Then matrix inversion gives

$$
\begin{bmatrix} a \\ b \\ c \end{bmatrix} = \begin{bmatrix} x_1 & y_1 & 1 \\ x_2 & y_2 & 1 \\ x_3 & y_3 & 1 \end{bmatrix}^{-1} \begin{bmatrix} \zeta_1 \\ \zeta_2 \\ \zeta_3 \end{bmatrix}, \quad
\begin{bmatrix} d \\ e \\ f \end{bmatrix} = \begin{bmatrix} x_1 & y_1 & 1 \\ x_2 & y_2 & 1 \\ x_3 & y_3 & 1 \end{bmatrix}^{-1} \begin{bmatrix} \eta_1 \\ \eta_2 \\ \eta_3 \end{bmatrix}.
$$

These transformations may be written in a more compact form. In one coordinate,

$$
\mathbf{q} = \mathbf{D}\,\mathbf{p}, \quad \text{so} \quad \mathbf{p} = \mathbf{D}^{-1}\mathbf{q},
$$

where

$$
\mathbf{p} = \begin{bmatrix} a \\ b \\ c \end{bmatrix}, \quad
\mathbf{q} = \begin{bmatrix} \zeta_1 \\ \zeta_2 \\ \zeta_3 \end{bmatrix}, \quad
\mathbf{D} = \begin{bmatrix} x_1 & y_1 & 1 \\ x_2 & y_2 & 1 \\ x_3 & y_3 & 1 \end{bmatrix},
$$

and the point set $\mathbf{D}$ is the data matrix.

General Linear Fit

Usually these data points are determined by measurement and are accompanied by random, normally distributed measurement errors. When more than the minimum three points are specified, the transformation is overdetermined. The additional information may be used to find a "best" (in the least-squares sense) statistical fit. The least-squares method minimizes the squares of the differences between the actual transformations and those values predicted by the equations. The predicted values are

$$\hat{\zeta} = ax + by + c,$$
$$\hat{\eta} = dx + ey + f \quad \text{for } i = 1, 2, 3.$$

The three equations to be minimized, for $i = 1, 2, \ldots, n$, are

$$\sum_i (\zeta_i - \hat{\zeta}_i)^2 + \sum_i (\eta_i - \hat{\eta}_i)^2,$$

$$\min \sum (\zeta_i - \hat{\zeta}_i)^2 = \min \sum (\zeta_i - ax_i - by_i - c)^2,$$
$$\min \sum (\eta_i - \hat{\eta}_i)^2 = \min \sum (\eta_i - dx_i - ey_i - f)^2.$$

Minimize these quantities by differentiating with respect to a, b, and c (and again for d, e, and f), set each to zero, and solve the system. For all n data points, this step gives a covariance matrix, $\mathbf{M}$, well-known to methods of statistical regression (Vandergraft 1983):

$$\mathbf{M} = \begin{bmatrix} \sum x_i^2 & \sum x_i y_i & \sum x_i \\ \sum x_i y_i & \sum y_i^2 & \sum y_i \\ \sum x_i & \sum y_i & n \sum 1 \end{bmatrix} = \mathbf{D}^{\mathrm{T}} \mathbf{D}.$$

The solutions are

$$\begin{bmatrix} a \\ b \\ c \end{bmatrix} = \mathbf{M}^{-1} \begin{bmatrix} \sum x_i \zeta_i \\ \sum y_i \zeta_i \\ \sum \zeta_i \end{bmatrix} = \mathbf{M}^{-1} \left(\mathbf{D}^{\mathrm{T}} \begin{bmatrix} \zeta_1 \\ \zeta_2 \\ \zeta_3 \end{bmatrix} \right) \quad \text{and}$$

$$\begin{bmatrix} d \\ e \\ f \end{bmatrix} = \mathbf{M}^{-1} \begin{bmatrix} \sum x_i \eta_i \\ \sum y_i \eta_i \\ \sum \zeta_i \end{bmatrix} = \mathbf{M}^{-1} \left(\mathbf{D}^{\mathrm{T}} \begin{bmatrix} \eta_1 \\ \eta_2 \\ \eta_3 \end{bmatrix} \right).$$

General Quadratic Fit

In practice, a second-order or higher fit may be desired because of slightly nonconstant scale factors, for example. An exact second-order fit requires six data points using the transformation equations

$$\zeta = a_5 x^2 + a_4 y^2 + a_3 x + a_2 y + a_1 xy + a_0,$$
$$\eta = b_5 x^2 + b_4 y^2 + b_3 x + b_2 y + b_1 xy + b_0.$$

Each row, i, of the data matrix $\mathbf{D}$ now becomes $[x_i^2 \quad y_i^2 \quad x_i \quad y_i \quad x_iy_i \quad 1]$, for $i = 1, 2, \ldots, 6$, and the solutions are

$$\begin{bmatrix} a_5 \\ \vdots \\ a_0 \end{bmatrix} = \mathbf{D}^{-1} \begin{bmatrix} \zeta_1 \\ \vdots \\ \zeta_6 \end{bmatrix} \quad \text{and} \quad \begin{bmatrix} b_5 \\ \vdots \\ b_0 \end{bmatrix} = \mathbf{D}^{-1} \begin{bmatrix} \eta_1 \\ \vdots \\ \eta_6 \end{bmatrix}.$$

Generalizing this second-order scheme to a least-squares fit, minimize

$$\sum(\zeta_i - a_5 x_i^2 - a_4 y_i^2 - a_3 x_i - a_2 y_i - a_1 x_i y_i - a_0)^2,$$
$$\sum(\eta_i - b_5 x_i^2 - b_4 y_i^2 - b_3 x_i - b_2 y_i - b_1 x_i y_i - b_0)^2.$$

This gives the coefficient matrix, $\mathbf{M}$:

$$\mathbf{M} = \begin{bmatrix} \sum x_i^4 & \sum x_i^2 y_i^2 & \sum x_i^3 & \sum x_i^2 y_i & \sum x_i^3 y_i & \sum x_i^2 \\ \sum x_i^2 y_i^2 & \sum y_i^4 & \sum x_i y_i^2 & \sum y_i^3 & \sum x_i y_i^3 & \sum y_i^2 \\ \sum x_i^3 & \sum x_i y_i^2 & \sum x_i^2 & \sum x_i y_i & \sum x_i^2 y_i & \sum x_i \\ \sum x_i^2 y_i & \sum y_i^3 & \sum x_i y_i & \sum y_i^2 & \sum x_i y_i^2 & \sum y_i \\ \sum x_i^3 y_i & \sum x_i y_i^3 & \sum x_i^2 y_i & \sum x_i y_i^2 & \sum x_i^2 y_i^2 & \sum x_i y_i \\ \sum x_i^2 & \sum y_i^2 & \sum x_i & \sum y_i & \sum x_i y_i & n \end{bmatrix} = \mathbf{D}^\mathrm{T}\mathbf{D}, \text{ as before.}$$

The solutions are

$$\begin{bmatrix} a_5 \\ a_4 \\ a_3 \\ a_2 \\ a_1 \\ a_0 \end{bmatrix} = \mathbf{M}^{-1} \begin{bmatrix} \sum x_i^2 \zeta_i \\ \sum y_i^2 \zeta_i \\ \sum x_i \zeta_i \\ \sum y_i \zeta_i \\ \sum x_i y_i \zeta_i \\ \sum \zeta_i \end{bmatrix} \quad \text{and} \quad \begin{bmatrix} b_5 \\ b_4 \\ b_3 \\ b_2 \\ b_1 \\ b_0 \end{bmatrix} = \mathbf{M}^{-1} \begin{bmatrix} \sum x_i^2 \eta_i \\ \sum y_i^2 \eta_i \\ \sum x_i \eta_i \\ \sum y_i \eta_i \\ \sum x_i y_i \eta_i \\ \sum \eta_i \end{bmatrix}.$$

Note that operations on each coordinate take place completely independently. This allows a Gaussian elimination upon matrix $\mathbf{M}$ to take place, transforming $\mathbf{M}$ augmented by the column vector on the right-hand side into the solution vector. This technique is implemented in the program code; other methods could also be used.

More generally, a weighted set of input data may be employed, as some of the data points have positions whose accuracies are trusted with a higher degree of confidence than others. To use weighted values, each summation in the coefficient matrix and in the right-hand column vector would include a factor w_i for a relative weight.

For practical graphics applications, the coordinate transformations described here are based upon simple models that prove useful. Related methods such as the SVD (Golub and Van Loan 1989) as used in a somewhat related gem (Wu 1992) generalize the technique, but the requisite mathematical subroutine libraries are overkill for solving the task at hand. The program presented below is both fully self-contained and carefully designed.

◇   **C Code**   ◇

```c
#include <stdio.h>
#include <stdlib.h>

#define SQR(a)  ((a)*(a))

typedef double MATX[10][10];
typedef double VECT[10];
typedef struct {double x; double y;} Point2;

Point2 pt[1023];                    /* From coordinates */
       zeta[1023], eta[1023];       /* To   coordinates */
int    npoints;

int Gauss(MATX ain, VECT bin, int n, VECT v)
/*  Gaussian elimination by converting to upper triangular system.
    Row interchanges are done via re-indexing sub[]. See Vandergraft:
    Intro. Numerical Methods, 2ed, Academic Press, 1983, Chapter 6. */
{   MATX a;   VECT b;
    int  i, j, k, last, index;
    double big, absv;
    int  sub[21];

    for(k=0; k < n; k++) {          /* make local copies */
        for(j=0; j < n; j++) a[k][j] = ain[k][j];
        b[k]  = bin[k];
        }

    last= n-1;
    for (k= 0; k <= last; k++) sub[k]= k;
    for (k= 0; k <= last-1; k++) {
        big= 0.0;
        for (i= k; i <= last; i++) {
            absv= abs(a[sub[i]][k]);
            if (absv > big)
                { big= absv; index= i; }
            }
```

```
            if (big == 0.0) return 0;
            j- sub[k];
            sub[k]= sub[index];
            sub[index]= j;
            big= 1.0/a[sub[k]][k];
            for (i= k+1; i <= last; i++) {
                a[sub[i]][k]= -a[sub[i]][k]*big;
                for (j= k+1; j <= last; j++)
                    a[sub[i]][j] += a[sub[i]][k] * a[sub[k]][j];
                b[sub[i]]    += a[sub[i]][k] * b[sub[k]];
                }
            }
            v[last]= b[sub[last]] / a[sub[last]][last];
            for (k= last-1; k >= 0; k--) {
                v[k]= b[sub[k]];
                for (i= k+1; i <= last; i++)
                    v[k] = v[k] -a[sub[k]][i] * v[i];
                v[k] = v[k] /a[sub[k]][k];
                }
            return 1;
}

void PrintMatrix(MATX a, VECT v, int size)
{   int r, c;
    for(r= 0; r < size; r++) {
        for(c= 0; c < size; c++) printf("%14.6lf  ",a[r][c]);
        printf(" %14.6lf\n", v[r]);
        }
     printf("\n");
}

void PrintSolution(VECT v, int vectorsize, char which)
/*  Print the solution vector */
{   int k;
    printf("Solution vector %c\n", which);
    for(k = 0; k < vectorsize; k++)
        if (abs(v[k]) < 1.0E6) printf("%14.6f  ",v[k]);
        else printf("%14.6e  ", v[k]);
    printf("\n");
}

void FirstOrderExact(VECT xv, VECT yv)
{   int k, ok;   VECT b;   MATX c;
    for(k= 0; k<=2; k++) b[k] = zeta[k];
    for(k= 0; k<=2; k++) {
        c[k][0] = pt[k].x;
        c[k][1] = pt[k].y;
        c[k][2] = 1.0;
        };
```

```
        printf("Augmented matrix:\n");
        PrintMatrix(c, b, 3);
        ok =Gauss(c, b, 3, xv);
        PrintSolution(xv, 3, 'X');

        for(k= 0; k<=2; k++) b[k] = eta[k];
        for(k= 0; k<=2; k++) {
            c[k][0] = pt[k].x;
            c[k][1] = pt[k].y;
            c[k][2] = 1.0;
            };

        PrintMatrix(c, b, 3);
        ok =Gauss(c, b, 3, yv);
        PrintSolution(yv, 3, 'Y');
}

void SecondOrderExact(VECT xv, VECT yv)
{   int k, ok;   VECT b;   MATX c;
    for(k= 0; k<=5; k++) b[k] = zeta[k];
    for(k= 0; k<=5; k++) {
        c[k][0] = pt[k].x*pt[k].x;
        c[k][1] = pt[k].y*pt[k].y;
        c[k][2] = pt[k].x;
        c[k][3] = pt[k].y;
        c[k][4] = pt[k].x*pt[k].y;
        c[k][5] = 1;
        }

    printf("Augmented matrix:\n");
    PrintMatrix(c, b, 6);
    ok =Gauss(c, b, 6, xv);
    printf("x = a5*x√2 + a4*y√2 + a3*x + a2*y + a1*x*y + a0:\n");
    PrintSolution(xv, 6, 'X');

    for(k= 0; k<=5; k++) b[k] = eta[k];
    for(k= 0; k<=5; k++) {
        c[k][0] = SQR(pt[k].x);
        c[k][1] = SQR(pt[k].y);
        c[k][2] = pt[k].x;
        c[k][3] = pt[k].y;
        c[k][4] = pt[k].x*pt[k].y;
        c[k][5] = 1;
        }

    printf("Augmented matrix:\n");
    PrintMatrix(c, b, 6);
    ok =Gauss(c, b, 6, yv);
    printf("y = b5*x√2 + b4*y√2 + b3*x + b2*y + b1*x*y + b0:\n");
    PrintSolution(yv, 6, 'Y');
}
```

```
void FirstOrderLeastSquares(int npoints, VECT xv, VECT yv)
{   MATX c;  VECT b;
    double sumx= 0, sumxx= 0, sumy= 0, sumyy= 0, sumxy= 0,
           sumd= 0, sumdx= 0, sumdy = 0;
    int k, ok;
    double xt, yt;
    for(k=0; k < npoints; k++) {
        sumx  += pt[k].x;
        sumxx += SQR(pt[k].x);
        sumy  += pt[k].y;
        sumyy += SQR(pt[k].y);
        sumxy += pt[k].x*pt[k].y;
        sumd  += zeta[k];
        sumdx += pt[k].x*zeta[k];
        sumxy += pt[k].y*zeta[k];
        }

    c[0][0] = sumxx;   c[0][1] = sumxy;   c[0][2] = sumx;
    c[1][0] = sumxy;   c[1][1] = sumyy;   c[1][2] = sumy;
    c[2][0] = sumx;    c[2][1] = sumy;    c[2][2] = npoints;

    b[0] = sumdx;       b[1] = sumdy;       b[2] = sumd;
    ok = Gauss(c, b, 3, xv);

    sumd = sumdx = sumdy = 0;

    for(k=0; k < npoints; k++) {
        sumd += eta[k];
        sumdx+= pt[k].x*eta[k];
        sumxy+= pt[k].y*eta[k];
        };

     b[0] = sumdx;  b[1] = sumdy; b[2] = sumd;
     ok = Gauss(c, b, 3, yv);
     printf("residuals\n");
     for(k=0; k < npoints; k++) {
         xt = zeta[k] -(pt[k].x*xv[0] + pt[k].y*xv[1] + xv[2]);
         yt =  eta[k] -(pt[k].x*yv[0] + pt[k].y*yv[1] + yv[2]);
         printf("%4d   %12.6   %12.6\n", xt, yt);
         }
}

void SecondOrderLeastSquares(MATX c, int npoints, VECT xv, VECT yv)
{   int j, k, ok;
    MATX c; VECT b;
    double sumd=0, sumdx=0, sumdx2=0, sumdy=0,
                   sumdy2=0, sumdxy =0;
    double px2, py2, xt, yt;

    for(j=0; j<= 5; j++)
        for(k=0; k<= 5; k++) c[j][k] = 0;
```

```
for(k =0; k < npoints; k++) {
    px2 = SQR(pt[k].x);
    py2 = SQR(pt[k].y);
    c[0][0] += px2 *px2;     /* coefficients for normal equations */
    c[0][1] += px2 *py2;
    c[0][2] += px2 *pt[k].x;
    c[0][3] += px2 *pt[k].y;
    c[0][4] += px2 *pt[k].x *pt[k].y;
    c[0][5] += px2;
    c[1][1] += py2 *py2;
    c[1][2] += pt[k].x *py2;
    c[1][3] += pt[k].y *py2;
    c[1][4] += pt[k].x *py2 *pt[k].y;
    c[1][5] += py2;
    c[2][2] += px2;
    c[2][3] += pt[k].x *pt[k].y;
    c[2][4] += px2 *pt[k].y;
    c[2][5] += pt[k].x;
    c[3][3] += py2;
    c[3][4] += pt[k].x *py2;
    c[3][5] += pt[k].y;
    c[4][4] += px2 *py2;
    c[4][5] += pt[k].x *pt[k].y;

    sumd    += zeta[k];
    sumdx   += pt[k].x *zeta[k];
    sumdx2  += px2 *zeta[k];
    sumdy   += pt[k].y *zeta[k];
    sumdy2  += py2 *zeta[k];
    sumdxy  += pt[k].x *pt[k].y *zeta[k];
    }

c[1][0] =c[0][1]; /* Coefficient matrix is symmetric about diagonal */
c[2][0] =c[0][2];  c[2][1] =c[1][2];
c[3][0] =c[0][3];  c[3][1] =c[1][3];  c[3][2] =c[2][3];
c[4][0] =c[0][4];  c[4][1] =c[1][4];  c[4][2] =c[2][4];
                                      c[4][3] =c[3][4];
c[5][0] =c[0][5];  c[5][1] =c[1][5];  c[5][2] =c[2][5];
                                      c[5][3] =c[3][5];
c[5][4] =c[4][5];  c[5][5] =npoints;

b[0] =sumdx2;    b[1] =sumdy2;    b[2] =sumdx;   /* new vector */
b[3] =sumdy;     b[4] =sumdxy;    b[5] =sumd;

printf("Augmented matrix:\n");
PrintMatrix(c, b, 6);
ok =Gauss(c, b, 6, xv);
printf("x = a5*x√2 + a4*y√2 + a3*x + a2*y + a1*x*y + a0:\n");
PrintSolution(xv, 6, 'X');

sumd = sumdx = sumdx2 = sumdy = sumdy2 = sumdxy =0;
```

```
for(k =0; k < npoints; k++) {
    sumd   += eta[k];
    sumdx  += pt[k].x *eta[k];
    sumdx2 += px2 *eta[k];
    sumdy  += pt[k].y *eta[k];
    sumdy2 += py2 *zeta[k];
    sumdxy += pt[k].x *pt[k].y *eta[k];
    }

/* Coefficient matrix must remain unchanged. */

    b[0] =sumdx2;    b[1] =sumdy2;    b[2] =sumdx;   /* New vector */
    b[3] =sumdy;     b[4] =sumdxy;    b[5] =sumd;

    ok =Gauss(c, b, 6, yv);
    printf("y = b5*x√2 + b4*y√2 + b3*x + b2*y + b1*x*y + b0:\n");
    PrintSolution(yv, 6, 'Y');

    printf("Residuals:\n");
    for(k =0; k < npoints; k++) {
        xt = SQR(pt[k].x)*xv[0] + SQR(pt[k].y)*xv[1] +
                pt[k].x *xv[2] + pt[k].y*xv[3] +
                pt[k].x *pt[k].y*xv[4] +xv[5];
        xt = zeta[k] -xt;
        yt = SQR(pt[k].x)*yv[0] + SQR(pt[k].y)*yv[1] +
                pt[k].x*yv[2] + pt[k].y*yv[3] +
                pt[k].x *pt[k].y*yv[4] +yv[5];
        yt = eta[k] -yt;
        printf("%4d %12.6f  %12.6f\n", (k+1), xt, yt);
        }
}
```

◇ **Bibliography** ◇

(Golub and Van Loan 1989) G. H. Golub and Charles F. Van Loan. *Matrix Computations*, 2nd edition, Chapter 8.3, Computing the SVD, pages 427–436. Johns Hopkins University Press, Baltimore, Maryland, 1989.

(Vandergraft 1983) James S. Vandergraft. *Introduction to Numerical Computations*, 2nd edition, Chapter 6. Academic Press, New York, 1983.

(Wu 1992) Xiaolin Wu. A linear-time simple bounding volume algorithm. In David Kirk, editor, *Graphics Gems III*. AP Professional, Boston, 1992.

◇ III.5

A Walk through BSP Trees

Norman Chin
Department of Computer Science
Columbia University
New York, New York
nc@cs.columbia.edu

◇ Introduction ◇

Binary space-partitioning (BSP) trees are data structures that allow for fast visible-surface determination in environments where the viewer moves while the polygonal objects remain static, as in interactive walkthroughs. This gem describes the construction of BSP trees and their traversal, which generates polygons in a sorted order suitable for rendering. It concludes with an efficient viewer/object collision detection algorithm based upon this versatile data structure.

◇ Background ◇

One solution to the visible-surface problem is to render a scene's polygons in back-to-front order[1] so that polygons nearer to the viewer overwrite those farther away. Unfortunately, this simple painter's algorithm offers no consistent means of identifying polygon depth; choosing either the extreme vertices or the centroid as the sorting key fails in certain cases. As seen from above in Figure 1, polygon B is more distant than A using either key, but will be incorrectly rendered before A. This algorithm also fails in cases of cyclic overlaps and interpenetrating polygons (Figure 2). Here, no polygon can be drawn first without incorrectly overwriting what should be in front of it. The depth sort algorithm (Newell *et al.* 1972) solves all of these problems, but in a view-dependent way.

The BSP-tree visible-surface algorithm (Fuchs *et al.* 1980) provides a simple, elegant, and efficient solution to these problems in a view-independent way. A BSP tree is a binary tree that represents a recursive partitioning of n-space, based upon an earlier algorithm (Schumacker *et al.* 1969). In three-space, arbitrarily oriented planes partition the scene. (A less general method employing axis-aligned planes in the context of ray tracing was presented as a previous gem (Sung and Shirley 1992).) The back-to-front rendering order is then determined by a tree traversal governed solely by the position of

---

[1]This order is also useful in some transparency and antialiasing algorithms (Foley *et al.* 1990).

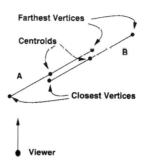

Figure 1. "Back-to-front" ambiguity.

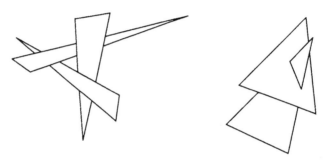

Figure 2. Cyclic overlaps and penetration.

the viewer; no sorting key is needed. The BSP-tree algorithm deals with the problem of cyclic overlaps and polygon interpenetration by splitting the offending polygons during the initial construction of the BSP tree, described below.

◇ **BSP-Tree Construction** ◇

The BSP tree is constructed only once for a given static scene. First, a polygon is selected. Any one will do. Its plane partitions the scene into two half-spaces. One half-space contains all remaining polygons in the positive side of this root polygon, relative to its plane equation; the other contains all polygons in its negative side. Polygons that straddle the plane are split by the plane, and their positive and negative pieces are assigned to the appropriate half-space. (A related gem (Chin 1992) provides an implementation for this operation for convex polygons.) This process recurs within each half-space until that space is empty. The pseudocode for the BSP-tree construction follows.

```
BSPnode *BSPconstructTree(POLYGON *polygonList)
{
    /* choose a polygon's plane from a list of polygons */
    plane= BSPchoosePlane(polygonList);

    /* partition a list of polygons by the plane into 4 separate lists:
     * -lists of polygons in negative/positive sides of the plane
     * -lists of coplanar polygons facing in same/opposite directions as plane
     */
    BSPpartitionFaceListWithPlane(plane,polygonList,&negativeList,&positiveList,
                            &sameList,&oppList);
    /* create node and save lists of polygons */
    newBSPnode= allocate();
    newBSPnode->sameList= sameList; newBSPnode->oppList= oppList;

    /* recursively process remaining polygons, if any, on either side */
    if (negativeList == NULL) newBSPnode->negativeSide= NULL;
    else newBSPnode->negativeSide= BSPconstructTree(negativeList);
    if (positiveList == NULL) newBSPnode->positiveSide= NULL;
    else newBSPnode->positiveSide= BSPconstructTree(positiveList);

    return(newBSPnode);
} /* BSPconstructTree() */
```

A sample construction (Figure 3) shows both the geometry and its BSP tree at successive steps. The scene begins in Figure 3(a) with six polygons, depicted in 2D as lines. Arrows represent their surface normals with the arrowhead indicating the direction of the positive half-space. The − and + signs represent the respective negative and positive BSP-tree branches. The circled letters represent polygons yet to be processed for that half-space, that is, unassigned nodes.

First, select polygon E to define a root partitioning plane. It partitions the scene into two half-spaces as indicated by the thin line in Figure 3(b). One half-space contains all the remaining polygons in its positive side, i.e., B. The other half-space contains all the remaining polygons in its negative side, i.e., A, A, and D. Since C straddles the partitioning plane, it is split into C_1 and C_2. Deposit each portion of C into the appropriate half-space (Figure 3(b)). Node E becomes the root; its two branches (ellipses) each contain a list of polygons yet to be processed for its corresponding half-space.

This process is continued recursively by choosing another plane within each half-space to partition the remaining polygons. This continues until no planes remain, as in Figures 3(c) and (d). Note that polygons coplanar to the selected partitioning plane are kept in the same node under two separate lists: One list contains polygons facing the same direction as the partitioning plane, and the other contains those facing the opposite direction, that is, A and $\bar{A}$ respectively in Figure 3(c).

Whereas all polygons exhibiting cyclic overlaps or interpenetration will be appropriately split during the building of the BSP tree, additional splitting of other polygons

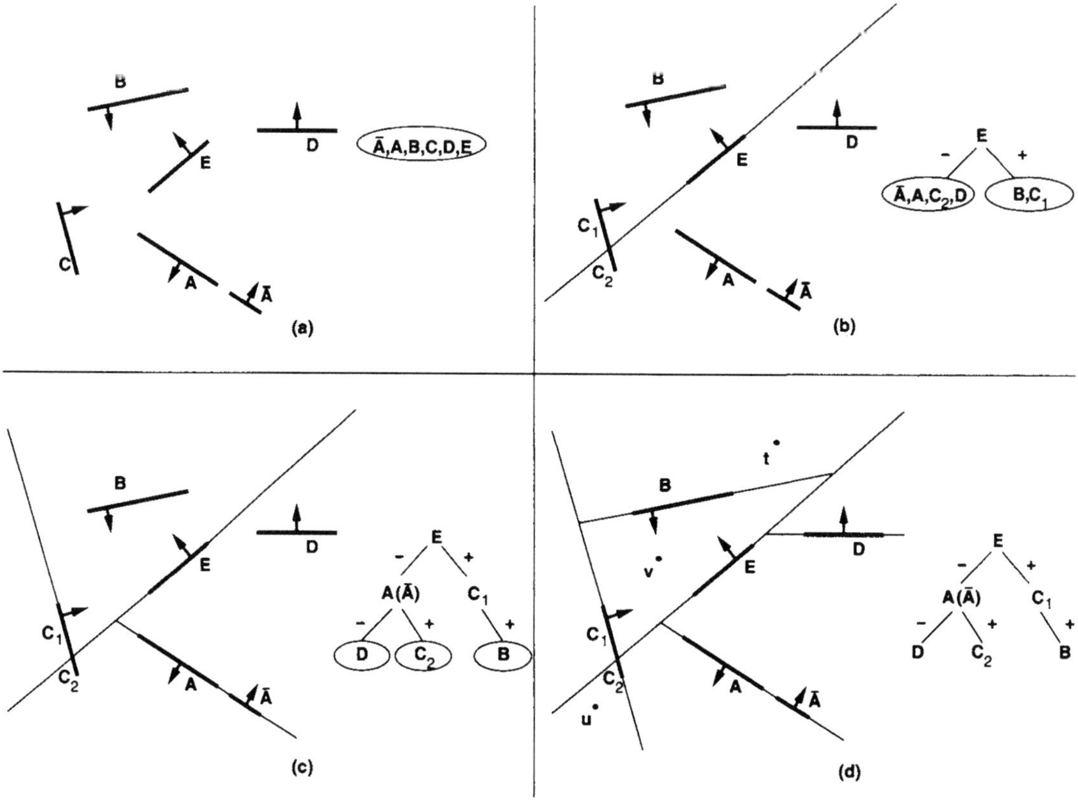

Figure 3. Example of BSP-tree construction.

may also occur. For example, C did not exhibit any problems yet was still partitioned. Note that all splitting occurs independent of the viewer's position and direction.

Partitioning Plane Selection

Different BSP trees can result depending on which polygon's plane was selected at each step. As an example, consider the alternative BSP tree shown in Figure 4. This BSP tree is one node smaller because no polygon was split during its construction. Therefore, it is preferable to select that polygon which minimizes the amount of splitting. Floors and walls are good candidates in typical scenes since they tend not to split other objects. One heuristic examines the first n polygons at each step and selects the one whose plane splits the least number of other polygons in the list (Fuchs *et al.* 1983).

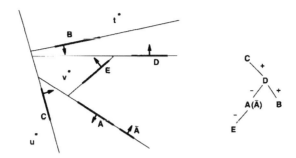

Figure 4.   Alternative BSP tree of scene in Figure 3.

◇   BSP-Tree Traversal   ◇

The BSP tree's greatest advantage is that a special in-order traversal of it provides for an $O(n)$ back-to-front ordering of polygons from an arbitrary viewpoint. This traversal recursively does the following. To render polygon P, first all of the polygons in P's half-space opposite the viewer are rendered, then P is rendered, then all of the polygons in P's half-space containing the viewer are rendered. The pseudocode for the BSP-tree traversal follows.

```
void BSPtraverseTreeAndRender(bspNode,position)
{
    if (bspNode == NULL) return;

    /* in which side of the plane is the viewer? is it the + side? */
    if (BSPisViewerInPositiveSideOfPlane(bspNode->plane,position)) {
        /* yes, recurse on - side, render this node, and recurse on + side */
        BSPtraverseTreeAndRender(bspNode->negativeSide,position);
        /* transform, clip and project polygons in this node to display */
        render(bspNode->sameList);
        render(bspNode->oppList); /* comment out for back-face culling */
        BSPtraverseTreeAndRender(bspNode->positiveSide,position);
    }
    else { /* viewer is in  side or on plane */
        /* recurse on + side, render this node, and recurse on - side */
        BSPtraverseTreeAndRender(bspNode->positiveSide,position);
        /* transform, clip and project polygons in this node to display */
        render(bspNode->oppList);
        render(bspNode->sameList); /* comment out for back-face culling */
        BSPtraverseTreeAndRender(bspNode->negativeSide,position);
    }
} /* BSPtraverseTreeAndRender() */
```

A sample traversal follows for viewpoint t appearing in Figure 3(d). First, t is on the positive side of node E, so traverse the negative side of node E. Next, t is on the negative side of node A so A's positive side is traversed. Render C_2 since it is the only polygon there. Next, render node A's polygons: $\bar{A}$ and A. (Coplanar polygons in the

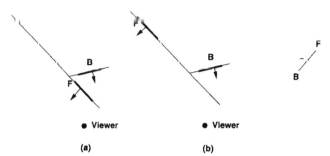

Figure 5. "Back-to-front" ordering is independent of distance.

same node can be rendered in any order.) After that, traverse the negative side of node A, rendering D. Next, traverse the positive side of node E. As C_1's negative half-space is empty, render C_1. Finally, traverse the positive side of node C_1, rendering B.

The complete back-to-front ordering is $[C_2, \bar{A}, A, D, E, C_1, B]$. A similar BSP-tree traversal for viewpoint u is $[B, C_1, E, D, A, \bar{A}, C_2]$. Continuing to the BSP tree in Figure 4, viewpoints t and u yield the orderings $[C, \bar{A}, A, E, D, B]$ and $[B, D, E, A, \bar{A}, C]$ respectively. Note that these orderings are different despite an identical viewpoint and scene, since their BSP trees differ.

It is interesting that this "back-to-front" ordering is independent of distance to the viewer. For example, in Figure 5(a), polygon B lies in the half-space opposite the viewer and is rendered first; F then overwrites it. However, in Figure 5(b), B is still rendered first even though F is clearly much farther away from the viewer. This is also apparent in Figure 3(d) from viewpoint u. Although C_1 is second only to B in the sorted list in line 5 above, E and D (which are rendered immediately after C_1) are actually farther away from u than C_1.

More remarkably, this "back-to-front" ordering is independent not only of distance, but of direction as well. That is, a given position generates the same ordering regardless of viewer direction. Therefore, only the viewing positions, not directions, need be shown in Figures 3(d) and 4. For example, if viewer t pivots in place to face away from the scene, the BSP tree will still be traversed in its entirety, yielding again the same back-to-front ordering. However, none of the polygons will be visible after sending them down the graphics pipeline where they are ultimately transformed, clipped, and projected onto the display (Foley *et al.* 1990).

If the viewer is surrounded by polygons, as in the case of viewpoint v in Figure 3(d), the "back-to-front" ordering is generated as follows. First, v lies in the positive side of node E, so traverse its negative side toward node A. Since v is in A's negative side, traverse A's positive side, rendering C_2. Return to render $\bar{A}$ and A. Traverse A's negative side, rendering D. Return to render E. Next, traverse the positive side of E. Since v is in the positive side of C_1 and its negative branch is empty, render C_1. Traverse C_1's positive side, finally rendering B. The ordering is $[C_2, \bar{A}, A, D, E, C_1, B]$. Similarly, the ordering for v in Figure 4 yields $[C, B, D, \bar{A}, A, E]$. Even though the viewer

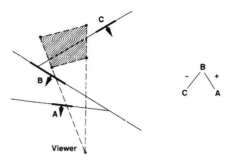

Figure 6.   View-frustum culling.

is surrounded by polygons, no polygons are eliminated from the sorted list. They still need to be rendered by sending them down the graphics pipeline. Therefore, when using BSP trees as a visible-surface algorithm, there is no advantage in balancing the BSP tree since the entire tree is traversed.

Note that the traversal returns merely an ordering; it does not reveal which polygons are actually within the view frustum. It guarantees only that when polygons are sent down the graphics pipeline in this "back-to-front" order, any polygon that should be obscured by another will be, with respect to the viewer.

The next two sections discuss two optimizations to the BSP-tree traversal: back-face culling and view-frustum culling.

Back-Face Culling

Back-face culling can be done at no cost during this traversal as indicated in the traversal pseudocode. Whenever the viewer is in the negative half-space of the polygon to be rendered, that polygon can be culled. For example, from viewpoint t in Figure 3(d), polygons A and B are tagged as back-facing. Similarly, $\bar{A}$, C_1, C_2, D, and E are marked as such with respect to u. Likewise, A and D may be back-face culled with respect to v. Note that even with back-face culling, the entire BSP tree is traversed.

View-Frustum Culling

In addition to supporting back-face culling, BSP trees can be used to accomplish view-frustum culling (Foley *et al.* 1990). If all of the view frustum's eight vertices lie completely on one side of a polygon's plane, then the entire subtree on the opposite side can be eliminated from further traversal. (Determining which side of a plane a point is in has been discussed in a previous gem (Chin 1992).) For example, the view frustum, shown as a filled quadrilateral in Figure 6, lies completely in the negative side of polygon B's plane. Thus, B and its positive subtree consisting of A can be completely pruned. The traversal is called recursively with B's negative subtree, which contains C. Since the view-frustum straddles C's plane, it is not culled; the ordered list consists merely of $[C]$. By comparison, without view-frustum culling the sorted list is $[C, B, A]$. Note that view-frustum culling does not guarantee that all polygons outside the view frustum are omitted. For example, C remains in the ordered list, though it lies outside the view frustum. As mentioned previously, the graphics pipeline ultimately clips C during final rendering.

The following pseudocode incorporates view-frustum culling into the BSP-tree traversal.

```
void BSPtraverseTreeAndCullViewFrustum(bspNode,position)
{
    if (bspNode == NULL) return;

    side= whichSideIsViewFrustum(bspNode->plane,viewFrustum);
    if (side == POSITIVE)
        BSPtraverseTreeAndCullViewFrustum(bspNode->positiveSide,position);
    else if (side == NEGATIVE)
        BSPtraverseTreeAndCullViewFrustum(bspNode->negativeSide,position);
    else { assert(side == BOTH);
        /* insert 2nd if-statement of BSPtraverseTreeAndRender() and
         * replace BSPtraverseTreeAndRender() with
         * BSPtraverseTreeAndCullViewFrustum()
         */
    }
} /* BSPtraverseTreeAndCullViewFrustum() */
```

◇ A Viewer Collision Detection Algorithm ◇

A desirable addition to interactive walkthroughs is the ability to detect collisions between the viewer and the objects in the scene. This is easily added by modifying the BSP-tree data structure to represent solid models (Thibault and Naylor 1987). The main difference between this and the previous BSP-tree data structure is the addition of "in" and "out" leaf nodes which correspond to convex regions that are either inside some object or outside all objects respectively. Figure 7 depicts a BSP-tree solid-modeling representation of a scene containing two concave objects with outward-pointing normals. There are six "in" leaf nodes and eight "out" leaf nodes, corresponding to the same number of "in" and "out" regions in the scene. **BSPconstructTree()** can be made to generate this BSP-tree variant by simply modifying the following two statements from

```
    if (negativeList == NULL) newBSPnode->negativeSide= NULL;
    ...
    if (positiveList == NULL) newBSPnode->positiveSide= NULL;
```

to

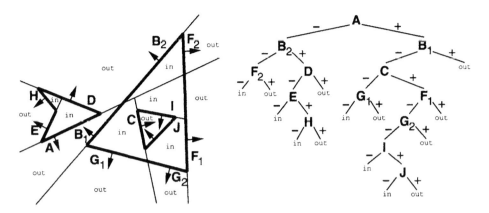

Figure 7. BSP-tree solid-modeling representation of two concave objects.

```
if (negativeList == NULL) newBSPnode->negativeSide= allocate(IN);
...
if (positiveList == NULL) newBSPnode->positiveSide= allocate(OUT);
```

The BSP-tree traversal operates as before except that leaf nodes are ignored.

Given this BSP-tree solid-modeling representation, collision detection between the viewer and the objects in the scene is simple. First, the viewer's path from one frame to the next is modeled as a line segment. Next the endpoints are classified as "on" an object, "in" an object, or "out"(side) all objects. The classifier filters each point down the BSP tree toward the leaves to determine the point's state (described below). A collision is detected if at least one endpoint is "on" or if the endpoints have dissimilar states. If the test fails, a collision is still possible since objects may lie between the endpoints. In this case a line segment is classified next by filtering it down the BSP tree toward the leaves. A collision occurs if and only if the line segment fragments have dissimilar states.

Point and Line Segment Classification

A point is classified as follows. First it is compared with the root's plane. It is then filtered down the branch for the side in which it lies. The process continues recursively until it reaches a leaf node, whereupon the point is classified as "in" or "out." If it is on the plane, it is filtered down both sides and the classifications are compared. If the two classifications differ, the point is "on" since it is on a boundary; otherwise, it is classified by the common value (Thibault and Naylor 1987). Classifying a line segment is similar except that if a line segment straddles a plane, it is split and filtered down the corresponding sides to be classified separately.

Note that all planes are assigned a small tolerance to determine if a primitive is on the plane. Balancing the tree, in this case, will result in a more efficient classification since primitives are filtered down to the leaves (Thibault and Naylor 1987).

◇   **Implementation**   ◇

The routines `BSPconstructTree()` and `BSPtraverseTreeAndRender()` contain the C code for the BSP-tree solid-modeling construction and traversal procedures, respectively. The input format of the polygons for `BSPconstructTree()` is detailed in a prior gem (Chin 1992) along with the splitter, `BSPpartitionFaceListWithPlane()`, which has been slightly modified for this gem. A heuristic that selects a "good" partitioning plane is implemented in `BSPchoosePlane()`. The function `BSPdidViewerCollideWith Scene()` supplies the viewer collision detection algorithm which calls `BSPclassifyPoint()` and `BSPclassifyLineInterior()` to classify their corresponding primitives. Left as an exercise is `BSPtraverseTreeAndCullViewFrustum()`. Most of the core routines are listed at the end of this gem; the complete source code resides on the accompanying disk. Pseudocode for a sample driver for these routines follows.

```
void main()
{
    POSITION position= NULL, newPosition= NULL;
    /* construct BSP tree for a given scene */
    BSPnode *bspTree= BSPconstructTree(getScene());

    do {
        /* display scene for a given viewpoint */
        BSPtraverseTreeAndRender(bspTree,position);

        newPosition= wait for viewer's new position;
        /* check for a collision */
        if (BSPdidViewerCollideWithScene(bspTree,position,newPosition))
            print "Collision!"
        position= newPosition;

    } while (user does not exit);

    BSPfreeTree(bspTree);
} /* main() */
```

◇   **Conclusion**   ◇

The BSP tree was presented as an efficient data structure used to interactively render polygons in correct back-to-front[2] order. Close study showed that the order is not pre-

---

[2]Rendering in front-to-back order is an alternative (Gordon and Chen 1991).

cisely "back-to-front," but is functionally equivalent to it. Optimizations were described that further cull the polygon list. Finally, the BSP-tree framework supports additional methods, including viewer collision detection, Boolean operations (Thibault and Naylor 1987) and shadow generation (Chin and Feiner 1989, Chin and Feiner 1992).

◇ **Acknowledgments** ◇

I would like to thank Alan Paeth and George Wolberg for their many suggestions on improving this gem. A special thanks goes to my advisor Steve Feiner for his comments and for his encouragment in implementing the BSP-based solid modeler, which ultimately resulted in my deeper understanding of the field.

◇ **C Code** ◇

bsp.h

```
/* bsp.h: header file for BSP tree algorithm
 * Copyright (c) Norman Chin
 */
#ifndef _BSP_INCLUDED
#define _BSP_INCLUDED

#include <stdio.h>
#include <stdlib.h>             /* exit() */
#include <assert.h>            /* assert() */
#include <math.h>             /* fabs() */
#include <values.h>           /* MAXINT */
#include "GraphicsGems.h"

typedef struct { float rr,gg,bb; } COLOR;
typedef struct { float xx,yy,zz; } POINT;
typedef struct { float aa,bb,cc,dd; } PLANE;

typedef struct vertexTag {
    float xx,yy,zz;
    struct vertexTag *vnext;    /* vertex position */
                                /* pointer to next vertex in CCW order */
} VERTEX;
#define NULL_VERTEX ((VERTEX *) NULL)

typedef struct faceTag {
    COLOR color;                /* color of face */
    VERTEX *vhead;              /* head of list of vertices */
    PLANE plane;                /* plane equation of face */
    struct faceTag *fnext;      /* pointer to next face */
} FACE;
#define NULL_FACE ((FACE *) NULL)
```

```
typedef enum {PARTITION_NODE= 'p', IN_NODE= 'i', OUT_NODE= 'o'} NODE_TYPE;

typedef struct partitionnodeTag {
    FACE *sameDir, *oppDir;        /* pointers to faces embedded in node */

    struct bspnodeTag *negativeSide, *positiveSide; /* "-" & "+" branches */
} PARTITIONNODE;
#define NULL_PARTITIONNODE ((PARTITIONNODE *) NULL)

typedef struct bspnodeTag {
    NODE_TYPE kind;                /* kind of BSP node */

    PARTITIONNODE *node; /* if kind == (IN_NODE || OUT_NODE) then NULL */
} BSPNODE;
#define NULL_BSPNODE ((BSPNODE *) NULL)

#define TOLER 0.0000076
#define IS_EQ(a,b) ((fabs((double)(a)-(b)) >= (double) TOLER) ? 0 : 1)
typedef enum {NEGATIVE= -1, ZERO= 0, POSITIVE= 1} SIGN;
#define FSIGN(f) (((f) < -TOLER) ? NEGATIVE : ((f) > TOLER ? POSITIVE : ZERO))

/* external functions */
BSPNODE *BSPconstructTree(FACE **faceList);
boolean BSPisViewerInPositiveSideOfPlane(const PLANE *plane,const POINT *position);
void BSPtraverseTreeAndRender(const BSPNODE *bspNode,const POINT *position);
boolean BSPdidViewerCollideWithScene(const POINT *from, const POINT *to,
                                     const BSPNODE *bspTree);
/* the complete file is on disk */
#endif  /* _BSP_INCLUDED */
```

bspTree.c

```
/* bspTree.c: module to construct and traverse a BSP tree.
 * Copyright (c) Norman Chin
 */
#include "bsp.h"

/* local functions */
static void BSPchoosePlane(FACE *faceList,PLANE *plane);
static boolean doesFaceStraddlePlane(const FACE *face,const PLANE *plane);

/* Returns a BSP tree of scene from a list of convex faces.
 * These faces' vertices are oriented in counterclockwise order where the last
 * vertex is a duplicate of the first, i.e., a square has five vertices.
 *
 * faceList - list of faces
 */
BSPNODE *BSPconstructTree(FACE **faceList)
{
    BSPNODE *newBspNode; PLANE plane;
    FACE *sameDirList,*oppDirList, *faceNegList,*facePosList;
```

```
    /* choose plane to split scene with */
    BSPchoosePlane(*faceList,&plane);
    BSPpartitionFaceListWithPlane(&plane,faceList,&faceNegList,&facePosList,
                                  &sameDirList,&oppDirList);
    assert(*faceList == NULL_FACE); assert(sameDirList != NULL_FACE);

    /* construct the tree */
    newBspNode= allocBspNode(PARTITION_NODE,sameDirList,oppDirList);

    /* construct tree's "-" branch */
    if (faceNegList == NULL_FACE)
     newBspNode->node->negativeSide= allocBspNode(IN_NODE,NULL_FACE,NULL_FACE);
    else newBspNode->node->negativeSide= BSPconstructTree(&faceNegList);

    /* construct tree's "+" branch */
    if (facePosList == NULL_FACE)
     newBspNode->node->positiveSide=allocBspNode(OUT_NODE,NULL_FACE,NULL_FACE);
    else newBspNode->node->positiveSide= BSPconstructTree(&facePosList);

    return(newBspNode);
} /* BSPconstructTree() */

/* Traverses BSP tree to render scene back-to-front based on viewer position.
 *
 * bspNode  - a node in BSP tree
 * position - position of viewer
 */
void BSPtraverseTreeAndRender(const BSPNODE *bspNode,const POINT *position)
{
    if (bspNode == NULL_BSPNODE) return;

    if (bspNode->kind == PARTITION_NODE) {
        if (BSPisViewerInPositiveSideOfPlane(&bspNode->node->sameDir->plane,position)){

            BSPtraverseTreeAndRender(bspNode->node->negativeSide,position);
            drawFaceList(stdout,bspNode->node->sameDir);
            drawFaceList(stdout,bspNode->node->oppDir); /* back-face cull */
            BSPtraverseTreeAndRender(bspNode->node->positiveSide,position);

        }
        else {

            BSPtraverseTreeAndRender(bspNode->node->positiveSide,position);
            drawFaceList(stdout,bspNode->node->oppDir);
            drawFaceList(stdout,bspNode->node->sameDir); /* back-face cull */
            BSPtraverseTreeAndRender(bspNode->node->negativeSide,position);

        }
    }
    else assert(bspNode->kind == IN_NODE || bspNode->kind == OUT_NODE);
} /* BSPtraverseTreeAndRender() */
```

```
/* Chooses plane with which to partition.
 * The algorithm is to examine the first MAX_CANDIDATES on face list. For
 * each candidate, count how many splits it would make against the scene.
 * Then return the one with the minimum amount of splits as the
 * partitioning plane.
 *
 * faceList - list of faces
 * plane    - plane equation returned
 */
static void BSPchoosePlane(FACE *faceList,PLANE *plane)
{
    FACE *rootrav; int ii;
    int minCount= MAXINT;
    FACE *chosenRoot= faceList;  /* pick first face for now */

    assert(faceList != NULL_FACE);
    /* for all candidates... */
#define MAX_CANDIDATES 100
    for (rootrav= faceList, ii= 0; rootrav != NULL_FACE && ii< MAX_CANDIDATES;
            rootrav= rootrav->fnext, ii++) {
        FACE *ftrav; int count= 0;
        /* for all faces in scene other than itself... */
        for (ftrav= faceList; ftrav != NULL_FACE; ftrav= ftrav->fnext) {
            if (ftrav != rootrav)
                if (doesFaceStraddlePlane(ftrav,&rootrav->plane)) count++;
        }
        /* remember minimum count and its corresponding face */
        if (count < minCount) { minCount= count; chosenRoot= rootrav; }
        if (count == 0) break; /* can't do better than 0 so return this plane */
    }
    *plane= chosenRoot->plane;   /* return partitioning plane */
} /* BSPchoosePlane() */


/* Returns a boolean to indicate whether the face straddles the plane
 *
 * face  - face to check
 * plane - plane
 */
static boolean doesFaceStraddlePlane(const FACE *face, const PLANE *plane)
{
    boolean anyNegative= 0, anyPositive= 0;
    VERTEX *vtrav;

    assert(face->vhead != NULL_VERTEX);
    /* for all vertices... */
    for (vtrav= face->vhead; vtrav->vnext !=NULL_VERTEX; vtrav= vtrav->vnext) {
        float value= plane->aa*vtrav->xx + plane->bb*vtrav->yy +
                    plane->cc*vtrav->zz + plane->dd;
        /* check which side vertex is on relative to plane */
        SIGN sign= FSIGN(value);
        if (sign == NEGATIVE) anyNegative= 1;
        else if (sign == POSITIVE) anyPositive= 1;
```

```
        /* if vertices on both sides of plane then face straddles else it no */
        if (anyNegative && anyPositive) return(1);
    }
    return(0);
} /* doesFaceStraddlePlane() */

/* Returns a boolean to indicate whether or not point is in + side of plane.
 *
 * plane     - plane
 * position  - position of point
 */
boolean BSPisViewerInPositiveSideOfPlane(const PLANE *plane,const POINT *position)
{
    float dp= plane->aa*position->xx + plane->bb*position->yy +
              plane->cc*position->zz + plane->dd;
    return( (dp > 0.0) ? 1 : 0 );
} /* BSPisViewerInPositiveSideOfPlane() */
/* the complete file is on disk */
/*** bspTree.c ***/
```

bspCollide.c

```
/* bspCollide.c: module to detect collisions between the viewer and static
 * objects in an environment represented as a BSP tree.
 * Copyright (c) Norman Chin
 */
#include "bsp.h"

/* flags to indicate if any piece of a line segment is inside any polyhedron
 *     or outside all polyhedra
 */
static boolean anyPieceOfLineIn, anyPieceOfLineOut;

/* local functions - see function definition */
static int BSPclassifyPoint(const POINT *point, const BSPNODE *bspNode);
static void BSPclassifyLineInterior(const POINT *from, const POINT *to,
                                    const BSPNODE *bspNode);

/* Returns a boolean to indicate whether or not a collision had occurred
 * between the viewer and any static objects in an environment represented as
 * a BSP tree.
 *
 * from     - start position of viewer
 * to       - end position of viewer
 * bspTree   BSP tree of scene
 */
boolean BSPdidViewerCollideWithScene(const POINT *from, const POINT *to,
                                     const BSPNODE *bspTree)
{
    /* first classify the endpoints */
    int sign1= BSPclassifyPoint(from,bspTree);
```

```
    int sign2= BSPclassifyPoint(to,bspTree);

    /* collision occurs iff there's a state change between endpoints or
     * either endpoint is on an object
     */
    if (sign1 == 0 || sign2 == 0 || sign1 != sign2) return(1);
    else {
        anyPieceOfLineIn= anyPieceOfLineOut= 0; /* clear flags */
        /* since we already classified the endpoints, try interior of line */
        /*    this routine will set the flags to appropriate values */
        BSPclassifyLineInterior(from,to,bspTree);

        /* if line interior is inside and outside an object, collision detected*/
        /* else no collision detected */
        return( (anyPieceOfLineIn && anyPieceOfLineOut) ? 1 : 0 );
    }
} /* BSPdidViewerCollideWithScene() */


/* Classifies point as to whether or not it is inside, outside or on an object
 * represented as a BSP tree, where inside is -1, outside is 1, on is 0.
 *
 * point   - position of point
 * bspNode - a node in BSP tree
 */
static int BSPclassifyPoint(const POINT *point,const BSPNODE *bspNode)
{
    if (bspNode == NULL_BSPNODE) return(1); /* point is out since no tree */

    if (bspNode->kind == PARTITION_NODE) { /* compare point with plane */
        const PLANE *plane= &bspNode->node->sameDir->plane;
        float dp= plane->aa*point->xx + plane->bb*point->yy +
                  plane->cc*point->zz + plane->dd;
        if (dp < -TOLER)         /* point on "-" side, filter down "-" branch */
            return(BSPclassifyPoint(point,bspNode->node->negativeSide));
        else if (dp > TOLER)     /* point on "+" side, filter down "+" branch */
            return(BSPclassifyPoint(point,bspNode->node->positiveSide));
        else {
            /* point is on plane, so classify the neighborhood of point by
             * filtering the same point down both branches.
             */
            int sign1= BSPclassifyPoint(point,bspNode->node->negativeSide);
            int sign2= BSPclassifyPoint(point,bspNode->node->positiveSide);
            /* if classification is same then return it otherwise it's on */
            return( (sign1 == sign2) ? sign1 : 0 );
        }
    }
    else if (bspNode->kind == OUT_NODE) return(1); /* point is outside */
    else { assert(bspNode->kind == IN_NODE); return(-1); } /* point is inside */
} /* BSPclassifyPoint() */

/* Classifies interior of line segment (not including endpoints) as to whether
 * or not any piece is inside or outside an object represented as a BSP tree.
 * If it's on, it's recursively called on both half-spaces to set the flags.
```

```
 * There is no explicit on condition like we have with BSPclassifyPoint().
 *
 * from       endpoint of line segment
 * to       - other endpoint of line segment
 * bspNode - a node in BSP tree
 */
static void BSPclassifyLineInterior(const POINT *from,const POINT *to,
                                    const BSPNODE *bspNode)

{
    if (bspNode->kind == PARTITION_NODE) { /* compare line segment with plane */
        float ixx,iyy,izz;
        const PLANE *plane= &bspNode->node->sameDir->plane;
        float dp1= plane->aa*from->xx + plane->bb*from->yy +
                   plane->cc*from->zz + plane->dd;
        float dp2= plane->aa*to->xx + plane->bb*to->yy +
                   plane->cc*to->zz + plane->dd;
        SIGN sign1= FSIGN(dp1); SIGN sign2= FSIGN(dp2);

        if ( (sign1 == NEGATIVE && sign2 == POSITIVE) ||
             (sign1 == POSITIVE && sign2 == NEGATIVE) ) { /* split! */
            SIGN check= anyEdgeIntersectWithPlane(from->xx,from->yy,from->zz,
                                                  to->xx,to->yy,to->zz,
                                                  plane,&ixx,&iyy,&izz);
            POINT iPoint;
            assert(check != ZERO);

            /* filter split line segments down appropriate branches */
            iPoint.xx= ixx; iPoint.yy= iyy; iPoint.zz= izz;
            if (sign1 == NEGATIVE) { assert(sign2 == POSITIVE);
                BSPclassifyLineInterior(from,&iPoint,bspNode->node->negativeSide);
                BSPclassifyLineInterior(to,&iPoint,bspNode->node->positiveSide);
            }
            else { assert(sign1 == POSITIVE && sign2 == NEGATIVE);
                BSPclassifyLineInterior(from,&iPoint,bspNode->node->positiveSide);
                BSPclassifyLineInterior(to,&iPoint,bspNode->node->negativeSide);
            }
        }
        else {                       /* no split, so on same side */
            if (sign1 == ZERO && sign2 == ZERO) {
                BSPclassifyLineInterior(from,to,bspNode->node->negativeSide);
                BSPclassifyLineInterior(from,to,bspNode->node->positiveSide);
            }
            else if (sign1 == NEGATIVE || sign2 == NEGATIVE) {
                BSPclassifyLineInterior(from,to,bspNode->node->negativeSide);
            }
            else { assert(sign1 == POSITIVE || sign2 == POSITIVE);
                BSPclassifyLineInterior(from,to,bspNode->node->positiveSide);
            }
        }
    }
    else if (bspNode->kind == IN_NODE) anyPieceOfLineIn= 1; /* line inside */
    else { assert(bspNode->kind == OUT_NODE); anyPieceOfLineOut= 1; }
```

```
} /* BSPclassifyLineInterior() */
/*** bspCollide.c ***/
```

◇ **Bibliography** ◇

(Chin and Feiner 1989) Norman Chin and Steven K. Feiner. Near real-time shadow generation using BSP trees. *Computer Graphics (SIGGRAPH '89 Proceedings)*, 23(3):99–106, July 1989.

(Chin and Feiner 1992) Norman Chin and Steven K. Feiner. Fast object-precision shadow generation for area light sources using BSP trees. *Computer Graphics (1992 Symposium on Interactive 3D Graphics)*, pages 21 30, March 1992.

(Chin 1992) Norman Chin. Partitioning a 3-D convex polygon with an arbitrary plane. In David Kirk, editor, *Graphics Gems III*, pages 219–222,502–510. AP Professional, Boston, 1992.

(Foley *et al.* 1990) J. D. Foley, A. van Dam, S. K. Feiner, and J. F. Hughes. *Computer Graphics: Principles and Practice*. Addison-Wesley, Reading, MA, 1990.

(Fuchs *et al.* 1980) H. Fuchs, A. M. Kedem, and B. F. Naylor. On visible surface generation by a priori tree structures. *Computer Graphics (SIGGRAPH '80 Proceedings)*, 14(3):124–133, July 1980.

(Fuchs *et al.* 1983) H. Fuchs, G. D. Abram, and E. D. Grant. Near real-time shaded display of rigid objects. *Computer Graphics (SIGGRAPH '83 Proceedings)*, 17(3):65–72, July 1983.

(Gordon and Chen 1991) D. Gordon and S. Chen. Front-to-back display of BSP trees. *IEEE Computer Graphics and Applications*, 11(5):79–85, September 1991.

(Newell *et al.* 1972) M. E. Newell, R. G. Newell, and T. L. Sancha. A solution to the hidden surface problem. *Proceedings of the ACM National Conference '72*, pages 443–450, 1972.

(Schumacker *et al.* 1969) R. Schumacker, B. Brand, M. Gilliland, and W. Sharp. Study for applying computer-generated images to visual simulation. Technical Report AFHRL-TR-69-14, USAF Human Resources Laboratory, 1969.

(Sung and Shirley 1992) K. Sung and P. Shirley. Ray tracing with the BSP tree. In David Kirk, editor, *Graphics Gems III*, pages 271–274. AP Professional, Boston, 1992.

(Thibault and Naylor 1987) W. C. Thibault and B. F. Naylor. Set operations on polyhedra using BSP trees. *Computer Graphics (SIGGRAPH '87 Proceedings)*, 21(4):153–162, July 1987.

III.6

Generic Implementation of Axial Deformation Techniques

Carole Blanc
Laboratoire Bordelais de Recherche en Informatique (LaBRI)
Talence, France
blanc@labri.u-bordeaux.fr

◇ Introduction ◇

Global deformation techniques were first introduced to extend the set of primitives that may be used in constructive solid modeling (Barr 1984, Sederberg and Parry 1986). In fact, these techniques are more general and have been consequently adapted to tessellated surfaces or parametric patches as well. This gem proposes a generic implementation of several of these global deformation techniques. The term "generic" focuses on the fact that the implementation depends neither on a given geometric model for surfaces nor on specific data structures for internal representation.

The principle of global deformation is to map each point (x, y, z) in the Euclidian space $\mathbf{R}^3$ onto another point (x', y', z') under a deformation function $f(x, y, z, a, b, c, \ldots)$. The additional parameters $(a, b, c, \ldots)$ used by the deformation function are either constants or values returned by *shape functions*. Moreover, according to the way these shape functions are defined, global deformation techniques may be further classified as procedural or interactive.

There is a subset of global deformation techniques for which the shape functions operate upon only one coordinate (typically z) of the initial point P. For this and related reasons (Lazarus *et al.* 1992), such techniques are called *axial deformation techniques* in what follows. Although they are relatively specific compared to more general techniques such as FFD (Sederberg and Parry 1986) or EFFD (Coquillart 1990), axial deformations have been found useful in many computer graphics applications; for instance, all the procedural techniques proposed in Barr's original work on global deformations (Barr 1984) were axial deformations.

◇ Description ◇

The general mapping function for axial deformations may be expressed by

$$(x', y', z') = f(x, y, z, a(z), b(z), c(z), \ldots). \tag{1}$$

The axial deformations proposed here are defined with a simplified form of Equation (1) that uses only two additional parameters:

$$(x', y', z') = f(x, y, z, s(z), a), \tag{2}$$

where $s(z) : \mathbf{R} \rightarrow [0, 1]$ is the shape function and $a \in \mathbf{R}$ is the amplitude of the deformation. The role of both parameters may be understood intuitively: When the shape function $s(z)$ is null for a given point (x, y, z), it means that this point will be unchanged by the deformation; similarly, when the amplitude a is null, the whole object remains undeformed.

In the generic implementation proposed here, each deformation routine acts only on points: It takes the coordinates of a point on the original object, computes its displacement according to the deformation function, and finally returns the new coordinates of the point. A complete implementation of axial deformations should include some interactive tools for defining the shape function. Such a tool lies outside the scope of this gem, but many interesting procedural deformations may be obtained by using general-purpose functions, such as the *wave generators* described elsewhere in this volume (gem VII.1).

Six different axial deformations are provided (pinch, taper, mold, twist, shear, bend), which differ only by the function f that is applied on each point. Figure 1 shows several objects that may be obtained with the six deformation operators, starting from a parallelepiped. In fact, two kinds of operators are used here: The first kind (pinch, shear, bend) takes the Cartesian coordinates (x, y, z) of the point in the local frame, whereas the second kind (taper, mold, twist) acts on the cylindrical coordinates (r, θ, z). The following lines give an overview of the work that is done by each operator:

pinch: The x coordinate is scaled according to a and $s(z)$.
taper: The r coordinate is scaled according to a and $s(z)$.
mold: The r coordinate is scaled according to a and $s(\theta)$.
twist: The θ coordinate is scaled according to a and $s(z)$.
shear: The z axis is translated according to a and $s(z)$.
bend: The z axis is rotated according to a and $s(z)$.

For each deformation technique, two routines are provided. The first (`local_*`) assumes that the coordinates of the incoming point are already expressed in the local frame where the deformation is defined (i.e., the frame for which the z coordinate is used by the shape function). The second one (`world_*`) takes the coordinates of the point in the world frame and returns the coordinates in the same frame. For this, it needs an additional parameter defining the local frame and performs the deformation within this frame. The implementation uses the toolbox of macro functions given on the distribution disk (Schlick 1995) which provides the frame conversion routines.

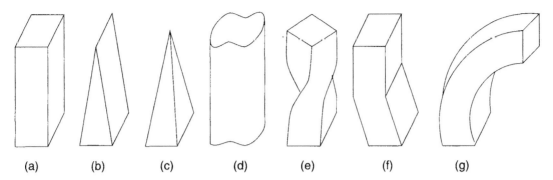

Figure 1. (a) Original object, (b) pinch, (c) taper, (d) mold, (e) twist, (f) shear, (g) bend.

Finally, note that a *unit-cube frame* (Blanc and Schlick 1994) may be employed instead of the traditional frame having unit vectors, because it facilitates the deformation of objects independently of their position, orientation, and size.

◇ Source Files ◇

```
/* ------------------------------------------------------------------------ *\
   AXD.H : Carole Blanc (4 June 1994)

   This package provides an implementation of 6 different algorithms
   for doing axial deformations.

   "Generic Implementation of Axial Deformation Techniques"
   in Graphics Gems V (edited by A. Paeth), Academic Press
\* ------------------------------------------------------------------------ */

#ifndef _AXD_
#define _AXD_

/*
** This package uses the "Toolbox of Macros Functions for Computer Graphics"
** which provides files : tool.h, real.h, uint.h, sint.h, vec?.h and mat?.h
*/

#include "real.h"

typedef real (*shape) (real);

extern void local_pinch (rv3 *Point, shape Shape, real Ampli);
extern void world_pinch (rv3 *Point, frame3 Frame, shape Shape, real Ampli);
extern void local_taper (rv3 *Point, shape Shape, real Ampli);
extern void world_taper (rv3 *Point, frame3 Frame, shape Shape, real Ampli);
extern void local_mould (rv3 *Point, shape Shape, real Ampli);
extern void world_mould (rv3 *Point, frame3 Frame, shape Shape, real Ampli);
```

```
extern void local_twist  (rv3 *Point, shape Shape, real Ampli);
extern void world_twist  (rv3 *Point, frame3 Frame, shape Shape, real Ampli);
extern void local_shear  (rv3 *Point, shape Shape, real Ampli);
extern void world_shear  (rv3 *Point, frame3 Frame, shape Shape, real Ampli);
extern void local_bend   (rv3 *Point, shape Shape, real Ampli);
extern void world_bend   (rv3 *Point, frame3 Frame, shape Shape, real Ampli);

#endif

/* ----------------------------------------------------------------------- *\
   AXD.C : Carole Blanc (4 June 1994)

   This package provides an implementation of 6 different algorithms
   for doing axial deformations.

   "Generic Implementation of Axial Deformation Techniques"
   in Graphics Gems V (edited by A. Paeth), Academic Press
\* ----------------------------------------------------------------------- */

#include "axd.h"
#include "mat3.h"

/*
** Each "local_*" routines inputs/outputs the following arguments
**
** Input:  Point = coordinates of the point in the local frame
**         Shape = shape function of the deformation
**         Ampli = amplitude of the deformation
** Output: Point = coordinates of the deformed point in the local frame
**
** Each "world_*" routines inputs/outputs the following arguments
**
** Input:  Point = coordinates of the point in the world frame
**         Frame = local frame in which the deformation is applied
**         Shape = shape function of the deformation
**         Ampli = amplitude of the deformation
** Output: Point = coordinates of the deformed point in the world frame
**
** Note: The "Frame" argument must be initialized by MAKE_FRAME3 (see "mat3.h")
*/

/*
** pinch : Scale the x coordinate of the object according to z
*/

void local_pinch (realvec3 *Point, shape Shape, real Ampli)
{
  Point->x *= 1.0 - Ampli * Shape (Point->z);
}
```

```
void world_pinch (realvec3 *Point, frame3 Frame, shape Shape, real Ampli)
{
  LOCAL_FRAME3 (Point, Framc);
  local_pinch  (Point, Shape, Ampli);
  WORLD_FRAME3 (Point, Frame);
}

/*
** taper : Scale the polar radius of the object according to z
*/

void local_taper (realvec3 *Point, shape Shape, real Ampli)
{
  register real Tmp;

  Tmp = 1.0 - Ampli * Shape (Point->z); Point->x *= Tmp; Point->y *= Tmp;
}

void world_taper (realvec3 *Point, frame3 Frame, shape Shape, real Ampli)
{
  LOCAL_FRAME3 (Point, Frame);
  local_taper  (Point, Shape, Ampli);
  WORLD_FRAME3 (Point, Frame);
}

/*
** mould : Scale the polar radius of the object according to the polar angle
*/

void local_mould (realvec3 *Point, shape Shape, real Ampli)
{
  register real Tmp;

  Tmp = atan2 (Point->y, Point->x) / PI;
  Tmp = 1.0 - Ampli * Shape (Tmp); Point->x *= Tmp; Point->y *= Tmp;
}

void world_mould (realvec3 *Point, frame3 Frame, shape Shape, real Ampli)
{
  LOCAL_FRAME3 (Point, Frame);
  local_mould  (Point, Shape, Ampli);
  WORLD_FRAME3 (Point, Frame);
}

/*
** twist : Scale the polar angle of the object according to z
*/
```

```
void local_twist (realvec3 *Point, shape Shape, real Ampli)
{
  register real Tmp, Cos, Sin;

  Tmp = PI * Ampli * Shape (Point->z);
  Cos = cos (Tmp); Sin = sin (Tmp); Tmp = Point->x;
  Point->x = Cos * Tmp - Sin * Point->y;
  Point->y = Sin * Tmp + Cos * Point->y;
}

void world_twist (realvec3 *Point, frame3 Frame, shape Shape, real Ampli)
{
  LOCAL_FRAME3 (Point, Frame);
  local_twist  (Point, Shape, Ampli);
  WORLD_FRAME3 (Point, Frame);
}

/*
** shear : Translate the z axis of the object along x according to z
*/

void local_shear (realvec3 *Point, shape Shape, real Ampli)
{
  Point->x += Ampli * Shape (Point->z);
}

void world_shear (realvec3 *Point, frame3 Frame, shape Shape, real Ampli)
{
  LOCAL_FRAME3 (Point, Frame);
  local_shear  (Point, Shape, Ampli);
  WORLD_FRAME3 (Point, Frame);
}

/*
** bend : Rotate the z axis of the object around y according to z
*/

void local_bend (realvec3 *Point, shape Shape, real Ampli)
{
  register real Tmp, Cos, Sin;

  Tmp = PI * Ampli * Shape (Point->z);
  Cos = cos (Tmp); Sin = sin (Tmp); Tmp = Point->z;
  Point->z = Cos * Tmp - Sin * Point->x;
  Point->x = Sin * Tmp + Cos * Point->x;
}

void world_bend (realvec3 *Point, frame3 Frame, shape Shape, real Ampli)
{
  LOCAL_FRAME3 (Point, Frame);
  local_bend   (Point, Shape, Ampli);
  WORLD_FRAME3 (Point, Frame);
}
```

◇ **Bibliography** ◇

(Barr 1984) A. Barr. Global and local deformations of solid primitives. *Computer Graphics*, 18(3):21–30, 1984.

(Blanc and Schlick 1994) C. Blanc and C. Schlick. Easy transformations between cartesian, cylindrical and spherical coordinates. Technical Report 832/94, LaBRI, 1994.

(Coquillart 1990) S. Coquillart. Extended free form deformations: A sculpturing tool for 3D geometric modeling. *Computer Graphics*, 24(4):187–196, 1990.

(Lazarus *et al.* 1992) F. Lazarus, S. Coquillart, and P. Jancene. Interactive axial deformations (in French). In *Proc. of Groplan 92 (Nantes, France)*, pages 117–124, 1992.

(Schlick 1995) C. Schlick. A toolbox of macro functions for computer graphics. In *Graphics Gems V*. Academic Press, 1995.

(Sederberg and Parry 1986) T. Sederberg and S. Parry. Free-form deformations of solid geometric models. *Computer Graphics*, 20(4):151–160, 1986.

◊ **IV** ◊

Curves and Surfaces

The gems in this section describe curves and surfaces. This is the book's largest contributed section. The gems chosen support a straightforward machine implementation of the methods presented.

In the first two gems, Goldman catalogs the identities that underlie the univariate and bivariate Bernstein (IV.1) and the B-spline (IV.2) basis functions. The entries include historical citations. Their compact notation (and the parallel treatment in IV.1) add further value by better revealing the deep structure of these important models. Turkowski (IV.3) derives an equation for circular arc "bending" of arcs bisected from a parent of known bend. By this equation, recursive binary subdivision may be directly employed in order to render these curves using a compact and efficient routine. de Figueiredo (IV.4) employs a related nonuniform curve subdivision in order to solve problems of curve length, rendering, and point on curve testing. Ahn (IV.5) provides an efficient computation of the vertices of any ellipsoid. The code minimizes trigonometric evaluations and produces the edge and face lists used to describe these polyhedral approximations. Bajaj and Xu (IV.6) derive conditions for curves through a sparse(st) set of points. They apply the formulas to join parametric cubic curves using a reduced data set while preserving continuity (pseudocode included). Data thinning of digitized font descriptions is one immediate application. Gravesen (IV.7) estimates the length of Bézier curves using six related subdivision methods. Extensive empirical data summarizes their behavior in reference to a large number of curves (not shown), while two representative curves provide worthwhile benchmarks for such estimators. Miller (IV.8) describes the efficient rendering of Bézier curves by applying continuously evaluated subexpressions to the factorial and exponential terms that describe such curves. The section closes with a tutorial by Shoemake (IV.9) that describes a broad class of univariate and multivariate curves and surfaces in terms of simple linear interpolation. This grand unification helps demythologize the field while simultaneously presenting compact formulas in terms of one underlying function.

147

IV.1

Identities for the Univariate and Bivariate Bernstein Basis Functions

Ronald N. Goldman
Department of Computer Science
Rice University
Houston, Texas
rng@cs.rice.edu

◇ Introduction ◇

Bézier curves and surfaces are essential to a wide variety of applications in computer graphics and geometric modeling, and the Bernstein basis functions play a central role in the construction and analysis of these curve and surface schemes. Here we shall adopt the standard notation $B_k^n(t), 0 \leq k \leq n$, and $B_{i,j}^n(s,t), 0 \leq i+j \leq n$, to represent the univariate and bivariate Bernstein basis functions of degree n.

Let $\{P_k\}$ and $\{P_{i,j}\}$ be arrays of control points. Then Bézier curves and surfaces are defined in the following fashion.

Bézier Curve

$$C(t) = \sum_k B_k^n(t)P_k, \quad t \in [0,1]$$

Tensor Product Bézier Surface

$$P(s,t) = \sum_i \sum_j B_i^m(s)B_j^n(t)P_{i,j}, \quad s,t \in [0,1]$$

Triangular Bézier Surface

$$T(s,t) = \sum_{0 \leq i+j \leq n} B_{i,j}^m(s,t)P_{i,j}, \quad (s,t) \in \Delta^2 = \{(s,t) \mid s,t \geq 0 \text{ and } s+t \leq 1\}$$

The purpose of this gem is to assemble in one place those identities involving the univariate and bivariate Bernstein basis functions that help to facilitate the symbolic and numeric manipulation of Bézier curves and surfaces. This gem presents these identities in a consistent framework and may serve both as a compact reference and as a subject for further study.

The formulas are organized into twenty-five categories. In general, each category begins with the formulas for the univariate bases and then lists the corresponding formulas for the bivariate bases, though in some cases no direct univariate (xvii) or bivariate (xi) analogues exist.

Currently these identities are widely scattered throughout the literature. For all of the more complicated identities, citations have been provided where proofs of these formulas or analogous formulas may be found. However, some of the simpler identities are so well known or so easy to derive from other identities that no citation is supplied.

◇ Identities for the Bernstein Basis Functions ◇

(i) Definitions

(a)

$$B_k^n(t) = \binom{n}{k} t^k (1 - t)^{n-k}, \quad 0 \le k \le n$$

$$\binom{n}{k} = \frac{n!}{k!\,(n-k)!}$$

(b)

$$B_{i,j}^n(s,t) = \binom{n}{i\ \ j} s^i t^j (1 - s - t)^{n-i-j}, \quad 0 \le i + j \le n$$

$$\binom{n}{i\ \ j} = \frac{n!}{i!\,j!\,(n-i-j)!}$$

(ii) Non-negativity

(a)

$$B_k^n(t) \ge 0, \quad 0 \le t \le 1$$

(b)

$$B_{i,j}^n(s,t) \ge 0, \quad (s,t) \in \Delta^2$$

(iii) Symmetries

(a)

$$B_k^n(t) = B_{n-k}^n(1 - t)$$

(b)

$$B_{i,j}^{n}(s,t) = B_{i,n-i-j}^{n}(s,1-s-t)$$

(c)

$$B_{i,j}^{n}(s,t) = B_{n-i-j,j}^{n}(1-s-t,t)$$

(d)

$$B_{i,j}^{n}(s,t) = B_{j,i}^{n}(t,s)$$

(iv) Corner Values

(a)

$$B_{k}^{n}(0) = 0, k \neq 0$$
$$= 1, k = 0$$

(b)

$$B_{k}^{n}(1) = 0, k \neq n$$
$$= 1, k = n$$

(c)

$$B_{i,j}^{n}(0,0) = 0, (i,j) \neq (0,0)$$
$$= 1, (i,j) = (0,0)$$

(d)

$$B_{i,j}^{n}(1,0) = 0, (i,j) \neq (n,0)$$
$$- 1, (i,j) - (n,0)$$

(e)

$$B_{i,j}^{n}(0,1) = 0, (i,j) \neq (0,n)$$
$$= 1, (i,j) = (0,n)$$

(v) Boundary Values

(a)

$$B_{i,j}^{n}(s,0) = 0, \qquad j \neq 0$$
$$= B_{i}^{n}(s), \quad j = 0$$

(b)

$$B^n_{i,j}(0,t) = 0, \qquad i \neq 0$$
$$= B^n_j(t), \quad i = 0$$

(c)

$$B^n_{i,j}(s,1-s) = 0, \qquad i+j \neq n$$
$$= B^n_i(s), \quad i+j = n$$

(vi) Partitions of Unity (Farin 1988)

(a)

$$\sum_k B^n_k(t) = 1$$

(b)

$$\sum_i \sum_j B^n_{i,j}(s,t) = 1$$

(vii) Alternating Sums

(a)

$$\sum_k (-1)^k B^n_k(t) = (1-2t)^n$$

(b)

$$\sum_i \sum_j (-1)^{i+j} B^n_{i,j}(s,t) = (1-2s-2t)^n$$

(viii) Conversion to Monomial Form (Polya and Schoenberg 1958)

(a)

$$B^n_k(t)/(1-t)^n = \binom{n}{k} u^k, \quad u = t/(1-t)$$

(b)

$$B^n_k(t)/t^n = \binom{n}{k} u^{n-k}, \quad u = (1-t)/t$$

(c)

$$B_{i,j}^n(s,t)/(1-s-t)^n = \binom{n}{i\ \ j}u^iv^j, \quad u = s/(1-s-t), v = t/(1-s-t)$$

(d)

$$B_{i,j}^n(s,t)/s^n = \binom{n}{i\ \ j}u^{n-i-j}v^j, \quad u = (1-s-t)/s, v = t/s$$

(e)

$$B_{i,j}^n(s,t)/t^n = \binom{n}{i\ \ j}u^iv^{n-i-j}, \quad u = s/t, v = (1-s-t)/t$$

(ix) Representation in Terms of Monomials (Farouki and Rajan 1988)

(a)

$$B_k^n(t) = \sum_{k \le j \le n}(-1)^{j-k}\binom{n}{k}\binom{n-k}{j-k}t^j$$

(b)

$$B_{i,j}^n(s,t) = \sum_{k \ge i}\sum_{l \ge j}(-1)^{i+j+k+l}\binom{n}{i\ \ j}\binom{n-i-j}{k-i\ \ l-j}s^kt^l, \quad 0 \le k+l \le n$$

(x) Representation of Monomials (Farouki and Rajan 1988)

(a)

$$t^j = \sum_{j \le k \le n}\frac{\binom{k}{j}}{\binom{n}{j}}B_k^n(t), \quad 0 \le j \le n$$

(b)

$$s^it^j = \sum_{k \ge i}\sum_{l \ge j}\frac{\binom{k}{i}\binom{l}{j}}{\binom{n}{i\ \ j}}B_{k,l}^n(s,t), \quad 0 \le i+j \le n$$

(xi) Linear Independence

(a)

$$\sum_k c_k B_k^n(t) = 0 \Longleftrightarrow c_k = 0 \text{ for all } k$$

(b)

$$\sum_i \sum_j c_{i,j} B_{i,j}^n(s,t) = 0 \Longleftrightarrow c_{i,j} = 0, \text{ for all } i,j$$

(xii) Descartes' Law of Signs (Polya and Schoenberg 1958)

(a)

$$\text{Zeros in } (0,1) \text{ of } \left\{ \sum_k c_k B_k^n(t) \right\} \leq \text{Sign alternations of } (c_0, c_1, \dots, c_n)$$

(b) There is no known analogous formula for the bivariate Bernstein basis functions.

(xiii) Recursion (Farin 1988)

(a)

$$B_k^n(t) = (1 - t)B_k^{n-1}(t) + t B_{k-1}^{n-1}(t)$$

(b)

$$B_{i,j}^n(s,t) = (1 - s - t)B_{i,j}^{n-1}(s,t) + s B_{i-1,j}^{n-1}(s,t) + t B_{i,j-1}^{n-1}(s,t)$$

(xiv) Discrete Convolution

(a)

$$(B_0^n(t), \dots, B_n^n(t)) = \underbrace{\{(1-t), t\} * \cdots * \{(1-t), t\}}_{n \text{ factors}}$$

(b)

$$(B_{0,0}^n(t), \dots, B_{0,n}^n(t)) = \underbrace{\{(1 - s - t), s, t\} * \cdots * \{(1 - s - t), s, t\}}_{n \text{ factors}}$$

(xv) Subdivision (Goldman 1982, 1983)

(a)

$$B_i^n(rt) = \sum_{i \le k \le n} B_i^k(r) B_k^n(t)$$

(b)

$$B_i^n((1-t)r + t) = \sum_{0 \le k \le i} B_{i-k}^{n-k}(r) B_k^n(t)$$

(c)

$$B_i^n((1-t)r + ts) = \sum_k \left\{ \sum_{p+q=i} B_p^{n-k}(r) B_q^k(s) \right\} B_k^n(t)$$

(d)

$$B_{i,j}^n(su, sv + t) = \sum_k \sum_l B_{i,j-l}^k(u,v) B_{k,l}^n(s,t)$$

(e)

$$B_{i,j}^n(tu + s, tv) = \sum_k \sum_l B_{i-k,j}^l(u,v) B_{k,l}^n(s,t)$$

(f)

$$B_{i,j}^n((1-s-t)u + s, (1-s-t)v + t) = \sum_k \sum_l B_{i-k,j-l}^{n-k-l}(u,v) B_{k,l}^n(s,t)$$

(g)

$$B_{i,j}^n((1-s-t)u_1 + sv_1 + tw_1, (1-s-t)u_2 + sv_2 + tw_2)$$

$$= \sum_k \sum_l \left\{ \sum_{a+c+e=i,b+d+f=j} B_{a,b}^{n-k-l}(u_1,u_2) B_{c,d}^k(v_1,v_2) B_{e,f}^l(w_1,w_2) \right\} B_{k,l}^n(s,t)$$

(xvi) Partial Derivatives (Farin 1988)

(a)

$$dB_k^n(t)/dt = n\{B_{k-1}^{n-1}(t) - B_k^{n-1}(t)\}$$

(b)

$$d^{\nu}B_k^n(t)/dt^{\nu} = \frac{n!}{(n-p)!}\sum_{0\le j\le p}(-1)^{p-j}\binom{p}{j}B_{k-j}^{n-p}(t)$$

(c)

$$\partial B_{i,j}^n(s,t)/\partial s = n\{B_{i-1,j}^{n-1}(s,t) - B_{i,j}^{n-1}(s,t)\}$$

(d)

$$\partial B_{i,j}^n(s,t)/\partial t = n\{B_{i,j-1}^{n-1}(s,t) - B_{i,j}^{n-1}(s,t)\}$$

(e)

$$\partial^{p+q}B_{i,j}^n(s,t)/\partial s^p \partial t^q$$

$$= \frac{n!}{(n-p-q)!}\sum_{\alpha}\sum_{\beta}(-1)^{p+q+\alpha+\beta}\binom{p}{\alpha}\binom{q}{\beta}B_{i-\alpha,j-\beta}^{n-p-q}(s,t)$$

(xvii) Directional Derivatives (Farin 1986)

(a)

$$D_{\boldsymbol{u}}\{B_{i,j}^n(s,t)\} = n\{u_1 B_{i-1,j}^{n-1}(s,t) + u_2 B_{i,j-1}^{n-1}(s,t) - (u_1+u_2)B_{i,j}^{n-1}(s,t)\}$$

(b)

$$D_{\boldsymbol{u}}^m\{B_{i,j}^n(s,t)\}$$

$$= \frac{n!}{(n-m)!}\sum_{\alpha}\sum_{\beta}\binom{m}{\alpha\ \beta}u_1^{\alpha}u_2^{\beta}\{-u_1-u_2\}^{m-\alpha-\beta}B_{i-\alpha,j-\beta}^{n-m}(s,t)$$

($D_{\boldsymbol{u}}^m$ denotes the mth directional derivative in the direction $\boldsymbol{u} = (u_1, u_2)$.)

(xviii) Integrals (Farin 1988)

(a)

$$\int_0^t B_k^n(\tau)d\tau = \sum_{k+1\le j\le n+1}\frac{B_j^{n+1}(t)}{n+1}$$

(b)

$$\int_t^1 B_k^n(\tau)d\tau = \sum_{0\le j\le k}\frac{B_j^{n+1}(t)}{n+1}$$

(c)

$$\int_0^1 B_k^n(\tau)d\tau = \frac{1}{n+1}$$

(d)

$$\int_0^s B_{i,j}^n(\sigma,t)d\sigma = \sum_{h\geq i+1} \frac{B_{h,j}^{n+1}(s,t)}{n+1}$$

(e)

$$\int_s^{1-t} B_{i,j}^n(\sigma,t)d\sigma = \sum_{h\leq i} \frac{B_{h,j}^{n+1}(s,t)}{n+1}$$

(f)

$$\int_0^{1-t} B_{i,j}^n(\sigma,t)d\sigma = \frac{B_j^{n+1}(t)}{n+1}$$

(g)

$$\int_0^t B_{i,j}^n(s,\tau)d\tau = \sum_{k\geq j+1} \frac{B_{i,k}^{n+1}(s,t)}{n+1}$$

(h)

$$\int_t^{1-s} B_{i,j}^n(s,\tau)d\tau = \sum_{k\leq j} \frac{B_{i,k}^{n+1}(s,t)}{n+1}$$

(i)

$$\int_0^{1-s} B_{i,j}^n(s,\tau)d\tau = \frac{B_i^{n+1}(s)}{n+1}$$

(j)

$$\iint_{\Delta^2} B_{i,j}^n(\sigma,\tau)d\sigma d\tau = \frac{1}{(n+1)(n+2)}$$

(xix) Degree Elevation (Farin 1988)

(a)

$$(1-t)B_k^n(t) = \frac{n+1-k}{n+1}B_k^{n+1}(t)$$

(b)

$$tB_k^n(t) = \frac{k+1}{n+1}B_{k+1}^{n+1}(t)$$

(c)

$$B_k^n(t) = \frac{n+1-k}{n+1}B_k^{n+1}(t) + \frac{k+1}{n+1}B_{k+1}^{n+1}(t)$$

(d)

$$(1-s-t)B_{i,j}^n(s,t) = \frac{n+1-i-j}{n+1}B_{i,j}^{n+1}(s,t)$$

(e)

$$sB_{i,j}^n(s,t) = \frac{i+1}{n+1}B_{i+1,j}^{n+1}(s,t)$$

(f)

$$tB_{i,j}^n(s,t) = \frac{j+1}{n+1}B_{i,j+1}^{n+1}(s,t)$$

(g)

$$B_{i,j}^n(s,t) = \frac{n+1-i-j}{n+1}B_{i,j}^{n+1}(s,t)$$
$$+ \frac{i+1}{n+1}B_{i+1,j}^{n+1}(s,t) + \frac{j+1}{n+1}B_{i,j+1}^{n+1}(s,t)$$

(xx) Products and Higher-Order Degree Elevation (Farouki and Rajan 1988)

(a)

$$B_j^m(t)B_k^n(t) = \frac{\binom{m}{j}\binom{n}{k}}{\binom{m+n}{j+k}}B_{j+k}^{m+n}(t)$$

(b)

$$B_k^n(t) = \sum_{0 \le j \le m} \frac{\binom{m}{j}\binom{n}{k}}{\binom{m+n}{j+k}} B_{j+k}^{m+n}(t)$$

(c)

$$B_{i,j}^m(s,t)B_{k,l}^n(s,t) = \frac{\binom{m}{i\ j}\binom{n}{k\ l}}{\binom{m+n}{i+k\ j+l}} B_{i+k,j+l}^{m+n}(s,t)$$

(d)

$$B_{k,l}^n(s,t) = \sum_i \sum_j \frac{\binom{m}{i\ j}\binom{n}{k\ l}}{\binom{m+n}{i+k\ j+l}} B_{i+k,j+l}^{m+n}(s,t)$$

(xxi) Generating Functions

(a)

$$\sum_k B_k^n(t)x^k = \{(1-t) + tx\}^n$$

(b)

$$\sum_{k} B_k^n(t)e^{ky} = \{(1-t) + te^y\}^n$$

(c)

$$\sum_i \sum_j B_{i,j}^n(s,t)x^i y^j = \{(1-s-t) + sx + ty\}^n$$

(d)

$$\sum_i \sum_j B_{i,j}^n(s,t)e^{ix}e^{jy} = \{(1-s-t) + se^x + te^y\}^n$$

(xxii) Marsden Identities (Cavaretta and Micchelli 1992, Marsden 1970)

(a)

$$(x - t)^n = \sum_k \frac{(-1)^k}{\binom{n}{k}} B_{n-k}^n(x) B_k^n(t)$$

(b)

$$(sx + ty + 1)^n = \sum_i \sum_j (x + 1)^i (y + 1)^j B_{i,j}^n(s, t)$$

(xxiii) de Boor–Fix Formulas
(de Boor and Fix 1973, Lodha and Goldman 1994, Zhao and Sun 1988)

(a)

$$\left\{ \frac{1}{n!} \binom{n}{i} \right\} \sum_p (-1)^{j+p} \{ B_i^n(t) \}^{(p)} \{ B_{n-j}^n(t) \}^{(n-p)} = \delta_{i,j} = \begin{cases} 0 & i \neq j \\ 1 & i = j \end{cases}$$

(b)

$$\left(\frac{1}{n!} \right) \sum_p \sum_q \binom{i}{p} \binom{j}{q} (n - p - q)! \, \partial^{p+q} B_{k,l}^n(0, 0) / \partial s^p \partial t^q = \delta_{i,k} \delta_{j,l}$$

(xxiv) Relationships between Univariate and Bivariate Basis Functions
(Goldman and Filip 1987, Goldman 1983)

(a)

$$B_i^n(s) = \sum_{0 \leq j \leq n-i} B_{i,j}^n(s, t)$$

(b)

$$B_j^n(t) = \sum_{0 \leq i \leq n-j} B_{i,j}^n(s, t)$$

(c)

$$B_k^n(s + t) = \sum_{i+j=k} B_{i,j}^n(s, t)$$

(d)

$$B_{i,j}^n(s,t) = \sum_p \sum_q (-1)^{n-p-q} \begin{pmatrix} n \\ p \quad q \end{pmatrix} B_i^p(s) B_j^q(t)$$

(e)

$$B_{i,j}^n(su,tv) = \sum_k \sum_l B_i^k(u) B_j^l(v) B_{k,l}^n(s,t)$$

(xxv) Conversion between Bivariate and Tensor Product Bases
(Goldman and Filip 1987, Brueckner 1980)

(a)

$$B_i^m(s) B_j^n(t) = \sum_k \sum_l \frac{\begin{pmatrix} k \\ i \end{pmatrix} \begin{pmatrix} l \\ j \end{pmatrix} \begin{pmatrix} m+n-k-l \\ m-i+j-l \end{pmatrix}}{\begin{pmatrix} m+n \\ n \end{pmatrix}} B_{k,l}^{m+n}(s,t)$$

(b)

$$B_{i,j}^n(s,t) = \sum_{k,l} \sum_{p,q} (-1)^{n-p-q} \frac{\begin{pmatrix} n \\ p \quad q \end{pmatrix} \begin{pmatrix} p \\ i \end{pmatrix} \begin{pmatrix} q \\ j \end{pmatrix} \begin{pmatrix} n-p \\ k-i \end{pmatrix} \begin{pmatrix} n-q \\ l-j \end{pmatrix}}{\begin{pmatrix} n \\ k \end{pmatrix} \begin{pmatrix} n \\ l \end{pmatrix}} B_k^n(s) B_l^n(t)$$

◇ **Acknowledgment** ◇

This work was partially supported by NSF grant CCR-9113239.

◇ **Bibliography** ◇

(de Boor and Fix 1973) C. de Boor and G. Fix. Spline approximation by quasi-interpolants. *J. Approx. Theory*, 8:19–45, 1973.

(Brueckner 1980) I. Brueckner. Construction of Bézier points of quadrilaterals from those of triangles. *Computer-Aided Design*, 12:21–24, 1980.

(Cavaretta and Micchelli 1992) A. Cavaretta and C. Micchelli. Pyramid patches provide potential polynomial paradigms. In T. Lyche and L. Schumaker, editors, *Mathematical Methods in CAGD II*, pages 69–100. Academic Press, Boston, 1992.

(Farin 1986) G. Farin. Triangular Bernstein–Bézier patches. *Computer Aided Geometric Design*, 3:83–127, 1986.

(Farin 1988) G. Farin. *Curves and Surfaces for Computer Aided Geometric Design: A Practical Guide*. Academic Press, Inc., New York, 1988.

(Farouki and Rajan 1988) R. T. Farouki and V. T. Rajan. Algorithms for polynomials in Bernstein form. *Computer Aided Geometric Design*, 5:1–26, 1988.

(Goldman 1982) R. N. Goldman. Using degenerate Bézier triangles and tetrahedra to subdivide Bézier curves. *Computer-Aided Design*, 14(6):307–311, 1982.

(Goldman 1983) R. N. Goldman. Subdivision algorithms for Bézier triangles. *Computer-Aided Design*, 15(3):159–166, 1983.

(Goldman and Filip 1987) R. N. Goldman and D. Filip. Conversion from Bézier rectangles to Bézier triangles. *Computer-Aided Design*, 19(1):25–28, 1987.

(Lodha and Goldman 1994) S. Lodha and R. N. Goldman. A multivariate generalization of the de Boor–Fix formula. In Pierre-Jean Laurent, Alain Le Mehaute, and Larry Schumaker, editors, *Curves and Surfaces in Geometric Design*, pages 301–310. A.K. Peters, Ltd., 1994.

(Marsden 1970) M. J. Marsden. An identity for spline functions with applications to variation-diminishing spline approximation. *J. Approx. Theory*, 3:7–49, 1970.

(Polya and Schoenberg 1958) G. Polya and I. Schoenberg. Remarks on De La Vallee Poussin means and convex conformal maps of the circle. *Pacific Jour. of Math.*, 8:296–334, 1958.

(Zhao and Sun 1988) K. Zhao and J. Sun. Dual bases of multivariate Bernstein–Bézier polynomials. *Computer Aided Geometric Design*, 5:119–125, 1988.

IV.2

Identities for the B-Spline Basis Functions

Ronald N. Goldman

Department of Computer Science
Rice University
Houston, Texas
rng@cs.rice.edu

◇ Introduction ◇

The purpose of this gem is to collect in one place those properties and identities of the B-spline basis functions that are most helpful for understanding and investigating B-spline curves and tensor product B-spline surfaces. This gem presents these identities in a consistent framework and may serve both as a compact reference and as a source for additional investigation. Further discussion and proofs of most of these identities can be found in general references books on splines (Bartels *et al.* 1987, de Boor 1978, Schumaker 1981). Citations are provided for some of the less common identities.

◇ Notation ◇

The kth B-spline basis function, $N_{k,n}(t)$, of degree n over the knot vector $t_0, t_1, \ldots, t_m$ is a piecewise polynomial of degree n with breakpoints at the knots and support in the interval $[t_k, t_{k+n+1}]$. The smoothness at each knot depends on its multiplicity. Usually the B-spline basis functions are defined recursively, though explicit formulas in terms of divided differences are also known (see below).

B-spline curves and surfaces are constructed by setting

$$C(t) = \sum_k N_{k,n}(t) P_k \qquad \text{(curves)}$$
$$S(u,v) = \sum_i \sum_j N_{i,m}(u) N_{j,n}(v) P_{i,j} \qquad \text{(tensor product surfaces)}.$$

NURBS curves and surfaces are defined similarly by introducing a collection of scalar weights, multiplying the control points by the weights, and scaling by a denominator that is the sum of the weights times the basis functions. Thus,

$$C(t) = \frac{\sum_k N_{k,n}(t) w_k P_k}{\sum_j w_j N_{j,n}(t)} \qquad \text{(NURBS curves)}$$

$$S(u,v) = \frac{\sum_i \sum_j N_{i,m}(u) N_{j,n}(v) w_{i,j} P_{i,j}}{\sum_p \sum_q w_{p,q} N_{p,m}(u) N_{p,n}(v)} \qquad \text{(tensor product NURBS surfaces)}.$$

When there is no confusion about the location of the knots, the notation $N_{k,n}(t)$ denotes the B-spline basis function of degree n with support in the interval $[t_k, t_{k+n+1}]$. Otherwise, knots are made explicit:

$$N_{k,n}(t \mid t_k, \ldots, t_{k+n+1}) = \text{the B-spline basis function of degree } n \text{ with}$$
$$\text{breakpoints at the knots } t_k, \ldots, t_{k+n+1} \text{ and support}$$
$$\text{in the interval } [t_k, t_{k+n+1}].$$

In several formulas it is necessary to normalize by dividing each B-spline by the length of its support. An abbreviated (and easier to remember) notation may be used:

$$N_{k,n}(t)/\text{Support} = N_{k,n}(t)/(t_{k+n+1} - t_k).$$

Finally, the notation $F[x_0, \ldots, x_n]$ denotes the divided difference of a function F evaluated at the parameters $x_0, \ldots, x_n$; Δ^n denotes the simplex

$$\{(v_1, \ldots, v_{n+1}) \mid v_1, \ldots, v_{n+1} \geq 0 \text{ and } \sum v_k = 1\}, \quad \text{and}$$

$$(x - t)_+^n = \begin{cases} (x - t)^n & x > t \\ 0 & x \leq t \end{cases}.$$

◇   Algebraic Identities for B-Spline Basis Functions   ◇

(i) Compact Support

$$\text{Support}\{N_{k,n}(t)\} = [t_k, t_{k+n+1}]$$

(ii) Smoothness at the Knots

$$\tau \text{ appears } \mu \text{ times in the sequence } t_k, \ldots, t_{k+n+1} \implies N_{k,n}(t) \text{ is } C^{n-\mu} \text{ at } \tau$$

(iii) Interpolation at the Knots

$$t_{j+1} = \cdots = t_{j+n} \implies N_{j,n}(t_{j+1}) = 1$$

(iv) Evaluation at the Knots

$$N_{k,n}(t_{k+j} \mid t_k, \ldots, t_{k+n+1}) = N_{k,n-1}(t_{k+j} \mid t_k, \ldots, t_{k+j-1}, t_{k+j+1}, \ldots, t_{k+n+1})$$

(v) Non-negativity

$$N_{k,n}(t) \geq 0$$

(vi) Partition of Unity

$$\sum_k N_{k,n}(t) = 1$$

(vii) Recursion

$$N_{k,n+1}(t) = \{(t - t_k)/(t_{k+n+1} - t_k)\}N_{k,n}(t)$$
$$+ \{(t_{k+n+2} - t)/(t_{k+n+2} \quad t_{k+1})\}N_{k+1,n}(t)$$
$$N_{k,n+1}(t) = (t - t_k)N_{k,n}(t)/\text{Support} + (t_{k+n+2} - t)N_{k+1,n}(t)/\text{Support}$$

(viii) Differentiation

$$dN_{k,n}(t)/dt = n\{N_{k,n-1}(t)/(t_{k+n} - t_k) - N_{k+1,n-1}(t)/(t_{k+n+1} - t_{k+1})\}$$
$$dN_{k,n}(t)/dt = n\{N_{k,n-1}(t)/\text{Support} - N_{k+1,n-1}(t)/\text{Support}\}$$

(ix) Integration

$$\int_{\text{Support}} \left\{ \frac{N_{k,n}(t)}{\text{Support}} \right\} dt = \frac{1}{(n+1)}$$

$$\int_{\text{Support}} \left\{ \frac{N_{k,n}(t)}{\text{Support}} \right\} \left\{ \frac{F^{(n+1)}(t)}{n!} \right\} dt = F[t_k, \ldots, t_{k+n+1}]$$

$$\int_{\text{Support}} \left\{ \frac{N_{k,n}(t)}{\text{Support}} \right\} \left\{ \frac{F^{(n+1)}(t)}{n!} \right\} dt = \int_{\Delta^n} F^{(n+1)}\left(\sum_j v_j t_{k+j} \right) dv_1 \ldots dv_{n+1}$$

$$\int_{-\infty}^{\infty} \left\{ \frac{N_{i,m}(t)}{\text{Support}} \right\} \left\{ \frac{N_{j,n}(t)}{\text{Support}} \right\} dt = \left\{ (-1)^{m+1} \frac{m!\,n!}{(m+n+1)!} \right\} (y-x)_+^{m+n+1}$$
$$[t_j, \ldots, t_{j+n+1}]_y [t_i, \ldots, t_{i+m+1}]_x$$

(Here the subscripts x and y denote the variable with respect to which to compute the divided difference.)

(x) Linear Independence

$$\sum_k c_k N_{k,n}(t) = 0 \iff c_k = 0 \text{ for all } k$$

(xi) Variation Diminishing Property

$$\text{Sign alternations in } (t_n, t_{m-n}) \text{ of } \left[\sum_k c_k N_{k,n}(t) \right] \le \text{Sign alternations } (c_0, \ldots, c_m)$$

(xii) Nodes

$$t - \sum_{k}[(t_{k+1} + \cdots + t_{k+n})/n]N_{k,n}(t)$$

(xiii) Representation of the Monomials

$$\frac{n!}{j!\,(n-j)!}t^j = \sum_{k}\left\{\sum_{\sigma}(t_{k+\sigma(1)}\cdots t_{k+\sigma(j)})\right\}N_{k,n}(t)\ (\sigma = \text{permutation of } \{1,\ldots,n\})$$

(xiv) Divided Difference Formula

$$N_{k,n}(t) = (-1)^{n+1}(t_{k+n+1} - t_k)(t - x)^n_+[t_k,\ldots,t_{k+n+1}]$$

$$\frac{N_{k,n}(t)}{\text{Support}} = (-1)^{n+1}(t - x)^n_+[t_k,\ldots,t_{k+n+1}]$$

(xv) Marsden Identity (Marsden 1970)

$$(x - t)^n = \sum_{k} N_{k,n}(x)(t_{k+1} - t)\ldots(t_{k+n} - t)$$

(xvi) de Boor–Fix Formula (de Boor and Fix 1973)

$$\sum_{r}\left\{\frac{(-1)^{(n-r)}}{n!}\right\}\{N_{j,n}(\tau)\}^{(r)}\{(t_{k+1} - \tau)\ldots(t_{k+n} - \tau)\}^{(n-r)} = \delta_{j,k} = \begin{cases} 0 & j \neq k \\ 1 & j = k \end{cases}$$

for all $\tau \in (t_{k+1}, t_{k+n})$

(xvii) Knot Insertion (Boehm 1980)

$$N_{k,n}(t|t_k,\ldots,t_{k+n+1}) = \left\{\frac{\tau - t_k}{t_{k+n} - t_k}\right\}N_{k,n}(t \mid t_k,\ldots,\tau,\ldots t_{k+n})$$

$$+ \left\{\frac{t_{k+n+1} - \tau}{t_{k+n+1} - t_{k+1}}\right\}N_{k+1,n}(t \mid t_{k+1},\ldots,\tau,\ldots,t_{k+n+1})$$

(xviii) Degree Elevation (Prautzsch 1984)

$$N_{k,n}(t \mid t_k,\ldots,t_{k+n+1}) = \sum_{j} N_{k,n+1}(t \mid t_k,\ldots,t_{k+j},t_{k+j},\ldots t_{k+n+1})/(n + 1)$$

(xix) Continuous Convolution Formula for Uniform B-splines

$$N_{0,n}(t \mid 0,\ldots,n + 1) = \int_{-\infty}^{\infty} N_{0,n-1}(t - x \mid 0,\ldots,n)dx$$

$$N_{0,n}(t \mid 0,\ldots,n + 1) = \chi_{[0,1]} * \cdots * \chi_{[0,1]}\ (n \text{ factors})$$

$$\chi_{[0,1]} = \text{characteristic function on } [0, 1]$$

◇ **Acknowledgment** ◇

This work was partially supported by NSF grant CCR-9113239.

◇ **Bibliography** ◇

(Bartels *et al.* 1987) R. Bartels, J. Beatty, and B. Barsky. *An Introduction to Splines for Use in Computer Graphics and Geometric Modeling.* Morgan Kaufmann Publishers, Inc., 1987.

(Boehm 1980) W. Boehm. Inserting new knots into B-spline curves. *Computer-Aided Design,* 12:199–201, 1980.

(de Boor 1978) C. de Boor. *A Practical Guide to Splines.* Springer, 1978.

(de Boor and Fix 1973) C. de Boor and G. Fix. Spline approximation by quasi-interpolants. *J. Approx. Theory,* 8:19–45, 1973.

(Marsden 1970) M. J. Marsden. An identity for spline functions with applications to variation-diminishing spline approximation. *J. Approx. Theory,* 3:7–49, 1970.

(Prautzsch 1984) H. Prautzsch. Degree elevation of B-spline curves. *Computer Aided Geometric Design,* 1:193–198, 1984.

(Schumaker 1981) L. Schumaker. *Spline Functions: Basic Theory.* John Wiley and Sons, New York, 1981.

IV.3

Circular Arc Subdivision

Ken Turkowski

Apple Computer, Inc.
Cupertino, California
turk@apple.com

◇   **Introduction**   ◇

This gem presents an algebraic solution to the rendering problem of circular arcs. These forms commonly arise in graphic design. For instance, well-designed typefaces may apply a very slight curvature on a portion of a letterform to produce a profound aesthetic effect.[1]

A circular arc may be represented in terms of the center and radius of its parent circle, plus the starting and ending angles θ_{st} and θ_{end}. This suggests a first-principles solution that generates successive points on the arc by evaluating the sine and cosine of a series of intermediate angles:

$$x = x_0 + r \cos\theta \qquad \text{with}$$
$$y = y_0 + r \sin\theta, \qquad \theta_{st} \leq \theta \leq \theta_{end}.$$

Clearly, this approach is computationally intensive. Moreover, the method has numerical problems if the radius is large, the circle's center is remote, or the values have limited precision (e.g., fixed-point or even single-precision floating point). All these undesirable conditions arise for any arc having a very small bend, as its radius of curvature rapidly grows to infinity.

An algebraic, vector-based approach instead subdivides the arc into two halves until the (inverse radius of) curvature goes to zero and a vector suffices. This suggests a recursive implementation that can also terminate when a sufficient number of intermediate vertices have been produced (i.e., the length of the intermediate vector is very small, independent of curvature). This approach avoids both trigonometric operations and ill-conditioned formulas. The method is derived from related work (Karow 1987) based upon a suggestion. Both the expressions and an error analysis are presented below.

---

[1]Hermann Zapf's *Optima* is such an example, resembling his well-known *Helvetica* save for a slight curve on otherwise vertical strokes.

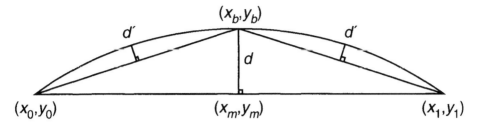

Figure 1. Bisecting and quad-secting the arc.

◇   **Derivation**   ◇

The circular arc is represented by its endpoints and the chordal deviation:

$$(x_0, \ y_0, \ x_1, \ y_1, \ d).$$

The sign of d is used to distinguish between the two arcs that lie on either side of the chord that joins the endpoints (in Figure 1, d is positive).

The bisection point of each arc is used as an endpoint for each half arc:

$$x_b = \frac{x_0 + x_1}{2} - d\frac{y_1 - y_0}{L},$$

$$y_b = \frac{y_0 + y_1}{2} + d\frac{x_1 - x_0}{L},$$

where

$$L = \sqrt{(x_1 - x_0)^2 + (y_1 - y_0)^2}$$

is the length of the chord.

The chordal deviation d', or *sagitta*, of the bisected arc can be approximated by

$$d' \approx \frac{d}{4}.$$

In other words, when an arc is divided into congruent "sub-arc" halves, their chordal deviation is divided by about four.

By repeated bisection of the arc, the chordal deviation is reduced with *quadratic* convergence. The arc is then replaced with a series of sub-arcs until a tolerance is reached. This approximation works well for arcs subtending less than about 75°; however, this depends upon the resolution and arc radius (estimated by d).

◇ **Proof** ◇

The ratio between the two chordal deviations can be expressed as

$$\frac{d}{d'} = \frac{1 \quad \cos\theta}{1 - \cos\frac{\theta}{2}},$$

where θ is the angle subtended by the smaller arc. Substituting $\cos\theta = 2\cos^2\frac{\theta}{2} - 1$ yields

$$\frac{d}{d'} = \frac{1 - \left(2\cos^2\frac{\theta}{2} - 1\right)}{1 - \cos\frac{\theta}{2}} = 2\frac{1 - \cos^2\frac{\theta}{2}}{1 - \cos\frac{\theta}{2}} = 2\left(1 + \cos\frac{\theta}{2}\right).$$

This is an exact representation. Expanding its reciprocal as a Taylor series about zero gives

$$\frac{d'}{d} = \frac{1}{2(1 + \cos\frac{\theta}{2})} = \frac{1}{4} + \frac{\theta^2}{64} + \frac{\theta^4}{1536} + O(\theta^6),$$

the desired result.

The error in the approximation of d' can be approximated well by retaining terms through the quadratic, $\frac{\theta^2}{64}$. The exact error is

$$\epsilon = d' - \tilde{d}' = d\left(\frac{1 - \cos\frac{\theta}{2}}{1 - \cos\theta} - \frac{1}{4}\right).$$

◇ **C Implementation** ◇

```
/* arcdivide.c - recursive circular arc subdivision (FP version) */

#define DMAX 0.5    /* max chordal deviation = 1/2 pixel */

#include <math.h>
#include <GraphicsGems.h>

/* Function prototype for externally defined functions */
void DrawLine(Point2 p0, Point2 p1);

void
DrawArc(Point2 p0, Point2 p1, double d)
{
    if (fabs(d) <= DMAX) DrawLine(p0, p1);
    else {
        Vector2 v;
        Point2  pm, pb;
```

```
    double   dSub;

    v.x = p1.x - p0.x;        /* vector from p0 to p1 */
    v.y = p1.y   p0.y;

    pm.x = p0.x + 0.5 * v.x;  /* midpoint */
    pm.y = p0.y + 0.5 * v.y;

    dSub = d / 4;
    V2Scale(&v, dSub);        /* subdivided vector */

    pb.x = pm.x - v.y;        /* bisection point */
    pb.y = pm.y + v.x;

    DrawArc(p0, pb, dSub);    /* first half arc */
    DrawArc(pb, p1, dSub);    /* second half arc */
    }
}
```

◇   **Discussion**   ◇

This method quickly produces a polyline that inscribes the circular arc. It should be faster than a previous gem (Musial 1991), which employs a secant-based root finder and trigonometric functions to maintain arc length while splitting errors between the outside and inside of the arc.

A variant method (Paeth 1988) uses a nonuniform chord subdivision to locate the point where the sagitta has dropped to half its height. Given a chord on the interval $[-1 \ldots +1]$ along the x-axis having sagitta s, the points of half-sagitta descent lie at $\pm\frac{1}{2}\sqrt{2+s}$. These converge to a constant offset for $s \approx 0$ — a parabola then approximates the circle. This formulation adds floating-point overhead to account for the nonuniform subdivision.

For IEEE-based (radix 2) floating-point representations, halving operations are almost free.

A fixed-point implementation of this uniform subdivision algorithm will be faster on many machines than a floating-point implementation. Multiplication by two and four can be accomplished by a right shift, and a fixed-point square root (see page 22) can be used to help rescale the vector.

Given d_{max}, the maximum chordal deviation allowed by approximating a circular arc by a series of line segments, the number of arc bisections n can be computed as

$$n = \left\lceil \frac{|d_0|}{4d_{max}} \right\rceil,$$

where d_0 is the initial chordal deviation and $\lceil \cdots \rceil$ is the *ceiling* function. This fact can be used to write a faster implementation that uses iteration instead of recursion, as advocated for parametric curves in another gem (Lindgren *et al.* 1992) that also uses maximum chordal deviation as a subdivision criterion.

◇ **Bibliography** ◇

(Karow 1987) Peter Karow. *Digital Formats for Typefaces*, pages 236–251. URW Verlag, Hamburg, Germany, 1987.

(Lindgren *et al.* 1992) Terence Lindgren, Juan Sanchez, and Jim Hall. Curve tessellation criteria through sampling. In David Kirk, editor, *Graphics Gems III*, pages 262–265. AP Professional, Boston, 1992.

(Musial 1991) Christopher Musial. A good straight-line approximation of a circular arc. In James Arvo, editor, *Graphics Gems II*, pages 435–439. AP Professional, Boston, 1991.

(Paeth 1988) Alan Paeth. Lemming editor. *IRIS Software Exchange*, 1(17), Summer 1988.

◊ IV.4

Adaptive Sampling of Parametric Curves

Luiz Henrique de Figueiredo
IMPA, Instituto de Matemática Pura e Aplicada
Rio de Janeiro, Brasil
lhf@visgraf.impa.br

◊ Introduction ◊

Approximating a parametric curve by a polygonal curve is a practical undertaking, involving a sampling of the parameter domain. A first-principles *uniform* sampling strategy remains the most popular. Unfortunately, it can prove very inefficient if high precision is required.

This gem presents an *adaptive* method for sampling the domain with respect to local curvature. Samples concentration is in proportion to this curvature, resulting in a more efficient approximation—in the limit, a flat curve is approximated by merely two endpoints. Applications of this sampling strategy, including rasterization and arc length parametrization, are also discussed.

◊ Uniform Sampling ◊

Let $\gamma\colon [0,1] \to \mathrm{R}^d$ describe a curve lying in d-dimensional space (typically, $d \leq 3$). To approximate γ, choose n equally spaced sample points $0 = t_1 < t_1 < \cdots < t_n = 1$, which define the vertices $v_0, v_1, \ldots, v_n$, where $v_i = \gamma(l_i)$. The challenge is to choose sample points $t_1 \ldots t_n$ that induce a good approximation while keeping n small. Methods of uniform sampling most often choose n by trial and error (trading accuracy for efficiency), though automated heuristic tests are available (Lindgren *et al.* 1992).

◊ Adaptive Sampling ◊

Ideally, a nonuniform parametric sampling gives rise to a "uniform" vertex precision, leading to increased sampling density in regions of high curvature. The general method described here is based upon the following strategy:

1. Choose a criterion for refining samples
2. Evaluate the criterion on the interval.
3. If the curve is almost flat in the interval, then the sample is given by its two extremes.
4. Otherwise, divide the interval into two parts and recursively sample the two parts.

This strategy is similar to using the de Casteljau algorithm for Bézier curves, stopping when the control polygon is almost flat. There are a number of heuristic refinement criteria applicable to general curves.

Refinement Criteria

The refinement criterion employed here, termed *probing*, chooses an intermediate point m within the interval of consideration $[a, b]$. Next, it tests the three candidate vertices for (approximate) collinearity, that is, $\overline{v_a v_m} \parallel \overline{v_m v_b}$ is evaluated with $v_a = \gamma(a)$, $v_m = \gamma(m)$ and $v_b = \gamma(b)$. This flatness (parallel vector) test may take a number of forms:

- the area of the triangle $v_a v_m v_b$ is small;
- the angle $\angle v_a v_m v_a$ is close to $180°$;
- v_m lies near the chord $\overline{v_a v_b}$;
- $|v_a - v_m| + |v_m - v_b|$ is approximately equal to $|v_a - v_b|$;
- the curve's tangents at $\gamma(a)$, $\gamma(m)$ and $\gamma(b)$ are approximately parallel.

(The last is of value when a closed-form expression for γ's derivative is available.)

Although they are not equivalent in theory, empirical practice shows that these tests are equally effective in locating regions of low curvature. The area criterion is the algorithm's method of choice, as it requires no square roots.

Choosing the Interior Point

The intuitive choice for the interior point m is the interval's midpoint, $m = \frac{1}{2}(a + b)$. A subtle form of sampling error, or *aliasing*, arises: The probing strategy considers a curve "flat" throughout the interval $a \leq t \leq b$ when a flatness test is satisfied. In fact, the heuristic fails should the curve undulate along the interval under consideration. The sinusoid curve $[t, \sin(t)]$ with t sampled at $\pm i\pi$ is a ready example. Here, every vertex v_i lies along the x-axis. In general, any deterministic probing is vulnerable to aliasing.

Random probing along the interval avoids aliasing sampling due to such symmetries in γ. Since sampling near the interval's midpoint is desirable, a uniform distribution may be biased toward this interior. In this implementation, a uniform distribution on the restricted interval $[0.45, 0.55]$ is employed. Other variations may substitute Gaussian distributions (easily found by summing random variables, by virtue of the central limit theorem) or use multiple probes. Vertices having the greatest deviation may then be chosen preferentially or otherwise used in a recursive evaluation of higher order (Chandler 1990). In practice, the binary recursion scheme presented next provides adequate results.

The Algorithm

For the sake of efficiency, arrange the sampling so that the interior vertex used for the flatness test is also the point of subdivision, should recursion take place. This ensures that γ is evaluated exactly once at each sample point. The pseudocode for the algorithm is

```
sample(a, b, va, vb):
    m ← random point in [a, b]
    vm ← γ(m)
    if flat(va, vm, vb)
        line(va, vb)
    else
        sample(a, m, va, vm)
        sample(m, b, vm, vb)
```

Invoking the function $\texttt{sample}(0, 1, \gamma(0), \gamma(1))$ initiates the procedure on the complete domain $0 \le t \le 1$. The function **flat** implements one of the refinement criteria suggested earlier; **line** is the basic line-drawing operation.

Note that this algorithm generates points in the exact order that they occur along the curve, as the recursive implementation performs a depth-first search of the interval "tree." With proper adaptation, the algorithm performs a direct rasterization of the curve, as when **line(va,vb)** describes coincident pixels or the test **flat(va,vm,vb)** evaluates adjacent pixels. Here, (discrete) Γ substitutes for its continuous counterpart γ. The pseudocode is

```
raster(a, b, va, vb):
    if neighbors(va, vb)
        plot(va)
    else
        m ← random point in [a, b]
        vm ← Γ(m)
        raster(a, m, va, vm)
        raster(m, b, vm, vb)
```

Invoking the function $\texttt{raster}(0, 1, \Gamma(0), \Gamma(1))$ initiates the procedure on the complete domain $0 \le t \le 1$, though the final pixel $\Gamma(1)$ must be plotted explicitly. Note that this implementation requires neither a tolerance test nor a **line** function; recursion depth is determined by the display resolution.

◇ **Applications** ◇

Adaptive sampling strategies may be adopted to solve problems in related fields of numerical integration, quadrature of explicit functions, line integration, or arc length parametrization. The pseudocode for computing the length of a curve is

```
length(a, b, va, vb):
    m ← random point in [a, b]
    vm ← γ(m)
    if flat(va, vm, vb)
        return |vb − va|
    else
        return length(a, m, va, vm) + length(m, b, vm, vb)
```

Functions may also be evaluated based upon methods of binary descent. The arc length parametrization of a curve locates the parameter value t having the corresponding vertex v_t at a desired length along a curve. This calculation is of value in digital animation (Guenter and Parent 1990).

Finally, polygonal lines digitized either manually or automatically (e.g., using an image edge detection algorithm) usually have a large number of vertices. Here, the refining criterion may be used to thin (remove) any redundant vertex v_m collinear with bracketing vertices $\overline{v_a v_b}$. The size of the bracketing interval can once again be computed in adaptive fashion using binary recursion. In this guise, an adaptive sample "running in reverse" rederives a method commonly employed in digital cartography (Visvalingam and Whyatt 1990).

◇ **Implementation** ◇

An implementation of the adaptive sampling method is now presented. Created for use with three-dimensional curves, the code is easily modified to arbitrary dimension, or reworked to provide direct rasterization as in the second pseudocode example.

The data structure `Point` is a `struct` containing the parameter value t and the coordinates x, y, z of $\gamma(t)$. It is used to ensure that γ is never evaluated more than once at any point. Macros providing efficient access to this structure are also provided; these macros also increase program clarity.

The code's core is the recursive sampling function `sample`, which calls two user-defined functions: `gamma`, which computes the coordinates of the point on the curve corresponding to a parameter value, and `line`, which performs the line segment rendering. The function `flat` implements a refinement criterion based on triangle area, using the cross product (the user-supplied tolerance `tol` is used within this code).

The code has been written for simplicity and presentation. A production version passes the functions `gamma`, `line`, and `tol` as parameters to the top-level entry point

aspc, allowing generic operation. In all cases, invoking $\mathbf{aspc}(a, b)$ begins the adaptive sampling of the curve along the interval $[a, b]$.

```
/* aspc.c -- generic adaptive sampling of parametric curves */

typedef struct point { double t,x,y,z; } Point;

#define T(p)      ((p)->t)
#define X(p)      ((p)->x)
#define Y(p)      ((p)->y)
#define Z(p)      ((p)->z)

extern void gamma(Point* p);              /* user supplied */
extern void line(Point* p, Point* q);     /* user supplied */

static void sample(Point* p, Point* q)
{
 Point rr, *r=&rr;
 double t = 0.45 + 0.1 * (rand()/(double) RAND_MAX);
 T(r) = T(p) + t*(T(q)-T(p));
 gamma(r);
 if (flat(p,q,r)) line(p,q); else { sample(p,r); sample(r,q); }
}

static int flat(Point* p, Point* q, Point* r)
{
 extern double tol;                       /* user supplied */
 double xp = X(p)-X(r); double yp = Y(p)-Y(r); double zp = Z(p)-Z(r);
 double xq = X(q)-X(r); double yq = Y(q)-Y(r); double zq = Z(q)-Z(r);
 double x =  yp*zq-yq*zp;
 double y =  xp*zq-xq*zp;
 double z =  xp*yq-xq*yp;
 return (x*x+y*y+z*z) < tol;              /* |pr x qr|√2 < tol */
}

void aspc(double a, double b)             /* entry point */
{
 Point pp, *p = &pp;
 Point qq, *q = &qq;
 srand(time(0));                          /* randomize */
 T(p)= a; gamma(p); T(q)=b; gamma(q);     /* set up */
 sample(p,q);                             /* sample */
}
```

◇ **Bibliography** ◇

(Chandler 1990) R. E. Chandler. A recursive technique for rendering parametric curves. *Computers and Graphics*, 14(3/4):477–479, 1990.

(Guenter and Parent 1990) B. Guenter and R. Parent. Computing the arc length of parametric curves. *IEEE Computer Graphics and Applications*, 10(3):72–78, May 1990.

(Lindgren *et al.* 1992) T. Lindgren, J. Sanchez, and J. Hall. Curve tesselation criteria through sampling. In D. Kirk, editor, *Graphics Gems III*, pages 262–265. AP Professional, Boston, 1992.

(Visvalingam and Whyatt 1990) M. Visvalingam and J. D. Whyatt. The Douglas–Peucker algorithm for line simplification: Re-evaluation through visualization. *Computer Graphics Forum*, 9(3):213–228, September 1990.

◇ IV.5

Fast Generation of Ellipsoids

Jaewoo Ahn
Systems Engineering Research Institute, KIST
Yusong, Daejon, South Korea

◇   Introduction   ◇

Among the many methods for generating a polygonal approximation to an ellipse in standard position (of the form $x^2/a^2 + y^2/b^2 = 1$) (Anton 1984), the one shown in Figure 1 is simple and common. The idea is to subdivide the angles in plane around the center of the unit circle equally, forming a polygonal approximation to the unit circle, which is then scaled by a in the x axis, and by b in the y axis.

Note that vertices get denser around the sharper-axis direction of the ellipse rather than around the smoother-axis one, which is a merit of the method. When the degree of approximation n is given and the approximation is to yield a symmetric polygon of $4 \cdot n$ vertices, the whole $4 \cdot n$ vertices on the unit circle need not actually be computed. Only the first half of the vertices in the first quadrant need to be computed; the cosine and sine values corresponding to the angles $i/n \cdot \pi/2$, $i = 0, 1, \ldots, \lfloor n/2 \rfloor$ are computed [Figure 1(a)]. The other half in the first quadrant are found by knowing that $\cos(\pi/2 - \theta) = \sin\theta$ [Figure 1(b)]. The first quadrant of the ellipse is obtained by scaling [Figure 1(c)], and the remaining quadrants are obtained by reflecting it in the x and the y axis [Figure 1(d)].

The idea for 2D ellipse generation is directly generalized to 3D ellipsoid generation. Vertices on the surface of the unit sphere are generated by subdividing the angles in space around the center of the unit sphere regularly, forming a polyhedral approximation to the unit sphere, which is then scaled appropriately in each of the x, y, and z axes. Triangular faces are also generated with vertices ordered counterclockwise when viewed from the outside. Ellipsoids are symmetric with respect to each of the xy, yz, and zx planes. Thus, we need to compute vertices only in the first octant of the ellipsoid, and the vertices in the other octants can be found by reflections. In fact, as will be discussed, many fewer cosine and sine evaluations are made than is usually thought, even for the initialization of the first octant of the unit sphere.

A regular subdivision of the angles in space around the center of the unit sphere is shown in Figures 2(a) and 2(b). Here, $n \geq 1$ is the degree of subdivision, and (i, j), $j = 0, 1, \ldots, i$, $i = 0, 1, \ldots, n$, corresponds to the vertex with the azimuthal angle $\theta = j/i \cdot \pi/2$ and the incidence angle $\phi = i/n \cdot \pi/2$ (with the convention that $0/0 = 0$). The number of vertices and faces generated under this subdivision are $1 + 4 \cdot (1 + 2 + $

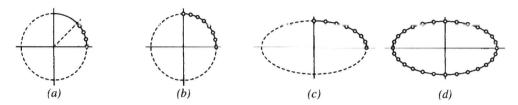

Figure 1. A polygonal approximation to an ellipse ($n = 7$). (a) $(\cos\theta, \sin\theta)$, $\theta = i/n \cdot \pi/2$, $i = 0, 1, \ldots, \lfloor n/2 \rfloor$. (b) The first quadrant of the unit circle. (c) The first quadrant of the ellipse. (d) A polygonal approximation to the ellipse, $(a\cos\theta, b\sin\theta)$, $\theta = i/n \cdot \pi/2$, $i = 0, 1, \ldots, 4 \cdot n - 1$.

$\cdots + n - 1 + n + n - 1 + \cdots + 2 + 1) + 1 = 4 \cdot n^2 + 2$ and $4 \cdot (1 + 3 + \cdots + 2 \cdot n - 1) \cdot 2 = 8 \cdot n^2$, respectively. Incidentally, these numbers are the same as those from the octahedral subdivision method (Angel 1990, Koenderink 1990), which starts from the unit octahedron, subdivides each of the eight original triangular faces into smaller ones, and then projects the vertices of the subdivided triangular faces onto the surface of the unit sphere, forming a refined polyhedral approximation to the unit sphere.

Specifically, three steps are involved in generating a polyhedral approximation to an ellipsoid using the current method, now called the *angular subdivision method*:

1. Initialization of trigonometric values: Cosine and sine values are evaluated corresponding to the azimuthal and the incidence angles of vertices in the first octant of the unit sphere.

2. Generation of the first octant of the ellipsoid: The first octant of the unit sphere is scaled appropriately in each axis direction.

3. Generation of the ellipsoid: Vertices and their unit normals are generated from reflections of those in the first octant, and triangular faces are generated.

In what follows, assume that an ellipsoid is in standard position (of the form $x^2/a^2 + y^2/b^2 + z^2/c^2 = 1$) (Anton 1984), and that its parameters of axis length along the x, y, and z axes are a, b, and c, respectively. Assume also that $n \geq 1$ denotes the degree of subdivision, θ the azimuthal angle measured from the zx plane counterclockwise when viewed from the positive z axis onto the origin, and ϕ the incidence angle measured from the positive z axis.

◇ Ellipsoid Generation ◇

Step 1: Initialization of Trigonometric Values

The cosine and sine arguments needed for the angular subdivision method are the angles belonging to the vertices on the first octant of the unit sphere. Figure 2(a) is a projection of the first octant of the unit sphere having vertices generated by the angular

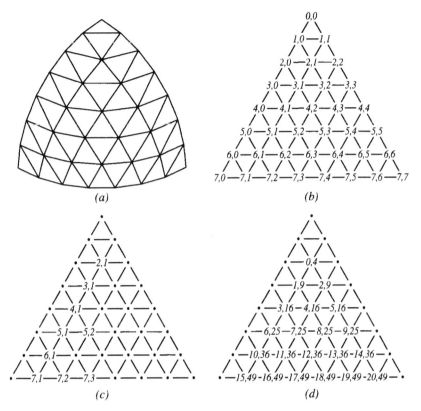

Figure 2. The first octant of the unit sphere ($n = 7$). (a) Vertices on the first octant. (b) (i, j), $j = 0, 1, \ldots, i$, $i = 0, 1, \ldots, n$, corresponding to the vertex with $(\theta, \phi) = (j/i \cdot \pi/2, i/n \cdot \pi/2)$. (c) (i, j)'s with $0 < j < i$, $\gcd(i, j) = 1$. (d) (k, l)'s for finding the slots of (i, j)'s with $\gcd(i, j) > 1$.

subdivision method with $n = 7$. Figure 2(b) draws the relationship between the vertices and their azimuthal angle θ and incidence angle ϕ, where $\theta = j/i \cdot \pi/2$ and $\phi = i/n \cdot \pi/2$.

A minimal set of angles for which the cosine and sine values need to be evaluated may now be found. First, only the azimuthal angles need to be considered, since $\phi = i/n \cdot \pi/2$, $0 < i < n$, is the same as $\theta = j/i \cdot \pi/2$, $0 < j < i$, $i = n$. Second, the angles when $j = 0$ or $j = i$ are trivial and do not need real evaluations for cosine and sine values, nor do the angles corresponding to $(h \cdot i, h \cdot j)$ for $h = 2, \ldots, \lfloor n/i \rfloor$, since they are the same as the angle corresponding to (i, j). Moreover, $(\cos \theta, \sin \theta)$ for $\theta = (i - j)/i \cdot \pi/2$ is the same as $(\sin \theta, \cos \theta)$ for $\theta = j/i \cdot \pi/2$. Therefore, we need to evaluate cosine and sine values only for the angles $j/i \cdot \pi/2$, where $\gcd(i, j) = 1$, $1 \leq j \leq \lfloor i/2 \rfloor$, $i = 2, \ldots, n$. Figure 2(c) shows those (i, j)'s corresponding to these angles.

For the other (i, j)'s that are not trivial and $\gcd(i, j) > 1$, $1 < j < i$, $i = 2, \ldots, n$, their corresponding cosine and sine values are copied from those of $(i/\gcd(i, j), j/\gcd(i, j))$ or from those of $(i, i - j)$ in step 2. In practice, an array of $1 + 2 + \cdots + n - 1$

$= (n-1) \cdot n/2$ slots for $(\cos\theta, \sin\theta)$'s corresponding to the vertices (i, j), $0 < j < i$, $2 \le i \le n$ is initialized (see Figure 3(a)). Figure 2(d) associates a pair (k, l) to each of the nontrivial (i, j)'s of Figure 2(b), where $k = (i-2) \cdot (i-1)/2 + j - 1$ and $l = i^2$. Incidentally, k is the same as the index of the array of slots for $(\cos\theta, \sin\theta)$, where $\theta = j/i \cdot \pi/2$ (see Figure 3(a)). Then, the index of the slot for $(h \cdot i, h \cdot j)$, $h \ge 2$ is $(h \cdot i - 2) \cdot (h \cdot i - 1)/2 + h \cdot j - 1$, or equivalently, $h \cdot k + ((h-1) \cdot h/2) \cdot l$. The latter form directly shows us that the indices for $(h \cdot i, h \cdot j)$, $h \ge 1$ are k, $2 \cdot k + l$, $3 \cdot k + 3 \cdot l$, $4 \cdot k + 6 \cdot l$, $5 \cdot k + 10 \cdot l$, etc. The indices advance successively by $k + l$, $k + 2 \cdot l$, $k + 3 \cdot l$, $k + 4 \cdot l$, etc. That is, knowing $(\cos\theta, \sin\theta)$ of the slot for (i, j) with $\gcd(i, j) = 1$, the indices of the slots for $(h \cdot i, h \cdot j)$, $2 \le h \le \lfloor n/i \rfloor$, that have the same $(\cos\theta, \sin\theta)$ values are $k + \sum_{d=1}^{h-1}(k + d \cdot l)$.

```
struct slot { float cos, sin; enum { None, Only, Done } flag; };
```

The `flag` field of each slot for (i, j) marks the status of the slot. `None` marks that `cos` and `sin` are not set yet. `Only` marks that they are set, but still need to be copied to $(h \cdot i, h \cdot j)$, $h = 2, \ldots, \lfloor n/i \rfloor$, and `Done` marks that nothing need be done. Note that the initialization does not need to be done for every invocation of the angular subdivision method; once it is initialized for some maximum degree of subdivision n_{max}, no further initialization is necessary for any degree of subdivision $n \le n_{max}$. In other words, as long as the degree of subdivision does not exceed n_{max}, no further cosine and sine evaluations are necessary in generating ellipsoids. Step 1 is implemented by the routine `ellipsoid_init()`.

Step 2: Construction of the First Octant of the Ellipsoid

The position (p_x, p_y, p_z) and the unit normal (n_x, n_y, n_z) of a vertex on an ellipsoid are computed by

$$
\begin{aligned}
p_x(\theta, \phi) &= \cos\theta \cdot \sin\phi \cdot a, \\
p_y(\theta, \phi) &= \sin\theta \cdot \sin\phi \cdot b, \\
p_z(\theta, \phi) &= \cos\phi \cdot c, \\
n_x(\theta, \phi) &= \cos\theta \cdot \sin\phi \cdot a^{-1}, \\
n_y(\theta, \phi) &= \sin\theta \cdot \sin\phi \cdot b^{-1}, \\
n_z(\theta, \phi) &= \cos\phi \cdot c^{-1}.
\end{aligned}
$$

Note that all the necessary cosine and sine values have been computed and stored in a table in step 1. Figure 3(a) shows the indices of the table [cf. Figure 2(d)]. Figure 3(b) shows the first octant of an ellipsoid that is to be generated in step 2. This is called the *base* octant to avoid any confusion with the first octant of the eight octants of the

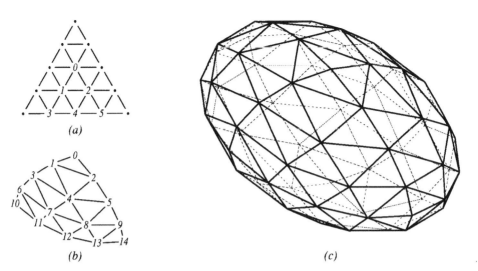

Figure 3. Generation of an ellipsoid ($n = 4$). (a) Indices of the cosine and sine table. (b) Indices of the base octant of the ellipsoid. (c) An approximation to the ellipsoid as generated through reflections of the base octant.

ellipsoid that are to be generated from this base octant in step 3. Step 2 is implemented by the routine `ellipsoid_octant()`.

Step 3: Generation of the Ellipsoid

After the base octant is constructed, it is reflected through the three coordinate planes to produce an array of all vertices. An array of all triangular faces is also produced by finding all the appropriate ordered sets of three indices of the vertex array. Figure 4 shows the indices of the vertex array and the face array. Step 3 is implemented by both sequential and parallel means, by `ellipsoid_seq()` and `ellipsoid_par()`, respectively.

◇ Timing Comparisons ◇

Table 1 lists execution times for generating ellipsoids using this angular subdivision method. The *depth* column denotes the degrees of subdivision, and *#v* and *#f* the numbers of vertices and triangular faces generated, respectively. Execution times are measured in microseconds using the UNIX system call *gettimeofday*(3B) in the SGI's Onyx™ system with four R4400 150 MHz CPUs. Those in the *init* column are for step 1, and those in the *seq* and *par* columns are for steps 2 and 3 in sequential and parallel means, respectively. Note again that the initialization need be done only for the largest degree of subdivision that will be used, once and for all, [see `ellipsoid_init()`]. In

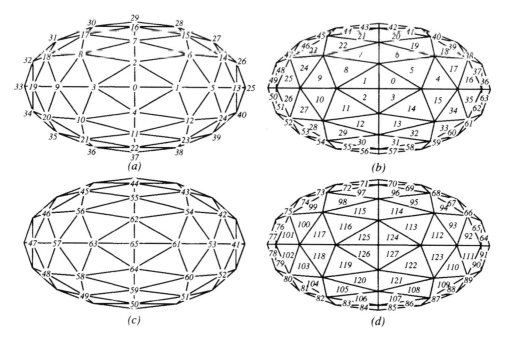

Figure 4. Indices of arrays of vertices and faces ($n = 4$) as viewed from the positive z axis for (a), (b) the first, second, third, and fourth octants, and (c), (d) the fifth, sixth, seventh, and eighth octants.

Table 1. Approximate timing of angular subdivision method.

depth	#v	#f	init	seq	par	libsphere	depth	#v	#f	init	seq	par
1	6	8	3	8	10	417	35	4902	9800	805	4490	3601
2	18	32	9	25	30	1263	40	6402	12800	1068	5861	4581
3	38	72	12	42	50	2640	45	8102	16200	1345	7390	5644
4	66	128	15	65	78	4569	50	10002	20000	1659	9123	6966
5	102	200	21	95	113	7322	55	12102	24200	2044	11117	8323
6	146	288	28	129	154	10782	60	14402	28800	2476	13240	9701
7	198	392	36	169	198	14834	65	16902	33800	2955	15509	11279
8	258	512	45	218	250	19661	70	19602	39200	3457	19107	13100
9	326	648	57	275	305	25395	75	22502	45000	4004	23182	14802
10	402	800	69	352	386	31422	80	25602	51200	4552	28830	17084
15	902	1800	151	845	898	72538	85	28902	57800	5132	34814	18758
20	1602	3200	265	1490	1381	127640	90	32402	64800	5751	41147	21827
25	2502	5000	415	2312	2013	209728	95	36102	72200	6404	47758	24489
30	3602	7200	595	3308	2738	312108	100	40002	80000	7097	54646	26944

the parallel means, the four processors in the machine are utilized by compiling only the `ellipsoid_par()` routine with some simple compiler directives specified in the code for independent loops. It could be tuned further for better performances. Those in the *libsphere* column denote the times for generating spheres using the Sphere Library provided in the SGI's IRIS GL™ system. The comparisons may not be too accurate, however, since the internal operations of the library may not be properly counted, although the author tried to be quite reasonable.

◇   Conclusions   ◇

An efficient angular subdivision of the unit sphere used to model ellipsoid data is described. Unit normals for vertices are also computed accurately from their defining equations. A minimal number of trigonometric functions are evaluated, and parallel constructions may be employed. (Code for both sequential and parallel implementations is provided.)

The initialization of the base octant (steps 1 and 2) may be done using other methods such as the octahedral subdivision method and then reflections (step 3) may be applied to change the schemes and degrees of approximation.

An ellipsoid in nonstandard position can be modeled by an appropriate transformation of its corresponding ellipsoid in standard position. Since a sphere of radius r is an ellipsoid with $a = b = c = r$, the method can be adjusted to model sphere's data more efficiently. Other objects exhibiting (eightfold) symmetry, such as quadratic surfaces and tori, may be modeled efficiently using methods adapting reflections, and they are extensions worthy of additional study.

◇   Acknowledgment   ◇

The author thanks the editor for his valuable comments and criticisms.

◇   An Efficient Implementation in C   ◇

```
/*-< ellipsoid.h >-------------------------------------------------------------*/

#ifndef ellipsoid_H
#define ellipsoid_H

typedef struct point { float x, y, z; } point;
typedef struct vertex {
    point p, n;          /* point and unit normal */
} vertex;
typedef struct face {
    int v0, v1, v2;      /* indices of vertex array for a triangular face */
} face;
```

```
typedef struct object {
    int nv, nf,          /* numbers of elements in v and f */
    vertex *v; face *f; /* arrays of vertices and faces */
} object;

void ellipsoid_init (int n);
void ellipsoid_seq (object *ellipsoid, int n, float a, float b, float c);
void ellipsoid_par (object *ellipsoid, int n, float a, float b, float c);

#endif /* ellipsoid_H */

/*-< ellipsoid.c >-------------------------------------------------------------*/

#include <stdio.h>
#include <math.h>
#include <malloc.h>
#include "ellipsoid.h"

typedef struct slot { float cos, sin; enum { None, Only, Done } flag; } slot;

static int n_max = 0;          /* current maximum degree of subdivision */
static slot *table = NULL;     /* an array of slots */
static vertex *octant = NULL; /* the base octant of the ellipsoid */

#define SetP(p,px,py,pz) (p).x=(px), (p).y=(py), (p).z=(pz)
#define SetV(v,px,py,pz,nx,ny,nz) SetP((v)->p,px,py,pz), SetP((v)->n,nx,ny,nz)
#define SetF(f,i0,i1,i2) (f)->v0 = i0, (f)->v1 = i1, (f)->v2 = i2

/*
// Compute the necessary cosine and sine values for generating ellipsoids
// with the degree of subdivision n, and initialize the array table[].
// The largest n becomes n_max, and calls with n <= n_max return immediately.
// The memory for the base octant is allocated to cope with any n <= n_max.
*/
void ellipsoid_init (int n)
{
    int n_table, i, j, k, l, m, h, d;
    slot *t0, *t1, *t2;
    float theta;

    if (n > n_max) {
        n_max = n;
        if (table) free (table);
        if ((n_table = ((n-1)*n)/2) == 0) table = NULL;
        else table = (slot *) malloc (n_table * sizeof(slot));
        if (octant) free (octant);
        octant = (vertex *) malloc (((n+1)*(n+2))/2 * sizeof(vertex));

        for (t0 = table, k = n_table; k > 0; k--, t0++) t0->flag = None;
        for (t0 = table, k = 0, l = 1, m = 3, i = 2; i <= n_max; i++) {
            l += m, m += 2, h = n_max / i - 1;
            for (t1 = t0+i - 2, j = 1; j < i; j++, k++, t0++, t1--) {
                if (t0->flag == None) {
```

```
                theta = (M_PI_2 * j) / i;
                t0->cos = t1->sin = cos (theta);
                t0->sin = t1->cos = sin (theta);
                t0->flag = t1->flag = Only;
            }
            if (t0->flag == Only) {
                t0->flag = Done;
                for (d = k+1, t2 = t0; h > 0; h--) {
                    t2 += d, d += 1;
                    t2->cos = t0->cos;
                    t2->sin = t0->sin;
                    t2->flag = Done;
                }
            }
        }
    }
}
}

/*
// Construct the base octant of the ellipsoid whose parameters are a, b, and c,
// with the degree of subdivision n using the cosine and sine values in table[].
// It is assumed that n <= n_max.
*/
static void ellipsoid_octant (int n, float a, float b, float c)
{
    int i, j;
    float a_1, b_1, c_1;
    float cos_ph, sin_ph, px, py, pz, nx, ny, nz, nznz, rnorm, tmp;
    vertex *o = octant;
    slot *table_th, *table_ph;

    a_1 = 1.0 / a; b_1 = 1.0 / b; c_1 = 1.0 / c;
    o = octant;
    table_th = table;
    table_ph = table + ((n-1)*(n-2))/2;

    SetV (o, 0.0, 0.0, c, 0.0, 0.0, 1.0), o++;        /* i = 0, j = 0 */
    for (i = 1; i < n; i++, table_ph++) {
        cos_ph = table_ph->cos;
        sin_ph = table_ph->sin;
        pz = cos_ph * c;
        nz = cos_ph * c_1;
        nznz = nz * nz;

        px = sin_ph * a;
        nx = sin_ph * a_1;
        rnorm = 1.0 / sqrt (nx*nx + nznz);            /* 0 < i < n, j = 0 */
        SetV (o, px, 0.0, pz, nx*rnorm, 0.0, nz*rnorm), o++;
        for (j = i; --j > 0; table_th++) {
            tmp = table_th->cos * sin_ph;
            px = tmp * a;
            nx = tmp * a_1;
```

```
            tmp = table_th->sin * sin_ph;
            py = tmp * b;
            ny = tmp * b_1;
            rnorm = 1.0 / sqrt (nx*nx + ny*ny + nznz);    /* 0 < i < n, 0 < j < i */
            SetV (o, px, py, pz, nx*rnorm, ny*rnorm, nz*rnorm), o++;
        }
        py = sin_ph * b;
        ny = sin_ph * b_1;
        rnorm = 1.0 / sqrt (ny*ny + nznz);                /* 0 < i < n, j = i */
        SetV (o, 0.0, py, pz, 0.0, ny*rnorm, nz*rnorm), o++;
    }
    SetV (o, a, 0.0, 0.0, 1.0, 0.0, 0.0), o++;            /* i = n, j = 0 */
    for (j = i; --j > 0; table_th++) {
        tmp = table_th->cos;
        px = tmp * a;
        nx = tmp * a_1;
        tmp = table_th->sin;
        py = tmp * b;
        ny = tmp * b_1;
        rnorm = 1.0 / sqrt (nx*nx + ny*ny);               /* i = n, 0 < j < i */
        SetV (o, px, py, 0.0, nx*rnorm, ny*rnorm, 0.0), o++;
    }
    SetV (o, 0.0, b, 0.0, 0.0, 1.0, 0.0);                 /* i = n, j = i */
}


/*
// Note the following conventions in ellipsoid_seq() and ellipsoid_par():
// the north pole:         th =   0,      ph =   0,
// the 1st octant:    0 <= th <  90,   0 < ph <=  90,
// the 2nd octant:   90 <= th < 180,   0 < ph <=  90,
// the 3rd octant:  180 <= th < 270,   0 < ph <=  90,
// the 4th octant:  270 <= th < 360,   0 < ph <=  90,
// the 5th octant:    0 <= th <  90,  90 < ph <= 180,
// the 6th octant:   90 <= th < 180,  90 < ph <= 180,
// the 7th octant:  180 <= th < 270,  90 < ph <= 180,
// the 8th octant:  270 <= th < 360,  90 < ph <= 180, and
// the south pole:         th =   0,      ph = 180.
*/


/*
// Generate the vertices for the ellipsoid with parameters a, b, and c
// with the degree of subdivision n, by reflecting the base octant.
// Also generate triangular faces of the ellipsoid with vertices ordered
// counterclockwise when viewed from the outside.
*/


/* sequential version */
void ellipsoid_seq (object *ellipsoid, int n, float a, float b, float c)
{
    vertex *v, *o;
    face *f;
    int i, j, ko, kv, kw, kv0, kw0;
```

```
    /* Check parameters for validity. */
    if (n <= 0 || n_max < n || a <= 0.0 || b <= 0.0 || c <= 0.0) {
        ellipsoid->nv = 0; ellipsoid->v = NULL;
        ellipsoid->nf = 0; ellipsoid->f = NULL;
        return;
    }

    /* Initialize the base octant. */
    ellipsoid_octant (n, a, b, c);

    /* Allocate memories for vertices and faces. */
    ellipsoid->nv = 4*n*n + 2;
    ellipsoid->nf = 8*n*n;
    ellipsoid->v = (vertex *) malloc (ellipsoid->nv * sizeof(vertex));
    ellipsoid->f = (face *) malloc (ellipsoid->nf * sizeof(face));

    /* Generate vertices of the ellipsoid from octant[]. */
    v = ellipsoid->v;
    o = octant;
#define op o->p
#define on o->n
    SetV (v, op.x, op.y, op.z, on.x, on.y, on.z), v++; /* the north pole */
    for (i = 0; ++i <= n;) {
        o += i;
        for (j = i; --j >= 0; o++, v++)                      /* 1st octant */
            SetV (v, op.x, op.y, op.z, on.x, on.y, on.z);
        for (j = i; --j >= 0; o--, v++)                      /* 2nd octant */
            SetV (v, -op.x, op.y, op.z, -on.x, on.y, on.z);
        for (j = i; --j >= 0; o++, v++)                      /* 3rd octant */
            SetV (v, -op.x, -op.y, op.z, -on.x, -on.y, on.z);
        for (j = i; --j >= 0; o--, v++)                      /* 4th octant */
            SetV (v, op.x, -op.y, op.z, on.x, -on.y, on.z);
    }
    for (; --i > 1;) {
        o -= i;
        for (j = i; --j > 0; o++, v++)                       /* 5th octant */
            SetV (v, op.x, op.y, -op.z, on.x, on.y, -on.z);
        for (j = i; --j > 0; o--, v++)                       /* 6th octant */
            SetV (v, -op.x, op.y, -op.z, -on.x, on.y, -on.z);
        for (j = i; --j > 0; o++, v++)                       /* 7th octant */
            SetV (v, -op.x, -op.y, -op.z, -on.x, -on.y, -on.z);
        for (j = i; --j > 0; o--, v++)                       /* 8th octant */
            SetV (v, op.x, -op.y, -op.z, on.x, -on.y, -on.z);
    }
    o--, SetV (v, -op.x, -op.y, -op.z, -on.x, -on.y, -on.z); /* the south pole */
#undef op
#undef on

    /* Generate triangular faces of the ellipsoid. */
    f = ellipsoid->f;
    kv = 0, kw = 1;
```

```
for (i = 0; i < n; i++) {
    kv0 = kv, kw0 = kw;
    for (ko = 1; ko <= 3; ko++)                   /* the 1st, 2nd, 3rd octants */
        for (j = i;; j--) {
            SetF (f, kv, kw, ++kw), f++;
            if (j == 0) break;
            SetF (f, kv, kw, ++kv), f++;
        }
    for (j = i;; j--) {                           /* the 4th octant */
        if (j == 0) { SetF (f, kv0, kw, kw0), kv++, kw++, f++; break; }
        SetF (f, kv, kw, ++kw), f++;
        if (j == 1) SetF (f, kv, kw, kv0), f++;
        else SetF (f, kv, kw, ++kv), f++;
    }
}
for (; --i >= 0;) {
    kv0 = kv, kw0 = kw;
    for (ko = 5; ko <= 7; ko++)                   /* the 5th, 6th, 7th octants */
        for (j = i;; j--) {
            SetF (f, kv, kw, ++kv), f++;
            if (j == 0) break;
            SetF (f, kv, kw, ++kw), f++;
        }
    for (j = i;; j--) {                           /* the 8th octant */
        if (j == 0) { SetF (f, kv, kw0, kv0), kv++, kw++, f++; break; }
        SetF (f, kv, kw, ++kv), f++;
        if (j == 1) SetF (f, kv, kw, kw0), f++;
        else SetF (f, kv, kw, ++kw), f++;
    }
}
}

/* parallel version */
void ellipsoid_par (object *ellipsoid, int n, float a, float b, float c)
{
/* Code for this is included on on-line version of current graphics gems. */
}
```

◇ **Bibliography** ◇

(Angel 1990) Edward Angel. *Computer Graphics.* Addision-Wesley, Boston, 1990.

(Anton 1984) Howard Anton. *Elementary Linear Algebra,* 4th edition. John Wiley & Sons, New York, 1984.

(Koenderink 1990) Jan J. Koenderink. *Solid Shape.* MIT Press, Cambridge, MA, 1990.

 IV.6

Sparse Smooth Connection between Bézier/B-Spline Curves

Chandrajit Bajaj
Purdue University
West Lafayette, Indiana

Guoliang Xu
Computing Center, Academia Sinica
Beijing, China

◇ Introduction ◇

Often in interactive font design, free-form sketching, and input path specification for graphics animation, one is faced with the problem of connecting two Bézier or B-spline polynomial curves with a piecewise transition polynomial curve achieving prescribed continuity at the two endpoints. Furthermore, one desires the transition polynomial curve to have the fewest number of (sparse) pieces. This issue is addressed by first identifying the degrees of freedom[1] needed to achieve the conditions for smoothness and sparseness, described below, by solving the following two problems:

Conditions for Smooth Connection. Given two polynomials $P : [a, b] \to I\!R$ and $Q : [c, d] \to I\!R$ of degree n with $b < c$, find a piecewise polynomial $R : [b, c] \to I\!R$ also of degree n, such that

$(1°)$ R is $C^{n-\mu}$ continuous in (b, c) for any integer μ with $1 \le \mu \le n$,
$(2°)$ P and R join at b with $C^{n-\mu_1}$ continuity for any integer μ_1 with $1 \le \mu_1 \le n$,
$(3°)$ R and Q joint at c with $C^{n-\mu_2}$ continuity for any integer μ_2 with $1 \le \mu_2 \le n$.

Conditions for Sparse (Smooth) Connection. In addition to the preceding conditions $(1°)$, $(2°)$, and $(3°)$, it is required that $(4°)$ R has the fewest number of segments.

As an example, the composite function (P, R, Q) may be a single B-spline. It is obvious that there are potentially infinite ways to join any two polynomials with prescribed continuity. The goal here is not only to achieve a smooth join, but also to make the join as *simple* as possible. Here *simple* means that the polynomial R is to determined, as far as possible, from P and Q.

The solution to both the foregoing problems is derived by the use of blossoming (Ramshaw 1989, Seidel 1989). For a given degree n polynomial $F : I\!R \to I\!R$, the blossom of F, denoted as $f = B(F)$, is an n-affine symmetric function satisfying $f(u, \dots, u) = F(u)$. A function $f : I\!R \to I\!R$ is called *affine* if it preserves affine combinations, that

---

[1]The succesive degrees of freedom form a hierarchy and use the notation $(1°)$ to $(3°)$.

IBM ISBN 0-12-543455-3
Macintosh ISBN 0-12-543457-X

is, if f satisfies $f(\sum_i a_i u_i) = \sum_i a_i f(u_i)$ for all real numbers $a_1, \ldots, a_k, u_1, \ldots, u_k \in \mathbb{R}$ with $\sum_i u_i = 1$. A function $f : \mathbb{R}^n \to \mathbb{R}$ is called *n-affine* if it is an affine function on each individual argument with the others held fixed. Finally, a function $f : \mathbb{R}^n \to \mathbb{R}$ is called *symmetric* if f keeps its value under any permutation of its arguments.

◇ Solution of Smooth Connections ◇

Lemma 1. *Let AS_n be the set of all n-affine symmetric functions, $t_1 \le \cdots \le t_n < t_{n+1} \le \cdots \le t_{2n}$. Then the map $M : f \in AS_n \to \{f(t_\ell, t_{\ell+1}, \ldots, t_{\ell+n-1})\}_{\ell=1}^{n+1} \in \mathbb{R}^{n+1}$ is a one to one map between AS_n and $\mathbb{R}^{n+1}$.*

Proof: It is obvious that M is a linear map, and by $M(f) = (0, \ldots, 0)$ it can be proved that $f = 0$. In fact, by the progressive de Casteljau algorithm (Ramshaw 1989), $f(x_1, \ldots, x_n) = 0$, i.e., $f = 0$. Now, the only thing left to be proved is that M is invertible, that is, given $(b_1, b_2, \ldots, b_{n+1}) \in \mathbb{R}^{n+1}$, there exists an $f \in AS_n$, such that $M(f) = (b_1, \ldots, b_{n+1})$. This $f = f_1^n$ can be constructed by the following progressive de Casteljau algorithm:

$$f_i^0() = b_i, \quad i = 1, 2, \ldots, n+1,$$

$$f_i^r(x_1, \ldots, x_r) = \frac{t_{n+1} - x_r}{t_{n+i} - t_{i+r-1}} f_i^{r-1}(x_1, \ldots, x_{r-1})$$

$$+ \frac{x_r - t_{i+r-1}}{t_{n+i} - t_{i+r-1}} f_{i+1}^{r-1}(x_1, \ldots, x_{r-1}), \quad i = 1, 2, \ldots, n+1-r,$$

for $r = 1, \ldots, n$ (see Theorem 7.1, Ramshaw 1989).   ◇

Lemma 2. *The smooth connection conditions can always be met.*

Proof: This lemma is proved constructively as follows.

(i) If $n + 1 \le \mu_1 + \mu_2$, then the piecewise polynomial R to be determined degenerates to a single segment, and R can be determined by using the Hermite interpolation conditions:

$$R^{(i)}(b) = P^{(i)}(b), \quad i = 0, 1, \ldots, n - \mu_1,$$
$$R^{(i)}(c) = Q^{(i)}(c), \quad i = 0, 1, \ldots, n - \mu_2. \tag{1}$$

If $n+1 = \mu_1 + \mu_2$, the solution is unique. If $n+1 < \mu_1 + \mu_2$, there is no uniqueness. If R is of degree $2n - \mu_1 - \mu_2 + 1 (< n)$, then we have uniqueness.

(ii) If $n + 1 > \mu_1 + \mu_2$, Equation (1) has no solution in general. Here a B-spline $F(x) : [a, d] \to \mathbb{R}$ is constructed such that

$$F(x)|_{[a,b]} = P(x), \qquad F(x)|_{[c,d]} = Q(x), \tag{2}$$

and $R(x) = F(x)|_{[b,c]}$ satisfies the smooth conditions $(1°)$, $(2°)$, and $(3°)$. Let

$$T = (t_0 = \cdots = t_n) < (t_{n+1} = \cdots = t_{n+\mu_1}) < t_{n+\mu_1+1} \leq \cdots$$
$$\leq t_{2n-\mu_2+1} < t_{2n-\mu_2+2} = \cdots = (t_{2n+1} < t_{2n+2} = \cdots = t_{3n+2}),$$

where $t_n = a$, $t_{n+1} = b$, $t_{2n+1} = c$, $t_{2n+2} = d$ and $t_{n+\mu_1+1}, \ldots, t_{2n-\mu_2+1}$ are chosen so that each of them has multiplicity $\leq \mu$ in T. Let $\{N_\ell^n(x)\}_{\ell=0}^{2n+1}$ be the normalized B-spline bases over T, and let

$$d_\ell = f_1(t_{\ell+1}, \ldots t_{\ell+n}), \quad \ell = 0, 1, \ldots, n,$$
$$d_\ell = f_2(t_{\ell+1}, \ldots t_{\ell+n}), \quad \ell = n+1, \ldots, 2n+1.$$

where $f_1 = B(P)$, $f_2 = B(Q)$ are the *blossoms* of P and Q, respectively. Then $F(x) = \sum_{\ell=0}^{2n+1} d_\ell N_\ell^n(x)$ is the required B-spline (see Theorem 3.4, (Seidel 1989)). In fact, $F(x)$ is $C^{n-\mu_1}$ and $C^{n-\mu_2}$ continuous at b and c, respectively, since b has multiplicity μ_1 and c has multiplicity μ_2. Furthermore, since $t_{n+\mu_1+1}, \ldots, t_{2n-\mu_2+1}$ have multiplicity $\leq \mu$, $f(x)$ is $C^{n-\mu}$ continuous on (b, c). Now it only remains to show that condition (2) is satisfied. From Theorem 3.4 (Seidel 1989), we have

$$d_\ell = B(F|_{[a,b]})(t_{\ell+1}, \ldots, t_{\ell+n}), \quad \ell = 0, 1, \ldots, n,$$
$$d_\ell = B(F|_{[c,d]})(t_{\ell+1}, \ldots, t_{\ell+n}), \quad \ell = n+1, \ldots, 2n+1.$$

Hence,

$$f_1(t_{\ell+1}, \ldots, t_{\ell+n}) = B(F|_{[a,b]})(t_{\ell+1}, \ldots, t_{\ell+n}), \quad \ell = 0, 1, \ldots, n,$$
$$f_2(t_{\ell+1}, \ldots, t_{\ell+n}) = B(F|_{[c,d]})(t_{\ell+1}, \ldots, t_{\ell+n}), \quad \ell = n+1, \ldots, 2n+1.$$

Since f_1, f_2, $B(F|_{[a,b]})$ and $B(F|_{[c,d]})$ are in AS_n, it follows from Lemma 1 that $f_1 = B(F|_{[a,b]})$, $f_2 = B(F|_{[c,d]})$, and then $P = F|_{[a,b]}$, $Q = F|_{[c,d]}$. ◇

Thus, a total of $n + 1 - (\mu_1 + \mu_2)$ knots are inserted in (b, c), leaving R with at most $n + 2 - (\mu_1 + \mu_2)$ pieces. Since the $t_{n+\mu_1+1}, \ldots, t_{2n-\mu_2+1}$ knots can be arbitrarily chosen under the required conditions, R is not unique.

Corollary 3. *The sparse (smooth) connection conditions can always be met.*

◇   The Computation of the Sparse Connection Polynomial   ◇

The proof of Lemma 2 already provides a way to compute the transition polynomial R. Furthermore, this uses only the information that comes from P and Q and some inserted knots. However, the number of pieces of R may not be minimal. In order to get a sparse connection polynomial, the intention is to insert the least number of knots. As in the discussion above, there are two possible cases.

(i) If $n + 1 \leq \mu_1 + \mu_2$, the problem is reduced to a Hermite interpolation problem as before. One segment is enough to connect the two given polynomials. Then the number of segments is minimum. Now we give a B-spline representation of the composite function. Let

$$T = (t_0 = \cdots = t_n < t_{n+1} = \cdots = t_{n+\mu_1} < t_{n+\mu_1+1}$$
$$= \cdots = t_{n+\mu_1+\mu_2} < t_{n+\mu_1+\mu_2+1} = \cdots = t_{2n+\mu_1+\mu_2+1}) \tag{3}$$

and $\{N_\ell^n(x)\}_{\ell=0}^{n+\mu_1+\mu_2}$ be the normalized B-spline bases over T. Then $F(x) = \sum_{\ell=0}^{n+\mu_1+\mu_2} d_\ell N_\ell^n(x)$ is the required function, where

$$\begin{aligned} d_\ell &= f_1(t_{\ell+1}, \ldots t_{\ell+n}), &\ell &= 0, 1, \ldots, n, \\ d_\ell \text{ are free}, & &\ell &= n+1, \ldots, \mu_1+\mu_2-1, \\ d_\ell &= f_2(t_{\ell+1}, \ldots t_{\ell+n}), &\ell &= \mu_1+\mu_2, \ldots, n+\mu_1+\mu_2. \end{aligned} \tag{4}$$

(ii) If $n + 1 > \mu_1 + \mu_2$, then the computation of the inserted knots proceeds as follows, with i increasing from 0 to $n + 1 - (\mu_1 + \mu_2)$:

(a) Let

$$T_i = (t_0 = \cdots = t_n < t_{n+1} = \cdots = t_{n+\mu_1} < x_1 \leq \cdots \leq x_i < t_{n+\mu_1+i+1}$$
$$= \cdots = t_{n+\mu_1+\mu_2+i} < t_{n+\mu_1+\mu_2+i+1} = \cdots = t_{2n+\mu_1+\mu_2+i+1}), \tag{5}$$

where $t_n = a$, $t_{n+1} = b$, $t_{n+\mu_1+\mu_2+i} = c$, $t_{n+\mu_1+\mu_2+i+1} = d$ and $x_1, \ldots, x_i$ are the knots to be determined and satisfying the following conditions:

$$\begin{aligned} &b < x_j < c, \\ &x_j \text{ has multiplicity} \leq \mu \text{ in } T_i. \end{aligned} \tag{6}$$

(b) For $\ell = i + \mu_1 + \mu_2, \ldots, n$, the de Boor points (Seidel 1989) d_ℓ are determined satisfying conditions from both P and Q. These double conditions leads to the following equations for unknowns $x_1, \ldots, x_i$:

$$B(P)(t_{\ell+1}, \ldots, t_{n+\mu_1}, x_1, \ldots, x_i, t_{n+\mu_1+i+1}, \ldots, t_{\ell+n})$$
$$= B(Q)(t_{\ell+1}, \ldots, t_{n+\mu_1}, x_1, \ldots, x_i, t_{n+\mu_1+i+1}, \ldots, t_{\ell+n})$$

for $\ell = i + \mu_1 + \mu_2, \ldots, n$, or

$$g_\ell(x_1, \ldots, x_i) = B(P - Q)(t_{\ell+1}, \ldots, t_{n+\mu_1}, x_1, \ldots, x_i, t_{n+\mu_1+i+1}, \ldots, t_{\ell+n}) = 0$$

for $\ell = i + \mu_1 + \mu_2, \ldots, n$. There are $n + 1 - (i + \mu_1 + \mu_2)$ equations and i unknowns. The ideal cases (a unique solution is expected) are $i = n + 1 - (i + \mu_1 + \mu_2)$ or $i = \frac{n+1-(\mu_1+\mu_2)}{2}$. Comparing this with the proof of Lemma 2, in which $n + 1 - (\mu_1 + \mu_2)$

knots are inserted, this ideal case will reduce the number of the inserted knots to half. For example, if $n = 3$ (cubic), $\mu_1 = \mu_2 = 1$ (C^2 continuity), then $i = 1$. If $\mu_1 = \mu_2 = 2$ (C^1 continuity), then $i = 0$. If $n = 5$, $\mu_1 = \mu_2 = 2$ (C^3 continuity), $i = 1$. If $\mu_1 = \mu_2 = 1$ (C^4 continuity), $i = 2$.

Let $P(x) = \sum_{j=0}^{n} a_j x^j$, $Q(x) = \sum_{j=0}^{n} b_j x^j$. Then $B(P - Q)(u_1, \ldots, u_n) = \sum_{j=0}^{n} (a_j - b_j)/\binom{n}{j} \sigma_{jn}(u_1, \ldots, u_n)$, where $\sigma_{jn}(u_1, \ldots, u_n)$ is the jth n-variable elementary symmetric function (Chrystal 1964). Therefore, $g_\ell(x_1, \ldots, x_i)$ can be written as $g_\ell = \sum_{j=0}^{i} a_j^{(\ell)} \sigma_{ji}(x_1, \ldots, x_i)$. Let $\sigma_j = \sigma_{ji}(x_1, \ldots, x_i)$ be the unknowns, $j = 1, 2, \ldots, i$, $\sigma_0 = 1$. Thus, the following system of linear equations is obtained:

$$
\begin{bmatrix}
a_1^{(i+\mu_1+\mu_2)} & a_2^{(i+\mu_1+\mu_2)} & \cdots & a_i^{(i+\mu_1+\mu_2)} \\
a_1^{(i+\mu_1+\mu_2+1)} & a_2^{(i+\mu_1+\mu_2+1)} & \cdots & a_i^{(i+\mu_1+\mu_2+1)} \\
\vdots & \vdots & & \vdots \\
a_1^{(n)} & a_2^{(n)} & \cdots & a_i^{(n)}
\end{bmatrix}
\begin{bmatrix}
\sigma_1 \\
\sigma_2 \\
\vdots \\
\sigma_i
\end{bmatrix}
= -
\begin{bmatrix}
a_0^{(i+\mu_1+\mu_2)} \\
a_0^{(i+\mu_1+\mu_2+1)} \\
\vdots \\
a_i^{(n)}
\end{bmatrix}.
$$

(7)

(c) If Equation (7) has no solution, increase i by 1, until it has a solution (it may have many solutions). Let $[\sigma_1, \ldots, \sigma_i]^T$ be a solution of (7). Form a polynomial equation

$$
h(x) := \sum_{k=0}^{i} (-x)^{i-k} \sigma_k = 0.
$$

(8)

If all the roots x_j of $h(x)$ are real, and they satisfy (6), then the required knots x_j are obtained. Otherwise, i is increased until the required knots are obtained. If (7) has many solutions, a closed form of the solution of (8) is helpful to get the required solution. If $i < 5$, the closed form of the root x_j is available.

The case $i = 0$ needs separate consideration, since Equations (7) and (8) are degenerate. In this case g_ℓ are constants. If they are all zero, then do not insert knots in (b, c) and compute the de Boor points (4), but no degree of freedom is left. If not all g_ℓ are zero, the next i must be considered.

Since the solution x_j's that satisfy condition (6) are desired, Equation (8) is solved for σ_k that satisfies the following necessary condition:

$$
\binom{i}{k} b^k < \sigma_k < \binom{i}{k} c^k, \quad k = 1, 2, \ldots, i.
$$

(9)

(d) Let $t_{n+\mu_1+j} = x_j$ for $j = 1, \ldots, i$. Let

$$
d_\ell = f_1(t_{\ell+1}, \ldots t_{\ell+n}), \quad \ell = 0, 1, \ldots, n,
$$

(10)

$$
d_\ell = f_2(t_{\ell+1}, \ldots t_{\ell+n}), \quad \ell = n + 1, \ldots, n + \mu_1 + \mu_2 + i.
$$

(11)

Then, as in the proof of Lemma 2, the B-spline function $F(x) = \sum_{\ell=0}^{n+\mu_1+\mu_2+i} d_\ell N_\ell^n(x)$ is required, where $\{N_\ell^n(x)\}_{\ell=0}^{n+\mu_1+\mu_2+i}$ are the normalized B-spline bases over T_i.

◇ Pseudocode of the Algorithm ◇

Pseudocode of the preceding algorithm is presented here. Standard library procedures for solving a linear equation and for finding the real roots of a polynomial are assumed.

Sparse Connection Algorithm
Input
P, Q *coefficients arrays of the polynomial P and Q in power bases.*
A, B *endpoints of interval [a,b].*
C, D *endpoints of interval [c,d].*
N *degree of the given polynomials.*
MU1, MU2 *continuity at b and c, respectively.*
MU *continuity in (b, c).*

Output
D *coefficients array of the de Boor points d_l.*
Knots *is inserted knots in (b, c) .*
I *number of inserted knots.*

```
    I = 0
    for j = 0 to N do
        P(j) = P(j)/(N choose j)   Q(j) = Q(j)/(N choose j)   C(j) = P(j) − Q(j)
    endloop
    for j = 0 to 2N+MU1 + MU2 +1 do
        if j ≤ N then      T(j) =A
        else  if j ≤ N + MU1 then       T(j) =B
        else  if j ≤ N + MU1 + MU2 then      T(j) =C
        else   T(j) =D
        end if
    endloop
    if N + 1 ≤ MU1 + MU2 then
        for l = 0 to N+MU1 + MU2 do
            for j = 1 to N do Point(j) = T(l+j) endloop
            if l ≤ N then
                call EVALUATE(P, N, Point, N, Coeffout)
                D(l) = Coeffout(0)
```

```
        else if l ≥ MU1 + MU2 then
          call EVALUATE(Q, N, Point, N, Coeffout)
          D(l) = Coeffout(0)
        else   D(l) are free , set to zero
        end if
      endloop
else
    for i = 1 to N + 1 − (MU1 + MU2) do
      for l = i + MU1 + MU2 to N do
        for j = 1 to N − i do Point(j) = T(l+j) endloop
        call EVALUATE(C, N, Point, N−i, Coeffout)
        for k = 1 to i do Matrix(l − i − MU1 − MU2, k − 1) = Coeffout(k)
        endloop
        Lefthand(l − i − MU1 − MU2) = − Coeffout(0)
      endloop
      call LINEARSOLVER(Matrix, Lefthand, Solution)
      call POLYSOLVER(Solution, i, Knots)
      if all Knots satisfy the condition (6) then goto L
    endloop
  L: I = i
    for j = 0 to 2N+MU1 + MU2 + i + 1 do
      if j ≤ N then      T(j) =A
      else  if j ≤ N + MU1 then      T(j) =B
      else  if j ≤ N + MU1 + i then      T(j) = Knots(j − N − MU1)
      else  if j ≤ N + MU1 + MU2 + i then      T(j) =C
      else   T(j) = D     end if
    endloop
    for l = 0 to N do
      for j = 1 to N do    Point(j) = T(l | j)   endloop
      call EVALUATE(P, N, Point, N, Coeffout)
      D(l) = Coeffout(0)
    endloop
    for l = N+1 to N + MU1 + MU2 + i do
      for j = 1 to N do    Point(j) = T(l+j)    endloop
      call EVALUATE(Q, N, Point, N, Coeffout)
      D(l) = Coeffout(0)
    endloop
end if
finish
```

Procedure to evaluate an n-affine symmetric function
procedure EVALUATE(Coeffin, N, Point, M, Coeffout)
Coeffin *is the input coefficients array.* N − 1 *is the number of coefficients. Point is the* *input evaluating points array.* M *is the number of evaluating points . Coeffout is the* *output coefficients array.*

    for j = 0 **to** N **do** Coeffout(j) = Coeffin(j) **endloop**
    for k = 0 **to** M − 1 **do**
        for j = 1 **to** N − k **do** Coeffout(j−1) = Coeffout(j−1) + Point(k)*Coeffout(j)
        endloop
    endloop
    return

◇   **Bibliography**   ◇

(Chrystal 1964) C. Chrystal. *Algebra, Part I,* 7th ed. Chelsea Publishing Company, New York, 1964.

(Ramshaw 1989) L. Ramshaw. Blossoms are polar forms. *Computer-Aided Geometric Design*, 6:323–358, 1989.

(Seidel 1989) Seidel, H.-P. A new multiaffine approach to B-splines. *Computer-Aided Geometric Design*, 6:23–32, 1989.

◇ IV.7

The Length of Bézier Curves

Jens Gravesen
Mathematical Institute
Technical University of Denmark
Lyngby, Denmark

◇   Introduction   ◇

It is an often-used fact that the control polygon of a Bézier curve approximates the curve and that repeated subdivision produces a sequence of control polygons that converge to the curve (Farin 1988). The length of these control polygons converges to the arc length of the Bézier curve, and with the use of a certain convex combination of the length of the control polygon and the length of the chord between the endpoints of the segments, the convergence becomes much faster. This gem derives and implements an adaptive method for the calculation of the arc length based on this result. Previously, Gaussian quadrature has been combined with adaptive subdivision to find the arc length of arbitrary parametric curves (Guenter and Parent 1990).

◇   Background   ◇

Given an nth-degree Bézier curve $b(t)$ with control points $Q_0, Q_1, \ldots, Q_n$, define the lengths

$$\text{arc length:} \qquad L(b) = \int_0^1 b'(t)\, dt,$$

$$\text{polygon length:} \quad L_p(b) = \sum_{i=1}^{n} |Q_i - Q_{i-1}|,$$

$$\text{chord length:} \qquad L_c(b) = |Q_n - Q_0|,$$

with $L_c(b) \leq L(b) \leq L_p(b)$. As suggested above, subdividing any curve takes place at its parametric midpoint. De Casteljau's algorithm (Farin 1988) yields

$$
\begin{aligned}
Q_i^0 &= Q_i, & i &= 0, \ldots, n, \\
Q_i^k &= \tfrac{1}{2} Q_i^{k-1} + \tfrac{1}{2} Q_{i+1}^{k-1}, & i &= 0, \ldots, n-k, \quad k = 1, \ldots, n.
\end{aligned}
$$

From the algorithm we get the control polygon $Q_0^0, Q_0^1, \ldots, Q_0^n$ for the first half of the curve $b_1^1(t) = b\left(\frac{1}{2}t\right)$ and the control polygon $Q_0^n, Q_1^{n-1}, \ldots, Q_n^0$ for the second half of the curve $b_2^1(t) = b\left(\frac{1}{2} + \frac{1}{2}t\right)$. After k repetitions we obtain 2^k Bézier curves $b_1^k, \ldots, b_{2^k}^k$, where $b_i^k(t) = b\left(2^{-k}(i - 1 + t)\right)$.

Now define

$$L_p^k(b) = \sum_{i=1}^{2^k} L_p\left(b_i^k\right) \quad \text{and} \quad L_c^k(b) = \sum_{i=1}^{2^k} L_c\left(b_i^k\right).$$

As described previously (Gravesen 1993), this gives

$$L_p^k(b) \searrow L(b) \quad \text{and} \quad L_p^k(b) - L(b) = O(2^{-2k}),$$
$$L_c^k(b) \nearrow L(b) \quad \text{and} \quad L_c^k(b) - L(b) = O(2^{-2k}).$$

The length of the curve is bounded below by L_c^k and above by L_p^k, so we may expect some combination of the two to give a better approximation. Indeed, if one defines the weighted averages

$$L_a(b) = \frac{2}{n+1} L_c(b) + \frac{n-1}{n+1} L_p(b),$$
$$L_a^k(b) = \sum_{i=1}^{2^k} L_a(b_i^k) = \frac{2}{n+1} L_c^k(b) + \frac{n-1}{n+1} L_p^k(b),$$

then

$$L_a^k(b) \to L(b) \quad \text{and} \quad L_a^k(b) - L(b) = O(2^{-4k}),$$

indicating a high rate of convergence (Gravesen 1993).

◇ **The Algorithms** ◇

Consider evaluating the length of a curve that has already undergone partial subdivision. The order statistics just given indicate that as each new subdivision halves the curve, the related error of the length of the segment will be $\frac{1}{16}$ of the previous error. To keep the total number of subdivisions (which is proportional to the cost) as small as possible, do not subdivide the segments that have a small error. This suggests an adaptive scheme: Either use L_a, or, if the error is too large, subdivide the segment and calculate the length of the two halves. The principle is illustrated by the pseudocode in Figure 1. Similar use of adaptive subdivision can be found on page 173 and elsewhere (Chandler 1990, Guenter and Parent 1990, Lindgren *et al.* 1992).

```
BezierLength(b, eps): real
      b: record of BezierCurve;              degree, control points, etc.
      eps : real;                            Error tolerance.
begin
      Lp ← poly_length(b);                   The length of the control polygon.
      Lc ← chord_length(b);                  The length of the chord.
      n ← degree(b);                         The degree of b.
      err ← error();                         The error estimate.
      if err < eps then return (2*Lc+(n-1)*Lp)/(n+1);
      else begin
            b1, b2 ← subdivide(b);           The two halves of b.
            eps1, eps2 ← tolerance();        The tolerances on the two halves.
            return length(b1, eps1) + length(b2, eps2);
            end;
end BezierLength
```

Figure 1.   Pseudocode for adaptive calculation of the arc length of a Bézier curve.

The code makes use of the following functions.

degree(b) returns the degree of the curve b.

poly_length(b) returns the length of the control polygon of the curve b.

chord_length(b) returns the length of the chord of the curve b.

subdivide(b) returns the two halves of b. Presently, the point of division is always $t = \frac{1}{2}$; exploration of other values of t might prove worthwhile.

error() is the error estimate. The following three methods are suggested.

1. $L_p - L_c$. This is in fact an error bound, but $L_p - L_c = O(2^{-2k})$, while the error is $O(2^{-4k})$, so it will be a gross overestimate for small errors.
2. $(L_p - L_c)^2$. This estimate has order $O(2^{-4k})$ and hence the proper asymptotic behavior.
3. $\frac{1}{15}|L_a^0 - L_a^1|$. Here one assumes an error of the form $c2^{-4k}$; solving for c gives $c = \frac{16}{15}(L_a^0 - L_a^1)$ and $L = L_a^1 - \frac{1}{15}(L_a^0 - L_a^1)$. This yields both an estimate of the absolute value of the error and an estimate of the error *per se*. One can then perform the usual "error correction," and for the length use $L_a^1 - \frac{1}{15}(L_a^0 - L_a^1)$ instead of merely L_a^1. This gives a better approximation, but the error will be overestimated for small error values.

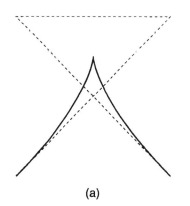 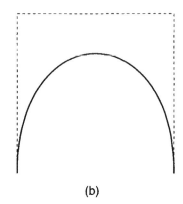

(a) (b)

Figure 2. (a) A cubic curve with a cusp, and (b) a curve with arc length equal to L_a^0.

tolerance() is the error tolerance. Given a segment with an error tolerance ϵ, if subdivision is required, then determine error tolerances ϵ_1 and ϵ_2 for the two new segments. The simple estimate $\epsilon_i = \epsilon/2$ is used to control the absolute error and $\epsilon_i = \epsilon$ is used for the relative error.

The error estimates can be used not only when calculating the length of a Bézier curve, but in any situation that makes use of adaptive subdivision of Bézier curves.

◇ Empirical Tests ◇

Empirical study of the algorithms on a number of sample curves suggests that (1) a precision of 0.1% can be obtained by subdividing the curve into four to twelve segments and that (2) cubic curves need only be divided into approximately four segments to obtain this accuracy.

The error estimates have been checked by comparing the given tolerance ϵ with the real error **err**. Ideally one should have $\mathrm{err}/\epsilon \approx 1$, and under no circumstances $\mathrm{err}/\epsilon \gg 1$. As expected, the error estimate $L_p - L_c$ is a gross overestimate, and $\mathrm{err}/\epsilon \ll 1$ holds even for moderate ϵ, so $L_p - L_c$ should not be used unless it is absolutely vital to have an error bound.

For most curves, both $(L_p - L_c)^2$ and $|\frac{1}{15}(L_a^0 - L_a^1)|$ behave well, but practice shows that $(L_p - L_c)^2$ fails when the curve has a cusp [Figure 2(a)]. Quantitative performance is given in Table 1. Special attention should be given to values when using error estimate $(L_p - L_c)^2$, as the factor in underestimation may be as large as forty-five.

Consider now the curve whose control points are the corners of a square [Figure 2(b)]. Its length can be calculated exactly: It is half the square's perimeter. This is the same as $L_a^0 = (L_p + L_c)/2$ and fools the estimate $|\frac{1}{15}(L_a^0 - L_a^1)|$. The performance of the algorithms for this curve is summarized in Table 2. Note that $\frac{1}{15}|L_a^1 - L_a^0|$ underestimates the error by a factor of fifteen in the worst case.

Table 1. Results for the curve with the cusp. The number ϵ is the error bound, err/ϵ is the absolute error divided by the error bound, and n is the total number of subdivisions.

error estimate $L_p - L_c$

ϵ	0.1	0.01	0.001	0.0001	0.00001
err/ϵ	0.082	0.049	0.031	$2 \cdot 10^{-3}$	$1 \cdot 10^{-3}$
n	3	13	47	119	445

error estimate $(L_p - L_c)^2$

ϵ	0.1	0.01	0.001	0.0001	0.00001
err/ϵ	0.902	0.820	7.138	6.747	48.805
n	1	3	5	7	13

error estimate $\frac{1}{15}|L_a^1 - L_a^0|$

ϵ	0.1	0.01	0.001	0.0001	0.00001
err/ϵ	0.027	0.273	0.173	0.011	$9 \cdot 10^{-3}$
n	3	3	7	19	31

Table 2. Results for the curve with arc length equal to L_a^0. The number ϵ is the error bound, err/ϵ is the absolute error divided by the error bound, and n is the total number of subdivisions.

error estimate $L_p - L_c$

ϵ	0.1	0.01	0.001	0.0001	0.00001
err/ϵ	$5 \cdot 10^{-4}$	$2 \cdot 10^{-5}$	$6 \cdot 10^{-6}$	$5 \cdot 10^{-7}$	$2 \cdot 10^{-8}$
n	7	31	107	255	1023

error estimate $(L_p - L_c)^2$

ϵ	0.1	0.01	0.001	0.0001	0.00001
err/ϵ	$8 \cdot 10^{-3}$	$5 \cdot 10^{-3}$	0.046	0.030	0.066
n	3	7	9	15	29

error estimate $\frac{1}{15}|L_a^1 - L_a^0|$

ϵ	0.1	0.01	0.001	0.0001	0.00001
err/ϵ	0.158	1.581	15.812	$1 \cdot 10^{-3}$	$3 \cdot 10^{-5}$
n	7	7	7	7	15

For both curves (and all other tested curves) it is clear that the first estimate $L_p - L_c$ forces far too many subdivisions.

◇ **Implementation** ◇

When calculating L_c and L_p one can replace the control points Q_i with the forward differences $\Delta Q_i = Q_{i+1} - Q_i$. This lowers both the degree (by one) and the cost of subdivision. Instead of $b(t) = \sum_{i=0}^{n} Q_i B_i^n(t)$ we consider the curve $nb'(t) = \sum_{i=0}^{n-1} \Delta Q_i B_i^{n-1}(t)$. Then

$$L_p = \sum |\Delta Q_i|,$$

that is, the length of the control polygon of b is the sum of the length of the control vectors of nb', and

$$L_c = |\sum \Delta Q_i|,$$

that is, the length of the chord of b is the length of the sum of the control vectors of nb'. However, added care is required during subdivision. The first half of the curve is merely $b_1^1(t) = b\left(\frac{1}{2}t\right)$, hence $b_1^{1'}(t) = \frac{1}{2}b'\left(\frac{1}{2}t\right) = \frac{1}{2}b'_1^1(t)$, and similarly for the second half. Thus, when working with nb' one should divide every control vector by two after each subdivision, or equivalently divide the length by two.

◇ **Program Code** ◇

The actual implementation makes use of the following functions:

degree(b) as in the pseudocode.

sum_of_length(b) replaces poly_length(b).

length_of_sum(b) replaces chord_length(b).

destructive_subdiv(b) replaces subdivide(b). Subdivision is most efficient if the original control points are allowed to be overwritten, and as the code does not operate upon the original control points, but with the forward differences, this does no harm.

DiffBezierCurve(b) returns a curve with control points equal to the forward differences of the original control points.

FreeBezierCurve(b) frees the memory occupied by the curve b.

Six implementations are presented on the floppy disk accompanying this volume. These are based on the three error estimates with two variations (relative and absolute) and have the name `BezierLength`nv, in which n is the method number (1,2,3) and n is the variation r or a.

◇ **Bibliography** ◇

(Chandler 1990) R. E. Chandler. A recursive technique for rendering parametric curves. *Computers and Graphics*, 14(3/4):477–479, 1990.

(Farin 1988) Gerald Farin. *Curves and Surfaces for Computer Aided Geometric Design. A Practical Guide.* Academic Press, London, 1988.

(Gravesen 1993) Jens Gravesen. Adaptive subdivision and the length of Bézier curves. DACMM-report 472, The Danish Center for Applied Mathematics and Mechanics, Technical University of Denmark, 1993.

(Guenter and Parent 1990) B. Guenter and R. Parent. Computing the arc length of parametric curves. *IEEE Computer Graphics and Applications*, 10(3):72–78, May 1990.

(Lindgren *et al.* 1992) T. Lindgren, J. Sanchez, and J. Hall. Curve tesselation criteria through sampling. In D. Kirk, editor, *Graphics Gems III*, pages 262–265. Academic Press, 1992.

IV.8

Quick and Simple Bézier Curve Drawing

Robert D. Miller
East Lansing, Michigan

◇ **Abstract** ◇

This gem describes a simple and efficient method for drawing Bézier curves. The method requires neither the subdivisions nor the attendant complexity of the de Casteljau algorithm (Farin 1993). Instead, calculations are reorganized to support the computation of factorials and integral powers, yielding a straightforward implementation.

◇ **Method** ◇

The general equation for a point $\mathbf{q}(t)$ on a Bézier curve (Mortenson 1985) is

$$\mathbf{q}(t) = \mathbf{p}_k \mathbf{B}_{k,n}(t),$$

where

$$t \quad \text{is the curve's parameter; } 0 \leq t \leq 1,$$

$$\mathbf{p}_k \quad \text{is the } k\text{th vertex of the control polygon,}$$

$$\mathbf{B}_{k,n} = \binom{n}{k} t^k (1-t)^{n-k}, \text{ and}$$

$$\binom{n}{k} = \frac{n!}{k!(n-k)!} \quad (n \text{ choose } k).$$

The terms $\mathbf{q}$, $\mathbf{p}$, and $\mathbf{B}$ are written as vectors, indicating that they have components for each spatial dimension.

Writing out the first equation gives

$$\mathbf{q}(t) = \sum_{k=1}^{n} \mathbf{p}_k \binom{n}{k} t^k (1-t)^{n-k}.$$

The calculations are performed in two steps. The first step (procedure `BezierForm`) evaluates $\mathbf{p}_k \binom{n}{k}$ for each spatial dimension and each kth control vertex. Successive binomial coefficients may be evaluated in a loop body that contains two additions, one multiplication, and one integer division by employing the following recurrence relation:

$$\binom{n}{k} = \frac{n-k+1}{k} \binom{n}{k-1}$$

To generate points along the curve, merely evaluate the remaining terms, $t^k (1-t)^{n-k}$, as a second step (procedure `BezierCurve`). The implementation utilizes two loops. The first loop computes

$$\mathbf{B}_k = C_k \times t^k.$$

The second loop sums terms giving

$$\mathbf{q}(t) = C_k (1-t)^{n-k},$$

represented in the array q.

Each loop computes successive powers using integer multiplication. The loop counter runs from $n-1$ down to zero, forming the factors that scale $(1-t)$.

The curve is evaluated using the parameter t, where $0 \le t \le 1$. As t moves from zero to one, in steps of dt, the length of the resulting curve segment is not, in general, proportional to dt. In other words, the curve is not traced with constant velocity as t changes.

Advantages of this method are its speed and ease of implementation. These routines work well with higher-order curves, not just the common cubic (four-point) curve. A strong benefit of curves of order higher than three is that the shape of the curve may be modified without changing the endpoints or the tangents of the curve at those points.

The Bézier curve may be redrawn with higher resolution simply by calling `BezierCurve`, specifying a smaller step size, as the results from `BezierForm` need not be recalculated. In practice, as within an interactive curve editor, a curve may first need to be drawn, modified, then redrawn in the original form to restore the background color (Paeth 1992). The routines described next make this an especially simple task.

◇ **Code** ◇

```
/* Quick and Simple Bezier Curve Drawing --- Robert D. Miller
 * This 2-D planar Bezier curve drawing software is 3-D compliant ---
 * redefine Point and change the commented lines as indicated.
 */
```

```c
#include <stdio.h>
#define MaxCtlPoints  12

typedef struct {float x; float y;} Point;         /* for 2-D curves */
                                                  /* for 3-D space curves */
/* typedef struct {float x; float y; float z;} Point; */
typedef Point PtArray[99];
typedef Point BezArray[MaxCtlPoints];

void BezierForm(int NumCtlPoints, PtArray p, BezArray c)
/*    Setup Bezier coefficient array once for each control polygon. */
{
    int k; long n, choose;
    n= NumCtlPoints -1;
    for(k = 0; k <= n; k++) {
        if (k == 0) choose = 1;
        else if (k == 1) choose = n;
        else choose = choose *(n-k+1)/k;
        c[k].x = p[k].x *choose;
        c[k].y = p[k].y *choose;
     /* c[k].z = p[k].z *choose; */    /* use for 3-D curves */
        };
}


void BezierCurve(int NumCtlPoints, BezArray c, Point *pt, float t)
/*  Return Point pt(t), t <= 0 <= 1 from C, given the number
    of Points in control polygon. BezierForm must be called
    once for any given control polygon. */
{   int k, n;
    float t1, tt, u;
    BezArray b;

    n = NumCtlPoints -1;   u =t;
    b[0].x = c[0].x;
    b[0].y = c[0].y;
 /* b[0].z = c[0].z; */      /* for 3-D curves */
    for(k =1; k <=n; k++) {
        b[k].x = c[k].x *u;
        b[k].y = c[k].y *u;
     /* b[k].z = c[k].z *u */  /* for 3-D curves */
        u =u*t;
        };

    (*pt).x = b[n].x;   (*pt).y = b[n].y;
    t1 = 1-t;          tt = t1;
    for(k =n-1; k >=0; k--) {
        (*pt).x += b[k].x *tt;
        (*pt).y += b[k].y *tt;
     /* (*pt).z += b[k].z *tt;  */   /* Again, 3-D */
        tt =tt*t1;
        }
}
```

```
float u;
int   k;
PtArray pn;
BezArray bc;
Point pt;
void main ()
{
    pn[0].x = 100;  pn[0].y = 20;
    pn[1].x = 120;  pn[1].y = 40;
    pn[2].x = 140;  pn[2].y = 25;
    pn[3].x = 160;  pn[3].y = 20;
    BezierForm(4, pn, bc);

    for(k =0; k <=10; k++) {
        BezierCurve(4, bc, &pt, (float)k/10.0);
        printf("%3d  %8.4f  %8.4f\n",k, pt.x, pt.y);
     /* draw curve  */
     /* if (k = 0) MoveTo(pt.x, pt.y);
        else LineTo(pt.x, pt.y);  */
        }
}
```

◇ **Bibliography** ◇

(Farin 1993) Gerald Farin. *Curves and Surfaces for CAGD*, 3rd ed. Academic Press, Boston, 1993.

(Mortenson 1985) Michael E. Mortenson. *Geometric Modeling*. John Wiley & Sons, New York, 1985.

(Paeth 1992) Alan Wm Paeth. A generic pixel selection mechanism. In David Kirk, editor, *Graphics Gems III*, Chapter 2.6, pages 77–79. AP Professional, Boston, 1992.

IV.9

Linear Form Curves

Ken Shoemake

University of Pennsylvania
Philadelphia, Pennsylvania
shoemake@graphics.cis.upenn.edu

◇ Introduction ◇

Straight lines are simple curves: easy to understand, and easy to manipulate. A generalization, the multilinear form, underlies the common curves of computer graphics (Ramshaw 1987, Barry and Goldman 1988). This gem uses multilinearity and symmetry to explain Lagrange polynomials, Bézier and B-spline curves, the de Casteljau and de Boor algorithms, and Catmull–Rom splines; and it unites all these in a single routine. Though space prevents it here, these methods can also be applied to other curves, to rectangular and triangular surface patches, and to geometric continuity.

◇ Curves from Two Points ◇

Through every pair of distinct points there is a unique line; this is an axiom of Euclidean geometry. But use of points and lines in computer graphics is impossible without a numerical representation. Points are commonly represented using (x, y, z) coordinates. Lines, however, may be represented in a variety of ways—Plücker coordinates, implicit equations, parametric equations—depending on the task. The developments below use a parametric function of the form $F(t)$, where t is a real-valued parameter and the result is a point on the line.

Among the various forms of such a function, one is particularly convenient. Suppose point p_0 has coordinates (x_0, y_0, z_0) and point p_1 has coordinates (x_1, y_1, z_1). Since the unique vector translating p_0 to p_1 is $v_{01} = (x_1 - x_0, y_1 - y_0, z_1 - z_0)$, a simple parametric function for the line though points p_0 and p_1 is $F(t) = p_0 + tv_{01}$. With a little manipulation, this gives

$$F(t) = ((1 - t)x_0 + tx_1, (1 - t)y_0 + ty_1, (1 - t)z_0 + tz_1)$$

or, more succinctly, $F(t) = (1 - t)p_0 + tp_1$.

Although the above computations may seem pedantic, weighted sums of points should be used with caution. While adding a vector to a point—performing a translation—is fine, adding a point to a point is not. The vector v_{01} is a difference of points, $p_1 - p_0 =$

$(1)p_1 + (-1)p_0$, a weighted sum in which the weights alone sum to 0. Any scalar multiple of a vector is still a vector, and it gives scaled weights that still sum to 0. So adding to a point any expression giving a vector must give a weighted sum of points in which the weights alone sum to 1. Algebraic rearrangements will not alter that fact, as the expression in question shows.

Use of $\mathbf{t} = (t_0, t_1)$, with $t_0 + t_1$ either 0 or 1, allows a more general line function:

$$\text{line}(\mathbf{t}; p_0, p_1) = [p_0 \quad p_1] \cdot \mathbf{t}$$

$$= \begin{bmatrix} x_0 & x_1 \\ y_0 & y_1 \\ z_0 & z_1 \end{bmatrix} \cdot \begin{bmatrix} t_0 \\ t_1 \end{bmatrix}$$

$$= t_0 \begin{bmatrix} x_0 \\ y_0 \\ z_0 \end{bmatrix} + t_1 \begin{bmatrix} x_1 \\ y_1 \\ z_1 \end{bmatrix}$$

$$= \begin{bmatrix} t_0 x_0 + t_1 x_1 \\ t_0 y_0 + t_1 y_1 \\ t_0 z_0 + t_1 z_1 \end{bmatrix}.$$

When $t_0 + t_1 = 1$, this still gives a point; but when $t_0 + t_1 = 0$, it gives a vector. For convenience, define the mapping $\bar{t} = (1 - t, t)$ and the constant $\delta = (-1, 1)$. Then $\mathbf{t} = \bar{0}$ gives p_0; $\mathbf{t} = \bar{1}$ gives p_1; and $\mathbf{t} = \bar{t}, t \in [0, 1]$ gives points in between. Clearly $\text{line}(\bar{t}; p_0, p_1)$ gives the earlier $F(t)$, but now $\mathbf{t} = \delta$ gives $p_1 - p_0$.

This vector result is significant, since $\frac{d}{dt}\bar{t} = \delta$ and the "line" function is linear. Thus, $\frac{d}{dt}F(t) = \frac{d}{dt}\text{line}(\bar{t}; p_0, p_1) = \text{line}(\delta; p_0, p_1)$. More generally, suppose the interval $[a_0, a_1]$ should parameterize the line segment from p_0 to p_1. Define

$$\text{bary}(t; a_0, a_1) = \frac{1}{a_1 - a_0} \begin{bmatrix} a_1 - t \\ t - a_0 \end{bmatrix}$$

and consider $f(t) = \text{line}(\text{bary}(t; a_0, a_1); p_0, p_1)$. Then $f(a_0) = p_0$, $f(a_1) = p_1$, and $\frac{d}{dt}f(t) = \text{line}(\delta; p_0, p_1)/(a_1 - a_0)$. Of course, letting $a_0 = 0$ and $a_1 = 1$ again gives the previous simpler line function, $F(t)$.

Incidentally, the name "bary" refers to barycentric coordinates, and this entire discussion fits within the discipline of affine geometry. With minimal changes barycentric coordinates can describe planes instead of lines. That is a tempting digression, but it is time to turn to curves that bend.

◇ Curves from Three Points ◇

Starting with two points, weighted sums with a single free parameter generate a line. With three points, there are more interesting possibilities. Unless the points happen to be collinear, a line is unlikely. We will consider four options, but notice that any option must give a curve that lies in the plane of the three points, p_0, p_1, and p_2.

Polylines

The easiest option, but the least satisfactory, is a polyline. That is, use the line segment from p_0 to p_1 when t is between a_0 and a_1, and use the line segment from p_1 to p_2 when t is between a_1 and a_2. For this to make sense, necessarily $a_0 < a_1 < a_2$. Polylines need only one trivial piece of new machinery: an interval selector. Binary search, comparing t to a_1, would be a natural implementation.

Polylines are easy, but not smooth. Technically, they have position continuity (C^0), but not derivative continuity (C^1). Other options are smoother, but if the points are close to each other or nearly collinear, polylines *look* smooth because their angles are not visible—a feature of great practical utility.

One interesting subtlety shows up even in these elementary curves. Suppose the control points are collinear. Then the two pieces of the curve must lie together on a line, but the curve is not C^1, even though the derivative of the second segment is a multiple of the derivative of the first segment. A picture of the curve looks perfectly smooth, but an object translating along the curve jerks as it crosses p_1—where it abruptly changes speed. This situation is known as geometric continuity, and the polyline generated by collinear points (with p_1 between p_0 and p_2) is said to have G^1 continuity. This simply means that a different parameterization of the curve (changing a_2, for instance) does give C^1 continuity. (In fact, this example has G^∞ continuity.)

Smooth Interpolation

Polylines have only C^0 continuity because they abruptly change direction. To get a C^1 curve, a smooth transition is needed. That, however, is easily accomplished with a doubly weighted sum built by nesting line functions.

Consider two unrelated line segments, through p_0 and p_1 in the first case, and p_0' and p_1' in the second. Now find points p and p' on each, and combine the results using the line function again. A smooth curve that goes through p_0 at $t = a_0$, p_1 at $t = a_1$, and p_2 at $t = a_2$ uses this approach with a judicious choice of points and parameters. (See Figure 1(a).) A suitable curve definition is

$$F(t) = \text{line}(\text{bary}(t; a_0, a_2); \text{line}(\text{bary}(t; a_0, a_1); p_0, p_1), \text{line}(\text{bary}(t; a_1, a_2); p_1, p_2)),$$

which simplifies to

$$F(t) = \frac{(t - a_1)(t - a_2)}{(a_0 - a_1)(a_0 - a_2)} p_0 + \frac{(t - a_0)(t - a_2)}{(a_1 - a_0)(a_1 - a_2)} p_1 + \frac{(t - a_0)(t - a_1)}{(a_2 - a_0)(a_2 - a_1)} p_2.$$

This method, called divided differences, goes back hundreds of years (Dahlquist and Björck 1974). The weight functions, $(t - a_1)(t - a_2)/(a_0 - a_1)(a_0 - a_2)$ and so on, are Lagrange polynomials. As expected, the weight for p_i is 1 when $t = a_i$, and 0 when $t = a_j$, $j \neq i$. Equal a_i can be used for fitting derivatives (Hermite interpolation).

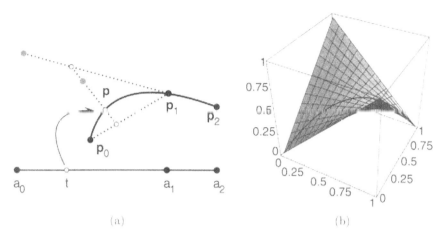

Figure 1. (a) Lagrange interpolation. (b) Lines between lines.

Interpolation looks appealing at first, but experience reveals a serious drawback. Like a rebellious child, it tends to behave very badly when one is not looking—between the interpolation points. More cooperation is possible.

Bézier Curves

Interpolating curves use a different interval for each line of the construction. Beautiful simplification and better behavior come from using the same interval for all. So let every $\mathbf{t}_i$ be obtained using some fixed interval $[a_0, a_1]$.

Now again consider line segments (p_0, p_1) and (p_0', p_1'). Find points p and p' at $\mathbf{t}_1$ on each, then combine them using $\mathrm{line}(\mathbf{t}_2; p, p')$. Alternatively, find $p_0'' = \mathrm{line}(\mathbf{t}_2; p_0, p_0')$ and $p_1'' = \mathrm{line}(\mathbf{t}_2; p_1, p_1')$, then use $\mathrm{line}(\mathbf{t}_1; p_0'', p_1'')$. The result is the same either way. When the first segment is from p_0 to p_1 and the second is from p_1 to p_2, an ancient theorem by Menelaus permits even more freedom of evaluation: $\mathbf{t}_1$ can swap with $\mathbf{t}_2$ (Seidel 1991). The resulting function

$$f(\mathbf{t}_1, \mathbf{t}_2) = \mathrm{line}(\mathbf{t}_2; \mathrm{line}(\mathbf{t}_1; p_0, p_1), \mathrm{line}(\mathbf{t}_1; p_1, p_2)),$$

under the condition that $\mathbf{t}_1 = \mathbf{t}_2 = \bar{t} = (1 - t, t)$, simplifies to

$$f(\bar{t}, \bar{t}) = (1 - t)^2 p_0 + 2(1 - t)t p_1 + t^2 p_2.$$

The function $F(t) = f(\bar{t}, \bar{t})$ is, in fact, the degree two Bézier curve determined by p_0, p_1, and p_2. The three weight polynomials, $(1 - t)^2$, $2(1 - t)t$, and t^2, are the degree two Bernstein polynomials, defined for degree n as

$$B_i^n(t) = \binom{n}{i} t^i (1 - t)^{n-i},$$

where $\binom{n}{i}$ means the binomial coefficient $n!/i!\,(n - i)!$.

Since $F(0) = p_0$ and $F(1) = p_2$, this form of curve interpolates the end control points. It does not, however, go through the middle control point, p_1. That requires the bilinear f, the polar form or *blossom* (Ramshaw 1987) of F. In Figure 1(b), the graph of a degree two blossom, the bilinear nature of f is evident from the two families of lines. The control points are $f(\bar{0}, \bar{0}) = p_0$, $f(\bar{0}, \bar{1}) = f(\bar{1}, \bar{0}) = p_1$, and $f(\bar{1}, \bar{1}) = p_2$.

Rational Curves

Parametric polynomial curves have a major limitation: They cannot exactly describe a circle (or an ellipse or hyperbola). Yet these are much-needed curves, and they have a simple degree two implicit form. Unfortunately, implicit curves of degree at least three generally have no parametric form (Sederberg 1983). For example, the plane curve $y^2 + x - x^3 = 0$ is clearly impossible to parameterize because it consists of two separate pieces. Fortunately, for degree two there is a way around the problem. Consider the curve with control points $(1, 0, 1)$, $(1, 1, 1)$, and $(0, 2, 2)$, namely

$$F(t) = (1 - t^2, 2t, 1 + t^2).$$

Its perspective projection from the origin using z as depth is

$$F(t) = \left(\frac{1 - t^2}{1 + t^2}, \frac{2t}{1 + t^2} \right).$$

As t varies from 0 to 1, this sweeps out the first quadrant of a unit circle[1] (Paeth 1991). Although the interval $[-1, 1]$ gives a semicircle, a full circle requires $[-\infty, \infty]$, which is not practical. Thus, a full circle requires two or more rational Bézier curves and consequently incurs some amount of parametric discontinuity. Once again, modelers get their desired geometric continuity, but animators are left unhappy. (The only way to completely satisfy animators who want steady circular motion is to use sine and cosine.)

Because of the difficulties of manipulating 4D points (and for other reasons), rational curves are usually managed in a slightly different way. Ordinary 3D control points are supplemented by weights to control a curve in space. This makes it easy to place a quarter-circle perpendicular to, say, the y axis by using the points and weights $(1, 0, 0; 1)$, $(1, 0, 1; 1)$, and $(0, 0, 1; 2)$. The weighted point $(x, y, z; w)$ is treated as (wx, wy, wz, w), and the resulting 4D curve is projected by dividing out the w component (instead of the z component). Notice that the 4D point (wx, wy, wz, w), from the weighted 3D point $(x, y, z; w)$, projects to (x, y, z) for any (nonzero) w.

The quarter-circle is still not in standard form, however. It is always possible to have the end weights be 1, with only the center weight varying. The standard form (in the x–y plane) has control points $(1, 0, 0; 1)$, $(1, 1, 0; \sqrt{2}/2)$, $(0, 1, 0; 1)$. Altering just the center weight gives a whole family of conics (circle, ellipse, hyperbola, parabola).

---

[1] Readers may confirm that the sum of the squares of the projected x and y components is 1.

◇ **Simple Curves from Many Points** ◇

Each of these curves defined by three points has a generalization to any number of points, with four points being used often, and larger numbers rarely. Polylines through $n + 1$ points, p_0 to p_n, need $n + 1$ real values, a_0 to a_n. A t in any interval $[a_i, a_{i+1}]$ is mapped onto a line segment from p_i to p_{i+1}.

Interpolating curves that take the same data can be built by overlapping larger and larger intervals. For example, to go from three points to four points, build the curve over p_0, p_1, and p_2 and the curve over p_1, p_2, and p_3, then use the interval $[a_0, a_3]$ to go between them. As before, the interior points agree, and the ends get all the weight at the right time. Explicitly, the four-point interpolating curve [see Figure 2(b)] is

$$F(t) = \text{line}(\text{bary}(t; a_0, a_3);$$
$$\text{line}(\text{bary}(t; a_0, a_2);$$
$$\text{line}(\text{bary}(t; a_0, a_1); p_0, p_1),$$
$$\text{line}(\text{bary}(t; a_1, a_2); p_1, p_2)),$$
$$\text{line}(\text{bary}(t; a_1, a_3);$$
$$\text{line}(\text{bary}(t; a_1, a_2); p_1, p_2),$$
$$\text{line}(\text{bary}(t; a_2, a_3); p_2, p_3)))$$

Bézier curves use the same points, but require only a single interval, $[a_0, a_1]$ (and that is often implicitly $[0, 1]$). They build up in much the same way as interpolating curves. For example,

$$f(\mathbf{t}_1, \mathbf{t}_2, \mathbf{t}_3) = \text{line}(\mathbf{t}_3;$$
$$\text{line}(\mathbf{t}_2; \text{line}(\mathbf{t}_1; p_0, p_1), \text{line}(\mathbf{t}_1; p_1, p_2))$$
$$\text{line}(\mathbf{t}_2; \text{line}(\mathbf{t}_1; p_1, p_2), \text{line}(\mathbf{t}_1; p_2, p_3)))$$

These, plus their rational versions, are the simple possibilities. For small numbers of points they are fine, but for large numbers of points spline curves are better. Fortunately, splines can be constructed in this same fashion. And the best way to understand splines is to look closer at blossoms.

◇ **Blossoms** ◇

The blossom of a degree n polynomial function $F(t)$ is a symmetric multilinear polynomial function[2] $f(\mathbf{t}_1, \dots, \mathbf{t}_n)$. Multilinearity means that, considered as a function of $\mathbf{t}_i$, f is linear for each i, $1 \le i \le n$. Symmetry means that $f(\dots, \mathbf{t}_i, \dots, \mathbf{t}_j, \dots) = f(\dots, \mathbf{t}_j, \dots, \mathbf{t}_i, \dots)$, for all $1 \le i, j \le n$. Also connecting F and f is the "diagonal equivalence" $F(t) = f(\bar{t}, \dots, \bar{t})$, which, with symmetry and linearity, gives a unique correspondence. Since uniqueness still holds when F has degree *at most* n, or when f

---

[2]For convenience, this includes the logically separate "homogenization," $t \mapsto \bar{t}$.

has *at least* n arguments, we can elevate the degree of a curve at will. For example, given a two-argument f_2, the equivalent three-argument f_3 is

$$f_3(t_1, t_2, t_3) = \frac{1}{3} f_2(t_1, t_2) + \frac{1}{3} f_2(t_1, t_3) + \frac{1}{3} f_2(t_2, t_3)$$

De Casteljau Evaluation

The Bézier curve construction given previously is called the de Casteljau algorithm (Farin 1993), and it springs directly from blossom properties. From the values $f(\bar{0}, \bar{0})$ and $f(\bar{0}, \bar{1})$, blossom linearity leads to $f(\bar{0}, \bar{t})$, computed with the line function. Likewise, $f(\bar{0}, \bar{1})$ and $f(\bar{1}, \bar{1})$ give $f(\bar{t}, \bar{1})$, which by symmetry equals $f(\bar{1}, \bar{t})$. Now from $f(\bar{0}, \bar{t})$ and $f(\bar{1}, \bar{t})$ linearity gives $f(\bar{t}, \bar{t})$, which by diagonal equivalence is $F(t)$. Even the debris is useful: The points $f(\bar{0}, \bar{0})$, $f(\bar{0}, \bar{t})$, and $f(\bar{t}, \bar{t})$ are the control points for the portion of the curve parameterized by $[0, t]$; and the points $f(\bar{t}, \bar{t})$, $f(\bar{t}, \bar{1})$, and $f(\bar{1}, \bar{1})$ are the control points for the portion of the curve parameterized by $[t, 1]$.

Derivatives

Blossoms' symmetry and linearity simplify many calculations. Derivative calculations are of special interest, since they are prominent in spline discussions. If f_n is the blossom of a degree n polynomial function F, then the derivative at a, $\frac{d}{dt}F(a)$, is just $n\, f_n(\delta, \bar{a}, \bar{a}, \ldots, \bar{a})$. Linearity accounts for the δ, while symmetry accounts for the factor of n. The second derivative, $\frac{d^2}{dt^2}F(a)$, substitutes a second δ and appends a factor of $n-1$, giving $n(n-1)\, f_n(\delta, \delta, \bar{a}, \ldots, \bar{a})$. Higher derivatives follow suit. Thus, with suitable arguments, the de Casteljau algorithm will compute derivatives as well as points.

◇ **Splines** ◇

Splines add polynomial smoothness to polyline seams. In fact, polylines and Bézier curves are both extreme members of the family of B-spline curves. B-spline curves do not interpolate their control points, but Catmull–Rom splines do, and Lagrange interpolants can be treated as a degenerate case. Since spline curves are composed of multiple polynomials joined end to end, evaluation begins by localizing t to an appropriate interval—just like polylines.

B-Spline Curves

The construction of a B-spline curve by lines reverses the pattern used for Lagrange interpolation. Interpolation begins with small intervals that grow by unions. B-spline curves begin with large intervals that shrink by intersections. The initial intervals for a degree n spline are n atomic intervals wide. That is, they are of the form $[a_k, a_{k+n}]$. The intervals chosen are all those that include t.

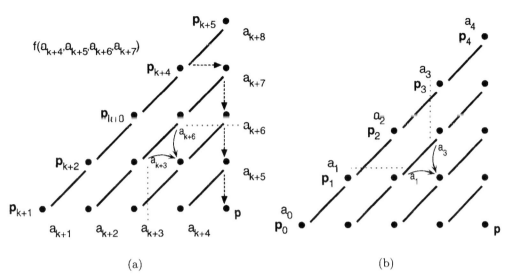

Figure 2.   (a) De Boor algorithm. (b) Divided difference algorithm.

Consider a degree two curve evaluated at $t \in [a_{k+2}, a_{k+3}]$. The initial intervals will be $[a_{k+1}, a_{k+3}]$ and $[a_{k+2}, a_{k+4}]$; these are mapped onto (p_{k+1}, p_{k+2}) and (p_{k+2}, p_{k+3}). This gives two new points for another line. Now map $[a_{k+2}, a_{k+3}]$, the intersection of the first two intervals, onto this segment, and evaluation is complete. A degree three case would expand as follows, this time for $t \in [a_{k+3}, a_{k+4}]$.

$$
\begin{aligned}
F(t) = \ &\text{line}(\text{bary}(t; a_{k+3}, a_{k+4}); \\
&\quad \text{line}(\text{bary}(t; a_{k+2}, a_{k+4}); \\
&\qquad \text{line}(\text{bary}(t; a_{k+1}, a_{k+4}); p_{k+1}, p_{k+2}), \\
&\qquad \text{line}(\text{bary}(t; a_{k+2}, a_{k+5}); p_{k+2}, p_{k+3})), \\
&\quad \text{line}(\text{bary}(t; a_{k+3}, a_{k+5}); \\
&\qquad \text{line}(\text{bary}(t; a_{k+2}, a_{k+5}); p_{k+2}, p_{k+3}), \\
&\qquad \text{line}(\text{bary}(t; a_{k+3}, a_{k+6}); p_{k+3}, p_{k+4})))
\end{aligned}
$$

The process for a degree four curve is depicted in Figure 2(a). This is the celebrated de Boor algorithm (Farin 1993). For comparison, Figure 2(b) shows interpolation. One important difference is that each intermediate point generated by the de Boor algorithm lies between the segment ends, and so the final point must lie within the region enclosed by the control points used. This "convex hull" property suggests the curve is well behaved; it is also of great benefit in geometric operations such as intersection.

For degree n, if a_{k+1} through a_{k+n} are 0 and a_{k+n+1} through a_{k+2n} are 1, the de Boor algorithm reduces to the de Casteljau algorithm. This validates the claim that Bézier curves are a special case. Alternatively, degree one B-spline curves are simply polylines.

Once again the Menelaus theorem applies, and so the de Boor algorithm computes blossom values if different arguments are used at each step. Careful study of the algorithm shows that, for any k, p_{k+1} is the blossom value $f(\bar{a}_{k+1}, \ldots, \bar{a}_{k+n})$ for any segment of the curve to which it contributes. This fact is of great practical benefit, facilitating many of the same operations we saw for Bézier curves. Probably the single most important operation is knot insertion. Using blossoms, it is simple to derive the Boehm knot insertion algorithm (Boehm 1980), which is just one de Boor step.

Since the de Boor algorithm computes blossom values, it also computes derivatives. This makes it easy to compare adjacent curve segments and prove that degree n B-spline curves are C^{n-1} smooth: The two polynomials meeting at a_k have all but one control point in common, and so give the same result for all blossom values of the form $f(\bar{a}_k, \mathbf{t}_1, \mathbf{t}_2, \ldots, \mathbf{t}_{n-1})$. Thus, their first $n-1$ derivatives agree, as claimed.

Use of weighted control points and projection gives non-uniform rational B-spline curves (NURBS). Repeating the control points (and a little more) leads to periodic B-spline curves, which are closed and continuous (Farin 1993).

Catmull–Rom Splines

Finally, consider Catmull–Rom splines. Catmull and Rom originally described a method for generating splines of many kinds, not just cubic C^1 interpolating splines (Catmull and Rom 1974). Among the possibilities are interpolating splines of arbitrary smoothness. Such a family is readily generated by combining Lagrange interpolation with B-splines. (See Figure 3.) For C^n continuity, take n Lagrange steps followed by $n+1$ de Boor steps (Barry and Goldman 1988). The first de Boor step is actually equivalent to another Lagrange step. Readers familiar with the C^1 curves may wish to compare their algorithm with this one.

◇ **Linear Systems** ◇

Beyond the basic curve methods discussed so far lies a larger world of linear possibilities. Polynomials of a given degree form a linear space (a vector space), and admit many different sets of basis polynomials (such as basis vectors) (de Boor 1978). This gives another way to look at the relationships among Bézier curves (Bernstein basis), interpolating curves (Lagrange basis), and standard polynomial expressions (power basis). Splines—which are a collection of polynomial pieces—also form a linear space, for which B-splines are a basis. Thus, by solving a linear system, it is possible to convert a spline in Catmull–Rom form to one in B-spline form.

Linear systems allow many other possibilities. The foregoing degree three splines gave either C^1 continuity with interpolation, or C^2 continuity without interpolation. A linear system that depends on every control point can give a spline with both C^2 continuity

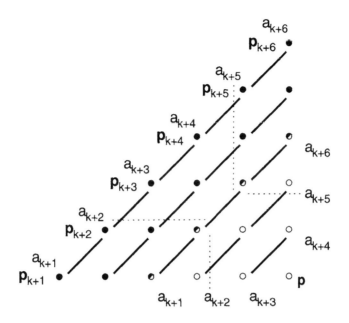

Figure 3.   Catmull–Rom algorithm.

and interpolation (de Boor 1978). Unfortunately, this spline changes shape everywhere if any point is moved, and it requires a solution time proportional to the total number of control points to do so.

A less extreme approach allows manipulation of a curve and its derivatives (and thus, say, curvature) at a given point (Welch and Witkin 1992). This is again a matter of solving a linear system relating the desired values to the control points. It is sometimes more convenient to manipulate a curve "directly" like this, moving control points indirectly. The linear systems involved are underdetermined, but there are standard methods (such as pseudo-inverses) to handle them.

◇   **Conclusions**   ◇

As this gem demonstrates, linear forms unify the construction of many common curves (and some uncommon ones) and clarify operations on them. While special circumstances often allow more efficient calculations, unity and clarity are lost. Remarkably, there is more waiting (Farin 1993). Triangular patches can be generated using the de Casteljau algorithm on triangles instead of line segments. Rectangular patches can be generated by splining curves instead of points. (These are the "tensor product" surfaces.) And n-sided patches (S patches) can be generated by mating n-sided polygons with Bézier simplices, the multidimensional generalization of Bézier curves and triangular patches (Loop and DeRose 1989).

Blossoms, tensor products, and S patches are all examples of a more general concept. Complexity can be reduced by factoring one large problem into many small pieces, perhaps working in a higher dimension. Geometric continuity, only briefly touched upon here, also yields nicely to this approach (Seidel 1993).

The code that follows will generate curves of many different flavors. Specific possibilities include Lagrange interpolants, Bézier curves, B-spline curves, and C^n Catmull–Rom splines. With a suitable wrapper, it can also manage rational versions of all these.

◇ **Code** ◇

```
/****** lincrv.h ******/
/* Ken Shoemake, 1994 */

#define MAXDIM 2
typedef float Vect[MAXDIM];
typedef float Knot;
typedef int Bool;

int DialASpline(Knot t, Knot a[], Vect p[], int m, int n, Vect work[],
                unsigned int Cn, Bool interp, Vect val);


/****** lincrv.c ******/
/* Ken Shoemake, 1994 */

#include "lincrv.h"

/* Perform a generic vector unary operation. */
#define V_Op(vdst,gets,op,vsrc,n) {register int V_i;\
    for(V_i=(n)-1;V_i>=0;V_i--) (vdst)[V_i] gets op ((vsrc)[V_i]);}

static void lerp(Knot t, Knot a0, Knot a1, Vect p0, Vect p1, int m, Vect p)
{
    register Knot t0=(a1-t)/(a1-a0), t1=1-t0;
    register int i;
    for (i=m-1; i>=0; i--) p[i] = t0*p0[i] + t1*p1[i];
}

/* DialASpline(t,a,p,m,n,work,Cn,interp,val) computes a point val at parameter
   t on a spline with knot values a and control points p. The curve will have
   Cn continuity, and if interp is TRUE it will interpolate the control points.
   Possibilities include Langrange interpolants, Bezier curves, Catmull-Rom
   interpolating splines, and B-spline curves. Points have m coordinates, and
   n+1 of them are provided. The work array must have room for n+1 points.
 */
int DialASpline(Knot t, Knot a[], Vect p[], int m, int n, Vect work[],
                unsigned int Cn, Bool interp, Vect val)
```

```
{
    register int i, j, k, h, lo, hi;

    if (Cn>n-1) Cn = n-1;        /* Anything greater gives one polynomial */
    for (k=0; t> a[k]; k++);     /* Find enclosing knot interval */
    for (h=k; t==a[k]; k++);     /* May want to use fewer legs */
    if (k>n) {k = n; if (h>k) h = k;}
    h = 1+Cn - (k-h); k--;
    lo = k-Cn, hi - k+1+Cn;

    if (interp) {                /* Lagrange interpolation steps */
        int drop=0;
        if (lo<0) {lo = 0; drop += Cn-k;
                    if (hi-lo<Cn) {drop += Cn-hi; hi = Cn;}}
        if (hi>n) {hi = n; drop += k+1+Cn-n;
                    if (hi-lo<Cn) {drop += lo-(n-Cn); lo = n-Cn;}}
        for (i=lo; i<=hi; i++) V_Op(work[i],=,,p[i],m);
        for (j=1; j<=Cn; j++) {
            for (i=lo; i<=hi-j; i++) {
                lerp(t,a[i],a[i+j],work[i],work[i+1],m,work[i]);
            }
        }
        h = 1+Cn-drop;
    } else {                     /* Prepare for B-spline steps */
        if (lo<0) {h += lo; lo = 0;}
        for (i=lo; i<=lo+h; i++) V_Op(work[i],=,,p[i],m);
        if (h<0) h = 0;
    }
    for (j=0; j<h; j++) {
        int tmp = 1+Cn-j;
        for (i=h-1; i>=j; i--) {
            lerp(t,a[lo+i],a[lo+i+tmp],work[lo+i],work[lo+i+1],m,work[lo+i+1]);
        }
    }
    V_Op(val,=,,work[lo+h],m);
    return (k);
}

/*** lincrvtest.c ***/

#include <stdlib.h>
#include <stdio.h>
#include <math.h>
#include "lincrv.h"

#define TRUE 1
#define FALSE 0
#define BIG (1.0e12)

static Vect work[4];
static Vect ctlPts[] = { {0,0}, {1,1}, {1,0}, {0,0}, };
static float *knots;
static float bezKts[] = {0, 0, 0, 1, 1, 1, BIG};
```

```
static float lagKts[] = {0.00, 0.25, 0.75, 1.00, BIG};
static float catKts[] = {-1, 0, 1, 2, BIG};
static float bspKts[] = {-2, -1, 0, 1, 2, 3, BIG};
static int m = MAXDIM;
static int n = 3;
static int Cn = 1;
static Bool interp = FALSE;
static Vect val = {0.84375, 0.0};
static float t = 0;
static int eh = 0;

enum Flavor{PLY, LAG, BEZ, CAT, BSP, NFLAVORS};
char fnames[][4] = {"PLY", "LAG", "BEZ", "CAT", "BSP"};

void main(void)
{
    int i, j, k;
    int flavor = PLY;

    for (flavor=0; flavor<NFLAVORS; flavor++) {
        switch (flavor) {
        case PLY:    knots = lagKts; interp = TRUE;  Cn = 0; break;
        case LAG:    knots = lagKts; interp = TRUE;  Cn = 2; break;
        case BEZ:    knots = bezKts; interp = FALSE; Cn = 2; break;
        case CAT:    knots = catKts; interp = TRUE;  Cn = 1; break;
        case BSP:    knots = bspKts; interp = FALSE; Cn = 2; break;
        default:     knots = bspKts; interp = FALSE; Cn = 0; break;
        }
        printf("Flavor %s: interp=%d, Cn=%d\n", fnames[flavor],interp,Cn);
        for (t=0.0; t<=1.0; t+=0.125) {
            eh = DialASpline(t, knots, ctlPts, m, n, work, Cn, interp, val);
            printf("(%6.3f) ", t);
            for (i=0; i<MAXDIM; i++) printf("%9.6f ",val[i]); printf("\n");
        }
    }
}
```

◇ Bibliography ◇

(Barry and Goldman 1988) Phillip J. Barry and Ronald N. Goldman. A recursive evaluation algorithm for a class of Catmull–Rom splines. *Computer Graphics (SIG-GRAPH '88 Proceedings)*, 22(4):199–204, August 1988.

(Boehm 1980) W. Boehm. Inserting new knots into B-spline curves. *Computer-Aided Design*, 12(4):199–201, 1980.

(Catmull and Rom 1974) Edwin Catmull and Raphael Rom. A class of local interpolating splines. In R. E. Barnhill and R. F. Riesenfeld, editors, *Computer Aided Geometric Design*, pages 317–326. Academic Press, New York NY, 1974.

(Dahlquist and Björck 1974) Germund Dahlquist and Åke Björck. *Numerical Methods.* Prentice-Hall, Englewood Cliffs, NJ, 1974.

(de Boor 1978) Carl de Boor. *A Practical Guide to Splines.* Springer-Verlag, 1978.

(Farin 1993) Gerald Farin. *Curves and Surfaces for Computer Aided Geometric Design,* 3rd ed. Academic Press, San Diego, , 1993.

(Loop and DeRose 1989) Charles Loop and Tony DeRose. A multisided generalization of Bézier surfaces. *ACM Transactions on Graphics,* 8(3):204–234, July 1989.

(Paeth 1991) Alan W. Paeth. A half-angle identity for digital computation: The joys of the halved tangent. In James Arvo, editor, *Graphics Gems II,* Chapter 8.5, pages 381–386. AP Professional, Boston, 1991.

(Ramshaw 1987) Lyle Ramshaw. Blossoming: A connect-the-dots approach to splines. SRC Research Report 19, Digital, 130 Lytton Avenue, Palo Alto, CA 94301, June 1987.

(Sederberg 1983) Thomas Warren Sederberg. *Implicit and Parametric Curves and Surfaces for Computer Aided Geometric Design.* PhD thesis, Purdue University, August 1983.

(Seidel 1991) Hans-Peter Seidel. Menelaus's theorem. In James Arvo, editor, *Graphics Gems II,* Chapter 9.5, pages 424–427. AP Professional, Boston, 1991.

(Seidel 1993) Hans-Peter Seidel. Polar forms for geometrically continuous spline curves of arbitrary degree. *ACM Transactions on Graphics,* 12(1):1–34, January 1993.

(Welch and Witkin 1992) William Welch and Andrew Witkin. Variational surface modeling. *Computer Graphics (SIGGRAPH '92 Proceedings),* 26(3):157–166, July 1992.

◇ V ◇
Ray Tracing and Radiosity

The gems in this section describe methods of ray tracing and radiosity. While a few entries could be classified equally well under either computational geometry or modeling, these gems have all been crafted with higher-speed photorealistic rendering in mind.

In the first gem (V.1), Shene generalizes his previous cylindrical intersection test gem to include cones. (A cylinder is a cone with its apex at infinity.) Schlick (V.2) examines the mathematical and computational pros and cons of ray tracing a surface described by quadrangle tessellation versus the traditional triangular mesh. Quadrangles clearly have merit and application. Möller (V.3) presents a set of object–scan line intersection heuristics and their related equations. These are easily retrofitted to most ray tracing software and provide for generous speed-ups. Leipelt (V.4) fully derives the equations of a ray intersecting a sphere swept through space along an arbitrary parametric curve and having a modulated radius. (This class of objects is truly tubular to the max.) Márton (V.5) provides a welcome and extensive treatment of Voronoi diagrams. To better spatially classify objects for faster ray intersection tests, the code implementation is provided as a fully general and freestanding work. Zimmerman (V.6) derives an radiosity illumination model in which cylindrical lamps replace a point sources, allowing added photorealism while only slightly increasing the computational load for a constant number of fixed sources. Finally, Feda (V.7) introduces directional light to intermediate radiosity. This provides an added degree of photorealism, as seen in the gem's related color plates.

◇ V.1

Computing the Intersection of a Line and a Cone

Ching-Kuang Shene
Northern Michigan University
shene@nmu.edu

◇ Introduction ◇

Computing the intersection of a line and an object is a common operation in computer graphics, for example, when ray tracing. Computation of the intersection of a line and a cylinder has been treated in previous gems (Cychosz and Waggenspack 1994, Shene 1994). This gem extends the latter work by computing the intersection of a line and a cone through geometric means.

◇ Definitions ◇

The notation and defining formulas are presented for three geometric objects:

- $\ell(\mathbf{B}, \mathbf{d})$: the line defined by base point $\mathbf{B}$ and direction vector[1] $\mathbf{d}$.
- $\mathcal{P}(\mathbf{B}, \mathbf{n})$: the plane defined by base point $\mathbf{B}$ and normal vector $\mathbf{n}$.
- $\mathcal{C}(\mathbf{V}, \mathbf{v}, \alpha)$: the cone defined by vertex $\mathbf{V}$, axis direction $\mathbf{v}$, and cone angle α.

In these definitions, bold-face roman type indicates a vector quantity. Moreover, upper (lower)-case vectors are position (direction) vectors. Position vectors are sometimes referred to as points. Therefore, $\mathbf{P}$ and P are equivalent. The normalized cross product $\mathbf{u} \otimes \mathbf{v} = \mathbf{u} \times \mathbf{v} / \|\mathbf{u} \times \mathbf{v}\|$ is also employed.

◇ Problem Statement ◇

Given a test line $\ell(\mathbf{D}, \mathbf{d})$ and cone $\mathcal{C}(\mathbf{V}, \mathbf{v}, \alpha)$, determine the point of intersection by computing a t such that point $\mathbf{D} + t\mathbf{d}$ lies on $\mathcal{C}(\mathbf{V}, \mathbf{v}, \alpha)$ or show that no intersection exists.

---

[1]In this exposition, $\|\mathbf{d}\| = 1$ holds for any direction vector $\mathbf{d}$.

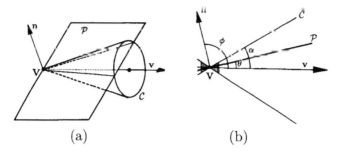

(a)   (b)

Figure 1.   The normal vector **n** of plane $\mathcal{P}$.

◇   **The Algorithm**   ◇

If $\mathbf{V} \in \ell$, the intersection point is $\mathbf{V}$. Therefore, in what follows, $\mathbf{V} \notin \ell$ holds.

Consider the plane $\mathcal{P}$ determined by $\mathbf{V}$ and ℓ. Its normal vector is $\mathbf{n} = \mathbf{d} \otimes \overrightarrow{DV}$. However, if $\mathbf{v} \cdot \mathbf{n} > 0$, $\mathbf{n}$ is reversed. This ensures that $\mathcal{P}$ lies "between" $\mathbf{n}$ and $\mathbf{v}$ (Figure 1). Therefore, the desired plane is $\mathcal{P}(\mathbf{V}, \mathbf{n})$. Since $\mathcal{P}$ contains $\mathbf{V}$, $\mathcal{P} \cap \mathcal{C}$ is either a point (i.e., $\mathbf{V}$), or consists of one or two lines. In the following, the computation of $\ell \cap \mathcal{C}$ will be reduced to the computation of $\ell \cap (\mathcal{P} \cap \mathcal{C})$. In other words, the intersection lines of $\mathcal{P} \cap \mathcal{C}$ will be computed and intersected with ℓ. However, prior to the intersection computation, a disjoint test is needed.

Checking for Intersection

Let θ be the angle between $\mathbf{v}$ and $\mathcal{P}$ [Figure 1(a)]. By trichotomy exactly one of the following conditions is true:

- $\theta > \alpha$: $\mathcal{P} \cap \mathcal{C}$ is $\mathbf{V}$, and $\ell \cap \mathcal{C}$ is empty.
- $\theta = \alpha$: $\mathcal{P} \cap \mathcal{C}$ is the tangent line of $\mathcal{P}$ and $\mathcal{C}$, and $\ell \cap \mathcal{C}$ consists of at most one point.
- $\theta < \alpha$: $\mathcal{P} \cap \mathcal{C}$ consists of two lines, and $\ell \cap \mathcal{C}$ consists of at most two points.

However, using θ directly is not as efficient as using $\cos \theta$, since the latter can be obtained easily as follows. Let $\phi = \theta + 90°$ be the angle between $\mathbf{n}$ and $\mathbf{v}$ [Figure 1(b)]. Therefore, $\cos \phi = \mathbf{n} \cdot \mathbf{v}$ and

$$\cos \theta = \cos(\phi - 90°) = \sin \phi = (1 - \cos^2 \phi)^{1/2} = (1 - (\mathbf{n} \cdot \mathbf{v})^2)^{1/2}.$$

Since the cosine function is monotonically decreasing between $0°$ and $90°$, $\cos(x) > \cos(y)$ if and only if $x < y$ for $0° \leq x, y \leq 90°$. Therefore, with $\cos \alpha$ and $\cos \theta$, tests $\theta > \alpha$, $\theta = \alpha$, and $\theta < \alpha$ can be replaced by $\cos \theta < \cos \alpha$, $\cos \theta = \cos \alpha$, and $\cos \theta > \cos \alpha$, respectively.

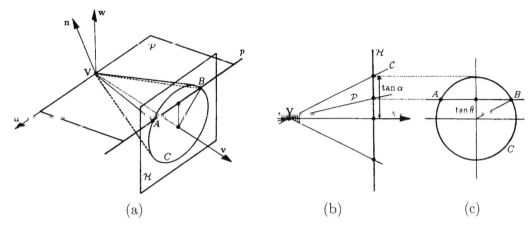

Figure 2. The *u-v-w* coordinate system and related information.

Solving for Intersection

Assuming $\cos\theta \geq \cos\alpha$, two steps are required to compute $\ell \cap \mathcal{C}$: (1) computing $\mathcal{P} \cap \mathcal{C}$, and (2) computing $\ell \cap (\mathcal{P} \cap \mathcal{C})$. For the first step, a well-chosen coordinate system is vital. Since **n** and **v** are not parallel, $\mathbf{v} \times \mathbf{n}$ is well defined. Let vectors **u** and **w** be defined as follows:

$$\mathbf{u} = \mathbf{v} \otimes \mathbf{n},$$
$$\mathbf{w} = \mathbf{u} \otimes \mathbf{v} = (\mathbf{v} \otimes \mathbf{n}) \otimes \mathbf{v}.$$

Then **u**, **v**, and **w** are perpendicular to each other and form a right-handed *u-v-w* coordinate system with origin at **V** [Figure 2(a)]. Since $\mathbf{n} \perp \mathbf{u}$ and $\mathbf{V} \in \mathcal{P}$, $\mathcal{P}$ contains the *u*-axis and is perpendicular to the *vw*-plane.

Using this coordinate system, the direction vectors of $\mathcal{P} \cap \mathcal{C}$ are computed as follows. Consider a plane $\mathcal{H}$ with $v = 1$ in the *u-v-w* coordinate system. $\mathcal{H} \cap \mathcal{C}$ is a circle C, while $\mathcal{H} \cap \mathcal{P}$ is a line p. Let p and C intersect at A and B. Then the intersection of $\mathcal{P}$ and $\mathcal{C}$ consists of two lines, $\overrightarrow{VA}$ and $\overleftrightarrow{VB}$. Thus, if their direction vectors, $\delta_1 = \overrightarrow{VA}$ and $\delta_2 = \overrightarrow{VB}$, can be found, $\mathcal{P} \cap \mathcal{C}$ will be determined.

To compute A and B, first note that their *w*-coordinates are both equal to $\tan\theta$, and that $\frac{1}{2}\overline{AB} = (\tan^2\alpha - \tan^2\theta)^{1/2}$, where $\tan\alpha$ is the radius of circle C [Figure 2(b) and (c)]. Since $\overleftrightarrow{AB}$ is parallel to the *u*-axis, direction vectors $\delta_1 - \overrightarrow{VA}$ and $\delta_2 = \overrightarrow{VB}$ can be computed as follows:

$$\delta_1 = \mathbf{v} + (\tan\theta)\mathbf{w} + (\tan^2\alpha - \tan^2\theta)^{1/2}\mathbf{u},$$
$$\delta_2 = \mathbf{v} + (\tan\theta)\mathbf{w} - (\tan^2\alpha - \tan^2\theta)^{1/2}\mathbf{u}.$$

Therefore, the intersection lines of $\mathcal{P}$ and $\mathcal{C}$ are simply $\ell_1(\mathbf{V}, \delta_1)$ and $\ell_2(\mathbf{V}, \delta_2)$. Without loss of generality, assume $\|\delta_1\| = \|\delta_2\| = 1$. Note that if $\mathcal{P}$ is tangent to $\mathcal{C}$, $\alpha = \theta$, and $\ell_1 = \ell_2$.

Finally, computing $\ell_1 \cap \ell$ and $\ell_2 \cap \ell$ yields the desired result. Determining the intersection point of two coplanar lines is not difficult. If δ_1 and $\mathbf{d}$ have the same or opposite direction (i.e., $\mathbf{d} \times \delta_1 = \mathbf{0}$, or equivalently $\|\mathbf{d} \cdot \delta_1\| = 1$), ℓ_1 and ℓ are parallel to each other and there is no intersection point. Otherwise, there exist r and s such that $\mathbf{D} + r\mathbf{d} = \mathbf{V} + s\delta_1$. Since $\mathbf{g} \times \mathbf{g} = \mathbf{0}$ holds for any nonzero vector $\mathbf{g}$, computing the cross product with δ_1, the preceding formula gives

$$r\mathbf{d} \times \delta_1 = (\mathbf{V} - \mathbf{D}) \times \delta_1.$$

Computing the inner product with $\mathbf{d} \times \delta_1$ yields

$$r = \frac{[(\mathbf{V} - \mathbf{D}) \times \delta_1] \cdot (\mathbf{d} \times \delta_1)}{\|\mathbf{d} \times \delta_1\|^2}.$$

Thus, $\ell_1 \cap \ell$ is computed. Replacing δ_1 with δ_2 yields $\ell_2 \cap \ell$.

In practice, the computation for r could be simpler. Let $\pi_i(\mathbf{x})$ be the ith component of vector $\mathbf{x}$. Then

$$r = \frac{\pi_i((\mathbf{V} - \mathbf{D}) \times \delta_1)}{\pi_i(\mathbf{d} \times \delta_1)},$$

where $\pi_i(\mathbf{d} \times \delta_1)$ is a nonzero component of vector $\mathbf{d} \times \delta_1$.

Remark. Since a cylinder is a cone with its vertex at infinity, the algorithm presented here provides another way of computing the intersection of a line and a cylinder. In this case, $\mathcal{P}$ is the plane that is parallel to the cylinder axis and contains the given line, and $\mathcal{P} \cap \mathcal{C}$ degenerates to a pair of parallel lines. Consequently, the computation is reduced to computing the intersection points of this pair of lines with the given one.

◇ Acknowledgment ◇

This work was supported in part by a faculty research grant of Northern Michigan University.

◇ Bibliography ◇

(Cychosz and Waggenspack 1994) J. M. Cychosz and W. N. Waggenspack, Jr. Intersecting a ray with a cylinder. In Paul Heckbert, editor, *Graphics Gems IV*, pages 356–365. AP Professional, Boston, 1994.

(Shene 1994) Ching-Kuang Shene. Computing the intersection of a line and a cylinder. In Paul Heckbert, editor, *Graphics Gems IV*, pages 353–355. AP Professional, Boston, 1994.

V.2

Ray Intersection of Tessellated Surfaces: Quadrangles versus Triangles

Christophe Schlick
Laboratoire Bordelais de Recherche
  en Informatique (LaBRI)
Talence, France
schlick@labri.u-bordeaux.fr

Gilles Subrenat
Laboratoire Bordelais de Recherche
  en Informatique (LaBRI)
Talence, France
subrenat@labri.u-bordeaux.fr

◇   **Introduction**   ◇

Tessellating a surface into triangular facets for manipulation or visualization has become a very popular technique in computer graphics. Several reasons explain this popularity. First, a triangle in three-dimensional space is always convex and necessarily planar, whereas this does not hold for a facet having four or more vertices. Second, fast triangulation techniques have been developed both for implicit surfaces and parametric surfaces (Preparata 1985); see, for instance several previous gems (Lischinsky 1994, Bloomenthal 1994, Peterson 1994). Last, triangular facets are well suited to specific optimization techniques proposed for ray tracing (Snyder and Barr 1987).

In contrast, this gem presents an algorithm that computes the intersection between a ray and a quadrangle. It is particularly valuable for tessellating parametric surfaces, and may be considered as an extension to a previous gem (Badouel 1990) that employed a triangular decomposition. A comparison of both algorithms in terms of cost and precision is also presented.

◇   **Triangular Facets**   ◇

In review, compute the precise intersection point between a ray and a triangular facet ABC. A point M that belongs to the ray starting from P and going in direction $\mathbf{V}$ is expressed by

$$\mathbf{AM} = \mathbf{AP} + t\,\mathbf{V}, \quad \text{where } t \geq 0 \text{ is the parameter defining position.} \quad (1)$$

IBM ISBN 0-12-543455-3
Macintosh ISBN 0-12-543457-X

First, the intersection point with the plane of the facet must be established. Calling **N** the normal vector of the facet, the parameter of intersection is

$$t = -\frac{\mathbf{AP} \cdot \mathbf{N}}{\mathbf{V} \cdot \mathbf{N}} \quad \text{with} \quad \mathbf{N} = \frac{\mathbf{AB} \times \mathbf{AC}}{\|\mathbf{AB} \times \mathbf{AC}\|}. \tag{2}$$

If M is inside the triangle, it obeys

$$\mathbf{AM} = u\,\mathbf{AB} + v\,\mathbf{AC} \quad \text{with} \quad 0 \le u \le 1 \quad 0 \le v \le 1 \quad 0 \le u+v \le 1. \tag{3}$$

Equation (3) is a *linear system* of three equations (one for each coordinate), where one of them is redundant because it can be obtained by a linear combination of the two others. To avoid numerical overflows (division by a number close to zero), discard the equation k that corresponds to the greatest absolute component of the normal vector (Snyder and Barr 1987):

$$k \in \{x, y, z\} \quad \text{with} \quad |\mathbf{N_k}| = \max\left(|\mathbf{N_x}|, |\mathbf{N_y}|, |\mathbf{N_z}|\right). \tag{4}$$

To simplify notations, introduce the operator $*$ defined by $U * V = (U \times V)_k$ to easily determine the values u and v:

$$u = \frac{\mathbf{AM} * \mathbf{AC}}{\mathbf{AB} * \mathbf{AC}} \quad \text{and} \quad v = \frac{\mathbf{AB} * \mathbf{AM}}{\mathbf{AB} * \mathbf{AC}}. \tag{5}$$

Thus, to find if M belongs to ABC, compute u and v by (5) and check if $0 \le u \le 1$, $0 \le v \le 1$, and $0 \le u + v \le 1$. The advantage of this intersection algorithm is that it yields directly the parameters u and v, which are subsequently reused to interpolate between points A, B, and C. In particular, if the three points have corresponding normal vectors $\mathbf{N_A}$, $\mathbf{N_B}$, and $\mathbf{N_C}$, then the normal vector $\mathbf{N_M}$ at point M is given by

$$\mathbf{N_M} = (1 - u - v)\,\mathbf{N_A} + u\,\mathbf{N_B} + v\,\mathbf{N_C}. \tag{6}$$

When a surface is defined by its parametric equation, approximating facets may be fit by sampling the isoparametrics in u and v to obtain quadrangles $ABCD$ [Figure 1(a)]. With such a tessellation, the previous intersection process can be used again by dividing $ABCD$ into two triangles, ABD and CDB [Figure 1(b)]. In this way, one obtains the values of u and v for a point M inside the quadrangle with the following definition:

$$\begin{cases} \text{Triangle } ABD : & \mathbf{AM} = u\,\mathbf{AB} + v\,\mathbf{AD}, \\[2ex] \text{Triangle } CDB : & \mathbf{CM} = (1 - u)\,\mathbf{CD} + (1 - v)\,\mathbf{CB}. \end{cases} \tag{7}$$

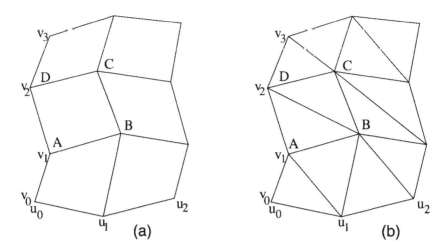

Figure 1. Tessellation of a parametric surface: (a) in quadrangles, (b) in triangles.

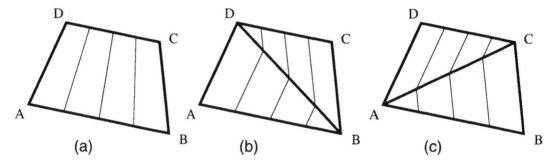

Figure 2. Isoparametric segments on quadrangular facet for parameter $u = \frac{1}{4}, \frac{1}{2}$, and $\frac{3}{4}$. (a) Quadrangle. (b) Triangles $ABD + CDB$. (c) Triangles $BCA + DAC$.

Then the normal vector $\mathbf{N_M}$ may be obtained as the bilinear interpolation between the four points A, B, C, and D:

$$\mathbf{N_M} = (1-u)(1-v)\,\mathbf{N_A} + u(1-v)\,\mathbf{N_B} + uv\,\mathbf{N_C} + (1-u)v\,\mathbf{N_D}. \quad (8)$$

There are two drawbacks to this artificial quadrangle subdivision. First, the result depends on the choice of the triangles, and second, the isoparametric segments of the quadrangle ($u = constant$ or $v = constant$) are not preserved. For instance, Figure 2(a) shows the quadrangle $ABCD$ having three isoparametric segments ($u = \frac{1}{4}$, $u = \frac{1}{2}$ and $u = \frac{3}{4}$), defining line segments nearly parallel to $\overline{AD}$ and $\overline{BC}$. Now consider two possible triangulations. Splitting the quadrangle along $\overline{BD}$ and $\overline{AC}$ is shown in Figures 2(b) and 2(c), respectively, with isoparametric segments also drawn. Note that the split necessarily disturbs the orientation of these segments. This modification of the isoparametric directions can induce visible artifacts such as distorted texture mappings.

This defect can be removed if all four vertices $ABCD$ are used when computing u and v. This requires a method based upon quadrangular faceting, described next.

◇ **Quadrangular Facets** ◇

A point M belongs to a planar and convex quadrangle $ABCD$ iff

$$\mathbf{AM} = u\mathbf{AB} + v\mathbf{AD} + uv\mathbf{AE} \tag{9}$$

with $\quad \mathbf{AE} = \mathbf{DC} + \mathbf{BA} = \mathbf{DA} + \mathbf{BC} \qquad 0 \le u \le 1 \qquad 0 \le v \le 1.$

Equation (9) is a *quadratic system* of three equations. As before, one can be obtained by linear combination of the other two. By analogy to (4), eliminate the equation k corresponding to the largest absolute component of the normal vector. The final system can be solved either in terms of u or v:

$$u^2 \left(\mathbf{AB} * \mathbf{AE} \right) + u \left(\mathbf{AB} * \mathbf{AD} + \mathbf{AE} * \mathbf{AM} \right) + \mathbf{AD} * \mathbf{AM} = 0; \quad v = \frac{\mathbf{AM} - u\,\mathbf{AB}}{\mathbf{AD} + u\,\mathbf{AE}} \tag{10}$$

$$v^2 \left(\mathbf{AD} * \mathbf{AE} \right) + v \left(\mathbf{AD} * \mathbf{AB} + \mathbf{AE} * \mathbf{AM} \right) + \mathbf{AB} * \mathbf{AM} = 0; \quad u = \frac{\mathbf{AM} - v\,\mathbf{AD}}{\mathbf{AB} + v\,\mathbf{AE}}. \tag{11}$$

To find if M lies within the quadrangle, compute u and v by (10) or (11) and check that $0 \le u \le 1$ and $0 \le v \le 1$. These parameters allow for a proper four-point interpolation (8), which preserves the facets' true isoparametrics [Figure 2(a)].

All the previous computations are valid only for planar, convex quadrangles. Thus, quadrangles obtained by parametric sampling might not qualify. However, the small size of the facets created by such a sampling process allows them to be considered both planar and convex. Moreover, the *planar and convex condition* may be directly enforced in certain adaptive sampling schemes (Snyder and Barr 1987, Peterson 1994), thereby preventing the generation of unvalid quadrangles. Empirical testing has not revealed any distinguishable visual artifacts when using this method.

◇ **Trapezoid** ◇

When $ABCD$ defines a trapezoid (at least two opposite sides are parallel), the quadratic term appearing in (10) or (11) is zero, greatly simplifying computation. Without loss

Table 1. Costs of each computation.

	Plane intersection	UV triangle	UV trapezoid	UV quadrangle
Number of multiplications	9	6	14 (10)	17 (13)
Number of divisions	1	2	2	2
Number of square roots	—	—	—	1

(n) : number of multiplications if trapezoid/nontrapezoid information is stored offline.

Table 2. Global intersection costs.

	Triangle (twice)	Trapezoid	Quadrangle
Number of multiplications	30	23 (19)	26 (22)
Number of divisions	6	3	3
Number of square roots	—	—	1

(n) : number of multiplications if trapezoid/nontrapezoid information is stored offline.

Table 3. Time measurements.

	Quadrangle method	Triangle method
Trapezoids	60	100
Quadrangles	76	100

of generality, the solution for the case[1] $\overline{AB} \parallel \overline{DC}$ is now presented. The u coordinate is computed by (10), which is now a linear equation. In this trapezoid, all isoparametrics in v are exactly parallel to $\overline{AB}$ and $\overline{CD}$. Therefore, v is obtained simply by dividing the distance from M to $\overline{AB}$ (or $\overline{CD}$) by the distance from D to $\overline{AB}$ (or $\overline{CD}$):

$$u = \frac{\mathbf{AM} * \mathbf{AD}}{\mathbf{AB} * \mathbf{AD} + \mathbf{AE} * \mathbf{AM}} \quad \text{and} \quad v = \frac{\mathbf{AM} * (\mathbf{AB} + \mathbf{DC})}{\mathbf{AD} * (\mathbf{AB} + \mathbf{DC})}. \tag{12}$$

In the source code concluding this gem, the *trapezoid versus nontrapezoid test* is done on-the-fly by the intersection routine. To speed computation, this test can be computed offline for each quadrangle and the result can be stored in the quadrangle structure, costing two bits per quadrangle but saving four multiplications per routine call.

◇ **Comparison** ◇

Table 1 presents the number of numerical operations for different parts of the algorithm. Table 2 compares intersection costs for the three facet types. Table 3 compares timings between the triangle and quadrangle algorithms. Intuitively, the intersection

---

[1]Notice that a degenerated quadrangle (i.e., $A = B$ or $C = D$) is only a particular case of a trapezoid, and so the same solution can be applied.

of a ray with a quadrangle (one quadratic equation and one linear equation) appears *a priori* more expensive than the intersection with a triangle (two linear equations). But in fact, for a given quadrangle $ABCD$, the triangle-based ray intersection must be computed twice (except in the few situations where the ray hits the first triangle). Moreover, when the quadrangle is a trapezoid, the square root is removed by optimization and the quadrangle algorithm easily outperforms its rival. Note: to obtain maximal efficiency, algorithms used for time trials employed both macro-based vector functions and a precomputed (non)trapezoid flag. The code listed below uses the toolbox of macro functions defined in the present volume (page 402); on the distribution disk, there is also the code using the Graphics Gems library (Glassner 1990).

Finally, note that trapezoids are frequently obtained when tessellating classical surfaces used in computer graphics, which include ruled surfaces, surfaces of revolution, extrusion surfaces (without torsion), and even large regions of many free-form surfaces. This makes quadrangle- and trapezoid-based ray intersection algorithms, as described here, the method of choice.

◇ **Source Code** ◇

```
/* ---------------------------------------------------------------------- *\
   QUAD.H : Christophe Schlick and Gilles Subrenat (15 May 1994)

   "Ray Intersection of Tessellated Surfaces : Quadrangles versus Triangles"
   in Graphics Gems V (edited by A. Paeth), Academic Press
\* ---------------------------------------------------------------------- */

#ifndef _QUAD_
#define _QUAD_

#include <math.h>
#include "tool.h"
#include "real.h"
#include "vec2.h"
#include "vec3.h"

/*
** Type definitions
*/
typedef struct {
    realvec3  A,B,C,D;    /* Vertices in counter clockwise order */
    realvec3  Normal;     /* Normal vector pointing outwards     */
} QUAD;

typedef struct {
    realvec3  Point;      /* Ray origin                          */
    realvec3  Vector;     /* Ray direction                       */
} RAY;
```

```
typedef struct {
    realvec3  Point;     /* Intersection point                             */
    real      Distance;  /* Distance from ray origin to intersection point */
    real      u, v;      /* Parametric coordinates of the intersection point */
} HIT;

/*
** External declarations
*/
extern bool ray_hit_quad (RAY *, QUAD *, HIT *);

#endif



/* ------------------------------------------------------------------------ *\
   QUAD.C : Christophe Schlick and Gilles Subrenat (15 May 1994)

   "Ray Intersection of Tessellated Surfaces : Quadrangles versus Triangles"
    in Graphics Gems V (edited by A. Paeth), Academic Press
\* ------------------------------------------------------------------------ */

#include "quad.h"

/*
** Macro definitions
*/
#define MY_TOL              ((real) 0.0001)

#define LARGEST_COMPONENT(A)  (ABS((A).x) > ABS((A).y) ? \
                              (ABS((A).x) > ABS((A).z) ? 'x' : 'z') : \
                              (ABS((A).y) > ABS((A).z) ? 'y' : 'z'))

/*
** Compute parametric coordinates of the intersection point
*/
static bool point_in_quad (QUAD *Quad, HIT *Hit)
{
    char     LargestComponent;              /* of the normal vector          */
    realvec2 A, B, C, D;                    /* Projected vertices            */
    realvec2 M;                             /* Projected intersection point  */
    realvec2 AB, BC, CD, AD, AM, AE;        /* Miscellanous 3D-vectors       */
    real     u, v;                          /* Parametric coordinates        */
    real     a, b, c, SqrtDelta;            /* Quadratic equation            */
    bool     Intersection = FALSE;          /* Intersection flag             */
    realvec2 Vector;                        /* Temporary 2D-vector           */

    /*
    ** Projection on the plane that is most parallel to the facet
    */
    LargestComponent = LARGEST_COMPONENT(Quad->Normal);

    if (LargestComponent == 'x') {
        A.x = Quad->A.y; B.x = Quad->B.y; C.x = Quad->C.y; D.x = Quad->D.y;
```

```
        M.x = Hit->Point.y;
    }
    else {
        A.x = Quad->A.x; B.x = Quad->B.x; C.x = Quad->C.x; D.x = Quad->D.x;
        M.x = Hit->Point.x;
    }

    if (LargestComponent == 'z') {
        A.y = Quad->A.y; B.y = Quad->B.y; C.y = Quad->C.y; D.y = Quad->D.y;
        M.y = Hit->Point.y;
    }
    else {
        A.y = Quad->A.z; B.y = Quad->B.z; C.y = Quad->C.z; D.y = Quad->D.z;
        M.y = Hit->Point.z;
    }
    SUB_VEC2 (AB, B, A); SUB_VEC2 (BC, C, B);
    SUB_VEC2 (CD, D, C); SUB_VEC2 (AD, D, A);
    ADD_VEC2 (AE, CD, AB); NEG_VEC2 (AE, AE); SUB_VEC2 (AM, M, A);

    if (ZERO_TOL (DELTA_VEC2(AB, CD), MY_TOL))              /* case AB // CD */
    {
        SUB_VEC2 (Vector, AB, CD);
        v = DELTA_VEC2(AM, Vector) / DELTA_VEC2(AD, Vector);
        if ((v >= 0.0) && (v <= 1.0)) {
            b = DELTA_VEC2(AB, AD) - DELTA_VEC2(AM, AE);
            c = DELTA_VEC2 (AM, AD);
            u = ZERO_TOL(b, MY_TOL) ? -1.0 : c/b;
            Intersection = ((u >= 0.0) && (u <= 1.0));
        }
    }
    else if (ZERO_TOL(DELTA_VEC2(BC, AD), MY_TOL))          /* case AD // BC */
    {
        ADD_VEC2 (Vector, AD, BC);
        u = DELTA_VEC2(AM, Vector) / DELTA_VEC2(AB, Vector);
        if ((u >= 0.0) && (u <= 1.0)) {
            b = DELTA_VEC2(AD, AB) - DELTA_VEC2(AM, AE);
            c = DELTA_VEC2 (AM, AB);
            v = ZERO_TOL(b, MY_TOL) ? -1.0 : c/b;
            Intersection = ((v >= 0.0) && (v <= 1.0));
        }
    }
    else                                                   /* general case */
    {
        a = DELTA_VEC2(AB, AE); c = - DELTA_VEC2 (AM,AD);
        b = DELTA_VEC2(AB, AD) - DELTA_VEC2(AM, AE);
        a = -0.5/a; b *= a; c *= (a + a); SqrtDelta = b*b + c;
        if (SqrtDelta >= 0.0) {
            SqrtDelta = sqrt(SqrtDelta);
            u = b - SqrtDelta;
            if ((u < 0.0) || (u > 1.0))          /* we want u between 0 and 1 */
                u = b + SqrtDelta;
            if ((u >= 0.0) && (u <= 1.0)) {
```

```
                    v = AD.x + u * AE.x;
                    if (ZERO_TOL(v, MY_TOL))
                        v = (AM.y - u * AB.y) / (AD.y + u * AE.y);
                    else
                        v = (AM.x - u * AB.x) / v;
                    Intersection = ((v >= 0.0) && (v <= 1.0));
                }
            }
        }
        if (Intersection) {
            Hit->u = u;
            Hit->v = v;
        }
        return (Intersection);
    }


    /*
    ** Search for an intersection between a facet and a ray
    */
    bool hit_ray_quad (RAY *Ray, QUAD *Quad, HIT *Hit)
    {
        realvec3    Point;

        /* if the ray is parallel to the facet, there is no intersection */
        Hit->Distance = DOT_VEC3 (Ray->Vector, Quad->Normal);
        if (ZERO_TOL(Hit->Distance, MY_TOL)) return (FALSE);

        /* compute ray intersection with the plane of the facet */
        SUB_VEC3 (Point, Quad->A, Ray->Point);
        Hit->Distance = DOT_VEC3 (Point, Quad->Normal) / Hit->Distance;
        MULS_VEC3 (Hit->Point, Ray->Vector, Hit->Distance);
        INC_VEC3 (Hit->Point, Ray->Point);

        /* is the point in the facet ? */
        return (point_in_quad(Quad, Hit));
    }
```

◇ **Bibliography** ◇

(Badouel 1990) Didier Badouel. An efficient ray–polygon intersection. In Andrew S. Glassner, editor, *Graphics Gems*, pages 390–393. AP Professional, Boston, 1990.

(Bloomenthal 1994) Jules Bloomenthal. An implicit surface polygonizer. In Paul S. Heckbert, editor, *Graphics Gems IV*, pages 324–349. AP Professional, Boston, 1994.

(Glassner 1990) Andrew Glassner. 2D and 3D vector library. In Andrew S. Glassner, editor, *Graphics Gems*, pages 629–642. AP Professional, Boston, 1990.

(Lischinsky 1994) Dani Lischinsky. Incremental Delauney triangulation. In Paul S. Heckbert, editor, *Graphics Gems IV*, pages 47–59. AP Professional, Boston, 1994.

(Peterson 1994) John W. Peterson. Tessellation of NURB surfaces. In Paul S. Heckbert, editor, *Graphics Gems IV*, pages 286–320. AP Professional, Boston, 1994.

(Preparata 1985) F.P. Preparata. *Computational geometry: An introduction.* Springer Verlag, 1985.

(Snyder and Barr 1987) J.M. Snyder and A.H. Barr. Ray tracing complex models containing surface tessellations. *Computer Graphics (ACM SIGGRAPH '87 Proceedings)*, 21(4):119–128, July 1987.

V.3

Faster Ray Tracing Using Scanline Rejection

Tomas Möller
Lund Institute of Technology
Lund, Sweden
d91tm@efd.lth.se

◇ **Introduction** ◇

Ray tracing speeds may be improved (Weghorst *et al.* 1984) by testing the primary ray intersections. A preprocessing phase uses a hidden surface algorithm to find a visible object for each pixel. This gem presents a scanline-based *first-hit speedup* technique. Its added advantage lies in its reuse of geometry-based intersection testing, making for a more uniform implementation. It also works with different kinds of supersampling.

Figure 1 shows an overview of a simple viewing geometry. Assume that the picture is rendered one scanline at the time with increasing scanline number. Now consider all first-hit intersections for a particular scanline. All lie within a common plane defined by the eyepoint E and the scanline. Any object that does not intersect the plane cannot intersect a ray; all nonintersecting objects can be rejected for further intersection testing during the processing of the scanline. This is depicted in Figure 2. Formally, consider two points A and B, which are positioned on a particular scanline in space. The normal of the plane is then $N_s = (B - E) \times (A - E)$. Normalize N_s so $|N_s| = 1$ and then $d_s = -N_s \cdot E$. The equation of the scanline plane (where P is any point on the plane) is

$$N_s \cdot P + d_s = 0. \tag{1}$$

The following subsections present rejection tests for spheres, boxes, and polygons, then methods of extension. Each test assumes that only one ray is shot per pixel and that this ray passes through the center of the pixel. Each object/scanline test returns a status code taken from the set {*OnScanline*, *OffScanline*, *Interval*, *NeverAgain*}. Additional heuristic information may also be produced. At the conclusion of all subsections, the scanline-rejection technique is generalized to support methods of supersampling, adaptive supersampling, and stochastic sampling.

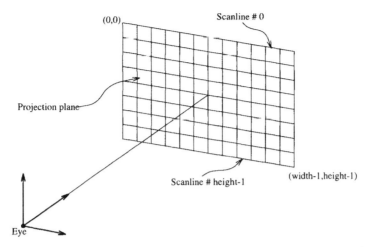

Figure 1. The viewing geometry. Horizontal lines define the scanline center; pixels lie at line crossings.

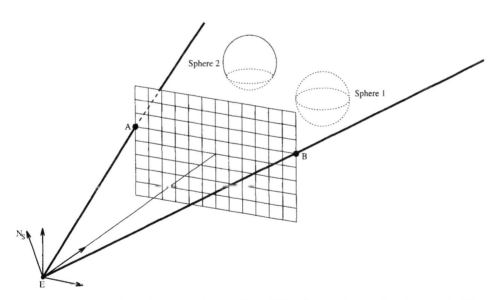

Figure 2. The scanline plane through points *A*, *B*, and *E*. Sphere 2 lies on the plane and will be tested further; sphere 1 lies below the plane and will not be tested further.

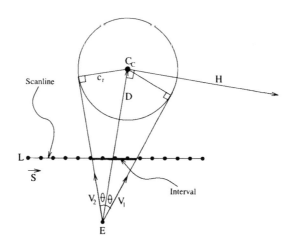

Figure 3. The circle of intersection common to sphere and scanline plane. Its scanline projection is the interval of guaranteed intersection. S is the vector between two pixels on the (dotted) scanline.

◇ **Spheres** ◇

The sphere is the basic ray tracing object. Their simplicity makes them useful even for an advanced ray tracer. They are, for example, often used as bounding volumes for more complex objects.

Given a sphere with center S_c and radius s_r and a scanline plane, first compute the shortest distance between the plane and the center of the circle. Intersection occurs *iff* this is less than or equal to the radius s_r. Cost of evaluation is reduced by using a distance calculation described in a previous gem (Georgiades 1992). Formally, the signed distance t is

$$t = N_s \cdot S_c + d_s. \tag{2}$$

If $|t| \leq s_r$ then the status of that sphere is *OnScanline*. This means that a first-hit test must potentially be computed for every pixel on that scanline. If $|t| > s_r$ then no intersection occurs and the status code returned is *OffScanline*. This means that no additional first-hit tests on that scanline are required for that sphere. Since (2) provides a *signed* distance (side of plane), all first-hit tests on subsequent scanlines may be rejected should these scanlines further increase this distance. In this case $|t| > s_r$ and S_c lies on the same side of the plane as previous scanlines, and code *NeverAgain* is set.

If the sphere intersects the plane, an even more efficient rejection can be made. The intersection of a plane and a sphere is a circle whose projection onto the scanline is an interval of intersection (Figure 3). Here, code *Interval* is set; its endpoints are now determined. Given the center of the circle C_c and its radius c_r, then c_r is easily computed using the Pythagorean relation: $s_r^2 = c_r^2 + t^2$ and $C_c = S_c - tN_s$. Using the notation in Figure 3, compute the interval of intersection by finding vectors V_1 and V_2. Let $D = C_c - E$ and $d = |D|$, which gives $\sin\theta = c_r/d$ and the vector $H = D \times N_s$. Since $|D| = |H|$, V_1 and V_2 can be computed as

$$V_1 = \sin(\theta)H + \cos(\theta)D - \frac{c_r}{d}H + \sqrt{1 - \left(\frac{c_r}{d}\right)^2}D,$$

$$V_2 = -\sin(\theta)H + \cos(\theta)D = -\frac{c_r}{d}H + \sqrt{1 - \left(\frac{c_r}{d}\right)^2}D.$$

The desired interval is called [*Interval.min*,*Interval.max*] and these values are integers representing pixel offsets. They are found by computing the intersection between the scanline in space and the lines $E + \beta_1 V_1$ and $E + \beta_2 V_2$. The leftmost point on the scanline is called L, and the vector between two adjacent pixels in space is called S, which gives us the scanline $L + \alpha S$. α_1 and α_2 are computed using the two systems of equations below:

$$L + \alpha_1 S = E + \beta_1 V_1 \tag{3}$$

$$L + \alpha_2 S = E + \beta_2 V_2 \tag{4}$$

To reduce these systems to two dimensions, simply project the lines onto an axis-parallel plane (the same projection normally performed on the points of a polygon during the point-in-polygon test), that is, throw away the coordinates that correspond to $\max(N_{s,x}, N_{s,y}, N_{s,z})$. Call the projection plane the *uv*-plane. Equation (3) reduces to the system below:

$$L_u + \alpha_1 S_u = E_u + \beta_1 V_{1,u}$$
$$L_v + \alpha_1 S_v = E_v + \beta_1 V_{1,v} \tag{5}$$

The linear system (5) has a unique solution (α_1, β_1) if V_1 is not parallell to S. The value of interest, α_1, is given by

$$\alpha_1 = \frac{V_{1,u} \cdot (E_v - L_v) - V_{1,v} \cdot (E_u - L_u)}{S_v \cdot V_{1,u} - S_u \cdot V_{1,v}}. \tag{6}$$

If V_1 is exchanged for V_2 in Equation (6), the solution for α_2 is obtained. Since S is the vector between two adjacent points (a point is here the center of a pixel), α_1 and α_2 are the (floating-point) horizontal pixel offsets for the projection of the sphere onto the scanline. The endpoints of the interval are then

$$Interval.min = \lceil \alpha_2 \rceil,$$
$$Interval.max = \lfloor \alpha_1 \rfloor, \tag{7}$$

in which the ceiling and floor functions produce a more conservative estimate that includes partially intersected pixels. These calculations guarantee that a ray outside the interval cannot intersect the sphere and that a ray inside must intersect the sphere.

If a sphere is used merely as a bounding volume, then the subsidiary interval computation may be omitted. (Should the test fail, all objects within the bounding volume are marked *OffScanline*. Alternatively, all objects can be marked by the common interval, though this information is of less value.) A bounding volume hierarchy traversal is a natural and productive extension. Intersection failure of any point within the tree implies failure within all subtrees.

The distance to the intersection point can also be estimated. The distance t to the first intersection is $d - c_r \leq t < d$ if the eyepoint is outside the sphere, else $0 < t < 2c_r$. This information can be used to further improve hierarchial traverse (Haines 1991).

There are some special cases that are all handled in the source code. If $d < c_r$, then the eyepoint E lies inside the sphere and the status of that sphere is set to *OnScanline* since every ray from the eye will hit the sphere. Another special case is when V_1 or V_2 are parallel to S. This simple problem is not discussed here but is treated in the code. Note also that the implementation assumes that all spheres that are completely behind the eyepoint E are set to *NeverAgain* before the ray tracing starts. All objects with status *NeverAgain* are immediately rejected from further testing when presented to any of the scanline intersection routines.

◇ **Polygons** ◇

The test for polygons is quite similar to the test just described. Compute the signed distance for each vertex of the polygon. Intersection occurs iff at least one is positive and one negative. As before, *NeverAgain* is returned if all points lie on the same side as previous scanlines.

If intersection occurs, an interval may again be constructed by projecting the set of intersections (page 386). Find adjacent vertices V_i and V_{i+1} that differ in sign. Then the point of intersection is found by computing the intersection between the line

$$V_i + t(V_{i+1} - V_i)$$

and the scanline plane. The t-value of the intersection is

$$t = \frac{-d_s - N_s \cdot V_i}{N_s \cdot (V_{i+1} - V_i)},$$

which in turn gives the point of intersection

$$P_i = V_i + t(V_{i+1} - V_i).$$

To project P_i onto the scanline, find the intersection between the two lines

$$L + \alpha_i S$$

and

$$E + \beta(P_i - E).$$

The interval is then given by

$$\begin{aligned}
Interval.min &= \lceil \min(\alpha_i) \rceil, \\
Interval.max &= \lfloor \max(\alpha_i) \rfloor.
\end{aligned} \tag{8}$$

If the polygon is convex and the pixel is inside the interval, then the intersection between the ray and the polygon is guaranteed and the point-in-polygon test omitted, saving considerable execution time. If the polygon is concave, then all pixels inside the interval potentially lie within the polygon, while all rays lying outside the interval miss.

Boxes are easily treated as special-case polygons using the preceeding methods.

◇ **Pseudocode** ◇

Given an object record that includes interval offsets, the pseudocode resembles the following:

```
for y ← 0, y < Ymax, y ← y + 1 do
    Compute Ns and ds for scanline number y.
    for obj ← object0 to objectm do
        FirstTest(obj,y);   /* this sets obj.status and obj.interval.min, max */
    endloop;
    for x ← 0, x < Xmax, x ← x + 1 do
        RayTrace loop
        for obj ← object0 to objectm do
            if obj.status==Interval then
            begin
                if obj.interval.min ≤ x ≤ obj.interval.max then
                    RayTrace(x,y,obj,true);   /* guaranteed hit */
            end
            else if obj.status==OnScanline then
                RayTrace(x,y,obj,false);   /* potential hit */
            else
                The ray misses the Object.
        endloop;
```

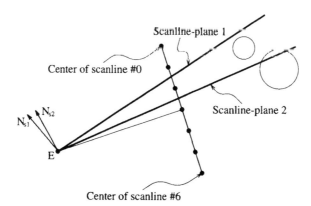

Figure 4. Stochastic supersampling showing scanline plane 1 and 2 for scanline #2. Note: an object may lie between the planes without intersecting them.

> **endloop;**
> **endloop;**

RayTrace(*x*,*y*,*obj*,*intersect*) is the original "RayTrace" function, now augmented by a third "object" parameter indicating the candidate object of intersection and by a fourth parameter *intersect*, which is set to *true* if intersection must occur and set to *false* if it is a potential hit.

◇ **Supersampling** ◇

The algorithm just described is well suited to $n \times n$ supersampling and adaptive supersampling tasks. The method is largely unchanged: For $n \times n$ supersampling, n planes are generated per scanline. Adaptive supersampling introduces new planes with each additional (fractional) scanline.

For stochastic supersampling, neither of these techniques can be used. Instead construct, for each scanline, two scanline planes: one through the uppermost part of the pixels and one through the bottommost part (Figure 4). To test a sphere for intersection, start with a signed distance test for both plane 1 and 2 in the figure. Call the distances d_1 and d_2. If $d_1 > s_r$ or $d_2 < -s_r$, then reject the sphere on that scanline. On the other hand, if any of the absolute values of d_1 or d_2 is less than the radius of the sphere, then an interval can be computed. Assuming the pixels are square, Equation (7) for the interval calculation changes to

$$
\begin{aligned}
Interval.min &= \lceil \min(\alpha_{2,1}, \alpha_{2,2}) - \tfrac{1}{2} \rceil, \\
Interval.max &= \lfloor \max(\alpha_{1,1}, \alpha_{1,2}) + \tfrac{1}{2} \rfloor,
\end{aligned}
\tag{9}
$$

where $\alpha_{i,j}$ is α_i for scanline plane j. But note that this test will not work for all spheres of subpixel size. When the radius s_r is smaller than the projected scanline spacing, it may lie between the two planes without intersecting either, requiring an additional test. If $d_1 < -s_r$ and $d_2 > s_r$, the sphere lies between the planes and it is possible that rays will hit it on that scanline. Project the sphere onto the projection plane to find the interval.

Observe that one cannot guarantee intersection inside this interval, but the risk of miss is small. Outside the interval no intersection will occur, as usual.

Roughly the same situation applies for polygons. If all points are above plane 1 or below plane 2, then the polygon is rejected. Otherwise, the polygon is a potential first-hit, but note that no interval can easily be computed for polygons. The status *OnScanline* is returned and no further heuristic testing occurs.

Observe that all objects behind the eyepoint must be rejected before any of these tests are done, since the orientation of the planes is inverted behind the eyepoint.

◇ **Optimizations** ◇

Before all ray tracing commences the five planes of the viewing pyramid can clip and reject (status *NeverAgain*) all objects outside it. These objects will never be considered.

Another optimization orders the objects using a linked list during the evaluation of each scanline. Every object that receives the *NeverAgain* status is placed last in the list. Objects with status *OffScanline* preface the *NeverAgain* objects. The *Interval* and *OnScanline* objects will thus be first in the list. This order will be changed for every scanline, but when traversing the list and finding an object with *OffScanline* or *NeverAgain* status, the **for** $obj \leftarrow object_0$ to $object_m$ enumeration loop for that pixel may immediately terminate. In the same fashion, the **for**-loop that calls **FirstTest** may terminate when an object with status *NeverAgain* is encountered.

The author welcomes the inclusion of additional intersection tests to the library. Quadrics (such as the cylinder or the cone) are likely first extensions.

◇ **Acknowledgment** ◇

Thanks to Alan Paeth, who turned this article into a beautifully cut gem.

◇ **Source Code** ◇

scanline.cc

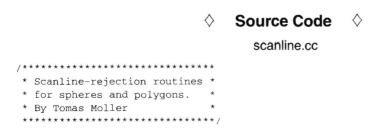

```
/*******************************
 * Scanline-rejection routines *
 * for spheres and polygons.   *
 * By Tomas Moller             *
 *******************************/
```

```c
#include "vector.h"

#define EPSILON 1e-6            /* a small number */
#define INFINITY 1e8            /* a large number */
enum StatusFlag {OnScanline,OffScanline,Interval,NeverAgain};

struct FirstHitStatus
{
        StatusFlag Flag;                    /* se enum above */
        short IntervalMin,IntervalMax;   /* the interval */
};

/*******************************************************************
* SphereComputeFirstHitStatus - computes the first hit status      *
*    for a sphere and the Interval (if any) for the scanline-plane *
*    given by the first two parameters.                            *
*                                                                  *
* Entry:                                                           *
*   Ns - normal of the scanline-plane                             *
*   ds - "d-value" for the scanline-plane                          *
*   LeftMost - the leftmost point on the scanline. Referred to     *
*       as L in the text.                                          *
*   ScanLineDir - the direction of the scanline in space.          *
*       Observe that it is constructed by subtracting two          *
*       adjacent points on the scanline from each other.           *
*   width - number of pixels per scanline                          *
*   Ui,Vi - the indices to the uv-plane. 0==x,1==y,2==z            *
*   Eyepos - the positition of the eye (or camera)                 *
*   Sphcen - the centre of the sphere                              *
*   Sr -  the radius of the sphere                                 *
*                                                                  *
* The function returns a struct FirstHitStatus with all            *
* necessary information.                                           *
*******************************************************************/
struct FirstHitStatus SphereComputeFirstHitStatus(Vector &Ns,float ds,
        Vector LeftMost,Vector ScanLineDir,int width,int Ui,int Vi,
        Vector Eyepos,Vector Sphcen,float Sr)
{
    struct FirstHitStatus FHstatus;
    float signed_dist=Ns*Sphcen+ds;
    if(signed_dist>Sr) FHstatus.Flag=NeverAgain;     /* sphere is above plane */
    else if(signed_dist<-Sr) FHstatus.Flag=OffScanline; /* below plane */
    else
    {
        Vector D,H,Cc,Nd;                            /* Cc=Circle Origo */
        float sintheta,costheta,centerdist;
        float cr2,d2,t1,t2,t3,V1v,V1u,V2v,V2u;       /* squared circle radius */
        Cc=Sphcen-Ns*signed_dist;
        cr2=Sr*Sr-signed_dist*signed_dist;           /* the * is dot-product */
        D=Cc-Eyepos;
        d2=D*D;                                       /* D dot D=squared length of D */
        if(d2<=cr2)
        {                                             /* we are inside the sphere */
```

```
            FHstatus.Flag=OnScanline;
            return FHstatus;
        }
        H=D%Ns;                                        /* % = cross product */
        t1=cr2/d2;
        sintheta=sqrt(t1);
        costheta=sqrt(1-t1);
        t1=H[Ui]*sintheta;
        t2=D[Ui]*costheta;
        V1u=t1+t2;                                     /* compute V1 and V2 */
        V2u=-t1+t2;
        t1=H[Vi]*sintheta;
        t2=D[Vi]*costheta;
        V1v=t1+t2;
        V2v=-t1+t2;
        t1=LeftMost[Ui]-Eyepos[Ui];                    /* some constants */
        t2=Eyepos[Vi]-LeftMost[Vi];
        t3=V1u*ScanLineDir[Vi]-V1v*ScanLineDir[Ui];
        if(t3!=0.0)                                    /* V1 parallel to ScanLineDir ? */
        {
            FHstatus.IntervalMax=(int)floor((V1v*t1+V1u*t2)/t3);
            t3=V2u*ScanLineDir[Vi]-V2v*ScanLineDir[Ui];
            if(t3==0.0) FHstatus.IntervalMin=0;
            else FHstatus.IntervalMin=(int)ceil((V2v*t1+V2u*t2)/t3);
        }
        else                                           /* V1 parallel to ScanLineDir */
        {
            t3=V2u*ScanLineDir[Vi]-V2v*ScanLineDir[Ui];
            FHstatus.IntervalMin=(int)ceil((V2v*t1+V2u*t2)/t3);
            FHstatus.IntervalMax=width-1;
        }
        /* check if interval is valid and set status */
        if(FHstatus.IntervalMin>=width || FHstatus.IntervalMax<0)
            FHstatus.Flag=OffScanline;
        else
        {
            if(FHstatus.IntervalMax>=width) FHstatus.IntervalMax=width-1;
            if(FHstatus.IntervalMin<0) FHstatus.IntervalMin=0;
            if(FHstatus.IntervalMin==0 && FHstatus.IntervalMax==width-1)
                FHstatus.Flag=OnScanline;
            else FHstatus.Flag=Interval;
        }
    }
    if(FHstatus.IntervalMin>FHstatus.IntervalMax) FHstatus.Flag=OffScanline;
    return FHstatus;
}


/* Macro used by PolyComputeFirstHitStatus. It projects
 * the point (x,y,z) onto the scanline and saves the
 * result in [realIntervalMin,realIntervalMax].
 */
```

```
#define PROJECTPOINT(x,y,z)                                                    \
    switch(Ui)                                                                 \
    {                                                                          \
        case Xi:u=x; break;                                                    \
        case Yi:u=y; break;                                                    \
        case Zi:u=z; break;                                                    \
    }                                                                          \
    switch(Vi)                                                                 \
    {                                                                          \
        case Xi:v=x; break;                                                    \
        case Yi:v=y; break;                                                    \
        case Zi:v=z; break;                                                    \
    }                                                                          \
    denom=ScanLineDir[Ui]*(Eyepos[Vi]-v)-ScanLineDir[Vi]*(Eyepos[Ui]-u); \
    if(denom==0.0)                                                             \
    {                                                                          \
        if(ScanLineDir[Ui]!=0.0) alpha=(u-Eyepos[Ui])/ScanLineDir[Ui]; \
        else alpha=(v-Eyepos[Vi])/ScanLineDir[Vi];                            \
        if(alpha>0.0) realIntervalMax=width-1;                                \
        else realIntervalMin=0;                                               \
    }                                                                          \
    else                                                                       \
    {                                                                          \
        alpha=(Eyepos[Ui]-LeftMost[Ui])*(Eyepos[Vi]-v);                       \
        alpha-=(Eyepos[Ui]-u)*(Eyepos[Vi]-LeftMost[Vi]);                      \
        alpha/=denom;                                                          \
        if(alpha>realIntervalMax) realIntervalMax=alpha;                      \
        if(alpha<realIntervalMin) realIntervalMin=alpha;                      \
    }                                                                          \


/*********************************************************************
 * PolyComputeFirstHitStatus - computes the first hit status for a *
 *   polygon and the Interval (if any) for the scanline-plane      *
 *   given by the first two parameters.                            *
 *                                                                 *
 * Entry:                                                          *
 *   Ns - normal of the scanline-plane                            *
 *   ds - "d-value" for the scanline-plane                        *
 *   LeftMost - the leftmost point on the scanline. Referred to   *
 *       as L in the text.                                        *
 *   ScanLineDir - the direction of the scanline in space.        *
 *       Observe that it is constructed by subtracting two        *
 *       adjacent points on the scanline from each other.         *
 *   width - number of pixels per scanline                        *
 *   Ui,Vi - the indices to the uv-plane. 0==x,1==y,2==z          *
 *   Eyepos - the positition of the eye (or camera)               *
 *   x,y,z - the points of the polygon                            *
 *   NrVert - Number of vertices                                  *
 *                                                                 *
 * The function returns a struct FirstHitStatus with all          *
 * necessary information.                                         *
 *********************************************************************/
```

```
struct FirstHitStatus PolyComputeFirstHitStatus(Vector Ns,float ds,
        Vector LeftMost,Vector ScanLineDir,int width,int Ui,int Vi,
        Vector Eyepos,float *x,float *y,float *z,short NrVert)
{
    struct FirstHitStatus FHstatus;
    Vector isect,dir;
    float dist,prevdist=0,denom,alpha,u,v;
    float realIntervalMax=-INFINITY,realIntervalMin=INFINITY;
    prevdist=Ns.X()*x[NrVert-1]+Ns.Y()*y[NrVert-1]+Ns.Z()*z[NrVert-1]+ds;
    /* start with last point */
    for(int i=0;i<NrVert;i++)
    {
        dist=Ns.X()*x[i]+Ns.Y()*y[i]+Ns.Z()*z[i]+ds;
        if(dist==0.0)
        {       /* point i is on the plane, project it on the scanline */
            PROJECTPOINT(x[i],y[i],z[i]);
        }
        else if((prevdist<0.0 && dist>0.0) || (prevdist>0.0 && dist<0.0))
        /* intersection */
        {
            isect.Set(x[i],y[i],z[i]);
            if(i==0)
            {
                dir.SetX(x[NrVert-1]-x[0]);
                dir.SetY(y[NrVert-1]-y[0]);
                dir.SetZ(z[NrVert-1]-z[0]);
            }
            else dir.Set(x[i-1]-x[i],y[i-1]-y[i],z[i-1]-z[i]);
            alpha=(-ds-Ns*isect)/(Ns*dir);
            isect+=dir*alpha;              /* intersection point calculated */
            PROJECTPOINT(isect.X(),isect.Y(),isect.Z());
        }
        prevdist=dist;
    }
    if(realIntervalMax==-INFINITY)          // no intersection
    {
        if(dist>0) FHstatus.Flag=NeverAgain;
        else FHstatus.Flag=OffScanline;
    }
    else if(realIntervalMax<0 || realIntervalMin>=width)
        FHstatus.Flag=OffScanline;
    else
    {
        FHstatus.IntervalMax=(int)floor(realIntervalMax);
        FHstatus.IntervalMin=(int)ceil(realIntervalMin);
        if(FHstatus.IntervalMax>=width) FHstatus.IntervalMax=width-1;
        if(FHstatus.IntervalMin<0) FHstatus.IntervalMin=0;
        if(FHstatus.IntervalMin==0 && FHstatus.IntervalMax==width-1)
            FHstatus.Flag=OnScanline;
        else FHstatus.Flag=Interval;
    }
```

```
        if(FHstatus.IntervalMin>FHstatus.IntervalMax) FHstatus.Flag=OffScanline;
        return FHstatus;
}
```

vector.h

```
/************************************************************
 * vector.h - a vector class written in c++                 *
 * functions for +, -, dotproduct, crossproduct, scaling,   *
 * length & normalizing, many of these are operators        *
 * By Tomas Moller                                          *
 ************************************************************/
#ifndef VECTOR_H
#define VECTOR_H

#include <stream.h>
#include <string.h>
#include <math.h>

#define Xi 0              // indices into vector
#define Yi 1
#define Zi 2

class Vector
{
    protected:
        float fx,fy,fz;
    public:
        Vector() {fx=0.0;fy=0.0;fz=0.0;}   // constructor with no argument
        Vector(float x,float y,float z);   // constructor with coords
        Vector(Vector& a);                 // constructor with vector
        void Set(float x,float y,float z); // assign new values to vector
        void SetX(float x);                // set x
        void SetY(float y);                // set y
        void SetZ(float z);                // set z;
        void SetIndex(int index,float value);
        // set x,y or z to value depending on index
        float X(void);                     // return fx
        float Y(void);                     // return fy
        float Z(void);                     // return fz
        void Add(float x,float y,float z); // addition to this vector
        void Sub(float x,float y,float z); // subtraction
        void Scale(float a);               // scaling of vector
        float Length(void);                // length of vector
        void Normalize(void);              // normalize vector

        void operator=(Vector& a);         // operator: assignment
        Vector operator*(float t);         // operator: scaling
        Vector operator+(Vector& a);       // operator: addition
        Vector operator-(Vector& a);       // operator: subtraction
        Vector operator+(void);            // unary +
        Vector operator-(void);            // unary -
        void operator+=(Vector& a);        // operator: +=
```

```
          void operator-=(Vector& a);         // operator: -=
          void operator*=(float t);           // operator: *= (scaling)
          float operator*(Vector& a);         // operator: dot product
          Vector operator%(Vector& a);        // operator: cross product
          float operator[](short index);
          // if short=0 then X, short=1 then Y, else Z, see constants above
};

/* here follows the inline functions and operators */

inline Vector::Vector(float x,float y,float z)
{ fx=x; fy=y; fz=z; }

inline Vector::Vector(Vector& a)
{ fx=a.fx; fy=a.fy; fz=a.fz; }

inline void Vector::Set(float x,float y,float z)
{ fx=x; fy=y; fz=z; }

inline void Vector::SetX(float x)
{ fx=x;}

inline void Vector::SetY(float y)
{ fy=y; }

inline void Vector::SetZ(float z)
{ fz=z; }

inline void Vector::SetIndex(int index,float value)
{
    switch(index)
    {
        case Xi: fx=value;
        case Yi: fy=value;
        case Zi: fz=value;
    }
}

inline float Vector::X(void)
{ return fx; }

inline float Vector::Y(void)
{ return fy; }

inline float Vector::Z(void)
{ return fz; }

inline void Vector::Add(float x,float y,float z)
{ fx+=x; fy+=y; fz+=z; }

inline void Vector::Sub(float x,float y,float z)
{ fx-=x; fy-=y; fz-=z; }
```

```
inline void Vector::Scale(float a)
{ fx*=a; fy*=a; fz*=a; }

inline float Vector::Length(void)
{ return sqrt((*this)*(*this)); // square root of Dot(this,this)
}

inline void Vector::Normalize(void)
{
    if(Length()==0.0) cout<<"Error:normalize\n";
    else Scale(1.0/Length());
}


/***************** Operators ********************/
inline void Vector::operator=(Vector& a)      // assignment
{ fx=a.fx; fy=a.fy; fz=a.fz; }

inline Vector Vector::operator+(void)         // unary +
{ return *this; }

inline Vector Vector::operator*(float t)        // scaling
{ Vector temp; temp.Set(fx*t,fy*t,fz*t); return temp; }

inline Vector Vector::operator+(Vector& a)
{ Vector sum; sum.Set(fx+a.fx,fy+a.fy,fz+a.fz); return sum; }

inline Vector Vector::operator-(Vector& a)
{ Vector sum; sum.Set(fx-a.fx,fy-a.fy,fz-a.fz); return sum; }

inline Vector Vector::operator-(void)             // unary -
{ Vector neg; neg.Set(-fx,-fy,-fz); return neg; }

inline void Vector::operator+=(Vector& a)
{ Set(fx+a.fx,fy+a.fy,fz+a.fz); }

inline void Vector::operator-=(Vector& a)
{ Set(fx-a.fx,fy-a.fy,fz-a.fz); }

inline void Vector::operator*=(float t)      // scaling
{ Set(fx*t,fy*t,fz*t); }

inline float Vector::operator*(Vector& a)         // dot product
{ return fx*a.fx+fy*a.fy+fz*a.fz; }

inline Vector Vector::operator%(Vector& a)        // cross product
{
    Vector cross;
    cross.Set(fy*a.fz-fz*a.fy,fz*a.fx-fx*a.fz,fx*a.fy-fy*a.fx);
    return cross;
}
```

```
inline float Vector::operator[](short index)
{
    switch(index)
    {
        case Xi: return fx;
        case Yi: return fy;
        case Zi: return fz;
    }
    return 0.0;                     // if invalid index
}
/************** End of Operators *****************/
#endif
```

◇   **Bibliography**   ◇

(Beatty *et al.* 1981) J. C. Beatty, K. S. Booth, and L. H. Matthies. Revisiting Watkins algorithm. In *Proceedings, 7th Canadian Man-Computer Communications Conference (CMCCS '81)*, June 1981.

(Georgiades 1992) Príamos Georgiades. Signed distance from point to plane. In David Kirk, editor, *Graphics Gems III*, pages 223–224. AP Professional, Boston, 1992.

(Glassner 1989) Andrew S. Glassner. *An Introduction to Ray Tracing*. AP Professional, London, 1989.

(Haines 1991) Eric Haines. Efficiency improvements for hierarchy traversal in ray tracing. In James Arvo, editor, *Graphics Gems II*, pages 267–272. AP Professional, London, 1991.

(Watkins 1970) G. S. Watkins. *A Real Time Visible Surface Algorithm*. PhD thesis, University of Utah, Salt Lake City, UT, June 1970.

(Weghorst *et al.* 1984) H. Weghorst, G. Hooper, and D. P. Greenberg. Improved computational methods for ray tracing. *ACM Trans. Graphics*, pages 52–69, 1984.

V.4

Ray Tracing a Swept Sphere

Andreas Leipelt

Mathematisches Seminar der Universität Hamburg
Hamburg, Germany
leipelt@GEOMAT.math.uni-hamburg.de

This gem presents the basic algorithms required for ray tracing the swept surface (Hanrahan 1989) generated by sweeping a sphere along a path. These surfaces look like wound tubes with varying thickness, resembling plant stems or exhaust pipes.

$\diamond$ **Introduction** $\diamond$

For ray tracing this interesting modeling primitive, one needs to solve the following problems:

- Compute the intersections with a ray.
- Determine the axis-aligned bounding box.
- Decide if a point is inside or not.
- Compute the surface normal at an intersection point.

In order to ease the computation, it is assumed that the sweep path is represented by a vector-valued polynomial $\vec{c}(t)$ of degree n parameterized by time t on the bounded interval $[a, b]$. Similarly, the sphere's radius is "modulated" during the sweep, defined by the nonnegative real-valued polynomial $r(t)$ of degree m.

The problems listed above, save for the normal computation, can be solved by using a common technique: finding the absolute or positive minima (maxima) of a function on an interval. Real analysis offers the following steps:

1. Calculate the first derivative of the given function.
2. Find all roots of the derivative, thereby locating the global extrema.
3. Evaluate the function at the roots and choose the smallest (largest) value.
4. Check the function at the interval's endpoints as it may take a larger (smaller) value there.

In all cases this will lead to a polynomial equation. For solving polynomial equations, refer to (Schwarze 1990) and (Hook and McAree 1990). Robust solution of cubics and quartics is treated on page 3.

◇ **Intersections with a Ray** ◇

To find the intersections with a ray, first intersect all spheres of the sweeping process with the ray. The t-depending spheres are given by the equation

$$\|\vec{c}(t) - \vec{x}\|^2 = r(t)^2, \qquad t \in [a \ldots b], \tag{1}$$

where $\|\ \|$ denotes the usual Euclidean distance in three-space. This ray is defined parametrically:

$$\vec{x} = \vec{a} + \lambda \vec{d}, \tag{2}$$

with normalized direction $\vec{d}$. Substituting the ray equation in Equation (1) gives

$$\|\vec{c}(t) - \vec{a}\|^2 - 2\lambda \vec{c}(t) \cdot \vec{d} + \lambda^2 - r(t)^2 = 0 \ . \tag{3}$$

Define

$$p(t) = \vec{c}(t) \cdot \vec{d} \qquad \text{and} \qquad q(t) = \|\vec{c}(t) - \vec{a}\|^2 - r(t)^2 \ . \tag{4}$$

The degree of the polynomial p is less than or equal to n, and the degree of q is less than or equal to $max\{2n, 2m\}$. With this notation, the quadratic equation for λ is obtained:

$$\lambda^2 - 2\lambda p(t) + q(t) = 0 \ . \tag{5}$$

The t-depending solutions of this equation are

$$\lambda(t) = p(t) \pm \sqrt{p(t)^2 - q(t)} \ . \tag{6}$$

This is in general a complex-valued function. Nevertheless, the described algorithm can be used in order to find the positive minimum of $\lambda(t)$, because a root t of the derivative with complex $\lambda(t)$ does not lead to an intersection point. Hence, in a bad case one computes more roots of the derivative than needed. The first derivative of $\lambda(t)$ is

$$\lambda'(t) = p'(t) \pm \frac{2p(t)p'(t) - q'(t)}{2\sqrt{p(t)^2 - q(t)}} \ . \tag{7}$$

Thus, the equation

$$p'(t) \pm \frac{2p(t)p'(t) - q'(t)}{2\sqrt{p(t)^2 - q(t)}} = 0 \tag{8}$$

is to be solved. This equation is equivalent to

$$p'(t) = \mp (2p(t)p'(t) - q'(t))(2\sqrt{p(t)^2 - q(t)})^{-1}$$

or

$$2p'(t)\sqrt{p(t)^2 - q(t)} = \mp(2p(t)p'(t) - q'(t)) \,. \tag{9}$$

Squaring Equation (9) results in

$$4p'(t)^2(p(t)^2 - q(t)) = 4p(t)^2p'(t)^2 - 4p(t)p'(t)q'(t) + q'(t)^2$$

or

$$0 = q'(t)^2 - 4p(t)p'(t)q'(t) + 4p'(t)^2q(t) \,. \tag{10}$$

Now generalize (10), giving

$$s(t) = q'(t)^2 + 4p'(t)(p'(t)q(t) - p(t)q'(t)) \,. \tag{11}$$

The polynomial $s(t)$ is of a degree less than or equal to $max\{4n - 2, 4m - 2\}$. Find all roots of $s(t)$ and evaluate λ at these roots. Accept only those values λ that are real and positive (an intersection only occurs for a positive parameter λ) and find the smallest one. Check the values $\lambda(a)$ and $\lambda(b)$, too.

The Axis-Aligned Bounding Box

The polynomial $\vec{c}$ has three components, $c_1(t), c_2(t)$, and $c_3(t)$. Build the polynomials

$$m_i(t) = c_i(t) - r(t), \qquad M_i(t) = c_i(t) + r(t), \qquad i = 1, \ldots, 3.$$

Now define min_i as the absolute minimum of $m_i(t)$, treated separably by component. That is, a unique time t_{min} need not exist for which $m_i(t_{min}) = min_i$, $i = 1, \ldots, 3$. Establish max_i as well. The vectors (min_1, min_2, min_3) and (max_1, max_2, max_3) form the lower-left and upper-right corner of the bounding box. These extrema are computable in the manner described, resulting in the best-fitting axis-aligned bounding box.

The Inside Test

A point P in three-space is inside the surface *iff* there exists a value $t_o \in [a \ldots b]$ such that

$$\|\vec{c}(t_o) - P\|^2 - r(t_o)^2 < 0.$$

Hence, find a negative minimum of the polynomial $\|\vec{c}(t) - P\|^2 - r(t)^2$. Reapply the algorithm to locate a minimum.

◇ **Computation of the Normal** ◇

An intersection point belongs to a parameter t of the surface. The normal at this point is only the normal of the sphere with center $\vec{c}(t)$ and radius $r(t)$. The calculation of a sphere's normal is straightforward and is described in the C++ implementation.

◇ **Hints** ◇

The degree of the polynomial s grows four times faster than that of $\vec{c}$ and r: $deg(s) = 4\max(deg(r), deg(\vec{c})) - 2$. For this reason, restricting the degree to $deg(r) \leq 3$ and $deg(\vec{c}) \leq 3$ is advised, suggesting the use of surface models based upon cubic splines. Both the polynomial root solver gem (Hook and McAree 1990), based upon the Sturm sequences, and most methods of (modified) regular Falsi encounter difficulties when the polynomial degree exceeds ten; substitution of other root solvers is recommended.

◇ **C++ Implementation** ◇

```
/*****************************************************
 *   POLY.H
 *   Andreas Leipelt, "Ray Tracing a Swept Sphere"
 *   from "Graphics Gems", Academic Press
 *
 */

#ifndef POLY_CLASS
#define POLY_CLASS

#define MAX_DEGREE 10
#define polyeps 1E-10   // tolerance for polynomial coefficients

class polynomial {
  public:

  int deg;
  double coef[MAX_DEGREE+1];

  polynomial();
  double      eval(double);
  int         roots_between(double,double,double*);
  double      min(double,double);
  double      max(double,double);
  polynomial derivative();
};

polynomial operator+(polynomial&, polynomial&);
polynomial operator-(polynomial&, polynomial&);
polynomial operator*(polynomial&, polynomial&);
```

```
polynomial operator*(double, polynomial&);

#endif



/*****************************************************
 * POLY.CPP
 * Andreas Leipelt, "Ray Tracing a Swept Sphere"
 * from "Graphics Gems", Academic Press
 *
 * Implementation of the polynomial class. The code is
 * not complete ! You need to insert a root solver in
 * the method 'root_between' .
 */

#include <math.h>
#include "poly.h"

// constructor of the polynomial class
polynomial::polynomial()
{
  deg = 0;
  for (double *fp = &coef[MAX_DEGREE]; fp >= coef; fp--) *fp = 0.0;
}

// evaluates the polynomial with Horner's scheme.
double polynomial::eval(double x)
{
  double *fp = &coef[deg], val;
  for (val = *fp--; fp >= coef; fp--) val = val*x + *fp;
  return val;
}

// returns the first derivative of the polynomial.
polynomial polynomial::derivative()
{
  polynomial ret;

  if (!deg) return ret;
  ret.deg = deg-1;
  for (int i=0; i <= ret.deg; i++) ret.coef[i] = (i+1)*coef[i+1];
  return ret;
}

// returns the absolute minimum of the given polynomial in the
// interval [a , b]
double polynomial::min(double a, double b)
{
  double roots[MAX_DEGREE], tmp, Min = eval(a);

  int n = derivative().roots_between(a, b, roots);
  roots[n] = b;
```

```
  for (int i=0; i <= n; i++) {
    tmp = eval(roots[i]);
    if (tmp < Min) Min = tmp;
  }
  return Min;
}

// returns the absolute maximum of the given polynomial in the
// interval [a ; b]
double polynomial::max(double a, double b)
{
  double roots[MAX_DEGREE], tmp, Max = eval(a);

  int n = derivative().roots_between(a, b, roots);
  roots[n] = b;
  for (int i=0; i <= n; i++) {
    tmp = eval(roots[i]);
    if (tmp > Max) Max = tmp;
  }
  return Max;
}

int polynomial::roots_between(double a, double b, double *roots)
{
  // This function should return the number of roots between
  // a  and  b  and the array 'roots' should contain these roots.
  // Refer to Hook and McAree, "Using Sturm Sequences to Bracket
  // Real Roots of Polynomial Equations" in "Graphics Gems I"
  return 0;
}

polynomial operator+(polynomial& p, polynomial& q)
{
  polynomial sum;

  if (p.deg < q.deg) sum.deg = q.deg;
  else sum.deg = p.deg;
  for (int i=0; i <= sum.deg; i++)
     sum.coef[i] = p.coef[i] + q.coef[i];
  if (p.deg == q.deg) {
    while (sum.deg > -1 && fabs(sum.coef[sum.deg]) < polyeps)
       sum.coef[sum.deg--] = 0.0;
    if (sum.deg < 0) sum.deg = 0;
  }
  return sum;
}

polynomial operator-(polynomial& p, polynomial& q)
{
  polynomial dif;

  if (p.deg < q.deg) dif.deg = q.deg;
  else dif.deg = p.deg;
```

```
   for (int i=0; i <= dif.deg; i++)
      dif.coef[i] = p.coef[i] - q.coef[i];
   if (p.deg == q.deg) {
     while (dif.deg > -1 && fabs(dif.coef[dif.deg]) < polyeps)
        dif.coef[dif.deg--] = 0.0;
     if (dif.deg < 0) dif.deg = 0;
   }
   return dif;
}

polynomial operator*(polynomial& p, polynomial& q)
{
   polynomial prod;

   prod.deg = p.deg + q.deg;
   for (int i=0; i <= p.deg; i++)
     for (int j=0; j <= q.deg; j++)
        prod.coef[i+j] += p.coef[i]*q.coef[j];
   return prod;
}

polynomial operator*(double s, polynomial& p)
{
   polynomial scale;

   if (s == 0.0) return scale;
   scale.deg = p.deg;
   for (int i=0; i <= p.deg; i++) scale.coef[i] = s*p.coef[i];
   return scale;
}


/****************************************************
 *   SWEEP.CPP
 *   Andreas Leipelt, "Ray Tracing a Swept Sphere"
 *   from "Graphics Gems", Academic Press
 *
 *   This file contains the code to handle a swept sphere in
 *   ray tracing
 */

#include <math.h>
#include "poly.h"

#define rayeps   1E-8  // tolerance for intersection test

// refer to  Andrew Woo, "Fast Ray-Box Intersection",
// "Graphics Gems I"
extern char HitBoundingBox(double*,double*,double*,double*);

// class of the swept sphere primitive
class swept_sph {
   polynomial m[3]; // center of the sphere
```

```
  polynomial r;      // radius of the sphere
  polynomial r2;     // r2 = r*r
  double a, b;       // the interval [a;b], where  m  and  r  live
  double minB[3],    // lower left corner of the bounding box
         maxB[3];    // upper right corner of the bounding box
  double param;      // parameter of last intersection, used for member
                     // 'normal'
  public:

  swept_sph() {}
  swept_sph(polynomial*,polynomial,double,double);
  int  intersect(double*,double*,double*);
  void normal(double*,double*);
  int  inside(double*);
};

// constructor of the swept_sph-class
swept_sph::swept_sph(polynomial *M, polynomial R, double A, double B)
// M : trajectory of the center of the moving sphere.
//     An array of polynomials, which is interpreted as a
//     vector valued polynomial.
// R : varying radius of the moving sphere. The radius is assumed
//     to be non-negative.
{
  for (int i=0; i < 3; i++) m[i] = M[i];
  r = R;
  r2 = r*r;
  a = A;  b = B;
  // Calculate the axis aligned bounding box
  for (i=0; i < 3; i++) {
    minB[i] = (m[i] - r).min(a, b);
    maxB[i] = (m[i] + r).max(a, b);
  }
}

int swept_sph::intersect(double *origin, double *dir, double *l)
// origin : origin of the ray
// dir    : unit direction of the ray
// t      : intersection parameter of the ray
{
  polynomial p, q, dp, dq, s;
  double save[3];
  double roots[MAX_DEGREE];
  double p_val, q_val, D, test;

  if (!HitBoundingBox(minB, maxB, origin, dir)) return 0;
  // save the constant term of the trajectory
  for (int i=0; i < 3; i++) {
    save[i] = m[i].coef[0];
    m[i].coef[0] -= origin[i];
  }
  p = dir[0]*m[0] + dir[1]*m[1] + dir[2]*m[2];
  q = m[0]*m[0] + m[1]*m[1] + m[2]*m[2] - r2;
```

```
  dp = p.derivative();
  dq = q.derivative();
  s = dq*dq | 4.0*dp*(dp*q - p*dq);
  int n = s.roots_between(a, b, roots);
  roots[n++] = a;
  roots[n]   = b;
  *l = 1E20;
  // test all possible values
  for (i=0; i <= n; i++) {
    // calculate the real solutions of the equation
    // l = p_val +- sqrt(p_val*p_val - q_val)
    p_val = p.eval(roots[i]);
    q_val = q.eval(roots[i]);
    D = p_val*p_val - q_val;
    if (D >= 0.0) {
      // check, if the candidate  roots[i]  leads to a better
      // intersection value  l
      D = sqrt(D);
      test = p_val - D;
      if (test < rayeps) test = p_val + D;
      if ((test >= rayeps) && (test < *l)) {
param = roots[i];
*l = test;
      }
    }
  }
  // restore the constant term of the trajectory
  for (i=0; i < 3; i++) m[i].coef[0] = save[i];
  if (*l < 1E20) return 1;
  else return 0;
}

void swept_sph::normal(double *IP, double* Nrm)
// IP  : intersection point
// Nrm : normal at IP
{
  double R = r.eval(param);
  // if the radius is zero, return an arbitrary normal.
  if (R < polyeps) {
    Nrm[0] = Nrm[1] = 0.0;
    Nrm[2] = 1.0;
    return;
  }
  for (int i=0; i < 3; i++) Nrm[i] = (IP[i] - m[i].eval(param))/R;
}

// returns 1, if the point P lies inside.
int swept_sph::inside(double *P)
{
  double save[3];
  int is_inside;

  for (int i=0; i < 3; i++) {
```

```
    save[i] = m[i].coef[0];
    m[i].coef[0] -= P[i];
  };
  is_inside =
    ((m[0]*m[0]+m[1]*m[1]+m[2]*m[2]-r2).min(a, b) < rayeps);
  for (i=0; i < 3; i++) m[i].coef[0] = save[i];
  return is_inside;
}
```

◇ **Bibliography** ◇

(Hanrahan 1989) Pat Hanrahan. A survey of ray-surface intersection algorithms. In Andrew S. Glassner, editor, *An Introduction to Ray Tracing*. AP Professional, Boston, 1989.

(Hook and McAree 1990) D. G. Hook and P. R. McAree. Using Sturm sequences to bracket real roots of polynomial equations. In Andrew S. Glassner, editor, *Graphics Gems*. AP Professional, Boston, 1990.

(Schwarze 1990) Jochen Schwarze. Cubic and quartic roots. In Andrew S. Glassner, editor, *Graphics Gems*. AP Professional, Boston, 1990.

V.5

Acceleration of Ray Tracing via Voronoi Diagrams

Gábor Márton
Department of Process Control
Technical University of Budapest
Budapest, Hungary
marton@seeger.fsz.bme.hu

Voronoi diagrams are among the most frequently studied structures in discrete and computational geometry. They are not only elegant but also very powerful, having an almost inexhaustible treasury of applications. A previous gem (Lischinski 1994) presents code for the two-dimensional case only. In this gem Voronoi diagrams are applied to methods of ray tracing. A *d*-dimensional diagram solver (coded in C++) is also provided.

◇   **Introduction**   ◇

Ray tracing, despite its unique simulation potentialities, is generally known as a time-consuming method of image synthesis. Although the method itself is classical (Whitted 1980), much research effort is still directed toward improving its effectiveness.

A survey of ray tracing acceleration techniques has been given (Arvo and Kirk 1989). Following their terminology, the method presented here is a *space subdivision technique*. Their common characteristic is the reduction of ray–object tests by subdividing the object scene. The operation is in two parts. First, a preprocessing phase decomposes the scene into disjoint territories called *cells*. A list associated with each cell contains references to those objects that have non-empty intersection with it. Last, the tracing phase enumerates, for each ray generated, the cells encountered successively by the ray. The object lists of the cells encountered are the only candidates for object intersection testing. This enumeration of cells in object space is called *voxel walking*.

Two different types of cell have been used up to this time:

1. *Regular Cubic Lattice*: These employ a regular grid of congruent cubic cells. The advantage of this choice is that voxel walking is easily performed—the original implementation used a three-dimensional DDA line generator (Fujimoto *et al.* 1986). The disadvantage is the lack of spatial adaptivity: The structure of the grid does not conform itself to the actual arrangement and shape of the objects.

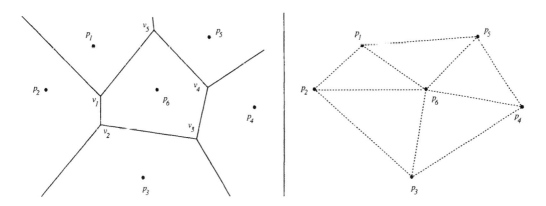

Figure 1. An example Voronoi diagram (solid) and its dual (dotted).

2. *Octree Spatial Partition*: This well-known data structure (Meagher 1982) was adapted to this task by Glassner and contemporaries (Glassner 1984). It may be regarded as a locally adaptive, eightfold Cartesian subdivision. Voxel walking becomes more complex, but there are fewer cells.
3. *Voronoi Diagrams* (new): These approach the ideal (impossible in practice) of placing exactly one object within each cell. The methods are reviewed and then applied to ray tracing in the following two sections.

◇ Voronoi Diagrams ◇

Given a set $p_1, \ldots, p_n$ of particles (points) in the d-dimensional Euclidean space $\mathcal{E}^d$, classify all space into distinct regions such that each region contains all points of $\mathcal{E}^d$ closest to its defining particle. Thus, the *Voronoi cell* $\mathcal{V}(p_i)$ corresponding to a particle p_i is defined as the set of points closer to p_i than to any other particle p_j. Figure 1 shows a (closest point) Voronoi diagram in two dimensions. Formally:

$$\mathcal{V}(p_i) \equiv \left\{ p \in \mathcal{E}^d\colon \forall j \neq i\colon \|p - p_i\| < \|p - p_j\| \right\}.$$

Let $\mathcal{B}(p_i, p_j)$ denote the *bisector plane* between p_i and p_j, that is, the set of points being at an equal distance from p_i and p_j:

$$\mathcal{B}(p_i, p_j) \equiv \left\{ p \in \mathcal{E}^d\colon \|p - p_i\| = \|p - p_j\| \right\},$$

and let $\mathcal{H}(p_i, p_j)$ denote the *half space* bounded by $\mathcal{B}(p_i, p_j)$ and containing p_i, that is, the set of points being closer to p_i than to p_j:

$$\mathcal{H}(p_i, p_j) \equiv \left\{ p \in \mathcal{E}^d\colon \|p - p_i\| < \|p - p_j\| \right\}.$$

Then $\mathcal{V}(p_i)$ is the region common to the half spaces defined by p_i and all the other particles p_j. Formally, this is the region of intersection,

$$\mathcal{V}(p_i) \equiv \bigcap_{j \neq i} \mathcal{H}(p_i, p_j),$$

also containing its defining particle p_i. The Voronoi cells are *convex and disjoint* territories and (their closure) *completely cover* the space. The cells corresponding to the particles on the convex hull of the set $p_1, \ldots, p_n$ are unbounded; the others are bounded. This aggregate of the cells is called the *Voronoi diagram* of the particle set (Voronoi 1908). Alternative names are *Dirichlet tesselation* (Dirichlet 1850) and *Thiessen tessellation* (Thiessen 1911).

If the particles $p_1, \ldots, p_n$ are in general position, then exactly $d+1$ cells meet at each vertex of each cell. Such a vertex, called a *Voronoi vertex*, is at equal distance from its *forming particles* contained by the meeting cells. In other words, it is the center of the *circumsphere* of the d-simplex formed by the $d + 1$ particles. These simplexes, called *Delaunay simplexes*, are also disjoint and completely cover the convex hull of the particle set. Their aggregate, which is the dual of the Voronoi diagram, is called the *Delaunay triangulation* of the particle set [Figure 1(b)]. This triangulation possesses the very important *empty circumsphere property*, that is, the circumspheres of the Delaunay simplexes contain no further particles beyond those forming the simplex (Preparata and Shamos 1985). This property is usually exploited when constructing Voronoi diagrams by a computer program.

The properties of Voronoi diagrams have been thoroughly investigated within geometric, combinatorial, and statistical contexts. The interested reader is referred to an extensive survey with companion bibliography (Aurenhammer 1991).

◇ Computing Multidimensional Voronoi Diagrams ◇

Constructing Voronoi diagrams by computer program is a rewarding challenge. A two-dimensional implementation appeared in the previous *Graphics Gems* volume (Lischinski 1994); a solution for arbitrary d-dimensional spaces is also known (Bowyer 1981, Watson 1981). Their general methods are elegant, relatively simple to implement, and worthy of greater attention. Though more efficient two-dimensional methods are possible, Bowyer's algorithm serves as the best starting point and is now reviewed.

The data structure used to represent the diagram is a spatial graph whose nodes are the Voronoi vertices and whose edges are the one-dimensional edges of the Voronoi cell boundaries (Voronoi edges). A node v is represented by a $2(d + 1)$-tuple:

$$v = \langle p_0, \ldots, p_d, v_0, \ldots, v_d \rangle, \tag{1}$$

where $p_0, \ldots, p_d$ are (references to) the forming particles and $v_0, \ldots, v_d$ are (references to) the neighboring nodes (vertices) along the Voronoi edges. Some vertex references

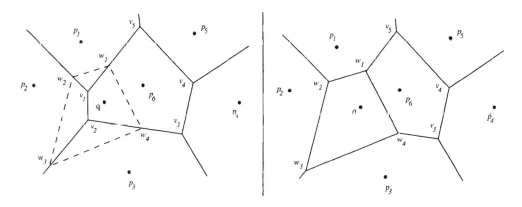

Figure 2. Inserting a new particle (q) into the Voronoi diagram.

may be empty. This occurs at those vertices that contribute to the convex hull of the particles. For example, in Figure 1 the vertex v_1 is formed by the particles p_1, p_2, p_6, and its neighbors are only v_2 and v_5. Two nodes v, w are neighbors iff the two sets of their forming particles contain exactly d identical ones:

$$w \in \{v_0(v), \dots, v_d(v)\} \quad \text{iff} \quad \| \{p_0(v), \dots, p_d(v)\} \cap \{p_0(w), \dots, p_d(w)\} \| = d.$$

These d particles form a *ring* around the Voronoi edge v, w from which they are situated at equal distance. The vertex representation in (1) has a normal form: The ring around each edge $v, v_i(v)$ outgoing from v must contain the particles $\{p_0(v), \dots, p_d(v)\} \backslash \{p_i(v)\}$. For example, in Figure 1 the correct representation of vertex v_1 is $\langle p_1, p_2, p_6, v_2, v_5, \emptyset \rangle$. This ensures that the forming particle $p_i(v)$ always "opposes" edge $v, v_i(v)$.

Bowyer's algorithm performs an *incremental construction* (based on this data structure). That is, the particles are inserted into the structure one by one. It is assumed furthermore that the new particle to be inserted always falls into the convex hull of the previous insertions. (This can always be achieved by bounding the original particles by a d-simplex spanned by $d + 1$ pseudo-particles. These form a single Voronoi vertex having no neighbors at the beginning. The real particles can then be inserted one by one in any order.) The insertion algorithm exploits the empty circumsphere property of Delaunay triangulations. Its main steps provide for the insertion of a new particle q. It is described as follows:

1. *Initial Vertex Location*: Find any vertex v_{i_1} in the current structure nearer to q than to its forming particles. (In Figure 2 it is v_2.) This search is best done by a linear walk through the Delaunay simplexes from the centroid of the structure to q (the circumsphere of the simplex containing q will also contain q). This vertex will definitely be among those which should be deleted from the structure.

2. *Tree Search:* Check the vertex structure, starting from v_{i_1}, to find all the other vertices to be deleted, that is, collect those vertices whose empty circumsphere property is hurt by q. This results in a list $v_{i_1}, \ldots, v_{i_D}$ of vertices. (In Figure 2 this list is v_2, v_1.)

3. *Create New Vertices:* For each of the vertices $v_{i_1}, \ldots, v_{i_D}$, consider its neighbors one by one. Let w denote any neighbor of v_{i_j}. If w itself has also to be deleted, then take the next one. Otherwise, the ring of particles around the edge v_{i_j}, w and the new particle q form a new vertex. Create this vertex and put it onto a list. (In Figure 2 the ring around the edge v_1, v_5 is p_1, p_6; thus, q, p_1, p_6 form a new vertex.) The result is a list $w_1, \ldots, w_N$ of new vertices.

4. *Link Insertion:* The new vertices $w_1, \ldots, w_N$ are linked to each other and to their neighbors from the original structure by identifying the *identical rings of particles* around the outgoing edges, updating the structure in place. (In Figure 2 w_1 and w_2 are mutually linked because both contain the ring q, p_1. For the same reason, w_1 is also connected to v_5 and w_4.)

Note that the particles $p_1, \ldots, p_n$ may occupy arbitrary position. Consequently, a number of *degenerate cases* can arise in the implementation. (They occur more frequently than one might think!) These are treated by Bowyer in his original article.

◇ Voronoi Subdivision for Ray Tracing ◇

Voronoi diagrams are very elegant, but the objects within the scene are not isolated points. The structure itself could be extended to accomodate point sets. [The power diagram (Aurenhammer 1991), for example, is one possible generalization of the Voronoi diagram, where the particles are spheres.] This possibility is, however, left for future research. A computationally less expensive solution is to choose the particle set $p_1, \ldots, p_n$ to be a set of some *representative points of the objects*, for example their centroids, and create a Voronoi diagram upon this set. Identifying optimal sets of representative particles is also a subject of further research.

The Voronoi data structure described in the previous section can be augmented to suit the task at hand. Voronoi vertices remain the same. The representation of a particle p (omitted above on account of its simplicity) now contains two lists in addition to its spatial coordinates:

$$p = \langle x, y, z, L, P \rangle,$$

where x, y, z are its coordinates, L contains references to those objects that have nonempty intersection with the Voronoi cell $\mathcal{V}(p)$, and P contains references to those particles that are *contiguous* to p in the diagram; that is, there is an edge between them in the Delaunay triangulation [in other words, P represents the union of the particles

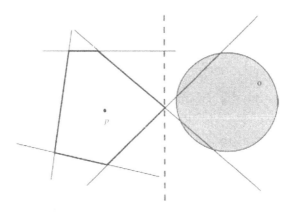

Figure 3.   A superfluous object appearing in the list $L(p)$.

forming the boundary of the cell $\mathcal{V}(p)$ minus p]. Both lists are built in the preprocessing phase and are used in the tracing phase during voxel walking.

The lists P are built after the diagram has been completed. A traversal is performed on the vertex structure, and for each vertex v, its forming particles $p_0(v), \ldots, p_d(v)$ are taken one by one. Taking $p_i(v)$, each of the other forming particles is added to the list $P(p_i(v))$, provided that it is not already there, since more simplexes share one edge in the triangulation.

The lists L can be built after the lists P are ready because these latter ones provide a more suitable representation of the Voronoi cells than the vertex structure: The cell $\mathcal{V}(p)$ is in fact the intersection of the half spaces defined by p and the contiguous particles:

$$\mathcal{V}(p) = \bigcap_{q \in P(p)} \mathcal{H}(p, q). \tag{2}$$

This property can be exploited when building the lists $L(p)$: If there is at least one among the half spaces $\mathcal{H}(p, q)$ that has empty intersection with an object o, then o is *not* put onto list $L(p)$; otherwise, it is. Note that the lack of such a half space does not necessarily imply that o intersects $V(p)$. As illustrated in Figure 3, superfluous objects may appear in the list $L(p)$. A more sophisticated solution could be a search for a *separating plane*, as shown by a dashed line in the figure, though the added expense might not justify this extension.

◇   **Voxel Walking**   ◇

A ray r is customarily represented by a pair,

$$r = \langle s, \delta \rangle, \tag{3}$$

where $s \in \mathcal{E}^3$ is the starting point and $\delta \in \mathcal{E}^3$ is the direction vector, so that the points of the ray are generated by the equation

$$r(\tau) = s + \tau \delta \quad (\tau \in \mathcal{R}), \tag{4}$$

where $\tau \geq 0$ is known as the *ray parameter*. The enumeration of the Voronoi cells along the path of the ray needs the following two kinds of steps:

1. *Voxel Initialization:* Locate the starting point of the ray in the structure, that is, find the cell $\mathcal{V}_1$ containing s. This cell contains the first *ray span.*
2. *Voxel Walk:* Provided that the cell $\mathcal{V}_i$ containing the ith ray span has already been found, the cell $\mathcal{V}_{i+1}$ containing the $(i+1)$th span should be identified.

Step 1 can be realized by the methods used in step 2: From an arbitrary point, say q, start a pseudo-ray $r' = \langle q, s - q \rangle$ toward s and perform step 2 along r' repeatedly until reaching s. This assumes that the location of q is known *a priori*. The centroid of the structure is a suitable first approximation; a more effective choice (exploiting image coherence) will be discussed later.

For step 2, assume that the ray parameter τ_i where r *enters* the cell $\mathcal{V}_i$ is known (τ_1 is set to zero). Then compute the *other* intersection point between the ray and the boundary of the cell, that is, where r *exits* $\mathcal{V}_i$. (From the convexity of Voronoi cells, there are at most two intersection points.) This results in the ray parameter τ_{i+1}, according to the inductive assumption, and $\mathcal{V}_{i+1}$ is the contiguous cell on the other side of the face containing the intersection point. The walk concludes when either there are no more cells (no τ_{i+1} is found because r exits the convex hull of the objects) or an intersection is found between r and an object on the list associated with the cell $\mathcal{V}_i$.

Note that the Voronoi cells are associated with the particles $p_1, \ldots, p_n$. Therefore, voxel walking is the enumeration of a corresponding sequence of particles. The intersection between the ray and the boundary of a cell can easily be computed since the lists $P(p_i)$ are available. According to Equation (2),

$$r \cap \mathcal{V}_i = r \cap \mathcal{V}(q_i) = \bigcap_{q \in P(q_i)} r \cap \mathcal{H}(q_i, q),$$

that is, the ray span contained by the cell is the intersection of the ray spans contained by the half spaces defined by q_i and the contiguous particles. The bisector plane $\mathcal{B}(q_i, q)$, which is the boundary of such a half space, is the set of points p satisfying the equation

$$(p - \tfrac{1}{2}(q_i + q)) \cdot (q - q_i) = 0,$$

where "$\cdot$" denotes scalar product. Substituting the ray equation (4) yields

$$\tau_q = \frac{(\tfrac{1}{2}(q_i + q) - s) \cdot (q - q_i)}{\delta \cdot (q - q_i)} \tag{5}$$

for the intersection point between the bisector plane and the ray. The ray parameter defining the point of exit is

$$\tau_{i+1} = \min_{\substack{q \in P(q_i) \\ \tau_q > \tau_i}} \tau_q,$$

and the next cell is the associated contiguous cell. Note that a negative denominator in (5) implies a backward step; such neighbors can immediately be excluded from consideration. Zero denominators should also be excluded (the ray is going parallel with the face).

Exploiting Image Coherence

The location of the starting point of the ray (step 1) can be more effectively performed by exploiting image coherence. For this reason, the representation of rays in (3) is augmented with a new item c, called the *ray code*:

$$r = \langle s, \delta, c \rangle .$$

The code c uniquely identifies a ray as reflective or transmissive, together with the identity of all ancestor rays, beginning with the main ray. With $\hat{r}$ denoting the ancestor of a ray r, this may be encoded as

$$c(r) = \begin{cases} 0, & \text{if } r \text{ is the main ray;} \\ 2c(\hat{r}) + 1, & \text{if } r \text{ is the reflective child of } \hat{r}; \\ 2c(\hat{r}) + 2, & \text{if } r \text{ is the transmissive child of } \hat{r}. \end{cases}$$

For a maximal depth of recurrence $D_{\max}$, an array $q_{\text{start}}[]$ of size $2^{D_{\max}+1} - 1$ can be built storing references to *possible starting cells*. If the starting point of a ray r is found to be in cell $\mathcal{V}(q)$, then a reference to q is put into the array at position $q_{\text{start}}[c(r)]$ (C-style indexing). When the next pixel of the image is evaluated, then the starting points of the rays are located by starting the walk from the cells referenced by the array q_{start}. In the majority of cases, no step needs to be done.

◇ **Implementation Details** ◇

The proposed method is used in an *object-oriented* implementation of the widely known ray tracer called *POV-Ray* (POV-Ray Team 1993). The implementation was written in C++ and was compiled by GNU C++ compiler (gcc, g++) under HP-UX. The source code of the parser and scanner was generated by yacc and lex from the grammar rules and token definitions.

voronoi.h

The most general part of the source code is located in the file `voronoi.h`. It contains the templates for computing Voronoi diagrams in a space of arbitrary dimension. The templates are parameterized by the dimension number denoted by D in the code. In order to declare the template `voronoi<D>`, which is the diagram itself, it is necessary to declare the templates `permutation<D>`, `vector<D>`, and `matrix<D>`, as they appear in this order in the header file. The constructor of `voronoi<D>` is responsible for building the diagram, and its `operator()` is used for traversal.

```
//      PERMUTATION TEMPLATE (USED IN GAUSSIAN ELIMINATION)

template <int D> class permutation {
        int n[D];                                       // ELEMENTS
public:
        permutation() {for(register int i=0; i<D; i++) n[i]=i;}
        int operator[](int i) {return n[i];}
        void operator()(int i, int j) {                 // SWAP
                if(i==j) return;
                register int t=n[i]; n[i]=n[j]; n[j]=t;
        }
};


//      D-DIMENSIONAL VECTOR TEMPLATE

template <int D> class vector {
        friend ostream& operator<<(ostream& o, vector<D>& v);
        double x[D];                                    // COORDINATES
public:
        vector() {for(register int i=0; i<D; i++) x[i]=0.;}
        vector(double x[D]) {for(register int i=0; i<D; i++) this->x[i]=x[i];}
        vector(double x[D], permutation<D>& p) {
                for(register int i=0; i<D; i++) this->x[i]=x[p[i]];
        }
        double operator[](int i) {return x[i];}
        void operator-=(vector<D>& v) {
                for(register int i=0; i<D; i++) x[i]-=v.x[i];
        }
        vector<D> operator*(double d) {
                vector<D> w; for(register int i=0; i<D; i++) w.x[i]=x[i]*d;
                return w;
        }
        vector<D> operator/(double d) {
                vector<D> w; for(register int i=0; i<D; i++) w.x[i]=x[i]/d;
                return w;
        }
        double operator*(vector<D>& v) {
                double d=0.; for(register int i=0; i<D; i++) d+=x[i]*v.x[i];
                return d;
        }
        vector<D> operator+(vector<D>& v) {
```

```
                vector<D> w; for(register int i=0; i<D;i++) w.x[i]=x[i]+v.x[i];
                return w;
        }
        vector<D> operator-(vector<D>& v) {
                vector<D> w; for(register int i=0; i<D;i++) w.x[i]=x[i]-v.x[i];
                return w;
        }
};


//      D-DIMENSIONAL SQUARE MATRIX TEMPLATE

template <int D> class matrix {
        friend ostream& operator<<(ostream& o, matrix<D>& A);
        vector<D> a[D];                                    // ROWS
public:
        matrix(vector<D> a[D]) {for(register int i=0;i<D;i++) this->a[i]=a[i];}
        matrix(double a[D][D]) {
                for(register int i=0; i<D; i++) this->a[i]=vector<D>(a[i]);
        }
        vector<D> operator*(vector<D>& x) {
                double y[D];
                for(register int i=0; i<D; i++) y[i]=a[i]*x;
                return vector<D>(y);
        }
        int operator()(vector<D>& x, vector<D>& b) {      // SOLVE (*this)x=b

//              GAUSSIAN ELIMINATION METHOD

                const double EPS=1e-10;
                vector<D> B[D]; double c[D]; permutation<D> p;
                register int i, j, k;
                for(i=0; i<D; i++) {B[i]=a[i]; c[i]=b[i];}      // COPY
                for(i=0; i<D; i++) {                            // THROUGH ROWS
                        double a, amax=0., e, emain;
                        for(j=i; j<D; j++)                     // MAIN ELEMENT
                                if((a=fabs(e=B[p[j]][i]))>amax)
                                        {emain=e; amax=a; k=j;}
                        if(amax<EPS) return 0;                 // SINGULAR
                        p(i,k);                                // SWAP
                        for(j=i+1; j<D; j++) {                 // NULL BELOW
                                double s=B[p[j]][i]/emain;
                                B[p[j]]-=B[p[i]]*s;
                                c[p[j]]-=c[p[i]]*s;
                        }
                }
                for(i=D-1; i>=0; i--) {                        // BUILD SOLUTION
                        for(j=D-1; j>i; j--) c[p[i]]-=B[p[i]][j]*c[p[j]];
                        c[p[i]]/=B[p[i]][i];
                }
                x=vector<D>(c,p); return 1;
        }
};
```

```
//      VORONOI-VERTEX TEMPLATE

template <int D> struct vertex {
        vector<D>* p[D+1];                              // FORMING POINTS
        vertex<D>* v[D+1];                              // CONTIGUOUS VERTICES
        vector<D> c;                                    // POSITION
        double rr;                                      // RADIUS SQUARE
        int b;                                          // BACK INDEX (WORK)
        int i;                                          // ACTUAL INDEX (WORK)
        long t;                                         // TRAVERSE CODE (WORK)
private:
        void initialize(vector<D>* f[D+1]) {
                register int i;
                for(i=0; i<D+1; i++) {p[i]=f[i]; v[i]=(vertex<D>*)0;}
                this->b=-1; this->i=0; this->t=0L;
                vector<D> A[D]; double b[D];
                for(i=0; i<D; i++) {
                        A[i]=(*f[i+1])-(*f[i]);
                        b[i]=(((*f[i+1])+(*f[i]))*0.5)*A[i];
                }
                if(!matrix<D>(A)(c,vector<D>(b))) {     // EQUATION A*c=b
                        rr=-1.;                         // DEGENERATE
                        return;
                }
                rr=(*p[0]-c)*(*p[0]-c);
        }
public:
        vertex(vector<D>* f[D+1]) {initialize(f);}      // FORMING POINTS
        vertex(vector<D> *q, vertex<D> *v, int i) {     // POINT q AND RING i
                vector<D> *f[D+1]; f[0]=q;
                for(register int j=1; j<D+1; j++) f[j]=v->p[(j+i)%(D+1)];
                initialize(f);
        }
};


//      VORONOI-DIAGRAM TEMPLATE

template <int D> class voronoi {
        friend ostream& operator<<(ostream& o, voronoi<D>& v);
        vector<D> C;                                    // CENTROID
        vector<D> *b[D+1];                              // BOUNDING SIMPLEX
        vertex<D> *c;                                   // CLOSEST TO CENTROID
        double ll(vector<D>& v) {return v*v;}           // LENGTH SQUARE
        double dd(vector<D>& v, vector<D>& w) {         // DISTANCE SQUARE
                vector<D> d=v-w; return d*d;
        }
        void normals(int d, double n[D+1][D]) { // NORMAL VECTORS FOR bound()
                register int i, j;
                if(d==2) {
                        n[0][0]=1.0; n[0][1]=1.0;
                        n[1][0]=-1.0; n[1][1]=1.0;
                        n[2][0]=0.0; n[2][1]=-1.0;
                        return;
```

```
                    }
                    normals(d-1, n);
                    for(i=0; i<d; i++) n[i][d-1]=1.0;
                    for(i=0; i<d-1; i++) n[d][i]-0.0;
                    n[d][d-1]=-1.0;
            }
        void bound(list<vector<D>*>* l);         // BUILD BOUNDING SIMPLEX
        vector<D>* q;                             // ACTUAL POINT
        list<vertex<D>*> *ld;                     // VERTICES TO DELETE
        void find();                              // FIND A VERTEX TO DELETE
        void search();                            // FIND ALL VERTICES TO DELETE
        list<vertex<D>*> *ln;                     // NEW VERTICES
        void create();                            // CREATE NEW VERTICES
        int samering(vertex<D>*v, int iv, vertex<D>*w, int iw) {
                for(register int i=(iv+1)%(D+1);i!=iv;i=(i+1)%(D+1)) {
                        vector<D> *p=v->p[i];
                        for(register int j=(iw+1)%(D+1);j!=iw;j=(j+1)%(D+1))
                                if(w->p[j]==p) {j=-1; break;}
                        if(j>=0) return 0;
                }
                return 1;
        }
        void link();                              // LINK NEW VERTICES TO EACH O.
        void build(list<vector<D>*>* l) {         // DISJOINT PARTICLES
                traverse=0L;
                bound(l);
                for(vector<D>* p=l->first(); p; p=l->next())
                        {q=p; find(); search(); create(); link();}
        }
        long traverse;                            // TRAVERSE CODE
        static void free(vertex<D>*v){delete v;}// FOR DESTRUCTOR
        static void donothing(vertex<D>*v){}     // FOR REINITIALIZE traverse
public:
        voronoi(list<vector<D>*>* l) {
                for(register int i=0; i<D+1; i++) b[i]=new vector<D>;
                build(l);
        }
        voronoi(list<vector<D>*>* l, vector<D> *b[D+1]) {
                for(register int i-0; i<D+1; i++) this->b[l]=b[l];
                build(l);
        }
        void operator()(void (*f)(vertex<D>* v));    // TRAVERSE VERTICES
        fvoronoi() {                                 // TRAVERSE AND DELETE
                (*this)(free);
                for(register int i=0;i<D+1;i++) delete b[i];
        }
};

template <int D> void voronoi<D>::bound(list<vector<D>*>* l) {
        register int i, j;

//      NORMAL VECTORS FOR FACES OF BOUNDING SIMPLEX
```

```
        double a[D+1][D]; normals(D, a);
        vector<D> n[D+1];
        for(i=0; i<D+1; i++) n[i]=vector<D>(a[i])/sqrt(ll(vector<D>(a[i])));

//      MAXIMAL DISTANCES IN DIRECTION OF NORMALS

        double d, dmax[D+1], dmin[D+1]; register int first=1;
        for(vector<D>* p=l->first(); p; p=l->next()) {
                for(i=0; i<D+1; i++) {
                        d=n[i]*(*p);
                        if(first || d>dmax[i]) dmax[i]=d;
                        if(first || d<dmin[i]) dmin[i]=d;
                }
                first=0;
        }

//      VERTICES OF BOUNDING SIMPLEX (INTERSECT FACES CYCLICALLY)

        for(i=0; i<D+1; i++) dmax[i]+=(dmax[i]-dmin[i])*.5;      // INACCURACY
        vector<D> A[D]; double t[D];
        for(i=0; i<D+1; i++) {
                for(j=0; j<D; j++) {
                        A[j]=n[(i+j)%(D+1)];
                        t[j]=dmax[(i+j)%(D+1)];
                }
                (void)matrix<D>(A)(*b[i],vector<D>(t)); // EQUATION A*b[i]=t
        }

//      CENTRAL VERTEX AND CENTROID

        c=new vertex<D>(b);
        for(i=0; i<D+1; i++) C=C+(*b[i]);
        C=C*(1./(double)(D+1));
}

template <int D> void voronoi<D>::find() {
        register int i, j;
        double P[D+1][D+1]; for(j=0; j<D+1; j++) P[D][j]=1.;
        double q[D+1]; for(j=0; j<D; j++) q[j]=(*this->q)[j]; q[D]=1.;
        vertex<D> *v=c;
        vector<D+1> a;                          // BARICENTRIC COORDINATES OF q
        for(;;) {
                for(i=0; i<D; i++) for(j=0; j<D+1; j++) P[i][j]=(*v->p[j])[i];
                (void)matrix<D+1>(P)(a,vector<D+1>(q));         // SOLVE P*a=q
                double aminus=0.;
                for(j=0; j<D+1; j++) if(a[j]<aminus) {aminus=a[j]; i=j;}
                if(aminus<0.) {v=v->v[i]; continue;}
                break;                                          // q INSIDE
        }
        ld=new list<vertex<D>*>; *ld+=v;
}
```

```
template <int D> void voronoi<D>::search() {
        vertex<D> *vstart=ld->first(), *v=vstart; v->b=-1;
        register int back=0;
        for(;;) {
                register int go=0, i; vertex<D> *n;
                do {
                        if(back) {                          // STEP BACKWARDS
                                *ld+=v;
                                i-v->b; v->b=-1; v=v->v[i]; back=0; continue;
                        }
                        if(v->i==v->b) continue;
                        if(v->v[v->i]==(vertex<D>*)0) continue;
                        n=v->v[v->i];                       // NEIGHBOR
                        if(n->b>=0) continue;               // ALREADY TRAVERSED
                        if((*ld)[n]) continue;              // ALREADY ON LIST
                        if(dd(*q,n->c)<n->rr) go=1;         // GO IF q IN SPHERE
                        if(go) break;
                } while((v->i=(v->i+1)%(D+1))!=0);
                if(go) {                                    // STEP FORWARDS
                        for(i=0; i<D+1; i++)                // COMPUTE BACK INDEX
                                if(v==n->v[i]) {n->b=i; break;}
                        v=n; continue;
                }
                if(v==vstart) break;
                back=1;
        }
}

template <int D> void voronoi<D>::create() {
        vertex<D> *v;
        ln=new list<vertex<D>*>;
        for(v=ld->first(); v; v=ld->next()) {               // TAKE VERTICES
                for(register int i=0; i<D+1; i++) {         // TAKE NEIGHBORS
                        vertex<D> *n=v->v[i];
                        if((*ld)[n]) continue;              // ALSO DELETED
                        vertex<D> *m=new vertex<D>(q,v,i);  // POINT q + RING i
                        if(m->rr<0.)
                                {delete m;*ld+=n;continue;} // DEGENERACY
                        *ln+=m;                             // STORE
                        register int j;
                        for(j=0; j<D+1; j++)
                                if(m->p[j]==q) m->v[j]=n;   // OUTER LINK
                        if(n==(vertex<D>*)0) continue;      // NO REAL NEIGHBOR
                        for(j=0; j<D+1; j++)
                                if(n->v[j]==v) n->v[j]=m;   // BACK LINK
                }
        }
        if((*ld)[c]) {                                      // NEW c NEEDED
                double d, ddmin; register int first=1;
                for(v=ln->first(); v; v=ln->next()) {
                        d=dd(v->c,C);
                        if(first || d<ddmin) {c=v; ddmin=d;}
                        first=0;
```

```
                  }
           }
       }
       for(v=ld->first(); v; v=ld->next()) {delete v;} // DELETE VERTICES
       delete ld;
}

template <int D> void voronoi<D>::link() {
       register int i, j, n, iv, iw;
       vertex<D> *v, *w;
       n=0; for(v=ln->first(); v; v=ln->next()) n++;
       vertex<D> *N[n];
       n=0; for(v=ln->first(); v; v=ln->next()) N[n++]=v;
       for(i=0; i<n-1; i++) {
              v=N[i];
              for(j=i+1; j<n; j++) {
                     w=N[j];
                     for(iv=0; iv<D+1; iv++) {
                            for(iw=0; iw<D+1; iw++) {
                                   if(samering(v,iv,w,iw))
                                          {v->v[iv]=w; w->v[iw]=v;}
                            }
                     }
              }
       }
       delete ln;
}

template <int D> void voronoi<D>::operator()(void (*f)(vertex<D>* v)) {
       traverse++;
       if(traverse==-1L) {                              // OVERFLOW
              traverse=-2L; (*this)(donothing);         // REINITIALIZE
              traverse=0L;
       }
       vertex<D> *v=c; v->b=D+1;                        // PARTICULAR CASE
       register int back=0;
       for(;;) {                                        // ITERATIVE TRAVERSE
              v->t=traverse;                            // MARK AS TRAVERSED
              register int go=0;                        // DON'T GO YET
              vertex<D> *n;                             // ACTUAL NEIGHBOR
              do {                                      // ACTION ON ACTUAL v
                     if(back) {                         // STEP BACKWARDS
                            vertex<D>*n=v->v[v->b];      // FROM WHERE WE CAME
                            v->b=-1;                    // FOR NEXT USAGE
                            f(v);                       // PERFORM ACTION
                            v=n; back=0; continue;      // TAKE BACK VERTEX
                     }
                     if(v->i==v->b) continue;           // DON'T STEP BACK YET
                     if(v->v[v->i]==(vertex<D>*)0)
                            continue;                   // NO REAL NEIGHBOR
                     n=v->v[v->i];                      // WHERE WE SHOULD GO
                     if(n->t==traverse) continue;       // ALREADY TRAVERSED
                     go=1; break;                       // GO ON
```

```
        } while((v->i=(v->i+1)%(D+1))!=0);     // UNTIL NOT ALL DONE
        if(go) {                               // STEP FORWARDS
                for(register int i=0;i<D+1;i++) // FIND BACK LINK
                        if(v==n->v[i])
                                {n->b=i;break;} // BOOK
                v=n; continue;                 // LET'S GO
        }
        if(v==c) break;                        // RETURNED
        back=1;                                // GO BACK IF NO BETTER
    }
    f(c); c->b=-1; c->t=traverse;              // THE LAST ONE
}
```

◇ **Bibliography** ◇

(Arvo and Kirk 1989) James Arvo and David Kirk. A survey of ray tracing acceleration techniques. In Andrew S. Glassner, editor, *An Introduction to Ray Tracing*, pages 201–262. Academic Press, London, 1989.

(Aurenhammer 1991) Franz Aurenhammer. Voronoi-diagrams — a survey of a fundamental geometric data structure. *ACM Computing Surveys*, 23(3):346–405, 1991.

(Bowyer 1981) A. Bowyer. Computing Dirichlet tessellations. *The Computer Journal*, 24(2):162–166, 1981.

(Dirichlet 1850) G. L. Dirichlet. Über die Reduction der positiven quadratischen Formen mit drei unbestimmten ganzen Zahlen. *J. Reine u. Angew. Math.*, (40):209–227, 1850.

(Fujimoto *et al.* 1986) Akira Fujimoto, Tanaka Takayuki, and Iwata Kansei. Arts: Accelerated ray-tracing system. *IEEE Computer Graphics and Applications*, 6(4):16–26, 1986.

(Glassner 1984) Andrew S. Glassner. Space subdivision for fast ray tracing. *IEEE Computer Graphics and Applications*, 4(10):15–22, 1984.

(Lischinski 1994) Dani Lischinski. Incremental Delaunay triangulation. In Paul S. Heckbert, editor, *Graphics Gems IV*, pages 47–59. Academic Press, Boston, 1994.

(Meagher 1982) D. Meagher. Geometric modelling using octree encoding. *Computer Graphics and Image Processing*, 20(4):129–147, 1982.

(POV-Ray Team 1993) POV-Ray Team. Persistence of vision ray tracer (POV-Ray), version 2.0, user's documentation, 1993. anonymous ftp from `alfred.ccs.carleton.ca` in `/pub/pov-ray/POV-Ray2.0`.

(Preparata and Shamos 1985) Franco P. Preparata and Michael Ian Shamos. *Computational Geometry: An Introduction*. Springer-Verlag, New York, 1985.

(Thiessen 1911) A. H. Thiessen. Precipitation average for large area. *Monthly Weather Rev.*, (39):1082–1084, 1911.

(Voronoi 1908) M. G. Voronoi. Nouvelles applications des parametres continus a la theorie des formes quadratiques. *J. Reine u. Angew. Math.*, (134):198–287, 1908.

(Watson 1981) D. F. Watson. Computing the n-dimensional Delaunay tessellation with application to Voronoi polytopes. *The Computer Journal*, 24(2):167–172, 1981.

(Whitted 1980) Turner Whitted. An improved illumination model for shaded display. *Communications of the ACM*, 23(6):343–349, 1980.

◇ V.6

Direct Lighting Models for Ray Tracing with Cylindrical Lamps

Kurt Zimmerman

Indiana University
Bloomington, Indiana
kuzimmer@cs.indiana.edu

Fluorescent lights are used for many lighting applications, such as classrooms and shopping centers, and neon lights are again becoming popular for advertising signs and cosmetic lighting. Fluorescent and neon luminaires[1] can be modeled as diffuse emitting cylinders with associated spectral distributions. The following gem presents a method for performing the direct lighting computations for cylindrical luminaires in distribution ray tracing.

This gem extends a previous entry (Wang 1992) that presents physically correct methods for computing the contribution of spherical and triangular luminaires. The reader is referred to recent publications (Wang 1994), which provide more detailed accounts of these methods.

◇ Direct Lighting Computations ◇

Suppose that a point x is illuminated by a luminaire E. The radiance reflected in direction ω towards x is defined by the rendering equation (Kajiya 1986)

$$L(x,\omega) = \int_{x' \in E} g(x,x')\rho(x,\omega,\omega')L_E(x',\omega')\cos\theta \frac{\cos\theta' dx'}{\|x'-x\|^2}, \qquad (1)$$

where x' is a point on the luminaire E, $g(x,x') = 1$ if x' is visible from x and zero otherwise, ω' is the direction from x' to x, ρ is the bidirectional reflectance distribution function (BRDF), θ is the angle between the vector $-\omega'$ and the surface normal at x, θ' is the angle between ω' and the surface normal at x', and $L_E(x',\omega')$ is the emitted radiance from the luminaire point x' in direction ω'. The geometry for this equation with respect to a cylindrical luminaire is shown in Figure 1.

---

[1]The term "luminaire" refers to a light, lamp, or generic light source.

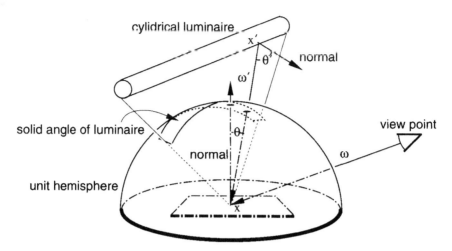

Figure 1. Calculating radiance.

Monte Carlo integration may be used to obtain an accurate approximation to (1). A set of n points $x_1, \ldots, x_n$ then estimates the integral

$$\int_{x \in \Omega} f(x) \, dx \approx \frac{1}{n} \sum_{i=1}^{n} \frac{f(x_i)}{p(x_i)},$$

where $p(x)$ is any probability density function that is positive when $f(x)$ is nonzero and x is distributed by $p(x)$, written $x \sim p(x)$.

In traditional distribution ray tracing (Cook *et al.* 1984), $n = 1$. This means that each luminaire is sampled with one shadow ray, giving the Monte Carlo estimate

$$L(x, \omega) = g(x, x') \rho(x, \omega, \omega') L_e(x', \omega') \frac{\cos \theta \cos \theta'}{p(x') \|x' - x\|^2}, \tag{2}$$

which can now be generalized for $n > 1$.

The following steps determine $L(x, \omega)$:

1. Select a probability density function p.
2. Choose x' on the luminaire such that $x' \sim p$.
3. Compute $g(x, x')$ by sending a shadow ray to determine if there is an obstruction.
4. If $g = 1$, then compute $L(x, \omega)$ by Equation (2); else set $L(x, \omega) = 0$.

The most difficult part lies in determining x' and $p(x')$. The following offers, without derivation, a good p and the associated method for generating x'.

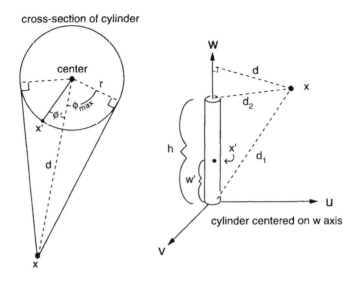

Figure 2.   Two views of the generated luminaire point x' in relation to the illuminated point x.

◇   Sampling Cylindrical Luminaires   ◇

For spherical and triangular luminaires, previous research (Wang 1992) suggests a sampling based on the estimated subtense (solid angle) of the luminaire as a good strategy. However, for a cylinder this angle can be difficult to characterize (Figure 1). Therefore, an alternative approach is taken, which follows from the observation that an approximation to solid-angle-based sampling can be obtained by choosing p such that the luminaire point x' is more likely to be generated nearer to the illuminated point x. This approach provides a reasonable approximation because x' subtends a greater differential solid angle as it moves nearer to x. The probability density function p is then designed to produce sample positions in which the distance $\|x - x'\|$ is weighted toward the value $(d - r)$ (Figure 2). The suggested p generates sample positions with these characteristics by selecting w' according to an appropriate linear function along the height of the cylinder and by selecting ϕ' with a cosine distribution about the vector defined by x and the center of the cylinder.

The following steps assume a uvw coordinate system where the cylinder center is the w axis and the base is at the coordinate origin (Figure 2). This simplifies calculations and requires the use of only a simple coordinate transformation. It is further assumed that cylindrical luminaires are diffuse, since fluorescent tubes and neon tubes are nearly diffuse, and that the ends of the cylinder do not emit light. Sample positions are generated in the following manner.

1. Generate (ϕ', w'). Let ξ_1 and ξ_2 be random numbers such that $\xi_1, \xi_2 \in [0, 1)$ and let $D = \frac{d_2 - d_1}{d_2 + d_1}$ with d_1 the distance from the origin to x and d_2 the distance from the point $(0, 0, h)$ to x:

$$(\phi', w') = \left(\sin^{-1} \left[\frac{2\xi_1 - 1}{d} \sqrt{d^2 - r^2} \right], \left(\frac{h}{2D} \right) \left[1 + D - \sqrt{(-1 - D)^2 - 4D\xi_2} \right] \right).$$

2. Find x'. Let $x = (x_u, x_v, x_w)$. Then

$$x' = (x'_u, x'_v, x'_w)$$
$$= \left(\frac{r}{d}(x_u \cos \phi' - x_v \sin \phi'), \; \frac{r}{d}(x_v \cos \phi' + x_u \sin \phi'), \; w' \right).$$

3. Return x' and $p(x')$:

$$p(x') = \left(\frac{-2D}{h^2} w' + \frac{1 + D}{h} \right) \frac{d \cos \phi'}{2r \sqrt{d^2 - r^2}}.$$

It should be noted that as the distance between x and the luminaire becomes large, simpler strategies can be utilized with similar results. Simpler strategies should be used when possible because they require less computation per sample, provided that the strategy does not introduce too much error. For example, an acceptable simplification of the preceding strategy would set $w' = \xi_2 h$. This would in turn simplify the probability density function to

$$p(x') = \frac{d \cos \phi'}{2rh \sqrt{d^2 - r^2}}.$$

Determining when to use a simple or complex strategy is subject to statistical analysis.

It should also be noted that these strategies have been designed for diffuse environments. Because the Monte Carlo estimates are unbiased, they will work for environments with more complex reflective properties, but many samples may then be required.

◇ **Bibliography** ◇

(Cook *et al.* 1984) Robert L. Cook, Thomas Porter, and Loren Carpenter. Distributed ray tracing. *Computer Graphics (ACM SIGGRAPH '84 Proceedings)*, 18(4):165–174, July 1984.

(Kajiya 1986) James T. Kajiya. The rendering equation. *Computer Graphics (ACM SIGGRAPH '86 Proceedings)*, 20(4):143–150, August 1986.

(Wang 1992) Changyaw Wang. Physically correct direct lighting for distribution ray tracing. In David Kirk, editor, *Graphics Gems III*, pages 307–313. AP Professional, Boston, 1992.

(Wang 1994) Changyaw Wang. *The Direct Lighting Computation in Global Illumination Methods*. PhD thesis, Indiana University, 1994.

V.7

Improving Intermediate Radiosity Images Using Directional Light

Martin Feda
Technical University of Vienna
Vienna, Austria
feda@cg.tuwien.ac.at

This gem describes a simple extension of ambient light to directional light for the improvement of progressive refinement radiosity images (Cohen *et al.* 1988). Directional light gives the user a much better impression of the scene geometry than ambient light, for only a little additional expense. The approach described here exploits the same approach as ambient light to estimate the final illumination, but includes a directional component. Although the new technique presented here is simple and gives much better results than the conventional ambient light, surprisingly it has been neither described in literature nor implemented.

◇ Background ◇

The most commonly used radiosity method is the progressive refinement approach (Cohen *et al.* 1988). It starts with an initial radiosity solution of low accuracy, which is then continuously improved, converging to the final solution. Intermediate images can be displayed after each iteration step. However, the illumination of the environment is usually inadequate during early iterations. The visual feedback can be improved by ambient light, which provides an *a priori* estimate of the final illumination. The ambient light depends on the unshot radiosities and the reflectivity of the environment. Although the estimate itself is quite good, the quality of early intermediate images using ambient light is still unsuitable in most cases. Since ambient light does not account for surface orientation, there are no contrasts between surfaces of uniform material, such as walls in a room. This makes it impossible to see the shape of objects and their distance from the viewing position. In fact, the user typically does not have the impression of viewing a three-dimensional scene during early iterations, especially in regions occluded from all shooting patches. The problem is especially troublesome for complex scenes, where the progressive refinement algorithm converges very slowly.

◇ Illumination Estimation by Ambient Light ◇

The difference between the current radiosity values and the complete solution can be estimated based on the amount of radiosity that has not yet been "shot," that is, radiosity not distributed to the environment (Cohen *et al.* 1988). The estimate uses the average unshot radiosity of all patches in the scene, given by

$$\Delta B_{av} = \frac{\sum \Delta B_i \cdot A_i}{\sum A_i} \; , \tag{1}$$

where ΔB_i denotes the unshot radiosity and A_i the area of patch i. On average, without knowing where unshot radiosity will arrive, a fraction ρ_{av} will be reflected, where ρ_{av} denotes the average reflectance in the scene,

$$\rho_{av} = \frac{\sum \rho_i \cdot A_i}{\sum A_i} \; . \tag{2}$$

From the reflected radiosity, some fraction will be rereflected, and so on. The global interreflections can therefore be approximated by an infinite sum,

$$R = 1 + \rho_{av} + \rho_{av}^2 + \rho_{av}^3 + \cdots = \frac{1}{1 - \rho_{av}} \; . \tag{3}$$

The amount of radiosity that will be received by a patch at later iterations can be estimated by

$$B_{estimate} = R \cdot \Delta B_{av} \; . \tag{4}$$

Since the incoming direction is not known in advance, $B_{estimate}$ is used to represent ambient light (Cohen *et al.* 1988). For display purposes, the following estimate of the final radiosity of patch or element i is conventionally used:

$$B_i^{display} = B_i + \rho_i \cdot B_{estimate} \; . \tag{5}$$

◇ Illumination Estimation by Directional Light ◇

Although the incoming direction of radiosity that will be received at later iterations is not known, it is not necessary to use $B_{estimate}$ as purely ambient light. It can also be assumed to be directional, falling onto a patch or element i from an arbitrary direction. If L is the normalized vector pointing to this incoming direction, and N is the surface normal, the diffuse illumination of the patch due to the estimated directional light can be computed by the dot product $(N \cdot L)$, as in simple illumination models (Phong 1975). In practice, $B_{estimate}$ should be used as partly ambient and partly directional light. Therefore the displayed radiosity can be computed by the following formula:

$$B_i^{display} = B_i + \rho_i \cdot B_{estimate} \cdot [(1 - d) + d \cdot \max(0,(N \cdot L))] \ . \qquad (6)$$

The parameter d determines the fraction of directional light. If $d = 1$, $B_{estimate}$ is used as purely directional illumination; for $d = 0$, it is purely ambient. The parameter d can be interactively changed by the user after each image. Typically, $d \approx 0.5$ gives best results. There exist several possibilities in choosing the incoming direction of the estimated directional light. A good choice is to use the point of view as a virtual light source, so that L points to the virtual camera. The advantage of this choice is that the directional light illuminates all parts of the scene seen by the user. This enables the user to perceive the orientation of all visible surfaces. However, if walkthroughs are performed with this technique during early iterations, the directional component of estimated illumination will change from image to image. Another possibility is to use several virtual point light sources distributed in the scene, or several predefined incoming directions specified by the user. In both cases, the directional component has to be split up among the light sources or incoming directions. Bad choices are using the light sources or the patches with the most unshot energy as virtual light sources. In the first case, the effect of direct illumination is increased, which is computed during the first iterations anyhow, while regions in shadow are not improved. In the second case, the incoming direction would change at each iteration step, thus irritating the user.

◇ **Results** ◇

Radiosity images generated with the method described here give a much better impression of the scene geometry than with pure ambient light, especially during early iteration steps, maintaining a useful approximation of the correct illumination. Examples appear as Color Plates V.7a–V.7c. The contribution of estimated directional illumination decreases at each progressive refinement iteration in the same manner as the classical ambient light, so that the generated images converge continuously to the correctly illuminated image. The additional expense of the new method—the computation of the dot product—is insignificant and can be performed by the graphics hardware.

◇ **Bibliography** ◇

(Cohen *et al.* 1988) Michael F. Cohen, Shenchang Eric Chen, John R. Wallace, and Donald P. Greenberg. A progressive refinement approach to fast radiosity image generation. *Computer Graphics (ACM SIGGRAPH '88 Proceedings)*, 22(4):75–84, August 1988.

(Phong 1975) Bui-Tuong Phong. Illumination for computer generated images. *Communications of the ACM*, 18(6):311–317, June 1975.

◇ VI ◇

Halftoning and Image Processing

The gems in this section describe methods used either to create scenes having a discrete structure (halftoning) or to analyze them, thus reconstructing a continuous model where possible (image processing).

The gem by Tobler, Purgathofer, and Geiler (VI.1) showcases state-of-the-art research in constructing ordered dither matrices used for digital halftoning. The book's color plates and monochromatic images illustrate their success; a full description of the methods is the subject of a journal article, published concurrently. Wong and Hsu describe a new variation upon precipitation-based halftoning, itself an emerging topic. Their method (VI.2) produces demonstrably superior results, with illustrations accompanying the stepwise refinements they describe. Eker (VI.3) presents a screen-coordinate line-clipping algorithm that produces an invariant set of "on" pixels independent of endpoint position along the line that underlies the segment. The problem is common to window-based systems; he provides a newer method of solution. Doué and Rubio describe an algorithm (VI.4) that reconstructs bitmap shapes into vector motion chains. Their pattern-based method of attack is closely related to the theory of cellular automata. Along similar lines, Hsu and Lee (VI.5) provide an exact and reversible inverse to the popular Bresenham line-drawing algorithm. Careful attention is paid to the best placement of endpoints common to two vectors, creating a method that produces coordinate pairs from a bitmap scene. Both methods are well suited to lossless, high-ratio compression of fax documents as well as to bitmap magnification by way of coordinate transformation. Sharma (VI.6) reconsiders adaptive image refinement. Here, images are sampled at lower resolution when full detail is not required (as in browsing). His sampling heuristic is based upon object priority; extensions to this early work might ultimately offer animated display at low data rates by minimizing the computations associated with perceptually unimportant scene features. Finally, Cross (VI.7) provides a random point sampling pattern having the minimum statistical correlation to a set of edges at arbitrary slope. His highly concise results represent many CPU hours spent "distilling" scene data with the aid of neural networks. (Note: the book's floppy disk and associated FTP mirrors offer his latest vintages.)

◇ VI.1

Improved Threshold Matrices for Ordered Dithering

Werner Purgathofer
Technical University of Vienna
Vienna, Austria

Robert F. Tobler
Technical University of Vienna
Vienna, Austria

Manfred Geiler
Technical University of Vienna
Vienna, Austria

This gem presents an improved halftoning technique using dispersed dots.[1] This corresponds to finding a microdot distribution that approximates the intensity levels that have to be rendered. An improved threshold matrix for ordered dithering is presented that avoids unwanted low-frequency portions without introducing too much random noise. Since the new method produces images of high quality, it is ideally suited for output generation in high-end image processing systems.

◇ Introduction ◇

Ordered dithering is a digital halftoning technique (Ulichney 1987) that generates microdot distributions by using a so-called threshold matrix. This matrix of threshold values is replicated and put on top of the image. If the intensity of the pixel is lower than its corresponding threshold value, a microdot is set in the output image. Thus, neighboring pixels are compared to different threshold values.

There are two major variants of ordered dithering:

- *Dispersed Dot Dithering* (Lippel and Kurland 1971, Bayer 1973): If consecutive threshold values are placed far from each other within the matrix, halftoning of an image of constant intensity will produce a number of dispersed microdots. Since current threshold matrices are almost always based on regular orderings of the threshold values, the resulting output image will display highly visible patterns.

---

[1]Based on "Forced Random Dithering: Improved Threshold Matrices for Ordered Dithering" by W. Purgathofer, R. F. Tobler, and M. Geiler, which appeared in the *Proceedings of the First IEEE Conference on Image Processing*, November 13–16, 1994, Austin, Texas, pp. 1032–1035.

- *Clustered Dot Dithering*: If consecutive threshold values are placed in a special sequence within the matrix, the microdots will join to create larger dots. The larger dots will result in a visible raster that is superimposed on the output image. This method will produce images similar to those found in cheap newspapers.

To overcome these artifacts, various improvements have been suggested that distribute the quantization error made at each pixel (Knuth 1987, Lippel and Kurland 1971). All of these methods reduce the performance of the original algorithm. A different method that does not introduce regular patterns, *random threshold dithering*, can be achieved by comparing each pixel to a random value between 0 and 1 that is generated anew for each pixel of the input. But this method, also known under the name *dithering with white noise* (Ulichney 1988), introduces a great deal of noise into the output image.

Random threshold dithering can also be done with the ordered dithering algorithm, by using a huge matrix with the threshold values placed in random ordering. Thus, random threshold dithering and ordered dithering with completely regular matrices can be viewed as the two extreme cases of a whole range of dithering matrices with various degrees of randomness in the distribution of threshold values.

◇   **Improved Threshold Matrices**   ◇

Since ordered dithering has very good characteristics in terms of performance and achievable parallelism, our goal was to find threshold matrices for this algorithm that have improved characteristics compared to previously known matrices. A threshold matrix used for ordered dithering has to satisfy the following criteria:

- It should not introduce all-too-obvious regular patterns into the dithered image. A certain degree of randomness is useful to avoid this kind of artifact.
- It should not be too random, so that the amount of noise introduced by the dithering process does not degrade the image information too much.
- It should not introduce artifacts at the boundaries between replicated threshold matrices. Thus, the algorithm to generate the matrix has to compensate for these boundaries.

A New Way to Generate the Matrices

In order to derive the computation of such in-between matrices, it is useful to think about a different algorithm for generating these matrices: selecting positions for the threshold values one by one, starting with the lowest value. This corresponds to adding microdots to a dot distribution as the desired intensity level slowly changes from white to black. Additional constraints can be specified to influence the emerging pattern of values. If the microdots (points) are thrown in randomly according to an equal distribution, and the matrix is made as large as the image, a matrix for random threshold dithering can be generated. The other extreme can be achieved by using the following rule: Put each new point in the position farthest away from all previous points. This rule specifies a set of matrices that contains the completely regular matrices for ordered dithering (Bayer 1973). After introducing a repulsive force field generated by all points already included in the matrix, new values can be thrown in randomly, and their position can be changed according to the force field. The force-field function used can be arbitrarily chosen to influence the resulting dot distribution.

The Force-Field Function

In order to produce isotropic images, the force-field function should be radially symmetric. The function should also discourage additional points from being placed close to already-existing points to avoid clustering. Therefore, the following function for generating the force field of points thrown into the threshold matrix has been chosen:

$$f(r) = \exp\left(-\left(\frac{r}{s}\right)^p\right). \tag{1}$$

Here $r = \sqrt{x^2 + y^2}$ is the distance from the point, and p and s are parameters to control the function. As new points are added, their force fields are added to a force-field matrix. To avoid problems at the boundaries of the repeatedly used threshold matrix, the top and bottom edge and the left and right edge of the force-field matrix are joined, changing it topologically to a torus.

Selecting Positions for Threshold Values

In order to avoid being caught in local minima of the force-field matrix, a large number of empty positions from the matrix are randomly selected, and the force-field intensities at these positions are compared. The new point is then fixed at the randomly selected position having minimum value. Here the number of selected positions governs the precision with which the global minimum is found. Selecting half of all free positions for finding the minimum and choosing the parameter values $s = 0.5$ and $p = 0.5$ for the force-field function yields dithering matrices that are best suited for generating dithering patterns without too many artifacts.

The Size of the Matrix

Nowadays most images use pixel values in the range $[0 \ldots 255]$. In order to achieve the same resolution in the number of intensity levels, the matrix has to be at least 16 by 16 points: A matrix of size n by n can generate $n^2 + 1$ dot patterns of different density if images with constant intensity levels are used. In general, bigger matrices are better than smaller matrices. Not only is the resolution in the number of intensity levels higher, but they also introduce less obvious recurring patterns of dots, which can be

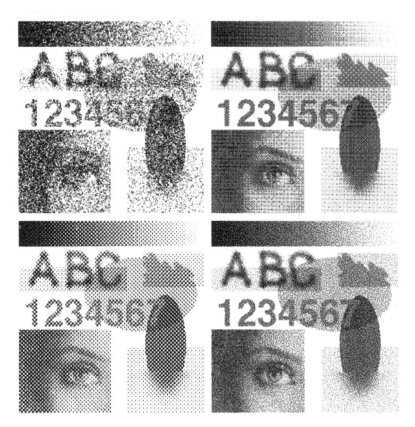

Figure 1. A 150 dpi image rendered using (top left to bottom right) random threshold dithering, ordered dithering with regular matrix, clustered dot dithering, ordered dithering with improved matrix.

quite visible for small matrices. Bigger matrices use more memory; therefore, the upper limit is given by the amount of fast memory that is available. A matrix with a size of 300×300 pixels seems to be a realistic value, since there are almost no artifacts due to recognizable repeating patterns. For this size of matrix, the memory requirements are ninety kilobytes (if the input image has intensity levels in the range $[0 \ldots 255]$), which is small enough for the matrix to completely reside in the secondary caches of current hardware. The resulting algorithm is therefore extremely fast.

Using Multiple Matrices for Color Images

In color printing, three or four color channels are overlaid to produce intermediate colors by subtractive color mixing. A lot of methods introduce highly visible moiré patterns into the output image, since they produce very regular dot distributions (Roetling 1976). In conventional printing this problem is solved by twisting the channel patterns by a few

Plate VI.1a. Random dithering.

Plate VI.1b. Ordered dithering.

Plate VI.1c. Clustered dot dithering.

Plate VI.1d. Ordered dithering (improved).

PlateV.7a. Original scene under an ambient light.

Plate V.7b. Directional illumination under ambient sources.

Plate V.7c. Final convergence to a radiometric solution.

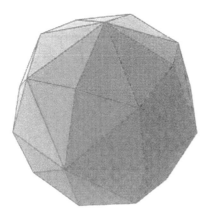

Plate II.7. Hexakis octahedron approximating the unit sphere.

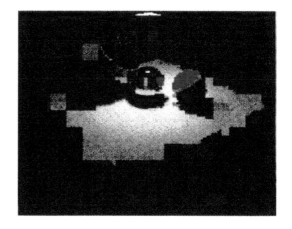

Plate VI.6. Adaptive progressive refinement (8000 rectangles).

degrees against each other, a technique not applicable in computer-generated images. The new method can avoid this problem, if different matrices are used for each channel (or the same matrix with different offsets). The overlaid matrices are then completely uncorrelated and therefore not subject to any interference.

◇ Results ◇

Figure 1 (Color Plate VI.1a–d) shows the results of applying a few different algorithms on the same image. The improved matrices avoid too much random noise (compare random threshold dithering) and regular dot distributions introduced by threshold patterns (compare ordered dithering with regular matrix and clustered dot dithering).

The presented method is very fast since it is derived from ordered dithering (the time for generating the threshold matrix does not need to be considered, since this is a one-time operation), can be parallelized easily, and generates dot distributions for dithering that do not exhibit too many artifacts. Although the contrast of the produced images is a little low, this can be overcome by proper image preparation.

◇ Bibliography ◇

(Bayer 1973) B. E. Bayer. An optimum method for two-level rendition of continuous-tone pictures. In *IEEE Conference on Communication, Conference Record*, pages (26–11)–(26–15), 1973.

(Knuth 1987) D. E. Knuth. Digital halftones by dot diffusion. *ACM Transactions on Graphics*, 6(4):245–273, 1987.

(Lippel and Kurland 1971) J. O. Lippel and M. Kurland. The effect of dither on luminance quantization of pictures. *IEEE Transactions on Communications and Technology*, 19(4):879–888, 1971.

(Roetling 1976) Paul G. Roetling. Halftone method with edge enhancement and Moiré suppression. *Jour. Opt. Soc. Amer.*, 66(10):985–989, October 1976.

(Ulichney 1987) Robert Ulichney. *Digital Halftoning*. MIT Press, Cambridge, MA, 1987.

(Ulichney 1988) R. A. Ulichney. Dithering with blue noise. In *Proc. IEEE*, 76;56–79, 1988.

VI.2

Halftoning with Selective Precipitation and Adaptive Clustering

Tien-tsin Wong
Computer Science Department
The Chinese University of Hong Kong
Shatin, Hong Kong
ttwong@cs.cuhk.hk

Siu-chi Hsu
Creature House, Ltd.
Hong Kong
schsu@acm.org

Halftoning techniques are used to display continuous tone pictures on bilevel displays and printers (or on those with a very limited number of shades). The most popular and well-known techniques are ordered dither and error diffusion. The latter produces aperiodic patterns with limited low-frequency components, a useful property (Ulichney 1987), but its dispersed dots suffer from an excessive smudging, which is especially objectionable on high-resolution devices. Ordered dither, on the other hand, is capable of clustering the dots produced by using a properly designed dither matrix. However, a regular dither pattern is then clearly visible in the output picture. A comparison of most digital halftoning techniques can be found in the literature (Schumacher 1991, Ulichney 1987).

Recently, researchers have been investigating new halftoning techniques that traverse images along a space-filling curve (Cole 1990, Velho and de Miranda Gomes 1991, Zhang and Webber 1993), based upon a Peano curve algorithm of the last decade (Witten and Neal 1982). The space-filling curve halftoning is attractive because of the pleasant smooth grains in the resultant image and the aperiodicity of the halftone pattern. Velho and de Miranda Gomes (*op. cit.*) further proposed a clustered-dot space-filling curve halftoning algorithm that reduces the smudging problem. However, clustering the dots naïvely would blur the image excessively. This gem presents two improvements, *selective precipitation* and *adaptive clustering*, used to minimize blurring.

◇ Selective Precipitation ◇

The first improvement is to precipitate black dots selectively. The original clustered-dot space-filling curve halftoning algorithm precipitates the black dots at a fixed location, say, at the beginning of each cluster. This results in a poor approximation to the original image when the original gray values in a particular cluster are not gathered around that

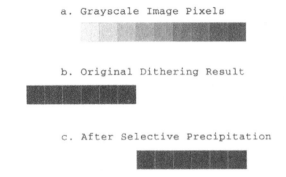

Figure 1.   Halftoning (a 1D continuous tone image) using precipitation.

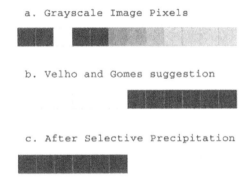

Figure 2.   Halftoning using selective precipitation.

fixed location (Figure 1). Although Velho and de Miranda Gomes have briefly suggested that the white subregion can be centered at the pixel with the highest intensity in order to preserve details, this may still result in a poor approximation (Figure 2).

By placing the black output dots over the area with the highest *total* gray value, a better approximation can be obtained. This technique is called *selective precipitation.* The number of black dots to be output in the current cluster is determined by summing all gray values inside the cluster. This number is then used as the length of a moving window that shifts within the halftone cluster. The objective is to find the position of the moving window having the highest summed gray pixel value. The black dots are then precipitated at that position.

In essence, spatial offsets are applied to localize the position of maximum dot density. This approach advances the original ARIES technique researched extensively at Xerox (Roetling 1976). The basic algorithm is sketched below.

Input

1. `input[]`: a one-dimensional array of continuous tone pixels on the range $[0 \ldots 1]$ presented as a one-dimensional array in the order of the space-filling traverse.
2. `clustersize`: the cluster size.
3. `clusterstart`: the index of the current cluster's first element.
4. `graysum`: cumulative gray sum within the current cluster.

```
winlen := ⌊graysum⌋
graysum := graysum - winlen
winsum := 0
maxsum := 0
winstart := clusterstart
for i := winstart to (winstart+winlen-1) do
begin
    winsum := winsum + input[i]
end
while (winstart+winlen) - clusterstart < clustersize
begin
    if maxsum < winsum
    begin
        maxsum := winsum
        rightplace := winstart
    end
    winsum := winsum - input[winstart] + input[winstart+winlen]
    winstart := winstart + 1
end
```

Output

1. Black dots are produced at `rightplace` for `winlen` positions.
2. The final quantization error is in `graysum`.

The time complexity of this process is clearly linear.

◇ **Adaptive Clustering** ◇

Another factor that causes the blurring is the rigid grouping of output black dots (Figure 3). Here, the original gray values are grouped at opposite ends of the cluster. Presented with such data, selective precipitation can generate black dots only at the one end having a higher total gray value. A better approximation can be obtained by dividing the cluster into two smaller clusters and performing the selective precipitation process in both clusters.

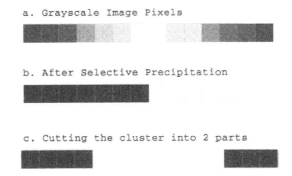

a. Grayscale Image Pixels

b. After Selective Precipitation

c. Cutting the cluster into 2 parts

Figure 3. Selective precipitation with adaptive clustering.

One method of locating the point of subdivision is finding the sharp edges. Since human eyes are more sensitive to high-frequency changes, blurring phenomena on sharp edges are more noticeable. A partitioning of clusters at sharp edges therefore preserves sharp details. This approach is used; the improvement is called *adaptive clustering.*

Since the space-filling curve goes through each pixel in the image exactly once, it effectively scales down the 2D edge detection problem into a 1D problem. It is therefore sufficient to employ merely a 1D filter along the space-filling curve in order to detect sharp edges. That is, the curve's traverse constitutes a continuous image signal. Applying the standard 1D negative of the Laplacian of the Gaussian filter (Jain 1989) can detect these sharp edges along the chain (signal). The formula of the filter is

$$\frac{\exp(-x^2/2\sigma^2)}{\sigma^3\sqrt{2\pi}}\left(1 - \frac{x^2}{\sigma^2}\right),$$

where σ is the standard deviation and x is the input signal. A filter kernel with a width of seven pixels ($\sigma = 1$) is sufficient.

The adaptive clustering algorithm is now outlined. Traverse the image pixels along a chosen space-filling cover, forming a cluster whenever N (the maximum cluster size) pixels have been traversed or a sharp edge is encountered, whichever comes first. Perform selective precipitation upon the current cluster. The pseudocode follows.

Input

1. N: maximum cluster size.
2. T: threshold.
3. M: number of input pixels.
4. input[1..M]: 1D pixel data in preselected order.

```
graysum := 0
clustersize := 0
clusterindex := 0
lastconvol := 0
for index := 0 to M-1 do
begin
     convol := InvLaplGaussian(input, 7, index-3)
                                   Convolve array with seven sample window
                                   centered about current pixel.
     graysum := graysum + input[index]    Accumulate total gray.
     clustersize := clustersize + 1    Increase current cluster.
     if |convol-lastconvol| > T or clustersize > N
     begin
          precipitate(input, graysum, clustersize, clusterindex);
                                   Perform selective precipitation outlined
                                   in the previous pseudocode.
          clustersize := 0    Begin next cluster.
          clusterindex := index
     end
     lastconvol := convol
end
```

The sensitivity of the edge detection filter affects the resulting halftone image and may be controlled with a user-defined threshold T. This value can also be determined automatically using previous techniques (Schlag 1991). A lower threshold detects additional edges, resulting in potentially smaller clusters.

Figures 4 and 5 show the performance of the improved halftoning method. Note the excessive blurring, seen as a loss of floor texture [Figure 4(b)] or of fine image detail [Figure 5(b)]. This blurring phenomenon is significantly reduced when selective precipitation and adaptive clustering is employed [Figures 4(c) and 5(c), respectively].

◇ C Implementation ◇

```
/*========================================================================*
 * Halftoning using Space Filling Curve with adaptive clustering and      *
 * selective precipitation                                                *
 *                                                                        *
 * Limitation:                                                            *
 * Only process image with size 2√n x 2√n where n is positive integer.    *
 *========================================================================*/

unsigned char **path;    /* space-filling curve path */
/*
 * path[] is a global array storing the information to move along
 *        the space-filling curve.
```

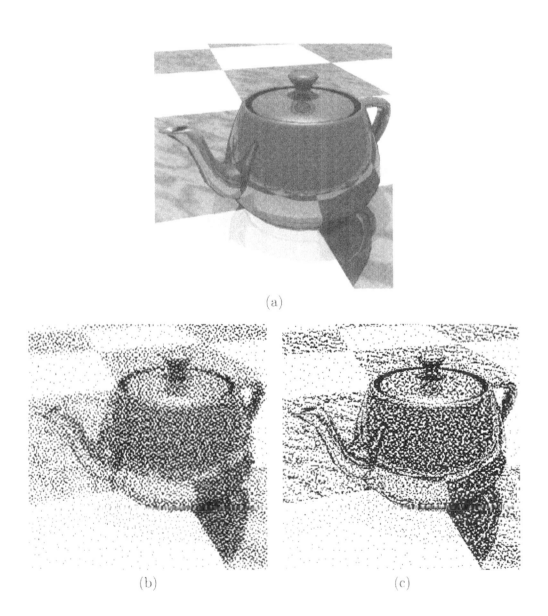

Figure 4. Teapot. (a) Original grayscale image (256x256). (b) Space-filling dithering; cluster size $N = 9$ pixels. (c) Selective precipitation with adaptive clustering; $N = 9$.

(a)

(b)   (c)

Figure 5. F16 factory. (a) Original grayscale image (256x256). (b) Space-filling dithering; cluster size $N = 9$ pixels. (c) Selective precipitation with adaptive clustering; $N = 9$.

```
 * genspacefill() is a function to generate the information in path[].
 *         This function is implemented based on a gem in Graphics Gems II,
 *         Ken Musgrave, "A Peano Curve Generation Algorithm".
 * move() is a macro to move along the space-filling curve using the
 *         the information stored in path[].
 */
#define TRUE    1
#define FALSE   0
#define BLACK   255
#define WHITE   0
#define LEFT    0
#define RIGHT   1
#define UP      2
#define DOWN    3
#define END     255
#define move(x,y)  switch (path[x][y])            \
                   {                              \
                     case UP:    y++; break;      \
                     case DOWN:  y--; break;      \
                     case LEFT:  x--; break;      \
                     case RIGHT: x++; break;      \
                   }


/*
 * Description of parameters:
 *   picture,        2D array holding the grayscale image.
 *   out,            2D array holding the dithered image.
 *   maxclustersize, Max cluster size, N.
 *   thresh,         Edge detection threshold T.
 *   do_sp,          Flag to switch on/off selective precipitation.
 *                   To switch off the selective precipitation,
 *                   set do_sp = FALSE.
 *   do_ac,          Flag to switch on/off adaptive clustering.
 *                   To switch off the adaptive clustering, set do_ac=FALSE
 */
void spacefilterwindow(int **picture, int **out, int maxclustersize,
                       int thresh, char do_sp, char do_ac)
{
  char edge;              /* Flag indicates sudden change detected */
  char ending;           /* flag indicates end of space-filling curve */
  int accumulator;       /* Accumulate gray value */
  int currclustersize;   /* Record size of current cluster */
  int frontx, fronty;    /* Pointer to the front of the cluster */
  int windowx, windowy;  /* Pointer to first pixel applied with filter */
  int clusterx, clustery;/* Pointer to first pixel in current cluster */
  int windowlen;         /* Size of the moving window */
  int winnum;            /* Current moving window's sum */
  int maxsum;            /* Maximum moving window's sum recorded */
  int rightplace;        /* Position of the moving window with max sum */
  int *cluster;          /* An array hold the pixel of current cluster */
  int last, i,j, tempx, tempy, currx, curry;    /* temp variables */
  long filter[7] = {-1, -5, 0, 13, 0, -5, -1};  /* 1D -ve Lap. Gauss. filter */
```

```
long convolution;       /* Convolution value in this turn */
long lastconvolution;   /* Convolution value in last turn */
/*
 * Description of the pointer along the space-filling curve.
 *
 * clusterx,                        windowx,   currx,    frontx,
 * clustery                         windowy    curry     fronty
 *    |                                |         |          |
 *    v                                v         v          v
 *    +------------------------------------------------------------+
 *    |                      Cluster                               |
 *    +------------------------------------------------------------+
 *                          |                              |
 *                          |                              |
 *                          |              /\              |
 *                          |            /    \            |
 *                          |___       /        \       ___|
 *                          |    \/              \/   |
 *                          -ve Laplacian of Gaussian Filter
 */

if ((cluster=malloc(sizeof(int)*maxclustersize))==NULL)
{
  fprintf(stderr,"not enough memory for cluster\n");
  return;
}
genspacefill();     /* generates the spacefilling path */

convolution=0;
currclustersize=0;
accumulator=0;
for (frontx=0, fronty=0, i=0 ; i<7 ; i++)
{
  if (i<3)
  {
    cluster[currclustersize] = picture[frontx][fronty];
    accumulator += cluster[currclustersize];
    currclustersize++;
  }
  if (i==3)
  {  currx = frontx;  curry = fronty;   }
  convolution += filter[i]*(long)(picture[frontx][fronty]);
  move(frontx,fronty);  /* assume the image has at least 7 pixels */
}
lastconvolution = convolution;
clusterx=0;    clustery=0;
windowx=0;     windowy=0;
edge=FALSE;
ending=FALSE;
```

```
while (TRUE)
{
  if (do_ac) /* switch on/off adaptive clustering */
  {
    /* do convolution */
    convolution = 0;
    for (tempx=windowx, tempy=windowy, i=0 ; i<7 ; i++)
    {
      convolution += filter[i]*picture[tempx][tempy];
      move(tempx,tempy);
    }

    /* detect sudden change */
    if ( (convolution >= 0 && lastconvolution <=0
          && abs(convolution-lastconvolution)>thresh)
       ||(convolution <= 0  && lastconvolution >=0
          && abs(convolution-lastconvolution)>thresh))
      edge=TRUE; /* force output dots */
  }

  /* Output dots if necessary */
  if (edge || currclustersize >= maxclustersize || ending)
  {
    edge=FALSE;

    /* Search the best position within cluster to precipitate */
    rightplace = 0;
    if (do_sp) /* switch on/off selective precipitation */
    {
      windowlen = accumulator/BLACK;
      winsum = 0;
      for (i=0; i<windowlen; i++)
        winsum += cluster[i];
      for (maxsum=winsum, last=0; i<currclustersize; i++, last++)
      {
        winsum+= cluster[i] - cluster[last];
        if (winsum > maxsum)
        {
          rightplace=last+1;
          maxsum=winsum;
        }
      }
    }

    /* Output dots */
    for (i=0 ; currclustersize!=0 ; currclustersize--, i++)
    {
      if (accumulator>=BLACK && i>=rightplace)  /* precipitates */
      {
        out[clusterx][clustery]=BLACK;
        accumulator-=BLACK;
      }
```

```
   else
     out[clusterx][clustery]=WHITE;
   move(clusterx,clustery)
 } /* for */

 if (ending)
   break;
} /* if */

cluster[currclustersize] = picture[currx][curry];
accumulator += cluster[currclustersize];
currclustersize++;
if (path[currx][curry]==END)
  ending = TRUE;
move(currx,curry);
move(windowx,windowy);
move(frontx,fronty);
} /* while */
}
```

◇ **Bibliography** ◇

(Cole 1990) A. J. Cole. Naïve halftoning. In T. S. Chua and Kunii, editors, *Proceedings of CG International '90*, pages 203–222. Springer-Verlag, 1990.

(Jain 1989) Anil K. Jain. *Fundamentals of Digital Image Processing*. Prentice Hall, 1989.

(Roetling 1976) Paul J. Roetling. Halftone method with edge enhancement and moiré suppression. *Journal of the Optical Society of America*, 66(10):985–989, October 1976.

(Schlag 1991) John Schlag. Noise thresholding in edge images. In James Arvo, editor, *Graphics Gems II*, page 105. AP Professional, Boston, 1991.

(Schumacher 1991) Dale A. Schumacher. A comparsion of digial halftoning techniques. In James Arvo, editor, *Graphics Gems II*, pages 57–77. AP Professional, Boston, 1991.

(Ulichney 1987) R. Ulichney. *Digital Halftoning*. MIT Press, Cambridge, MA, 1987.

(Velho and de Miranda Gomes 1991) Luiz Velho and Jonas de Miranda Gomes. Digital halftoning with space filling curves. In Thomas W. Sederberg, editor, *Computer Graphics (SIGGRAPH '91 Proceedings)*, Volume 25, pages 81–90, July 1991.

(Witten and Neal 1982) I. H. Witten and R. M. Neal. Using Peano curves for bilevel display of continuous-tone images. *IEEE Computer Graphics and Applications*, 2:47–52, May 1982.

(Zhang and Webber 1993) Yuefeng Zhang and Robert E. Webber. Space diffusion: An improved parallel halftoning technique using space-filling curves. In James T. Kajiya, editor, *Computer Graphics (SIGGRAPH '93 Proceedings)*, Volume 27, pages 305–312, August 1993.

VI.3

Faster "Pixel-Perfect" Line Clipping

Steven Eker
Brunel University
Uxbridge, United Kingdom

◇ **Introduction** ◇

This gem considers the problem of "pixel-perfect" line clipping. The task is to generate precisely those pixels of a rasterized line that lie within a given clipping rectangle. This requirement arises naturally in window systems when redrawing an exposed rectangle containing part of a rasterized line. Any pixel imperfection will show up as a discontinuity in the line. Clipping the line to the rectangle, rounding each clipped endpoint to the nearest pixel, and rasterizing the resulting line is not an adequate solution (Figure 1). Rasterizing the line and then clipping the pixels is inefficient; an improved method is known (Pike 1983). In comparison to other clippers, it avoids missing pixels at the ends of the clipped segment by using a more sophisticated rounding technique, and avoids off-by-one errors in the positions of the generated pixels by adjusting the starting conditions of the line rasterizer (Bresenham 1965).

The solution presented here is based on Pike's method but with several refinements: integer clipping tests in the style of Dörr (Dörr 1990) are used, and the calculation of subsequently unused products is avoided, as suggested by Krammer (Krammer 1992). Also, a novel idea is introduced: that of choosing at which end to start drawing the line in order to minimize the number of multiplications and divisions required for clipping. In fact, the algorithm requires at most one division that is used to establish algebraically the intersection of the line and rectangle at the point where pixel production commences. Termination occurs when the final in-rectangle pixel is generated and is detected by discrete methods.

◇ **Algorithm** ◇

Without loss of generality, assume that the clipping rectangle is specified by bottom-left and top-right corners (x_l, y_b) and (x_r, y_t) with $x_l \leq x_r$, $y_b \leq y_t$, and the line is specified by endpoints (x_1, y_1) and (x_2, y_2). Then put $\Delta_x = x_2 - x_1$; $\Delta_y = y_2 - y_1$.

314

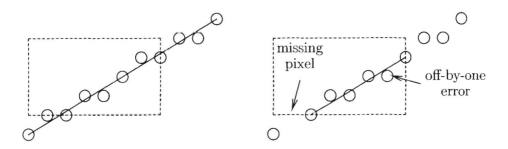

Figure 1. Improper line rasterization when clipping endpoints to the nearest pixel.

The algorithm produces a set of pixels. Ambiguity in pixel choice occurs when the line passes exactly midway between two pixels. A uniform rounding (bias) based on octants is one solution (Bresenham 1987). This is often impractical: Most implementations "fold" this symmetry into one octant or quadrant. In practice there are two choices: either round toward (x_1, y_1) or round toward (x_2, y_2). Here the algorithm takes a flag, allowing the user to select between endpoints. If, after comparing the endpoints against the clipping rectangle, it is advantageous to exchange the endpoints and draw the line starting from the other end, this flag is inverted to preserve the rounding direction and ensure that the same set of pixels is generated.

For the sake of exposition, consider merely the case $\Delta_x \geq 0$, $\Delta_y \geq 0$, $\Delta_x \geq \Delta_y$ with rounding toward (x_2, y_2). With a careful consideration of symmetry, the other fifteen cases can be implemented cheaply. The pixels (x, y) in the rasterization of the unclipped line are given by

$$y = y_1 + \left\lfloor \frac{\Delta_y}{\Delta_x}(x - x_1) + \frac{1}{2} \right\rfloor \tag{1}$$

for $x = x_1, x_1 + 1, \ldots, x_2$, and the Bresenham error term r at each pixel (x, y) is given by

$$r = 2\Delta_y(x - x_1 + 1) - 2\Delta_x(y - y_1) - \Delta_x.$$

Outcode Computation

Rectangle–object intersection tests traditionally employ a "space partitioning" defined by the extension of the rectangle's edges. The classic Cohen–Sutherland line-clipping algorithm (Newman 1979) computes an *outcode* using (at most) four comparisons for each endpoint. The outcode encodes the endpoint's half-plane membership as a four-bit number. Here a *type* which is the number of bits set in an endpoint's outcode is also computed. The half-planes, outcodes, and types are shown in Figure 2. In the usual

$$
\begin{array}{c|c|c}
\begin{matrix}1001\\ \underline{2}\end{matrix} & \begin{matrix}1000\\ \underline{1}\end{matrix} & \begin{matrix}1010\\ \underline{2}\end{matrix} \\
\hline
\begin{matrix}0001\\ \underline{1}\end{matrix} & \begin{matrix}0000\\ \underline{0}\end{matrix} & \begin{matrix}0010\\ \underline{1}\end{matrix} \\
\hline
\begin{matrix}0101\\ \underline{2}\end{matrix} & \begin{matrix}0100\\ \underline{1}\end{matrix} & \begin{matrix}0110\\ \underline{2}\end{matrix}
\end{array}
$$

Figure 2.   Outcode and type computation for endpoints.

way, a line that lies completely within one half-plane can be rejected. This occurs when a bitwise-and of its outcodes is nonzero.

Clipping the First Endpoint

If the first endpoint is of type $\underline{0}$, no clipping is necessary. Otherwise, if it is of type $\underline{2}$ and (under the previous assumptions) must lie outside the left and bottom edges, the edge to which it should be clipped must be determined. Remember, however, that it is the pixel set and not the line that must be clipped: The line may intersect one edge while the pixel set may need to be clipped to the other. Using Equation (1), the pixel set must be clipped along the bottom edge if

$$
y_1 + \left\lfloor \frac{\Delta_y}{\Delta_x}(x_l - x_1) + \frac{1}{2} \right\rfloor < y_b,
$$

and otherwise along the left edge. This inequality can be simplified, giving

$$
2\Delta_y(x_l - x_1) + \Delta_x < 2\Delta_x(y_b - y_1).
$$

As a result of this test, one of the two set bits in the outcode can reset to zero.

The (adjusted) outcode now indicates the proper clipping edge. For clipping to the left edge, the starting coordinates (x_s, y_s) will be $x_s \leftarrow x_l$ and $y_s \leftarrow y_1 + t$, where

$$
t = \left\lfloor \frac{\Delta_y}{\Delta_x}(x_l - x_1) + \frac{1}{2} \right\rfloor = \left\lfloor \frac{2\Delta_y(x_l - x_1) + \Delta_x}{2\Delta_x} \right\rfloor.
$$

One must test the y_s against y_t. If y_s is greater, the line lies entirely above the clipping rectangle and is rejected. Otherwise, the Bresenham error term at (x_s, y_s) can be calculated from the Bresenham error term at (x_1, y_1) by adding

$$
2\Delta_y(x_l - x_1) - 2\Delta_x t.
$$

For clipping to the bottom edge, the starting coordinates (x_s, y_s) will be $y_s \leftarrow y_b$, and x_s will be the least x such that

$$y_1 + \left\lfloor \frac{\Delta_y}{\Delta_x}(x - x_1) + \frac{1}{2} \right\rfloor = y_b.$$

It can be shown that $x_s = x_1 + t$, where

$$t = \left\lfloor \frac{2\Delta_x(y_b - y_1) - \Delta_x + 2\Delta_y - 1}{2\Delta_y} \right\rfloor.$$

One must test x_s against x_r. If x_s is greater, the line lies entirely to the right of the clipping rectangle and is rejected. Otherwise, the Bresenham error term at (x_s, y_s) can be calculated from the Bresenham error term at (x_1, y_1) by adding

$$2\Delta_y t - 2\Delta_x(y_b - y_1).$$

Clipping the Second Endpoint

The key idea when clipping the second endpoint is that the line–rectangle intersection need not be computed algebraically. Instead, the Bresenham line-drawing algorithm is terminated when it encounters an edge of the clipping rectangle. The extra tests required to detect this may be removed from the pixel drawing loop by precomputing the number of repetitions. This requires that one determine which edge is (first) hit.

If the second endpoint is of type $\underline{0}$, no clipping is necessary. Otherwise, if it is of type $\underline{2}$ and (under the previous assumptions) must lie outside of the top and right edges, the edge to which it should be clipped must be determined. Using Equation (1), the pixel set must be clipped along the top edge if

$$y_1 + \left\lfloor \frac{\Delta_y}{\Delta_x}(x_r - x_1) + \frac{1}{2} \right\rfloor > y_t,$$

and otherwise along the right edge. This inequality can be simplified, giving

$$2\Delta_x(y_t - y_1) + \Delta_x \;<\; 2\Delta_y(x_r - x_1) + 1.$$

As a result of this test, one of the two set bits in the outcode can reset to zero.

The (adjusted) outcode now indicates the proper clipping edge. For clipping to the right edge, the Bresenham algorithm must terminate after it has completed $n = x_r - x_s$ steps to the right.

For clipping to the top edge, the Bresenham algorithm must terminate after it has completed $n = y_t - y_s$ steps upwards. Here the loop repeats until the conditional y-step is executed for the $(n+1)$th time. An alternative version of Bresenham's algorithm is used where the loop counter is only decremented and tested inside the conditional y-step.

Which Way Around to Draw the Line?

Allowing for common subexpressions, one can count the multiplications and divisions needed to clip the first endpoint and update the Bresenham error term depending on its type. The results are summarized in the following table.

Type	Multiplications	Divisions
0	0	0
1	2	1
2	3	1

For the second endpoint, two multiplications are needed if it has type 2, and none otherwise. Clearly it is advantageous to swap the endpoints whenever the second endpoint has type 0 and the first endpoint has a nonzero type. Less obviously, a multiplication is saved by swapping the endpoints when the first endpoint has type 1 and the second endpoint has type 2.

◇ Putting It All Together ◇

The biggest difficulty in implementing this approach is finding an elegant and efficient way of handling all sixteen cases. Note that the rounding direction for integer division in ANSI C is only defined for positive numbers. Some implementors get around this difficulty by using a preprocessor flag to select different fragments of code depending on whether the target architecture has symmetric or asymmetric rounding (Dörr 1990). The approach taken here is to ensure that division is applied only to positive operands. Therefore, the absolute value of Δ_x (Δ_y) is taken, and the sign is stored in a separate variable s_x (s_y). This divides the number of cases by four and is also convenient for implementing Bresenham's algorithm.

It turns out that all the expressions used in tests and for calculating clipped coordinates change by at most one if the opposite rounding direction is assumed [toward (x_1, y_1)] for rasterization. Thus, four cases can be collapsed to two by incorporating a 0-1 flag, *dir*, or its complement into such expressions.

The remaining two cases are distinguished by whether the slope of the line is less than or equal to 45° (the "semihorizontal" case) or greater than 45° (the "semivertical" case). These two cases cannot be collapsed easily, so separate code is used for each case; however, the most complex part of the algorithm is written as a preprocessor macro that is expanded once for each case.

Further Refinements

There are a couple of changes that can be made to the basic implementation to optimize it for specific circumstances and hardware.

First, if a large proportion of the lines are expected to be rectilinear ($\Delta_x = 0$ or $\Delta_y = 0$), it is advantageous to detect such lines when Δ_x and Δ_y are computed and use the obvious fast clipping and drawing algorithms for them.

In clipping the second endpoint when it has type $\underline{2}$, two multiplications are used to determine which of two candidate edges will be hit when rasterizing the line. This is done so that only a single exit condition is needed for the Bresenham algorithm loop. If multiplications are prohibitively expensive on the target architecture while lines are expected to be relatively short, it may be advantageous to use a modified Bresenham algorithm with two loop counters and two exit conditions and avoid the two multiplications.

◇ C Implementation of the Line Clipper ◇

```
#define LEFT            1
#define RIGHT           2
#define BOTTOM          4
#define TOP             8

#define SWAP(x, y)      { int _t = x; x = y; y = _t; }

#define OUTCODE(x, y, outcode, type)                                    \
{                                                                       \
  if (x < xl) outcode = LEFT, type = 1;                                 \
  else if (x > xr) outcode = RIGHT, type = 1;                           \
  else outcode = type = 0;                                              \
  if (y < yb) outcode |= BOTTOM, type++;                                \
  else if (y > yt) outcode |= TOP, type++;                              \
}

#define CLIP(a1, a2, b1, da, da2, db2, as, bs, sa, sb,                  \
             amin, AMIN, amax, AMAX, bmin, BMIN, bmax, BMAX)           \
{                                                                       \
  if (out1) {                                                           \
    if (out1 & AMIN) { ca = db2 * (amin - a1); as = amin; }            \
    else if (out1 & AMAX) { ca = db2 * (a1 - amax); as = amax; }       \
    if (out1 & BMIN) { cb = da2 * (bmin - b1); bs = bmin; }            \
    else if (out1 & BMAX) { cb = da2 * (b1 - bmax); bs = bmax; }       \
    if (type1 == 2)                                                     \
      out1 &= (ca + da < cb + !dir) ? f(AMIN | AMAX) : f(BMAX | BMIN); \
    if (out1 & (AMIN | AMAX)) {                                        \
      cb = (ca + da - !dir) / da2;                                     \
      if (sb >= 0) { if ((bs = b1 + cb) > bmax) return; }              \
      else { if ((bs = b1 - cb) < bmin) return; }                     \
      r += ca - da2 * cb;                                              \
```

```
      }                                                                    \
      else {                                                               \
        ca = (cb   da + db2 - dir) / db2;                                  \
        if (sa >= 0) { if ((as = a1 + ca) > amax) return; }               \
        else { if ((as = a1 - ca) < amin) return; }                       \
        r += db2 * ca - cb;                                               \
      }                                                                    \
    }                                                                      \
    else { as = a1; bs = b1; }                                            \
    alt = 0;                                                               \
    if (out2) {                                                           \
      if (type2 == 2) {                                                   \
        ca = db2 * ((out2 & AMIN) ? a1 - amin : amax - a1);               \
        cb = da2 * ((out2 & BMIN) ? b1 - bmin : bmax - b1);               \
        out2 &= (cb + da < ca + dir) ? f(AMIN | AMAX) : f(BMIN | BMAX);   \
      }                                                                    \
      if (out2 & (AMIN | AMAX)) n = (out2 & AMIN) ? as - amin : amax - as; \
      else { n = (out2 & BMIN) ? bs - bmin : bmax - bs; alt = 1; }        \
    }                                                                      \
    else n = (a2 >= as) ? a2 - as : as - a2;                              \
}


void clip(int dir, int x1, int y1, int x2, int y2,
          int xl, int yb, int xr, int yt)
/*
 *      If dir = 0, round towards (x1, y1)
 *      If dir = 1, round towards (x2, y2)
 */
{
  int adx, ady, adx2, ady2, sx, sy;
  int out1, out2, type1, type2;
  int ca, cb, r, diff, xs, ys, n, alt;

  OUTCODE(x1, y1, out1, type1);
  OUTCODE(x2, y2, out2, type2);
  if (out1 & out2) return;
  if ((type1 != 0 && type2 == 0) || (type1 == 2 && type2 == 1)){
    SWAP(out1, out2);
    SWAP(type1, type2);
    SWAP(x1, x2);
    SWAP(y1, y2);
    dir √= 1;
  }
  xs = x1;
  ys = y1;
  sx = 1;
  adx = x2 - x1;
  if (adx < 0) { adx = -adx; sx = -1; }
  sy = 1;
  ady = y2 - y1;
  if (ady < 0) { ady = -ady; sy = -1; }
  adx2 = adx + adx;
```

```
  ady2 = ady + ady;
  if (adx >= ady) {
/*
 *      line is semi-horizontal
 */
    r = ady2 - adx - !dir;
    CLIP(x1, x2, y1, adx, adx2, ady2, xs, ys, sx, sy,
         xl, LEFT, xr, RIGHT, yb, BOTTOM, yt, TOP);
    diff = ady2 - adx2;
    if (alt) {
      for (;; xs += sx) {        /* alternate Bresenham */
        plot(xs, ys);
        if (r >= 0 ) {
          if (--n < 0) break;
          r += diff;
          ys += sy;
        }
        else r += ady2;
      }
    }
    else{
      for (;; xs += sx) {        /* standard Bresenham */
        plot(xs, ys);
        if (--n < 0) break;
        if (r >= 0 ) { r += diff; ys += sy; }
        else r += ady2;
      }
    }
  }
  else {
/*
 *      line is semi-vertical
 */
    r = adx2 - ady - !dir;
    CLIP(y1, y2, x1, ady, ady2, adx2, ys, xs, sy, sx,
         yb, BOTTOM, yt, TOP, xl, LEFT, xr, RIGHT);
    diff = adx2 - ady2;
    if (alt) {
      for (;; ys += sy) {        /* alternate Bresenham */
        plot(xs, ys);
        if (r >= 0 ) {
          if (--n < 0) break;
          r += diff;
          xs += sx;
        }
        else r += adx2;
      }
    }
    else {
      for (;; ys += sy) {        /* standard Bresenham */
        plot(xs, ys);
        if (--n < 0) break;
        if (r >= 0 ) { r += diff; xs += sx; }
```

```
        else r += adx2;
      }
    }
  }
}
```

◇ **Bibliography** ◇

(Bresenham 1965) Jack E. Bresenham. Algorithm for the control of a digital plotter. *IBM Systems Journal*, 4(1):106–111, May 1965.

(Bresenham 1987) Jack E. Bresenham. Ambiguities in incremental line rastering. *IEEE Computer Graphics and Applications*, 7(5):31–43, May 1987.

(Dörr 1990) Michael Dörr. A new approach to parametric line clipping. *Computers & Graphics*, 14(3/4):449–464, 1990.

(Krammer 1992) Gergely Krammer. A line clipping algorithm and its analysis. *Computer Graphics Forum (Eurographics '92)*, 11(3):253–266, 1992.

(Newman 1979) W. M. Newman. *Principle of Interactive Computer Graphics*. McGraw-Hill, New York, 1979.

(Pike 1983) Rob Pike. Graphics in overlapping bitmap layers. *ACM Transactions on Graphics*, 2(2):135–160, April 1983.

◇ VI.4

Efficient and Robust 2D Shape Vectorization

Jean-François Doué
HEC
Paris, France

Ruben Gonzalez Rubio
University of Sherbrooke
Canada

◇ Introduction ◇

In computer graphics applications, it is often convenient to be able to convert a shape from its bitmap representation to a vectorized form. Indeed, a vectorized form has many advantages over a bitmap: It can be transformed without loss of resolution, and it is sometimes better suited for the needs of computer vision. This gem presents an algorithm to perform the vectorization of arbitrary 2D shapes (a shape is defined here as "a set of contiguous pixels of the same color"). We developed the algorithm for a computer vision application: The purpose was to study how to train a neural network to recognize arbitrarily scaled handwritten digits and required the network to be presented with a more meaningful representation of the data than just a raw bitmap (Michaud *et al.* 1993).

The first part of this gem summarizes the problem, explains how it is usually solved, and shows the limits of this technique. The second part presents a simple yet very useful extension of the algorithm, based on pattern matching, that solves the limitations raised in the first part. It uses postprocessing rules somewhat similar to the production rules found in formal systems. Finally, a third section makes some remarks about vectorization that can be useful.

◇ Summary of the Problem ◇

Vectorization transforms a shape into a collection of vectors that delimits its boundaries. Since vectorization starts from a coarse approximation of the shape (its rasterization on a grid of pixels), it can only produce a limited number of vectors, which can be encoded as integers in the [0, 7] range (see Figure 1). The collection is also sometimes

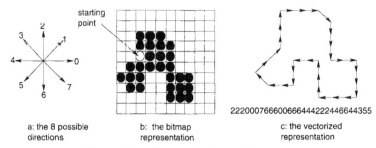

a: the 8 possible   b: the bitmap   c: the vectorized
directions   representation   representation

Figure 1.   The original algorithm.

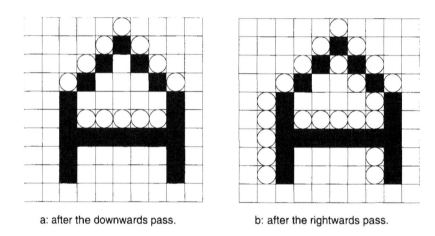

a: after the downwards pass.   b: after the rightwards pass.

Figure 2.   Generating the contour.

called "chain code." The encoding process has already been described by others (Plaziac 1991, Ballard and Brown 1992), but deserves some explanation.

The Usual Algorithm

First, the algorithm generates the boundaries. It does so in four phases, scanning the bitmap in a particular direction (leftward, rightward, upward and downward) at each phase. Each phase adds a layer of pixels to the shape any time it comes across a boundary, a bit as if it were "snowing" on the shape. Figure 2 shows how each of the first two phases adds pixels to the bitmap to progressively determine the contour of the shape. The other two passes work exactly the same way.

Finally, the algorithm finds a pixel of the contour of the shape and may now enter its main loop (see the following pseudocode).

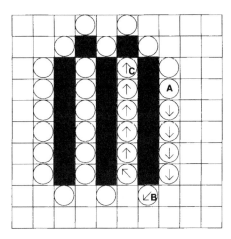

Figure 3. A dead end.

```
loop
    mark(p)                         // Mark present location.
    for idelta = 0 to 7             // Index of neigbor offsets, ccw.
    delta = ccw[idelta]             // Get unit offset vector.
    if boundary(p+delta)            // Found neighboring boundary.
        addChain(delta)             // Record motion.
        p := p + delta              // Update location (vector add).
        endif
while movesRemain()
```

Limitations

This algorithm, though it sets the ground rules of chain code generation, is not perfect. It especially has problems with thin bitmaps or bitmaps that present very narrow canyons. Following are two examples of the kind of problems that usually arise.

Problem 1. In the first example, the algorithm is applied to a small, lower-case m (see Figure 3). The algorithm starts normally at point A, then comes close to a very narrow canyon (only one pixel wide), at point B. Since it is checking the directions counterclockwise, it falls into the canyon. However, as it continues deeper into the canyon, marking the pixels along its way, it does not notice that it is blocking its exit. The algorithm terminates at the bottom of the canyon (point C), leaving two-thirds of the m unvectorized!

Problem 2. In the second example, the algorithm is applied to a 1, starting at point A (see Figure 4). Theoretically, a good algorithm should walk up a vertical line until

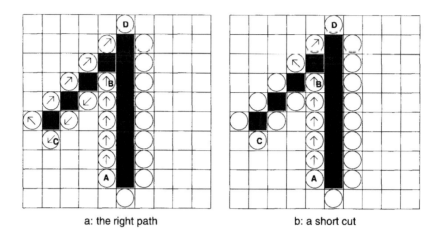

a: the right path   b: a short cut

Figure 4.   A leak.

point B, then take the "staircase" leftward until point C and then go back up until point D. However, as it reaches point B, the standard algorithm takes a short cut, and goes directly to point D. This comes from the fact that it checks all the directions counterclockwise: For thin 45° lines, it has no way of knowing whether route C or route D is the best one.

◇   The New Algorithm   ◇

A very simple extension will solve the two problems. The trick is to subdivide every pixel of the bitmap into a 4×4 grid of "smaller" pixels, as shown in Figure 5 (anything greater than 2×2 (3×3 and beyond) would work too, requiring less memory). However, four is a more practical number, since computers can multiply and divide by four very easily using bit-shifts.

At the new scale, problem 1 simply disappears. In a 4×4 world, there are no more narrow canyons. All canyons are at least four pixels wide. There is no risk of getting stuck.

Problem 2 still persists, but becomes simpler. In the 4×4 world, the straight moves (left, right, up, down) always have priority over the oblique moves (left-up, right-up, left-down, right-down). Oblique routes should only be taken as a last resort, when no straight route is possible. Therefore, problem 2 is easily solved by changing the order in which the directions are checked. The rightward, upward, leftward, and downward directions should always be checked first, and only then the oblique directions.

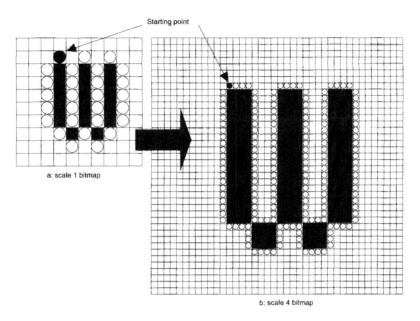

Figure 5. The new algorithm.

Shortcomings

The reader will have at least three objections regarding the new method:

1. The new algorithm generates a chain code at 4× that is much longer than the chain code at 1× and very different from it.
2. The chain code is wrong. Suppose the algorithm is applied to an oblique 45° line at 1×. Then at 4× one will end up with the chain code for a big staircase instead of the chain code for an oblique line.
3. The new algorithm will be extremely slow. Given a scale factor of 4×, there are sixteen times as many pixels to process.

Two Additional Tricks

It turns out that two rather simple tricks will overcome most of the problems raised by these three remarks.

1. The first trick is based on an interesting property of the chain code at 4× and solves the first two objections. The chain code can be *very* easily postprocessed to obtain a 1× chain code, using three simple rules of pattern searching. Using C to indicate a code value, if the input is a code at 4× and the desired output is a code at 1×, then the reduction rules are as follows:

$$
\begin{array}{rcl}
\text{CCCC} & \rightarrow & \text{C} \qquad \text{reduce to one copy,} \\
\text{CCC} & \rightarrow & \{\} \qquad \text{eliminate,} \\
\text{CC} & \rightarrow & \text{CC} \qquad \text{(ignored),} \\
\text{C} & \rightarrow & \text{C} \qquad \text{identity,}
\end{array}
$$

in which the fourth pattern rule (identity) subsumes the third.

A simple example will prove the efficiency and the simplicity of this postprocessing technique (see Figure 5). Scanning manually from Figure 5(a), one naturally obtains the following code:

76666222217666622221766655353322221

A good algorithm should be able to achieve the same results. The original algorithm would certainly fail, since the figure presents both problems 1 and 2. The new algorithm applied to the shape yields the following results:

4× chain code [Figure 5(b)]:
000 7 6666 6666 6666 6666 666 000 2222 2222 2222 2222 222 1
000 7 6666 6666 6666 6666 666 000 2222 2222 2222 2222 222 1
000 7 6666 6666 6666 6666 666 5 444 666 5 444 3 222 444 666 5
444 3 222 444 3 2222 2222 2222 2222 222 1

After postprocessing the 4× code, one obtains the exact result.

Postprocessed 1× chain code [Figure (5a)]:
76666222217666622221766655353322221

2. The second trick does not completely solve the last objection (there is truly more processing to do), but it helps considerably. The original algorithm spent most of its time blindly testing the eight possible directions of motion, which was not very efficient. The reader will notice that the chain code at 4× presents many long segments of identical continuous values, meaning that the algorithm often keeps on moving in the same direction for at least a few steps. By keeping track of the last direction in which it was moving and using it as a first guess for the next move, the new algorithm can save many computations.

◇ **Additional Remarks** ◇

Computing the Derivative

It is often interesting to compute the (discrete) derivative of the chain code, since it is invariant under boundary rotations. The derivative of the chain code reflects the change in the orientation of the tangent to the contour as one moves from one point of the contour to the next. The derivative cannot simply be the difference between two consecutive direction codes, since this would imply many discontinuities. For instance, if the current direction is 7 and the next one is 0, the change should not be recorded as $0 - 7 = -7$, but rather as -1, the shortest path on the trigonometric circle. To do this, we will use the following implementation:

$$C'_k \leftarrow (C_k - C_{k-1} + 12) \bmod 8 - 4. \tag{1}$$

The reader should be careful with the mod function, which is here meant as the genuine modulo function for relative integers (i.e., $-2 \bmod 8 \equiv 6$ and not -2, as some math packages will compute. The $a \bmod b$ function should return the smallest integer r in the $[0, b - 1]$ range such that $bq + r = a$).

The Problem of the Starting Point

A difficult problem to solve is that of the starting point. Since the chain code reflects the contour of the object, it is indeed cyclic. A suitable starting point must be found. Ideally, the behavior of the algorithm should be invariant under boundary rotation. A canonical form is quite important for certain applications such as optical character recognition (OCR). The C++ code presented below chooses the contour pixel closest to the upper-left corner of the bounding box of the shape. However, this is just a convention and certainly not the perfect choice.

Extensions

Though the present method finds merely the contours of 2D objects, voids can be identified following the generation of the shape's contour. The postprocessing of the chain code using a simple pattern matcher is a powerful technique worthy of further study. Extended rules sets, particularly those useful for different scale factors, deserve attention. The interested reader is directed to standard treatments (Olson 1992, Schneider 1990, Feldman 1992, Freeman 1961) for supplementary information.

◇ **C Code** ◇

pt2.H

```
typedef struct pt2struct{
  int x,y;
} pt2;

extern pt2* addPt2(pt2 *a, pt2 *b, pt2 *c);
extern pt2* subPt2(pt2 *a, pt2 *b, pt2 *c);
```

pt2.C

```
#include "pt2.h"

/******************************************************************/
/*                                                                */
/* Two utility functions to add and subtract 2D integer points.*/
/*                                                                */
/******************************************************************/

pt2* addPt2(pt2 *a, pt2 *b, pt2 *c)
{ c->x = a->x + b->x; c->y = a->y + b->y; return c; }

pt2* subPt2(pt2 *a, pt2 *b, pt2 *c)
{ c->x = a->x - b->x; c->y = a->y - b->y; return c; }
```

chainCode.H

```
#define DEFAULT_CODE_LENGTH 512
#define SCALE 4

class chainCode{
    public:
        char* code;
        int   length;

        chainCode();
        fchainCode();
        void add(char c);
        chainCode* postProcess();
        void printSelf();
};




\paragraph{chainCode.C}
\begin{codingeightpt}
#include <stdlib.h>
#include <stdio.h>
#include "chainCode.h"

/******************************************************************/
/*                                                                */
/* Class constructor.                                             */
/*                                                                */
/******************************************************************/

chainCode::chainCode()
{
code = malloc(DEFAULT_CODE_LENGTH * sizeof(char));
```

```
code[0] = '\0';
length = DEFAULT_CODE_LENGTH;
}


/****************************************************************/
/*                                                          */
/* Class destructor.                                        */
/*                                                          */
/****************************************************************/

chainCode::ƒchainCode()
{ free(code); }



/****************************************************************/
/*                                                          */
/* This method appends a new code to the chain. If there    */
/* is not enough memory left, the function doubles the size  */
/* of the chain code.                                       */
/* It receives as a parameter the new code to be added (c). */
/*                                                          */
/****************************************************************/

void chainCode::add(char c)
{
int l = strlen(code);

if (l >= length-1){
    length *= 2;
    code = realloc(code, length);
    }
code[l] = c;
code[l+1] = '\0';
}



/****************************************************************/
/*                                                          */
/* This method post processes a 4x chain code to generate a 1x */
/* chain code. A pointer to the 1x code is returned. The method */
/* uses the 4 following rules:                              */
/* CCCC ->  C :  reduce to one copy                         */
/*  CCC -> {} :  eliminate                                  */
/*   CC -> CC :  (ignored)                                  */
/*    C ->  C :  identity                                   */
/*                                                          */
/****************************************************************/

chainCode* chainCode::postProcess()
{
int        i = 0, j;
chainCode  *filtCode;
```

```
filtCode = new chainCode();
while (i<length){
    if (i+SCALE 1 < length){
        for (j=0; j<SCALE-1; j++)
            if (code[i+j] != code[i+j+1])
                break;
        if (j == SCALE-1){
            filtCode->add(code[i]);
            i += SCALE;
            continue;
            }
        }

    if (i+SCALE-2 < length){
        for (j=0; j<SCALE-2; j++)
            if (code[i+j] != code[i+j+1])
                break;
        if (j == SCALE-2){
            i += SCALE-1;
            continue;
            }
        }
    filtCode->add(code[i]);
    i++;
    }
return filtCode;
}


/******************************************************************/
/*                                                                */
/* A utility method to display the chain code                     */
/*                                                                */
/******************************************************************/

void chainCode::printSelf()
{ printf("\n%s", code); }
```

vectorize.C

```
#include <string.h>
#include <stdlib.h>
#include <limits.h>
#include "chainCode.h"
#include "pt2.h"

/* DEFINITION OF THE CONSTANTS */

#define CONTOUR 'c'
#define VISITED 'v'
#define BLACK '1'
#define WHITE '0'
```

```
/* DEFINITION OF THE MACROS */

#define PIX(a,b) ((b) * t_size.x + (a))
#define PIX2(a,b) ((b) * size->x + (a))
#define MIN(x,y) ((x)<(y) ? (x) : (y))
#define MAX(x,y) ((x)>(y) ? (x) : (y))


/***************************************************************/
/*                                                           */
/* This is the main function. It receives as a parameter a   */
/* bitmap image of size 'size' and outputs a chain code.     */
/* The following constraints are placed on the bitmap:       */
/* + Each pixel is encoded as a char.                        */
/* + Only white (0) and black (1) pixels are taken into      */
/*   account.                                                */
/* + The shape to encode should have no holes and should be  */
/*   in a single piece.                                      */
/*                                                           */
/***************************************************************/

chainCode* encode(pt2 *size, char *bitmap)
{
static pt2    contour_dir[8] = {{ 1,  0},
                                { 0, -1},
                                {-1,  0},
                                { 0,  1},
                                { 1, -1},
                                {-1, -1},
                                {-1,  1},
                                { 1,  1}};
chainCode    *code1,
             code4;
char         *fatmap,
             direction_code[8] = {'0','2','4','6','1','3','5','7'};
int          i,j,u,v,
             flag,
             d, distance,
             last_dir;
pt2          pixel,
             test_pixel,
             start_pixel,
             f_size,
             bbox[2] = {{INT_MAX,  INT_MAX},
                       {-INT_MAX, -INT_MAX}};

/* CREATE AN EMPTY CHAIN CODE TO RETURN THE RESULT */
code1 = new chainCode();

/* RESCAN THE BITMAP AT A GREATER RESOLUTION (4x4 GREATER) */
/* ADD TWO BLANK LINES TO THE LEFT, RIGHT, TOP AND BOTTOM  */
/* OF THE FATMAP. THESE COULD BE NECESSARY TO AVOID THE    */
/* CONTOUR TO BE DRAWN OUTSIDE OF THE BOUNDS OF THE MATRIX */
```

```
f_size.x = 2 + SCALE*size->x + 2;
f_size.y = 2 + SCALE*size->y + 2;
fatmap = malloc(f_size.x * f_size.y * sizeof(char));
for (i=0; i<f_size.x * f_size.y; i++)
    fatmap[i] = WHITE;
for (j=0; j<size->y; j++)
    for (i=0; i<size->x; i++)
        if (bitmap[PIX2(i,j)] == BLACK)
            for(v=0; v<SCALE; v++)
                for(u=0; u<SCALE; u++)
                    fatmap[PIX(2+4*i+u, 2+4*j+v)] = BLACK;

/* GENERATE THE CONTOUR OF THE BITMAP USING 4 SUCCESSIVE */
/* PASSES: FOR EACH DIRECTION, WE SCAN EACH LINE UNTIL   */
/* WE REACH A BLACK PIXEL: THE PIXEL JUST BEFORE IT IS A */
/* CONTOUR PIXEL                                         */

/* PASS 1: LEFTWARDS */
for (j=0; j<f_size.y; j++)
    for(i=1; i<f_size.x; i++)
            if (fatmap[PIX(i,j)] == BLACK){
                if (flag == 0) {
                    fatmap[PIX(i-1, j)] = CONTOUR;
                    flag = 1;
                    }
                }
            else
                flag = 0;

/* PASS 2: RIGHTWARDS */
for (j=0; j<f_size.y; j++)
    for (i=f_size.x - 1; i>=0; i--)
            if (fatmap[PIX(i,j)] == BLACK){
                if (flag == 0) {
                    fatmap[PIX(i+1, j)] = CONTOUR;
                    flag = 1;
                    }
                }
            else
                flag = 0;

/* PASS 3: DOWNWARDS */
flag = 0;
for (i=0; i<f_size.x; i++)
    for (j=0; j<f_size.y; j++)
            if (fatmap[PIX(i,j)] == BLACK){
                if (flag == 0) {
                    fatmap[PIX(i, j-1)] = CONTOUR;
                    flag = 1;
                    }
                }
            else
```

```
                      flag = 0;

/* PASS 4: UPWARDS */
flag = 0;
for (i=0; i<f_size.x; i++)
    for (j=f_size.y - 1; j>=0; j--)
            if (fatmap[PIX(i,j)] == BLACK){
                if (flag == 0) {
                    fatmap[PIX(i, j+1)] = CONTOUR;
                    flag = 1;
                    }
                }
            else
                flag = 0;


/* COMPUTE THE BOUNDING BOX OF THE CHARACTER (L,T,R,B) */
for (j=0; j<f_size.y; j++)
    for(i=1; i<f_size.x; i++)
        if (fatmap[PIX(i,j)]==CONTOUR){
            bbox[0].x = MIN(i, bbox[0].x);
            bbox[0].y = MIN(j, bbox[0].y);
            bbox[1].x = MAX(i, bbox[1].x);
            bbox[1].y = MAX(j, bbox[1].y);
            }

/* DETERMINE THE CONTOUR PIXEL CLOSEST TO THE UPPER LEFT CORNER */
/* OF THE BOUNDING BOX                                          */

distance = INT_MAX;
for (j=0; j<f_size.y; j++)
    for(i=1; i<f_size.x; i++)
        if (fatmap[PIX(i,j)]==CONTOUR){
            d = (i-bbox[0].x) * (i-bbox[0].x) + (j-bbox[0].y) * (j-bbox[0].y);
            if (d < distance) {
                distance = d;
                start_pixel.x = i;
                start_pixel.y = j;
                ]
            }


/* BEGIN THE ENCODING PROCEDURE */
pixel.x = start_pixel.x;
pixel.y = start_pixel.y;
fatmap[PIX(pixel.x, pixel.y)] = VISITED;
last_dir = 4;
while(0 < 1) {
    /* AT FIRST, CHECK THE PIXEL IN THE LAST KNOWN DIRECTION */
    addPt2(&pixel, &contour_dir[last_dir], &test_pixel);
    if (fatmap[PIX(test_pixel.x, test_pixel.y)] == CONTOUR){
        pixel.x = test_pixel.x;
        pixel.y = test_pixel.y;
```

```
            fatmap[PIX(pixel.x, pixel.y)] = VISITED;
            code4.add(direction_code[last_dir]);
            }
    /* CHECK ALL THE POSSIBLE DIRECTIONS, CLOCKWISE */
    for (i=0;i<8;i++) {
        addPt2(&pixel, &contour_dir[i], &test_pixel);
        if (fatmap[PIX(test_pixel.x, test_pixel.y)] == CONTOUR){
            pixel.x = test_pixel.x;
            pixel.y = test_pixel.y;
            fatmap[PIX(pixel.x, pixel.y)] = VISITED;
            code4.add(direction_code[i]);
            last_dir = i;
            break;
            }
        }
    if (i == 8)
        break;
    }

/* WRITE THE LAST MOVE TO THE OUTPUT VECTOR */
for (i=0; i<8; i++) {
    subPt2(&start_pixel, &pixel, &test_pixel);
    if (test_pixel.x==contour_dir[i].x && test_pixel.y==contour_dir[i].y){
        code4.add(direction_code[i]);
        break;
        }
    }

/* POST-PROCESSING LOOP:                              */
/* GO BACK TO A LOWER RESOLUTION BY FILTERING THE 4x CODE */

code1 = code4.postProcess();
return code1;
}
```

◇ **Bibliography** ◇

(Ballard and Brown 1992) Dana H. Ballard and Christopher M. Brown. *Computer Vision*. Prentice Hall, 1992.

(Feldman 1992) Tim Feldman. Generating isovalue contours from a pixmap. In David Kirk, editor, *Graphics Gems III*. AP Professional, Boston, 1992.

(Freeman 1961) H. Freeman. On the encoding of arbitrary geometric configurations. *IRE Transactions on Electronic Computers*, EC-10(2), 1961.

(Michaud *et al.* 1993) François Michaud, Ruben Gonzalez Rubio, and Alain Berkane. Etude de l'interdépendance des paramètres d'apprentissage avec la rétropropagation standard. To appear, 1993.

(Olson 1992) John Olson. Smoothing enlarged monochrome images. In Andrew Glassner, editor, *Graphics Gems*. AP Professional, Boston, 1992.

(Plaziac 1991) Nathalie Plaziac. Reconnaissance de caractères par les réseaux neuronaux. Master's thesis, Institut National de la Recherche Scientifique, Montréal, Canada, 1991.

(Schneider 1990) Philip J. Schneider. An algorithm for automatically fitting digitized curves. In David Kirk, editor, *Graphics Gems III*. AP Professional, Boston, 1990.

◊ VI.5

Reversible Straight Line Edge Reconstruction

S. C. Hsu
Computer Science Department
The Chinese University of Hong Kong
schsu@acm.org

I. H. H. Lee
Creature House, Ltd.
Hong Kong
creature@acm.org

◊ Introduction ◊

Jagged edges, appearing in digitized images due to aliasing, are often magnified when images are being manipulated (e.g., enlarged or rotated). To eliminate this nuisance, many techniques have been developed to reconstruct analytical representations of jagged edges (Chryssafis 1986), also described in other gems and/or cited below. Edge reconstruction techniques are also employed in commercial graphics packages to extract outlines from scanned artwork. This "vectorization" is an essential step when subsequent processing involves clipping frames, enlargement, or producing high-resolution output.

Published techniques include least-squares minimization (Cantoni 1971), the construction of regions of bounded precision (Williams 1981), edge following (Roth 1982), an edge inference algorithm (Bloomenthal 1983) based on the recognition of repeated jag patterns, and the use of simple templates for smoothing staircase patterns (Olsen 1990).

Some of these methods (Cantoni 1971, Williams 1981) need quadratic time to render (in the worst case), since the original data has to be traced more than once. Pattern-based techniques generate more lines than are needed, should no obvious jag patterns be identified. Finally, none of these methods is designed with an underlying digitization model in mind.

This gem presents an algorithm for fitting a sequence of line segments to the jagged edge contour formed by a chain of pixels. Only a single trace through the pixel edges is required. The algorithm is based on the inverse process of Bresenham's midpoint line algorithm (Bresenham 1965). Only integer arithmetic is required in the reconstruction process, and the time complexity of the algorithm is $O(N)$, where N is the number of raster edges in the given image. The efficiency of the algorithm makes it useful as a preprocessing pass used to locate the sharp corners prior to employing conventional curve fitting techniques, as are described in a previous gem (Schneider 1990). Furthermore, the straight lines resulting have a valuable property: They can perfectly reconstruct the

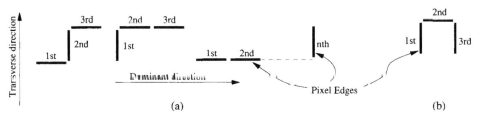

Figure 1. (a) Pixel edge patterns exhibiting dominant and transverse directions (three-edge patterns, symmetric cases omitted). (b) The U-turn case forcing a quick stop.

original jagged pattern if re-rasterized using Bresenham's algorithm. This reversibility makes it possible to use the fitted edges as a lossless data representation of the original.

◇ Outline Reconstruction ◇

Given an image in bitmap form, the positions of pixel edges can be extracted by simple comparison of adjacent pixels, described in a previous gem (Feldman 1992).

Assume that the existence of jagged edges is a result of having applied Bresenham's algorithm to a set of imaginary line segments, the set that is the objective. It follows that all the possible line segments that could be fitted to a jagged edge must fall within ± 0.5 pixel length from their corresponding pixel edges. A line segment is allowed to start or end at any position along a pixel edge or along the normal to the midpoint of that pixel edge (within ± 0.5 pixel length from the midpoint). The reason for this shall be apparent later.

Establishing the Dominant and Transverse Directions

By examining the first few consecutive pixel edges, one can establish a dominant direction (toward which more pixel edges point) and a transverse direction (toward which fewer pixel edges point) of the intended line segment. This in effect classifies the direction of the intended line segment into one of the octants as in Bresenham's algorithm. The possible patterns of the first few pixel edges are shown in Figure 1.

Inverse Midpoint Algorithm

The line extending (in the transverse direction) 0.5 pixel length on either side from the midpoint of a pixel edge is called the bounding window of that pixel edge. Now for the first pixel edge we could extend two lines from the starting point to the ± 0.5 pixel length positions on the bounding window. The slopes of these lines correspond to the maximum and minimum gradient limits for the set of possible line segments that could have produced the jagged pattern so far (Figure 2).

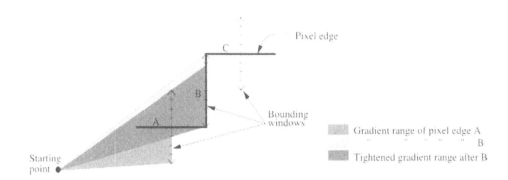

Figure 2. The bounding windows of the pixel edges. Corresponding gradient ranges are shaded.

Similarly, each subsequent pixel edge has its own bounding window and gradient limits. Therefore, in stepping onto a new pixel edge, the gradient limits are tightened. The minimum gradient limit becomes the larger of the previous and the current minimum gradient limits. Similarly, the updated maximum gradient limit is the smaller of the previous and the current maximum gradient limits.

To avoid the use of floating-point coordinates to represent the endpoints, coordinates with a predefined subpixel resolution are used. Hence, any gradient limit can be represented as a pair of integers, that is, the components of the gradient vector, dx and dy. Thus, a comparison between two gradient limits involves only a test of the sign of the cross product of the gradient vectors: $dx_1 \times dy_2 - dx_2 \times dy_1$. Note that only two integer multiplications and one integer comparison are required.

Termination Criteria

Consideration of pixel edge extension stops on meeting any of the following conditions:

1. The orientation of the next pixel edge is neither dominant nor transverse.
2. Two consecutive transverse pixel edges are encountered.
3. The maximum gradient limit no longer exceeds the minimum gradient limit.

Now the bounding window on the preceding pixel edge is the last consecutive bounding window through which one can "see" from the starting point. The fitted line segment shall end here, at a position (on the bounding window) closest to the midpoint of the last successful pixel edge; hence the assumption of the position of the starting point.

It is important that the fitted line segment does not touch any edges of the bounding windows. Otherwise, one cannot uniquely identify the appropriate pixel edge when recovering the jagged pattern.

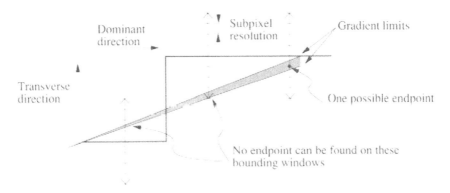

Figure 3. Establishing final location of an endpoint that cannot be located in the initial windows.

Locating the Endpoint

Because of the finite resolution of endpoint coordinates, it is possible that no endpoint can be established even before the gradient limits cross over. Three solutions to this problem are considered. The first is to introduce an extra test on the tightening of gradient limits: If there is no point within the new bounding window (under the subpixel resolution) that can satisfy the gradient limits, then the new pixel edge will not be considered. Instead, the line will end within the last bounding window. Using this method means that an extra test is needed for each pixel edge. The line segments fitted are also not the longest possible (Figure 3). This method was rejected, as it would results in many more line segments than are necessary.

The second method of solution proceeds irrespective of resolution until the gradient limits cross over. It then backtracks along previous pixel edges until an endpoint beneath the level of subpixel resolution can be found. This method finds line segments of maximum length. In practice, backtracking beyond one pixel edge is rarely required given a subpixel resolution of 1/16 pixel.

The first two methods terminate the line segments at an arbitrary point within the bounding window, for example, the one closest to the midpoint, and restart from that point. This occasionally results in shorter fitted lines having a more ragged appearance. The third method overcomes this problem by testing all the feasible ending positions within the last bounding window to determine which gives the longest continuing line. This gives the best results and increases the execution time by only a constant factor proportional to the subpixel resolution.

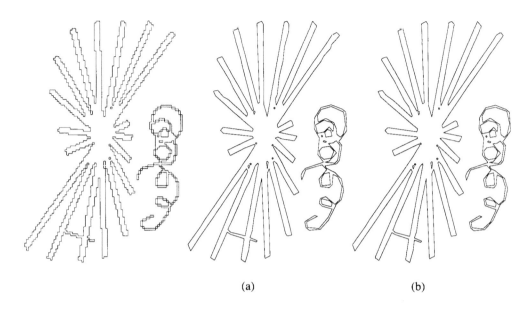

(a)   (b)

Figure 4. A test image reconstructed exactly using line segments. (a) With backtracking (276 line segments; 0.071 sec). (b) With exhaustive endpoint testing (261 line segments; 0.776 sec).

◇ Reconstructing the Jagged Edges ◇

To recover the original jagged pattern from the line segments fitted, one need only apply Bresenham's midpoint line algorithm (Heckbert 1990). Since our line segments neither start nor end at the midpoints of any pixel edge, the initial value of the *decision variable* must be preloaded with the offset having a precision scaled in proportion to the subpixel resolution. A sample implementation is presented below.

◇ C Implementation ◇

```
/* revfit.h: definitions for reversible straight line reconstruction routines */
#include "GraphicsGems.h"
#define HRZ            1
#define VRT            2
/* Watch out for the precision of `int' type. Make sure that the max */
/* coordinate value * SUBPIXRES can be stored in an `int'.            */
#define SUBPIXRES      32


/*******************************************************************/
/* typedef for Edgelist: the list of edges where lines are to be fitted */
/*******************************************************************/
```

```
typedef struct {
 int x,y;              /* in bitmap resolution         +ve      */
 int dir;              /*            --- <-- H edge      √       */
} PixelEdge;           /* (x,y)-->  * | <   V edge      | --> +ve */

typedef struct {
 int Nedges;           /* number of edges in the list            */
 int current;          /* current edge being visited             */
 PixelEdge *list;      /* the list of edges found from the pixmap */
} Edgelist;

int fitlines(Edgelist el, boolean Pretest, boolean TryAllEndPts,
             IntPoint2 *lines, int MaxLines);
void linestojagged(int Nlines, IntPoint2 *lines);

/*
 * revfit.c : edge reconstruction and the inverse process.
 */
#include <stdio.h>
#include "GraphicsGems.h"
#include "revfit.h"

#define HalfSUBPIXRES  (SUBPIXRES/2)
#define ESTABLISHED    127
#define MAXRUN         2000          /* max no of pixel edges in a line */

extern DrawPixelEdge(int x, int y, int V_H); /* a user supplied function */
                                             /* for drawing a PixelEdge  */

/*********************************************************************\
 * typedef's for sub-pixel resolution pixel edges and gradient bounds *
\*********************************************************************/
typedef struct {
    int x1,y1;   /* from (coordinates multiplied by sub-pixel resolution) */
    int x2,y2;   /* to   (coordinates multiplied by sub-pixel resolution) */
} Pedge;

typedef struct {
    int ly,lx;   /* lower limit */
    int uy,ux;   /* upper limit */
} Bound;

#define MidX(e) (((e).x1+(e).x2)/2)        /* midpt coordinates of a Pedge  */
#define MidY(e) (((e).y1+(e).y2)/2)
#define Is_Horizontal(d) (abs(d)==HRZ)  /* a horizontal direction? (1, -1) */
#define Is_Vertical(d)   (abs(d)==VRT)  /* a vertical direction?   (2, -2) */
#define Against(a,b) (!((a)|(b)))        /* whether two directions are opp. */
#define Bound_OK(b) (slopecmp((b).uy,(b).ux,(b).ly,(b).lx))
#define WithinBound(dy,dx,b) (slopecmp((dy),(dx),(b).ly,(b).lx) &&\
                             slopecmp((b).uy,(b).ux,(dy),(dx)))
```

```
/*************************************************************************
 *   Get_Pedge(): Returns a pointer to the current Pedge from the list el. *
 *                The position of the cursor of list is not modified.     *
 *                Returns NULL if no more edges in the list.              *
 *                Coordinates multiplied by sub-pixel resolution.         *
 *************************************************************************/
static Pedge *Get_Pedge(Edgelist el) {
 static Pedge e;
 int dir;
   if (el.current>=el.Nedges) return NULL;
   if (Is_Horizontal(dir=(el.list[el.current].dir))) {
    e.y1=e.y2=el.list[el.current].y*SUBPIXRES + HalfSUBPIXRES;
    e.x1=el.list[el.current].x*SUBPIXRES
         - (dir>0 ? HalfSUBPIXRES : -HalfSUBPIXRES);
    e.x2=e.x1 + (dir>0 ? SUBPIXRES : -SUBPIXRES);
 }
 else {
    e.x1=e.x2=el.list[el.current].x*SUBPIXRES + HalfSUBPIXRES;
    e.y1=el.list[el.current].y*SUBPIXRES
         - (dir>0 ? HalfSUBPIXRES : -HalfSUBPIXRES);
    e.y2=e.y1 + (dir>0 ? SUBPIXRES : -SUBPIXRES);
 }
 return &e;
} /* Get_Pedge() */

/*************************************************************************
 *       forward(): Update the cursor of the list to the next edge.      *
 *************************************************************************/
#define forward(el) (((el).current)++)

/*************************************************************************
 *       backward(): Move back the cursor of the list one place so that  *
 *                   the previous edge can be visited again.             *
 *************************************************************************/
#define backward(el) (((el).current)--)

/*************************************************\
 *       wayof(): return a direction.             *
\*************************************************/
/* the directions no.s are chosen s.t. d1==-d2 if d1,d2 are opp. */
static int wayof(Pedge e) {
 int d=e.x2-e.x1;
   return d ? d/SUBPIXRES                /* 1 or -1 for horizontal edge */
            : (e.y2 - e.y1)/HalfSUBPIXRES; /* 2 or -2 for vertical edge   */
} /* wayof() */

/*************************************************************************
 * slopecmp(): True if grad vector of the 1st is on the counter-clockwise *
 *             side of the 2nd one                                        *
 *************************************************************************/
static int slopecmp(int dy1,int dx1, int dy2,int dx2) {
   return (long)dx2*dy1 > (long)dx1*dy2;
} /* slopecmp() */
```

```
/*********************************************************************\
* calcbound(): calc the bounds (the pair of gradient limits) for the Pedge  *
\*********************************************************************/
void calcbound(int dominantdir, Pedge e, int Sx, int Sy,
               Bound* b, IntPoint2 *gradU, IntPoint2 *gradL) {
/* gradU and gradL shall be filled with the gradients just within the limits */
 int dy,dx;
    if (Is_Horizontal(dominantdir)) { /* horizontal dominant direction */
        b->uy = (e.y1+e.y2+SUBPIXRES)/2 Sy;
        b->ux = (e.x1+e.x2)/2          -Sx;
        b->ly = (e.y1+e.y2-SUBPIXRES)/2-Sy;
        gradU->x = gradL->x = b->lx = b->ux;
        gradU->y = b->uy-1; gradL->y = b->ly+1;
    }
    else { /* up or down dominant direction */
        b->uy = (e.y1+e.y2)/2          -Sy;
        b->ux = (e.x1+e.x2+SUBPIXRES)/2-Sx;
        gradU->y = gradL->y = b->ly = b->uy;
        b->lx = (e.x1+e.x2-SUBPIXRES)/2-Sx;
        gradU->x = b->ux-1; gradL->x = b->lx+1;
    }
    if (!Bound_OK(*b)) {     /* swaps the bounds if necessary */
     IntPoint2 p;
        dx=b->ux;    dy=b->uy;
        b->ux=b->lx; b->uy=b->ly;
        b->lx=dx;    b->ly=dy;
        p=*gradU; *gradU=*gradL; *gradL=p;
    }
} /* calcbound() */


/*********************************************************************
 * fitlines() : The reversible straight line edge reconstruction routine      *
 *********************************************************************/
int fitlines(Edgelist el, boolean Pretest, boolean TryAllEndPts,
             IntPoint2 *lines, int MaxNLine) {
/*-------------------------------------------------------------------*
 * el          : The supplied list of PixelEdges.
 * Pretest     : 1=perform pre-test on each pixel edge, i.e., stop as soon as
 *                  a valid end pt cannot be found on a pixel edge.
 *               0=Allows stepping back.
 * TryAllEndPts: 1=Try all possible end-pts, 0=Use the one closest to mid-pt.
 * lines[]      : A preallocated array to be filled with end pts of fitted lines
 *               Note: Coordinates of the end pts are multiplied by SUBPIXRES.
 * MaxNLine     : The size of the lines[] array.
 *-------------------------------------------------------------------*/
int i,linescount,startp,Nendpt,Nstartpt,NPedges,Nbound;       /* counters */
int Sx,Sy,Ex,Ey,  Ux,Uy,Lx,Ly,  maindir,transvrsc,dnow,  ndir,dir[J];
flag breaktrace, starttrace;                                  /* flags    */
int currentsave, bestpt, maxlen, bestpt_currentsave, bestpt_Nendpt;
IntPoint2 startpts[SUBPIXRES],endlist[SUBPIXRES],bestpt_endlist[SUBPIXRES];
Pedge Pedgehistory[MAXRUN],e,last,*nextp,estartsave,bestpt_last;
Bound bound[MAXRUN];
```

```
el.current=0;                          /* set cursor to the first edge */
e = *Get_Pedge(el);                    /* first edge                    */
Sx = MidX(e);
Sy = MidY(e);

if (!TryAllEndPts)  {
  lines[0].x = Sx;                     /* record the 1st starting pt.  */
  lines[0].y = Sy;
  linescount=1;
}
else  {
 flag hori = Is_Horizontal(wayof(e));
 Nstartpt=0;
 startpts[0].x = Sx;
 startpts[0].y = Sy;
 for (i=1;i<HalfSUBPIXRES;i++) { /* the list of possible init. starting pts */
   startpts[Nstartpt  ].x =  hori ? Sx-i : Sx;
   startpts[Nstartpt++].y = !hori ? Sy+i : Sy;
   startpts[Nstartpt  ].x =  hori ? Sx-i : Sx;
   startpts[Nstartpt++].y = !hori ? Sy+i : Sy;
 }
 startp=0;   /* counter for the list of possible starting pts (startpts[]) */
 bestpt_currentsave=currentsave=el.current;   /* save these for rewinding */
 estartsave=e;
 maxlen=bestpt=-1;                     /* no best starting pt (bestpt) yet */
 linescount=0;
} /* if (!TryAllEndPts) .. else .. */

for (starttrace=TRUE;;) {              /* loop for all PixelEdges */
 if (starttrace) {                     /* beginning of a new line segment  */
 dir[0]=wayof(e);    ndir=1;           /* no.of distinct directions so far */
 starttrace=0;  breaktrace=0;
 Pedgehistory[0]=e;                    /* the first Pedge traced */
 NPedges=1;                            /* reset the counters      */
 Nbound=0;
 } /* if (starttrace) */

 last=e;
 forward(el);                          /* go on to the next PixelEdge */
 if ((nextp=Get_Pedge(el))!=NULL) {    /* get a new Pedge             */
  Pedgehistory[NPedges++]=*nextp;
  e=*nextp;
  dnow=wayof(e);                       /* direction of the current edge    */
 }

 if (nextp==NULL || ndir==ESTABLISHED){ /* maindir and trnsvrse established */
 Bound b;
 IntPoint2 gradU,gradL;
 flag lowerupdated, upperupdated;

 if (nextp!=NULL) {
  calcbound(maindir,e,Sx,Sy,&b,&gradU,&gradL);
```

```
bound[Nbound]=bound[Nbound-1];

lowerupdated-upperupdated=FALSE;
if (slopecmp(bound[Nbound-1].uy,bound[Nbound-1].ux,
             b.uy,b.ux)) {              /* update the upper limit */
 bound[Nbound].uy=b.uy;
 bound[Nbound].ux=b.ux;
 upperupdated=TRUE;
}
if (slopecmp(b.ly,b.lx,
             bound[Nbound-1].ly,
             bound[Nbound-1].lx)) { /* update the lower limit */
 bound[Nbound].ly=b.ly;
 bound[Nbound].lx=b.lx;
 lowerupdated=TRUE;
}
} /* if (nextp!=NULL) */

if (nextp==NULL ||                              /* no more PixelEdge */
    (dnow!=trnsvrse && dnow!=maindir)    ||     /* U-turn            */
    (dnow==trnsvrse && dnow==wayof(last)) ||    /* 2 trnsvrse edges  */
    !Bound_OK(bound[Nbound]) ||                 /* not within limits */
    (Pretest &&    /* if Pretest, check if there is any pt within limits */
     ((lowerupdated && !WithinBound(gradU.y,gradU.x,bound[Nbound])) ||
      (upperupdated && !WithinBound(gradL.y,gradL.x,bound[Nbound]))))) {
            /* now we shall calculate the starting pt for the next trace */
 for (;;) {/* loop until the endpoint lies within the gradient limits  */
  int dx,dy,tmp;         flag exact,EndptOK;

  Ex=MidX(last); Ey=MidY(last);
  if (Nbound==0) { /* i.e. first few PixelEdges. therefore mid-pt is ok  */
   if (TryAllEndPts){
    endlist[0].x=Ex; endlist[0].y=Ey;
    Nendpt=1;
   }
   break;              /* end pt found */
  }

  b = bound[Nbound-1];

  dx= Ex - Sx;              /* the slope of the mid-pt of the last Pedge  */
  dy= Ey - Sy;

  if (TryAllEndPts && el.current-currentsave>maxlen) {
  /* find all possible end pts only if length longer than maxlen so far  */
    int h,addy,addx;

    if (abs(maindir)==1) { addy=1; addx=0; } else {addy=0; addx=1;}
    if (WithinBound(dy,dx,b)) {                /* check mid-pt first  */
     endlist[0].x=Ex; endlist[0].y=Ey; Nendpt=1;
    }
```

```
     else Nendpt=0;
     for (h=1; h<SUBPIXRES/2; h++) {                    /* offset from mid pt  */
       if (WithinBound(dy+addy*h,dx+addx*h,b)) {
        endlist[Nendpt  ].x = Ex + addx*h;
        endlist[Nendpt++].y = Ey + addy*h;
       }
       else if (WithinBound(dy-addy*h,dx-addx*h,b)) {
        endlist[Nendpt  ].x = Ex - addx*h;
        endlist[Nendpt++].y = Ey - addy*h;
       }
     } /* for (h) */
     Ex=endlist[0].x; Ey=endlist[0].y;
     EndptOK = Nendpt>0;
   }
   else { /* TryAllEndPts==FALSE. just calc the pt closest to the mid-pt  */
    if (!slopecmp(dy,dx,b.ly,b.lx)) {
     /*
      * dy dx is equal or below the lower limit.
      * i.e. the slope just above the lower limit should be taken.
      * if the lower gradient limit hits exactly on a sub-pixel res point,
      *   the truncation of the integer division has done part of the job.
      */
     if (Is_Horizontal(maindir)) {
      tmp= dx*b.ly;   exact= (dx==0 || tmp%b.lx==0);
      Ey = tmp/b.lx + Sy + (b.lx>0 ? (b.ly>0 ? 1        : exact)
                                   : (b.ly>0 ? -exact : -1    ));
     }
     else {
      tmp= dy*b.lx;   exact= (dy==0 || tmp%b.ly==0);
      Ex = tmp/b.ly + Sx + (b.ly>0 ? (b.lx>0 ? -exact : -1    )
                                   : (b.lx>0 ? 1        : exact));
     }
     EndptOK = Pretest || WithinBound(Ey-Sy,Ex-Sx,b);
    }
    else if (!slopecmp(b.uy,b.ux,dy,dx)) {
     /*
      * dy dx is equal or above the upper limit.
      * i.e. the slope just below the upper limit should be taken.
      * if the upper gradient limit hits exactly on a sub-pixel res point,
      *   the truncation of the integer division has done part of the job.
      */
     if (Is_Horizontal(maindir)) {
      tmp= dx*b.uy;   exact= (tmp%b.ux==0);
      Ey = tmp/b.ux + Sy + (b.ux>0 ? (b.uy>0 ? -exact :-1     )
                                   : (b.uy>0 ? 1        : exact));
     }
     else {
      tmp= dy*b.ux;   exact= (tmp%b.uy==0);
      Ex = tmp/b.uy + Sx + (b.uy>0 ? (b.ux>0 ? 1        : exact)
                                   : (b.ux>0 ? -exact :-1     ));
     }
     EndptOK = Pretest || WithinBound(Ey-Sy,Ex-Sx,b);
    }
```

```
    else       /* dy,dx is within the limits. i.e. midpoint is taken. */
     EndptOK=1;
    } /* if (TryAllEndPts)..else.. */

   if (EndptOK) break;     /* if Pretest is TRUE, EndptOK always TRUE */
   else {     /* no valid endpoint can be found, step back one edge */
    backward(el);
    last = Pedgehistory[--NPedges-2];
    Nbound--;
   }
  } /* for (;;) */                         /* until a valid end pt is found */
  breaktrace=TRUE;                         /* one line segment found.        */
 }
 else {                                    /* limits not crossed over yet    */
  Nbound++;                                /* one more new valid bound       */
  continue;                                /* continue to get another Pedge */
 } /* if (various trace breaking conditions) */
} /* if (nextp==NULL || ndir==ESTABLISHED) */
else {  /* i.e. dominant and trnsvrse direction not yet established */
  breaktrace = FALSE;
  if (ndir<3) {
   for (i=0;i<ndir;i++) {                 /* compare with previous dir's   */
    if (against(dnow,dir[i])) {           /* there is a `U' turn ...         */
     breaktrace = TRUE;                   /* therefore an early stop         */
     Ex=MidX(last);   Ey=MidY(last);
     if (TryAllEndPts) {
       endlist[0].x=Ex; endlist[0].y=Ey;
       Nendpt=1;
     } /* if (TryAllEndPts) */
    } /* for () */
   }
   if (ndir<2 || dnow!=dir[1] || dir[0]!=dir[1]) {
    dir[ndir]=dnow;
    ndir++;
   }
  }

  if (ndir==3)                 /* now we can establish the directions... */
  {                            /* _      |  */
   if (dir[0]!=dir[1]) {       /* _|  or _| */
    maindir=dir[2];                                       /*   | */
    if (dir[1]==dir[2]) {                                 /*  _| */
     trnsvrse=dir[0];          /* the 1st dir is the trnsvrse dir        */
     if (Is_Horizontal(maindir)) {
      Ux = Lx = MidX(e) - Sx;
      Uy = (Ly = e.y1-Sy-HalfSUBPIXRES) +SUBPIXRES;
     }
     else {
      Uy = Ly = MidY(e) - Sy;
      Ux = (Lx = e.x1-Sx-HalfSUBPIXRES) +SUBPIXRES;
     }
    }
```

```
     else {                                                  /*   _    */
      trnsvrse=dir[1];                                        /*  _|    */
      if (Is_Horizontal(maindir)) {
       Lx = Ux = MidX(e)-Sx;
       Ly = (Uy = MidY(e)+HalfSUBPIXRES-Sy) -SUBPIXRES;
      }
      else {
       Ly = Uy = MidY(e)-Sy;
       Lx = (Ux = MidX(e)+HalfSUBPIXRES-Sx) -SUBPIXRES;
      }
     }
    }
    else {                                                   /* __.....| */
     maindir=dir[0];
     trnsvrse=dir[2];
     if (Is_Horizontal(maindir)) {
      Lx = e.x1 + (maindir>0 ? -HalfSUBPIXRES : HalfSUBPIXRES) - Sx;
      Ux = Lx + (maindir>0 ? SUBPIXRES : -SUBPIXRES);
      Uy = Ly = MidY(e) - Sy;
     }
     else {
      Ly = e.y1 + (maindir>0 ? -HalfSUBPIXRES : HalfSUBPIXRES) - Sy ;
      Uy = Ly + (maindir>0 ? SUBPIXRES : -SUBPIXRES);
      Ux = Lx = MidX(e) - Sx;
     }
    }
    if (slopecmp(Ly,Lx,Uy,Ux)) {        /* swap the grad limits if necessary */
     bound[0].uy=Ly; bound[0].ux=Lx;   /* Ly Lx larger */
     bound[0].ly=Uy; bound[0].lx=Ux;
    }
    else {
     bound[0].uy=Uy; bound[0].ux=Ux;   /* Uy Ux larger */
     bound[0].ly=Ly; bound[0].lx=Lx;
    }
    Nbound=1;                          /* first bound established */
    ndir = ESTABLISHED;
   } /* if (ndir==3) */
 } /* if (ndir==ESTABLISHED)...else... */
                                           /*-------------------------*/
if (breaktrace) {                          /*      one line ended     */
                                           /*-------------------------*/
 backward(el);     /* last pixel edge shall be the start of another line.   */

 if (TryAllEndPts) {
  if (maxlen < (el.current-currentsave))  {   /* longer than the longest */
   maxlen = el.current-currentsave;           /* longest distance so far */
   bestpt_last=last;                          /* save the last edge      */
   bestpt=startp;                             /* update the best pt so far*/
   bestpt_currentsave=el.current;             /* save the cursor for el  */
   for (i=0; i<Nendpt; i++) bestpt_endlist[i]=endlist[i]; /* save end pts */
   bestpt_Nendpt=Nendpt;                      /* save the no. of end pts */
  }
```

```
       startp++;                            /* next starting pt in startpts[]    */
       if (startp >= Nstartpt) {            /* all starting pts have been tried  */
        currentsave=el.current=bestpt_currentsave;    /* save the ending pos    */
        estartsave=e=bestpt_last;                      /* save the ending Pedge  */
        lines[linescount++] = startpts[bestpt];        /* record the best pt     */
        if (linescount>=MaxNLine) return -1;           /* too many lines         */
        if (bestpt_currentsave>=el.Nedges-1) {         /* no more Pixel edges ?  */
         lines[linescount++]=bestpt_endlist[0];        /* record end pt as well  */
         return linescount>=MaxNLine ? -1 : linescount;/* done                   */
        }

        Nstartpt=bestpt_Nendpt;        /* use the list of end pts as starting pts */
        for (i=0; i<bestpt_Nendpt; i++) startpts[i]=bestpt_endlist[i];

        startp=0;                      /* consider the first one in the new list  */
        Sx=startpts[0].x; Sy=startpts[0].y;
        maxlen=bestpt=-1;              /* reset maxlen and bestpt to undefined    */
       }
       else { /* i.e. startp<Nstartpt.  try next starting point                   */
        Sx=startpts[startp].x; Sy=startpts[startp].y; /* next starting pt         */
                                                      /* rewind and start again   */
        el.current=currentsave;
        e=last=estartsave;
       } /* if (startp>=Nstartpt) ... else ... */
      }
      else { /* i.e. TryAllEndPts==FALSE.  simply start at the end pt again       */
       Sx=Ex; Sy=Ey; e=last;
       lines[linescount].x=Ex; lines[linescount++].y=Ey;
       if (linescount>=MaxNLine) return -1;           /* too many lines           */
       if (el.current>=el.Nedges-1) return linescount;/* no more Pedges, done     */
      }
      starttrace=TRUE;                                /* start again              */
     } /* if (breaktrace) */
   } /* for (starttrace=TRUE;;) infinite loop */
 } /* fitlines() */

/*********************************************************************************\
 *              T H E    I N V E R S E    P R O C E S S                           *
 \*********************************************************************************/
#define divisible(a,b) ((a)%(b)==0)
#define ishori(x,y) (divisible(x,SUBPIXRES)||\
                     divisible(y+HalfSUBPIXRES,SUBPIXRES))
#define isvert(x,y) (divisible(y,SUBPIXRES)||\
                     divisible(x+HalfSUBPIXRES,SUBPIXRES))
#define sign(x) ((x)>=0 ? 1 : -1)
#define Trunc(n) ((n)/SUBPIXRES*SUBPIXRES)
static int lastx,lasty,lastdir;             /* to avoid duplicated pixel edges */

static void drawHPedge(int x, int y) {    /* draw a horizontal pixel edge      */
 if (lastx==x && lasty==y && lastdir==HRZ) /* starting edge==last ending edge  */
   return;
```

```
 lastx=x; lasty=y; lastdir=HRZ;
 DrawPixelEdge(x/SUBPIXRES, y/SUBPIXRES, HRZ);    /* call the user function   */
} /* drawHPedge() */

static void drawVPedge(int x, int y) {     /* draw a vertical pixel edge      */
 if (lastx==x && lasty==y && lastdir==VRT) /* starting edge==last ending edge */
   return;
 lastx=x; lasty=y; lastdir=VRT;
 DrawPixelEdge(x/SUBPIXRES, y/SUBPIXRES, VRT);    /* call the user function    */
} /* drawVPedge() */

/*************************************************************************
 * makejaggedline(): A modified Bresenham's midpoint algorithm. Based on *
 *    the code from the original Graphics Gem.  Neither the starting pt  *
 *    nor the ending pt need to be at the mid-pt of a pixel edge.        *
 *    The decision variable has been scaled by SUBPIXRES and preloaded   *
 *    with the offset from a `proper' starting pt, i.e. the mid-pt of the *
 *    first pixel edge pointing to the dominant direction.               *
 *************************************************************************/
static makejaggedline(int x1, int y1, int x2, int y2) {
 int d, x, y, ax, ay, sx, sy, dx, dy, finaltrnsvrse;

 dx = x2-x1;  ax = abs(dx)*SUBPIXRES;  sx = sign(dx)*SUBPIXRES;
 dy = y2-y1;  ay = abs(dy)*SUBPIXRES;  sy = sign(dy)*SUBPIXRES;
                                           /*============*/
 if (ax>ay)                                /* x dominant */
 {                                         /*============*/
  if (isvert(x1,y1)) /* 1st edge is trnsvrse. skip to the mid-pt   */
  {                    /* of the next dominant dir edge.           */
   y=Trunc(y1 + HalfSUBPIXRES) + sy/2;
   x=Trunc(x1) + HalfSUBPIXRES + sx/2;
   drawVPedge(x-sx/2,y-sy/2);             /* draw the skipped edge */
  }
  else { /* 1st edge is dominant. shift to the mid-pt */
   x=Trunc(x1 + HalfSUBPIXRES);
   y=Trunc(y1) + HalfSUBPIXRES;
  }
  /* preload decision var `d' with offset x-x1, y-y1. (if any) */
  d = ay - (ax>>1) + ay*(x-x1)/sx - ax*(y-y1)/sy;
  for (;;)   {
   drawHPedge(x,y);
   if (abs(x-x2) < HalfSUBPIXRES) return; /* final edge is a dominant one */
   x += sx;
   finaltrnsvrse = dx>0 ? x>x2: x<x2;
   if (d>0 || finaltrnsvrse) {       /* if the final edge is a trnsvrse */
    drawVPedge(x-sx/2,y+sy/2);             /* one, draw it before stopping    */
    y += sy;
    d -= ax;
   }
   if (finaltrnsvrse) return;
   d += ay;
  } /* for (;;) */
```

```
    }                                       /*============*/
    else                                    /* y dominant */
    {                                       /*============*/
     if (ishori(x1,y1)) /* 1st edge trnsvrse. skip to the mid-pt  */
     {                    /* of the next dominant dir edge         */
      x=Trunc(x1 + HalfSUBPIXRES) + sx/2;
      y=Trunc(y1) + HalfSUBPIXRES + sy/2;
      drawHPedge(x-sx/2, y-sy/2);           /* draw the skipped edge */
     }
     else { /* 1st edge is dominant. shift to the mid-pt */
      x=Trunc(x1) + HalfSUBPIXRES;
      y=Trunc(y1 + HalfSUBPIXRES);
     }
     /* preload decision var `d' with offset x-x1, y-y1 (if any) */
     d = ax - (ay>>1) + ax*(y-y1)/sy - ay*(x-x1)/sx;
     for (;;) {
      drawVPedge(x,y);
      if (abs(y-y2) < HalfSUBPIXRES) return; /* final edge is a dominant one */
      y += sy;
      finaltrnsvrse = dy>0 ? y>y2 : y<y2;
      if (d>0 || finaltrnsvrse)  {          /* if the final one is a trnsvrse */
       drawHPedge(x+sx/2, y-sy/2);          /* one, draw it before stopping.  */
       x += sx;
       d -= ay;
      }
      if (finaltrnsvrse) return;
      d += ax;
     } /* for (;;) */
    } /* if (ax>ay)... else ...*/
} /* makejaggedline() */

/************************************************************************
 * linestojagged(): reconstruct a sequence of pixel edges from given lines *
 *                  by calling the makejaggedline() function.              *
 ************************************************************************/
void linestojagged(int Nlines, IntPoint2 *lines) {
 int from_x, from_y, i;
 lastdir=0;
 for (from_x=lines[0].x, from_y=lines[0].y, i=1; i<Nlines; i++) {
  makejaggedline(from_x,from_y,lines[i].x,lines[i].y);
  from_x=lines[i].x;     from_y=lines[i].y;
 }
} /* linetojagged() */
```

◇ **Bibliography** ◇

(Bloomenthal 1983) Jules Bloomenthal. Edge inference with applications to antialiasing. In *Computer Graphics (SIGGRAPH '83 Proceedings)*, Volume 17, pages 157–162, July 1983.

(Bresenham 1965) J. E. Bresenham. Algorithm for computer control of a digital plotter. *IBM Systems Journal*, 4(1):25–30, 1965.

(Cantoni 1971) A. Cantoni. Optimal curve fitting with piecewise linear functions. *IEEE Transactions on Computers*, C-20(1), January 1971.

(Chryssafis 1986) A. Chryssafis. Anti-aliasing of computer-generated images: A picture independent approach. *Computer Graphics Forum*, 5:125–129, 1986.

(Feldman 1992) Tim Feldman. Generating isovalue contours from a pixmap. In David Kirk, editor, *Graphics Gems III*, Chapter 1.6, pages 29–33. AP Professional, Boston, 1992.

(Heckbert 1990) Paul S. Heckbert. Digital line drawing. In Andrew Glassner, editor, *Graphics Gems*, Chapter 2.10, pages 99–100. AP Professional, Boston, 1990.

(Olsen 1990) John Olsen. Smoothing enlarged monochrome images. In Andrew Glassner, editor, *Graphics Gems*, pages 166–170. AP Professional, Boston, 1990.

(Roth 1982) Scott D. Roth. Ray casting for modeling solids. *Computer Graphics and Image Processing*, 18:109–144, 1982.

(Schneider 1990) Philip J. Schneider. An algorithm for automatically fitting digitized curves. In Andrew Glassner, editor, *Graphics Gems*, Chapter 11.8, pages 612–626. AP Professional, Boston, 1990.

(Williams 1981) Charles M. Williams. Bounded straight-line approximation of digitized planar curves and lines. *Computer Graphics and Image Processing*, 16:370–381, 1981.

VI.6

Priority-based Adaptive Image Refinement

Rajesh Sharma
Indiana University
Bloomington, Indiana
rsharma@cs.indiana.edu

◊ **Introduction** ◊

This gem presents an extension to image refinement algorithms by incorporating adaptive refinement: an image based on priority.

The generation of pixel values, whether by an abstract process (rendering) or by empirical sampling (scanning), is a sequential process. For interactive purposes, this does not provide the user a "thumbnail" preview of the entire image. Fast production of reduced-quality image is of value both in previewing systems and in production of frames whose objects show rapid, dynamic changes.

A previous gem (Hollasch 1992) addresses the issue of providing an overall image of reduced quality. His algorithm repeatedly subdivides the image into equal-size rectangles and displays each rectangle as a solid region whose uniform color is taken from the lower-left corner of that rectangle. It may be regarded as a low-resolution (point) sampling of the image rendered by a ray tracer. Subsequently, the pixel is replicated to the full size of the rectangle (Schumacher 1991). The main drawback of the technique is that it necessarily treats all the rectangles equally. Thus, it fails to exploit the homogeneity present, whose subdivision is better deferred.

In contrast, an adaptive algorithm prioritizes rectangles, providing demonstrably better results at an equivalent cost of execution (Figure 1; Color Plate VI.6). The main algorithm, which maintains and makes references to a heap-based priority queue, is described below.

◊ **Pseudocode** ◊

```
1.    insert(heap, first_rect);
2.    while !empty(heap) do {
3.        top_rect = top(heap);
4.        draw_rect(top_rect);
5.        if !((top_rect.width == 1) && (top_rect.height == 1)) {
```

```
6.              split(top_rect, sub_rect_A, sub_rect_B);
7.              new_sample(sub_rect_A);
8.              new_priority(sub_rect_A);
9.              insert(heap, sub_rect_A);
10.             new_sample(sub_rect_B);
11.             new_priority(sub_rect_B);
12.             insert(heap, sub_rect_B);
13.         }
14.     }
```

◇ Details ◇

Each heap entry represents a rectangular region containing the following information about the region: the lower-left and the upper-right corners, the color of the sample at the lower-left corner, and the priority of the region. Displaying a solid rectangle is platform-dependent and is assumed to be much faster than the sampling process. Splitting of a rectangle is always performed along the longest dimension of the rectangle, that is, if the length of the rectangle is more than its width, then the rectangle is divided vertically into two equal-size subrectangles; otherwise, the rectangle is divided horizontally.

There are various metrics for priority, ranging from the more complicated sequential probability test ratio (SPRT) (Maillot *et al.* 1992) to the simplistic area of the rectangle. [The algorithm then degenerates to a form similar to the method of an earlier gem (Hollasch 1992).] Here, we describe an easy-to-implement, fast metric to assign priorities, based on area and intensity variation of the region. The formula used for calculating priorities can be expressed as

$$P_{L,R} = a_1 * A + a_2 * I + a_3 * P_p, \tag{1}$$

where $P_{L,R}$ denotes the priority of the rectangle with lower-left and upper-right corners at L and R, respectively. A defines the fractional screen area:

$$A = (R_x - L_x + 1) * (R_y - L_y + 1)/(N_x * N_y), \tag{2}$$

where N_x and N_y are the width and height of the image, respectively. P_p is the priority of the parent rectangle, and I is the intensity variation of a region and is computed as follows. The average luminance value (sum of r, g, and b components) for each of the top, bottom, left, and right external boundaries of a rectangle are read from the frame buffer. The absolute difference with the luminance value of the rectangle color is then computed, and the maximum of these differences is used as a measure for intensity variation, after normalizing its range to $[0, 1]$. The parameters all lie on the unit interval: $0 \leq \{A, I, P\} \leq 1$. Then, a_1, a_2, and a_3 are constants that can be varied to give more

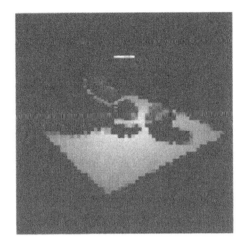

Nonadaptive (8000 rectangles)

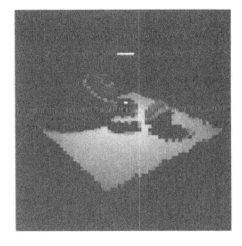

Nonadaptive (16,000 rectangles)

Adaptive (8000 rectangles)

Adaptive (16,000 rectangles)

Figure 1. Progressive refinement.

control over the refinement process. To keep the range of the priorities in $[0, 1]$, we have $\sum_{i=1}^{3} a_i = 1$, leaving two control parameters, as $a_3 = 1 - (a_1 + a_2)$.

Techniques suggesting a rectangle sampling at other than the lower-left corner of the pixel (rectangular) region exist (Chiu *et al.* 1994) (see also page 359) and can be incorporated into the algorithm at the cost of storing the location of the sample.

◇ **Bibliography** ◇

(Chiu *et al.* 1994) Kenneth Chiu, Peter Shirley, and Changyaw Wang. Multi-jittered sampling. In Paul Heckbert, editor, *Graphics Gems IV*, pages 9–19. AP Professional, Boston, 1994.

(Hollasch 1992) Steve Hollasch. Progessive image refinement via gridded sampling. In David Kirk, editor, *Graphics Gems III*, pages 358–361. AP Professional, Boston, 1992.

(Maillot *et al.* 1992) J-L Maillot, L. Carraro, and B. Peroche. Progessive ray tracing. In Alan Chalmers and Derek Paddon, editors, *Third Eurographics Workshop on Rendering*, pages 9–19. Consolidation Express, Bristol, 1992.

(Painter and Sloan 1989) James Painter and Kenneth Sloan. Antialiased ray tracing by adaptive progressive refinement. In Jeffrey Lane, editor, *Computer Graphics (SIGGRAPH '89 Proceedings)*, Volume 23, pages 281–288, July 1989.

(Schumacher 1991) Dale Schumacher. Fast anamorphic image scaling. In James Arvo, editor, *Graphics Gems II*, pages 78–79. AP Professional, Boston, 1991.

◊ VI.7

Sampling Patterns Optimized for Uniform Distribution of Edges

Robert A. Cross
Indiana University
Bloomington, Indiana
rcross@cs.indiana.edu

◊ Introduction ◊

This gem examines the results of an automated gradient search of optimized sampling patterns. The intent is to find a set of samples that perform better than other sampling patterns, yet require no evaluation as they are precomputed.

The present approach extends methods described in a previous gem (Chiu *et al.* 1994) whose introduction is restated below:

> Monte-Carlo integration is often used to compute pixel values. For every pixel, a set of sample points is generated. The radiances of each point are then computed and averaged. To avoid aliasing, the sample points must be generated randomly such that every point is equally likely to be selected. However, a sampling pattern that is "too random" can overemphasize some parts of the pixel, resulting in excessive noise unless the number of samples is very large.

◊ The Experiment ◊

The test images are a set of uniformly distributed anti-aliased lines, produced by exhaustive oversampling in order to produce an "exact" image (Figure 1). It is assumed that any sampling pattern that performs well on this test image will perform well on any pixels with a uniform edge orientation distribution. The optimal sampling patterns will then exhibit minimal mean-squared error relative to the test image.

A Monte-Carlo integration was conducted on the Silicon Graphics Onyx RealityEngine, taking advantage of its hardware accumulation buffer (Haeberli and Akeley 1990) as follows: For each sample, translate the viewpoint from the origin by the specified fraction of a screen pixel and scan-convert the line distribution; add the resulting image into the accumulation buffer. The contents of the accumulation buffer represent the final image scaled up by N_s (the number of samples). The mean-squared error is the sum of the squared difference between the generated image and the reference image, divided by the total pixels: $1/N_p \sum_{i,j} (\text{test}_{ij} - \text{exact}_{ij})^2$. This error measure defines the goodness of a set of samples.

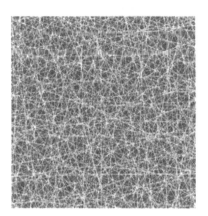

Figure 1. The goal of the gradient search, an image of 400 lines in a uniform distribution anti-aliased with 1000 samples.

Figure 2. Another reference image; a simple test scene sampled 1000 times.

A genetic algorithm performed the gradient search, combining portions of the best-performing sets of samples, with mutation introduced to avoid stagnation. The nature of a genetic algorithm requires a large population to ensure diversity; hardware support kept run times within reason.

The initial population was composed of *random*, *N-rooks* (Shirley 1991), *jittered* (Cook *et al.* 1984), and *multijittered* (Chiu *et al.* 1994) samples. In each successive generation, the sampling patterns were crossbred according to fitness to produce a new test set. The offspring were compared against the reference image to produce new fitness measures.

◇ Results ◇

Optimized sampling patterns of $N_s = 4$ and $N_s = 16$ are shown in Figures 3 and 4.

The per-pixel mean-squared error of the optimized samples is much better than even multijittered at four samples per pixel (Table 1); the advantage decreases with increasing samples per pixel. Time constraints restrict present results to $N_s \leq 64$; the trend suggests similar performance for larger sizes. A comparison of all methods against a

Table 1. Average mean-squared error in reproducing Figure 1 (maximum error is $255^2 = 65025$).

N_s	Random	N-Rooks	Jittered	Multijittered	**Optimized**
4	1457.60	1027.18	897.09	800.79	**501.87**
16	355.41	721.01	125.99	108.96	**96.16**
64	134.58	703.88	19.47	18.27	**23.93**
256	36.04	702.69	7.30	7.52	*no data*

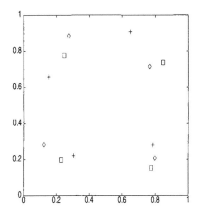

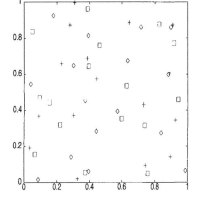

Figure 3. Three optimized sets of four samples.

Figure 4. Three optimized sets of sixteen samples.

simple test scene (Figure 2) appears in Table 2. The optimized sample sets are strongly competitive for $N_s \leq 16$. For larger sizes, while the accuracy of the optimized sets is finer than one bit per color component, the comparatively weaker performance indicates that these sample sets would benefit from further optimization.

◇ **Conclusions** ◇

Sampling patterns optimized for a uniform distribution of edges may be found using an experimental gradient search. The results of the experiment support the initial hypothesis that samples optimized for a uniform distribution of edges will produce low error for images in general; that is, one can use fewer samples. The speed of contemporary graphics hardware can generate a large set of samples quickly; a large static set of sampling patterns would be a useful tool.

Because of the size limitations, only sample sets of moderate size are reproduced on this volume's diskette; larger sample sets (and the software that produced them) are available on the Gems FTP servers and its mirrors.

Table 2. Average mean-squared error in reproducing the scene shown in Figure 2.

N_s	Random	*N* Rooks	Jittered	Multijittered	**Optimized**
4	12.3337	5.9019	7.7491	4.8132	**4.30309**
16	3.1280	2.9004	0.8900	0.5607	**0.88102**
64	0.6886	2.7522	0.1175	0.0783	**0.23542**
256	0.3170	2.7435	0.0210	0.0161	*no data*

◇ **Example Sampling Patterns** ◇

```
/* Example sample patterns appearing in Graphics Gems V
   ``Sampling Patterns Optimized for Uniform Distribution of Edges''
   Figures 3 and 4. */

typedef float sample[2];

sample foursamples[3][4]={
   {{0.274942,  0.884325},   {0.797099,  0.207128},
    {0.765063,  0.715779},   {0.122774,  0.282759}},

   {{0.152302,  0.657716},   {0.649413,  0.907929},
    {0.305133,  0.221223},   {0.784722,  0.280605}},

   {{0.775219,  0.152203},   {0.846312,  0.737633},
    {0.247618,  0.777035},   {0.228821,  0.197385}}};

sample sixteensamples[3][16]={
   {{0.755279,  0.0497319},  {0.384479,  0.688268},
    {0.666094,  0.868388},   {0.317172,  0.0331764},
    {0.729309,  0.43103},    {0.0867931, 0.368519},
    {0.322668,  1.0},        {0.442302,  0.572752},
    {0.889074,  0.606985},   {0.0343768, 0.191404},
    {0.910321,  0.872547},   {0.92479,   0.345332},
    {0.289126,  0.389783},   {0.896551,  0.141167},
    {0.23357,   0.678942},   {0.11281,   0.526939}},

   {{0.740161,  0.0942363},  {0.384479,  0.688268},
    {0.642662,  0.884825},   {0.324146,  0.0213393},
    {0.729309,  0.43103},    {0.0867931, 0.368519},
    {0.306925,  0.995787},   {0.442302,  0.572752},
    {0.889074,  0.606985},   {0.0343768, 0.191404},
    {0.910321,  0.872547},   {0.92479,   0.345332},
    {0.299325,  0.371848},   {0.896551,  0.141167},
    {0.226811,  0.658172},   {0.27796,   0.873217}},

   {{0.73534,   0.316016},   {0.755279,  0.0497319},
    {0.152649,  0.442638},   {0.917626,  0.771549},
    {0.0492709, 0.836601},   {0.0642901, 0.155284},
    {0.94238,   0.458705},   {0.392657,  0.644079},
    {0.626425,  0.534164},   {0.0918845, 0.468493},
    {0.372743,  0.0552449},  {0.217678,  0.319869},
    {0.460074,  0.759592},   {0.827202,  0.875453},
    {0.596844,  0.352386},   {0.387125,  0.96096}}};
```

◇ **Bibliography** ◇

(Chiu *et al.* 1994) Kenneth Chiu, Pete Shirley, and Changyaw Wang. Multi-jittered sampling. In Paul Heckbert, editor, *Graphics Gems IV*, pages 370–374. AP Professional, Boston, 1994.

(Cook *et al.* 1984) Robert L. Cook, Thomas Porter, and Loren Carpenter. Distributed ray tracing. In Hank Christiansen, editor, *Computer Graphics (SIGGRAPH '84 Proceedings)*, Volume 18, pages 137–145, July 1984.

(Haeberli and Akeley 1990) Paul E. Haeberli and Kurt Akeley. The accumulation buffer: Hardware support for high-quality rendering. In Forest Baskett, editor, *Computer Graphics (SIGGRAPH '90 Proceedings)*, Volume 24, pages 309–318, August 1990.

(Shirley 1991) P. Shirley. Discrepancy as a quality measure for sample distributions. In Werner Purgathofer, editor, *Eurographics '91*, pages 183–194. North-Holland, September 1991.

◇ **VII** ◇

Utilities

The gems in this section describe general graphics utilities. All place heavy emphasis on their underlying C code, which provides an extensive and proven solution to a well-known problem. In some cases, the emphasis is upon extensions, bug fixes, or refinements to previous gems. In nearly all cases additional code not otherwise appearing in print is included on the diskette.

Schlick (VII.1) provides a set of wave generators having adjustable waveform. The curve family and parameters are chosen to provide a wide range of effects using a manageable set of controls. Immediate applications include the noise-like functions used by Perlin to simulate texture. Green and Hatch (VII.2) provide a thorough solution to the intersection of a polygon and a cube. Their work updates a prior gem, includes a number of useful mathematical and procedural optimizations, and takes advantage of Hatch's library, surveyed below. Bouma and Vaněček offer a collision detection heuristic (VII.3) which is in turn based upon a generic and highly robust polygon–plane intersection routine (VII 4), derived from the second author's thesis research. This routine, while seldom invoked directly, provides the essential procedure central to nearly all 3D (polygon–polygon) intersection routines. Narkhede and Manocha (VII.5) implement a polygon triangulation procedure based upon Seidel's algorithm. The method offers both low computational complexity bounds plus a practical run-time performance, making it worthy of an audience beyond computational geometers. Karinthi (VII.6) provides a Z-buffer renderer assembled using "off-the-net" components capable of high-resolution color output given standard scene files. Finally, Paeth (VII.7) surveys four graphics libraries. The description includes excerpts from a primary work by Scheepers and May as well as discussions of the methods and code provided by authors whose related gem contributions appear elsewhere in this volume.

◇ VII.1

Wave Generators for Computer Graphics

Christophe Schlick
Laboratoire Bordelais de Recherche en Informatique (LaBRI)
Talence, France
schlick@labri.u-bordeaux.fr

◇   Introduction   ◇

The work of Perlin (Perlin 1985, 1989) shows that combining simple generic operators (e.g., noise, turbulence, bias, gain) allows the creation of complex specific visual effects such as marble, fire, or water. Though first presented as a procedural approach to texturing, the ideas have been generalized to many computer graphics applications (Upstill 1989), including modeling, deformation, rendering, and animation. This gem provides several wave generators that represent some basic tools for creating many regular or random visual effects in computer imagery.

◇   Noise   ◇

The most ubiquitous operator is the `noise` function. It generates a distribution having a user-controlled randomness while maintaining valuable statistical properties of invariance under translation or rotation and limited spectrum bandpass. Several implementations of the `noise` function have been proposed since its original development; a remarkably elegant recursive implementation appears in a previous gem (Ward 1991). Because the original `noise` routine was intended for solid texturing, it is often implemented as a 3D function that maps a point on the Euclidian space $\mathbf{R}^3$ onto a scalar value on the unipolar or bipolar interval[1] $[0, 1]$ or $[-1, 1]$.

Despite all its useful properties, the `noise` function also includes a few weaknesses. In many situations (for instance, in rendering or animation), there is a need only for 1D randomness; in such cases, using a 3D noise generator involves wasteful calculations. Another drawback of `noise` (at least with the usual implementations) is that it provides random signals that always have C^1 continuity. Therefore, many natural phenomena that involve C^0 and C^{-1} randomness (Peitgen and Saupe 1988) cannot be simulated by `noise` without specific post-treatment of the function.

---

[1]The first form is recommended, as transformation to the second is straightforward: "`t += t-1;`".

◇ **Description** ◇

This gem corrects the previous weaknesses by introducing *wave generators* as an addendum to the `noise` function. Three monodimensional operators are presented here: `Rwave` (rectangular wave), `Twave` (triangular wave), and `Swave` (sine wave). Each maps **R** onto $[0, 1]$ providing C^{-1}, C^0, and C^1 continuity, respectively. Each function `*wave` takes four parameters:

t	:	wave parameter	$(t \in \mathbf{R})$,
s	:	shape factor	$(-1 \le s \le 1)$,
f	:	frequency variance	$(0 \le f \le 1)$,
a	:	amplitude variance	$(0 \le a \le 1)$.

The default waves ($s = f = a = 0$) are shown in parts (a) of Figures 1–3. Following the idea of the integer lattice (Perlin 1985), the routines are implemented so that the extrema of the functions are located at integer values for t. In other words, the period of each function is 2:

$$\forall p \in \mathbf{N} \quad \texttt{Xwave}\,(2p, 0, 0, 0) = 1 \quad \text{and} \quad \texttt{Xwave}\,(2p+1, 0, 0, 0) = 0.$$

The shape factor s allows a stretch either toward low values ($s < 0$) or toward high values ($s > 0$). The resulting waves with three different values for the shape factor are shown respectively in parts (b), (c), and (d) of Figures 1–3. The stretching effect is obtained by using the rational bias function described elsewhere (Schlick 1994).

The frequency variance f and the amplitude variance a are used to introduce some noise to the waves, either in the frequency domain ($a = 0, f \ne 0$), in the amplitude domain ($a \ne 0, f = 0$), or in both ($a \ne 0, f \ne 0$). These AM, FM and hybrid AM+FM waves appear respectively in parts (b), (c), and (d) of Figures 4–6.

The amount of noise that may be introduced is strictly bounded to preserve the properties defined by Perlin. For instance, even with maximum frequency domain variance ($f = 1$), the pseudoperiod of the wave stays within the range $[1, 4]$. Similarly, maximum amplitude domain variance ($a = 1$) keeps the wave's local maximum (minimum) within $[\frac{1}{2}, 1]$ ($[0, \frac{1}{2}]$). Therefore, parameters f and a provide a double continuum between four kinds of waves:

$f = 0$	and	$a = 0$	:	constant-frequency/constant-amplitude,
$f = 0$	and	$a = 1$	:	constant-frequency/varying-amplitude,
$f = 1$	and	$a = 0$	:	varying-frequency/constant-amplitude,
$f = 1$	and	$a = 1$	:	varying-frequency/varying-amplitude.

◇ **Extensions** ◇

In the preceding description, no precision has been given about the relationship between the wave parameter t and the point (x, y, z) for which the wave function is computed. At least three different schemes may be used, giving three different visual effects:

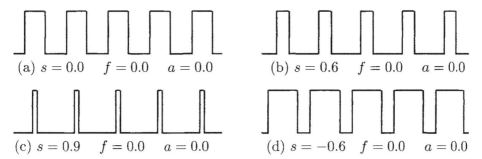

Figure 1. Rectangular-like waves for different shape factors.

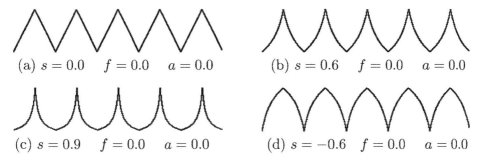

Figure 2. Triangular-like waves for different shape factors.

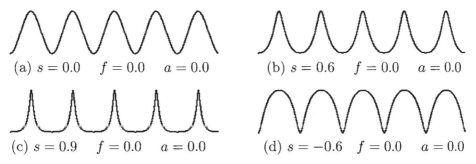

Figure 3. Sinusoidal-like waves for different shape factors.

- $t = ax + by + cz$, which provides *planar waves* (every point at a given distance from the plane $ax + by + cz = 0$ has the same wave value).
- $t = \sqrt{(ay - bx)^2 + (bz - cy)^2 + (cx - az)^2}$, which provides *cylindrical waves* (every point at a given distance from the axis directed by (a, b, c) has the same wave value).
- $t = \sqrt{x^2 + y^2 + z^2}$, which provides *spherical waves* (every point at a given distance from the origin has the same wave value).

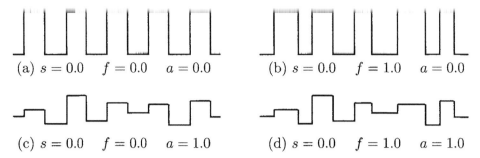

(a) $s = 0.0$ $f = 0.0$ $a = 0.0$ (b) $s = 0.0$ $f = 1.0$ $a = 0.0$

(c) $s = 0.0$ $f = 0.0$ $a = 1.0$ (d) $s = 0.0$ $f = 1.0$ $a = 1.0$

Figure 4. Rectangular-like waves for different frequency and amplitude variances.

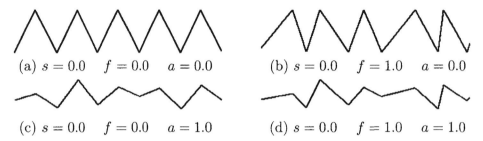

(a) $s = 0.0$ $f = 0.0$ $a = 0.0$ (b) $s = 0.0$ $f = 1.0$ $a = 0.0$

(c) $s = 0.0$ $f = 0.0$ $a = 1.0$ (d) $s = 0.0$ $f = 1.0$ $a = 1.0$

Figure 5. Triangular-like waves for different frequency and amplitude variances.

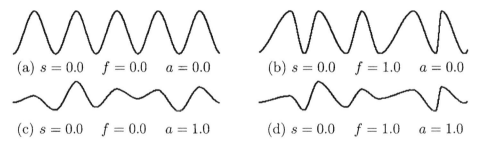

(a) $s = 0.0$ $f = 0.0$ $a = 0.0$ (b) $s = 0.0$ $f = 1.0$ $a = 0.0$

(c) $s = 0.0$ $f = 0.0$ $a = 1.0$ (d) $s = 0.0$ $f = 1.0$ $a = 1.0$

Figure 6. Sinusoidal-like waves for different frequency and amplitude variances.

Although using only monodimensional waves is sufficient in many cases, wave generators in higher dimensions (with similar shape and variance factors) would be a valuable extension. A naïve solution could be to create such waves by multiplying or averaging several orthogonal monodimensional waves. Unfortunately, such a process alters the statistical properties of the resulting waves. The only solution is to devise a specific scheme for each new dimension. The 2D case is already tricky but can be implemented with a reasonable effort (a future gem?). The 3D case appears to be much more difficult; volunteers are welcome.

◇ **Source Files** ◇

```
/* ------------------------------------------------------------------------ *\
    WAVE.H : Christophc Schlick (10 Septcmbcr 1993)

    This package provides 3 routines for generating rectangular-like,
    triangular-like and sine-like waves including specific features.

    "Wave Generators for Computer Graphics"
    in Graphics Gems V (edited by A. Paeth), Academic Press
\* ------------------------------------------------------------------------ */


#ifndef _WAVE_
#define _WAVE_

extern double Rwave (register double t, double s, double Fvar, double Avar);
extern double Twave (register double t, double s, double Fvar, double Avar);
extern double Swave (register double t, double s, double Fvar, double Avar);

#endif


/* ------------------------------------------------------------------------ *\
    WAVE.C : Christophe Schlick (10 September 1993)

    This package provides 3 routines for generating rectangular-like,
    triangular-like and sine-like waves including specific features.

    "Wave Generators for Computer Graphics"
    in Graphics Gems V (edited by A. Paeth), Academic Press
\* ------------------------------------------------------------------------ */

#include <math.h>
#include "wave.h"

/*
** Macro functions
*/

#define ABS(a)          ((a) < 0 ? -(a) : (a))
#define FLOOR(a)        ((a) < 0 ? (int) ((a)-1.0) : (int) (a))
#define MAX(a,b)        ((a) > (b) ? (a) : (b))
#define MIN(a,b)        ((a) < (b) ? (a) : (b))

/*
** rnd : Random function (adapted from Greg Ward in Graphics Gems II)
*/

static double rnd (register long s)
{
  s = s << 13 √ s;
  return (((s*(s*s*15731+789221)+1376312589) & 0X7FFFFFFF) / 2147483648.0);
}
```

```
#define FRND(a)          rnd (17*(a))
#dcfine ARND(a)          rnd (97*(a))

/*
** Rwave : Rectangular-like monodimensional wave
**
** Input : t = Wave parameter
**          s = Shape factor (in [-1,1])
**          f = Frequency variance (in [0,1])
**          a = Amplitude variance (in [0,1])
*/

double Rwave (register double t, double s, double f, double a)
{
  register int    i, j;
  register double a, b;

  i = j = FLOOR (t); t -= i; j++;

  if (f) {
    a = (FRND (i) - 0.5) * f;
    b = (FRND (j) - 0.5) * f + 1.0;
    t = (t-a) / (b-a);
  }

  if (i & 1) {i++; j--; t = 1.0-t;}
  t = (s < 0.0) ? (t+s*t) / (1.0+s*t) : (s > 0.0) ? t / (1.0-s+s*t) : t;
  t = t < 0.5 ? 0.0 : 1.0;

  if (a) {
    a = ARND (i) * a * 0.5;
    b = ARND (j) * a * 0.5;
    t = a + t * (1.0-a-b);
  }
  return (t);
}

/*
** Twave : Triangular-like monodimensional wave
**
** Input : t = Wave parameter
**          s = Shape factor (in [-1,1])
**          f = Frequency variance (in [0,1])
**          a = Amplitude variance (in [0,1])
*/

double Twave (register double t, double s, double f, double a) {
  register int    i, j;
  register double a, b;

  i = j = FLOOR (t); t -= i; j++;
```

```
  if (f) {
    a = (FRND (i) - 0.5) * f;
    b = (FRND (j)   0.5) * f + 1.0;
    if (t < a) {
      i--; j--; t++; a++;
      b = a; a = (FRND (i) - 0.5) * f;
    } else if (t > b) {
      i++; j++; t--; b--;
      a = b; b = (FRND (j) - 0.5) * f + 1.0;
    }
    t = (t-a) / (b-a);
  }

  if (i & 1) {i++; j--; t = 1.0-t;}
  t = (s < 0.0) ? (t+s*t) / (1.0+s*t) : (s > 0.0) ? t / (1.0-s+s*t) : t;

  if (a) {
    a = ARND(i) * a * 0.5;
    b = ARND(j) * a * 0.5;
    t = a + t * (1.0-a-b);
  }
  return (t);
}


/*
** Swave : sinusoidal-like monodimensional wave
**
** Input : t = Wave parameter
**         s = Shape factor (in [-1,1])
**         f = Frequency variance (in [0,1])
**         a = Amplitude variance (in [0,1])
*/

double Swave (register double t, double s, double f, double a)
{
  register int     i, j;
  register double a, b;

  i = j = FLOOR (t); t -= i; j++;

  if (f) {
    a = (FRND (i) - 0.5) * f;
    b = (FRND (j) - 0.5) * f + 1.0;
    if (t < a) {
      i--; j--; t++; a++;
      b = a; a = (FRND (i) - 0.5) * f;
    } else if (t > b) {
      i++; j++; t--; b--;
      a = b; b = (FRND (j) - 0.5) * f + 1.0;
    }
    t = (t-a) / (b-a);
  }
```

```
if (i & 1) {i++; j--; t = 1.0-t;}
t = (s < 0.0) ? (t+s*t) / (1.0+s*t) : (s > 0.0) ? t / (1.0-s+s*t) : t;
t *= t * (3.0-t-t);

if (a) {
  a = ARND(i) * a * 0.5;
  b = ARND(j) * a * 0.5;
  t = a + t * (1.0-a-b);
}
return (t);
}
```

◇ **Bibliography** ◇

(Peitgen and Saupe 1988) H. Peitgen and D. Saupe. *The Science of Fractal Images.* Springer Verlag, 1988.

(Perlin 1985) K. Perlin. An image synthesizer. *Computer Graphics*, 19(3):287–296, 1985.

(Perlin 1989) K. Perlin. Hypertexture. *Computer Graphics*, 23(3):253–262, 1989.

(Schlick 1994) C. Schlick. Fast alternatives to Perlin's bias and gain functions. In Paul Heckbert, editor, *Graphics Gems IV*, pages 401–404. AP Professional, Boston, 1994.

(Upstill 1989) S. Upstill. *The Renderman Companion.* Addison-Wesley, 1989.

(Ward 1991) G. Ward. A recursive implementation of the Perlin noise function. In James Arvo, editor, *Graphics Gems II*, pages 253–259. AP Professional, Boston, 1991.

◊ VII.2

Fast Polygon–Cube Intersection Testing

Daniel Green
Autodesk — Multimedia Division
San Rafael, California
daniel.green@autodesk.com

Don Hatch
Silicon Graphics, Inc.
Mountain View, California
hatch@sgi.com

◊ Overview ◊

This gem generalizes previous triangle–cube intersection methods (Voorhies 1992) to support arbitrary n-gons. Convex, concave, self-intersecting, and degenerate polygons are fully treated, and the new algorithm is more efficient and robust. The implementation uses the C vector macro library `vec.h` created by the second author (page 404).

◊ Background ◊

Efficient polygon–cube intersection testing is an important problem in computer graphics. Renderers can profit from fast polygon tests against display volumes, often avoiding the more expensive clipping operation. Likewise, bounding volume techniques can utilize such fast tests on the faces of polyhedral volumes.

The previous gem cited above gives an algorithm that tests whether a given triangle intersects the axially aligned cube of unit edge centered at the origin.

A related gem (Greene 1994) describes an efficient algorithm for testing convex polyhedra against axially aligned boxes. That algorithm works by attempting to find a plane separating the two figures. That work mentions that the intuitive approach is inefficient because of the number of possible intersection calculations. (The intuitive approach contains an intersection test of each polygon edge with each cube face, followed by intersecting each cube diagonal with the polygon body.)

◊ Description ◊

The approach presented here is a hybrid of the two previous techniques. It contains only a single intersection calculation, which is rarely performed because of the trivial tests that precede it. The rest of the calculations are of the same sort of fast inequality tests from the second work. This new implementation, however, is not restricted to convex figures.

375

Table 1. Intersection routines.

Function Name	File Name	Description
polygon_intersects_cube	pcube.c	low-level definitive test
fast_polygon_intersects_cube	fpcube.c	high-level wrapper test
trivial_vertex_tests	fpcube.c	trivial reject/accept test
segment_intersects_cube	pcube.c	low-level edge test
polygon_contains_point_3d	pcube.c	used internally, also generally useful

The top-level entry points of the implementation are described in Table 1. Further instructions appear within the heavily commented source code released with this book.

The previous triangle testing approach is elegant and sound, and the general approach has been retained, which proceeds from cheap trivial accept and reject tests through more expensive edge and face intersection tests. These individual tests have also been broken out into separate functions in order to allow higher-level routines to be built on top of them—such as general polyhedra and polygon mesh tests—without having to suffer redundant tests on shared vertices or edges.

The composite `fast_polygon_intersects_cube` function replaces Voorhies' original triangle–cube intersection function. It calls `trivial_vertex_tests` (essentially unchanged) and, failing classification, invokes the definitive `polygon_intersects_cube` function. This overall behavior is unchanged from the original code:

1. Trivial vertex tests.
2. If any edge intersects the cube, return TRUE.
3. If the polygon interior intersects the cube, return TRUE.
4. Return FALSE.

Step 1: Trivial Vertex Tests

The main algorithmic difference in the new point–plane tests is that in a number of places tests are no longer performed against planes that cannot possibly give useful information. For example, when the function determines that a point is located to the left of the cube, testing is not done against the cube's right face plane.

The `trivial_vertex_tests` function can be used to test an entire set of vertices for trivial rejection or acceptance. This test is useful for quickly classifying polyhedra or entire polygon meshes. Another useful application is in testing for trivial rejection of polyhedral bounding volumes against view volumes (described more fully in the next section).

The `trivial_vertex_tests` function stops testing vertices as soon as it determines that at least one vertex is to the inside of each plane. For example, suppose that at least one vertex has been found to be to the right of the left face plane, and one is found to be below the top face plane, and likewise for the other four face planes. There is then

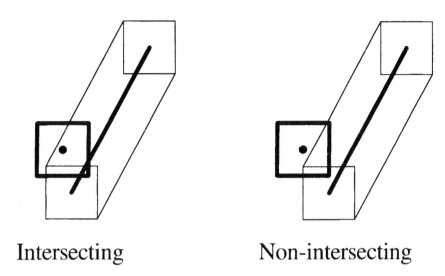

Intersecting   Non-intersecting

Figure 1.   Two-dimensional analogue of segment–cube intersection test.

no point in classifying any of the remaining vertices against the face planes because it is impossible that the vertices *as a set* all lie outside any one of those planes.

Step 2: Segment–Cube Intersection Test

A naïve implementation of this step consists of checking whether either endpoint of the segment is inside the cube, and, if not, checking whether the segment intersects any of the six cube faces. Such an implementation, however, is inherently error-prone: It gives a false negative when, due to floating-point roundoff error, the segment slips through the "cracks" between adjacent cube faces. In fact, the original gem's implementation suffers from exactly this problem.

The approach used here is to convert this part of the problem into a different problem space: Testing whether a line segment intersects the cube is equivalent to testing whether the origin is contained within the convex solid obtained by sweeping a unit cube from (being centered at) one segment endpoint to the other. This solid is a skewed rhombic dodecahedron. The code to implement this test consists of just twelve point–plane sidedness tests, so it is computationally more efficient than the original six line–plane intersections plus six point-within-polygon tests, in addition to being more robust.

Figure 1 shows the analogous situation in two dimensions, where the swept convex solid is simply a hexagon. The line segment intersects the square if and only if the hexagon contains the center of the square.

Any intersection test can be recast in this way. In general, testing whether two objects *A* and *B* have any points in common is equivalent to testing whether the origin is contained within the composite object:

$$\{a - b \mid a \subset A \ and \ b \subset B\}.$$

This reasoning can be applied to the entire original polygon–cube intersection problem by recasting it as a single point-within-solid test. However, in order to handle non-convexity or tiny facets in the composite solid, the analysis required is much more complex than simple sidedness tests. For this reason, that approach was specifically rejected, although the method is appropriate for the segment–cube intersection step.

Step 3: Polygon Interior–Cube Intersection Test

Since it is now known that no vertex or edge intersects the cube, this step only needs to test whether any of the four cube diagonals intersects the interior of the polygon. This observation was utilized in the original gem's implementation. The new implementation goes a step further and uses the fact that it is sufficient to test against only the one diagonal that comes closest to being perpendicular to the plane of the polygon; if the polygon intersects any of the cube diagonals, it will intersect that one. Finding that diagonal is trivial, so this part of the implementation is up to four times as fast as the original. Omitting the intersection tests with the other three diagonals avoids another case of numerical instability in the original gem's implementation: Calculating the intersection point of the polygon's plane with a cube diagonal that is almost parallel to that plane can result in a divide-by-zero or unstable solution.

The last part of this step is to test whether the polygon contains the point that is the intersection of the polygon's plane with the chosen diagonal. This test is performed by the function `polygon_contains_point_3d`, which is made externally visible since it may be useful for other applications.

◇ **Polyhedron–Cube Intersection Testing** ◇

When used to test polyhedra, the functions included in this module only test for intersections with points, edges, and surfaces, not volumes. If no such intersection is reported, the volume of a polyhedron could still contain the entire unit box. That condition would then need to be checked for with an additional point-within-polyhedron test. The origin would be a natural point to check in such a test. Below is C-like pseudocode that puts all the pieces together for a fast, complete polyhedron–cube intersection test.

```
switch(trivial_vertex_tests(verts))
{
    case  1: return TRUE  /* trivial accept */
    case  0: return FALSE /* trivial reject */
    case -1: for each edge
```

```
        if(segment_intersects_cube(edge))
            return TRUE
    for each face
        if(fast_polygon_intersects_cube(..., TRUE, TRUE))
            return TRUE
    return polyhedron_contains_point(polyhedron, origin)
}
```

Notice that when a box is used as a modeling-space bounding polyhedron, testing its intersection against a view volume can often be performed in either direction. In other words, not only can the box be transformed by the viewing transformation that takes the view volume to the unit cube and then tested there, but the view volume can also be transformed by the transformation that takes the bounding box to be the unit cube and the test performed there. In the latter case it is the world-space truncated pyramid of the view volume that becomes the polyhedron being tested.

◇   **Conclusions**   ◇

A set of highly optimized intersection tests was described that support a fast polygon–cube intersection test at the highest level. The latter supports operations upon general n-gons. All intersection routines are freestanding, making them good candidates for direct replacement of related routines described previously in this series. Production versions of this gem's code may be found in the subdirectory **pcube** on the accompanying diskette and FTP mirrors. The companion library may be found in **vec.h** and is described in gem VII.7 of this volume.

◇   **Bibliography**   ◇

(Greene 1994) Ned Greene. Detecting intersection of a rectangular solid and a convex polyhedron. In Paul S. Heckbert, editor, *Graphics Gems IV*, Chapter I.7, pages 74–82. AP Professional, Boston, 1994.

(Voorhies 1992) Douglas Voorhies. Triangle-cube intersection. In David Kirk, editor, *Graphics Gems III*, Chapter V.7, pages 236–239. AP Professional, Boston, 1992.

◊ VII.3

Velocity-based Collision Detection

William Bouma

Purdue University
Department of Computer Sciences
West Lafayette, Indiana
bouma@cs.purdue.edu

George Vaněček, Jr.

Purdue University
Department of Computer Sciences
West Lafayette, Indiana
http://www.cs.purdue.edu/people/vanecek

◊ Introduction ◊

This gem presents a simple method for speeding up collision detection between moving polyhedra (Vaněček, Jr. 1994). An inexpensive test based on the relative velocities of points will determine that a polygon cannot possibly be in collision. By applying the test to all polygons in an object, one can eliminate on average half of the candidate polygons. The algorithm is used as a preprocessing step to reduce the work of the full collision test, which generally requires computationally expensive operations such as polygon intersection. The technique can be employed when objects are in close proximity and applies to both convex and nonconvex polyhedra.

The procedure is based on the following intuitive principle: At any instant, roughly half of the polygons on a moving object will be facing in the general direction of motion, and the other half will be facing away. When considering the possibility of collision between pairs of objects, the polygons on one object that face backward in their relative direction of motion cannot collide with the other object. A dot product between the polygon normal and the relative velocity of a point in the polygon tests if that point is moving in a direction that could allow it to collide. The test extends cheaply to the entire polygon by applying it either to the vertices of the polygon, or merely to those of a simpler bounding polygon (e.g., a rectangle). The alert reader will notice the similarities between this method and the well-known back-face culling method often used when rendering polygons (Foley *et al.* 1990).

◊ Preliminaries ◊

Consider a polyhedron oriented in the global frame of reference with its local center indicated by the vector r. The *velocity* of the center is given as the time derivative $\dot{r}$ and the *angular velocity* about the center is given as ω. Using r, $\dot{r}$, and ω, any point

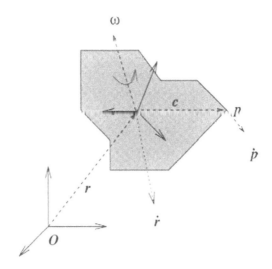

Figure 1. Instantaneous velocity $\dot{p}$ at point p.

$p = r + c$ has an *instantaneous velocity* (as shown in Figure 1) given by the equation

$$\dot{p} = \dot{r} + \omega \times c. \tag{1}$$

Given two polyhedra s_i and s_j in the same global frame of reference, the *relative velocity* at point p of object s_i as seen by an observer fixed on s_j is

$$\dot{p}_{ij} = \dot{p}_i - \dot{p}_j, \tag{2}$$

where the instantaneous velocities $\dot{p}_i$ and $\dot{p}_j$ are defined by Equation (1). Note that point p is expressed in terms of both s_i and s_j as

$$\dot{p} = \dot{r}_i + \dot{c}_i = \dot{r}_j + \dot{c}_j. \tag{3}$$

Expanding Equation (2) using Equation (1) and Equation (3), we obtain

$$\dot{p}_{ij} = a_{ij} + p \times \omega_{ji}, \tag{4}$$

where $a_{ij} = \dot{r}_i - \dot{r}_j - \omega_i \times r_i + \omega_j \times r_j$, and $\omega_{ji} = \omega_j - \omega_i$ are constants for a given time t. With this equation, we can compute the relative velocity for any point p without having to compute the points c_i or c_j in the coordinate space of either s_i or s_j.

◇ **Algorithm** ◇

Consider an object s_i moving in the presence of another object s_j. The instantaneous velocity vectors are obtained for the object at some time t. Given a face f of s_i in the

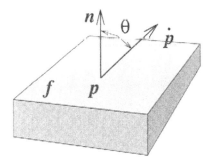

Figure 2. Point p, fixed on s_i, is moving away from face f when $\theta < \pi/2$.

global frame of reference, let $p \in f$. The angle θ between the normal vector $\boldsymbol{n}_f$ of face f and $\dot{\boldsymbol{p}}_{ij}$ describes whether p is moving toward the outside directly above f or not. It follows that if θ is less than $\pi/2$, then

$$\dot{\boldsymbol{p}}_{ij} \cdot \boldsymbol{n}_f \geq 0, \tag{5}$$

which indicates that in the local neighborhood of p, p is moving toward the empty space above f, and therefore p can possibly collide with some part of s_j within this local neighborhood (refer to Figure 2). It follows that $\forall p \in f$, $(\dot{\boldsymbol{p}}_{ij} \cdot \boldsymbol{n}_f < 0)$ implies that the entire face is moving away from any portion of s_j that may lie directly above it. Therefore, f cannot collide with s_j at the time t.

The task is simplified by the linear property of the relative velocity vector-space. The linearity implies that for any two points $p_1, p_2 \in f$ that fail Equation (5), all points along the line segment joining p_1 and p_2 must also fail it. Thus, it is sufficient to check just the vertices of some convex polygon that completely encloses the face. If all of the vertices satisfy $\dot{\boldsymbol{p}}_{ij} \cdot \boldsymbol{n}_f < 0$, then so does every point within the polygon.

Note that there is an efficiency trade-off depending on how the bounding polygon is chosen. The more area the polygon covers, the more likely it is that a vertex will satisfy Equation (5). Thus, the corresponding face may be kept even though no points in the face are moving in a direction of collision. Though one could apply the convex hull of the face as the bounding polygon, any performance gain might be outstripped given a face whose convex hull is not sparse. The speed could degrade significantly if the convex hull of a face has a large number of vertices. It is best to choose for each face the most tightly approximating polygon using a small constant number of vertices (Weghorst *et al.* 1984).

◇ **Implementation** ◇

Care must be taken in coding the algorithm to ensure that all variables lie within a common frame of reference. Object velocities are commonly kept as global coordinates, while object geometries remain local. The local reference frame for an object changes over time subject to the velocities incident upon it. The transformation

$$p = R_i p^L + r_i \tag{6}$$

maps a point p^L in the local frame to a corresponding point p in the global. The mapping uses a 3×3 rotational matrix, R_i, and the translation vector r_i. To get a common frame of reference, one can either apply Equation (6) to the polygon vertices of s_i and use Equation (4) in the global frame, or instead move the relative velocities into the local frame of s_i. Since there is only one linear component and one angular component to the velocity, but there are many polygon points, it is more efficient to do the latter. The modified Equation (4) then becomes

$$\dot{p}_{ij}^L = a_{ij}^L + p^L \times \omega_{ji}^L,$$

in the local frame of s_i, where $a_{ij}^L = R_i^{-1} a_{ij}$ and $\omega_{ji}^L = R_i^{-1} \omega_{ji}$.

◇ **The C++ Code** ◇

The C++ code provides a simple working example of the cull function that prints out the polygons that have been culled. The function is intended to be incorporated into an animation system as just one component of a collision detection package. For convenience, the code uses the vector and matrix definitions in the *algebra3.h* package from Gems IV.

```c++
// -*- C++ -*-
// by Bill Bouma and George Vanecek Jr. Aug, 1994.
// Compile by: g++ -O2 -s -o cull cull.cc algebra3.o -lm
#include "algebra3.h"          // See Graphics Gems IV, pg534-557
typedef vec3           Point;    // Points are not Vectors
typedef vec3           Vector;   // Vectors are not Points
typedef unsigned int   Index;    // Array Indices
typedef unsigned int   Counter;

class Polygon {
public:
  Polygon              ( const char      pId,
                         const Vector&   nV,
                         const Counter   nPs,
                         const Point* const p )
    : id(pId), pts(p), nPts(nPs), normalVector(nV) { }
  const Vector& normal( ) const { return normalVector; }
```

```
  char            name( ) const { return id; }
  Counter      nPoints( ) const { return nPts; }
  const Point&   point( const Index i ) const { return pts[i]; }
private:
  const char          id;            // Unique Id
  const Counter        nPts;         // pts[0..nPts-1]
  const Point*  const pts;           // Points around Polygon
  const Vector        normalVector;  // Unit Vector
};

class MovingPolyhedron {
public:
  MovingPolyhedron ( const char          pId,
                     const Vector&        rv,
                     const Vector&        vv,
                     const Vector&        wv,
                     const mat4&          m,
                     const Counter        nP,
                     const Polygon* const ps )
    : id(pId), r(rv), v(vv), w(wv), R(m), polys(ps), nPolys(nP) { }
  const Polygon&    polygon( const Index i ) const { return polys[i]; }
  void              cull( const MovingPolyhedron& ) const;
private:
  const char          id;        // Unique Id
  const Polygon* const polys;     // Points in local coordinates
  const Counter        nPolys;    // polys[0..nPolys-1]
  Vector               r;         // Center of Rotation (in world coords.)
  Vector               v;         // Linear Velocity (in world coords.)
  Vector               w;         // Angular Velocity (in world coords.)
  mat4                 R;         // Orientation Matrix
};

void MovingPolyhedron::cull( const MovingPolyhedron& j ) const
{
  const mat4   RIi = ((mat4&)R).transpose();
  const Vector aij = RIi * (v - j.v - (w √ r) + (j.w √ j.r));
  const Vector wij = RIi * (j.w - w);
  for( Index gi = 0; gi < nPolys; ++gi ) {
    const Polygon& g = polygon(gi);
    for( Index pi = 0; pi < g.nPoints(); ++pi )
      if( ( aij + (g.point(pi) √ wij )) * g.normal() > 0.0 )
        break;
    cout << "Polygon " << g.name() << " of Polyhedron " << id
         << " is" << ( pi == g.nPoints()  ? " " : " not ")
         << "culled." << endl;
  }
}

const Counter NPolyPoints = 4;
const Counter NFaces      = 6;
static const Point leftPoints[NPolyPoints]  = {
  Point(-1,-1,-1), Point(-1,-1, 1), Point(-1, 1, 1), Point(-1, 1,-1) };
static const Point rightPoints[NPolyPoints] = {
```

```
     Point( 1,-1,-1), Point( 1, 1,-1), Point( 1, 1, 1), Point( 1,-1, 1) };
static const Point topPoints[NPolyPoints]   = {
    Point(-1, 1,-1), Point(-1, 1, 1), Point( 1, 1, 1), Point( 1, 1,-1) };
static const Point bottomPoints[NPolyPoints]= {
    Point(-1,-1,-1), Point( 1,-1,-1), Point( 1,-1, 1), Point(-1,-1, 1) };
static const Point backPoints[NPolyPoints]  = {
    Point(-1,-1,-1), Point(-1, 1,-1), Point( 1, 1,-1), Point( 1,-1,-1) };
static const Point frontPoints[NPolyPoints] = {
    Point( 1, 1, 1), Point( 1,-1, 1), Point( 1, 1, 1), Point(-1, 1, 1) };
static const Polygon cube[NFaces]= {
    Polygon( 'a', Vector(-1, 0, 0), NPolyPoints, leftPoints   ),
    Polygon( 'b', Vector( 1, 0, 0), NPolyPoints, rightPoints  ),
    Polygon( 'c', Vector( 0, 1, 0), NPolyPoints, topPoints    ),
    Polygon( 'd', Vector( 0,-1, 0), NPolyPoints, bottomPoints ),
    Polygon( 'e', Vector( 0, 0,-1), NPolyPoints, backPoints   ),
    Polygon( 'f', Vector( 0, 0, 1), NPolyPoints, frontPoints  )
};

int main()
{
  MovingPolyhedron A( 'A',
                      Vector(10,10, 0 ), // Position
                      Vector( 0, 0, 0 ), // Velocity
                      Vector( 0, 0, 0 ), // Angular Velocity
                      identity3D(),
                      NFaces, cube );
  MovingPolyhedron B( 'B',
                      Vector(10,10,10 ), // Position
                      Vector( 0, 0,-1 ), // Velocity
                      Vector( 0, 1, 0 ), // Angular Velocity
                      identity3D(),
                      NFaces, cube );
  A.cull( B );
  B.cull( A );
}
```

◇ **Bibliography** ◇

(Foley *et al.* 1990) J. D. Foley, A. van Dam, S. K. Feiner, and J. F. Hughes. *Computer Graphics, Principles and Practice*, second edition. Addison-Wesley, Reading, MA, 1990.

(Vaněček, Jr. 1994) G. Vaněček, Jr. Back-face culling applied to collision detection of polyhedra. *Journal of Visualization and Computer Animation*, 5(1):55–63, January 1994.

(Weghorst *et al.* 1984) Hank Weghorst, Gary Hooper, and Donald P. Greenberg. Improved computation methods for ray tracing. *ACM Transactions on Graphics*, 3(1):52–69, January 1984.

◊ VII.4

Spatial Partitioning of a Polygon by a Plane

George Vaněček, Jr.
Purdue University
Department of Computer Sciences
West Lafayette, Indiana
vanecek@cs.purdue.edu

This gem presents an algorithm that partitions a polygon lying in 3D space by a plane, resulting in three lists of zero or more polygons. If the plane intersects the polygon transversely, the algorithm cuts the polygon by the plane and returns a list of new polygons that lie above and a list of new polygons that lie below the plane. This algorithm underpins many BSP tree and polygon intersection libraries. Splitting a polygon is a common problem encountered in many 3D geometric applications such as boundary representation (B-Rep) to BSP tree conversion (Thibault and Naylor 1987), B-Rep to MSP tree conversion (Vaněček, Jr. 1991), Boolean set operations on polyhedra (Vaněček, Jr. 1989), and convex decomposition. The algorithm presented here extends the convex-polygon splitting algorithm presented in Gems III (Chin 1992) to nonconvex polygons that may contain nonmanifold and adjacent, collinear vertices.

To illustrate the operation, consider as an example the polygon in Figure 1(a). The dashed line indicates the intersection with a transversal cut plane. When cut, the polygon splits into four polygons lying above the cut plane and four polygons below, as is shown in Figure 1(b).

The algorithm is implemented in C++ and developed under GNU's C++ compiler version 2.5.8. The C++ code presented here is a stand-alone code using minimally sufficient abstract data types defined as classes. It has been carefully crafted and thoroughly tested.

◊   The Representation of Polygons   ◊

A polygon is typically represented by a counterclockwise ordered sequence of points defining the line segments that border the polygon. This sequence of points is then represented either as an array of points or as a linked list of dynamically allocated points. The former is used when the shape of the polygon is fixed, while the latter is used when changes to the shape of the polygon are required.

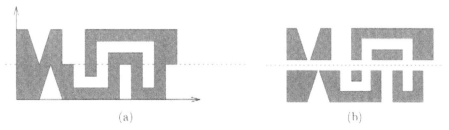

(a)   (b)

Figure 1.   A sample polygon with 30 points shown (a) before the cut and (b) after the cut. The dashed lines denote the transversal cut plane.

For our purpose, however, it is easier to operate on a representation of a polygon that is based on its bordering edges rather than one that is based only on the points. A `class DEdge` (a *directed edge* data type) is defined and forms a circular, doubly linked list of directed edges around the polygon.

```
class DEdge {
public:
  DEdge*          next ( ) const;
  DEdge*          prev ( ) const;
  const Point& srcPoint ( ) const;
  const Point& dstPoint ( ) const;
  Where          where ( ) const;
  Where&      srcWhere ( );
  Where&      dstWhere ( );
  double&   distFromRefP ( );
  //...
};
```

Although by itself there is no concept of a proper orientation, the orientation of the polygon is assumed so that in relation to the support plane of the polygon, the polygon is ordered counterclockwise when viewed from above the polygon, where above is in the direction of the support plane's normal. This is a common convention used by boundary representations for solids.

◇   The Algorithm   ◇

The problem of partitioning a polygon by a plane would be simpler if the polygon could be assumed to be convex. A single pair of directed edges would be inserted, and the polygon would split into two new polygons (Chin 1992). It would still be simple, if the edges of the polygon could be assumed to cleanly cross the cut plane. However, not only can edges with two different orientations lie on the cut plane, but the existence of inner holes connected by a bridge edge can cause a crossing that does not lead to a transition from the outside to the inside (or vice versa) of the polygon, and the polygon can also

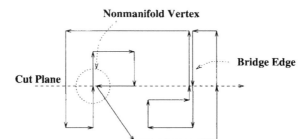

Figure 2. A polygon with a hole connected by a bridge edge (i.e., two oppositely oriented collinear and overlapping directed edges), and with a nonmanifold vertex.

contain nonmanifold vertices (a vertex that has more than two incident edges). These cases are illustrated in Figure 2.

For a polygon with manifold vertices, the introduction of new edges can be based purely on local topology (assuming that each vertex of the polygon contains a classification label). This label, having a value of either **ABOVE**, **ON**, or **BELOW**, gives the vertex's position relative to the cut plane. For a few cases involving nonmanifold vertices, geometrical information (i.e., the orientation and angle of the edges in relation to the cut) must be used to determine the appropriate places to insert the new edges.

The splitting of the polygon, ***g**, by the cut plane, **cut**, is performed by the following routine:

```
void split( Polygon*& g, const Plane& cut,
            List<Polygon>& above,
            List<Polygon>& on,
            List<Polygon>& below )
{
  Counter nOnDEdges = 0;
  DEdge*  onDEdges[g.nPoints()];
  switch( g->classifyPoints( cut, nOnDEdges, onDEdges ) ) {
  case ONABOVE:
  case ABOVE:
    above << g;
    break;
  case ON:
    on << g;
    break;
  case ONBELOW:
  case BELOW:
    on << g;
    break;
  default/* case CROSS */:
    assert( nOnDEdges >= 2 );
    g->complexCut( cut, nOnDEdges, onDEdges, above, below );
```

```
      collectFaces ( nOnDEdges, onDEdges, above, below );
      g->anchor  = NULL;
      g->nDEdges = 0;
      delete g;
   }
   g = NULL;
}
```

The routine returns three lists containing the new polygons partitioned into sets lying above, on, or below the cut plane. It also deletes ***g**.

The partitioning begins by classifying all the points against the cut plane and splitting any directed edges that cross the cut plane.

```
Where Polygon::classifyPoints( const Plane& cut,
                               Counter&      nOnDEdges,
                               DEdge*        onDEdges[] )
{
   first()->srcWhere() = cut.whichSide( first()->srcPoint() );
   Where polyW = first()->srcWhere();
   forEachDEdge( d ) {
      d->dstWhere() = cut.whichSide( d->dstPoint() );
      polyW = Where( polyW | d->dstWhere() );
      if( d->where() == ABOVEBELOW ) {
         split( cut, d );
         onDEdges[nOnDEdges++] = ( d = d->next() );
         d->srcWhere() = ON;
      } else if( d->srcWhere() == ON )
         onDEdges[nOnDEdges++] = d;
   }
   return polyW;
}
```

After the classification, no edge crosses the cut plane and each point is labeled as lying either **ABOVE**, **ON**, or **BELOW** the cut plane. Furthermore, the edges that have a source vertex on the cut plane are retained for further processing if needed. At this point it will be known if the polygon lies completely above, on, or below the cut plane, in which case the polygon is added to the proper list and the operation completes. If, on the other hand, the polygon crosses the cut plane, the polygon is split by calling the **Polygon::complexCut** method with the collected edges whose source vertices lie on the cut plane.

```
void Polygon::complexCut( const Plane& cut,
                          const Counter nOnDs, DEdge* const onDs[],
                          List<Polygon>& above, List<Polygon>& below)
{
   sortDEdges( nOnDs, onDs, cut.normal() √ plane().normal() );
   Index startOnD = 0;
   DEdge* srcD = NULL;
   while( srcD = getSrcD( onDs, startOnD, nOnDs ) ) {
      DEdge* const dstD = getDstD( onDs, startOnD, nOnDs );
```

```
      assert( dstD != NULL );
      addBridge( srcD, dstD );
      if( srcD->prev()->prev()->srcWhere() == ABOVE )
        useSrc = srcD->prev();
      else if( dstD->dstWhere() == BELOW )
        useSrc = dstD;
    }
  }
```

The first step sorts the directed edges (with source vertices that lie on the cut plane as returned by function `Polygon::classifyPoints`). The edges are ordered by their source vertex in increasing distance along a cut direction (e.g., left to right) by the method

```
void Polygon::sortDEdges( const Counter nOnDs, DEdge* const onDs[],
                          const Vector& cutDir )
{
  assert( nOnDs >= 2 );
  const Point& refP = onDs[0]->srcPoint();
  for( Index i = 0; i < nOnDs; ++i )
    onDs[i]->distFromRefP() = cutDir * ( onDs[i]->srcPoint() - refP );
  for( i = nOnDs-1; i > 0; --i )
    for( Index j = 0, k = 1; k <= i; j = k++ )
      if( onDs[j]->distFromRefP() > onDs[k]->distFromRefP() ||
          onDs[j]->distFromRefP() == onDs[k]->distFromRefP() &&
          onDs[j]->dstWhere() == ABOVE )
        swap( onDs[j], onDs[k] );
}
```

Typically, the number of these edges is small (e.g., two). Consequently, a bubble sort is used. The sorted edges are then scanned in left-to-right order and used to determine a source and a destination edge between whose source vertices new edges will be inserted. The next source directed edge is obtained by

```
static DEdge* useSrc = NULL;
static DEdge* getSrcD( DEdge* const onDs[],
                       Index& start, const Counter nOnDs )
{
  if( useSrc ) {
    DEdge* const gotIt = useSrc;
    useSrc = NULL;
    return gotIt;
  }
  while( start < nOnDs ) {
    const Where prevW = onDs[start]->prev()->srcWhere();
    const Where nextW = onDs[start]->dstWhere();
    if( prevW == ABOVE && nextW == BELOW ||
        prevW == ABOVE && nextW == ON &&
          onDs[start]->next()->distFromRefP() < onDs[start]->distFromRefP() ||
        prevW == ON && nextW == BELOW &&
          onDs[start]->prev()->distFromRefP() < onDs[start]->distFromRefP() )
      return onDs[start++];
```

```
      ++start;
    }
    return NULL;
  }
```

The next destination directed edge is obtained by

```
  static DEdge* getDstD( DEdge* const onDs[],
                         index& start, const Counter nOnDs )
  {
    while( start < nOnDs ) {
      const Where prevW = onDs[start]->prev()->srcWhere();
      const Where nextW = onDs[start]->dstWhere();
      if( prevW == BELOW && nextW == ABOVE ||
          prevW == BELOW && nextW == BELOW ||
          prevW == ABOVE && nextW == ABOVE ||
          prevW == BELOW && nextW == ON &&
            onDs[start]->distFromRefP() < onDs[start]->next()->distFromRefP() ||
          prevW == ON && nextW == ABOVE &&
            onDs[start]->distFromRefP() < onDs[start]->prev()->distFromRefP() )
        return onDs[start++];
      ++start;
    }
    return NULL;
  }
```

These two functions step through the ordered edges, **onDs**, using **start**, the index into the array. If a sector is defined to be the area on the inside of the polygon taken at a vertex, there are sixteen possible sector/cut-plane classifications. These are shown in Table 1. The table has four columns and sixteen rows. The first column shows a sector characterizing a class of such sectors. A sector of some directed edge g has three vertices, labeled for simplicity α, β, and γ. The second and third columns mark the sectors that are correspondingly the source and destination of a new edge. Of all sixteen possible sectors, only three sectors can cause an edge pair to be started, and only five can cause the new edges to terminate. The fourth column gives a condition that is used to recognize that sector. In the condition, $\alpha < \mathcal{P}$, $\alpha = \mathcal{P}$, and $\alpha > \mathcal{P}$ indicate that α is correspondingly below, on, and above the cut plane $\mathcal{P}$.

Given the source and destination edges, two new directed edges are created and spliced in between the source and the destination edges (as shown in the example of Figure 3) by the method

```
  void Polygon::addBridge( DEdge* const leftBelow, DEdge* const rghtAbove )
```

After all the new edges have been inserted, new polygon headers are created, and associated with the edge cycles. Since, however, it is not known how many times the edge cycle loops back and touches the cut plane, the constructor for the new polygon resets all the vertex classification labels to prevent the loop from belonging to more than one polygon header.

Table 1. $\sqrt{}$ marks possible source and destination sectors for a new edge. α, β and γ refer to the classification for the vertices of the sector. $\mathcal{P}$ is the cut plane. $\alpha < \mathcal{P}$ indicates that vertex α is below the cut plane.

α, β, γ	Src	Dst	Condition		α, β, γ	Src	Dst	Condition
		$\sqrt{}$	$\alpha < \mathcal{P}, \gamma > \mathcal{P}$					$\alpha = \mathcal{P}, \gamma < \mathcal{P}, \beta < \alpha$
		$\sqrt{}$	$\alpha < \mathcal{P}, \gamma = \mathcal{P}, \beta < \gamma$					$\alpha = \mathcal{P}, \gamma = \mathcal{P}, \alpha < \gamma$
			$\alpha < \mathcal{P}, \gamma = \mathcal{P}, \gamma < \beta$					$\alpha = \mathcal{P}, \gamma = \mathcal{P}, \gamma < \alpha$
		$\sqrt{}$	$\alpha < \mathcal{P}, \gamma < \mathcal{P}, \text{concave}$			$\sqrt{}$		$\alpha > \mathcal{P}, \gamma < \mathcal{P}$
			$\alpha < \mathcal{P}, \gamma < \mathcal{P}, \text{convex}$					$\alpha > \mathcal{P}, \gamma = \mathcal{P}, \beta < \gamma$
			$\alpha = \mathcal{P}, \gamma > \mathcal{P}, \alpha < \beta$			$\sqrt{}$		$\alpha > \mathcal{P}, \gamma = \mathcal{P}, \gamma < \beta$
		$\sqrt{}$	$\alpha = \mathcal{P}, \gamma > \mathcal{P}, \beta < \alpha$					$\alpha > \mathcal{P}, \gamma > \mathcal{P}, \text{convex}$
	$\sqrt{}$		$\alpha = \mathcal{P}, \gamma < \mathcal{P}, \alpha < \beta$				$\sqrt{}$	$\alpha > \mathcal{P}, \gamma > \mathcal{P}, \text{concave}$

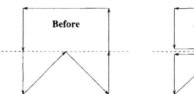
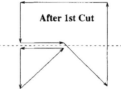

Figure 3. A polygon before and after one iteration of the edge insertion step. Each arrow indicates a directed edge and its orientation.

```
static void collectFaces( const Counter nOnDs, DEdge* const onDs[],
                          List<Polygon>& above, List<Polygon>& below )
{
  for( Index i = 0; i < nOnDs; ++i )
    if( onDs[i]->srcWhere() == ON )
      if( onDs[i]->dstWhere() == ABOVE )
        above << new Polygon( onDs[i], plane() );
      else if( onDs[i]->dstWhere() == BELOW )
        below << new Polygon( onDs[i], plane() );
}
```

Because of multiconnected polygons (i.e., with holes), the insertion of a pair of edges does not always split the polygon if the edge connects to an inner loop. Only after another edge pair is inserted on the other side of the hole does the polygon split into two. In general, inserting n edge pairs can split the polygon into as few as two polygons, or as many as $n + 1$ polygons.

Finally, here is a simple test-code fragment given `Polygon* g` and `const Plane cutPlane` showing how to split the polygon and print the result.

```
List<Polygon> above;
List<Polygon> on;
List<Polygon> below;
split( g, cutPlane, above, on, below);
printPolys( "Above", above);
printPolys( "On",    on);
printPolys( "Below", below);
```

For the sake of readability, the code presented for functions `getSrcD` and `getDstD` is written with the assumption of having vertices with at most two incident sectors. If nonmanifold vertices having more than two incident sectors fall on the cut plane, the two functions have to collect all coincident sectors and select from them the innermost sectors to be cut. This can be easily done by finding the sectors having the smallest angle between the cut vector and the out-edge.

◇ **Bibliography** ◇

(Chin 1992) N. Chin. Partitioning a 3D convex polygon with an arbitrary plane. In David Kirk, editor, *Graphics Gems III*, pages 219–222. AP Professional, Boston, 1992.

(Thibault and Naylor 1987) W. C. Thibault and B. F. Naylor. Set operations on polyhedra using binary space partitioning trees. *ACM Computer Graphics SIGGRAPH '87*, 21(4):153–162, July 1987.

(Vaněček, Jr. 1989) G. Vaněček, Jr. *Set Operations on Polyhedra Using Decomposition Methods*. PhD thesis, University of Maryland, College Park, Maryland, June 1989.

(Vaněček, Jr. 1991) G. Vaněček, Jr. Brep-index: A multidimensional space partitioning tree. *International Journal of Computational Geometry and Applications*, 1(3):243–262, September 1991.

VII.5

Fast Polygon Triangulation Based on Seidel's Algorithm

Atul Narkhede
Department of Computer Science
University of North Carolina
Chapel Hill, North Carolina
narkhede@cs.unc.edu

Dinesh Manocha
Department of Computer Science
University of North Carolina
Chapel Hill, North Carolina
manocha@cs.unc.edu

◇ Introduction ◇

Computing the triangulation of a polygon is a fundamental algorithm in computational geometry. In computer graphics, polygon triangulation algorithms are widely used for tessellating curved geometries, such as those described by splines (Kumar and Manocha 1994). Methods of triangulation include greedy algorithms (O'Rourke 1994), convex hull differences (Tor and Middleditch 1984) and horizontal decompositions (Seidel 1991).

This gem describes an implementation based on Seidel's algorithm (*op. cit.*) for triangulating simple polygons having no holes. It is an incremental randomized algorithm whose expected complexity is $O(n \log^* n)$. In practice, it is almost linear time for a simple polygon having n vertices. The triangulation does not introduce any additional vertices and decomposes the polygon into $n - 2$ triangles. Furthermore, the algorithm generates a query structure that can be used to determine the location of a point in logarithmic time. Related gems include incremental Delaunay triangulation of a set of points (Lischinski 1994) and polygonization of implicit surfaces (Bloomenthal 1994).

◇ Overview of the Triangulation Algorithm ◇

The algorithm proceeds in three steps as shown in Figure 1.

1. Decompose the Polygon into Trapezoids. Let S be a set of nonhorizontal, nonintersecting line segments of the polygon. The randomized algorithm is used to create the trapezoidal decomposition of the $X - Y$ plane arising from the segments of set S. This is done by taking a random ordering $s_1, \ldots, s_n$ of the segments in S and adding one segment at a time to incrementally construct the trapezoids. This divides the polygon into trapezoids (which can degenerate into a triangle if any of the horizontal segments of the trapezoid is of zero length). The restriction that the segments be nonhorizontal is necessary to limit the number of neighbors of any trapezoid. However, no generality

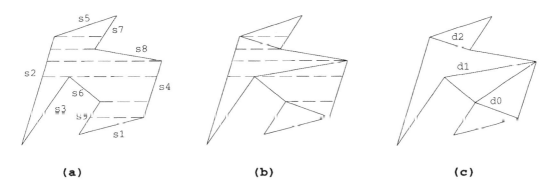

Figure 1. Generating monotone polygons from the trapezoid formation.

is lost because of this assumption, as it can be simulated using lexicographic ordering. That is, if two points have the same Y-coordinate, then the one with the larger X-coordinate is considered *higher*. The number of trapezoids is linear in the number of segments. Seidel proves that if each permutation of $s_1, \ldots, s_n$ is equally likely, then trapezoid formation takes $O(n \log^* n)$ expected time (*op. cit.*).

2. Decompose the Trapezoids into Monotone Polygons. A monotone polygon is a polygon whose boundary consists of two Y-monotone chains. These polygons are computed from the trapezoidal decomposition by checking whether the two vertices of the original polygon lie on the same side. This is a linear time operation.

3. Triangulate the Monotone Polygons. A monotone polygon can be triangulated in linear time by using a simple greedy algorithm that repeatedly cuts off the convex corners of the polygon (Fournier and Montuno 1984). Hence, all the monotone polygons can be triangulated in $O(n)$ time.

◇ **Data Structures for Implementation** ◇

All the data structures used in the implementation are statically allocated. The trapezoid formation requires a structure where the neighbors of each trapezoid and its neighboring segments can be determined in constant time. Therefore, for every trapezoid, the indices of its neighbors and the segments are stored in its table-entry T.

The query-structure Q, used to determine the location of a point, is implemented as described by Seidel. The same Q can be later used for fast point-location queries. Both Q and T are updated as a new segment is added into the existing trapezoid formation. This entails splitting in two the trapezoid(s) in which the endpoints of the segment lie, then traversing along the edge of the segment to merge in any neighboring trapezoids

Table 1. Performance on randomly generated polygons.

Number of Vertices	Running Time
10	0.9 ms
50	3.5 ms
100	6.7 ms
500	42.7 ms
1000	97.6 ms
5000	590.0 ms
10000	1.24 s
50000	7.3 s
100000	15.45 s

which both share the same left and right edges and also share a horizontal edge. All the monotone polygons are stored in a single linked list with pointers to the first vertex in the list stored in a table.

◇ Implementation Notes ◇

Table 1 shows the average running time of the algorithm for randomly generated data sets of various sizes. All the measurements were taken on an HP Series 735 with execution times averaged over one hundred repetitions.

Empirical testing has proven the method robust across wide classes of input data. The present implementation uses an ϵ (epsilon) tolerance when testing for floating-point equality. This computation occurs when determining whether a point lies to the left (right) of a segment or when detecting coincident points. This tolerance could potentially be removed by substituting a well-crafted point-in-polygon test (Haines 1994).

The triangulation code is invoked through the main interface routine,

```
int triangulate_polygon(n, vertices, triangles);
```

with an n-sided polygon given for input (the vertices are specified in canonical anti-clockwise order with no duplicate points). The output is an array of $n-2$ triangles (with vertices also in anticlockwise order). Once triangulated, point-location queries can be invoked as

```
int is_point_inside_polygon(vertex);
```

additional details appear in the C source code that accompanies this gem.

◇ **Bibliography** ◇

(Bloomenthal 1994) Jules Bloomenthal. An implicit surface polygonizer. In Paul Heckbert, editor, *Graphics Gems IV*, pages 324–349. AP Professional, Boston, 1994.

(Fournier and Montuno 1984) A. Fournier and D.Y. Montuno. Triangulating simple polygons and equivalent problems. *ACM Trans. on Graphics*, 3:153–174, 1984.

(Haines 1994) Eric Haines. Point in polygon strategies. In Paul Heckbert, editor, *Graphics Gems IV*, pages 24–46. AP Professional, Boston, 1994.

(Kumar and Manocha 1994) S. Kumar and D. Manocha. Interactive display of large scale NURBS models. Technical Report TR94-008, Department of Computer Science, University of North Carolina, 1994.

(Lischinski 1994) Dani Lischinski. Incremental Delaunay triangulation. In Paul Heckbert, editor, *Graphics Gems IV*, pages 47–59. AP Professional, Boston, 1994.

(O'Rourke 1994) J. O'Rourke. *Computational Geometry in C*. Cambridge University Press, 1994.

(Seidel 1991) R. Seidel. A simple and fast incremental randomized algorithm for computing trapezoidal decompositions and for triangulating polygons. *Computational Geometry: Theory and Applications*, 1(1):51–64, 1991.

(Tor and Middleditch 1984) S. B. Tor and A. E. Middleditch. Convex decomposition of simple polygons. *ACM Trans. on Graphics*, 3(4):244–265, 1984.

VII.6

Accurate Z-Buffer Rendering

Raghu Karinthi
West Virginia University
raghu@cs.wvu.edu

This gem describes the software implementation of a high-precision color Z-buffer renderer. The system is virtual: No frame-buffer hardware is assumed. Instead, a twenty-four-bit color model supported by a number of widely available Internet utilities (Fleischer and Salesin 1992, Foley *et al.* 1990) creates a desirable and highly portable system.

◇ Description ◇

The sequence of steps that map (in perspective) a scene description onto a raster file appears in Figure 1. This gem leverages off several freely available utilities to embody each function block. First, the input is presented using a slightly modified version of the Neutral File Format (NFF) used in the Standard Procedural Database (SPD) created as a universal means of scene description (Haines 1987). Twenty-four-bit color descriptors are used, which ultimately represent each output pixel. The matrix library underpinning both the viewing transformation plus other vector-based computation is taken from the SPHIGS package (Foley *et al.* 1990). Rasterization is based upon the fixed point methods whose routines appear in a previous gem (Fleischer and Salesin 1992); extensions include a 2D RGBZ interpolator. The pixel values are written in TARGA format using file write and display routines[1] taken from Paul Rivero's *LUG* library.

This gem is written in C and compiles under the Gnu C compiler on Unix platforms. Source code appears on the gems disk and FTP mirrors. The commands are:

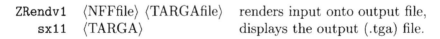

ZRendv1 ⟨NFFfile⟩ ⟨TARGAfile⟩   renders input onto output file,
   sx11 ⟨TARGA⟩   displays the output (.tga) file.

Figure 1.   The z-buffer rendering pipeline.

---

[1]The author thanks Todd Montgomery for his assistance.

◇   **Bibliography**   ◇

(Fleischer and Salesin 1992) K. Fleischer and D. Salesin. Accurate polygon scan conversion using half-open intervals. In David Kirk, editor, *Graphics Gems III*, Chapter 7.6, pages 362–365. AP Professional, Boston, 1992.

(Foley *et al.* 1990) J. Foley, A. van Dam, S. Feiner, and J. Hughes. *Computer Graphics: Principles and Practice, Second Edition*, Chapter 7, Object Hierarchy and Simple PHIGS (SPHIGS). Addison-Wesley, Reading, MA, 1990.

(Haines 1987) E. Haines. A proposal for standard graphics environments. *IEEE Computer Graphics and Applications*, 17(11):3–5, November 1987.

◊ VII.7

A Survey of Extended Graphics Libraries

Alan Wm. Paeth
Department of Computer Science
Okanagan University College
Kelowna, British Columbia, Canada
awpaeth@okanagan.bc.ca

Ferdi Scheepers & Stephen May
Department of Computer Science
Ohio State University
Columbus, Ohio
ferdi,smay@cgrg.ohio-state.edu

The very first source code appearing in *Graphics Gems* described a three-dimensional vector library. Written humbly in C and offered without an accompanying gem, it introduced that volume's first appendix.[1] From these simple beginnings it is fitting that Volume V should conclude with a cornucopia of extended graphics libraries. Four complete works are presented; full run-time details may be found in each library's sources.

◊   Overview   ◊

The libraries are a synthesis of many ideas appearing as full-fledged gems in Volume IV. The lineage of each entry may be traced to the revised C entry (Glassner and Haines 1994) and/or the related C++ library (Doué 1994). Methods of n-dimensional Euclidean geometry (Hanson 1994) provide a means of dimension extension, as does the perp-dot product (Hill 1994).

The libraries have both production and research application. For practical purposes, straightforward naming conventions assist both maintenance and a "correctness by construction" style of design. Utility functions support memory allocation, stream I/O, or assertion macros, thereby providing run-time diagnostics or otherwise ensuring proper operation. As research tools, they have been used to explore the regular polytopes, Rubik's hypercube, hyperplane rotation, and the mixed orthographic/perspective projections as is possible when viewing a scene in 4D world coordinates upon a 2D display.

The libraries are written in both C and C++ and offer a number of extensions. Operators in C++ allow a compelling polymorphism: v1 = v2 * f operates naturally upon vectors or scalars with equal facility; the elements in the right-hand side can commute.

---

[1] The library was revised by Bogart in Volume II.

Table 1.   Features of the extended graphics libraries.

Title, Contributor(s)	Source Directory	Macro-based	Maximum dimension	Additional comments
A Graphics Math Library Ferdi Scheepers & Stephen May	libgm C++ (all)	some inlines	3 (4)	The compleat C++ graphics library
A Toolbox of Macro Functions Christophe Schlick	mactbox C	yes, entirely	3 (4)	Elegant macros are gentle on the eyes
Penultimate Vector Macros Don Hatch	vec-h C,C++	yes (in C)	n (n+1)	C/C++ macros to go in any dimension
The C Vector Library in 4D Steve Hill	GG4D C	few	4 (5)	The 4D tour de force (includes 4D projections)

Macros[2] are used to advantage by all and by two exclusively [in C++ the `inline` may substitute (Lippman 1991)]. Macros support fast in-line evaluation of small routines without procedure overhead—their traditional use. They provide further leverage when used to redefine functions or even macros, thereby providing a means of "rewriting" a library at compile time for operation at increased dimension or with `double` precision operators substituting for `float`. The basic capabilities are summarized in Table 1.

Each complete library resides on disk in a private directory whose name appears in column two. The maximum dimension n (column four) lists the dimension of intended use; partial extention to dimension $(n + 1)$ is typically present to support the use of homogeneous coordinates.

◇   **A Graphics Math Library**   ◇

The C++ graphics library `libgm` (eight files) created by Scheepers and May supports a wide range of traditional vector- and scalar-based geometric operations. It is the largest library and of value as a direct C++ upgrade to previous entries in this series. It is production software in the best sense, employing the naming conventions' consistent and nonconflicting use typical of the genre (Anderson *et al.* 1991). Other features include scalar definitions at twenty-digit precision, `inline` versions of simple functions, and an `assert` macro used to verify expected function input values.

Standard vector operations through 3D are supported, with matrix support extended to basic 4×4 operations (including inversion). Utility operations include range clamps and linear and Hermite interpolators. Lower-level routines (macros) provide other useful functions, such as "fuzzy" floating-point equality, of value when (for instance) dealing

---

[2]An early macro-based graphics library by Hollasch appears as an appendix in Volumes II and III (Hollasch 1991, 1992).

Table 2. *libgm* vector operators.

Op	Description	Usage	Op	Description	Usage
[i]	access component i	f = v[0];	/=	destructive scalar divide	v1 /= f;
	2D: $i \in \{0,1\}$			requires: divisor $\not\approx 0$	
	3D: $i \in \{0,1,2\}$		+	addition	v1 = v2 + v3;
[i]	change component i	v[0] = f;	−	subtraction	v1 = v2 - v3;
	2D: $i \in \{0,1\}$		−	negation (unary)	v1 = -v2;
	3D: $i \in \{0,1,2\}$		*	scalar pre-multiply	v1 = f * v2;
=	assign	v1 = v2;	*	scalar post-multiply	v1 = v2 * f;
+=	destructive add	v1 += v2;	/	scalar divide	v1 = v2 / f;
-=	destructive subtract	v1 -= v2;		requires: divisor $\not\approx 0$	
*=	destructive scalar multiply	v1 *= f;	==	equality (fuzzy)	if (v1 == v2) ...
			!=	inequality (fuzzy)	if (v1 != v2) ...

with redundant vertices in space models which nonetheless differ slightly to the limits of machine precision.

As an illustration of style and use, a culled set of representative operations are presented in Tables 2 and 3. Further details on constructor use and additional operations and functions may be found in the prototypes **gm*.h** or the source **gmMatrix*.c**.

◇ A Toolbox of Macro Functions ◇

The C-language macro-based toolbox consists of ten ***.h** files, supporting more than three-hundred entries. The toolbox is based entirely on macros, hence the preference of the name "toolbox" over "library." Macros have zero function overhead, but this advantage is not without some cost. Local variables cannot be declared inside macros and (in six of the 300+) an additional parameter supplies a temporary variable.

An important feature of the toolbox is that even procedure-like macros return a value, allowing them to appear as expressions within assignment and **if** statements. This functional style of invocation is nicely supported within the macro bodies using the lesser-known , (comma) operator in C.

The kernel of the toolbox, **tool.h**, is based upon the original **GraphicsGems.h** and provides classical constants, and basic and extended functions. The latter includes clamping or rounding-off, floating-point comparison with tolerance, plus linear, cardinal, and Hermite interpolation. The file also provides general-purpose macros for memory handling, text file manipulation, and run-time error management in the respective macros ***_MEM**, ***_FILE**, and ***_ERROR**.

The essential files **sint.h**, **uint.h**, and **real.h** define scalar operations upon values having type **int**, **unsigned int**, and **float/double**. These scalar macros are used to derive the types **sintvec2** through **realmat4** that support 2D, 3D, and 4D operations on vectors and matrices. The related I/O macros **GET_SINT**, **PUT_REALVEC2**, and

Table 3. *libgm* utility functions.

Function	Description	Usage
gmAbs(f)	absolute value of f	f1 = gmAbs(f2);
gmCeil(f)	least integer greater than or equal to f	f1 = gmCeil(f2);
gmClamp(f,f1,f2)	clamp f to [f2,f3]	gmClamp(f,f1,f2);
gmCube(f)	f^3	f1 = gmCube(f2);
gmDegrees(f)	convert angle in radians, f, to angle in degrees	f1 = gmDegrees(f2);
gmFloor(f)	greatest integer less than or equal to f	f1 = gmFloor(f2);
gmFuzEQ(f1,f2)	true iff f1 is fuzzy equal to f2	if (gmFuzEQ(f1,f2)) ...
gmFuzGEQ(f1,f2)	true iff f1 is fuzzy greater than or equal to f2	if (gmFuzGEQ(f1,f2)) ...
gmFuzLEQ(f1,f2)	true iff f1 is fuzzy less than or equal to f2	if (gmFuzLEQ(f1,f2)) ...
gmInv(f)	inverse of f, $f \not\approx 0$	f1 = gmInv(f2);
gmIsZero(f)	true iff f is fuzzy equal to 0	if (gmIsZero(f)) ...
gmLerp(f,f1,f2)	linear interpolation from f1 (when $f = 0$) to f2 (when $f = 1$)	f3 = gmLerp(f,f1,f2);
gmMax(f1,f2)	maximum of f1 and f2	f = gmMax(f1,f2);
gmMax(f1,f2,f3)	maximum of f1 and f2 and f3	f = gmMax(f1,f2,f3);
gmMin(f1,f2)	minimum of f1 and f2	f = gmMin(f1,f2);
gmMin(f1,f2,f3)	minimum of f1 and f2 and f3	f = gmMin(f1,f2,f3);
gmRadians(f)	convert angle in degrees, f, to angle in radians	f1 = gmRadians(f2);
gmRound(f)	f rounded to nearest integer	f1 = gmRound(f2);
gmSign(f)	sign of f (-1 iff $f < 0$)	f1 = gmSign(f2);
gmSlide(f,f1,f2)	hermite interpolation from f1 (when $f = 0$) to f2 (when $f = 1$)	f3 = gmSlide(f,f1,f2);
gmSmooth(f)	smooth hermite interpolate of f	f1 = gmSmooth(f2);
gmSqr(f)	f^2	f1 = gmSqr(f2);
gmSwap(f1,f2)	swap f1 and f2	gmSwap(f1,f2);
gmSwap(i1,i2)	swap i1 and i2	gmSwap(i1,i2);
gmTrunc(f)	f truncated	f1 = gmTrunc(f2);
gmZSign(f)	zero or sign of f (-1, 0, or 1)	f1 = gmZSign(f2);

GET_UINTMAT3 also lend support. This methodology allows complete type substitution simply by setting a compiler switch, for example, -DSINGLE_SINT, or adding a #define SINGLE_SINT, thereby redefining all macros.

The remaining five *.h files provide an exhaustive set of vector and matrix manipulation tools. Their macros support operations including creation, duplication, arithmetic operations, comparison with tolerance, interpolations, dot or cross products, matrix determinant, transposition, and inversion.

The name of any macro takes the form **action_type** where "action" describes the macro operation and "type" the parameter type, for example, MIN_VEC2(V,A,B). This helps memorization of names and facilitates an eventual extension of the toolbox. Note that while the macros are defined in all cases, some cannot provide meaningful results, for example, matrix inversion upon the integers.

(Editor's note: The root solver QUADRATIC(a,b,c) requiring no temporaries and returning the number of roots is a work of art. Although it will not affect calculations at double precision, please note the last two digits of #define PI.)

◇ **Penultimate Vector Macros** ◇

This entry provides a major step in the direction of an ideal and hence "ultimate" macro library. In practice, the utility of even the most carefully crafted graphics library is lost when confronted with vectors having dimensional or type mismatch. This library's reason for existence is compelling: support code reuse in its broadest sense. This is achieved in an ironic fashion: Here it is the source code (the C program vec_h.c) that rewrites the macro file vec.h for given dimension n.

A machine-produced macro library has numerous advantages. Automatically produced files are easily tailored to their target application, are not prone to spurious typos, and can easily provide a uniform naming convention. The method works with a flourish: The vec.h file appearing in the distribution accompanying a companion gem (page 375) was created by executing the command vec_h 4.

The library supports garden-variety vector and matrix arithmetic operations upward through cross product and inversion, respectively. The former are generalized by using Hanson's definition (*op. cit.*) in preference to other alternatives (Goldman 1992); inversion is performed using Cramer's rule, taking advantage of macros that compute determinant and adjoints. Hill's "perp-dot" (*op. cit*) is also employed.

Finally, the library supports conformality in a highly extended sense. For instance, multiplying a 4×4 matrix by a 3×3 matrix produces a 4×4 result in a natural way. (In theory, the smaller matrix is augmented, placing 1's on the diagonal and 0's on the off-diagonal of the added row and column. In practice, the multiplications by zero and one are elided in the macro's definition, further increasing run-time efficiency.) As a last example of extended operation, the matrix operations support both row vector premultiplication and column vector postmultiplication. (Accordingly, the table of operations gives mathematical names only; parameter considerations are a nonissue.)

Table 4. Generic operations supported by vec.h.

assign	add	subtract	scalar multiply	scalar divide
dot product	cross product	transpose	determinant	adjoint
trace	assign	round to integer	fill with constant	set to zero
set to identity	compare	compare with zero	square of magnitude	squared difference
linear interpolation				

◇ **The C Vector Library in 4D** ◇

This library's emphasis is on 4D graphics in its broadest generality. The C++ library by Doué (*op. cit.*) was recoded in C and the scope of operation widened to support 5 × 5 matrices. The traditional (and bulky) matrix procedures which, for example, assign all elements *en masse* are largely absent. Replacing them are the affine matrix operations (rotation, translating, and scaling) which operate on coordinates (x, y, z, w) in homogeneous coordinates. Beyond simplifying coding style, this makes the library a useful research vehicle in the interactive exploration and visualization of 4D Euclidean space. Two affine matrices appear below.

$$\mathbf{S}(s_x, s_y, s_z, s_w) = \begin{pmatrix} s_x & 0 & 0 & 0 & 0 \\ 0 & s_y & 0 & 0 & 0 \\ 0 & 0 & s_z & 0 & 0 \\ 0 & 0 & 0 & s_w & 0 \\ 0 & 0 & 0 & 0 & 1 \end{pmatrix} \quad \mathbf{R}_{yw}(\theta) = \begin{pmatrix} 1 & 0 & 0 & 0 & 0 \\ 0 & \cos\theta & 0 & -\sin\theta & 0 \\ 0 & 0 & 1 & 0 & 0 \\ 0 & \sin\theta & 0 & \cos\theta & 0 \\ 0 & 0 & 0 & 0 & 1 \end{pmatrix}$$

The first supports independent (anamorphic) scaling given four parameters presented as a four-vector. The second rotates a matrix about the $y - w$ hyperplane by an amount θ. (There are six hyperplanes of rotation in 4D, an extension of the three axes of rotation in 3D.)

Perspective operations in 4D (which become orthographic projection in the limit) can be defined by analogy to their 3D counterparts; representative matrices appear in the source listings.

◇ **Contributors** ◇

One library was created by authors not appearing elsewere in this volume. These contributors are Ferdi Scheepers and Stephen May (Ohio State University, Columbus, Ohio), ferdi@cgrg.ohio-state.edu, and smay@cgrg.ohio-state.edu.

The editor wishes to thank those contributing to this and related works for their cooperation and patience in providing additional material on short notice.

◇ **Bibliography** ◇

(Anderson *et al.* 1991) E. Anderson, Z. Bai, C. Bischof, J. Demmel, J. Dongarra, J. Du Croz, A. Greenbaum, S. Hammarling, A. McKenney, and D. Sorensen. Preliminary LAPACK users' guide. Technical report, LAPACK Project, Computer Science Department, University of Tennessee, Knoxville, 1991.

(Doué 1994) Jean-François Doué. C++ vector and matrix algebra routines. In Paul Heckbert, editor, *Graphics Gems IV*, pages 534–557. Academic Press, Boston, 1994.

(Glassner and Haines 1994) Andrew Glassner and Eric Haines. C header file and vector library. In Paul Heckbert, editor, *Graphics Gems IV*, pages 558–570. Academic Press, Boston, 1994.

(Goldman 1992) Ronald Goldman. Cross product in four dimensions and beyond. In David Kirk, editor, *Graphics Gems III*, pages 84–88. Academic Press, Boston, 1992.

(Hanson 1994) Andrew J. Hanson. Geometry for n-dimensional graphics. In Paul Heckbert, editor, *Graphics Gems IV*, pages 149–170. Academic Press, Boston, 1994.

(Hill 1994) F. S. Hill, Jr. The pleasures of "perp dot" products. In Paul Heckbert, editor, *Graphics Gems IV*, pages 138–148. Academic Press, Boston, 1994.

(Hollasch 1991) Steve Hollasch. Useful C macros for vector operations. In James Arvo, editor, *Graphics Gems II*, pages 405–407. Academic Press, Boston, 1991.

(Hollasch 1992) Steve Hollasch. Useful C macros for vector operations. In David Kirk, editor, *Graphics Gems III*, pages 467–469. Academic Press, Boston, 1992.

(Lippman 1991) Stanley Lippman. *C++ Primer*. Addison-Wesley, Reading, MA, 1991.

◊ Index

A

Adaptive clustering (halftoning), 302
Adaptive image refinement, 355, *plates*
Algorithm
    Bresenham, exact clipping, 317
    Bresenham, inverse, 338
    Cohen-Sutherland, 315
    de Boor, 217
    de Casteljau, 199, 217
    Descartes-Euler-Cardano, 8
    Ferrari, 7
    Neumark, 9
    Seidel, 394
    Sutherland-Hodgman, 51
Ambiguous face, 99
Angle subdivision, *see* Ellipsoid generation
Arcs
    chord subdivision, nonuniform, 171
    chordal deviation, 169
    circular, 168
    de Casteljau subdivision, variant, 174
    radius of curvature, 168
    vertex deviation, 170, 174
Area
    polygon, 35
    quadrilateral, 37
    spherical triangle, 44
    vectors, 35
ARIES technique (halftoning), 303
Axial deformation, 139

B

B-spline curves
    de Boor algorithm, 217
    divided difference interpolation, 213, 217
    identities of basis functions, 163
    nonuniform rational, 216
    smooth connecting, 191
Back to front polygon rendering, 126
Back-face culling, 127
Bernstein basis functions, 149
Bézier curves
    arc length of, 199
    blossoms of, 191, 215
    control polygon, 204
    de Boor points, 194

    identities of Bernstein basis functions, 149
    interpolating form, linear, 213
    Gaussian quadrature, 199
    knot insertion, 194
    rendering of, 206
    smooth connection, 191
    subdivision, parametric, *see* de Casteljau
        algorithm
    vertex deviation, 174
Bidirectional reflectance distribution function, 285
Binary space-partitioning trees, 121
Body centered cubic lattice (bcc), 68, *see also* Truncated octahedron
BRDF, *see* Bidirectional reflectance distribution function
Bresenham algorithm (pixel rendering)
    exact clipping, 317
    inverse algorithm, pixel to vector, 338
BSP trees, *see* Binary space-partitioning trees

C

Catmull-Rom interpolation, 107
Catmull-Rom splines, 218
Cell ambiguity, 98
Chain code, 324, *see also* Edge contour
Characteristic matrix, *see* Conic sections
CIELAB, CIELUV color spaces, 62
Circumspheres (space packing), 67, 270
Clipping
    scanline-object, 242
    Sutherland-Hodgman, 51
    vector-viewport, 314
    view frustum, 127
Cohen-Sutherland clipping algorithm, 315
Collision testing, viewpoint
    moving polyhedra, 380
    static polygons, 128
Cone-line intersection, 227
Conic sections, 72
Continued fractions, 26
Contours
    edge, 338
    surface, 99
Coordinate
    barycentric, 211
    homogeneous, 112, 214

407

transformation, 111
unit cube frame representation, 141
Covariance matrix, 113
Cubic
    lattice, body centered, 68, *see also* Truncated octahedron
    lattice, face centered, 68, *see also* Rhombic dodecahedron
    symmetric polyhedra, 78, 83
    marching cubes, 98
    tricubic interpolation, 107
Cubic equations
    Descartes-Euler-Cardano, 8
    Ferrari's, 7
    Neumark's, 9
Cubic lattices, 62
Cuboctahedron, 70
Culling
    back-face, 127
    view-frustum, 127
Cylindrical luminaire, 285

D

de Boor algorithm, 217
de Boor-Fix formulas, 160, 166
de Casteljau algorithm, 199, 217
Decomposition
    into parallelohedra (space packing), 67
    quotient space, 61
    Seidel's algorithm (trapezoids, triangles), 394
    singular value, 115
Delaunay triangulation, 270
Descartes-Euler-Cardano algorithm, 8
Descartes' law of signs, 154
Directional light, 290
Dirichlet cell, 62, 270
Distance approximations, 78
Dithering, *see* Ordered dithering
Divergence theorem, 40

E

Edge contours, 338
Ellipse intersections
    equations, 75
    figure, 6
Ellipsoid generation, 179
Euclidean geometry, n-D
    graphics libraries, extended, 400
    n-D rotation, 55, 405
    n-D solids, 79
Euclidean norm, *see* Distance approximations
Euler angles, *see* Quotient space decomposition

F

Face centered cubic lattice (fcc), 68, *see also* Rhombic dodecahedron
Ferrari's algorithm, 7
Fluorescent lights, *see* Cylindrical luminaire

G

Girard's formula, 44
Graphics libraries, 400
Green's theorem, 40

H

Halftoning, 297, 302
Hermite interpolation, 212, 401
Hexakis octahedron, 82, *plates*
Hierarchical traverse, 246

I

Interpolation
    B-spline, divided differences, 213, 217
    Bézier curves, 213
    Hermite, 212, 401
    RGBZ, 398
    slerp, 62
    tricubic, 107
Intersection
    cone–line, 227
    moving polyhedra–viewpoint, 80
    polygon–cube, 375
    quadrangle surface–line, 232
    scanline–object, 242
    swept sphere–line, 258

L

Lagrange polynomials, 210
Least-squares fit, linear, 92
Lie algebra, 59
Line parameterization, 92

M

Marching cubes, 98
Marsden identities, 160, 166
Mathematician's tea, 37
Menelaus' theorem, 213
Mensuration, *see* Area *and* Volume
Microdot distribution, 297
Moiré patterns, 300
Monte-Carlo integration, 359
Multilinearity, 215

N

Nearest neighbor, 3D, 65
Neumark's algorithm, 9
Neutral file format (NFF), 398
Noise function, *see* Wave generators
NURBS, *see* B-splines, nonuniform rational

O

Octahedral subdivision, *see* Ellipsoid
      generation
Optical character recognition (OCR), 329
Optimal sampling patterns, 359
Ordered dithering, 297, *plates*
Oriented lines, 50

P

Packing
    body centered cubic (bcc), 68
    face centered cubic (fcc), 68
    circumspherical, 67, 270
Painter's algorithm, *see* Back to front polygon
     rendering
Parallelohedron, 67
Perp-dot product, 400
Polygon partitioning
    concave, 50
    general 2D in 3D, 386
    by half-space membership, 122
    triangulation, 394
Polyhedra figures
    cube (hexahedron), 67
    elongated dodecahedron, 67
    hexagonal prism, 67
    hexakis octahedron, 83, *plates*
    octahedron, 83
    rhombic dodecahedron, 67, 68, 83
    trapezoidal icositetrahedron, 83
    truncated octahedron, 68
Polylines, 212
Polytopes, semiregular, 67, 78, 83
Progressing refinement, radiosity, 290,
     plates

Q

Quadric surfaces, 3
Quartic equations, 4
    Descartes-Euler-Cardano, 8
    Ferrari's, 7
    Neumark's, 9
Quaternions, as rotation groups, 62, 84
Quotient space decomposition, 61

R

Rational curves, 214
Rational numbers, 25
Rendering software
    Bézier curves, 206
    Bresenham algorithm, exact clipping, 317
    BSP tree based, 131
    Z-buffer based, 398
RGBZ interpolation, 398
Rhombic dodecahedron (bcc packing), 68
Rolling ball, 55
Rotation groups, 59

S

S-patch surfaces, 219
Sagitta, 169
Sampling
    Optimal patterns, 359
    Solid-angle based, 287
    Stochastic supersampling, 248
Scanline-object rejection, 242
Seidel's algorithm, 394
Selective precipitation (halftoning), 302
Sequential probability test ratio, 356
Shape vectorization, 323
Simplex object, 99
Singular value decomposition, 115
Slerp interpolation, 62
Software packages, *see* Rendering software *and*
     Graphics libraries
Space subdivision, Voronoi, 268
Spatial classification
    n-D semiregular cubic solids, 78
    n-D Voronoi cells, 270
    parallelohedral decomposition (space packing),
     67
Spherical polygons, 42
Spherical projection, 43
SPHIGS package, 398
SPRT, *see* Sequential probability test ratio
Square root
    fixed point, 22
    floating point, inverse, 16
Staircase patterns, 338
Stochastic supersampling, 248
Subdivision
    angle, *see* Ellipsoid generation
    arcs, circular, 168
    Bézier, parametric, *see* de Casteljau algorithm
    chord, nonuniform, 171
    curve, 174
    space (Voronoi), 268
    surface, 104

Surface description
  by *n*-D cubic cells, 98
  by quadrangle mesh, 235
  by triangular mesh, 232
  by voxel, 273
Surfaces
  cell ambiguity, 98
  contours, 99
  quadric, 3
  S-patch, 219
  subdivision, 104
  tensor-product, 219
  tessellated, 232
Sutherland-Hodgman clipping, 51
SVD, *see* Singular value decomposition
Swept spheres, 258

T

TARGA file format, 398
Tensor product surfaces, 219
Tessellated surfaces, 232
Theiessen tessellation, *see* Voronoi
      diagrams
Theorem
  divergence, 40
  Green's, 40
  Menelaus, 213

Threshold matrices, 297
Trapezoidal
  decomposition, from polygon, 394
  icositetrahedron, 83
  test, 236
Triangle, decomposition from polygon, 395
Tricubic interpolation, 107
Truncated octahedron (fcc packing), 68
Tubular extrusions, *see* Swept spheres

V

View-frustum culling, 127
Volume
  hexahedron, 39
  polyhedron, 37
  tetrahedron, 38
Voronoi diagrams, 269
Voxel walking, 273

W

Wave generators, 367

Z

Z-buffer, 398
zonotopes, 70

◇ Volume I–V Cumulative Index

Format: volume number.page number

A

Absorption coefficient, II.279–II.280
Absorption index, II.280
A-buffer, I.76
Active edge list, I.92–I.93
Adaptive clustering (halftoning), V.302
Adaptive image refinement, V.355
Adaptive meshing, radiosity, shadow boundary
  detection, II.311–II.315
Adaptive prediction–correction coders, II.94–II.95
Adaptive subdivision, of surface, IV.287
Addresses, precalculating, I.285–I.286
Adjacent facets, normals, II.239
Adjoint matrices, I.538
Affine matrix
  group, II.345
  inverse, II.348–II.349
Affine modeling transformations, normal vectors,
  I.539–I.542
Affine transformation, *see also* Transformation
  decomposing, III.116
  unit circle inscribed in square, III.170
Aggregate objects, II.264
Albers equal-area conic map projection,
  I.321–I.325
Algebra, *see* Matrix; Vector
Algorithm
  Bresenham, *see* Bresenham's algorithm
  Cohen–Sutherland, V.315
  de Boor, V.217
  de Casteljau, V.199, V.217
  Descartes–Euler–Cardano, V.8
  Ferrari, V.7
  Neumark, V.9
  Seidel, V.394
  Sutherland–Hodgman, V.51
Aliasing, narrow domains, II.123–II.124
Alpha blending, I.210–I.211
Alpha buffer, I.218
Alpha compositing operators, I.211
Alternating Bresenham edge-calculator,
  III.350–III.351
Altitudes, triangles, intersection, I.22
Ambiguous face, V.99
Angle-preserving matrix group, II.345

Angles
  encoding, bit patterns, I.442
  not uniform, III.128–III.129
  subdivision, *see* Ellipsoid generation
  sum and difference relations, I.16
Animation
  camera control, IV.230
  collision detection, IV.83
  morphing, IV.445
  recording, I.265–I.269
    double-framed order, I.265–I.266
  2 1/2-D depth-of-field simulation, III.36–III.38
Anti-aliased circle generation, II.445–II.449
Anti-aliased lines, rendering, I.105–I.106
Anti-aliasing, I.37, IV.370, IV.445, *see also* Area of
  intersection
  advanced, algorithm, I.194–I.195
  combining spatial and temporal, III.376–III.378
  edge and bit-mask calculations, III.345–III.354,
    III.586
  pixel, I.73
  polygon scan conversion, I.76–I.83
  triangular pixels, III.369–III.373
Anti-aliasing filters, I.143
  common resampling tasks, I.147–I.165
    box filter, I.149
    choices of filters, I.148
    comparative frequency responses, I.161
    comparison of filters, I.151–I.152
    continuous, sampled, and discrete signals,
      I.147
    decimation, I.147–I.148
      with Lanczos2 sinc function, I.160–I.161
    Gaussian filter, I.150–I.153
    Gaussian 1/2 filter frequency response, I.163
    Gaussian $1/\sqrt{2}$ filter frequency response,
      I.164
    half-phase filter frequency response,
      I.162–I.163
    interpolation, I.147–I.148
      by factor of two with Lanczos2 sinc
        function, I.158–I.159
      with Gaussian 1/2 filter, I.152–I.154,
        I.156
      with Gaussian $1/\sqrt{2}$ filter, I.154–I.156

Anti-aliasing filters (*cont.*)
    Lanczos2 sinc functions frequency response,
      I.164–I.165
    Lanczos-windowed sinc functions,
      I.156–I.158
    sinc function, I.156–I.157
    tent filter, I.149–I.150
    zero-phase filter frequency response, I.162
  cone plus cosine, I.145–I.146
  Gaussian filter, I.144–I.145
  minimizing bumpy sampling, I.144–I.146
Apple patent, II.31–II.32
Apollonius problem, solution, III.203–III.209
  10th problem, II.19–II.24
Approximation, IV.241
Arcball, IV.175
Archimedean solids, semi-regular, II.177
Archival media, II.165
Arcs
  chordal deviation, V.169
  circular, V.168
  de Casteljau subdivision, variant, V.174
  chord subdivision, nonuniform, V.171
  vertex deviation, V.170, V.174
  radius of curvature, V.168
Arctangent, approximation, II.389–II.391
Area
  computing, binary digital image, II.107–II.111
  planar polygon, IV.3, IV.141
  polygon, II.5–II.6, V.35
  quadrilateral, V.37
  spherical polygon, IV.132
  spherical triangle, V.44
  triangle, I.20, IV.140, IV.161
  vectors, V.35
Area of intersection
  circle and half-plane, I.38–I.39
  circle and thick line, I.40–I.42
  two circles, I.43–I.46
Area-to-differential-area form factor, II.313
ARIES technique (halftoning), V.303
Arithmetic
  complex, IV.139
  exponentiation, IV.385, IV.403
  floating point, IV.125, IV.422
  integer, IV.123, IV.449, IV.526
Asymmetric filter, II.52–II.53
Autumn terminator, II.440–II.441
Axes, transforming, I.456–I.459
Axial deformation, V.139
Axis-aligned bounding boxes, transformation,
  I.548–I.550
Axis-amount representation, conversion with
  matrix, I.466–I.467
Azimuthal equal-area projection, I.317

Azimuthal equidistant projection, I.316–I.317
Azimuthal projections, I.314–I.317

B

Backface culling, I.346–I.347, I.544–I.545, V.127
Back to front polygon rendering, V.126
Banding, I.263
Bartlett filter, III.13, III.15
Barycentric coordinates, IV.162
Bernstein basis, II.406, II.409
Bernstein basis functions, V.149
  integration, I.604–I.606
Bernstein–Bézier, equation conversion to,
  I.409–I.411
Bernstein polynomials, I.613–I.614, II.407,
  II.409–II.410, II.428
Betacam, II.154
Beta function, integral form, III.150–III.151
Beveling, I.107–I.113
Bézier control points, derivation, II.377
Bézier curve-based root-finder, I.408–I.415
  bounding box, I.413–I.414
  conversion to Bernstein–Bézier form,
    I.409–I.411
  finding roots, I.411–I.415
  root-finding algorithm, I.412–I.413
Bézier curves and surfaces, I.613–I.616,
  II.412–II.416, IV.256, IV.261, *see also*
  Cubic Bézier curves
  arc length of, V.199
  blossoms of, V.191, V.215
  control polygon, V.204
  de Boor points, V.194
  de Casteljau Evaluation Algorithm, I.587–I.589
  derivative formulas, II.429
  differentiation, I.589–I.590
  fitting to digitized curve, I.616–I.624
  Gaussian quadrature, V.199
  identities of Bernstein basis functions, V.149
  interpolating form, linear, V.213
  interpolation using, III.133–III.136
    code, III.468
    implementation, III.136
    numeric solution, III.134
    symbolic solution, III.134–III.135
  knot insertion, V.194
  least-squares approximations, II.406
  monomial evaluation algorithm, I.590–I.591
  multivariate approximation, II.409–II.411
  notation, I.587
  parametric surface, IV.278, IV.290
  parametric versus geometric continuity,
    II.430–II.431
  properties, I.587–I.593
  rendering of, V.206

smooth connection, V.191
subdivision, parametric, *see* de Casteljau
    algorithm
in terms of Bernstein polynomials,
    I.613–I.614
univariate approximation, II.406–II.408
vertex deviation, V.174
Bézier form, conversion, I.609–I.611
from monomial form, I.591–I.592
to monomial form, I.592–I.593
Bézier simplices, II.412
Bézier triangles, conversion to rectangular patches,
    III.256–III.261, III.536
Bias function, IV.401
Bidirectional reflectance distribution function,
    V.285
Bilinear interpolation, *see* Interpolation
Binary digital image, II.107
computing area, circumference, and genus,
    II.107–II.111
    algorithm, II.109–II.111
    method, II.107–II.109
Binary order, animation recording, I.266–I.269
Binary recursive subdivision, ray–triangle
    intersection, II.257–II.263
Binary space partitioning tree, III.226,
    V.121–V.138
ray tracing with, III.271–III.274, III.538
Bisection, Strum sequences, I.420–I.421
Bit arithmetic, *see also* Element exchanging
bit rotation (tables), II.84
counting under a mask, II.372
finding first on bit, II.366, II.374
reading a write-mask, I.219
palindrome generation, II.369
power of two, test, II.366
tallying on/off bits, II.374–II.376
BitBlt, IV.486
generalized, algorithm, I.193–I.194
Bitmap, IV.466, IV.486
black-and-white, compositing, III.34–III.35
scaling operations, optimization, III.17–III.19,
    III.425
stretching, III.4–III.7, III.411
Bitmap rotator, 90-degree, II.84–II.85
Bit-mask calculations, III.352–III.354, III.586
Bits
conversion with digits, I.435
interleaving, quad- and octrees, I.443–I.447
patterns, encoding angles, I.442
Black-and-white bitmaps, compositing,
    III.34–III.35
Blobby model, IV.324
Blue–green plane, domain, II.120–II.122

Blue scanlines, adjusting minimum and maximum,
    II.122–II.123
Blur, *see* Image, filter
Body centered cubic lattice (bcc), V.68
Body color model, II.277–II.282
theoretical basis, II.277–II.278
Bottom-Up, II.206, II.208–II.209
Boundary generator, composited regions,
    III.39–III.43, III.441
Bounding box, IV.26, IV.74
axis-aligned, transformation, I.548–I.550
fifth-degree polynomial, I.413–I.414
radiosity, II.304–II.305
Bounding method, torus, II.254–II.255
Bounding sphere, I.301–I.303
Bounding volume algorithm
linear-time, III.301–III.306
worst case, III.302
Bounding volumes
cone, III.297
cube, III.295–III.296
cylinder, III.296–III.297
linear-time simple, III.301–III.306
polygon, III.296
rectangular, primitives, III.295–III.300, III.555
sorting, II.272
sphere, III.298–III.299
torus, III.299
Box, I.326
intersection with ray, fast, I.395–I.396
Kuhn's triangulation, III.246–III.247,
    III.252–III.253
Box filter, I.149, I.180, II.51–II.52, III.13, III.15
Box-sphere intersection testing, I.335–I.339
Branching, I.558–I.561
BRDF, V.285
Bresenham's algorithm, I.101 *see also* Line
    drawing
exact clipping, V.317
inverse algorithm, pixel to vector, V.308
line drawing algorithm, I.105–I.106,
    III.4–III.5
spheres-to-voxels conversion, I.327–I.329
Bresenham's circles, II.448–II.449
Brightness mapping, IV.415
B-spline curves, IV.252
de Boor algorithm, V.217
divided difference interpolation, V.213, V.217
identities of basis functions, V.163
non-uniform rational, IV.256, IV.286, V.216
smooth connecting, V.191
B-splines, II.377–II.378
cubic, knot insertion, II.425–II.427
parametric surface, IV.286

BSP trees, *see* Binary space-partitioning trees
Bump mapping, II.106, IV.433
Bumpy sampling, anti-aliasing filters that
  minimize, I.144–I.146
Butz's algorithm, II.25

C

Cache performance, increasing, II.87
Caching, II.268
Camera transformation, IV.230
Canonical fill algorithm, I.279
Cardano's Formula, I.405
Cartesian color cubes, I.254–I.255
Cartesian products
  color pixels, I.254–I.256
  extensions, I.256
Cartesian triple, factoring into, I.255–I.256
Cartography, *see* Map projections
Catmull–Rom interpolation, V.107
Catmull–Rom splines, V.218
Cell ambiguity, V.98
Cell occupancy, for different grid sizes,
  I.262
Center of gravity, triangles, I.20–I.21
Center of mass, superquadrics, III.139
Central projection, I.315
Centroid of a polygon, IV.3
Chain code, V.324, *see also* Edge contours
Chain rule, II.184
Change matrix, iteration, I.468–I.469
Change-of-focus simulation, III.38
Channel, frame buffer, I.217–I.218
Characteristic matrix, V.72
C header file, III.393–III.395
Chebychev polynomials, I.60
Chord-length parameterization, I.617, I.621
Chrominance, II.150
Cibachrome, II.164–II.165
Cibatrans, II.164–II.165
CIELAB, CIELUV color spaces, V.62
Circle
  anti-aliased generation, II.445–II.449
  area of intersection
    with half-plane, I.38–I.39
    with thick line, I.40–I.42
    two circles, I.43–I.46
  bounding, II.14–II.16
  Bresenham's algorithm, I.327–I.329
  circumscribing a triangle, IV.47, IV.143
  containing intersection of two circles,
    II.17–II.18
  drawing, shear algorithm, I.192 I.193
  inscribing a triangle, IV.145
  integral radius, on integral lattices,
    I.57–I.60

intersection
    with line, 2D, I.5–I.6
    with rectangle, fast checking, I.51–I.53
  with radials, II.383
  tangent line
    perpendicular to line, I.8–I.9
    to two circles, 2D, I.7–I.8
    2D, I.5
  touching three given circles, II.19–II.24
    2D, I.4–I.5
Circle clipping algorithm, III.182–III.187, III.487
Circular arc, straight-line approximation,
    II.435–II.439
Circular arc fillet, joining two lines,
    III.193–III.198, III.496
Circumcenter, triangles, I.20–I.23
Circumcircle, IV.47, IV.143
Circumference, computing, binary digital image,
    II.107–II.111
Circumradius, triangles, I.20–I.23
Circumspheres (space packing), V.67, V.270
C^1 joint, between cubic Bézier curves, II.432
CLAHE (contrast limited adaptive histogram
    equalization), IV.476
Class numbers, I.115–I.116
Clipping
  complex, II.44
  generic convex polygons, I.84–I.86
  line
    n-dimensional, IV.159
    in 2D and 4D, IV.125
  scanline-object, V.242
  Sutherland–Hodgman, V.51
  3D homogeneous, triangle strips,
    II.219–II.231
  2D, *see* Two-dimensional clipping
  vector-viewport, V.314
  view frustum, V.127
Closed loops, cubic spline interpolation formulas,
    I.580–I.582
Clustered-dot dither, II.63
C macros, vector operations, III.405
Cohen-Sutherland clipping algorithm, V.315
Coherence, II.26
  measure, II.28, II.30
Collision detection, IV.83
Collision testing, viewpoint
  moving polyhedra, V.380
  static polygons, V.128
Color
  image display, IV.415
  quantization, IV.422
  subroutines useful for RBG images, IV.534
Color cube, I.233–I.234, I.254–I.255
Color descriptor table, II.144

Color dithering, II.72–II.77
  conventions, II.72
  error-propagation dithering, II.75–II.77
  gamma correction, II.72–II.73
  ordered dithering, II.73–II.75
Color hardcopy, frame buffer, II.163–II.165
Color maps (LUTS), I.216–I.218, IV.401, IV.413
  animation, random algorithm, II.134–II.137
  basic architecture, I.215
  geometrically determined, I.233, II.143
  interpolation, II.138
  manipulation, 1-to-1 pixel transforms, I.270–I.274
  pseudo, PHIGS PLUS, II.138–II.140
  visible selections, III.77, IV.413
Color pixels, Cartesian products, I.254–I.256
Color printers, II.165
Color quantization, *see also* Octree quantization
  algorithm details and analysis, II.131–II.132
  based on variance minimization, II.127
  Cartesian, I.254
  color statistic computations, II.128–II.131
  error, II.126–II.128
  experimental results, II.133
  onto fourteen values, I.233
  inverse color mapping, II.116
  octree based, I.287
  optimal, statistical computations, II.126–II.133
  onto sixteen values, II.143
  variance minimizing, optimal, II.126
Color reduction filter, III.20–III.22, III.429
Color reference frame, II.148
Color rendering, linear, III.343–III.348, III.583
Color solid, four-bit, I.235–I.236
Color statistics, computations, II.128–II.131
Color television monitor, calibration, II.159–II.162
Combinatorics, inclusion–exclusion, II.129–II.130
Compact cubes, III.24–III.28
Compaction algorithm, II.89
Compact isocontours, III.23–III.28
  compact cubes, III.24–III.28
  cube-based contouring, III.23–III.24
Complex clipping, II.44
Complexity analysis, RGB triples, I.244
Complex number, IV.139
Composited regions, boundary generator,
    III.39–III.43, III.441
Compositing stage, III.37
Compression, II.49
  image file, II.93–II.100
Compression ratios, II.97, II.100
Compression techniques, II.89
Computational cost, jitter generation, I.67–I.68
Concave polygon
  scan conversion, I.87–I.91
  testing for, IV.7

Conducting medium, light reflection, II.286
Cone
  bounding volume, III.297
  equation for, IV.321
  intersection of ray with, IV.355
Cone–ellipsoid intersection, I.321–I.322
Cone–line intersection, V.227
Cone plus cosine, I.145–I.146
Conformal mapping, *see* Map projections
Conic sections, V.72
Conjugate diameters, III.169–III.171
Connection algorithm, 2-D drawing,
    III.173–III.181, III.480
  definitions, III.173–III.174
  overcrossing correction, III.179–III.180
  translate and rotate algorithm, III.174–III.179
Constants, full precision, I.434
Constraints for interactive rotation, IV.177
Continued fractions, V.26
Continuity conditions, cubic Bézier curves,
    I.615–I.616
Continuous image, I.246
Continuous signals, I.147
Contour data, defining surfaces from, I.558–I.561
Contours
  defining, I.554
  edge, V.338
  surface, V.99
  swept, I.562–I.564
Contrast
  cursor, IV.413
  display of high, IV.415
  enhancement, IV.401, IV.474
Contrast enhancement transform, I.197–I.198,
    I.201–I.202, I.270–I.271, I.274
Convex
  polygon, IV.7, IV.25, IV.141
  polyhedron, collision detection, IV.83
Convex decompositions, polygons, I.97
Convolution, IV.447
Convolution kernel, II.50–II.51
Coordinate frames, I.522–I.532
  matrix representation, I.524
  problem solving examples, I.527–I.532
  vectors and points, I.522–I.523, I.526
Coordinate Rotation Digital Computer, *see*
    CORDIC
Coordinates
  barycentric, V.211
  homogeneous, I.523, V.112, V.214
  nonhomogeneous, I.523
  transformation, V.111
  unit-cube frame representation, V.141
Coplanar sets, of nearly coplanar polygons,
    III.225–III.230, III.512

CORDIC, vector rotation, I.494–I.497
Corner rounding, IV.145
Corner value, I.553–I.554
Cosine
    angles between lines, 2D, I.11
    in exponentials, I.15
Covariance matrix, V.113
C-Print, II.164–II.165
Crack prevention, IV.292
    space packing lattices, II.174
Cramer's Rule, I.538, IV.90, IV.142, IV.164
Cross product, II.333–II.334
    in four dimensions and beyond, III.84–III.88
    identity, IV.158, IV.397
    matrix, I.473
    n-dimensional, IV.156, IV.167
    sign calculation, II.392–II.393
    in 2D, IV.140
Cross-section, positioning and orienting, I.570
Cube
    bounding volume, III.295–III.296
    dihedral, II.174–II.175
    intersection with triangle, III.236–III.239,
        III.521
Cube-based contouring, III.23–III.24
Cubic, *see also* Cubic lattices
    symmetric polyhedra, V.78, V.83
    marching cubes, V.98
    tricubic interpolation, V.107
Cubic Bézier curves, I.579, I.614, II.428–II.429
    continuity conditions, I.615–I.616
    forward differencing, I.600–I.601, I.603
    geometrically continuous, II.428–II.434
Cubic B-spline, III.14–III.15
Cubic curve, II.413
    planar, I.575–I.578
Cubic equations
    Descartes–Euler–Cardano, V.8
    Ferrari's, V.7
    Neumark's, V.9
Cubic lattices, V.62
    body centered, V.68
    face centered, V.68, *see also* Rhombic
        dodecahedron
Cubic roots, I.404–I.407
Cubic spline interpolation formulas, I.579–I.584
    closed loops, I.580–I.582
    open curves, I.582–I.583
Cubic tetrahedral algorithm, delta form-factor
        calculation, III.324–III.328, III.575
Cubic tetrahedron, adaptation of hemi-cube
        algorithm, II.299–II.302

Cubic triangle, II.413
    conversion to rectangular patches,
        III.260–III.261
Cuboctahedron, I.237, V.70
Culling
    backface, I.346–I.347, I.544–I.545, V.127
    view-frustum, V.127
Cumulative transformation matrix, III.295
Current object area, II.28
Cursor, IV.413
Curvature vector, I.568
Curves and surfaces, II.405, *see also* Surfaces
    anti-aliased circle generation, II.445–II.449
    Bézier, *see* Bézier curves and surfaces
    B-spline, IV.252
    fitting, *see* Digitized curve fitting
    great circle plotting, II.440–II.444
    interpolation with variable control point
        approximation, II.417–II.419
    intersection of cubic, IV.261
    knot insertion, IV.252
    Menelaus's theorem, II.424–II.427
    number of segments, II.435–II.436
    open, cubic spline interpolation formulas,
        I.582–I.583
    Peano, II.25–II.26
    polynomials, symmetric evaluation,
        II.420–II.423
    rational, IV.256
    reparametrization, IV.263, IV.441
    smoothing, IV.241
    straight-line approximation of circular arc,
        II.435–II.439
    subdivision, IV.251
Curve tessellation criteria, III.262–III.265
Cyclic sequences, fast generation, III.67–III.76,
        III.458
    $N = 2$, III.67–III.68
    $N = 3$, III.68–III.70
    $N = 3, 4, 6$, III.70–III.71
    $N = 6$ derivation, III.71–III.73
    $N = 6$ triggering, III.73–III.74
    $N = 7$, III.74–III.75
    $N = 24$, III.75–III.76
Cylinder
    bounding volume, III.296–III.297
    with changing cross-sections, I.570–I.571
    equation for, IV.321
    generalized, reference frames, I.567
    intersection of ray with, IV.353, IV.356
    normal vector, IV.359
Cylindrical equal area, I.318–I.319
Cylindrical equirectangular map, I.310
Cylindrical luminaire, V.285
Cylindrical maps, I.310–I.311

D

Darklights, III.366–III.368
Databases, direct charting, I.309–I.310
Data smoothing, IV.241
Data structure, *see also* Grid
    octree, IV.74
    scanline coherent shape algebra, II.32–II.34
Data value, I.30
DDA, *see* Line drawing
DDA algorithm, I.595
de Boor algorithm, V.217
de Boor–Fix formulas, V.160, V.166
de Casteljau algorithm, V.199, V.217
de Casteljau Evaluation Algorithm, I.587–I.589,
    I.604–I.605
Decimation, I.148, *see also* Resampling
    Gaussian 1/2 filter, frequency response, I.163
    Gaussian 1/√2 filter, frequency response, I.164
    Lanczos2 sinc functions, frequency response,
        I.164–I.165
        by factor of four, I.161
        by factor of three, I.160
        by factor of two, I.158–I.159
    by two, frequency response
        half-phase filters, I.162–I.163
        Lanczos2 sinc functions, I.164–I.165
        zero-phase filters, I.162
Decision tree, III.176–III.177
Decomposition
    into parallelohedra (space packing), V.67
    quotient space, V.61
    Seidel's algorithm (trapezoids, triangles), V.394
    singular value, V.115
Delauney triangulation, IV.47, V.270
Del operator, I.594–I.595, I.598
Delta form factor, II.313
    calculation, cubic tetrahedral algorithm,
        III.324–III.328, III.575
DeMoivre's Theorem, I.15
Density, superquadrics, III.139–III.140
Depth buffer, I.218
Depth cuing, I.365
Depth of field, III.36
2 1/2-D Depth-of-field simulation, computer
    animation, III.36–III.38
Descartes–Euler–Cardano algorithm, V.8
Descartes' law of signs, V.154
Destination pixel, contributors to, III.12
Determinant, IV.154, IV.167
Diagram layout, IV.497, IV.505
Diameters, conjugate, III.169–III.171
Dielectric materials, fresnel formulas, II.287–II.289
Difference, scanline coherent shape algebra,
    II.39–II.40

Difference equation, IV.245
Differentiation algorithm, Bézier curves,
    I.589–I.590
Diffuse reflection, II.233
Digital cartography, *see* Map projections
Digital computation, half-angle identity,
    II.381–II.386
Digital dissolve effect, I.221–I.232
    case study, I.229–I.231
    faster mapping, I.227–I.228
    first attempt, I.223–I.224
    further research, I.231–I.232
    optimizations, I.230–I.231
    randomly traversing 2D array, I.221–I.222
    scrambling integers, I.222–I.223
Digital filtering, *see* Discrete convolution
Digital generation, sinusoids, III.167–III.169
Digital halftoning, II.57–II.71, IV.489, V.297,
    V.302
    clustered-dot dither, II.63
    contrast adjustment during, II.63–II.64
    error diffusion dithering, II.65–II.71
    horizontal lines, II.60–II.61
    magic-square dither, II.60–II.62
    to multiple output levels, II.64–II.65
    ordered dither matrix, II.58–II.60
    threshold dithering, II.58–II.63
Digital images, color hardcopy, II.163–II.165
Digital line drawing, I.99–I.100
Digitized curve fitting, automatic, algorithm,
    I.612–I.626
    chord-length parameterization, I.617, I.621
    implementation notes, I.624–I.625
    Newton–Raphson iteration, I.621–I.623
    scalar curves, I.616
Digits, conversion with bits, I.435
Directional light, V.290
Direction ratios, I.456–I.457
Direct lighting, distribution ray tracing,
    III.307–III.313, III.562
Dirichlet cell, V.62, V.270
Discrete convolution, image smoothing and
    sharpening, II.50–II.56
Discrete image, I.246
Discrete laplacian filter, II.53–II.54
Discrete signals, I.147
Discriminator, I.101
Display, high fidelity, IV.415
Dissolve algorithm, I.225–I.227
Distance approximations, I.423, V.78
Distance
    between two polyhedra, IV.83
    to an ellipsoid, IV.113
    to a hyperplane, IV.161
    to a line, IV.143

Distance (*cont.*)
  n-dimensional, IV.120
  3D, fast approximation, I.432–I.433
Distance measures
  approximate vector length, I.429
  equations of unit distance, I.428
  fast approximation to 3D Euclidian distance,
    I.432–I.433
  fast approximation to hypotenuse, I.427
  full-precision constants, I.434
  high speed, low precision square root,
    I.424–I.426
Distance variable, I.105
Distribution check, III.131–III.132
Distribution ray tracing, direct lighting,
  III.307–III.313, III.562
Dither, IV.489
Dithering, *see* Ordered dithering
Dithering matrix, I.177
Divergence theorem, V.40
Dodecahedron, II.176
  dihedrals, II.175, II.177
  transformation of sphere, II.241
Dot products
  n-dimensional, IV.158
  for shading, I.348–I.360
    direct algorithm, I.351–I.352, I.359
    directing vectors, I.348
    new algorithm, I.351–I.352, I.359–I.360
    reflection of light, I.349–I.352
    refraction, I.353–I.354
    Snell's law, I.353–I.354
  in 2D, IV.140
Double-angle relations, I.17
Double-framed order, I.265–I.266
Double speed Bresenham's, I.101–I.102
Dual solids, I.236–I.237
Duff's formulation, II.418
Duratrans, II.164–II.165
Dymaxion gnomonic projection, I.316
Dynamic range of image, IV.415, IV.422
Dynamic simulation, mass and spring model,
  IV.506

E

Earth, ellipsoidal approximation, I.309, IV.135
Edge calculations, anti-aliasing, III.345–III.354,
  III.586
Edge contours, V.338
Edge detectors, II.105
Edge images, noise thresholding, II.105–II.106
Edge preservation, IV.61
Edge-sharpening convolutions, II.55
  applied before halftoning, II.70–II.71
Edge structure, II.86–II.87

Eigenvalues, II.324–II.325, *see also* Matrix,
  eigenvalues
Element exchanging, *see also* Cyclic sequences
  subtraction-based, I.172
  of three or more values, III.67
  XOR-based, I.171, I.436
Ellipse intersections
  equations, V.75
  figure, V.6
Ellipsoid, IV.113
  box-sphere intersection testing, generalizing,
    I.338–I.339
  equation, III.276
  intersection with cone, I.321–I.322
  superquadric
    inertia tensor, III.140–III.144
    "inside–outside" function, III.148
    normal vectors, III.148
    parametric surface functions, III.147
    shells, III.154–III.157
    volume, III.140
Ellipsoid generation, V.179
  Euclidean geometry, n-D
    graphics libraries, extended, V.400
    n-D rotation, V.55, V.405
    n-D solids, V.79
Elliptical arc, parametric, *see* Parametric elliptical
  arc algorithm
Elliptical cone, equation, III.277
Elliptical cylinder, equation, III.276
Elliptical hyperboloid, equation, III.277
Elliptical paraboloid, equation, III.277
Elliptical torus
  cross section, II.251–II.252
  equation, II.251–II.252
  intersection with ray, II.251–II.256
Embedding plane, intersection with ray,
  I.390–I.391
Embossing, IV.433
Encoded image data, rotation, II.86–II.88
Encoding, adaptive run-length, II.89–II.91
Energy balance criterion, III.320
Enlargement, monochrome images, smoothing,
  I.166–I.170
Error diffusion dithering, II.65–II.71
  blue noise added, II.70
  edge-enhanced, II.70–II.71
  introduction of random noise, II.69
  serpentine raster pattern, II.67, II.69
Error-propagation dithering, II.75–II.77
Euclidean dimensions, four, III.58–III.59
Euclidean distance, *see* Distance
Euclidean norm, I.423, V.78
Euler angle, IV.222, *see also* Quotient space
  decomposition

Evolute, IV.116
Exact computation of 2-D intersections, III.188–III.192, III.491
    Apollonius problem solution, III.203–III.209
Excircle, IV.47, IV.143
Exponentiation, IV.385, IV.403

F

Face centered cubic lattice (fcc), V.68, *see also* Rhombic dodecahedron
Face-connected line segment generation, *n*-dimensional space, III.89–III.91
Face dihedrals, II.174–II.175
Faceted shading, II.234, II.236
Factorial polynomials, I.595–I.596
Fast anamorphic image scaling, II.78–II.79
Fast fill algorithm, precalculating addresses, I.285–I.286
Fast Fourier transform algorithms, II.368–II.370
Fast lines, rendering on raster grid, I.114–I.120
    Hobby's polygonal pens, I.114–I.117
    software implementation, I.117–I.120
Fast memory allocator, III.49–III.50
Fat curve, generation, II.43
Fat lines, rendering on raster grid, I.114–I.120
Fence shading, IV.404
Fermat primes, I.18
Ferrari's algorithm, V.7
Feuerbach circle, III.215–III.218, IV.144
Fiber bundle, IV.230
Fill algorithms, I.278–I.284
    canonical, I.279
    optimal, I.281–I.282
    processing shadows, I.280–I.281
Fillet, IV.145
Filter, *see* Image, filter
Filtered image rescaling, III.8–III.16, III.414
    magnification, III.9
    minification, III.9–III.11
Filter post processing stage, III.37
Filter windows, I.194–I.195
Finite difference, IV.241
First decomposition algorithm, III.99–III.100
First derivative filters, II.105
First fundamental matrix, I.543–I.544
Fixed-point trigonometry, CORDIC, I.494–I.497
Flipped bit count, II.368
Floating point arithmetic, IV.125, IV.422
Floating point pixel format, II.81–II.82
Floyd–Steinberg error propagation, II.75–II.76
Floyd–Steinberg filter, II.68
Fluorescent lights, *see* Cylindrical luminaire
Fog, simulating, I.364–I.365
Font rendering, three-pass algorithm, I.193

Form factor
    accurate computation, III.329–III.333, III.577
    vertex-to-vertex, III.318–III.323
Forms
    differences with vectors, I.533–I.535
    triangular interpolants, I.535–I.538
Forward differencing, I.594–I.603, IV.251
    Bézier cubics implementation, I.000
    DDA algorithm, I.595
    Del operator, I.594–I.595, I.598
    factorial polynomials, I.595–I.596
    locally circular assumption, I.599–I.600
    Newton's formula, I.596–I.598
    step size determination, I.599–I.601
    subdividing, I.601–I.603
4 × 4 matrices, II.351–II.354
Fourier transform, II.368–II.370
Frame buffer, I.215–I.216, II.115, *see also* Image
    associated color map, I.217
    color hardcopy, II.163–II.165
    color quantization statistical computations, II.126–II.133
    fill algorithms, I.278–I.284
    inverse color map, computation, II.116–II.125
    mapping RGB triples, II.143–II.146
    PHIGS PLUS, II.138–II.142
    plane, I.217–I.218
    random color map animation algorithm, II.134–II.137
    setting monitor white point, II.159–II.162
    television color encoding, II.147–II.158
Free-form surface, *see* Surfaces, parametric
Frenet frame, I.567–I.568
Fresnel formulas
    approximations for applying, II.287–II.289
    dielectric materials, II.287–II.289
    wavelength-dependent reflection and refraction, II.286–II.287
Fresnel reflectance curve, II.284, II.289
Fresnel transmission curve, II.284, II.288–II.289
Frexp, II.82
Full-precision constants, I.434

G

Gain function, IV.401
Gamma correction, IV.401, IV.423
    color dithering, II.72–II.73
Gamma correction function, I.199, I.203–I.206, I.270, I.273
Gamma function, computation, III.151–III.152
Gaussian filter, I.144–I.145, I.150–I.153
Gaussian 1/2 filter
    frequency response, I.163
    interpolation, I.152–I.154, I.156

Gaussian $1/\sqrt{2}$ filter
    frequency response, I.164
    interpolation, I.154–I.156
Gaussian random numbers, II.136
Gaussians, uniform rotations from, III.129
Gaussian weighted filter, II.51–II.53
Gauss–Jordan elimination, II.349
General direction ratios, I.457
Genus, computing, binary digital image,
        II.107–II.111
Geodesics, I.315, II.440
Geometric constructions, interpolation of
        orientation with quaternions, II.377–II.380
Geometric continuity, I.615–I.616, II.430–II.431
Geometry
    n-dimensional, IV.83, IV.149
    2D, IV.138
Girard's formula, *see* Spherical triangle area
G^2 joint, between cubic Bézier curves, II.432
Gnomonic projection, I.315
n-gon, I.18
Gouraud renderer, III.345–III.347
Gouraud shading, I.84, II.235–II.236, IV.60,
        IV.404, IV.526
Gram–Schmidt orthogonalization procedure,
        III.108–III.109
    modified, III.112–III.113, III.116
Graph, display of, IV.505
Graphic design, IV.497, IV.505
Graphics libraries, V.400
Graphics workstations, motion blur,
        III.374–III.382, III.606
Graph labels, nice numbers, I.61–I.63
Gray interior points, I.244
Gray ramp, II.163–II.164
Great circle, IV.132
    arc, code to draw, IV.178
    plotting, II.440–II.444
Green's theorem, V.40
Grid
    for fast point search, IV.61
    for faster point-in-polygon testing, IV.29
    interpolating in a, IV.521
    iso-surface of grid data, IV.326
    traversing a 3D, IV.366
Gridded sampling, progressive image refinement,
        III.358–III.361, III.597
Group theory, II.343–II.344
    of infinitesimal rotations, III.56–III.57

H

Haar test, III.125
Half-angle identity, digital computation,
        II.381–II.386
Half-angle relations, I.16

Half-open intervals, polygon scan conversion,
        III.362–III.365, III.599
Half-phase filters, frequency response, decimation
        by two, I.162
Half-plane, area of intersection, with circle,
        I.38–I.39
Half-space testing, I.240–I.241
Half-tangent, II.381–II.386
Halftoning, *see* Digital halftoning
Halftoning matrix, II.58
Hardware, scrambling integers in, I.222–I.223
Hashing, for point search, IV.61
Hashing function, 3D grid, I.343–I.345
Hash tag, III.386–III.387
Haze, simulating, I.364–I.365
HDTV, II.154–II.155
Heckbert's algorithm, II.127
Hemi-cube algorithm, II.299, III.324
    cubic tetrahedral adaptation, II.299–II.302
Hemispherical projection, triangle, III.314–III.317,
        III.569
Hermite interpolation, V.212, V.401
Hermite polynomial, II.398–II.399
Hexagonal construction, I.238
Hexakis octahedron, V.82
Hidden-surface removal stage, III.37
Hierarchical traverse, V.246
Hierarchy traversal, II.267–II.272
    bottom-up method, II.270–II.271
    caching, II.268
    combining top-down and bottom-up
        approaches, II.270–II.271
    top-down list formation, II.268–II.269
High coherence, II.28, II.30
High dimensional, *see* N-dimensional
Highlight, *see* Specular reflection
Hilbert curve, II.27–II.28
    coherence of transversal sequences, II.28–II.30
Histogram equalization, IV.474
Hobby's polygonal pens, I.114–I.117
Hollow objects, box-sphere intersection testing,
        I.337–I.338
Homogeneous coordinates, I.523
    clipping lines using, IV.128
    n-dimensional, IV.154
    subroutine library for 2D and 3D, IV.534
Homogeneous media, light absorption,
        II.278–II.280
Hopf fibration, IV.232
Horner's rule, II.420–II.421
Hot colors, II.147, II.152–II.153
Hot pixels
    repairing, II.155–II.156
    test, II.155–II.157
Householder matrix, III.118

HSL Saturation, I.449
HSL-to-RGB transform, fast, I.448–I.449
HSV Saturation, I.448
Hue Saturation Value, I.239–I.240
Hybrid predictor, II.97–II.100
Hypercones, II.117
Hyperface, III.89–III.91
Hyperlattice, III.89–III.90
Hyperplane, parametric formula, IV.162
Hyperspace, *see* *N*-dimensional
Hypertexture procedural volume model, IV.401
Hypervoxel, III.89
Hypotenuse
    fast approximation, I.427–I.431
        derivation, I.427–I.429
        error analysis, I.429–I.431
    triangles, I.57–I.59

I

Icosahedron, dihedrals, II.175, II.177
Identity, matrix, I.473
IEEE fast square root, III.48, III.446
IEEE floating point, IV.125
Illumination, Phong model, IV.385, IV.388
Image
    display, high fidelity, IV.415
    enhancement, IV.474
    filter
        bilinear/trilinear reconstruction, IV.445,
            IV.521
        color reduction, code, III.429
        convolution, IV.447
        embossing, IV.433
        first derivative, II.105
        nonuniform quadratic spline, II.101–II.102
    quantization, IV.422
    resampling, IV.440, IV.449, IV.527
    thinning, IV.465
    warping, IV.440
Image file compression, II.93–II.100
    hybrid predictor, II.97–II.100
    prediction–correction coding, II.93–II.94
        adaptive, II.94–II.95
Image processing, II.49, III.3, *see also* Digital
        halftoning
    adaptive run-length encoding, II.89–II.91
    bitmap scaling operation optimization,
        III.17–III.19, III.425
    color dithering, II.72–II.77
    color reduction filter, III.20–III.22, III.429
    compact isocontours, III.23–III.28
    compositing black-and-white bitmaps,
        III.34–III.35
    fast anamorphic image scaling, II.78–II.79
    fast bitmap stretching, III.4–III.7, III.411

fast boundary generator, composited regions,
        III.39–III.43, III.441
    filtered image rescaling, III.8–III.16, III.414
    image file compression, II.93–II.100
    image smoothing and sharpening by discrete
        convolution, II.50–II.56
    isovalue contours from pixmap, III.29–III.33,
        III.432
    90-degree bitmap rotator, II.84–II.85
    noise thresholding in edge images, II.105–II.106
    optimal filter for reconstruction, II.101–II.104
    pixels, II.80–II.83
    run-length encoded image data rotation,
        II.86–II.88
    2 1/2-D depth-of-field simulation for computer
        animation, III.36–III.38
Image reconstruction, optimal filter, II.101–II.104
Image refinement, progressive, gridded sampling,
        III.358–III.361, III.597
Image rescaling, filtered, III.8–III.16, III.414
Image scaling, fast anamorphic, II.78–II.79
Image sharpening, by discrete convolution,
        II.50–II.56
Image smoothing, by discrete convolution,
        II.50–II.56
Implicit surface, *see* Surfaces, implicit
Importance sampling, III.309
In center, triangles, I.20–I.21
Incircle, IV.145
Inclusion–exclusion, combinatorics, II.129–II.130
Inclusion isotony, III.64
Inclusion testing, *see* Polygon, point in polygon
        testing
Inertia tensor
    superquadric, III.140–III.145, III.153
    world coordinates, III.145
Infinitesimal rotations, group theory, III.56–III.57
Inhomogeneous media, light absorption,
        II.280–II.281
InputFace, II.196
InputVertex, II.196
In radius, triangles, I.20–I.21
InsertBridge, II.199–II.201
"Inside–outside" function, superquadrics,
        III.147–III.148
Integer arithmetic, IV.123, IV.449, IV.526
Integers, II.371–II.372
    counting through bits under mask, II.372–II.373
    scrambling, I.222–I.223
    tallying on bits, II.373–II.376
Integer square root algorithm, II.387–II.388
Intensity, II.233, II.278–II.279
    interpolation between adjacent pixels, II.445
Interactive
    camera control, IV.230

Interactive (*cont.*)
  cursor display, IV.413
  image warp control, IV.440
  orientation control, IV.175
Interlace artifacts, reduction, III.378–III.379
Interlacing, III.376
InterPhong shading, II.232–II.241
  analysis of formula, II.238–II.240
  applications, II.241
Interpolation, I.148
  Bézier curves, V.213
  bilinear interpolation in 2D array, IV.445,
      IV.475, IV.521
  B-spline, divided differences, V.213, V.217
  by factor of two, Lanczos2 sinc function,
      I.158–I.159
  formulas, cubic spline, I.579–I.584
  Gaussian filter, I.150–I.153
  Gaussian 1/2 filter, I.152–I.154, I.156
  Gaussian $1/\sqrt{2}$ filter, I.154–I.156
  Hermite, V.212, V.401
  of image, *see* Image, filter
  linear, III.122
      fast, IV.526
      versus splined, III.122
  logarithmic space, III.121
  of 1D data, IV.241
  quaternion, with extra spins, III.96–III.97,
      III.461
  RGBZ, V.398
  slerp, V.62
  tent filter, I.149–I.150
  tricubic, V.107
  trilinear interpolation in 3D array, IV.328,
      IV.521
  using Bézier curves, III.133–III.136,
      III.468
Interpolation coefficients
  closed loops, I.581
  open curves, I.583
Intersection
  box and polyhedron, IV.78
  cone-line, V.227
  cubic curves, IV.261
  line, *see* Line, intersections
  moving polyhedra-viewpoint, V.80
  plane-to-plane, III.233–III.236, III.519
  polygon-cube, V.375
  quadrangle surface-line, V.232
  ray with
      cone, IV.355
      cylinder, IV.353, IV.356
      hyperplane, IV.165
      implicit surface, IV.113
      polygon, IV.26

  quadric surface, III.275–III.283, III.547
  voxel grid, IV.308
  rectangle and polygon, IV.77
  scanline coherent shape algebra, II.37
  scanline-object, V.242
  swept sphere-line, V.258
  triangle–cube, III.236–III.239, III.521
  of two circles, circle containing, II.17–II.18
  two-dimensional, exact computation,
      III.188–III.192, III.491
  two polyhedra, IV.83
Interval arithmetic, III.61–III.66, III.454
Interval sampling, II.394–II.395
Inverse color map, II.116
  adjusting blue scanlines, II.122–II.123
  aliasing, II.123–II.124
  computation, II.116–II.125
  convexity advantage, II.119–II.124
  domain in blue–green plane, II.120–II.122
  incremental distance calculation, II.117–II.119
  ordering, II.124–II.125
Inverse of a matrix, *see* Matrix, inverse
IRE unites, II.152
Irradiance, III.319–III.320
Iso-surface, IV.324
Isotropic transformations, normal vector, I.542
Isovalue contours, from pixmap, III.29–III.33,
      III.432
Iteration, rotation tools, I.468

J

Jacobian matrix, II.184, III.155, III.158
Jarvis, Judice, and Nanke filter, II.68
Jell-O, IV.375
Jitter, generation, I.64–I.74
  computational cost, I.67–I.68
  error analysis, I.72
  sampling properties evaluation, I.69–I.72
Jittered sampling, IV.370
Jitter function
  use in ray tracing, I.72–I.74
  using look-up tables, I.65–I.67

K

Knot insertion, IV.252
  into B-splines, II.425–II.427
Kochanek–Bartels formulation, II.417–II.419
Kronecker delta function, IV.158, IV.167
Kuhn's triangulation, box, III.246–III.247,
      III.252–III.253

L

Label placement on maps, IV.497
Lagrange polynomials, V.210

Lambertian radiosity model, II.385
Lambert's law of absorption, II.279
Lanczos2 sinc function
    decimation, I.160–I.161
    frequency response, I.164–I.165
    interpolation by factor of two, I.158–I.159
Lanczos3 filter, III.14, III.16
Lanczos-windowed sinc functions, I.156–I.158
Lattice, integral, integral radius circle on, I.57–I.60
Law of cosines, I.13
Law of sines, I.13
Law of tangents, I.13
Layout, IV.497, IV.505
Ldexp, II.82–II.83
Least-squares approximations, Bézier curves and
    surfaces, II.406–II.411
Least-squares fit, linear, V.92
Length-preserving matrix group, II.344–II.345
Level set, I.552
Levi–Civita symbol, IV.158, IV.167
Lie algebra, V.59
Light
    absorption
        homogeneous media, II.278–II.280
        inhomogeneous media, II.280–II.281
        translucent media, II.277–II.282
    reflection, II.282
Lighting, *see also* Illumination
    computations, III.226
Light sensing device, II.161–II.162
Line
    area of intersection, thick, with circle, I.40–I.42
    clipping, *see* Clipping, line
    distance to point, I.10, II.10–II.13
    intersection, *see also* Scanline coherent shape
        algebra
        Apollonius's 10th problem, II.19–II.24
        bounding circle, II.14–II.16
        calculation, polygons, I.128
        with circle, I.5–I.6
        circle containing intersection of two circles,
            II.17–II.18
        distance from point to line, II.10–II.13
        of line segments, II.7–II.9, III.199–III.202,
            III.500
        Peano curve generation algorithm,
            II.25–II.26
        point of, 2D, I.11
        segments, II.7–II.9
        space-filling curve, II.27–II.28
        3D, I.304
        2D, IV.141
        traversal, II.26–II.27
    joining two with circular arc fillet,
        III.193–III.198, III.496

segment, face connected, generation in
    n-dimensional space, III.89–III.91,
    III.460
subsegment, III.189
tangent
    to circle, I.5
    to circle and perpendicular to line, I.8–I.9
    to two circles, I.7–I.8
    vertical distance to point, I.17–I.18
Linear color rendering, III.343–III.348, III.583
Linear congruential generators, I.67
Linear feedback shift register, I.222
Linear interpolation, *see* Interpolation
Linear transformations, II.335–II.337
    nonsingular, decomposing, III.108–III.112
    singular, decomposing, III.112–III.116
Line drawing, I.98
    anti-aliasing lines, I.105–I.106
    digital, I.99–I.100
    for fast linear interpolation, IV.526
    fat lines on raster grid, I.114–I.120
    filling in bevel joints, I.107–I.113
    symmetric double step line algorithm,
        I.101–I.104
    for 3D voxel traversal, IV.366
    two-dimensional clipping, I.121–I.128
Line-edge intersections, uniform grid, I.29–I.36
Line equation, III.190
Line parameterization, V.92
Line structures, 2D, I.3–I.4
Lissajous figure, III.166
Locally circular assumption, I.599–I.600
Lookup table (LUT), IV.424, IV.449, IV.468, *see
    also* Color maps
    color, II.139
    nonlinear pixel mappings, I.253
Logarithmic space, interpolation, III.121
Lorentz transformations, III.59–III.60
LU decomposition, II.349
Luminaires, power from, II.307
Luminance–color difference space, II.147
Luminance meter, II.159–II.160

M

M2, II.154
Mach band effect, II.235–II.236
Magic square
    dither, II.60–II.62
    as outer product, II.74
Magnification of image, IV.449
Mailbox, II.264
    algorithm, II.268
Mailbox technique, III.285–III.286
Manhattan distance, I.432, II.258–II.259
Map-making, IV.497

Mapping
  nonlinear pixels, I.251 I.253
  original colors onto representatives, I.291
  RGB triples, II.143–II.146
  3D, I.306
Map projections, I.307–I.320
  Alber's, I.321–I.325
  central (gnomonic), I.315, III.314
  cylindrical, I.310, II.440, III.290
  equal area, I.312, I.318, I.321
  Mercator's conformal, I.313, II.445
  orthographic, I.316
  Sanson's sinusoidal, I.314
  stereographic, I.316, II.385
Maps, cylindrical, I.310–I.311
Marching cubes, IV.325, V.98
Marsden identities, V.160, V.166
Martian panoramas, III.291–III.293
Mass, superquadric, III.139–III.140, III.152
Mathematician's tea, V.37
Matrix
  of central moments, IV.194
  decomposition, IV.207
    into simple transformations, II.320–II.323
  determinant, IV.154, IV.167
  eigenvalues
    3 × 3 matrix, IV.195
    4 × 4 matrix, IV.201, IV.209
  exponential, II.332–II.333
  inverse, IV.199, IV.534
  subroutine library for 3 × 3 and 4 × 4, IV.534
Matrix groups, II.344
  affine, II.345
  angle-preserving, II.345
  inverse, II.348–II.349
  length-preserving, II.344–II.345
  membership and privileges, II.346–II.347
  nonsingular, II.345
    inverse, II.350
  window-to-viewport, II.344
    inverse, II.348
Matrix identities, I.453–I.454
Matrix inversion, I.470–I.471, II.342–II.350
  elementary, II.347
  evaluation strategy, II.347–II.348
  problem statement, II.342
Matrix multiplication, fast, I.460–I.461
Matrix orthogonalization, I.464
Matrix techniques, II.319
  cross product, II.333–II.334
  data recovery from transformation matrix,
    II.324–II.331
  4 × 4 matrices, II.351–II.354
  linear transformations, II.335–II.337
  notation, II.338

  pseudo-perspective, II.340–II.341
  quaternions, II.351–II.354
  random rotation matrices, II.355–II.356
  shear, II.339–II.340
  small sparse matrix classification, II.357–II.361
  tensor product, II.333–II.334
  transformations as exponentials, II.332–II.337
Matrix–vector, II.360–II.361
Mechanical simulation, mass and spring model,
    IV.506
Median cut algorithm, I.288
Median finding, 3 × 3 and 5 × 5 grid, I.171–I.175
Medical imaging, contrast enhancement, IV.474
  volume data, IV.324, IV.366, IV.521
Memory allocator, III.49–III.50, III.448
Menelaus's theorem, II.424–II.427, V.213
Mensuration, see Area; Volume
Mercator projection, I.311–I.313
Meridians, I.310–I.311
Mesh
  computing normals for 3D, IV.60
  generation for 2D region, IV.47
Metric properties, transformations, I.543–I.544
Metric tensor, I.543–I.544
Microdot distribution, V.297
Mirror image, transformation matrices, I.474
  data recovery from, II.327
Mitchell filter, III.15–III.16
Modeling, see also Curves and surfaces; Polygon
  affine transformations, I.539–I.542
Modified cylindrical equidistant projection, I.311
Modified facet shading, II.236–II.237
Moiré patterns, III.339–III.340, V.300
Molecular graphics, IV.193
Mollweide's Formula, I.13
Monitor, white point, setting, II.159–II.162
Monochromatic triples, II.146
Monochrome enlargements, smoothing, I.166–I.170
  pattern within rules, I.169
  rules, I.166–I.167
Monomial evaluation algorithm, Bézier curves,
    I.590–I.591
Monomial form, conversion
  from Bézier form, I.592–I.593
  to Bézier form, I.591–I.592
Monte Carlo
  label placement, IV.498
  sampling, IV.370
Monte Carlo integration, III.80, V.359
  spectral radiance, III.308
Morphing, IV.445
Motion blur, graphics workstation, III.374–III.382
  code, III.606
  combining spatial and temporal anti-aliasing,
    III.376–III.378

computing on fields, III.375–III.376
    implementation tricks, III.380–III.382
    interlace artifact reduction, III.378–III.379
    pixel shifts, III.380–III.381
    supersampling in time, III.374–III.375
Multidimensional sum tables, I.376–I.381
    d-dimensional, I.380–I.381
    three-dimensional, I.378–I.380
    two-dimensional, I.376–I.377
Multi-indices, II.412
Multilinearity, V.215
Multiple-angle relations, I.17
Multiple output levels, halftoning to, II.64–II.65
Multivariate approximation, Bézier curves and
    surfaces, II.409

N

Narrow domains, aliasing, II.123–II.124
National Television Systems Committee, encoding
    basics, II.148–II.152
N-dimensional
    distance, IV.120
    extent, overlap testing, III.240–III.243, III.527
    geometry, IV.149
    space, face connected line segment generation,
        III.460
Nearest neighbor, V.3D, V.65
Nearest-point-on-curve problem, I.607–I.611
    Bézier form conversion, I.609–I.611
    problem statement, I.608–I.609
Nesting, I.467–I.468
Negative light, III.367
Neumark's algorithm, V.9
Neutral file format (NFF), V.398
Newell's method, plane equation of polygon,
    III.231–III.232, III.517
Newton–Raphson iteration, digitized curve fitting,
    I.621–I.623
Newton's Formula, I.14, I.596–I.598
NextFaceAroundVertex, II.195–II.196
Nice numbers, for graph labels, I.61–I.63
Nine-point circle, IV.143
Noise function, V.367
Noise thresholding, edge images, II.105–II.106
Nolid, I.238
Nonhomogeneous coordinates, I.523
Nonlinear pixel mappings, I.251–I.253
Nonlocality tension, II.238
Nonsingular matrix group, II.345
    inverse, II.350
Nonuniform random point sets, via warping,
    III.80–III.83
Normal buffer, I.257–I.258

Normal coding, I.257–I.264
    encoding methods, I.258–I.263
        improving, I.263–I.264
        index number, I.260
        principles, I.258–I.259
    normal buffer, I.257–I.258
Normal map, I.260
Normal vector, I.539–I.540
    of cylinder, IV.050
    of ellipsoid, IV.113–IV.114
    interpolation, IV.404
    n-dimensional, IV.156
    rotation, IV.168
    superquadrics, III.148
    in 2D, IV.138
    vertex, IV.60
Normals, *see* Surface normal
NTSC encoding, *see* Pixel encoding
Null transform, I.196–I.197
Numerical and programming techniques, II.365,
    III.47
    arctangent, approximation, II.389–II.391
    bit picking, II.366–II.367
    cross product, in four dimensions and beyond,
        III.84–III.88
    face-connected line segment generation,
        n-dimensional space, III.89–III.91,
        III.460
    fast generation of cyclic sequences,
        III.67–III.76, III.458
    fast memory allocator, III.49–III.50, III.448
    Fourier transform, II.368–II.370
    generic pixel selection mechanism, III.77–III.79
    half-angle identity, II.381–II.386
    IEEE fast square root, III.48, III.446
    integer square root algorithm, II.387–II.388
    interval arithmetic, III.61–III.66, III.454
    interval sampling, II.394–II.395
    nonuniform random point sets, via warping,
        III.80–III.83
    Perlin noise function, recursive implementation,
        II.396–II.401
    rolling ball, III.51–III.60, III.452
    sign of cross product calculation, II.392–II.393
    using geometric constructions to interpolate
        orientation with quaternions,
        II.377–II.380
NURBS (nonuniform rational B-spline), IV.256,
    IV.286, V.216

O

Object area, II.26–II.27
Object space partitioning, III.284–III.287
Object-space rendering, II.26
Octahedral subdivision, *see* Ellipsoid generation

Octahedron, dihedrals, II.174–II.175
Octree, I.288, IV.74
  bit interleaving, I.443–I.447
Octree quantization, I.287–I.293
  algorithm, I.289
  color table filling, I.290–I.291
  evaluation of representatives, I.289–I.290
  improvements, I.291–I.292
  mapping onto representatives, I.291
  memory and computational expense,
    I.292–I.293
  principle, I.288
Octree-to-Boundary conversion, II.214–II.218
Octree-to-PCS, II.214–II.215
Offset prints, II.165
1-to-1 pixel transforms, I.196–I.209
  color-map manipulation, I.270–I.274
  contrast enhancement transform, I.197–I.198,
    I.201–I.202, I.270–I.271, I.274
  gamma correction function, I.199, I.203–I.206,
    I.270, I.273
  null transform, I.196–I.197
  photo-inversion transform, I.196, I.198,
    I.270–I.271
  quantization transform, I.196–I.197, I.199,
    I.270, I.272
  sawtooth transform function, I.203, I.207–I.209
Opcode, II.36
Open curves, cubic spline interpolation formulas,
  I.582–I.583
Optical character recognition (OCR), V.329
Optimal sampling patterns, V.359
Ordered dithering, I.176–I.178, V.297
  color, II.73–II.75
  matrix, II.58–II.60
Orientation, of triangle, IV.144
Orientation control, IV.175
  mouse-driven, rolling ball, III.51–III.60, III.452
Oriented lines, V.50
Orthogonalization, matrix, I.464
Orthogonal loops, I.105
Orthogonal projection
  transformation matrices, I.475
  in 2D, IV.142
Orthogonal transformations, normal vectors,
  I.542–I.543
Orthographic projection, I.309, I.316
Orthonormal base
  movement from one to another, I.508
  3D viewing and rotation using, I.516–I.521
    general rotations, I.520–I.521
    new approach, I.517–I.520
    UVN coordinate system, I.518–I.519
    viewing transformation, pseudo-code, I.521

Overcrossing correction, III.179–III.180
Overlapping testing, *n*-dimensional extent,
  III.240–III.243, III.527

P

Packing
  body centered cubic (bcc), V.68
  face centered cubic (fcc), V.68
  circumspherical, V.67, V.270
Painter's algorithm, *see* Back to front polygon
  ordering
Paint program, IV.433
PAL encoding, II.153–II.154
Panoramic virtual screen, ray tracing,
  III.288–III.294, III.551
Parallel connected stripes representation,
  II.203–II.204
Parallelepiped, IV.155, IV.161
Parallelogram, IV.140
  approximation, I.183–I.184
Parallelohedron, V.67
Parallel projection, transformation matrices, I.475
Parametric continuity, I.616, II.430–II.431
Parametric elliptical arc algorithm
  code, III.478
  conjugate diameters, III.169–III.171
  digital generation of sinusoids, III.167–III.169
  quarter ellipse, III.164–III.165
  simplifying computation, III.171–III.172
Parametric surface, *see* Surfaces, parametric
Parametric surface functions, superquadrics,
  III.146–III.147
Partitioning
  object space, III.284–III.287
  3-D polygons, III.219–III.222, III.502
Patch, *see* Surfaces, parametric
Patch visibility index, II.313
Pattern mask, II.57
PCS-to-boundary conversion, II.205
PCS-to-Chain procedure, II.205–II.206
Peano curve, I.28, II.27–II.28
  coherence of transversal sequences, II.28–II.30
  generation algorithm, II.25–II.26
Perception
  of brightness, IV.416
  of texture patterns, IV.487
Perimeter, triangles, I.20
Periodic plane tesselation, I.129–I.130
Perlin noise function, recursive implementation,
  II.396–II.401
Perp-dot product, IV.139, V.400
Perpendicular bisector, IV.139
  intersection, triangles, I.22–I.23
Perpendicular vector, *see* Normal vector
Perspective, *n*-dimensional, IV.153

Perspective projection, transformation matrices, I.475
PHIGS PLUS, II.138–II.142, II.420
    implementation, II.141–II.142
    pseudo color
        interpolation, II.140–II.141
        mapping, II.138–II.140
Phong illumination (specular formula), IV.385, IV.388
Phong shading (normal vector interpolation), IV.60, IV.404
Phosphors
    chromaticity, II.151
        coordinates, II.161
    spectral emission curve, II.160–II.161
Photo-inversion transform, I.196, I.198, I.270–I.271
Physically based methods, for graph layout, IV.506
Pipeline accelerator, III.383–III.389
Pixel, II.80–II.83
    angular width, III.289
    band, anti-aliasing, II.445–II.446
    components, II.109–II.110
    destination, contributors to, III.12
    gamma-corrected byte storage, II.80
    locations, II.33–II.34
    nonlinear mappings, I.251–I.253
    remapping, II.78
    replication, II.79
    selection mechanism, III.77–III.79
    sub-sampling, II.79
    triangular, anti-aliasing, III.369–III.373
    unportable bits, II.81
Pixel coordinates, I.246–I.248
    continuous, I.246
    converting, I.247–I.248
    discrete, I.246
    along unit axis, I.250
Pixel encoding, *see also* Color quantization
    floating point, common exponent, II.80
    hyperbolic, IV.422
    logarithmic ($\mu - 255$ law), I.251–I.253
    non-linear luminance scaling, IV.415
    NTSC broadcasting, II.147
Pixel value, dynamic range, IV.415, IV.422
Pixmap, generating iso-value contours from, III.29–III.33, III.432
Planar cubic curves, I.575–I.578
Planar polygon, area, II.170
Planar rotations, III.124–III.126
Planar subdivision, IV.47
Plane
    arbitrary, partitioning 3D convex polygon with, III.219–III.222, III.502
    comparing two, III.229–III.230

crystallographic groups, I.129–I.133
    embedding, intersection with ray, I.390–I.391
    frame buffer, I.217–I.218
    intersection of three, I.305
    periodic tilings on raster grid, I.129–I.139
        wallpaper groups, I.129–I.133
    signed distance to point, III.223–III.224, III.511
Plane equation of polygon, Newell's method, III.231–III.232, III.517
Plane-to-plane intersection, III.233–III.236, III.519
Point
    distance to line, I.10, II.10–II.13
        vertical, I.47–I.48
    generating random, triangles, I.24–I.28
    generation equation, II.179
    mutual visibility, I.30–I.31
    signed distance to plane, III.223–III.224, III.511
    3D, I.522–I.523, I.526
Point distributions (uniform)
    interval (progressive), II.394–II.395
    sphere, I.320, III.117, III.126
    triangle, I.24
Point in polygon testing, IV.16, IV.24
Point-on-line test, I.49–I.50
Point–triangle intersection, II.259–II.261
Polar decomposition of matrix, IV.207
Polygon, *see also* Polyhedron
    area, II.5–II.6, IV.3, IV.141
        spherical, IV.132
    bounding volume, III.296
    centroid, IV.3
    convexity testing, IV.7, IV.25, IV.141
    intersection
        calculation, I.128
        fast scan conversion, I.96
        with ray, I.390–I.394
    nearly coplanar, grouping into coplanar sets, III.225–III.230, III.512
    plane equation, Newell's method, III.231–III.232, III.517
    point in polygon testing, IV.10, IV.24
    random point, I.24–I.28
    shading, IV.404
    Sutherland–Hodgman clipper, III.219–III.222
    texture-space images, I.366–I.367
    3-D, partitioning, III.219–III.222, III.502
    triangulation, IV.47
    from twisting reference frames, I.567–I.568
    user-provided display routines, radiosity, II.295–II.298
Polygonal pens, I.114–I.117
Polygonization
    implicit surface, IV.324
    parametric surface, IV.287
    planar region, IV.47

Polygon partitioning
  concave, V.50
    general 2D in 3D, V.386
    by half-space membership, V.122
    triangulation, V.394
Polygon scan conversion, I.76–I.83, IV.404
  algorithm, I.77–I.82
  arbitrary polygons, I.92–I.97
  background, I.76–I.77
  concave, I.87–I.91
  fast, I.92–I.97
    active edge lists, I.92–I.93
    convex decompositions, I.97
    intersecting polygons, I.96
    traffic between registers and memory, I.92
    x-transition table, I.93–I.95
    y extrema and memory requirements,
      I.95–I.96
  generic, and clipping, I.84–I.86
  half-open intervals, III.362–III.365, III.599
  implementation notes, I.82–I.83
  reducing code redundancy, I.84
  vertices during scan conversion, I.78–I.79
Polygon stretching, I.127–I.128
Polyhedra figures
  cube (hexahedron), V.67
  elongated dodecahedron, V.67
  hexagonal prism, V.67
  hexakis octahedron, 83
  octahedron, V.83
  rhombic dodecahedron, V.67–V.68, V.83
  trapezoidal icositetrahedron, V.83
  truncated octahedron, V.68
Polyhedron, *see also* Polygon
  collision detection, IV.78, IV.83
  convex, ray intersection, II.247–II.250
  exact dihedral metrics, II.174–II.178
  inferring topology, IV.61
  normal vector, IV.60
  regular, II.174–II.175
  3D, I.565–I.566
  volume, II.170–II.171
Polylines, V.212
  circular arc, II.435–II.437
Polynomial equations, bracketing real roots, *see*
  Strum sequences
Polynomials
  Horner's rule, II.420–II.421
  symmetric evaluation, II.420–II.423
Polytope, IV.84, IV.149
  semiregular, V.67, V.78, V.83
Pool, III.49
Popularity algorithm, I.288

Post-concatenation, transformation matrices,
  I.476–I.481
PostScript language, IV.145, IV.380
Power relations, I.15
Prediction–correction coding, II.93–II.94, *see also*
  Image file compression
Primitives, rectangular bounding volumes,
  III.295–III.300, III.555
Product relations, I.16
Programming techniques, *see* Numerical and
  programming techniques
Progressing refinement, radiosity, V.290
Progressive image refinement, gridded sampling,
  III.358–III.361, III.597
Projection
  Albers equal-area conic map, I.321–I.325
  azimuthal, I.314–I.317
  data recovery from transformation matrix,
    II.329–II.331
  equations, view correlation, II.182–II.183
  general, I.318
  hemispherical, triangle, III.314–III.317, III.569
  Mercator, I.311–I.313
  n-dimensional, IV.152
  properties, digital cartography, I.307–I.308
  Sanson–Flamsteed sinusoidal, I.312–I.314
  transformation matrices, I.475
  onto vector in 2D, IV.142
Projective transformations, decomposing,
  III.98–III.107
  first decomposition algorithm, III.99–III.100
  fourth decomposition algorithm, III.104–III.106
  second decomposition algorithm, III.100–III.102
  third decomposition algorithm, III.102–III.104
Proximity testing, I.237–I.239
Pseudo color
  interpolation, PHIGS PLUS, II.140–II.141
  mapping, PHIGS PLUS, II.138–II.140
Pseudo-perspective, II.340–II.341
Pyramid geometry, rendering with iterated
  parameters, II.186–II.187
Pythagorean relation, I.57
Pythagorean theorem, I.599
Pythagorean triangles, prime, I.58

Q

Quad-edge data structure, IV.48
Quadratic spline, nonuniform, II.101–II.102
Quadratic surface, equation, III.275–III.279
Quadratic triangles, conversion to rectangular
  patches, III.256–III.259, III.536
Quadric surface, V.3, *see also* Surfaces, implicit
  intersection with ray, III.275–III.283, III.547
  surface normal, III.282–III.283

Quadtree/octree-to-boundary conversion,
    II.202–II.218
    Bottom-Up, II.206, II.208–II.209
    Octree-to-Boundary conversion, II.214–II.218
    Octree-to-PCS, II.214–II.215
    parallel connected stripes representation,
        II.203–II.204
    PCS to boundary conversion, II.205
    PCS-to-Chain procedure, II.205 II.206
    quadtree-to-boundary conversion, II.211–II.213
    Quadtree-to-PCS, II.211–II.213
    Top-Down, II.206–II.208, II.210
Quadtrees, II.31
    bit interleaving, I.443–I.447
Quadtree-to-PCS, II.211–II.213
Quantization, *see also* Color quantization
    comparison of techniques, I.293
    logarithmic, IV.420, IV.422
Quantization transform, I.196–I.197, I.199, I.270,
    I.272
Quarter ellipse algorithm, III.164–III.165
Quartic equations, V.4
    Descartes–Euler–Cardano, V.8
    Ferrari's, V.7
    Neumark's, V.9
Quartic roots, I.406–I.407
Quaternions, I.498–I.515, II.351–II.354, IV.151,
    IV.175, IV.209, IV.222, IV.232
    algorithmetic implementation, I.509–I.515
    definition, I.499–I.500
    geometric construction interpolation of
        orientation, II.377–II.380
    interpolation with extra spins, III.96–III.97,
        III.461
    movements from one orthonormal base to
        another, I.508
    properties, I.501–I.502
    as rotation groups, V.62, V.84
    rotations, III.57
        in 3D space, I.503–I.506
    set of unit, properties, I.502–I.503
Quotient space decomposition, V.61

R

Radiosity, II.293–II.294, III.227, III.269–III.270
    accurate form-factor computation,
        III.329–III.333, III.577
    adaptive meshing, shadow boundary detection,
        II.311–II.315
    advantage, II.295
    extensions, II.308–II.309
    fast vertex update, II.303–II.305
    form factors, II.295

hemi-cube algorithm, cubic tetrahedral
        adaptation, II.299–II.302
    linear approximation, vertex-to-vertex form
        factors, III.318–III.323
    progressive, II.296–II.297
        implementation, II.297–II.298
        refinement, II.306–II.307
    ray-traced form factors, II.312–II.313
    by ray tracing, II.306–II.310
    sending power with rays, II.307–II.308
    user-provided polygon display routines,
        II.295–II.298
Random, *see also* Jitter
    integers, generation, I.438–I.439
    points in triangles, I.24–I.28
Random color map animation algorithm,
    II.134–II.137
Random distributions, *see also* Point distributions
    general equations, III.80
    interval (progressive), II.394–II.395
    jitter sampling, I.64, IV.370
    pseudo-random (PRN) sequences, I.222–I.225
    rotation matrices, II.355, *corrigendum:* III.117
Random noise function, II.396–II.401
Random-number generator, II.136
Random rotation matrices, II.355–II.356,
    III.117–III.120, III.463
Random rotations, uniform, III.124–III.132,
    III.465
    from Gaussians, III.129
Raster grid
    periodic tilings of plane, *see* Plane, periodic
        tilings on raster grid
    rendering fat lines, I.114–I.120
Raster image, 90-degree rotation, II.86
Rasterizing, *see* Scan conversion
Raster representation, II.111
Raster rotation, fast algorithm, I.179–I.195
    advanced anti-aliasing, I.194–I.195
    arbitrary rotation, I.186–I.187
    circle drawing, I.192–I.193
    comparisons, I.190–I.191
    font rendering, I.193
    further work, I.195
    generalized BitBlt, I.193–I.194
    history, I.191–I.192
    implementation, I.187–I.190
    parallelogram approximation, I.183–I.184
    rational rotation, I.184–I.186
    rotation through shearing, I.181–I.183
    statement of problem, I.180
Raster shearing, I.179, I.183–I.184
Rational curves, V.214
Rational numbers, V.25
Rational rotation, I.184–I.186

Ray
  definition, II.248
  intersection with
    elliptical torus, II.251–II.256
    object, eliminating calculations,
      III.284–III.287
    quadric surface, III.275–III.283, III.547
    sphere, I.388–I.389
Ray–box intersection, fast, I.395–I.396
Ray–convex polyhedron intersection, II.247–II.250
Ray equation, II.180
Rayleigh probability density function, II.106
Ray–object intersection, I.387
  tags, II.264–II.266
Ray–plane intersection, II.258–II.259
Ray–polygon intersection, I.390–I.394
Ray–polyhedron test, II.247–II.250
Ray rejection test, I.385–I.386, III.281–III.282
Rayshade, II.186, II.188–II.190
Ray tagging, voxel-based ray tracing, II.264–II.266
Ray tracing, II.245–II.246, III.269
  algorithm, I.64
  avoiding incorrect shadow intersections,
    II.275–II.276
  body color model, II.277–II.282
  with BSP tree, III.271–III.274, III.538
  code, IV.420, IV.534
  distribution, direct lighting, III.307–III.313,
    III.562
  eliminating ray–object intersection calculations,
    III.284–III.287
  hemispherical projection of triangle,
    III.314–III.317, III.569
  hierarchy traversal, II.267–II.272
  intersection
    ray and sphere, I.388–I.389
    ray with quadric surface, III.275–III.283,
      III.547
  intersection testing, *see* Intersection
  jitter function use, I.72–I.74
  linear-time simple bounding volume,
    III.301–III.306
  minimal, IV.375
  panoramic virtual screen, III.288–III.294,
    III.551
  radiosity by, II.306–II.310
  ray–convex polyhedron intersection,
    II.247–II.250
  ray–object intersection, I.387
  ray–polygon intersection, I.390–I.394
  ray rejection test, I.385–I.386
  recursive shadow voxel cache, II.273–II.274
  sampling, IV.370
  shadow attenuation, II.283–II.289

  transparent objects, shadow attenuation,
    I.397–I.399
  voxel-based, II.264–II.266
Ray–triangle intersection, I.393
  binary recursive subdivision, II.257–II.263
    constraints, II.257
    point–triangle intersection, II.259–II.261
    ray–plane intersection, II.258–II.259
    U, *V* computation, II.261–II.262
Real roots, bracketing, *see* Strum sequences
Reconstruction of continuous function from
    discrete samples, IV.521
Rectangle, intersection with circle, fast checking,
    I.51–I.53
Rectangular Bézier patches, conversion of Bézier
    triangles, III.256–III.261, III.536
Rectangular bounding volumes, primitives,
    III.295–III.300, III.555
Recursion property, Bernstein polynomials, I.614
Recursive shadow voxel cache, II.273–II.274
Reference frames
  calculation along space curve, I.567–I.571
  rotation minimizing frames, I.569
  twisting, polygons from, I.567–I.568
Reference geoid, I.309
Reflectance, IV.385, IV.388
Reflection, wavelength-dependent, II.286–II.287
Refraction
  Snell's law, I.353–I.354
  wavelength-dependent, II.286–II.287
Regions, I.560
Relative motion, transformations, III.122
Relaxation, IV.498, IV.506
RemoveEdge, II.198
Rendering, III.337, *see also* Illumination; Ray
    tracing; Shading
  anti-aliasing
    edge and bit-mask calculations for,
      III.349–III.354, III.586
    triangular pixels, III.369–III.373
  darklights, III.366–III.368
  fast linear color, III.343–III.348, III.583
  motion blur on graphics workstations,
    III.374–III.382, III.606
  pipeline accelerator, III.383–III.389
  polygon scan conversion, using half-open
    intervals, III.362–III.365, III.599
  shader cache, III.383–III.389
  shadow depth map, III.338–III.342, III.582
Rendering software
  Bézier curves, V.206
  Bresenham algorithm, exact clipping, V.317
  BSP tree based, V.131
  Z-buffer based, V.398
Rending equation, III.307

Representative color, II.116
Representative tree, III.228
Resampling, *see also* Anti-aliasing
    curve, IV.441
    image, IV.440, IV.449
Rescaling, filtered image, III.8–III.16, III.414
Residency masks, III.284–III.287
RGB, transform from HSL, I.448–I.449
RGB-to-YIQ encoding, II.151
RGB triples, mapping, II.143–II.146
    onto four bits, I.233–I.245
        algorithm design, I.241–I.242
        Cartesian quantization versus polyhedra,
            I.244–I.245
        complexity analysis, I.244
        cuboctahedron, I.237
        dual solids, I.236–I.237
        eight-point color cube, I.233–I.234
        four-bit color solid, I.235–I.236
        gray interior points, I.244
        half-space testing, I.240–I.241
        hexagonal construction, I.238
        nolid, I.238
        proximity testing, I.237–I.239
        related methods, I.239–I.240
        rhombic dodecahedron, I.236
        three versus four bits, I.243–I.244
RGB values
    gamma-corrected, II.157
    unencodable, II.147
RGBZ interpolation, V.398
Rhombic dodecahedron, I.236
    bcc packing, V.68
Rigid-body motion, equations, superquadric,
    III.149–III.150
Ritter's simple bounding sphere technique,
    III.305–III.306
RMS error, II.104
Roberts's method, II.96
Rolling ball, III.51–III.60, III.452, V.55
Rolling-ball algorithm
    extensions, III.56–III.60
    four Euclidean dimensions, III.58–III.59
    group theory of infinitesimal rotations,
        III.56–III.57
    implementation, III.54–III.56
    Lorentz transformations, III.59–III.60
    quaternion rotations, III.57
    using, III.53–III.54
Root finding, I.403
    Bézier curve-based, *see* Bézier curve-based
        root-finder
    cubic, I.404–I.407
    for polygonization, IV.326
    quartic, I.406–I.407

    ray tracing, *see* Intersection
    subroutines, IV.558
Root-finding algorithm, I.412 I.413
Rotation
    bit patterns for encoding angles, I.442
    data recovery from transformation matrix,
        II.326
    Euler angle, IV.222
    fast 2D–3D, I.440–I.441
    about general line, orthonormal bases,
        I.520–I.521
    geometrical representation, I.503–I.504
    interactive 3D, IV.175
    n-dimensional, IV.151
    quaternion, *see* Quaternions
    raster, *see* Raster rotation
    run-length encoded image data, II.86–II.88
    3D space, *see also* Orthonormal base
        quaternions, I.503–I.506
    transformation matrices, I.474
    twist control, IV.230
Rotation groups, V.59
Rotation matrix, I.180, *see also* Random rotation
    matrices
    homogeneous, II.352
    random, II.355–II.356
Rotation matrix methods, I.455
    fast matrix multiplication, I.460–I.461
    matrix inversion, I.470–I.471
    matrix orthogonalization, I.464
    rotation tools, I.465–I.469
    transforming axes, I.456–I.459
    virtual trackball, I.462–I.463
Rotation minimizing frames, I.569
Rotation tools, I.465–I.469
    converting between matrix and axis-amount
        representations, I.466–I.467
    iteration, I.468
    nesting, I.467–I.468
    transformation inverses, I.468
Rounded corners, IV.145
Run-length encoding, adaptive, II.89–II.91

S

Sagitta, V.169
Sampled data, defining surfaces from, I.552–I.557
Sampled signals, I.147
Sampling
    optimal patterns, V.359
    solid-angle based, V.287
    stochastic, IV.370
        supersampling, V.248
Sampling Theorem, I.147
Sanson–Flamsteed sinusoidal projection,
    I.312–I.314

Satellite, III.24

Sawtooth transform function, I.200, I.207–I.209

Scaling
  bitmap, optimization, III.17 III.19, III.425
  data recovery from transformation matrix,
    II.327–II.328
  transformation matrices, I.474–I.475

Scan conversion, I.75, *see also* Polygon scan
    conversion
  lines in 3D, IV.366

Scanline coherent shape algebra, II.31–II.45
  algorithm, II.34–II.37
  applications, II.41–II.44
  background, II.31–II.32
  data structures, II.32–II.34
  difference, II.39–II.40
  improvements, II.44–II.45
  intersection, II.37
  union, II.38–II.39
  utility functions, II.40–II.41

Scanline depth gradient, Z-buffered triangle,
    I.361–I.363

Scanline-object rejection, V.242

Scatterplot, IV.193, IV.497

Seed fill algorithm, I.275–I.277

Segment data structures, II.33–II.34

Seidel's algorithm, V.394

Selective precipitation (halftoning), V.302

Sequential probability test ratio, V.356

Serpentine raster pattern, II.67, II.69

SetWings, II.194–II.195

Shader cache, III.383–III.389
  effectiveness, III.388
  implementation, III.385–III.388
  logical arrangement, III.384
  results, III.388–III.389
  shading cache, III.385

Shading
  fast dot products, I.348 I.360
  fence, IV.404
  Gouraud, IV.60, IV.404, IV.526
  Phong, IV.60, IV.404
  from z-buffer, IV.433

Shading rays, caching, II.268

Shading techniques, incremental and empirical,
    II.233–II.236

Shading tension, II.238

Shadow algorithm, II.284–II.285

Shadow attenuation, II.283–II.289
  naive scheme, II.283–II.284
  wavelength-dependent reflection and refraction,
    II.286–II.287

Shadow boundaries
  detection, adaptive meshing in radiosity,
    II.311–II.315

  subdivision criteria, II.313–II.315
  visibility index, II.313

Shadow cache, II.273

Shadow depth map, III.338–III.342
  boundary case, III.340–III.341
  code, III.582
  Moiré pattern problem, III.339–III.340
  optimization, III.341

Shadow generation, approximations, II.283

Shadow object caching, II.268

Shadows, I.278
  attenuation for ray tracing transparent objects,
    I.397–I.399
  filling, I.280–I.281
  intersections, avoiding incorrect, II.275–II.276

Shadow voxel cache, II.273–II.274

Shaft culling, III.333

Shape
  algebra opcodes, II.36
  decomposition, II.32
  parameters, II.431, II.433

Shape-box routine, II.40–II.41

Shape construction, I.551

Shape representations, stored as linked lists, II.32

Shape vectorization, V.323

Shared chord, I.44

Sharpening filter, II.53–II.55

Shear, II.339–II.340, III.110–III.111, III.113
  data recovery from transformation matrix,
    II.328–II.329
  geometry, II.339

Shearing
  algorithm, I.188
  raster rotation through, I.181–I.183
  scan-line, I.187–I.190

Shear matrices, I.181

Short loops, unrolling, III.355–III.357, III.594

Shuffle generator, I.66

Signed distance, point to plane, III.223–III.224,
    III.511

Simplex
  dividing boxes into, III.252–III.253
  n-dimensional, IV.149
  polygonization with tetrahedra, IV.326
  splitting into simploid, III.253–III.255
  subdividing, III.244–III.249
    applications, III.248–III.249
    code, III.534
    recursively, III.244–III.246
    symmetrically, III.246–III.248

Simplex object, V.99

Simploids, III.250–III.255, *see also* Box; Simplex
  dividing boxes into simplices, III.252–III.253
  splitting simplices into, III.253–III.255

Simulated annealing, IV.498

Sinc function, I.156–I.157
  Lanczos2
    decimation by, I.160–I.161
    interpolation by factor of two, I.158–I.159
  Lanczos-windowed, I.156–I.158
Sine, in exponentials, I.15
Singular value decomposition, IV.209, V.115
Sinusoids, digital generation, III.167–III.169
Skeleton, image, IV.465
Slerp interpolation, V.62
Small sparse matrix, classification, II.357–II.361
Smoothing, II.53–II.54
  of data, IV.241
Smoothing algorithm, monochrome enlargements,
    I.166–I.170
Smooth shading, *see* Shading
Snell's law, refraction, I.353–I.354
Snub disphenoid, II.178
Snub figures, II.177–II.178
Sobel and Prewitt operators, II.105
Software, *see also* Rendering software
  graphics libraries, V.400
  scrambling integers in, I.223
  engineering, IV.377
Solid modeling, III.226
Solids
  box-sphere intersection testing, I.335–I.337
  quasi-regular, II.174–II.175
Space curve, reference frame calculation,
    I.567–I.571
Space-filling curves, II.3–II.4, II.27–II.28
Space packing lattices, crack prevention,
    II.174
Space subdivision, Voronoi, V.268
Span, I.278
  data structure, II.33
  processing, II.34–II.35
Span conversion, unrolling short loops,
    III.355–III.357, III.594
Sparse matrix
  classification, II.357–II.361
    zero structures, II.357–II.358
  multiplying a vector, II.360–II.361
S-patch surfaces, V.219
Spatial classification
  n-D semiregular cubic solids, V.78
  n-D Voronoi cells, V.270
  parallelohedral decomposition (space packing),
    V.67
Spatial data structure, *see* Bounding box; Grid;
    Octree
Spatial rotations, III.128
Special effects
  contrast enhancement, I.197–I.198, I.201–I.202,
    I.270–I.271, I.274

dissolve, *see* Digital dissolve effect
  photo-inversion, I.196, I.198, I.270–I.271
Spectral decomposition of matrix, IV.209
Spectral radiance, III.307
Specular reflection, II.234, IV.385, IV.388, IV.404
Sphere, I.326
  bounding volume, III.298–III.299
  box-sphere intersection testing, I.335–I.339
  intersection with ray, I.388–I.389
  moving on, II.172–II.173
Spheres-to-voxels conversion, I.327–I.334
Spherical
  arc, IV.132
    code to draw, IV.178
    polygon, IV.132
  excess, IV.132
Spherical coordinate transformation, I.317–I.318
Spherical distribution, uniform, III.126–III.127
Spherical luminaire, importance sampling,
    III.310–III.311
Spherical polygons, V.42
Spherical projection, V.43
SPHIGS package, V.398
Spinors, III.57
Splined interpolation, III.122
Splines, I.585–I.586, *see also* B-spline; Curves and
    surfaces
SplitEdge, II.197–II.198
SPRT, V.356
Square root
  fixed point, V.22
  floating point, inverse, V.16
  high speed, low-precision, I.424–I.426
  IEEE, III.48, III.446
Square root algorithm, II.387–II.388
Staircase patterns, V.338
State, code generation, II.35
Statistics, visualizing 3D data, IV.193
Stereographic map, I.316, II.385
Stipple, IV.487
Stirling's numbers, I.597
Stochastic sampling, IV.370
Stochastic supersampling, V.248
Storage-free swapping, I.436–I.437
Stretcher-algorithm, III.6
Stretching, bitmap, III.4–III.7, III.411
Strum sequences, I.416–I.422
  characteristics, I.420
  counting sign changes, I.419–I.420
  driving algorithm, I.418–I.419
  example, I.417–I.418
  method of bisection, I.420–I.421
  pseudo-division of polynomials, I.419
Strum's Theorem, I.416–I.417
Stucki filter, II.69

Subdividing motion, transformations, III.123
Subdivision
 angle, *see* Ellipsoid generation
 arcs, circular, V.168
 Bézier, parametric, *see* de Casteljau algorithm
 chord, nonuniform, V.171
 curve, V.174
 parametric curve, IV.251, IV.263
 parametric surface, IV.287
 simplices, III.244–III.249, III.534
 space (Voronoi), V.268
 surface, V.104
 triangulation, IV.47
Subgroup algorithm, III.129–III.131
Subpixel coordinates, I.77–I.78
Subtabulation, I.601
Sum tables, multidimensional, *see*
 Multidimensional sum tables
Superquadrics
 review, III.137–III.138
 rigid physically based, III.137–III.159, III.472
  center of mass, III.139
  derivation of volume, mass, and inertia
   tensor, III.152–III.159
  equations of rigid-body motion,
   III.149–III.150
  inertia tensor, III.140–III.145
  "inside–outside" function, III.147–III.148
  normal vectors, III.148
  parametric surface functions, III.146–III.147
  quantities, III.138–III.145
  volume, density, and mass, III.139–III.140
Surface description
 by n-D cubic cells, V.98
 by quadrangle mesh, V.235
 by triangular mesh, V.232
 by voxel, V.273
Surface normal
 quadric surface, III.282–III.283
 3D models, I.562–I.566
 torus, determination, II.256
Surface-normal transformations, I.539–I.547
 affine modeling transformations, I.539–I.542
 backface culling, I.544–I.545
 composition, I.543
 isotropic transformations, I.542
 orthogonal transformations, I.542–I.543
 shading, I.545–I.547
 transformations of metric properties,
  I.543–I.544
Surfaces, *see also* Curves and surfaces
 cell ambiguity, V.98
 contours, V.99
 defining
  from contour data, I.558–I.561

 from sampled data, I.552–I.557
  assumptions, I.552–I.553
  methods, I.553–I.557
implicit
 blob, IV.324
 cone, IV.321, IV.355
 cylinder, IV.321, IV.353, IV.356
 ellipsoid, IV.113
 hyperplane, IV.154
 polygonization, IV.324
parametric
 B-spline, IV.286
 Bézier, IV.278, IV.290
 bilinear Coons patch, IV.438
 biquadratic rectangular, IV.278
 ellipsoid, IV.114
 hyperplane, IV.162
 NURB (nonuniform rational B-spline),
  IV.286
 polygonization, IV.287
 quartic triangular, IV.278
 rational, IV.286
 reparametrization, IV.278
 subdivision, IV.287
polyhedron, *see* Polyhedron
quadric, V.3
S-patch, V.219
subdivision, V.104
tensor-product, V.219
tessellated, V.232
Surface shading, II.234
SU(2) spinors, III.57
Sutherland–Hodgman algorithm, II.220, II.231
Sutherland–Hodgman clipping, V.51
Sutherland–Hodgman polygon clipper,
 III.219–III.222
SVD, IV.209, V.115
Swapping, *see* Element exchanging
Swept contours, I.562–I.564
Swept spheres, V.258
Symmetric double step line algorithm, I.101–I.104
 double speed Bresenham's, I.101–I.102
 line drawing, I.101
 using symmetry, I.102–I.104
Symmetric evaluation, polynomials,
 II.420–II.423
Synthetic actor, II.241

T

TARGA file format, V.398
Television color encoding, II.147–II.158
 chrominance, II.150
 color reference frame, II.148
 component systems, II.154

HDTV, II.154–II.155
hot-pixel test, II.155–II.157
IRE unites, II.152
luminance color difference space, II.147
NTSC encoding basics, II.148–II.152
PAL encoding, II.153–II.154
unencodable RGB values, II.147
Temporal refinement, progressive, recording
    animation in binary order, I.265–I.269
Tensor
    modern view, I.533–I.535
    product, II.333–II.334, III.85
        matrix, I.473
        surfaces, V.219
Tent filter, I.149–I.150, II.51–II.52
Tessellated surfaces, V.232
Tessellation, *see* Polygonization
Tetrahedron, dihedrals, II.174–II.175
Text, placement on maps, IV.497
Texture
    bump mapping, IV.433
    environment mapping, IV.435
    synthesis, IV.401
Texture cell, I.366–I.367
    types, I.371–I.372
Textured cylinder, I.366–I.367
Texture map indices, interpretation, I.366–I.376
    algorithm, I.373–I.375
    decision tree, I.369–I.371
    replicating cells to create larger texture, I.369
    rigid transformation of square cell,
        I.374–I.375
    texture space as two-torus, I.367–I.368
    types of cells, I.371–I.372
Texture mapping, III.227
Texture-space images, polygons, I.366–I.367
Theiessen tessellation, II.117, IV.47, V.269
Theorem
    divergence, V.40
    Green's, V.40
    Menelaus, V.213
Thinning, image, IV.465
Thomas precession, III.60
3×3 matrix, zero structures for, II.358–II.359
Three-dimensional geometry, I.297–I.300, II.169,
    III.213, *see also* Digital cartography
    backface culling, I.346–I.347
    Bézier triangle conversion to rectangular
        patches, III.256–III.261, III.536
    boxes, I.326
    curve tessellation criteria, III.262–III.265
    fast n-dimensional extent, III.240–III.243,
        III.527
    grouping nearly coplanar polygons into
        coplanar sets, III.225–III.230, III.512

homogeneous clipping, triangle strips,
    II.219–II.231
InterPhong shading, II.232–II.241
intersection
    of three planes, I.305
    of two lines, I.304
mapping, I.306
moving on a sphere, II.172–II.173
Newell's method, III.231–III.232, III.517
planar polygon, area, II.170
plane-to-plane intersection, III.233–III.236,
    III.519
polyhedra
    exact dihedral metrics, II.174–II.178
    volume, II.170–II.171
quadtree/octree-to-boundary conversion,
    II.202–II.218
signed distance from point to plane,
    III.223–III.224, III.511
simploids, III.250–III.255
spheres, I.326
spheres-to-voxels conversion, I.327–I.334
subdividing simplices, III.244–III.249, III.534
3D grid hashing function, I.343–I.345
3D polygon partitioning, III.219–III.222,
    III.502
triangle–cube intersection, III.236–III.239,
    III.521
triangles, III.215–III.218
view correlation, II.181–II.190
viewing geometry, II.179–II.180
winged-edge model maintenance, II.191–II.201
Three-dimensional grid, defining surfaces from
    sampled data, I.552–I.557
Three-dimensional homogeneous clipping, triangle
    strips, II.219–II.231
    against non-normalized clipping volume,
        II.224–II.225
    algorithm study, II.220–II.223
    data study, II.219–II.220
    implementation, II.225–II.229
    memory considerations, II.223–II.224
Three-dimensional models, surface normals,
    I.562–I.566
Three-dimensional polygons, partitioning,
    III.219–III.222, III.502
Three-dimensional vector C, library, III.399
Threshold dithering, II.58–II.63
Thresholding matrix, II.57, V.207
Tick marks, I.61–I.63
Tilings, periodic, plane on raster grid, I.129–I.139
Top-Down, II.206–II.208, II.210
Topology
    polygon data, IV.61
    rotation space, IV.230

Toroids, superquadric
  inertia tensor, III.111
  "inside–outside" function, III.148
  normal vectors, III.148
  parametric surface functions, III.147
  shells, III.157–III.159
  volume, III.140
Torus
  bounding volume, III.299
  determining surface normal, II.256
  efficient bounding, II.254–II.255
Trackball, virtual, I.462–I.463
Transformation, III.95
  angle-preserving, IV.199
  axis-aligned bounding boxes, I.548–I.550
  decomposing linear and affine, III.108–III.116
  as exponentials, II.332–II.337
  fast random rotation matrices, III.117–III.120
  interpolation, using Bézier curves,
    III.133–III.136, III.468
  keyframing, III.121–III.123
  length-preserving, IV.199
  matrix, *see* Matrix
  projective, decomposing, III.98–III.107
  quaternion interpolation with extra spins,
    III.96–III.97, III.461
  relative motion, III.122
  rigid physically based superquadrics,
    III.137–III.159, III.472
  subdividing motion, III.123
  subroutines, IV.534, IV.558
  3D, coding, *see* Quaternions
  uniform random rotations, III.124–III.132,
    III.465
  for visualization, IV.193
Transformation identities, I.485–I.493
  anisotropic scaling following rotation, I.490
  commuting
    rotation and anisotropic scaling, I.490
    rotation and isotropic scaling, I.488
    skewing and isotropic scaling, I.489
  exchanging order
    of skews, I.491
    of translation and rotation, rules, I.487
  matrix representations of primitive
    transformations, I.492–I.493
  reversing order
    skewing and anisotropic scaling, I.489
    translation and scaling, I.487
    translation and skewing, I.488
  rotation expressed as
    combination of skews and scales, I.489
    three skews, I.489
  skew expressed as two rotations and a scale,
    I.491

Transformation inverses, I.468
Transformation matrix, I.472–I.475
  data recovery, II.324–II.331
    mirror image, II.327
    projection, II.329–II.331
    rotation, II.326
    scaling, II.327–II.328
    shear, II.328–II.329
    translation, II.326
  DDA coefficient conversion between-step sizes,
    I.602
  mirror image, I.473
  notation, I.472, I.485–I.486
  observations, I.472
  post-concatenation, I.476–I.481
    computational cost comparison, I.479–I.481
    direct, I.478–I.479
    implementation, I.476–I.477
  primitive transformations, I.492–I.493
  projection, I.474
  rotation, I.473
  scaling, I.473–I.474
  translation, I.472
Transforming axes, I.456–I.459
Transition table, I.93–I.95
Translate and rotate algorithm, III.174–III.179
Translation, transformation matrices, I.473
  data recovery from, II.326
Translucent media, light absorption, II.277–II.282
Translucent objects, ray tracing, shadow
    attenuation, II.283–II.289
Transmission coefficient, II.278
Transparent objects, ray tracing, shadow
    attenuation, I.397–I.399, II.283–II.289
Transpose of the inverse, I.541
Trapezoidal
  icositetrahedron, V.83
  test, V.236
  decomposition, from polygon, V.394
Traversal, II.26–II.27
  coherence, II.30
Triangle, I.20–I.23, III.215–III.218
  area, I.20
  in center, I.20–I.21
  center of gravity, I.20–I.21
  circumcenter, I.20–I.23
  circumradius, I.20–I.23
  decomposition from polygon, V.395
  generating random points, I.24–I.28
  hemispherical projection, III.314–III.317,
    III.569
  hypotenuse, I.57–I.59
  intersection
    of altitudes, I.22
    of perpendicular bisectors, I.22–I.23

with ray, I.393, II.257–II.263
perimeter, I.20
prime pythagorean, I.58
in radius, I.20–I.21
Triangle–cube intersection, III.236–III.239, III.521
Triangle filter, II.51–II.52, III.13, III.15
Triangle strips, three-dimensional homogeneous
    clipping, II.219–II.231
Triangular interpolants, I.535 I.538
Triangular luminaire, importance sampling,
    III.312–III.313
Triangular pixels, anti-aliasing, III.369–III.373
Triangulation, IV.47
Tricubic interpolation, V.107
Trigonometric formulas
    basic formulas, I.12–I.17
    dihedral, II.174
    halved tangent, I.184–I.185, II.381
    spherical, I.317, II.442–II.445
    values, closed-form expressions, I.18–I.19
Trigonometry
    angle sum and difference relations, I.16
    DeMoivre's Theorem, I.15
    double-angle relations, I.17
    fixed-point, CORDIC, I.494–I.497
    functions, I.18–I.19
        sums and differences, I.14
    half-angle relations, I.16
    inverse functions, I.14
    Law of Cosines, I.13
    Law of Sines, I.13
    Law of Tangents, I.13
    Mollweide's Formula, I.13
    multiple-angle relations, I.17
    Newton's Formula, I.14
    power relations, I.15
    product relations, I.16
    sines and cosines and exponentials,
        I.15
Trilinear interpolation, *see* Interpolation
Triple scalar product, IV.155
Tristimulus values, II.159–II.160
Truncated octahedron (fcc packing), V.68
Tubular extrusions, V.258
Twist reduction in animation, IV.230
Two-dimensional array, randomly traversing,
    digital dissolve effect, I.221–I.222
Two-dimensional clipping, I.121–I.128
    algorithm, I.124–I.126
    approximation error, I.186
    basic considerations, I.123–I.124
    implementation, I.126–I.127
    integers and vectors, I.121–I.122
Two-dimensional drawing, intersection, exact
    computation, III.188–III.192, III.491

Two-dimensional geometry, I.3–I.11, II.3–II.4,
    III.163, *see also* Triangle
    area, polygon, II.5 II.6
    circles, I.4–I.5
    connection algorithm, III.173–III.181, III.480
    cosine of angle between lines, I.11
    distance from point to line, I.10
    fast circle clipping algorithm, III.182–III.187,
        III.487
    intersection of circle and line, I.5–I.6
    lines tangent
        to circle and perpendicular to line, I.8–I.9
        to two circles, I.7–I.8
    line structures, I.3–I.4
    parametric elliptical arc algorithm,
        III.164–III.172, III.478
    point of intersection between lines, I.11
    point-on-line test, I.49–I.50
    triangles, I.20–I.23
Two-dimensional prediction, II.95
Two-dimensional rendering, circles of integral
    radius on integer lattices, I.57–I.60
Two-dimensional screen point, II.181
Two-dimensional template, minimum, II.95
Two-dimensional vector C, library, III.396

U

Uniform distributions, *see* Point distributions *and*
    Random distributions
Uniform grid, line-edge intersections, I.29–I.36
Uniform quantization, I.288
Unimodular transforms, I.135
Union, scanline coherent shape algebra, II.38–II.39
Unit quaternions, set, properties, I.502–I.503
Univariate approximation, Bézier curves and
    surfaces, II.406–II.407
Unrolling short loops, span conversion,
    III.355–III.357, III.594
Utility functions, scanline coherent shape algebra,
    II.40–II.41
UVN coordinate system, I.518–I.519
U, V values, II.261–II.262

V

Variable control point approximation, curve
    interpolation, II.417–II.419
Variance minimization, color quantization based
    on, II.127
Vector operations, C macros, III.405
Vector rotation, CORDIC, I.494–I.497
Vectors
    cross product, *see* Cross product
    differences with forms, I.533–I.535
    dot product, *see* Dot product
    norm, IV.120

Vectors (*cont.*)
    normal, *see* Normal vector
    subroutine library for 2D, 3D, and 4D, IV.534,
        IV.668
    3D, I.522–I.523, I.526
    triangular interpolants, I.535–I.538
Vertex dependence, II.238–II.239
Vertext normal, IV.60
    computing, I.563–I.565
Vertex-to-vertex form factors, linear radiosity
    approximation, III.318–III.323
Vertical distance, point to line, I.47–I.48
Vertical sampling, III.291
Video signal amplitudes, II.152
View correlation, II.181–II.190
    chain rule, II.184
    example, II.188–II.190
    implementation details, II.185–II.188
    iteration parameters, II.184–II.185
    mathematical basis, II.182–II.185
    projection equations, II.182–II.183
    pyramid geometry, rendering with iterated
        parameters, II.186–II.187
    2D screen point, II.181
View-frustum culling, V.127
Viewing, 3D, *see* Orthonormal base
Viewing geometry, II.179–II.180
Viewing transformation, pseudo-code, I.521
Virtual screen
    cylindrical, III.290–III.291
    panoramic, ray tracing, III.288–III.294, III.551
Virtual trackball, I.462–I.463
Visibility algorithm, I.30–I.31
Visibility index, II.313
Visualization
    of graph, IV.505
    of *n*-dimensional data, IV.149
    of 3D point data, IV.193
Visualization for Planetary Exploration Lab,
    III.291
Volume
    hexahedron, V.39
    n-dimensional parallelepiped, IV.155, IV.161
    n-dimensional simplex, IV.154
    polyhedron, V.37
    superquadrics, III.139–III.140, III.152
    tetrahedron, IV.162, V.38
Volume model, procedural "hypertexture", IV.401
Volume rendering, IV.324, V.366, IV.521
Voronoi diagram, II.117, IV.47, V.269
Voxel cache, II.273–II.274
Voxel subdivision, 3D grid hashing function,
    I.343
Voxel traversal, IV.366
Voxel walking, V.273

W

Wallpaper groups, tiling in raster grids,
    I.133–I.139
Warp, IV.440
Wave generators, V.367
Wavelength-dependent reflection and refraction,
    II.286–II.287
WEdgeData structure, II.192–II.194
Wedge product, III.85–III.88
Whitening filter, II.95
White point
    chromaticities, II.148–II.149
    monitor, setting, II.159–II.162
Wide line bevel joints, algorithm for filling in,
    I.107–I.113
Winding number, IV.22, IV.25
    transitions, I.94–I.95
Window data structure, II.42
Window-to-viewport matrix group, II.344
    inverse, II.348
Window tree, II.42
Winged-edge data structure, IV.48
Winged-edge library, fundamental operations,
    II.191
Winged-edge models, maintaining, II.191–II.201
    Euler operators, II.197
    inputFace, II.196
    inputVertex, II.196
    InsertBridge, II.199–II.201
    NextFaceAroundVertex, II.195–II.196
    RemoveEdge, II.198
    SetWings, II.194–II.195
    SplitEdge, II.197–II.198
    WEdgeData structure, II.192–II.194
World coordinates, inertia tensor, III.145
Write-only write mask, reading, I.219–I.220
WShape, II.192
Wu's algorithm, II.127
Wu's anti-aliased circles, II.448–II.449
    algorithm, II.447

X–Z

XOR cursor, III.77, IV.413
X-transition table, I.93–I.95
Y extrema, polygon fast scan conversion, I.95–I.96
Z-buffer, V.398
    shading from, IV.433
Z-buffered triangle, scanline depth gradient,
    I.361–I.363
Zero-phase filters, frequency response, decimation
    by two, I.162
Zero structures, II.357–II.358
    for 3×3 matrix, II.358–II.359
Zonotopes, V.70

Other AP PROFESSIONAL Titles of Interest

GRAPHICS GEMS PACKAGE
Special Package—Buy the First Three Hardcover Volumes for the Price of Two!
GRAPHICS GEMS - Edited by Andrew J. Glassner
GRAPHICS GEMS II - Edited by James Arvo
GRAPHICS GEMS III - Edited by David Kirk

The *GRAPHICS GEMS* Series was started in 1990 by Andrew Glassner. The vision and purpose of the Series was—and still is—to provide tips, techniques, and algorithms for graphics programmers. All of the gems are written by programmers who work in the field and are motivated by a common desire to share interesting ideas and tools with their colleagues. Each volume provides a new set of innovative solutions to a variety of programming problems.

ISBN: 0-12-270350-2   **ONLY $99.95**

FROM PIXELS TO ANIMATION: An Introduction to Graphics Programming
by James Alan Farrell

From Pixels to Animation: An Introduction to Graphics Programming will serve as an introduction to graphics programming as well as a complete graphics reference for the experienced graphics programmer. It covers the basics of graphics programming, from how a graphics monitor works to how to draw realistic 3-D images. The book thoroughly explains the history and inner workings of graphics theories and monitors, and includes advanced topics and tools—so that even experienced graphics programmers will benefit. A basic knowledge of C is assumed, but no prior graphics experience is necessary.

ISBN: 0-12-249710-4   **Paperback, $39.95**

TEXTURING AND MODELING: A Procedural Approach
by David Ebert, F. Kenton Musgrave, Darwyn Peachey, Ken Perlin, Steve Worley

This book contains a toolbox of procedures upon which programmers can build a library of procedural textures and objects. Procedural rendering, modeling, shading and texturing are of growing importance in computer graphics and animation, and, this is the first comprehensive book covering these topics. It also includes extensive explanations of how these functions work, and how to design new functions.

ISBN: 0-12-228760-6   **Hardcover, $49.95**

VIRTUAL REALITY EXCURSIONS
With Programs in C
by Christopher D. Watkins and Stephen R. Marenka

This book makes the current applications of virtual reality accessible to the PC user. The authors have developed software, the *3D World Editor*, and an *Architecture Visualizer* that enables readers to create their own virtual environments. The topical coverage is extensive and focuses on a few primary application areas: 3D CAD modeling and architectural modeling, flight simulation, and gaming. 3D Glasses Included!

ISBN: 0-12-737865-0 **Paperback, $39.95**

LEARNING WINDOWS™ PROGRAMMING WITH VIRTUAL REALITY
by Christopher D. Watkins and Russell J. Berube Jr.

This is an innovative book for teaching programming. Throughout the book, readers will develop a 3-D Virtual Reality game as they learn the Windows programming techniques. The 3-D engine provided with the book generates textured and interactive 3-D imagery like those found on two very popular shareware games—**Wolfenstein 3-D** and **Doom.** Explanations for development in both DOS and Windows (3.1 and higher) are included.

ISBN: 0-12-737842-1 **Paperback, $39.95**

RADIOSITY AND REALISTIC IMAGE SYNTHESIS
by Michael F. Cohen and John R. Wallace

This is the first book to provide a comprehensive look at the radiosity method for image synthesis and the tools required to achieve quality results. The book provides valuable assistance to professionals involved in creating realistic computer images— including architects and industrial designers, and to those in the entertainment and advertising industries, computer aided design, computer graphics (including virtual reality), and medical imaging fields. Includes 16 pages of full-color images.

ISBN: 0-12-178270-0 **Hardcover, $49.95**

3-D SOUND FOR VIRTUAL REALITY AND MULTIMEDIA APPLICATIONS
by Durand R. Begault

One of the key underlying technologies of immersive virtual reality (VR) is 3-D sound. This is **the first introduction to 3-D sound theory and applications aimed at the commercial engineer.** It will provide the reader with an understanding of the communication chain between source and listener. Special features include components of spatial auditory displays and psychoacoustics of spatial hearing. Begault overviews many different applications for spatialized sound, including: auditory feedback, communication systems, aeronautics, computer music, sonification, television and computer interfaces.

ISBN: 0-12-084735-3   **Hardcover, $49.95**

USING DIGITAL VIDEO
by Arch Luther

Digital motion video and sound are now available for any personal computer and can be installed inexpensively and easily by any PC user. This book teaches the principles of digital video and audio, and provides a comprehensive look at the technical aspects of both analog and digital video. It also provides all the information necessary to incorporate and distribute video and audio into existing applications, electronic presentations, and information, including production and postproduction.

ISBN: 0-12-460432-3   **Paperback, $34.95**

VIDEO COMPRESSION FOR MULTIMEDIA
by Jan Ozer

This book thoroughly covers and demonstrates the latest compression technologies including **JPEG, MPEG, Fractals, Vector Quantization** and **Wavelets**. Readers will learn how to apply **compression theory** during filming to create footage that compresses well on a digital platform. Ozer also explains how to optimize compression settings to achieve the highest possible compressed video quality and how to create and integrate video into windows applications.

ISBN: 0-12-531940-1   **Paperback, $39.95**

Printed and bound by CPI Group (UK) Ltd, Croydon, CR0 4YY

03/10/2024

01040321-0007